CREATIVITY

THEORIES AND THEMES:
RESEARCH, DEVELOPMENT, AND PRACTICE

SECOND EDITION

CREATIVITY

THEORIES AND THEMES: RESEARCH, DEVELOPMENT, AND PRACTICE

SECOND EDITION

MARK A. RUNCO

Torrance Center for Creativity and Talent Development, USA

ELSEVIER

AMSTERDAM • BOSTON • HEIDELBERG • LONDON
NEW YORK • OXFORD • PARIS • SAN DIEGO
SAN FRANCISCO • SINGAPORE • SYDNEY • TOKYO

Academic Press is an imprint of Elsevier

Academic Press is an imprint of Elsevier

32 Jamestown Road, London NW1 7BY, UK
225 Wyman Street, Waltham, MA 02451, USA
525 B Street, Suite 1800, San Diego, CA 92101-4495, USA

Notice
No responsibility is assumed by the publisher for any injury and/or damage to persons or property as
a matter of products liability, negligence or otherwise, or from any use or operation of any methods,
products, instructions or ideas contained in the material herein. Because of rapid advances in the
medical sciences, in particular, independent verification of diagnoses and drug dosages should be
made

British Library Cataloguing-in-Publication Data

A catalogue record for this book is available from the British Library

Library of Congress Cataloging-in-Publication Data

A catalog record for this book is available from the Library of Congress

ISBN: 978-0-12-410512-6

For information on all Academic Press publications
visit our website at elsevierdirect.com

Typeset by Scientific Publishing Services
www.sps.co.in

Printed and bound in United States of America
14 15 16 17   10 9 8 7 6 5 4 3 2 1

Working together
to grow libraries in
developing countries

www.elsevier.com • www.bookaid.org

Dedication

Psychologists often speak of people like me as part of the "sandwich generation," so named because our parents request our help while our children still need our support. Typically the sandwich generation implies a stressful life. What is not recognized nearly enough is that people like me, with parents and children actively involved in each and every day of our lives, are the luckiest people alive. I am enormously happy to be in the middle of the sandwich.

Contents

Preface

Creativity is an important and fascinating topic of study, but difficult to define. This difficulty is due in part to its diverse expression; creativity plays a role in technical innovation, education, business, the arts and sciences, and many other fields. Many famous people have earned their reputations from their creativity; it is sometimes related to expertise and fame. Other adults are highly creative, though perhaps in the everyday sense of coping, adapting, and solving novel problems. Although there is controversy about children, the view held in this textbook is that they, too, are creative. They may not be experts or even productive, but they are original and effectively expressive in their art, their dancing and singing, their imaginative play, and their perceptive questioning. It is even possible that children are more creative than adults, given their spontaneity and lack of inhibitions. Unlike adults, children do not rely on past experience, assumptions, and routines. One of the questions addressed in the current volume concerns age differences and developmental trajectories.

Another kind of diversity is apparent in that various cultures seem to have idiosyncratic modes and media for expressing creativity. Diverse expression is one reason that creativity is an important topic for investigation. Obviously it has the potential to be expressed in many different ways, so what exactly is creative potential? With its role in so many endeavors, we must attempt to answer this question. We have an obligation to make an attempt to fulfill creative potentials. Creativity is, in a phrase, a vital form of human capital. Creativity both contributes to the information explosion and helps each of us cope and adapt to the resulting challenges.

There are numerous approaches to the study of creativity. Most of these offer something useful, at least if they use reliable methods and sound scholarship. However, the creative process is multifaceted, and worse yet for those trying to define it, it is extremely complex. An eclectic approach is necessary. This textbook captures that eclectic approach to creativity.

EVERYDAY AND EMINENT CREATIVITY

Creativity plays a role in many everyday activities. Its role in some of these areas is easy to overlook, in part because the word "creativity" (or adjective "creative") is not often used when explaining these areas. Creativity plays a significant role in language, for example, and in fact this may be the best example of everyday creativity. It is the creativity of language that demonstrates that it is not entirely acquired through experience and learning. If language depended entirely on experience, we would have difficulty saying things we had not heard before. Very likely, our nervous system is sensitive to rules and linguistic conventions, and once we acquire a few rules (e.g., sentences should contain a noun and a verb), we can generate original expressions of our own. These are original (we have not heard them before) and useful; and as such fit the definition of creativity as original and useful.

It may be that creativity plays a role in each of our lives, every day. This surely sounds like a grand claim, but consider how frequently we use language or are faced with a problem. Think also how often problems are subtle and ill-defined. Vague and ill-defined but challenging situations can be defined using creative problem definition skills. The point is that creativity plays a role in each of our lives, and it does so very frequently. Admittedly, there is a debate about this, with some scholars focusing on eminent or unambiguous rather than everyday creativity. That debate is reviewed in the pages that follow, but for now suffice it to say that one premise of this particular volume is that creativity is a potential each of us shares and a talent each of us should employ, probably every day.

Creativity may sound a bit like adaptability, and these two things are related. They are not, however, one and the same. Creativity is associated with but distinct from intelligence, innovation, imagination, insight, and health. Each of these associations is reviewed herein. One of the most important messages found in the current volume is that creativity is a distinct and independent capacity. It plays a role in many things, including problem solving, adaptation, learning, coping, and so on, but it is clearly distinct from each of them.

THE FIELD OF CREATIVE STUDIES AND THE CREATIVITY COMPLEX

Creative studies are interdisciplinary. This is reflected in the present volume and its inclusion of behavioral, clinical, cognitive, developmental, economic, educational, evolutionary, historical, organizational, personality, and social perspectives.

Not surprisingly, creativity has been defined as a syndrome or complex. Both of these labels capture the idea that creativity can be expressed in diverse ways (e.g., art vs. science), and sometimes involves different processes (e.g., cognitive or social). It is also influenced by many different kinds of things, including personality, genetic make-up, social and environmental setting, and culture. The notion that creativity is a complex represents one of the most widely accepted views.

ORGANIZATION OF THE BOOK

Each of the major theoretical perspectives on creativity is reviewed in this volume. Some have entire chapters devoted to them. Others, such as evolutionary theory, are discussed within various chapters. The more important topics and issues, including those mentioned above (concerning age differences and everyday creativity) are also covered. The last two chapters do not focus on one theoretical perspective. The first of them (Chapter 12) focuses on enhancement issues. The second (Chapter 13) revisits the definition issues and explores how creativity is related to, but distinct from, other important human capacities and behaviors, including invention, innovation, imagination, and adaptability. This second edition of *Creativity* throws an even wider net around the topic of creativity than the first edition. It includes two new chapters. One is devoted to philosophy and creativity (Chapter 11), and the other politics and creativity (Chapter 10). The first of these may surprise some readers, given that creativity is often a topic for the social and behavioral sciences, and philosophy is not a science. Philosophy is, however, very relevant to the scientific study of creativity! Indeed, there is a moderately sized field devoted to "the philosophy of science." You might even say that all good science is creative. You might also say that all good philosophy is creative!

The second edition also updates the research, which is still booming. The value of creativity is even more widely recognized now than 5–10 years ago.

It was tempting to streamline parts of the book, and in particular to bring together sections from different chapters that deal with the same topic. Anxiety is, for example, discussed in the chapter on health (Chapter 4), but also in the chapter on personality (Chapter 9). The writer in me wanted to discuss anxiety in only one place, but because this is a textbook, I stuck with the rationale for displaced practice. That means that it is best, for learning, if there is exposure to a new idea, and then time away, and then another exposure to the same idea. I know displaced practice works well, and there are data to support it, some suggesting that it is the best, most effective method for learning of all! Other examples include discussions of domains and marginality.

This is primarily a textbook. It may, however, also be useful to researchers and practitioners, given the emphasis on scholarly, scientific, and objective research and the theories that are constructed from it. It is my hope that this volume will also capture at least some of the intrigue of the fascinating subject.

Mark A. Runco

La Habra, CA and Bishop, GA

Cognition and Creativity

You can only perceive beauty with a serene mind. **Henry David Thoreau**
Trouble with you is the trouble with me. Got two good eyes but still don't see. **Grateful Dead**

ADVANCE ORGANIZER

- Universals and Individual Differences
- Intelligence, IQ, and Threshold Theory
- Structure of Intellect and Associative Theory
- Creative Thinking as Problem Solving
- Problem Finding
- Stage Theories of the Creative Process
- Insight

- Componential Models
- Incubation and the Role of the Unconscious
- Logic
- Intuition
- Tactics and Metacognition
- Mindfulness
- Overinclusive Thinking

INTRODUCTION

Cognitive theories focus on thinking skills and intellectual processes. Cognitive perspectives are quite numerous; there may be more cognitive theories of creativity than any other kind of theory. This is because there is an intuitive connection between cognition and creativity (and evidence reviewed in this chapter suggests that intuition is a useful source of information), and because cognitive research is often very scientific. In other words, we can study the cognitive bases for creative problem solving, and we can often do so in reasonably valid and reliable ways, in a controlled laboratory setting or with paper-and-pencil tests. Some approaches to creativity do not allow such experimentation and rigorous research. No doubt the prevalence of cognitive research on creativity also reflects the fact that virtually all human behavior has a cognitive basis. Creative behavior must also have a basis in cognition.

The approaches to creative cognition are extremely varied. There are bridges between basic cognitive processes (e.g., attention, perception, memory, information processing) and creative problem solving, as well as connections with intelligence, problem solving, language, and other numerous individual differences. The basic cognitive processes are generally *nomo-thetic,* meaning that they represent universals. These are things shared by all humans. Individual differences represent the dimensions along which people vary. There are both cognitive universals and cognitive individual differences in creativity.

This chapter presents an overview of the available theories of creative cognition. We will begin by examining the relationship between creativity and traditional intelligence and then explore the possibility that creativity can sometimes be a kind of problem solving. We will also review research on the creativity of computers, incubation, insight, and expertise. As we will see, cognition is related to many kinds of creative behavior.

UNIVERSALS

Research on *universals* is sometimes described as *nomothetic,* but care should be taken when using this term. The word nomothetic is used to describe the kinds of laws that are found in a legal system, not laws in the sense that science defines them. Laws in the sciences refer to general rules, so there is a parallel, but it is only a parallel. Strictly speaking, it may be best to discuss universals in creativity and avoid the term nomothetic.

Similar confusion arises with the complementary term *idiographic.* An ideograph is a symbol, but idiographic has been used to describe the scientific emphasis on individual differences. This makes sense if you think about the more common term, idiosyncratic. The confusion here, then, is simply spelling (idiographic vs. ideographic). It certainly is useful to distinguish universals from individual differences.

CREATIVITY AND INTELLIGENCE

The relationship between IQ and creative potential was quite the controversy 50 years ago. In fact, the relationship of intelligence and creativity was *the* key question when the study of creativity was establishing itself. This question was key because the field of creativity needed to separate itself from other scientific topics and interests in the 1950s and 1960s, and this required empirical evidence that creativity was not the same thing as intelligence. It was the demonstrated separation of creativity from traditional intelligence that first gave this field its identity and respect.

Some of the earliest research on creativity was designed to test the possibility that creativity was distinct from intelligence. After all, if creativity was dependent on intelligence there would be little reason to study or encourage it. Intelligence could be studied or encouraged and creativity would follow along. But sure enough, the early research confirmed that creativity (in the research, defined in terms of divergent thinking or some paper-and-pencil measures) was not dependent on traditional intelligence.

The field of creative studies had a shaky start. Getzels and Jackson (1962), for example, reported that creativity was not clearly distinct from intelligence. This conclusion was based on empirical research with a sizeable group of students, each of whom had taken various tests of creative potential, and for whom there was information about traditional intellectual potential. Simplifying some, the measures of creative potential and the indicators of traditional intelligence were correlated. This does not support the conclusion of independence.

Wallach and Kogan (1965) questioned the creativity–intelligence correlation, and more precisely, questioned the methodology that led to it. They felt that the tests used by Getzels and Jackson (1962) were too diverse and tapped noncreative skills as well as creative talents. Significantly, they also suggested that creativity can easily be stifled in an educational or testing environment. With this in mind, they conducted their own investigation of the *Modes of Thinking in Young Children* (the title of their book). This investigation relied heavily on tests of divergent thinking. As described in detail later, these contain open-ended tasks (e.g., "List multiple uses for a broom"), and an individual can therefore produce original answers.

Wallach and Kogan (1965) also took great care with the testing environment. They spent a great deal of time in the schools before data were collected, for instance, and built rapport with the students. When the measures of divergent thinking finally were administered, they were described as games rather than tests. Children were told that no grades would be given, that spelling did not matter, that they did not need to think about "correct" answers but could instead list numerous ideas. They were told to have fun, for goodness sake, and apparently they did. The game-like and *permissive environment* paid off. The children were indeed quite original. They gave many answers to the various divergent thinking games, and those answers reflected a mode of thought that could not be predicted from traditional intelligence. The implication is that IQ, grade point average (GPA), and the convergent thinking that is required by them (Box 1.1) is independent of divergent and original thinking.

BOX 1.1

TESTS OF CONVERGENT AND DIVERGENT THINKING

Convergent thinking questions always have one (or very few) correct or conventional answers. Here are examples:

- Who was the first President of the United States?
- How far is it from New York City to London?
- How many dimes are in one dollar?
- Who won the 1988 World Series?

Divergent thinking requires open-ended questions for which there are multiple answers and solutions. Here are examples from the classic study of Wallach and Kogan (1965):

Instances tasks

- Make a list of things that move on wheels.

- List strong things.
- List square things.

Uses tasks

- Make a list of the different ways that you can use a brick.
- List uses for a shoe.
- List uses for a coat hanger.

Many other divergent thinking questions and tasks have been used. Wallach and Kogan (1965) had "visual" or figural tests called *pattern meanings* and *line meanings*. More recently, realistic questions have been developed (these are discussed in detail in Chapter 2).

That may sound like a statistical and scientific result—and it is!—but consider what the same conclusion means in the sense of identifying creative children. It means that if schools care about creativity and give children exercises and tests of creative potential, but these are given in a test-like academic atmosphere, then the children who always do well on academic tests will excel, and the children who do moderately or poorly on traditional tests will do only moderately or poorly. If those same tests are administered in the permissive atmosphere—even a classroom if it is carefully controlled—children who do only moderately well or even poorly in academic tests may do exceptionally well. We may find creative children who would otherwise be overlooked.

Wallach and Wing (1969) extended this line of work in an investigation of college students. Divergent thinking tests were again administered, but unlike the earlier investigation, Wallach and Wing also collected data on the extracurricular activities and accomplishments of the students. This allowed examination of the *predictive validity* of the divergent thinking tests. Predictive validity is the label given to tests that provide information about the future, or about performance beyond the testing environment. Very significantly, Wallach and Wing found that divergent thinking tests were moderately correlated with (i.e., predictive of) the extracurricular activities and achievements of the students (Box 1.2), whereas the measures of more traditional intelligence were not. This conclusion has been replicated many times over (Kogan & Pankove 1974; Runco 1986a). It does apply to some domains of accomplishment more than others, but that is as it should be, given domain differences in creativity (Albert 1980; Gardner 1983; Plucker 1998; Runco 1987a). The evidence for predictive validity is extremely important. It implies that creative thinking, as estimated from tests of divergent thinking, is more important in the natural environment than are tests of the IQ or academic tests. Consider this: What would you want to be able to predict, GPA or performance in the natural environment? If you had a child, would you prefer that he or she does better in school or in the natural environment?

Numerous other demonstrations of the predictive validity of creativity tests (divergent thinking exams, as well as a variety of others) are described elsewhere in this book. What is most important here is that *creative thinking may be very different from traditional intelligence.* When we practice one of them, we may not be improving the other at all.

BOX 1.2

EXAMPLES FROM THE CREATIVE ACTIVITY, ACCOMPLISHMENT, AND ACHIEVEMENT CRITERION

How often have you:

- Made candles (Craft domain)?
- Written poetry (Writing domain)?
- Designed any sort of experiment (Science domain)?

- Started a club (Social Leadership domain)?
- Composed music (Musical domain)
- Painted a picture (not as an assignment) (Artistic domain)
- Planned and kept a garden? (Natural domain)

What is practiced in our educational system? Traditional intelligence or creative problem solving? The distinction between divergent thinking (generating a number of ideas) and convergent thinking (finding or remembering one correct or conventional answer) helps to answer that: Most educational efforts emphasize convergent thinking and therefore may do very little, if anything, for creative potentials.

IQ tests can estimate the potential to do well in school, and although that is important in many ways, individuals in the United States are in school for 12 or so years. How long are they outside of school and in the natural environment? The rest of their lives!

Tests of creative potential are no doubt similarly limited to the skills that may be required by the test in question. Tests are always limited in some ways (see Chapter 6). Examinees may not be interested in the test, and thus not use their full potential. If this occurs, the individual will receive a test score that tells us only that the individual was uninterested in applying him- or herself. No wonder predictions from tests are rarely impressive. It is for this reason that it is best to refer to tests as indicators of *potential*. If the individual does well on the test, he or she may or may not do well in the natural environment. The test is probably only highly accurate when the individual is both interested in the test (and for that reason puts a great deal of effort into the examination) and interested in doing well in the natural environment.

Threshold Theory

Spearman (1927), the statistician who wrote so much about "g" and general ability (the basis for IQ), explicitly refuted the idea of creativity. He felt that all the evidence demonstrated

> that no such special creative power exists. All three "neo-genetic" processes ..., are generative of new mental content and of new knowledge; and no other cognitive generation can possibly be attained in any other way whatsoever, not even a Shakespeare, a Napoleon, and a Darwin were rolled into one. That which is usually attributed to such special imaginative or inventive operation can be simply resolved into a correlate eduction combined with mere reproduction. From this analytic standpoint, then, we must predict that all creative power—whether or not it be dubbed imagination—will at any rate involve g (p. 187).

Spearman cited some even older work by Hargreaves from the 1927 *British Journal of Psychological Monograph Supplement*, who found large correlations between tests of general ability and the following: inkblots, free-completion test, unfinished pictures, and unfinished stories. In this particular inkblot test, subjects had four minutes to look at a smudge and write down all the objects seen in them. It was a timed task, but not unlike a figural divergent thinking test. The free-completion test asked examinees to fill "gaps left in passages of prose" (p. 187). Unfinished pictures told examinees that "an artist had just begun a picture, had left it unfinished; you were to write down all of the things you would put into the picture if you were going to finish it" (p. 127). Unfinished stories gave examinees something like the following: "a small girl, after her first visit to the zoo, had a very strange dream. She dreamt that..." (pp. 187–188). Examinees were given 20 minutes to write a story.

Creative potential and intelligence may not be entirely independent. One very common perspective today is that there is a threshold of intelligence (basically, a minimal level) that is necessary for creative performance. It is probably more accurate to refer to a threshold of

---

BOX 1.3

CONCEPTIONS OF INTELLIGENCE

The term *intelligence* has changed dramatically over the years. It still is used in a wide variety of ways. The military, for instance, uses it as a synonym for useful information. Ten years ago John Keegan, military historian, for example, published a book titled, *Intelligence in War: Knowledge of the Enemy from Napoleon to al-Qaeda* (2003). His premise was that knowledge about one's enemy is of limited value in war, and that "objective force" is much more critical. For our purposes, his work simply exemplifies one definition of intelligence. Cognitive scientists are more likely to refer to useful knowledge of the sort Keegan describes simply as "knowledge," but implicit here is the distinction of

knowledge from information. Information is data; knowledge implies understanding (and hence the utility of "useful knowledge"). In that light, "useful knowledge" is a tautology, for knowledge is more than information precisely because it assumes understanding. Do not let this fool you, however, for cognitive scientists are far from agreeing about defining intelligence. For the present purposes intelligence is viewed as distinct from creative ability, but even there it is probably best to refer to *traditional* intelligence. Certain kinds of intelligence are, at certain levels and in particular domains, related to creativity. For this reason some theorists describe "creative intelligence."

"traditional" intelligence, because intelligence means many things to many different people (Box 1.3). Some people equate intelligence with academic performance, and others equate it with verbal aptitude or wit. Too often, children who are simply well informed are viewed as intelligent. In and of itself this is not so bad, but the corollary is that children who are not well informed are not intelligent. This is indeed a problem, called *experiential bias* (Runco et al. 2006; Runco & Acar 2010), for often information is picked up through experience, and thus associating intelligence with information leads directly to biases against children who may be capable but lack critical experiences.

Intelligence most often refers to the IQ or some similar kinds of abilities, yet even here it would be best to refer to a specific test. Different tests assess different intellectual skills. There is also the possibility that intelligence cannot be captured by a paper-and-pencil test.

Threshold theory suggests that there is a minimum level of intelligence (the lower threshold) below which the person cannot be creative. Instead of concluding that creativity and intelligence are one and the same, or that creativity and intelligence are entirely distinct, threshold theory describes the possibility that they are related, but only at certain levels of ability. One important implication of threshold theory is that intelligence is necessary but not sufficient for creative achievement. Thus, if an individual is below the threshold, they simply cannot think for themselves well enough to do manifestly creative work. Above the threshold, they have the potential for creativity, but there is no guarantee. They may be creative, but they may not be.

A scatterplot suggesting a triangle and lower threshold of intelligence is presented in Figure 1.1. One important implication of this theory is that some persons may have high levels of intelligence but low levels of creative potential. Intelligence and creativity are thus not

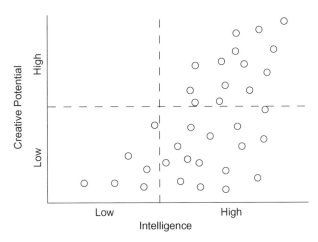

FIGURE 1.1   Scatterplot showing that creative potential is more likely to be high with high intelligence.

interdependent. Note also that no one has a low level of intelligence and a high level of creative potential. Finally, note that the data are from tests of creativity and intelligence. This theory is based on tested ability, not on creative or intelligent performances in the natural environment.

MUCH ADO ABOUT HETEROSCEDASTICITY

The relationship of creativity with traditional intelligence has been described with the idea of a threshold (e.g., Runco & Albert 1986b) and with triangular theory (Guilford 1968). The basic idea is that a minimum level of general intelligence is necessary for creative work. Truly creative work cannot be done below the threshold. The triangle is apparent in a scatterplot with intelligence on the abscissa and creativity on the ordinate (Figure 1.1). Regression analyses using quadratic predictors can be used to test the threshold. It is also accurate to describe the creativity–intelligence relationship using the notion of heteroscedasticity. This best describes the data and scatterplots and also captures what is suggested by the entire range of ability. Hollingworth's (1942) report implies that variability decreases at an IQ of 180, suggesting a second threshold. There was very little creativity in her sample of exceptionally high IQ individuals. The concept of heteroscedasticity implies different levels of variation at different levels of ability. It is consistent with the idea that no one with an extremely low IQ does highly creative work (low variation, high correlation), but above a moderate level of IQ some individuals are creative but others are not (high variation, low correlation). It also allows for the possibility that at the highest levels of IQ creativity is very difficult or even impossible (low variability, strong negative correlation).

Threshold theory apparently applies to some tests of intelligence better than others (Runco & Albert 1986b; Sligh, Conners, & Roskos-Ewoldsen 2005), but it is logical as well as consistent with the empirical research, and it is consistent as well with the general principle of creative performances as optimal. As detailed in Chapter 13, almost everything about creativity involves an optimum of some sort. There are many influences on creativity, such as divergent thinking, but only so much actually contributes. Beyond some point creative performances start to decline. If asked to name square things, "my dad's music" is both original and fitting— it is optimally divergent—but "basketball" may be past the optimal level of originality and is not fitting, not creative. We will revisit this principle of optima throughout this book (also see Runco & Sakamoto 1996) because it applies so broadly.

The most recent investigation of the threshold theory used sophisticated statistical procedures (segmented regression with iterative computational algorithms) and supported the original theory, but only with the measures of creative potential (Jauk et al. 2013). The threshold was absent in analyses with measures of actual creative performance. This of course fits well with a theme of the present textbook, namely that there is a big difference between creative achievement and creative potential (also see Runco 2008). Jauk et al. (2013) also reported that the threshold, when present, was around an IQ of 100, but only when originality was defined in a very liberal fashion. A liberal definition means that quite a few ideas are identified as original. When a stringent definition of originality was used, the cutoff was closer to an IQ of 120, which is the level first proposed, years ago, when the threshold was first identified. One final conclusion from Jauk et al. should be mentioned. They felt that when there was a threshold (and thus a relationship of general intelligence with creativity), personality was a significant influence on creativity. This might explain why, above the threshold of intelligence, some individuals are creative, but others are not.

Structure of Intellect

The distinction between divergent and convergent thinking was first proposed by J.P. Guilford. He was president of the American Psychological Association and devoted his 1949 Presidential Address to creativity (Guilford 1950). He argued that creativity is a natural resource and suggested that efforts to encourage creativity would pay high dividends to the whole of society. Guilford also suggested that creativity can be studied objectively. For the next 35 years he attempted to prove exactly this.

Guilford (1968, 1986) eventually identified 180 different aspects of the intellect. His view was, in this sense, about as far away from that of IQ theories as you can get. IQ tests typically assume that there is one general intelligence (or g) that underlies every intelligent act—every single one. Admittedly, Guilford's Structure of Intellect model was pointedly criticized, mostly because of the statistical methods used to separate the 180 cells (Carroll 1968). Yet even if Guilford's methods were questionable, his conception of divergent and convergent thinking has proven to be quite useful. Indeed, much of his thinking on creativity was, and remains, remarkably influential (see Runco 1999d).

Divergent thinking is employed when an individual is faced with an open-ended task (examples were given earlier—"How can a brick be used?"). From this perspective divergent thinking is a kind of problem solving. Unlike convergent thinking, where the individual gives the one correct or conventional response (e.g., "Who won the 1988 World Series?"), divergent thinking leads the individual to numerous and varied responses. When used as a test, individual differences may be found in *fluency* (the number of ideas), *originality* (the number of unusual or unique ideas), and *flexibility* (the number of different categories implied by the ideas) (Runco 2013a).

DIVERGENT THINKING BEFORE GUILFORD'S STRUCTURE OF INTELLECT

J.P. Guilford is usually given credit for distinguishing between convergent and divergent thinking, but a few earlier scientists did recognize the value of ideation. Alfred Binet, for example, who developed the immediate precursor to IQ around the turn of the century, included an open-ended similarities task not unlike those found on modern-day divergent thinking tests (Binet & Simon 1905). Here are sample items from Binet and Simon's (1905) first test of intelligence.

1. Unwrapping candy
2. Follow simple directions
3. Name objects
4. Name objects in pictures
5. Compare two weights
6. Compare two lines
7. Vocabulary
8. Repetition of sentences
9. Repetition of digits
10. Identify differences (e.g., fly and butterfly)
11. Identify similarities (e.g., blood and a poppy)
12. Order weights
13. Complete sentences
14. Cut paper
15. Define abstract terms
16. Visual tracking (i.e., follow moving object with head and eyes)
17. Tactile prehension (i.e., pick up particular object)
18. Distinguish edible and inedible objects

Adapted from Willerman (1979), pp. 85–86.

A Convergence–Divergence Continuum

The distinction between divergent and convergent thinking implies a dichotomy. Very likely, divergent thinking and convergent thinking are actually two ends of a continuum (Eysenck 2003). This may make the most sense, given we know about individual differences (they tend to fall along continua), and it is apparent when various divergent thinking questions are examined. Some are clearly more open-ended than others. Along the same lines, it is probably most accurate to think about problem solving as involving both divergent and convergent thinking. In the natural environment it is unusual to find a problem that relies completely on one or the other. Most often, both divergent and convergent thinking are useful.

Divergent thinking is not synonymous with creative thinking, but it does tell us something about the cognitive processes that sometimes lead to original ideas and solutions. No wonder divergent thinking tests are the most commonly used estimates of the potential for creative thought. They have a solid theoretical base, in both the Structure of Intellect model and in Associative Theory (outlined next); they have reasonable reliability and validity; and there is a vast literature available to assist interpretations. Divergent thinking tests can be used as exercises, rather than tests, in training studies and programs, in classrooms and in organizations (Runco & Basadur 1993). Chapter 6 presents a large number of exercises and tactics for original and flexible ideation.

More will be said about the reliability and validity of divergent thinking in Chapter 9. Of more relevance to cognition is the role of associative processes in divergent and creative thinking.

Associative Theory

Many theories of creative cognition look to associative processes. Associative theories focus on how ideas are generated and chained together. If you look back on the history of psychology, you will see that the associative view can be traced back hundreds of years, to John Locke, Alexander Bain, David Hume, and others (Marx & Hillix 1987; Roth & Sontag 1988). These theorists typically are described as philosophers, and certainly they were not scientists. They ocassional offered hypotheses but did not test them in any modern scientific sense. It was Mednick (1962) who brought the associative view into modern psychology. He proposed the "associative theory of the creative process" and offered several empirical tests of the theory. Perhaps most important was his finding that original ideas tend to be remote. The first things we think of are typically not very original. Instead, original ideas are found usually only after we deplete the most obvious ideas.

A very simple experimental technique for examining remote associates and ideational patterns—one you may choose to try—involves counting an examinee's responses to an open-ended task (e.g., a divergent thinking test question) (Box 1.1), and finding the half-way point. If you give 20 items to the question, "Name all of the things you can think of that are square," two sets of 10 ideas can be compared in terms of the number of the original and flexibility of the ideas. Results from several independent projects using this technique suggest that original ideas come later in a set of responses, though ideas are no more flexible and varied in the second half compared to the first (Mednick 1962; Milgram & Rabkin 1980; Runco 1985).

This line of research confirms that ideas can be counted in a reliable and objective fashion, and ideas can be used as an indication of how people generate solutions to solve problems. In fact, the notion that original ideas come late in the associative chain implies that we should take our time when faced with a problem, to insure that we get to those remote ideas. Mednick (1962) proposed that creative individuals are better at finding remote ideas. His device for the assessment of creative thinking was the Remote Associates Test (RAT). The RAT contains analogies with three given elements, and one blank (e.g., River:Blood:Note:). Empirical investigations of the RAT indicate that it lacks discriminant validity, with scores that often are moderately correlated with scores from tests of convergent thinking or verbal ability. Still, Mednick's theory of remote associates is laudable in its offering testable predictions about creative cognition. An example is Mednick's notion that "the greater the number of instances in which an individual has solved problems with given materials in a certain manner, the less the likelihood of his attaining a creative solution using these materials" (p. 223). Later in this chapter the potential inhibitive impact of experience and expertise will be explored (also see Runco, Dow, & Smith 2006).

The RAT presents questions verbally and the examinee responds verbally. As such it is open to a verbal bias. Earlier experiential biases were defined in the discussion of IQ tests. A *verbal bias* is similar, at least in the sense that the resulting scores are influenced significantly by something (e.g., verbal ability) that is unrelated to the skill targeted by the test (e.g., creativity). Behaviorally, this means that all individuals with moderate or high verbal abilities will do well on the RAT, and all individuals with low verbal abilities will do poorly on the RAT, even though the RAT was designed to test associative and creative potential, and not verbal ability. Several investigations of creativity have empirically determined how the RAT can provide useful information about creative potential (Bowman & Jung-Beeman 2003; Martindale 1980).

ANALOGICAL THINKING AND METAPHOR

Not everyone agrees that original ideas are found via associative processes. Some theories emphasize analogies and analogical thinking instead (e.g., Gick & Holyoak 1980; Harrington 1981; Hofstadter 1985). There are many examples of analogies being used for discovery (e.g., Velcro and weeds, steam engines and tea kettles), but not all of these are based on fact. Many of these—including the oft-cited case of Kékulé's discovering the structure of the benzene model, Archimedes, or even the planetary parallel of atoms (Finke 1995; Gruber 1988; Welling 2007)—are based on the inferences of a biographer or the ex post facto introspection of the creator or discoverer him- or herself. In either case there are potential problems of memory, honesty, subjectivity, self-promotion, and bias.

BOX 1.4

METAPHORICAL THINKING AND CREATIVITY

Gibbs (1999) suggested that people use approximately four *frozen metaphors* and two *novel metaphors* in every minute of discourse. Frozen metaphors are essentially those that are not novel. Novel metaphors of course require some creative thinking. The interesting thing is that when metaphors are used, something is gained (understanding, insight), but there is a cost as well. Information and detail about the original material is always lost (Runco 1991a). No doubt the benefits to communication and insight usually outweigh the loss.

BOX 1.5

ANALOGIES AND ANALOGICAL THINKING

Many creative insights seem to have benefitted from analogical thinking. Here are some examples described in the creativity literature:

- Cotton gin (Eli Whitney saw a cat trying to catch a chicken through a fence)
- Telegraph (Samuel Morse ostensibly put stations in the telegraph after thinking about stagecoaches changing their horses periodically)
- Benzene ring (a snake biting its own tail)
- Oil pump (brine pump)
- Steam engine (Figure 1.2) (tea kettle)
- Underwater tunnels (worm tunnels)
- Velcro (burs or weeds).

Note: Analogical thinking was not necessarily involved in the ideas and inventions listed above. It is often cited in introspective reports, but these are suspect given their subjectivity. In some instances, the analogical thinking is simply inferred, but again, it may very well be apocryphal.

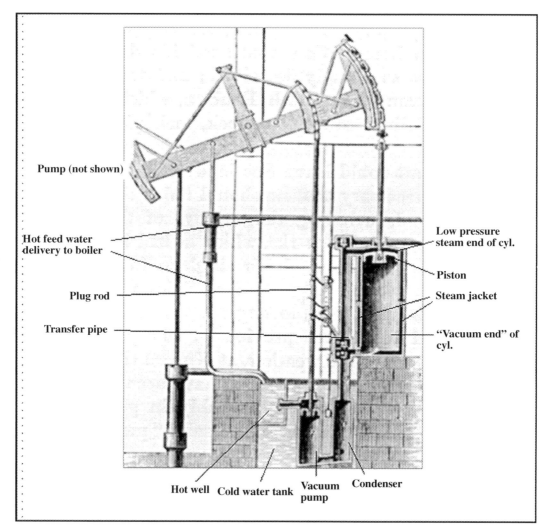

FIGURE 1.2   The steam engine was apparently conceived by Watt using analogical thinking. It is analogous to the tea kettle. *Source: Wikimedia Commons, http://en.wikipedia.org/wiki/File:Watt_steam_pumping_engine.JPG.*

Weisberg (1995a) identified a number of creative ideas and solutions where "information from a previous situation is transferred to the new situation that is analogous to the old" (p. 62). Even Picasso seems to have drawn heavily from previous work, some of which was his own, and some the work of other painters (Miller 1996; Weisberg 1995a, 1995b). Weisberg (1995b) suggested that most insights resulted from either a change in how the initial problem was interpreted, or from the use of an unconventional approach or representation of the problem.

Welling (2007) defined analogical thinking such that it "implies the transposition of a conceptual structure from one habitual context to another innovative context. The abstract relationship between the elements of one situation is similar to those found in the innovative context."

Dunbar (1995) focused on scientific analogies. He identified three different kinds:

- Local analogies (one part of one experiment is related to a second experiment).
- Regional analogies (involving "systems of relationships," which are applied in one domain and later used in a similar domain).
- Long-distance analogies (a system is found in one domain but applied in a dissimilar domain). Long-distance analogies might explain the benefits of what has also been called *marginality.* Freud, Darwin, and Piaget were each professionally marginal in the sense of being outside the mainstream. Marginality is discussed in detail in Chapter 7.

More recently, Dunbar (1997) offered evidence that, among research scientists, analogical ability is one of the more accurate predictors of creativity. Even more recently, Welling (2007) compared analogical, associative, and combinatorial thinking with abstraction. In doing so he pointed out that analogies are unique in that "no new cognitive structure is required" (Welling 2007). Some insights are dramatic shifts and can be explained in terms of cognitive restructuring. A person's thinking actually changes, and changes quickly, which is why insights may appear to be sudden. We will come back to this point later.

Welling (2007) also distinguished analogical thinking from combinatorial processes. In his words,

> combination is the merging of two or more concepts into one new idea. It differs from analogy in the sense that this operation requires the creation of a new conceptual structure. Concepts can be combined either spatially—concepts are applied simultaneously—or temporally in which the combination results from the sequential applications of existing ideas.

He cited Campbell's (1960) blind variation and selective retention model, Mednick's (1962) associative theory, Finke et al.'s (1992) geneplore theory, and Koestler's (1964) bisociation process as examples of combinatorial creative processes. Scott et al. (2005) reported a series of empirical studies on creative combinatorial processes.

Welling (2007) distinguished analogical thinking from *abstraction.* He defined abstraction as

> the discovery of any structure, regularity, pattern or organization that is present in a number of different perceptions that can be either physical or mental in nature. From this detection results. . . a conceptual entity, which defines the relationship between the elements it refers to on a lower, more concrete, level of abstraction.

This is not merely the identification of patterns. It is instead the creation of new concepts, new classes, new information. Welling gave Einstein's ideas of a continuity of space and time as an example of an abstraction. It represents a higher level of abstraction than had existed previously. Abstraction no doubt operates in the arts. Consider the work of Andy Warhol or Roy Lichtenstein, for example, each of whom stood back, so to speak, and asked the viewer to question "What is art?" Is it a tomato soup can, or as simple as a cartoon figure?

There are several issues. First is Welling's (2007) conclusion that "so-called high creativity is more readily associated with combination and abstraction operations, while everyday creativity is derived primarily from application and analogy operations." Clearly this is a simplification, but Welling admitted that "some contradictory findings can be explained by the fact that high creativity is often not the result of a single operation but results from a longer period in which several operations are put to use during the discovery process." The second issue reflects the possibility that "none of the [cognitive] operations generate entirely new knowledge because the result is always dependent on, or constructed with, previous knowledge. It may be tempting to assume that the ideas that result from abstraction are also the ones that are most impressive or revolutionary, but this is not the case." The more general question about analogical thinking concerns true originality. Is something truly original if it is similar to what came before it? We will return to this question in the last chapter of this book.

Many theories of creative thinking, including those that describe divergent thinking and associative processes, assume that creative ideas result from problem solving. Is creativity always a kind of problem solving?

TRANSFORMATIONAL CAPACITY

Creative insights may result from a capacity to transform one thing into another. Feldman and colleagues (1972) defined transformation as the "extent to which a given response represents the production of new forms rather than improves upon existing forms, the extent to which the apparent constraints of the stimulus situation are overcome, but overcome in highly appropriate fashion, and the extent to which the product generates additional thoughts in the observer." Feldman et al. (1972) attempted to operationalize transformation by creating an index of aesthetic reactions by judges for the Torrance Tests of Creative Thinking. Judges were instructed to concentrate on solutions that (a) seemed to break the constraints of the situation; (b) stimulated thinking and reflection about the possibilities generated by the response; and (c) caused them to accommodate their thinking to the "new reality" generated by the response. Participants included male and female middle-class high-school juniors ($n = 87$). Results indicated that about one in eight of the responses that were judged as "highly creative" were also judged to be transformational. Judges also identified the five participants who produced, overall, the most transformational ideas. Of these five students, three were also among the highest scores on the Torrance Test (ranked 2nd, 8th, and 11th for Torrance fluency + flexibility + originality score). These findings are interesting, but there were no external criteria of creative productivity in the study, so generalizations are not warranted.

Transformation was also recognized in the Structure of Intellect model (Guilford 1968; Michael 1999) and in a recent theory of *personal creativity* (Runco 2011). In the latter, creativity is the result of an individual's intentions, discretion, and capacity to construct original interpretations of experience. The last of these assumes a transformational capacity. Runco and Catalan (2013) took a first stab at testing this theory and operationalized transformation with four tests. The first was a test of visual divergent thinking. Individuals were asked to list things that a given visual image could represent. After they have plenty of time for this, they were given a distractor task, and then the same visual divergent thinking task. This time, however, examinees received explicit instructions to "Turn the figure upside down, make it bigger, or smaller, add something to it." In other words, they were asked to transform the stimulus and were given several methods for accomplishing it. They were asked to list ideas after the transformation, the assumption being that there would be a large discrepancy between the two testing conditions (before and after transformations) for individuals with high transformational capacities. A second measure used verbal divergent thinking tests and again had one experimental condition with only standard instructions ("Give as many ideas as you can") but a second condition (after a distractor task) that provided explicit instructions. These instructions provided tactics for transformation, and in particular for shifting one's perspective. Examples included "What would a child think in this situation? What would someone from history think? What would you think if you were a man instead of a woman (or woman instead of a man)?" Again, the premise was that there would be a large discrepancy between the standard and the explicit instructions conditions for individuals with notable transformational skills. The last task involved problem generation tasks (Runco et al. 1991a). Individuals were asked to list problems that could occur at work, at home, when dealing with other people, or result from one's financial situation. After problems were generated, individuals were asked to go back and choose one problem and then shift their perspective such that, instead of it being a problem, it was an opportunity! They were asked to list all of the good things that could occur in the situation which was initially viewed as problematic. This is presumably a very important type of creative transformation: turning a problem into a beneficial opportunity.

PROBLEM SOLVING

Cognitive theories of creativity often focus specifically on the problem-solving process. A *problem* can be defined as a situation with a goal and an obstacle. The individual wants or needs something (the goal) but must first deal with the obstacle. There are, of course, different kinds of problems. Divergent and convergent thinking were defined earlier, and they are easiest to contrast when you think about the two kinds of problems that elicit them. Open-ended problems allow divergent thinking, and closed-ended problems require convergent thinking. A similar distinction is between ill-defined problems and well-defined problems. Problems may also represent a dilemma, which is a specific kind of problem. If you have ever been "on the horns of a dilemma" (to repeat the old cliché), you know that it has two options (hence the prefix di-), neither of which completely resolves the problem. If you take one option—either one—you lose what the other option offers. Wakefield (1992) and numerous others have put great care into categorizing the many different kinds of problems.

Not everyone believes that creativity is merely a kind of problem solving. Some have taken the opposite point of view and suggested that problem solving is one kind of creativity. From this perspective there are creative acts and performances that are not attempts to solve a problem. It is not clear-cut, however, and it boils down to how "problem" is defined. After all, you might think that artists are not solving problems but are instead expressing themselves. Yet artists are sometimes attempting to find the best way to express themselves—and that implies that they have a problem. They may also be dealing psychologically with an issue from their past (Csikszentmihalyi 1988a; Jones, Runco, Dorinan, & Freeland 1997). Csikszentmihalyi referred to this as *abreactive catharsis*. Creative efforts are often cathartic, meaning that by being involved in the creative effort the individual releases tension.

A great deal depends on how "problems" are defined. Runco (1994a) stated,

> Creativity is by no means just problem solving. Creative thinking can help when solving problems (and finding and defining them), but there is more to it. Creative art (which is surely a tautology) is often

self-expressive, explorative, and aesthetic more than problem solving. Yet the separation of creativity from problem solving depends entirely on how *problem* is defined. If a problem is defined in terms of an obstacle between one's self and a goal, then much of activity of artists could be called problem solving. They may be solving the problem of finding a means to best express an idea or refine a technique. No one else would see it as a problem, especially because it is the artist's preferred activity, and he or she may be smiling and having a grand old time while doing the art. It may not look like an effort; the artist may not appear to have any problems whatsoever. This is the opposite case of what was described in the preceding paragraph. The problems that others saw were not felt as problems by the creator, but here no one sees the problem except the creator! This latter case is often described as *problem finding*. Problems are all that way; they are all personal interpretations. They are not givens, not objective entities.

This also shows the value of creativity—it is enormously helpful for solving problems but leaves us with a necessary ambiguity: creativity is sometimes a form of problem solving, but sometimes not.

Guilford (1965) offered a slightly different view: "I have come to the conclusion that wherever there is a genuine problem there is some novel behavior on the part of the problem solver, hence there is some degree of creativity. Thus, I am saying that all problem solving is creative. I leave the question open as to whether all creative thinking is problem solving."

It is probably best to accept that not all problem solving requires creativity, and creative performance is not always a solution to a problem. However, the work on problem solving does contribute to our understanding of some creative performances. This is especially true with the recognition that problems may be operationalized as well-defined or ill-defined, with the latter more common in the real world. This simply means that problems in the natural environment are often a bit ambiguous. They are not like problems we encounter in school, for instance, or on a test. Tests usually present problems in a very clear fashion in order to insure that the examinee focuses on the right goal. But in the natural environment problems may need to be identified as such, and defined in a workable fashion. Theories of problem *finding* take identification and definition into account. As we will see, it may be that problem finding can be separated from problem solving, and yet sometimes the quality of solutions depends on the quality of the problem.

PROBLEM FINDING

Nearly always, something must occur before a problem is ready to be solved. As was just suggested, sometimes the problem itself must be identified. This may sound silly—I know many of my problems slap me in the face and will not seem to go away!—but at times we may just have a hazy feeling that "something is wrong," but we do not know what it is. Indeed, anxiety and stress have both been interpreted as indicators that we have problems and concerns, even if we are not thinking about them (May 1996). Other times we think we know what the problem is, but we are wrong. (Why am I thinking of problems that occur in relationships?) We may have defined "the problem" too generally or too specifically, and therefore have not really identified the problem. It is almost as if we have not located the obstacle, at least not accurately.

Various problem-finding skills have been identified, including problem construction, problem identification (where a task is simply recognized but not manipulated or operationalized), problem definition (where the task is prepared for solution), problem discovery, problem perception, and problem generation (Getzels & Smilansky 1983; Mumford et al. 1991; Runco 1994a). Once again it may be best to use a continuum, with problems that are presented to us at one extreme (no identification or definition required), problems that do require discovery at the other extreme, and various moderate possibilities in between (Runco et al. 2006; Wakefield 1992).

A large body of research now indicates that individual differences exist, with some persons exceptionally capable at identifying or defining problems, but perhaps not as good at solving problems. Other people may be very good at solving problems, but the problems need to be given to them in a very unambiguous fashion. Interestingly, most people studying or experiencing problem finding believe that it is more important than skill in problem solving. Getzels (1975), for example, claimed that the quality of a problem determines the quality of a solution. Einstein seemed to hold this opinion. He often is quoted as saying: "The formulation of a problem is often more essential than its solution…. To raise new questions, new possibilities, to regard old problems from a new angle, requires imagination and marks real advance in science" (Einstein & Infeld 1938, p. 83). Not long after that, Wertheimer (1945/1982) pointed out that "often in great discoveries the most important thing is that a certain question is found. Envisaging, putting the productive question is often a more important, often a greater achievement than the solution of a set question" (p. 123). Guilford (1950) included "sensitivity to problems" in this seminal presidential speech presentation to the American Psychological Association in 1949, and Torrance (1962) emphasized "the process of *sensing gaps* or disturbing missing elements and formulating hypotheses" in his definition of creativity (p. 16, emphasis added).

In the arts, problem finding may be viewed as *problem expression*. Here the problem is not extrinsic, but more a matter of finding a way to capture a feeling or need. Recall here the problems (pun intended) involved in defining "a problem." The example given earlier was of an artist who might not be aware of the problem being addressed in his or her artwork. The work itself might seem to be exploratory, self-expression, or an attempt to refine technique. Yet if it is difficult to find the best expression, there is a problem.

Then again, artists are sometimes well aware that they are pinpointing problems. The novelist Kurt Vonnegut Jr., for example, felt "an urgency to be a good citizen, to draw people's attention to things, to function as a canary in a coal mine" (in Ulin 2005, p. E1). Ulin rephrased this and declared that the "writer's obligation [is] to make connections, to offer insights, to ask essential questions, *even (or especially) if the answer is to remain unknown*." The emphasis is added to that quotation because it confirms the idea that problem finding may be separate from problem solving.

TECHNOLOGY AND CREATIVITY: THE REAL CREATIVITY CRISIS

Much has been written about computers and creativity, and lately more and more is showing up to explore the impact of technology more generally, the Internet, and social media.

Technology contributes to life and culture advance in many different ways. It often makes a job easier to complete, and it expands human capacities in that it can magnify, and especially remember, so well. Certainly one of the best

(Continued)

things about technology is that computers, phones, and other devices contain memories—so we do not need to remember as much. In Chapter 12 we will see that technology sometimes "bites back," but realistically we should expect both good and bad to come from the Internet, social media, and technology.

Florida (2002) suggested that technology is one reason why certain places are more creative than others. The other reasons are talent and tolerance. Keep in mind that Florida's ideas are based on one kind of creativity. It might be called "big C" creativity, though that label can be quite misleading (Merrotsy 2013; Runco in press) and should probably be avoided. But the main point is that technology may be useful for particular kinds of creativity, including that of professionals, in design (they often use computers), science, and similar fields that depend heavily on computers and other forms of technology.

It may be that technology does not help "little c" creativity (another dubious label). This is nonprofessional creativity—the creativity of children, amateurs, and hobbyists.

Technology creates problems, as well. In fact, Runco (2013a) postulated that technology is causing a "creativity crisis" in America. He called this the "real creativity crisis" because Kim (2011) had sounded that alarm previously. Runco reinterpreted Kim's empirical findings and felt they were troubling but not of a crisis magnitude. Since technology is omnipresent, if it does indeed undermine creative behavior, then Runco felt that was a real crisis.

How does technology undermine and inhibit creativity? First, it emphasizes extrinsic concerns more than the intrinsic that are so important for creativity. It also imposes those extrinsic reactions ("Likes," "Comments," and so on) in a very powerful and quick fashion, which means that they are likely to have an impact. This of course relates to social media more than any other part of technology. It may also be a problem that the Internet provides factual information so easily, but that information is often lacking quality control. It used to be that there were editors and the like ("gatekeepers") who monitored what was published. This is why there is peer-review for academic journals. But it is all lacking in the Internet. Go ahead and Google something! But keep in mind, "garbage in, garbage out!"

A final problem is that the Internet is so compelling that it can keep us from exercising mindfulness. That means that we are less likely to attain the cognitive state that is the most conducive to creative thinking.

Are any of these real problems? The frequency of usage certainly suggests that they might be. Weinstein et al. (in press) reported that "In 2012, 63% of teens report texting every day, whereas in 2006 only roughly one quarter of teens even used text messaging as a way to communicate" and "The median American teen (14–17 years of age) sends 100 text messages per day." Weinstein and Katie felt that these figures imply "domain changes," given that youth are sending texts and email and not on the telephone or writing on paper nearly as much as they used to. They did see benefits, however:

> Online galleries offer unprecedented access to even the most renowned masterpieces. A simple Google search instantly produces art ranging from anonymous displays of graffiti to Klimt's The Kiss, providing contemporary teens with an impressive range of models from which to draw inspiration.... In addition, new technological

(Continued)

tools can facilitate the actualization of artistic vision. Digital programs for creating and editing art are available, many free of charge, and provide both novice and expert artists with myriad editing tools. Corel Painter 12, for example, is a digital art software that "opens up a world of creativity" thanks to "progressive drawing tools," including digitized paints, oils, and watercolors. … Graphics tablets facilitate speed drawing, speed painting and new methods for re-creating images like television cartoon characters with near perfection. Apps such as ArtStudio Procreate, and Instagram allow artists to create and edit work on-the-go with their cellphones or iPads…. Consequently, young people not only have a wealth of images from which to draw inspiration for their creations, but also unparalleled tools to help them create.

Problem finding has also been cited in the debate about computers and creativity (Box 1.6, Figure 1.3). A number of attempts have been made to program computers to be creative, and in fact they can frequently find the same high-quality solutions as humans (Simon 1988). This may not be truly creative, however, because unlike humans, computers need to be given a problem; they lack problem-finding skills.

Does a creative solution require a creative problem? Problems can be evaluated and their quality determined. Some can be evaluated for their originality—just as ideas are evaluated with divergent thinking tasks—in terms of statistical infrequency (Okuda et al. 1991; Runco & Chand 1995). Box 1.7 contains example tasks from the research on problem generation.

BOX 1.6

COMPUTERS AND CREATIVITY

Computers can solve problems, at least certain problems, quite well. They are fast and hold huge amounts of information. If creativity is simply a kind of problem solving, it would appear that computers can be creative (Simon 1995). Ohm's Law, Kepler's Law, and various other laws and discoveries in the hard sciences have been rediscovered by computers, once they are given the task and relevant information. Boden (1999) presented a thoughtful overview of the various computer programs.

Computers also offer useful metaphors. Consider a computer metaphor, with a distinction between hardware and software. Computer hardware is, of course, the computer itself, including the central processing unit (CPU). In humans, hardware can be viewed as the nervous system, and in particular both the central and peripheral systems. Hardware also would include specific receptors, such as the rods and cones of the eyes, and more centrally, neurons. What, then, is psychological software? The answer to this takes us to a definition of cognition. Cognition represents the software of the human brain. It represents the programs, or in cognitive terms, the concepts, scripts, structures, and processes of thinking.

Using this metaphor, individual differences can be taken as indicating that different persons have different programs available to them. Other "metaphors of mind" are given later in this chapter.

FIGURE 1.3 Can computers be creative?

Certainly, we can also take the long view, as is often done in research on famous creators. We can let posterity decide. Einstein seemed to have identified an excellent problem, for instance, as did Picasso, Freud, Frank Lloyd Wright, and other luminaries. We may be impressed by the solutions they offered to big problems, but in actuality they may have identified new problems, or redefined existing problems, as well as offering creative solutions. Curiously, individuals who only identify important problems but do not solve them are

---

BOX 1.7

EXAMPLE PROBLEM GENERATION TASKS

- List different problems in school that are important to you. You may write down problems about the campus itself, classes, professors, policies, classmates, or whatever. Try to be specific, and take your time. Think of as many problems as you can!

- Now list problems at work that are important to you. You may write down any problems about your boss, co-workers, clients, policies, or whatever. Be specific, and keep in mind that the more ideas, the better. Take your time!

probably much less likely to attain eminence when compared with individuals who successfully solve noteworthy problems.

STAGE MODELS OF CREATIVE COGNITION

The idea of problem finding implies that creative thinking can be delineated and its ingredients isolated. This is a debatable point, though entirely consistent with various lines of cognitive research (Shepard 1982). The same assumption of delineation led Wallas (1926) long ago to a four-stage description of the creative process. Wallas suggested that the creative process involves "preparation," "incubation," "illumination," and "verification." The preparation stage would include problem identification and problem definition, as well as information gathering and the like. The inclusion of verification is noteworthy in that it allows the creative individual to test and tinker. With creativity requiring both originality *and* effectiveness, verification is probably vitally important. It may be that problems are made the most effective during some sort of verification. The more recent extensions of this stage model have included *recursion*, the idea being that the individual may revisit early stages and cycle through the process as much as is needed. It is not a strictly linear affair.

The second stage, incubation, involves the unconscious processing of information. This is a relatively common requirement in models of the creative process (Rothenberg 1990; Smith & Amner 1997). Incubation is probably often recognized because it explains how progress can be made on a task, even if we are not consciously thinking of the problem. It is usually explained such that associative processes are at work and are free from the censorship of the conscious mind.

Incubation is not just respected by psychoanalysts and people who like to take naps. Guilford (1979), a psychometrician, respected incubation. He wrote, "My own hypothesis is aimed at accounting for the actual progress during an apparently inactive incubation interval. It attributes progress of this kind to transformation of information" (p. 2). Guilford felt that incubation allows promising associations to be formed by providing the time necessary for the cognitive transformations. Not surprisingly, then, Guilford directed his empirical efforts at the intervals between ideas given in response to divergent thinking tasks (Fulgosi & Guilford 1968, 1973).

Smith and Dodds (1999, p. 39) defined incubation as "a stage of creative problemsolving in which a problem is temporarily put aside after a period of initial work on the problem." They offered several explanations for the benefit of incubation:

- Intermittent conscious work occurs during the incubation problem.
- Incubation allows for a recovery from fatigue that has resulted from conscious work.
- Inappropriate mental states are forgotten and therefore no longer interfere with the problem solving or thinking.
- Remote associates may be found more easily.
- An individual is able to find and assimilate chance or serendipitous hints or data during incubation.
- Associations are broader and more extensive because the conscious mind has relaxed or is being focused elsewhere.

The third stage in Wallas' (1926) model, illumination, is best known because it leads to an "a-ha" experience (Gruber 1981b, 1988). Illumination is also known as *insight*. Importantly, most often insights are singular. We may have a problem, and one solution pops into our heads, like a lightbulb being turned on (Figure 1.4). In that light (another pun!), insightful thinking is unlike divergent thinking, where various ideas are generated. Insight usually leads to one solution. Take a look at the insight problem from Schilling (2005), given below, the nine-dot problem (Figure 1.5), and the two-string problem (Figure 1.6).

FIGURE 1.4   The lightbulb is often used to represent illumination or insight. The "a-ha" feels sudden but may, in fact, be protracted.

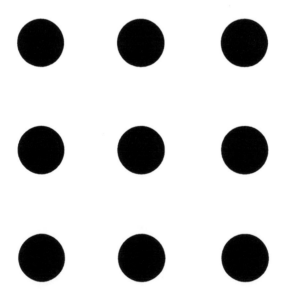

FIGURE 1.5   The nine-dot insight problem. Can you connect all dots with 3 straight connected lines? How about 2 lines, or 1?

FIGURE 1.6   The two-string insight problem. How can the strings be tied together if the person cannot reach them both?

EXAMPLE OF AN INSIGHT PROBLEM (FROM SCHILLING 2005)

Two men walking through the desert discover a third man, lying on the sand, dead. The dead man has a small pack that contains fresh food and water, a larger pack on his back, and a large ring on his index finger. Puzzled about the cause of his death, the two men proceed onward. Later, one of the men accidentally drops his handkerchief while mopping his brow, and as it flutters to the earth he suddenly realizes how the man had probably died: his parachute had broken, and he had plummeted to the ground. This example demonstrates how a partial representation with a gap (a dead man with a pack, food, water, and a large ring) may be suddenly filled in a way that completes the coherent structure of the representation (the large pack contained a parachute, and the ring was from its pull cord).

Insight is often contrasted with *trial and error*. Trial and error is step-by-step problem solving, where errors are made but corrected, each representing a small step forward, toward the solution. Insight, in contrast, is sudden, or at least feels that way. That is why a lightbulb is the common symbol of an insight. There is a sudden illumination. Yet insight may not actually depend on a discontinuous process. There is some controversy about that. Weisberg (1986), for example, wrote, "there seems very little reason to believe that solutions to novel problems come about in leaps of insight. At every step of the way, the process involves a small movement away from what is known" (p. 50).

It could be that insight just feels sudden because the processing that led up to it is beyond our awareness (Bowers et al. 1995; Runco 2006b). Bowers et al. found semantic similarities between guesses and answers, the idea being that on the semantic level there is continuity. Put differently, the unconscious processing leading up to an insight is smooth rather than discontinuous. The suddenness is just in the awareness of the solution, not in the discovery or construction of it. I recently attempted to describe the possibility that the processes occurring during incubation are simply beyond the comprehension of our conscious mind:

> the use of preconscious or unconscious processes allows the individual to utilize different reasoning processes, processes that, by virtue of their being beyond conscious awareness, are able to value and explore those things that allow original thinking. In this light the preconscious and unconscious are not actually irrational; they just have a rationality of their own (Runco 2006b, p. 109).

This view would help explain intuition, hunches, and the "feeling of knowing" that occurs when we know something but not *how* we know it (Metcalfe 1986). We may know something, or have a good idea, but the idea is in a form that is incompatible with conscious conventional logic or rationality. But we do have a good idea and we react emotionally to it, hence the feeling of knowing.

Wertheimer (1991) felt that insight represented a "discovery of the applicability of an existing schema to a new situation" (p. 190). More recently, Schilling (2005) defined insights in terms of "unexpected connection between disparate mental representations." She identified five explanations for insight, each of which involves some kind of unconscious process. Insight might occur in one of the following situations:

- A schema is completed. Schema refer to cognitive structures and information that is personally and meaningfully organized.
- Visual information is reorganized.
- A mental block is overcome.
- A "problem analog" is found.
- Information is randomly recombined.

The last of these may not seem all that scientific, and it is controversial. Nobel laureate Herbert Simon (1973), for example, suggested that our thinking follows systematic, logical, and rational processes, much like a computer searching all possible combinations. Not surprisingly, Simon was cited earlier in this chapter as the leading proponent of the idea that computers can be creative. The other side of the debate is probably more popular. Campbell's (1960) theory of blind variation and selective retention, for instance, is widely cited. It assumes that the variations of thought (the options considered) are blindly generated. Many others hold similar views about the random or at least asystematic nature of creative thinking (Simonton 2007). Keep in mind, however, that we are talking about one stage, and not the entire process. Part of the creative thinking process could draw on random subprocesses, whereas other stages might be entirely systematic and would thus be computable. Consider the various historical descriptions of thinking presented in Boxes 1.8 and 1.9.

RESTRUCTURING AND INSIGHT

Insight is often explained by the concept of *restructuring* (Ohlsson 1984a, 1984b). This occurs when the individual initially does not understand something because he or she is relying on one representation of the problem, but then the individual changes that

BOX 1.8

WILLIAM JAMES

William James (1880), often considered to be America's first psychologist, foresaw much of modern-day psychology. Here is his description of thinking, which suggests that ideas may come together for unexpected and unconscious reasons:

Instead of thoughts of concrete things patiently following one another in a beaten track of habitual suggestion, we have the most abrupt cross-cuts and transitions from one idea to another, the most rarefied abstractions and discriminations, the most unheard of combination of elements, the subtlest associations of analogy; in a word, we seem suddenly introduced into a seething cauldron of ideas, where everything is fizzling and bobbling about a state of bewildering activity, where partnerships can be joined or loosened in an instant, treadmill routine is unknown, and the unexpected seems only law. (p. 456, quoted by Schilling, 2005)

This is fairly consistent with the view that insights arise when the individual is able to explore various combinations of ideas, perhaps in a random fashion.

BOX 1.9

LOGIC AND CREATIVITY

Some forms of logic make creative thinking difficult. Deduction and induction, for example, sometimes constrain thinking such that it must move in a particular direction. This is only the case when logic demands one solution, however. Deduction and induction are both inferential processes, and as such may allow the individual to "go beyond the given information" (Bruner 1962a) and, perhaps, create something anew. Pribram (1999, p. 216) tied creative thinking to abduction, and in fact defined abduction by quoting the early psychologist Charles S. Peirce. Abduction is "the inspiration that produces the creative act" (Peirce, quoted by Pribram 1999).

And of course it is possible that all creative thinking requires some sort of logic, though perhaps it is logic operating on a preconscious, preverbal level.

There are different kinds of logic:

- **Deduction** involves reasoning from general (e.g., abstract concept or theory) to specific.
- **Induction** involves reasoning from specific(s) to general.
- **Transduction** involves reasoning about one object or case based on objects or cases within the same level (e.g., "That sports car is really fast, and there is another sports car! It must be fast too!").
- **Abduction** is "the inspiration that produces the creative act" (Peirce, quoted by Pribram 1999).
- **Eduction.** Spearman's (1927) description of the process is used to infer relationship among pieces of information.

representation—restructures it—such that it takes new information into account or in some way allows a better understanding and insight. (Representations are the cognitive analogs to understanding. You might say that information or experience is represented in the mind, and thus a person has representations.) Suppose you build a model of something out of Tinkertoys. Your model may be a map of some kind, or it may in fact represent some object. Suppose, further, that you discover something new about the place you have mapped or the thing you have represented. You might remove a few Tinkertoy pieces and add a few. You do not need to start from scratch, however, and in fact the restructuring may be fairly quick. Quick but dramatic changes are possible: Perhaps you built a model of a tall building but then decide it needs to be even taller. You add long legs to the structure. That may require very little work, but the result is dramatically different. The building may double in height. Restructuring is a bit like changing your model, and sometimes fairly quick changes offer a dramatically different representation.

The idea of restructuring has a long history (e.g., Duncker 1945; Kohler 1925; Wertheimer 1945, Wertheimer 1982). The concept is often tied to *gestalt* theory. The gestalt term for it is *Umstrukurierung.* A gestalt is essentially the result; it is a meaningful whole, as in a whole and complete understanding. Gestalt psychology has been used to describe the perceptual process, the key idea being that humans have a tendency to make sense of our experience and can often construct meaning from partial information. We may perceive a few stars, for instance, but impose meaning such that we see a bear, a Greek god, a dipper (big or little!). Our perceptual system completes the gestalt. More clinically oriented gestalt psychologists (Perls 1978) felt that humans have a need for meaning and are unhappy without it. We can, however, impose meaning on our lives—even when there is little to suggest it! A clinician will often help a client or patient find meaning and thereby happiness. This might even require an insight in the same sense that concept is used in the problem solving and creativity literature. The client's new understanding may be obtained quickly but with dramatic results.

An alternative explanation uses information processing theory and the idea of linear search (Newell & Simon 1972; Ohlsson 1984a; Weisberg & Alba 1981). As Ohlsson (p. 65) described this perspective, "to solve a problem is to proceed step-wise through the space of alternatives, until an action sequence is found which leads from the problem to the solution." Weisberg and Alba (1981) tested subjects with three insight problems—including the famous nine-dot problem (see Figure 1.5)—and concluded that the "spontaneous reorganization [restructuring or insight] of experience does not occur during problem solving" (p. 326). They rejected the ideas of insight, restructuring, and fixation.

Ohlsson (1984a, 1984b) suggested that the gestalt and the information-processing perspectives are compatible with one another. She acknowledged that the gestalt view is not as testable as it should be, for good science, and that it does not really help us to understand individual differences—or as she put it, "good" and "bad" thinking (Ohlsson 1984a, p. 72). Individual differences may be explained in terms of previous experience (Epstein 1990).

Schilling (2005) offered a *small network* explanation for insight. Here insight is defined as:

> a substantive shift or augmentation of a representation due to the addition or changing of either nodes (elements of information, or sets of information) or links (connections or relationships between nodes of information); ... such a shift may often be the result of forging connections along a path that the individual perceives as atypical; and ... the perceived significance or magnitude of the shift may be a function of both the unexpectedness of the connection, and the magnitude of change it creates in the network of representations.

Schilling relied on *small network theory*, which had been around since the 1950s but really came of age in the 1970s (cf. Watts & Strogatz 1998).

Insights seem to be quick and spontaneous. That is one reason the lightbulb often is used to characterize an "a-ha" moment: It illuminates quickly, seemingly all at once. Yet the evidence suggests that insights may actually be *protracted* (Gruber 1981b; Gruber 1988; Wallace 1991). They are not instantaneous but instead develop over time. Gruber (1981a, 1988) found protraction in a number of scientific insights, and Wallace (1991) found much the same in the writing of Dorothy Richardson, one of the writers who developed the "stream of consciousness" style of fiction.

EXPERIENCE, EXPERTISE, INFORMATION, AND INSIGHT

Wish I didn't know now what I didn't know then. *Bob Seger, Against the Wind*

The protraction of insight intimates that it may depend on information and experience. Then again, insights can be the most difficult when the individual has a great deal of experience in the problem domain (Wertheimer 1982). The individual may experience *einstellung* (Luchins 1942), which means there is a kind of mental block to one's thinking that keeps one from finding new and original ideas. It is similar to the *functional fixedness* that occurs when the individual sticks with previous experience and conventional thinking about the problem or situation at hand (Duncker 1945).

It is a bit puzzling that experts can sometimes understand things that others cannot, but at the same time may have difficulty thinking in an original fashion. There is a cost to expertise (Rubenson & Runco 1995). Langer (1989) described it as a blindness of knowledge.

The benefits of expertise usually are explained in terms of knowledge. Experts develop huge knowledge bases, much of it domain-specific knowledge, but at least as important is that they have an enormous number of interconnections among the bits and details of their knowledge. Experts' domain-specific knowledge, apparently, is also automatically activated when solving problems within their domains. The knowledge is probably better organized than that of a novice, perhaps being hierarchical, with concrete knowledge at the bottom of the hierarchy and abstract knowledge at the top. Keep in mind (no pun intended this time) that these characteristics of experts' knowledge are domain specific. Experts tend to outperform novices within their domains but not outside of them. Just think: your English might very well be better than Einstein's, or your mathematical skills better than those of Picasso.

Experts often make assumptions, because they know so much. This can preclude original and creative thinking. For that reason Piaget (see Gruber 1996) and Skinner (1956) both recommended reading *outside* one's own area of research. This kind of reading could easily give the individual a fresh perspective on his or her own field, and it could help the expert to avoid the saturation or rigidity that can result from having too much experience (Martinsen 1995).

Moving from one field to another creates a kind of professional *marginality*, and many famous creators have done this intentionally. Piaget himself did this, drawing from biology in his work on cognitive development. Freud drew heavily from physiology in his theory of psychoanalysis. Darwin studied geology extensively but contributed the most to evolutionary biology.

Martinsen (1995) and Epstein (1990) both demonstrated that specific experiences and information can either help or hinder insightful thinking. Martinsen's work suggests that for many of us there is an optimal level of information that can help us think creatively, but beyond that our thinking becomes less insightful.

INTUITION

No man clearly understands the sources of his own creativity. *Boring (1971, p. 55)*

I cannot always distinguish my own thoughts from those I read, because what I read becomes the very substance and texture of my mind. *Helen Keller (from Piechowski 1993a, p. 467)*

Intuition is probably the best example of unconscious processing. Anecdotal reports often pointed to intuition in creative insights, and case studies occasionally mention the famous person's intuitive capacity. In his study of Albert Einstein and Henri Poincare, Miller (1992) concluded that "aesthetics and intuition are notions that can be discussed in a well defined manner and are essential to scientific research as are mental imagery in descriptive and depictive modes."

EINSTEIN ON INTUITION

Einstein was very clear about the role of intuition and the scientific method. In his words, "from a systematic theoretical point of view, we may imagine the process of evolution of an empirical science to be a continuous process of induction. ...but this point of view by no means embraces the whole of the actual process; for it blurs over the important part played by intuition and deductive thought in the development of an exact science" (1961, p. 123).

Similar empirical evidence for intuition was provided by Hasenfus et al. (1983). They demonstrated that college students can infer the similarities among works of music, architecture, and art from different periods of history. Even if a student has not studied art history or the like, he or she may very well be able to see that Baroque music is related to Baroque architecture and painting, and that Classical art is related to Classical architecture and music. The students did not know how they know, but they did know.

The large body of research on insight is also relevant. As previously discussed, Gruber (1981b) demonstrated that creative insights frequently are protracted, which as just noted means that they cover a period of time. They are not sudden or immediate and quick. Instead, the creator is working with the problem or issue, albeit often on an unconscious level. As a matter of fact, that is what all of this research suggests—that the unconscious is very actively involved in many expressions of creativity, including those involving intuition or insight.

Langan-Fox and Shirley (2003) found discussions of intuition throughout history, going back at least to Spinosa, who felt that intuition was "the highest form of knowledge" (Langan-Fox & Shirley 2003, p. 3). Kant felt that it was an internal process "supplied by the mind itself" (Langan-Fox & Shirley 2003, p. 3). Bergson contrasted it with intelligence and felt it was more of an expression of instinct (cf. Barron 1995).

Remarkably, intuition can be studied using experimental methods. Bowers et al. (1990) did just that and concluded that intuition was an example of informed judgment. They described two stages involved in intuition: first is the guiding stage where a coherence or structure is unconsciously recognized and used, and second is an integrative stage where the coherence makes its way to the level of consciousness. The transition between the two stages very frequently leads to the sudden "a-ha" feeling. It may also explain a sudden closure, such as the ones seen in tasks of gestalt perceptions.

Bowers et al. (1990) developed several tests of intuition. First is the Dyads of Triads task (DOT). The second is the Waterloo Gestalt Closure Task. A third task is the Accumulated Clues Task or ACT. The ACT contains 16 items, each with a clue word that is an associate of the solution word. The last measure was a *faith in intuition* self-report scale. Items on this, as the name implies, attempted to capture an individual's confidence in his or her own feelings and decision making underlying actions. An example item asked about the individual's reliance on "gut feelings." A second example asked individuals to rate how frequently they have a feeling that they are right or wrong even if they cannot explain why.

The Myers–Briggs Type Indicator (MBTI; Myers & McCaulley 1985) was developed from Jung's (1964) work on feeling, thinking, sensing, and intuition. The MBTI asks examinees how they usually act or feel. It often is interpreted as behavioral rather than a cognitive measure of intuition. The MBTI intuition scale assesses the individual's perception of "possibilities, patterns, symbols, and abstractions" (Myers & McCaulley 1985, p. 207).

Briggs (2000) and Holton (1973) implied that intuition plays a strong role in the sciences. They referred to *themata,* which are essentially subjective themes and guides within the thinking and work of a scientist. *Nuances* may also play a role in scientific discovery, and they too are highly subjective guides, much like a gut feeling. They are not temporary, however, so the creator may experience a stable feeling guiding his or her work. Apparently nuances give the individual a basis for judging the worth of new ideas—his or her own, or ideas of another. They are in a sense criteria, and they allow the individual to judge the appropriateness and originality of new ideas (i.e., decide whether or not new ideas extend a line of thought in a worthy direction). These possibilities are entirely consistent with the larger cognitive sciences, and in particular with theories of tacit knowledge, implicit theories, *zeitgeist*, and "knowing more than we think we know" (Wilson 1975).

UNCONSCIOUS PROCESSES AND CREATIVE COGNITION

Theories of incubation and intuition suggest that there are benefits to the unconscious. One benefit has not yet been discussed, namely the possibility of reconciling opposites, contradictions, and seemingly incompatible ideas. Arieti (1976) referred to this kind of creative thinking as a *magic synthesis.* Similarly, Koestler (1964) felt that creative insights resulted from the bisociative process, the key feature of which is that discrepant ideas are synthesized. Interestingly,

Hoppe and Kyle (1990) used this theory to describe why the two hemispheres of the brain are both required for creative thinking. The associative view of creative thinking (Guilford 1979; Mednick 1962) also assumes an operative unconscious (see Suler 1980 for a review).

THE IDEA OF THE UNCONSCIOUS

The influence of the unconscious was recognized long before Freud. Tolstoy recognized it in *War and Peace* (Boring 1971, p. 55), as did Francis Galton, Charles Darwin, and Herbert Spencer (also see *The*

Unconscious Before Freud by Whyte, 1983). Admittedly, Freud most carefully delineated the unconscious and tested it in clinical studies. He was far more detailed and objective than his predecessors.

Rothenberg's (1990, 1999) research on creative cognition has implications for the unconscious. He has defined and manipulated two relevant processes, one labeled *Janusian*, named after the Roman God Janus, who could look in two directions at once (Figure 1.7), and the *homospatial* process, whereby two objects occupy one space. Rothenberg's experimental research demonstrates clear benefits to these processes, as well as individual differences in the capacity for them. Rothenberg cited existential philosophy (absurdity of life, but the possibility of happiness) and the Heisenberg Uncertainty Principle (the location and speed of a particle cannot both be determined) as exemplifying insights resulting from a creator's thinking about contradictions and opposites. I would add that chaos theory also exemplifies this, for chaos is "an orderly disorder" (Gleick 1987, p. 15).

Children are probably unable to employ these processes. They certainly have difficulty with dialectical thought (Smolucha & Smolucha 1986), and it resembles Janusian

FIGURE 1.7   The Roman God Janus, who could look in two directions at once.

and homospatial processes in the sense that opposites are considered simultaneously. The dialectical process starts with one perspective (a thesis) and the opposite perspective (an antithesis), and eventually produces a mixture of the two (a synthesis), even though the thesis and antithesis are ostensibly incompatible. That is no easy trick to bring opposites together! It is cognitively demanding and, not surprisingly, probably not possible until late adolescence (Smolucha & Smolucha 1986).

Componential Theories

Componential theories, like stage theories, delineate creative cognition. Componential theories do not require a stage-by-stage or step-by-step movement, and in general components are not as interdependent as stages. Usually, in stage models the assumption is that one stage must precede the next stage. Componential models allow for interactions but do not require this same kind of linear progression. Amabile (1990), for instance, presented a componential theory containing (a) task motivation, (b) domain-relevant skills, and (c) creativity-relevant processes. Motivation is often intrinsic (see Chapter 9), though it is for some people, or some of the time, extrinsic as well. Domain-relevant skills are often technical (e.g., knowing how to conduct research, for a scientist). Creativity-relevant skills are fairly general (e.g., a cognitive style that fits with a domain and tolerates originality and exploration).

Sternberg and Lubart (1996) proposed an investment model, with six kinds of resources: intelligence, knowledge, cognitive style, motivation, personality, and environmental context. They further defined each of the resources. Intellectual abilities, for example, allow synthesis, analysis, and a practical ability (e.g., selling the new idea).

Woodman and Schoenfeldt (1990) described the creative process as dependent on an interaction between antecedent conditions, personal characteristics, and situational circumstances. This model is described in Chapter 5 as it applies directly to the organizational setting.

Mumford et al. (1991) described problem construction, information encoding, category search, a specification of the most appropriate categories, combination and recombination of categories, idea evaluation, idea implementation, and process monitoring.

Finke (1997) outlined the *geneplore* model (*gen-* from generate and *-plore* from explore). The first phase generates a preinventive form, which is a kind of loosely formulated initial cognitive structure. These are then evaluated, extended, or elaborated, and tested during the exploration phase.

Runco and Chand (1995) presented a *two-tiered componential theory*. The first tier contains what might be called influences on the process, namely motivation (intrinsic and extrinsic) and knowledge (declarative/factual/conceptual and procedural). The second tier contains problem-finding skills, ideation, and evaluation.

Each of the components in the two-tiered model can be subdivided. Problem finding, for instance, represents a family of skills, including those mentioned earlier (e.g., problem identification, problem definition). Ideation also represents a family of skills, as is indicated by Guilford's (1968) and Torrance's (1995) theories of divergent thinking. Most often ideational fluency, ideational originality, and ideational flexibility are recognized.

Several aspects of this model should be emphasized. First is that the flexibility just mentioned may be particularly useful in creative thinking, given what was said earlier about functional fixedness. Flexibility will help the individual avoid ruts and fixedness. In addition to ideational flexibility, there is also a benefit to flexibility as manifested in the use of a "wide repertoire of cognitive styles" (Guastello et al. 1998, p. 77). Cognitive styles are defined in Box 1.10.

A second noteworthy aspect of the two-tier model is that it defines information and motivational influences on the creative thinking process. As noted earlier, motivation can be intrinsic (personally meaningful) or extrinsic (e.g., incentives and rewards). The influence of motivation must be recognized, for individuals will not put the effort into solving a problem unless they are somehow motivated to do so.

Information, which may be declarative (conceptual or factual) or procedural, is relevant in many ways, as is implied by the impact of experience on insight and the earlier discussion about experience. At least as important is that information can provide the individual with the know-how to be creative and solve problems in a creative fashion. Know-how seems like a casual term, but it is perfectly apt for procedural information. It reflects knowledge about how to get something done (in this case, how to find original and creative ideas and solutions). Another way to put this is that procedural knowledge provides *tactics* for creative thinking (Box 1.11).

Tactics depend on *metacognition*. In literal terms, metacognition is cognition about cognition. It reflects the individual's thinking about his or her own thinking. Metacognition allows the individual to monitor his or her own actions. It reflects the intentional actions taken to enhance one's own creativity. Tactics are highly practical precisely because they can be intentionally used. Indeed, they *must* be used intentionally. By definition the individual chooses which tactic to employ, and when, if in fact any is to be employed. Metacognition is, then, the basis for any tactical or strategic creative efforts.

Sticking with the literal approach, "tactics" are short-term procedures or maneuvers that are used to increase the probability of obtaining a goal. They differ from "strategies," which are more general and long-term. Strategies often lead to specific tactics (see Box 1.11). A number of tactics are presented in Chapter 12, which deals with the enhancement of creativity.

BOX 1.10

COGNITIVE STYLE

Cognitive style is supposedly independent of cognitive ability. From this perspective, individuals differ in their performances, not because they vary among some continuum reflecting levels of capacity or ability, but instead because of preferences and different cognitive "styles." Individuals will differ, then, not because one is better or worse than someone else, but instead because they are simply different. It is analogous to cross-cultural studies that would suggest that certain behavior patterns are not better or worse than other behavior patterns, but instead they are just different. This perspective implies qualitative individual differences rather than quantitative. Research on cognitive style addresses the question, "How do we explain individual differences in creativity?," which is a very different question from "How much do creative individuals differ on these important dimensions?" The fact that the first of these is qualitative and the second is quantitative does not keep the research on cognitive style from reliable assessments (cf. Martinsen & Diseth 2011; Wechsler et al. 2012).

BOX 1.11

TACTICS VS. STRATEGIES

The techniques and procedures used to insure or increase creativity often are described as strategies, but it is important to distinguish between tactics and strategies. Chandler (1962) put it this way: "strategy can be defined as the determination of the basic long-term goals and objectives of an enterprise, and the adoption of courses of action and the allocation of resources necessary for carrying out these goals" (pp. 15–16). Tactics, on the other hand, are specific processes for dealing with a particular situation or problem. Organizations often have strategies, especially if they are concerned about innovation (Lines & Grohaug, 2004), but individuals may employ specific tactics when, say, faced with an impasse. They may, for instance, "turn the problem on its head" or "put the problem aside for a short period." These two tactics do not refer to goals and objectives. Of course, organizations or individuals may have both strategies and tactics; it would be inaccurate to assign strategies only to organizations and tactics to individuals.

Metacognition develops only in adolescence (Elkind 1981). Children therefore cannot be tactical about their creativity (see Chapter 2). Then again, they do not need to be tactical: they are spontaneous and uninhibited and do not use as many assumptions and routines as adults. Adults rely on routine and may need tactics to solve problems in a creative fashion and to avoid fixedness.

PERCEPTION AND CREATIVITY

Two very different views of creative cognition have been described. One allows the creator to take intentional control of his or her work, often through tactics, and the other relies more on unintentional and unconscious processes. These views are not incompatible. Part of the creative process could be unconscious and random (or beyond the reasoning of our conscious mind), whereas another stage may be intentional and can be controlled. More will be said about the intentional processes in sections devoted to judgment, mindfulness, and personal creativity.

Another view distinguishes between random and unintentional processes ("blind variation") and systematic but unintentional processes. Perceptual processes play a role in certain kinds of creative thought, and they are anything but random. They are not, however, directed by our conscious mind nor are they in any sense intentional. Consider in this regard the process of *percept-genesis*. Smith et al. (1989; Smith & Amner 1997) gave this label to the process through which meaning is assigned, in a step-by-step fashion, to the information we perceive. It is similar to the *top-down processing model of cognition* (Lindsay & Norman 1977), which describes information processing as guided by one's thinking and expectations.

Bottom-up cognitive processing starts from experience and the mind reacts to it by determining what the experience means. Bottom-up processing is often a kind of recognition: We perceive something and react to it by searching our memory for similar objects or experiences.

We then label the new experience, based on what we found in our long-term memory. Top-down processing, on the other hand, may require less information because the individual is assigning meaning based on expectations. Of course we often find only what we are looking for, which is why top-down processing and a reliance on expectations can cause problems (Rosenthal 1991). Chapter 6 discusses several examples of the problems that may arise when working with creative students (e.g., they may not fit our expectations of ideal children). Smith's research on percept-genesis is one of the best examples of how the creative process can be empirically examined. This research shows that creative individuals assign meaning in a different fashion than less creative persons. Creative individuals tend to use ambiguous stimuli, or stimuli that have not yet been fully revealed. They can construct meaning based on very little information. Creativity here is very literal: It is the creation of meaning.

Khandwalla (1993) also focused on processes rather than product. He was particularly interested in sequential thinking as related to creative cognition. His method was called *protocol analysis*. It asks participants to "think aloud" while working on a divergent thinking task (i.e., "List objects that are green, liquid, and funny"). The participants are encouraged to express whatever comes to mind. Khandwalla was able to identify a number of distinct problem-solving categories and micromechanisms in the analysis of the 10 most detailed protocols. Very telling were the transitions, from one solution or idea to another. Five general solution categories were identified: ideation, problem structuring, search, feeling, and evaluating. Each had subcategories. Further analysis indicated that ideation was used most frequently (37.1% of the think-aloud reports). Next was evaluating (21.3%), search (15.9%), problem structuring (14.4%), and feeling (11.2%). Ideation was negatively correlated with feeling ($r = -.67$), structuring ($-.49$), and search ($-.31$) but positively associated with evaluations ($.24$). Khandwalla offered several suggestions. People in a rut and only using ideation, for instance, should recognize more of their feelings or restructure the problem.

Cupchik (1999) and Runco (2003b) detail ways that the human perceptual system may influence creative thinking. Perception represents one of the nomothetic processes mentioned briefly in the introduction to this chapter.

SYNAESTHESIA

Synaesthesia represents another unintentional but systematic perceptual and cognitive process. It occurs when information from one sensory modality (e.g., hearing) is translated to another sensory modality (taste). Domino (1989) found that 23% of his sample of 358 fine art students experienced synaesthesia, and did so consistently and spontaneously. These students apparently associated colors with music, tastes with certain vowels, and colors with numbers. Domino found the individuals who spontaneously experienced synaesthesia had higher scores on four creativity tests than did a control group.

MINDFULNESS

Langer (1989) believes that we can take control of our perceptual processes, and thereby fulfill our potential for creativity and even health. She suggested that creativity and health will flourish if we can avoid mindless (automatic) behaviors. We should also avoid relying on past routines and the categories of experience used in our personal pasts. We should instead look closely at new experiences and create new categories for those new experiences. We should also avoid relying on single perspectives and instead be alert to alternative perspectives. The last of these suggestions shows why mindfulness is related to creative behavior. Apparently, mindfulness and creativity are each related to flexibility. Flexibility will, for instance, allow us to avoid relying on routine and assumption and help us to consider various perspectives. Langer (1989) suggested that we remain open to new information, and "openness to experience," like flexibility, is often related to creative potential (McCrae 1987). Langer has demonstrated the benefits of mindfulness in the classroom (Langer et al. 1989) and various other institutions. Mindfulness can be enhanced, by one's self or by others (e.g., teachers, supervisors), and has profound effects on creativity and health.

There is no doubt of an optimal level of mindfulness. Indeed, assumption sometimes works well and makes our lives easier. When we make an assumption, we free up resources that can then be allocated to other concerns. Mindfulness is a very good thing, most of the time.

OVERINCLUSIVE THINKING

We can explore the idea of optima further, especially if we stand back and examine the concept of categorization (Box 1.12). This is one way we structure our thinking and make our lives easier: We classify people, objects, and experiences into categories and other cognitive structures (Piaget 1976). Usually this dramatically improves the efficiency of our thinking. It can be taken too far, however. If we rely on categories, we might err by assuming

---

BOX 1.12

CATEGORICAL AND HIERARCHICAL THINKING

Did you ever wonder how a letter finds its way to its addressee (the recipient)? The answer is probably obvious to you because you have no doubt addressed many a letter. (I know I have written every creditor in the known universe. They all confuse me with my evil twin.) The postal delivery method was, however, not so obvious when the United States was just getting started. The inventor was none other than Ben Franklin. The interesting thing about the postal delivery method is that it is a method. It is not a thing, a product, but is instead a means or procedure. We often do not think of methods as inventions, but they certainly are as creative as products. Consider Henry Ford's assembly line (and the later methodological changes, mostly in Asia, to make the auto industry more efficient and cost-effective), Thomas Edison's invention factory, or McDonald's fast food methods (Bryson 1994).

The other notable thing about the postal delivery method is that it relies on classification and hierarchical thinking. A letter is delivered by first identifying the country, then the state, then the city, and then the street

(Continued)

BOX 1.12   (*Continued*)

and house number. (Zip codes expedite this process further, but if you just used a zip code, your letter would not be delivered. It is not specific enough.) Categories, sometimes called concepts or classifications, develop as we acquire knowledge. They represent one way that knowledge is structured: the individual puts similar things in one category (cats and dogs are in the animal category), and infers and constructs hierarchies based on super- and subclassifications. Categories make our thinking much more efficient, for we can often judge something based on the general category. (To answer the question, "Do you like Siamese cats?" you do not even need to know anything specific about that breed, if you are allergic to all cats. Siamese cats represent one subclass in the class "Cats," which of course is a subclass of "Mammals," "Animals," and so on.) As a matter of fact the taxonomic system (Kingdom, phylum, class, order, family, genus, and species) represents another very useful hierarchy.

The up-side of categorical thinking is that our thinking is more efficient, and the down-side is that our thinking is too efficient. It is too efficient when we do not notice details in a mindful manner. This can create problems for creative thinking; it is really just another way of saying that when we rely on categories we are making assumptions. These problems—making assumptions, not looking at details, and mindless inattention—will each be examined in Chapter 12, for they all get in the way of original ideation and problem solving. In terms of the cognitive bases of creative thinking, the important points are that (a) our thinking is often structured, and often organized in a hierarchical fashion; (b) creative thinking sometimes results when we ignore the "conceptual boundaries" that define categories; and (c) thinking that completely ignores those same boundaries is overinclusive and sometimes related to psychosis (Eysenck, 1997a).

---

that each member of a category is identical. This can be seen when we stereotype people or groups and assume that everyone in one group is the same ("All lawyers are…"). We might also err in the manner that Langer (1989) described, in which case we rely too much on categories from our past experiences and do not notice the novelty and significance of new experiences.

Yet another theory of cognition suggests that sometimes categorization errors contribute to creative insights. I am referring to Eysenck's (1997a, 2003) theory of overinclusive thinking. Eysenck claimed that overinclusive thinking supplies the variations and options from which the individual may select useful and creative ideas. A great deal of attention indeed has been given to the production of variations and options (Campbell 1960; Simonton 2007), and no doubt using loose conceptual boundaries and including things in categories that others may not include could expand the range of options. There is also a modicum of experimental research that suggests that creative insights sometimes result from a loosening of conceptual boundaries (Martindale 1990).

CONCLUSIONS

The most fascinating thing about the cognitive research on creativity may be its diversity. It is tempting to borrow Minsky's (1988) metaphor of a society of mind, for societies are busy and a bit chaotic. Then again, the society metaphor may be anthropomorphic and imply undue homogeneity. Perhaps an *ecosystem of mind* is a better metaphor. An ecosystem implies diversity. In the natural world an ecosystem contains flora and fauna, and often extreme heterogeneity of each. And with the diverse species in an ecosystem, actions occur on various levels (from the treetops and sky to deep in the earth), at different speeds, sometimes interactively and systemically, and sometimes independently. An ecosystem contains not just one species and community, but many of them, as well as a physical environment. For creative cognition, the environment is the brain itself, and the mind it generates. But if you prefer a metaphor for mind and cognition, you are not alone (see Box 1.13).

Such cognitive diversity may be difficult to conceive. Yet this is the kind of thing that should be practiced, given that creative thinking sometimes requires an open mind and tolerance of ambiguity (Merrotsy 2013). The reader may need to practice just that—open-mindedness—while reading about cognition and creativity. Some of the research herein suggests that cognition depends on affect, for example, and the interplay with cognition is not always easy to grasp. Many people view cognition as "cold" and independent of emotions (Lazarus 1991). Even more challenging may be the idea of creative cognition sometimes involving a simultaneous consideration of opposites (Arieti 1976; Rothenberg 1999). This sounds a bit like "white is black" or "day is night." Then there is the idea of the unconscious! It is by definition untestable and many think it unscientific. But without a recognition of the unconscious, it would be very difficult to explain incubation, insight, percept-genesis, and the resolution of opposites. The best solution is to realize that the traditional scientific method, with objectivity as its centerpiece, does not apply perfectly to creative studies. By all means we need to be scientific about creativity, but not when extreme objectivity precludes a realistic understanding of the subject matter. It helps to be open-minded and tolerant.

Clearly there are different ways to be creative and different processes that can result in original and effective insights, ideas, or solutions. Some processes may be unconscious and out of our personal control. Yet others are entirely conscious and can be controlled. One of the best examples of a controllable process is simply knowledge acquisition. Knowledge is often

---

BOX 1.13

METAPHORS OF THE MIND

Every era seems to borrow from technology for its favored metaphor of the mind. Here are some examples:

- Telegraph
- Switchboard
- Computer
- Society
- Ecosystem
- Fractal
- Ocean

useful for creativity. No wonder there is a 10-year rule for many domains, where contributions to a field are beyond reach until the individual has invested 10 years (some say 20 000 hours) to its study. These 10 years allow the individual to master the prerequisite information. They then get to a point where they see the gaps and know what is important; they can then contribute in a meaningful way. There are domain differences in this regard (see Chapter 2) and exceptions—recall here the idea of *professional marginality*, where an individual from outside a field has an advantage in questioning assumptions and contributing in a creative fashion (Dogan & Pahre 1990; Runco 1994a)—but most of the time, information is helpful. What is most important is that the process of information acquisition is largely under our control. People who invest 20 000 hours mastering a field do so because they are fascinated by it; they are thrilled by it; so they decide to devote themselves to it. They often lose themselves and do not even realize that they are working at it. Time flies, as they say. Or as Thomas Edison put it, "genius is 10% inspiration and 90% perspiration."

Then there are processes that are seemingly beyond our control. All we can do with them is allow them to take place. Parnes (1967) suggested that we "let them happen," perhaps by taking a walk and providing the time and opportunity for incubation. That is, however, itself a tactical decision. Other tactics are more direct. Parnes referred to them as *make it happen* tactics. These are detailed in Chapter 6. I mention them here because it is very important that tactics for enhancing creative thinking and for fulfilling potentials have strong justification. That justification can be found in theories and research findings reported in this chapter and throughout the volume. That connection between theory or research and a tactic or strategy validates and justifies the tactics.

There are a number of additional connections between the concepts in the present chapter and those found elsewhere in this volume. Eysenck's (2003) theory of overinclusive thought, for example, is useful for our understanding of psychopathology (see Chapter 4), as is extremely low flexibility (a correlate of suicide ideation). Recall that Langer (1989) also looked at flexibility, and it is also an important part of the personality approach to creativity. Stein (1975), for instance, listed both flexibility and intuitive capacity in his summary of the creative personality. Cognition is also tied to social processes, as is evidenced by the research on brainstorming. These connections suggest a consensus about certain aspects of the creativity syndrome. We will explore these points of agreement, and various themes in the research, in the conclusion to this book.

2

Developmental Trends and Influences on Creativity

Being the third son of the family, and not bred to any trade, my head began to be filled very early with rambling thoughts. **Robinson Crusoe (Defoe, Robinson Crusoe, 1719, p. 1)**
He not busy being born is busy dying. **Bob Dylan**

ADVANCE ORGANIZER

- Developmental Trends
  - Stages of Conventionality
  - Piagetian Theory Applied to Creativity
    - Adaptability
    - Intrinsic Motivation
- Adversity During Childhood
- Family Influences
  - Birth Order
  - Family and Sibsize
- Peer Status of Creative Children
- Parental Influence
  - Divorce
- Parental Creativity
- Parental Personality
- Adult Development
- Postformal Operations and Problem Finding
- Old Age Style
- Choose to Live Long and Be Creative
- Box Inserts
  - Television
  - Crystallizing Experiences
  - Imaginary Companions

INTRODUCTION

Everyone has the potential to be creative, but not everyone fulfills that potential. Many people probably either do not have the experiences to fulfill their potential or do not exercise their creative talents. It is too easy to go through each day relying more on routine and assumption than on mindful and creative actions. The world could be a very different place—a more entertaining, productive, and efficient place—if we each used our full potential. Guilford (1975) put it this way: "If by any approach we could lift the population's problem solving skills by a small amount on the average, the summative effect would be incalculable" (p. 53).

Our potential depends a great deal on our *genotype*, our genetic inheritance. Our *phenotype*, or manifest talents, are the result of both nature (biology and genes) and nurture (experience). Thus biological factors contribute specifically to creative potential, and experience determines where within the range set by biological potentials the individual performs. Behavioral geneticists refer to this arrangement as a *range of reaction* (this is discussed more in Chapter 3). The present chapter discusses both nature and nurture, but the focus is on development. It describes typical developmental trends and trajectories (e.g., stages of development that characterize many individuals and relate to creative behavior) as well as influences on the developmental process. Special attention is given to the family, for it is a very significant developmental influence on creative potentials.

Potentials may be fulfilled during childhood, but it would be most accurate (though close to oxymoronic) to say that they are partially fulfilled. Many experiences are likely only after childhood; creative potential covers the lifespan. For this reason this chapter covers more than the family. In fact, creative expression shifts several times as the individual moves through childhood, adolescence, and adulthood. As we will see in this chapter, these shifts may involve *maturational processes*, which are defined as changes that reflect the unfolding of genetic potentials, or they may reflect changes in motivation or shifts in the environment that alter the support for creative efforts. It is useful to examine changes in creativity that occur through the lifespan; there are some fairly universal trends.

Clearly, it is best to describe creative development as the fulfillment of creative potentials. This allows both nature and nurture, and it implies that experiences, within or outside the family, can do only so much. Each of us has creative talents, but not everyone can be Einstein. Each of us has potentials to fulfill, but the range of potentials varies from individual to individual. That range, again, is the contribution of biology, genes, and nature. This biological contribution is very apparent in the trends and stages of development.

TRENDS AND STAGES OF DEVELOPMENT

Many theories of development describe stages. These are discontinuity theories, the discontinuities being the stages (Kohlberg 1987; Piaget 1970, 1976). Some theories of creativity also describe development as discontinuous. For the present purposes the most useful discontinuity theory is that which focuses on changes in *conventionality*. This theory was developed in studies of the development of moral reasoning (Kohlberg 1987) but has proven to be useful in work on art (Rosenblatt & Winner 1988), divergent thinking (Runco & Charles 1993), language (Gardner 1982), and various other areas with connections to creativity. Obviously it hinges on the concept of *conventions*—but what is a convention?

Broadly speaking, a convention involves normative or typical behavior. It is, for example, typical to wear shoes to school, and, therefore, accurate to say that it is conventional to wear footwear to school. Conventions may be formal or informal. Formal conventions take the form of rules (e.g., in a home or game), laws, traditions, and morals. These might be viewed as *explicit* conventions because they are articulated and shared. Informal conventions are apparent in conventional tendencies such as fashion and fads. These often influence what people do, and because many people do them (e.g., cut their hair a particular way), they are conventions. These might be considered *implicit* conventions, however, because sometimes we know what other people are doing but do not really talk about it or formalize it. In fact, it is tempting to tie this idea of informal conventions to the concept of *zeitgeist* (the "spirit of the times")—both occur without laws and articulated rules—but I will leave that for the chapter devoted to history and creativity.

Conventions define culture. They also direct thinking toward normative behavior, which means that they constrain thinking and can easily inhibit creativity. Conventions are, after all, indicative of something about which there is a consensus; creativity, on the other hand, requires originality, self-expression (not group expression), and unconventional thought or action. Conventions can be quite useful, but they can also mislead the individual, at least if accepted without being closely evaluated.

Kohlberg's (1987) theory of development describes young children in a *preconventional stage*. It is preconventional in that the children have yet to develop the thinking that allows them to understand and use conventions. Not only are they unaware of what is conventional (and therefore unable to conform to those conventions and the related expectations), but they also are incapable of thinking in a conventional fashion. Eventually the child (or preadolescent) enters the *conventional stage*. The youth now knows many conventions, often knows what is expected by others, and gives great weight to conventional and therefore typical normative behaviors. They often take this to the extreme. Such *hyperconventionality* is the easiest to see in the preadolescent's or adolescent's sensitivity to "what my friends are doing." Peer pressure is seemingly all-important in the conventional stage of development. With the right experiences the individual will develop *postconventional* thinking and at that point use conventions only as one source of information. The postconventional individual also thinks for him- or herself.

Certain kinds of creativity require postconventional capacities. This is especially true of creative products and discoveries that contribute to a formal field of study. A creative scientist, for example, is probably aware of existing scientific theories (and thus aware of what is conventional in his or her field), but also breaks away or extends the field by thinking in a postconventional and independent fashion. Even scientific rebellion tends to rebel against something; it is not entirely unconnected to the field.

Preconventional thinking also allows creative behavior. In this stage children are uninhibited by convention. They do not think about what is expected of them, nor even about what is socially appropriate. (That is why children can scream or cry at the top of their lungs, even in a public place, not caring what other people think.) Preconventional children play, use certain kinds of language, and draw and paint following only their own interests and inclinations. The artwork of a preconventional child is totally self-expressive, and usually is uninhibited, unconventional, and creative.

Children are often creative in their language, but then show an appreciation for conventions in the middle elementary school ages and grades. They can be entirely literal in the conventional stage. This is unfortunate for their creativity because there is little latitude in literal interpretations. Additionally, creative ideas are often metaphorical, or found via analogical thinking (see Chapter 1), and metaphor and analogy are antithetical to literal thinking.

What is most obvious is that children in the conventional stage have great difficulty being creative. This makes perfect sense, given that conventionality is a kind of conformity, and creativity requires nonconformity. It is impossible to be original if you are conforming, and originality is necessary though not sufficient for creativity (Runco & Jaeger 2012). The conventional child is a conformist in the sense that he or she follows social expectation and imitates typical behaviors of his or her peers. This inhibits self-expression and creativity. The lack of creativity in the conventional stage is apparent when children rely on a *literal stage* of language use (avoiding metaphors and other creative expressions), when they produce only *representational* art (which is recognizably like some object), and when they slump in terms of their original thinking (Torrance 1968b). Apparently, approximately half of the children at around age 9 experience this *fourth-grade slump* in original thinking.

Slumps in creativity also have been described as reflections of *U-shaped development.* This is really just a different terminology, however; U-shaped development describes children who are highly creative but stop behaving in that fashion at a particular age (the bottom of the U) only to regain their creative ways at some older age (e.g., Johnson 1985). An example of a U-shaped developmental trajectory is given in Figure 2.1.

A word of caution: Stages imply general tendencies, if not universals, but it is unwise to predict an individual's stage of development based on his or her chronological age. We develop at different rates and are not entirely consistent across settings with our conformity or nonconformity and conventionality and nonconventionality. In certain contexts, we all conform. Individuals tend to be preconventional once in a while, sometimes conventional, and postconventional other times. This kind of variation has been called a *trait × state interaction*, the idea being that behavior is a result of both traits (e.g., conventionality) and immediate states (e.g., a classroom, a social setting, the home, or workplace).

Not Everyone Slumps

The idea of slumps, including the fourth-grade slump, seems to grab everyone's attention. But slumps are not universal, nor are they inevitable. Indeed, Lau and Cheung (2010) uncovered a "substantial increase in fluency, flexibility, uniqueness, and unusualness elicited

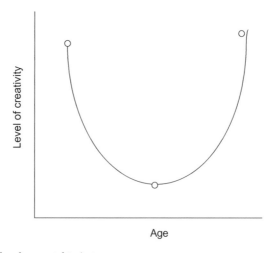

FIGURE 2.1   U-shaped developmental trajectory.

by figural stimuli." These increases were found in Grades 4–9, in a moderately large sample of students in Hong Kong. Lau and Cheung also found that

> the percentage gain in performance on fluency, flexibility, uniqueness, and unusualness over eight years (2002 vs 1994). ... Overall, the growth rate ranged from 25.83% to 72.86%. For fluency, the percentage gain ranged from 32.35% to 62.13%. For flexibility, it ranged from 25.83% to 48.80%. For uniqueness, it ranged from 42.86% to 72.86%. For unusualness, it ranged from 27.30% to 55.54%.

In other words, "the growth rate in creativity measures (fluency, flexibility, uniqueness, and unusualness) was like this: It was relatively high in Grade 4 and Grade 5; then a drop in Grades 6, 7, and 8; and a resurgence in Grade 9."

Recall here that uniqueness and unusualness of ideas are both indicators of originality. All scores were based on Wallach and Kogan (1965) type divergent thinking tests, most of which were administered via computer. Very importantly, the ideas elicited by verbal stimuli gave a much more ambiguous picture of growth and developmental trends. Lau and Cheung found only uniqueness, from the verbal divergent thinking stimuli, showed growth. The percentage gain for it was 35.91–92.87%, from grades 4 to 9. Unusualness also showed a moderate grain (14–59%), which makes sense because, like uniqueness, it is an index of original ideation.

The differences between the scores based on figural and verbal stimuli are consistent with a long-standing two-factor theory (Richardson 1986). Runco and Albert (1985) explained such differences in terms of familiarity, the idea being that the verbal stimuli are more familiar and thus more easily associated with rote and unoriginal ideas than the abstract figural stimuli. Lau and Cheung (2010) favored a psychoanalytic explanation for the differences.

Lau and Cheung (2010) also found sex differences, with rapid growth among boys in grades 4 and 5, a slump (or at least slowing) in the next three grades, and then a jump again in grade 9. Girls also had clear growth in divergent thinking in grades 4 and 5 and then a slump but they had no resurgence at grade 9. The low point for the girls was grade 6. Obviously this trough differs from earlier reports of a fourth-grade slump (Runco & Charles 1997; Torrance 1968b).

Then there are trends in adulthood. Reese and coworkers (2001), for instance, administered divergent thinking tests to young (17–22 years old), middle-aged (40–50), young-old (60–70), and "old-old" (75+) adults. The results indicated age differences in flexibility and some fluency scores, but none in originality nor one particular fluency score ("associational fluency"). Most readers will be happy to hear that the middle-aged group had the highest fluency, flexibility, and originality scores of all age groups. Other empirical investigations of adulthood changes in divergent thinking were reviewed by Runco and Charles (1997) and Runco and Cayirdag (2012a,b).

Piagetian Theory

Jean Piaget (1970, 1976) presented another discontinuity theory of development, and it too has been used to explain certain creative trends and tendencies. Mature classification is one of the Piagetian accomplishments of concrete operational stage (Katz & Thompson 1993; Runco 1994b) and it may play a role in some creative thinking. Creative problem solving, for example, may require classifications when an individual decides whether or not to explore a certain line of thought based on the judgment of its being socially appropriate or not.

That judgment is a classification, and if something is avoided because it is not socially appropriate, it has led to a kind of conformity or conventionality, and creative insight is unlikely. Recall here that classification is associated with categorization (see Box 1.12).

The Piagetian model also relies on *adaptation* to explain the process of development (Box 2.1). Adaptation (and adaptability) is one of the common near-synonyms of creativity (Cohen 1989). Moreover, adaptation is defined in terms of assimilation and accommodation in the

---

BOX 2.1

DIFFERENT VIEWS OF ADAPTION

Adaption plays a role in Darwinian theory, as well as in Piagetian theory. Not surprisingly, numerous Darwinian models of creativity have been proposed (e.g., Albert 2012; Campbell 1960; Lumsden & Findlay 1988; Simonton 1999c, 2007) (Figure 2.2). These are explored in Chapter 3. What may be most significant is the possibility that adaption may sometimes undermine creativity. Adaption is not always positively related to creative success. Consider

what happens, for example, if a highly adaptable individual finds him- or herself in an environment that reinforces conformity. The adaptable person will conform, and there goes the self-expression and originality that are required for creativity. Many biographies also suggest that adaptability and creativity do not always go hand in hand. Gedo's (1997) biography of the artist John Ensor demonstrates this very clearly.

FIGURE 2.2   Charles Darwin. Several theories of creativity have a Darwinian slant.

Piagetian model (also see Runco 1985) and the first of these can help us to understand the cognitive transformations that sometimes lead to creative ideas (Guilford 1968; Runco 1996d) while the latter can explain the sudden insights that characterize many creative "a-ha" moments (Gruber 1981b). Neither assimilation nor accommodation is considered, however, unless the individual feels the need for adaptation. In Piaget's own terms, adaptation occurs only when the individual experiences *disequilibrium*. This occurs when the person does not understand some experience or information (understanding is not in equilibrium with the information).

CRITICISM OF PIAGETIAN THEORY

Apparently there are various discontinuities in development. There are, however, continuity theories as well. These suggest that growth does not always start and stop, as is implied by stages. Instead, development is in some ways an ongoing and continuous process. Levine (1984) offered a criticism specifically of Piaget's stage theory as it applies to creativity.

Three other points bear emphasizing. First, the disequilibrium that sometimes motivates creative adaptions may be personal. One person may see a problem or gap that others do not. This often occurs; the creative person is the only one who is bothered by something and puts effort into resolving it. Problems are personal interpretations, after all, as is stress. Stress is not out there in the environment but is instead an individual's reaction to an experience. It, too, is an interpretation. Indeed, all challenges, problems, stressors, and adverse experiences depend on an individual's interpretation. Admittedly, some experiences are so adverse that everyone would agree on them, but many are not. The personal interpretation of adversity works in two ways: It may be that one person is overwhelmed by an experience that others do not notice, or that the individual does not care about something that creates great anxiety in others. As for motivation, it is quite possible that a creative person is challenged or intrigued by a particular problem; they view adversity as a challenge and are motivated to tackle it in a creative fashion. The problem is not a problem.

The related second point is that adversity can be subtle. It may not seem like adversity per se, but instead may be a very mild challenge. Indeed, it may be quite pleasant! People enjoy being challenged. Creative persons in particular often have an interest in complexity and intellectual activities (Barron 1995). No wonder the challenges that motivate creative work have been given different labels, including adversity, problems, gaps, tension, disequilibria, and challenges. Runco (1994c, 1999c) explored the variety of "discontents" that can instigate and motivate creative effort.

The third point is that we have a kind of controversy on our hands. There is plenty of evidence that creative work is a reaction to some challenge or adversity, but at the same time there is evidence that many of us are the most creative when we are in environments that are safe, nonevaluative, and nonjudgmental. Let's consider each of these alternatives in detail. This will help us with the topic of development.

Adversity

Adversity often is used to explain creative effort and high motivation. The individual may cope, for example, "in the face of adversity," or invent something only when it is necessary to do so—necessity being "the mother of invention." (See Chapter 13 for the differences between invention and creativity.) In one oft-cited study, Goertzel and Goertzel (1962) found adversity in an extraordinary proportion of the families in their study, *Cradles of Eminence*. In analyses of autobiographical and biographical data from 400 eminent persons, Goertzel and Goertzel found that most had "in their childhood experienced trauma, deprivations, frustrations and conflicts of the kind commonly thought to predispose one to mental illness or delinquency" (p. xii). Additionally, "only fifty-eight [of the 400] can be said to have experienced what is the stereotyped picture of the supportive, warm, relatively untroubled home. ... The comfortable and contented do not ordinarily become creative" (p. 131). There were notable differences among different forms of talent. Every single actor in the sample was, for example, raised in a "troubled home," as were the majority of novelists (89%), composers and musicians (86%), explorers and athletes (67%), and psychologists, philosophers and religious leaders (61%). Inventors, in contrast, rarely experienced family difficulties (or at least they rarely reported it); only 20% of the inventors reported familial conflict. Just to name one example, Charles Lindbergh was apparently "subject to terrific nightmares about falling off a roof or precipice" (p. 222). Note, however, that (a) the Goertzels relied on autobiographical and biographical reports, which means that there was quite a bit of room for interpretation, and (b) they examined eminent individuals, like Lindbergh, and there are differences between eminence (and fame, or high reputation) and creativity per se (Runco 1995c).

At about the same time, MacKinnon (1960) suggested that highly effective individuals very frequently experience trauma and deprivation during their childhoods. Fathers were often abusive and sometimes even sadistic. MacKinnon had special concerns about fathers and described how in "samples of highly creative subjects ... some endured the most brutal treatment at the hands of sadistic fathers". MacKinnon's work is notable in part because he not only identified the adversity but had an explanation for how it was related to creative efforts. In his words, "the creative individual has the capacity to tolerate the tension created in him by the strong opposing values, and in his life and work he effects some reconciliation of them". MacKinnon was well aware of the problems involved in doing research along these lines. He described how "ineffective" (uncreative) persons are often "motivated by their distress to reveal themselves". There is no doubt of the possibility of a *sampling bias*.

The emphasis on early childhood experiences is a bit Freudian. Freud felt that personality is developed early in life, certainly before mid-adolescence. Freud also described the role of the unconscious, and this too is very relevant for understanding how early experience, and especially adversity, may motivate a creative person. Csikszentmihalyi (1988a, 1988b) put it this way:

> The impressions artists work with come from many sources. One that is very prevalent among contemporary painters contains memories of childhood. Whether the viewer realizes it or not, and often also

unbeknown to the artist, the images that form the core of a great number of modern works represent the rage or the ecstasy of childhood which the artist tries to recapture in order to integrate it into current experience. … Such works occasionally achieve a magical synthesis of past and present, an abolition of objective time, a healing through the reactivation of former pain which can now be tolerated by the mature person. We might call such an achievement "abreactive originality," borrowing a term from psychoanalysis to describe the successful release of psychic tension through the symbolic reordering of repressed traumatic experiences (p. 219).

Albert (1978) used a similar logic to explain why parental loss (an early and surprisingly common form of adversity) is so common among gifted children. Later, Albert and Runco (1986) contrasted creative children with equally bright but less creative children and reported that the relationships between fathers and the "effective" (bright but not outstandingly creative) sons was "especially tolerable and harmonious … the creative child typically had more hostility to contend with than the equally bright but less creative child" (pp. 339–340). Albert and Elliot (1973) suggested that "preadolescent creative children are less likely to use repressive defense in recognizing a personal conflict, and, along with this, appear to have greater cognitive facility with and access to cognitive resources at different levels of consciousness than less creative people" (p. 177). Many theories of creativity emphasize this kind of preconscious process (e.g., Dudek & Verreault 1989; Kubie 1958; Rothenberg 1990).

Adversity may contribute to the creative individual's capacity for coping, but it may also lead to unusual preferences. Barron (1963b) explained how, after the experience of grief,

the motive is thus generated for searching out other situations which would seem to defy rational construction, with some degree of confidence that after much deprivation, tension, and pain a superior form of pleasure will be attained … the creative artist and scientist appear, when one reads biographical accounts, to have experienced an unusual amount of grief and ordeal in life and to have shouldered burdens of pain that most commonly disable the individual … the creative individual is one who has learned to prefer irregularities and apparent disorder and to trust himself to make a new order (p. 157).

The role of adversity should come as no surprise, given that there must be some motivation or the individual will not put the effort into adapting or creating (Runco 2005). In this regard we might look back at Piaget's theory again, for he tied adaption to *intrinsic motivation*. Given his biological training and perspective, it is likely that he felt that there was a genetic basis for the motivation to adapt. Regardless of the nature and nurture, the assumption is that humans do not like to feel disequilibrium and are motivated to put an end to it by adapting. Often these adaptations are creative (Cohen 1989; Runco 1994c). Piaget's tying adaptation to intrinsic motivation is significant because it helps us to understand why so many others have found intrinsic motivation to be necessary for creative work (see Chapter 9).

The alternative perspective in this controversy reflects humanistic theories of creativity, the crucial idea being that people can be themselves (and thereby spontaneous, uninhibited, creative, and self-actualized) when there are few or no pressures to conform and inhibit oneself. Harrington et al. (1987) applied this perspective to the home and found creativity to be associated with families that provide *unconditional positive regard*. Many others have applied the same logic to the organizational setting (Amabile 1990; Runco 1995a; Witt & Beorkrem 1989) and suggested that employees will be more creative when they can be themselves. This perspective may be quite attractive for it implies that parents should give children positive regard instead of creating an adverse home environment!

How can this controversy be resolved? We might accept both perspectives as useful, though at different times (and thus sometimes challenge but other times comfort), or we might find the optimal level of challenge such that creative potentials flourish. Albert (1978) seemed to prefer the first of these explanations:

> The creative person-to-be comes from a family that is anything but harmonious—one which has built into its relationships, its organization of roles, and its levels of communication a good deal of tension if not disturbance, what I term a "wobble." But along with these characteristics, there is a commitment to achievement as opposed to just "having fun," a special focus of interest and aspirations upon the indexed child, and a great deal of family effort to see that these aspirations are met (pp. 203–204).

Both the adversity that requires adaptation and creativity and the harmonious environment just described can be familial. No wonder developmental studies of creativity often focus directly on the family.

TELEVISION AS CATHARSIS

Television may be viewed as a *catharsis* (a release of tension) (Figure 2.3). It may also be a *catalyst* (and stimulate or initiate behavior). Most obviously it provides models for children. This is potentially problematic because there are very few good models on TV; most actors are busy entertaining. Even cartoons, though supposedly appropriate for children, are often violent and extremely unrealistic. Commercials may be the worst of all, for they are nothing but attempts to persuade and manipulate. *Parental mediation* may be employed (i.e., parents watch TV with their children and talk about the content of the shows), but adults may soon get bored with a child's show, or they may be intrigued and forget to mediate! Parents may allow only educational TV, but it is possible that these are the worse shows of all, because they justify themselves and allow parents to use TV as babysitter.

In actuality, all shows minimize thinking and self-expression. The TV really allows only passive behavior, but creativity requires interaction, reaction, evaluations, and self-expression. Even if you do not agree about educational TV shows, surely you will be frightened by the statistics: Many children in the United States watch 30 hours of TV each week. They do it during the formative years (approximately age 2–12 or 13); they watch TV more than anything else in their lives except sleep. Thus, even if TV shows could provide knowledge, perspective, entertainment, and other benefits, they displace children from activities (e.g., playing, socializing, reading) that are certainly developmentally healthful. This perspective is known as the *displacement theory* of TV viewing. That in and of itself should make parents think hard about what TV, and how much, their children watch.

FIGURE 2.3   Does television viewing influence creative potential?

The Family

The family exerts a very powerful influence on development. Cropley (1967a) put it this way:

> Whatever levels of [creative] potential are present in a child, the direction in which they are developed (towards convergence or divergence), will be … guided by the kinds of interactions the children have with their parents. In turn, the parents' thinking about how children should be treated is related to the way in which they themselves were reared, in fact, to the prevailing cultural notions about what is right and what [is] wrong behaviour in children. If a culture imposes severe negative sanctions against certain behaviours, most parents will try to suppress them in their children, while they will try to foster those behaviours of which the culture approves (p. 62).

The influence of the family is, however, difficult to describe. Some family processes, for example, are fairly private and therefore difficult to study. After all, "the home is a person's castle," to paraphrase an old saying. Additionally, family influences are typically longitudinal, and thus the effects can really be determined only with longitudinal research (Albert & Runco 1986). A number of longitudinal investigations were collected in a Special Issue of the *Creativity Research Journal*. This is not to say that the only effects are long term and require extensive periods of time; sometimes inspiration is the result of one single experience. These are known as *crystallizing experiences* (Box 2.2).

When it is a longitudinal influence, it may be longer than you think. That is because families are *intergenerational* (Albert 1980). This is especially true of family values, which are often passed from generation to generation. In part for this reason it is interesting to examine the genealogies of unambiguously creative persons. These show the intergenerational picture. Consider the genealogy of Johann Sebastian Bach (Simonton 1984). Clearly musical talent was common in the Bach family. Was this because of nature (a musical gene?), nurture (parents listened to and played music, so the children heard music and experienced the benefits), or both?

BOX 2.2

CRYSTALLIZING EXPERIENCES AS A PART OF DEVELOPMENT

Biographies of famous creators often mention family background, insights, and *crystallizing experiences*. These are specific experiences that have a huge influence on the individual's interests, motivations, and decisions. Einstein, for example, was apparently drawn to physics after he was given a compass by his uncle. He was fascinated by the invisible force at work, directing the compass needle. Raina (2003) described another example of a crystallizing experience, this one involving James Watson, who shared the Nobel Prize with Francis Crick for their work on DNA and the double helix. This experience was more mundane, for Watson referred to a book he read, *What Is Life?*, by Schrodinger (1992). Reading a book may sound like an everyday experience, but Watson gave it great weight: "from the moment I read *What Is Life?* I became polarized towards finding out the secret of the gene" (Raina 2003).

The influence of the family is *bidirectional*, as well as intergenerational (Runco & Albert 1985). Bidirectional effects are those that have the parents influencing the children (e.g., exposing children to the arts and valuing original thinking) *and* the children influencing the parents (e.g., a child may have special interests or talents, and the parents respond by seeking out the best experiences for the family, experiences that support those same interests or domains). A child may show musical talents, for example, and for that reason the parents buy tickets to concerts, arrange music lessons for the child, and buy a nice CD player for the home. Parents may do analogous things for children who show interests or talents in other creative domains as well, the important point being that the development of creativity is dynamic and often complicated.

Family Structure and Process

Much of the research on family influences on creativity fall into one of two categories: *family process* and *family structure*. Processes that might be relevant include discipline by parents who are somewhat lax but still give a sense of security for children, allowing them to explore, play, and experiment, all of which can contribute to practical but creative problem solving. Structural developmental variables include family size and birth order, both of which seem to be good predictors of creative potential. Individuals in large families seem to have high creative potential (Runco & Bahleda 1987a), perhaps because of their opportunities for frequent play or the lack of parental supervision. The finding about family size being positively related to creative potential is particularly interesting because almost the opposite seems to be true of IQ and GPA and scholastic achievement, where children from small families tend to excel.

Position within the family is an extremely accurate predictor of creative potential. Sulloway (1996) presented extensive support for the idea that middle children (and perhaps especially a second born child) are the most likely to develop a rebellious personality. This in turn allows the middle-born individual to behave in an unconventional and creative manner. The eldest child (the only offspring to be temporarily an only child) often develops a high need for achievement in conventional areas. The second-born child avoids competition with the eldest by finding another niche in the family. Since the conventional niche is taken, the easiest way to be unique and avoid competition is to take the unconventional (rebellious, creative) direction.

The separation of IQ and general intelligence from creative abilities is described in Chapter 1. This is a key issue because if general intelligence and creativity were strongly related, there would be no need to study creativity. We would know everything we needed to know by looking at general intelligence. We would not need to design environments to support creativity—we could just support intelligence and creativity would tag along. General intelligence and creativity, however, are distinct in terms of test scores (see Chapter 6). They are also distinct in the sense that one is more likely in large families, and the other is more likely in small families.

In general, it appears that the scholastic aptitude scores of children from larger families are lower than the scores of children from smaller families. The theory is that large families usually have a less stimulating *intellectual climate* than smaller families. The reason for this is that smaller families have proportionally more adult input than larger families, in which there may be two, three, four, or more children but only one or two contributing adults. Interestingly, only children tend to have lower scores than eldest children. At first blush, this is not consistent with the theory of intellectual climate, for by definition only children come from smaller families than eldest children. However, eldest children have some experiences that only children do not. In particular, eldest children can act as teachers for younger siblings.

The evidence for creativity is suggestive but less conclusive. On the one hand, only children and eldest children have been reported to have an advantage in terms of creativity, just as they do in terms of academic success. However, there are some data suggesting that eldest children, due to their dependence and conformity, are less creative than younger siblings. Finally, unlike academic success, creativity seems to flourish in larger families. The reason for this may be that children in larger families spend more time without supervision, and thus need to use their imaginative skills to remain entertained. Or perhaps it is a result of frequent and playful child–child interactions in larger families. The relationship may even be related to socioeconomic status (SES), for larger families tend to come from lower socioeconomic levels; they may then have fewer toys and environmental distractions. They could be creative in finding ways to play.

One interesting aspect of this involves the developmental research showing that divergent thinking is positively related to *sibsize* (number of siblings in a family). This finding was highlighted earlier because it is exactly the opposite of what we find for noncreative measures of talent. SAT scores, for example, are lowest in large families (Zajonc & Markus 1975). Although more research would need to investigate family dynamics and processes, it may be that having siblings leads to a particular kind of flexibility. The clearest case would be the only child, who may not need to be very flexible. (I am generalizing but only to keep the example as clear as possible.) They do not need to share, divide, or take into account the perspectives of others. If a child has siblings, he or she will be more likely to be required to share, divide, and take into account other perspectives. In short, sibsize may be specifically related to the flexibility that characterizes creative talents.

Recall here the relationship that exists between creativity and adaptability. Perhaps I should say "relationships," for adaptability may allow the individual to be flexible and creative, but it may also lead to conformity and preclude creativity. Adaptability is related to flexibility—more flexible individuals tend to be more adaptable—so the relationship of sib-size to flexibility may also apply to adaptability.

Socioeconomic Factors

Socioeconomic influences are not strictly familial; they are more general than that. Yet families can be classified, for research purposes, into SES categories, and there is research suggesting that SES is relevant to creativity and creative problem solving. It is likely that the most direct influence of economics on children's creative potentials is via the family. This is true of many things: Families communicate cultural values to their children, socialize children, and are responsible for their early enculturalization. In a sense, families channel and select culture for their children (Albert 1991). Families moderate culture and socioeconomic influences on children. Something might be a part of current *zeitgeist*, but if the family does not value it, it won't be emphasized to the children in that family. If something is out of fashion in a particular era or culture, the family might compensate and insure that it is still communicated to their children. Most music on the radio these days is pop, rap, or rock of some sort, but some children still hear classical music on the family stereo. Of course, this kind of family influence decreases with age. Many adolescents are independent enough to walk away from that audio system playing classical music or put on their headphones to get back to pop.

SES is relevant to creativity and its development in part because SES determines what kinds of experiences and resources are available. Additionally, parental education is correlated with family SES, and parental education by itself plays a large role in development. It determines communication patterns and content, for example, and conveys the idea that education is a valuable thing. SES may also determine how wide a range of experiences a child will have, in terms of travel, but also in terms of the books that may be available, the range of people who visit the home, and the cultural experiences (e.g., museums, theaters) the child visits.

Diverse experience is probably a good thing for the development of creativity; it is easy to see how it might be connected to the flexibility of thought that often is associated with creative talent, for example, although here again we should recognize an optimum. Too much diversity might very well be confusing. Note that this is essentially the same issue that is described in Chapter 1, though there, experience was defined as information. The conclusion about information is that it can help creative thinking, but it can also hinder it—there is an optimal level of information. The same thing applies to the experiences that may be determined by family and SES. Just to briefly mention one other example, it is likely that permissive environments are conducive to the independence that characterizes many creative efforts, but in the home, too much permissiveness may lead directly to insecurity. Research on attachment shows that children who are securely bonded with their parents explore in part because they have confidence that their parents will be waiting for them when the exploration is done.

Although family SES has itself been directly related to creativity (Bruininks & Feldman 1970; Dudek et al. 1994) and more generally to problem-solving strategies (Odom 1967), this is an area of research that is clearly incomplete. This may be because SES is an especially private aspect of the family ("We don't talk about money"), which can make it difficult to do research and may actually distort what research is conducted. Recall here that research on families is surprisingly complicated. To understand the influence of a family, you need to know about the parents (careers, values, education, divorces), family structure (birth order, sibsize, age gap, or interval among siblings), sex of the children, cultural background, and SES. There are other potentially relevant family influences, but even this list leads to literally hundreds of combinations and family types. That makes it difficult to isolate a particular influence, and difficult to conduct sound research on the topic.

Parental Variables

Several of the parents' personality traits are related to creative potential. In one recent demonstration of this, a study that was a part of a longitudinal investigation of exceptionally gifted boys, Runco and Albert (2005) administered the California Psychological Inventory (CPI; Gough 1975) to the boys themselves, as well as to the mothers and fathers. The CPI is an especially useful measure because it has extensive norms and gives a profile for each individual. The boys represented two distinct kinds of exceptional giftedness: one had a domain-specific skill (i.e., math–science), and the other, general intellectual ability (i.e., IQs in excess of 150). Profiles of the boys are given in Figures 2.4 and 2.5.

These profiles, like those of both parents (in both groups), are relatively flat, indicating that the participants did not deviate from normal on many scales. One deviation was that of the wellbeing scale, which is not included in the standard profiles (and thus not in the figures), but is necessary for calculation of the CPI's creativity index. Both groups of adolescents had low

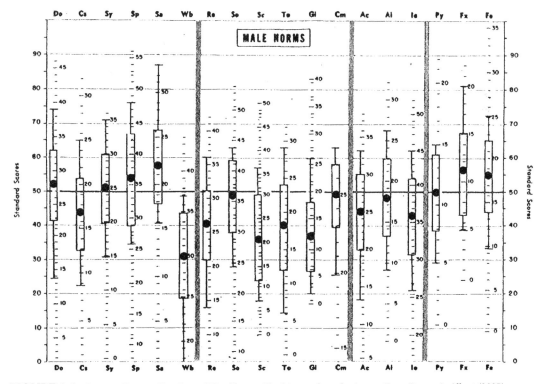

FIGURE 2.4 Personality profiles from CPI of boys gifted in math and science. *From Runco & Albert (2005).*

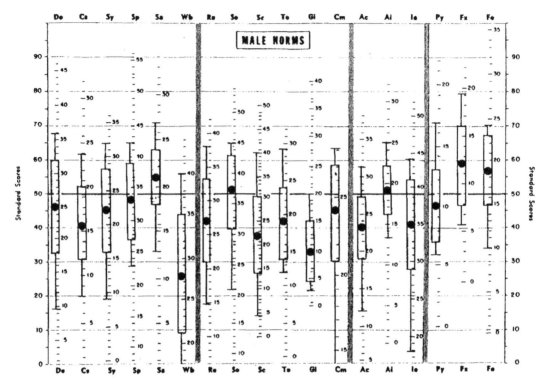

FIGURE 2.5 Personality profile of boys gifted in terms of exceptional general ability (IQ). *From Runco & Albert (2005).*

scores on this scale. There was also a hint of low sociability. In this particular research the differences between the exceptionally high IQ samples and the exceptionally high math–science samples were slight (cf. Runco & Albert 1985). Details about the creative personality are explored in Chapter 9, and what is most important here was that several of the CPI scales were correlated with creativity scores of the adolescent boys. The pattern of correlations was quite complicated, however, in part because there were various measures of creativity (the Biographical Inventory of Creativity, or BIC, divergent thinking tests, and even the CPI creativity index itself), and because the CPI supplies personality predictors in the form of composite scores, factor scores, and individual scale scores. There are also various ways to examine correlations, including product-moment, regression, and canonical analyses. The parents' capacity for independent thought, one of the individual scale scores from the CPI, was related to creativity, as was the masculinity/femininity index. There was also some indication that parents' conventionality was related to at least some of the creativity scores of their adolescent sons.

Runco and Albert (1985) looked specifically at the relationship between parental independence and the creativity of the children. Here independence was defined as an attitude, and parents actually rated how much independence was appropriate for children in various situations. The measure used to assess parental views of independence is presented (in adapted form) in Table 2.1.

TABLE 2.1 Measure Used to Estimate Parents' Views of Appropriate Levels of Independence

Directions to Parents: At what age do you think it is appropriate for a child to …

	Age (years)												
	4	5	6	7	8	9	10	11	12	13	14	15	16
1. Earn his or her own spending money?	4	5	6	7	8	9	10	11	12	13	14	15	16
2. Sleep overnight with a friend?	4	5	6	7	8	9	10	11	12	13	14	15	16
3. Play where he or she wants to play?	4	5	6	7	8	9	10	11	12	13	14	15	16
4. Make own friends and visit their homes?	4	5	6	7	8	9	10	11	12	13	14	15	16
5. Stay alone at night until midnight?	4	5	6	7	8	9	10	11	12	13	14	15	16
6. Make decisions about clothes or money?	4	5	6	7	8	9	10	11	12	13	14	15	16
7. Act as a babysitter in another home?	4	5	6	7	8	9	10	11	12	13	14	15	16
8. Go to bed on one's own?	4	5	6	7	8	9	10	11	12	13	14	15	16
9. Go to movies without parents?	4	5	6	7	8	9	10	11	12	13	14	15	16
10. Go on overnight trip?	4	5	6	7	8	9	10	11	12	13	14	15	16
11. Try new things without asking for help?	4	5	6	7	8	9	10	11	12	13	14	15	16
12. Do well in school without help from parents?	4	5	6	7	8	9	10	11	12	13	14	15	16
13. Entertain one's self?	4	5	6	7	8	9	10	11	12	13	14	15	16
14. Do well in competition?	4	5	6	7	8	9	10	11	12	13	14	15	16
15. Take part in parents' conversations?	4	5	6	7	8	9	10	11	12	13	14	15	16
16. Try new things without asking for help?	4	5	6	7	8	9	10	11	12	13	14	15	16

Adapted from Albert & Runco (1989).

Parental appreciation for the autonomy of their children is related to the actual independence of the children and to the creative and divergent thinking skills of the children. Parents who allow independence tend to have children who think creatively. The highly original children have parents who allow independence at an early age. Recall that independence is one of the important traits of creativity in the personality research. Independence may take many forms, including a tolerance of unconventional ideas and a tolerance of seemingly unrealistic perceptions. I am referring here to the imaginary friends and worlds that creative children sometimes construct. These may challenge a parent, for they are unrealistic (Boxes 2.3 and 2.4).

BOX 2.3

ON IMAGINARY COMPANIONS AND PARACOSMS

Imaginary companions and imaginary worlds (the latter known as *paracosms*) may be the most common in individuals with outstanding creative talents. Note the wording in this definition of imaginary companions: "During the preschool years, many children create imaginary companions that become a regular part of their daily routines" (Taylor et al. 1993, p. 276). The operative word is "create," as in "create imaginary companions."

Imaginary companions and paracosms seem to be the most common during the preschool years (Mackeith 1982; Taylor 1999). They are less frequent but have been found in school-aged children (Hurlock & Burstein 1932; Taylor 1999). Singer and Singer (1992, p. 110) seemed to feel that the same cognitive and emotional processes continue throughout life and that "the process of peopling one's private thoughts with companionable souls" continue throughout the lifespan. There are reports that imaginary companions sometimes endure until the individual is 18 years old (Taylor 1999). Taylor reported that 63% of the individuals in a sample of 100 persons had imaginary companions, a figure that is very close to the 65% reported by Singer and Singer (1992). Parents tend to report imaginary companions of their children much less frequently (perhaps 20%

of the time), but this is what you would expect, given that imaginary companions would be very obvious to the children playing with them but could easily escape notice or be forgotten by parents. The frequency of imaginary companions will also fluctuate depending on how imaginary companions are defined. Many researchers require that the companion be human, but others (e.g., Singer & Singer 1992) accept dolls and similar figures (e.g., teddy bears) as possible imaginary companions, but only if the doll is treated like an animate object—a true interactive companion.

One view of imaginary companions is essentially psychoanalytic (e.g., Sperling 1954) and posits that they are used as a defense mechanism (probably *projection*). Imaginary companions have also been explained as a sign of giftedness, indicative of narcissism or egocentricism, a reflection of some sort of deficit, or a result of poor impulse control. The last of these assumes that the imaginary playmate helps the child make the transition to mature and independent cognition. Most important for the present purposes is that imaginary companions may be indicative of creative potential. Simply put, the imaginary companion is the result of creative processes. Further, an

(Continued)

BOX 2.3 *(Continued)*

imaginary companion is often quite detailed. He or she is not hazy in the mind of the child but instead has stable characteristics, tendencies, and preferences. Each of these is a result of elaborative thinking. In this light the imaginary companion provides the child with a great deal of practice at thinking creatively.

In one of the more commonly cited studies of imaginary companions, Schaefer (1969) reported a significant association between imaginary companions and creativity. He did rely, however, on adolescents' recollections of their childhoods, which opens the door to the biases of self-reports. These include forgetting,

socially desirable responding, and fabrication. The association was the strongest for literary creativity. Manosevitz et al. (1977) were unable to replicate these findings.

Schaefer and Anastasi (1968) suggested that the presence of an imaginary companion is predictive of creative talent. They included a question about imaginary companions in their biographical measure of creativity. The assumption here is that creative persons tend to have imaginary companions, at least during their childhood. The incidence of imaginary companions among creative persons is unknown, however.

BOX 2.4

TOLERANCE OF CREATIVITY

Would you, if or when you have your own children, allow your offspring to play regularly with an imaginary friend? Hopefully you would, at least when your child is in his or her preschool years. It might not be as easy as it sounds. Your child, for example, might want an extra setting at the dinner table each night for the imaginary friend, which means extra work for you. Your preschool child may also create more than just an imaginary friend—perhaps an imaginary zoo, with a number of exotic animals that need special care. And if your child is indeed creative, he or she will have other tendencies, in addition to a vivid imagination, and some of these may also make your life more difficult than if you had a highly conventional, uncreative child. Just to mention one other tendency, it could be that your creative child is quite contrarian!

Taylor et al. (1993) pinpointed the preschool years. It may be acceptable, and even

developmentally stimulating, for a preschool child to have an imaginary companion, but what if an adult does? Very likely, the adult would be suspect and labeled something other than "creative." Consider Jimmy Stewart in the movie, *Harvey*, who was indeed nearly locked up for talking to an invisible friend named Harvey. Then again, Harvey was a six-foot rabbit (and for my money, Jimmy Stewart was the most normal individual in the movie).

Parents do not always tolerate creativity, and it does often require tolerance. It is one thing to agree that creativity is a desirable thing, and a trait that you admire and want to encourage in your children, but another thing to actually tolerate and support it. Brown's (1973) research on parents and children's language demonstrates the difficulties: He found that what was most important for parents in children's language was not grammar or

(Continued)

BOX 2.4　　*(Continued)*

complexity, but truthfulness. Parents did not want a child talking in a manner that reflected an inaccurate world view, and this is precisely what a creative child may invent! After all, what is an imaginary friend? How accurate is that?

Teachers also have difficulties with creative children. Consider in this regard the profiles of "the ideal child" provided by Torrance (1968a) and Raina (1975). Ideal children are polite, considerate, respectful, and punctual. They are not unconventional, nonconforming contrarians. Educators can be given some slack if we think about how we might like being in a classroom, six hours each day, five days a week, with 20 or 30 contrarians! Chapter 6 goes into detail about educational influences on creative potentials.

The personality studies of parents are meaningful in a very general way because they offer a kind of research and theoretical convergence on the creative complex. After all, there are cognitive studies that suggest that creativity benefits from divergence and originality (Guilford 1968), as well as personality studies that suggest much the same (perhaps in different terms).

Parental Implicit Theories of Creativity

Implicit theories are held by parents, teachers, and other nonresearchers. Researchers, in contrast, hold explicit theories. These are very easy to define: They are explicit because they must be articulated and shared. They are tested, presented, or published, and a part of the scientific community. Parents and teachers, on the other hand, do not need to share or test their ideas about creativity; they are in that sense implicit. These are not just ideas about creativity, however, but are also expectations. That may be the most important part of implicit theories: They lead to expectations, and expectations in turn lead to actual behavior. Clearly, a parent or teacher's expectations about children's creativity will determine how they react to the child and what opportunities they might provide. If a parent holds the implicit view that all creative children are artistic, for example, he or she will probably not expect much creativity from a child who can't draw. This particular mistake can be called an *art bias*.

Runco (1989a) examined the implicit theories held by parents about children's creativity, starting by administering the 300-item Adjective Check List (ACL; Gough & Heilbrun 1975) to one group of parents. They were asked to identify any traits from the list of 300 that they felt were indicative of children's creativity. The most frequently listed items were placed on the Parental Evaluation of Children's Creativity (PECC). (The Teachers' Evaluation of Students' Creativity is presented in Chapter 6.) Runco (1989a) compared the specific traits with those nominated in earlier research involving teachers (Runco 1984). There was some agreement between the parents and teachers: Both groups felt that the following traits were indicative of creativity: artistic, curious, imaginative, independent, inventive, original, and wide interests. Runco (1989a) collected additional data from additional groups of parents and teachers. The ratings from these groups were compiled so that several clusters of items were represented in composite scores. (It is never wise to compare groups or in any way rely on individual items from a test. Single items lack reliability.) These statistical comparisons of parents and teachers indicated a very low level of agreement. Runco was unsurprised by this, given the very different experiences parents and teachers have with children.

Runco and colleagues (1993) extended this work in order to examine both indicative and contraindicative traits. They also looked carefully at the social desirability of the items and traits that were related to creativity. The parents and teachers in this research had more similar views about creativity than did the groups in the earlier study. That may be because Runco et al. used exactly the same methodology with parents and teachers, whereas in the earlier research there were some methodological differences. This held the *method variance* constant for the two groups. Of course, the two groups were not in perfect agreement! Sixty-seven percent of the common items and traits (those nominated by at least 50% of the sample) were identical. But that leaves 33%, as well as items that were not commonly nominated (i.e., nominated by less than 50% of the sample). Both groups agreed that creative children are likely to be adaptable, imaginative, adventurous, clever, inventive, curious, daring, and dreamy. There was less agreement about contraindicative items, but nonetheless some consensus that the children who seemed to be less creative are likely to be cautious, aloof, conventional, fault-finding, and unambitious. Differences between the parents and teachers, when they occurred, suggested that parents were more concerned with personal and intellectual tendencies (i.e., enterprising, impulsive, industrious, progressive, resourceful, and self-confident), whereas the teachers seemed to be more concerned with traits that may be more apparent in social settings (i.e., cheerful, easy going, emotional, friendly, and spontaneous). Finally, there was some indication that the traits associated with creativity were socially desirable.

Johnson et al. (2003) used the social validation methodology to contrast the implicit theories of parents with those of teachers. They also compared a sample from the United States with a sample from India. This research also separated traits that are thought to be indicative of creativity and those that are contraindicative. The latter are negatively related to creativity; they inhibit it or at least are lacking in highly creative persons. A final objective of this research was to examine the relationship between creativity and social desirability.

Analyses indicated that both groups (parents and teachers) did indeed realize that there are both indicative and contraindicative traits for creativity. Additionally, most traits that were indicative of creativity were deemed socially desirable. This was not entirely true, however, for there were a few traits that were associated with creativity but not highly desirable. Differences between the adults from the United States and the adults from India were most apparent in intellectual traits and attitudinal traits. Examples of each are presented in Table 2.2.

Parental Creativity

The most direct assessment of the family focused on parental creativity. Not surprisingly, parental creativity is predictive of children's creativity. Parents who are original in their thinking have children with high divergent thinking skills. Correlations between parental divergent thinking test scores and those of their children, for example, may be in the .40 to .50 range (Runco & Albert 1986a). It is likely that the actual correlation varies in different samples, however. Runco and Albert found differences between children with exceptionally high IQs and children with mathematical and scientific talent in this regard (the relationship

TABLE 2.2 Attitudinal, Intellectual, and Motivational Traits

Attitudinal	Intellectual	Motivational
Changeable	Artistic	Active
Dreamy	Capable	Adventurous
Emotional	Clever	Alert
Excitable	Imaginative	Curious
Humorous	Interests wide	Determined
Independent	Inventive	Energetic
Individualistic	Original	Enthusiastic
	Resourceful	Impulsive
	Versatile	Spontaneous

Adapted from Johnson et al. (2003).

being stronger in the former), and all their participants were exceptionally talented. The relationship could be weaker in families with less talented children.

Modeling very likely occurs within the family, with children imitating the divergent thinking of their parents. *Valuation* would also be very important for divergent thinking and creativity, because parents who value original thinking presumably respect and appreciate creativity, including their children's divergent thinking. They may also explicitly value originality and reinforce their children's original thinking. Children may internalize the values, as well as learning the actual strategies for original thinking.

A statistically significant correlation between parental creativity and that of their children also was reported by Noble et al. (1993). This sample included families with alcoholics, families with a history of alcoholism, and families with no history of alcoholism. Interestingly, the correlation between parents and children was much stronger for the fathers than the mothers. There were group differences as well. Perhaps most surprising was the lack of association between the creativity test scores of the mothers and those of the fathers. The correlations were small and statistically insignificant, thus contrary to hypotheses about *assortive mating* (the tendency of similar people to marry). Although this study focused on exceptional samples, the correlations among fathers and their sons was apparent with various measures, including divergent thinking tests, the How Do You Think? test (Davis 1975), and an origence/intellectence index that is part of the ACL. (Alcoholism and creativity are discussed in detail in Chapter 4.)

Children spend less and less time in the home with the family as they grow older. In fact, as noted earlier in the discussion of conventionality, there is a period of development where peers are at least as important as the family in the life of a child, preadolescent, or adolescent. Some people believe that early experience is always the most significant influence on development and thus a child may distance him- or herself from the family and its values during the teenage years, but return to the earlier values at some point in adulthood. To my knowledge this kind of double-shift has not been empirically examined. There is, however, empirical research on the role of peers and the relationship between *peer status* and creative potential.

PEER STATUS AND CREATIVITY

Lau and Li (1996) examined the relationship of peer status and creativity in a large sample of Chinese students in Hong Kong. As is common in this kind of *sociometric* research, children were identified as popular, controversial, average, neglected, or rejected. These categorizations were based on peer nominations (e.g., the number of students within a class who were mentioned by their peers when asked who they liked the most and who they liked the least). Assessments of creativity were based on peer nominations and teachers' judgments.

Interestingly, the most popular children had the highest creativity ratings. The neglected group had very low creativity scores, as did the rejected group. The controversial group—which represented students who were liked by some peers but disliked by others—had higher creativity ratings than the average group. Differences among the five groups were found with both the teachers' ratings and the peer nominations. There were also minor sex differences, with boys having significantly higher scores than girls. This difference was not found in the teachers' ratings. Differences in creativity among the five groups were much more apparent in peer ratings than in the evaluations given by the teachers.

This last finding raises the possibility that children may be more sensitive to the creativity of their peers than are teachers. Of course it could be that their nominations are not as valid and accurate as those of teachers. There is, however, reason to think that the student ratings might be accurate (Runco et al. 1994). Runco et al. (1994) found students to be sensitive to differences, while adults were not. Their work, however, was with college students and art assignments, and the adults were professional artists. Nonetheless, they concluded that the student ratings, for many purposes, were more valid and useful than those given by the professional artists. It depends on what you are trying to predict. It may be that the same can be said of the ratings by the children involved in the research of Lau and Li (1996). In fact, it is not much of a stretch to suggest that some of the same reasons given for children being *more* creative than adults (Runco 1996a) could be applied here. Regardless, children's judgments about creativity may be at least as useful as those given by adults.

It really boils down to what you try to predict. The clearest example of this may be that children make fewer assumptions, and thus have fewer biases, than adults. Teachers may have certain biases toward academic work and conformity; these same things may be lacking in children, therefore not influencing their judgments. In that sense their judgments may be more a reflection of the actual originality of their peers. Torrance (1995) and Raina (1975) both described how teachers' views of an *ideal student* may preclude creative talents. The interpretation offered by Lau and Li was that "teachers were more conservative in rating children's creativity. This might be because teachers usually give primary attention to children's learning ability and behavioral conduct. Teachers may also be less sensitive than peers to children's creative thinking because of their schematic knowledge and higher expectation" (Lau and Li 1996, p. 350).

Lau and Li (1996) concluded that "creative children may have easier social development" (p. 350) than other children. The assumption here is that creativity is a kind of problem solving and adaptability that can be applied to social situations. Their explanation of how creativity is influenced by the status of children is very interesting: They suggested that a popular child who holds some sort of leadership position, perhaps informally, might produce new and original ideas and thereby earn respect. Lau and Li seemed to think that social status among peers may or may not be influenced by creativity, however, for they also described how a child who is not respected by his or her peers might produce original ideas but would not earn respect simply because it wasn't a leader or popular child who produced them. This possibility is quite consistent with what we know about interpersonal attributions (Kasof 1995; Runco 1995c) and the common misjudgment of creative thinking (Runco 1999b). Gibart-Eaglemont and Foddy (1994) also presented data on the relationship of social status creativity among children.

This line of work is intriguing, and differs in an important way from that which is typical in research on children's creativity. We should practice what we preach, which means that we should respect things that are different! The work on peer status among young students is different in the sense that the more common approach in studies of children's creativity is to focus on the process rather than the product or a person's persuasion. (These terms are used in the alliterative scheme for categorizing creativity research. The introduction to this book describes creative products, places, personalities, processes, and persuasion as the usual categories.) Research on adult or unambiguous (eminent) creativity often examine product and persuasion, the latter apparent whenever the creative person influences the thinking of other people. Lau and Li (1996) suggested that there is a parallel during childhood and that creative children may also manifest a social influence or kind of persuasion. Feldhusen and Goh (1995) offered a similar view and claimed that one part of creativity is the "ability to persuade others of the value of one's work" (p. 232).

Childhood is changing (Elkind 1981). Expectations are changing, as are opportunities and experiences. Children may be spending less time watching TV, just to name one example, but they are also using the Internet more and more. Do children growing up right now have enough time for creative self-expression and imaginative play?

Bowers et al. (2012) recently described how the creativity of children may no longer be given critical opportunities. They were specifically concerned about the loss of informal recreational activities and unstructured sports. They presented data showing that these are related to various indicators of creative potential. The data also showed that there is in fact less opportunity now than, say, 20 years ago, for children to be involved in informal and unstructured sports and recreation. Part of the problem may be that children are more likely to exhibit true play in unstructured settings, so play—which is clearly associated with the development of creativity—is less frequent now than every before. But another part of the problem is that the loss of unstructured experiences is the direct result of increases in structured experiences, such as formalized and organized sports. These usually have authority figures (e.g., coaches) and rules and, well, structure, each of which may preclude spontaneous play. The decrease in opportunities for spontaneity and for play cannot be good for the fulfillment of creative potentials.

ADULT DEVELOPMENT

Postformal Stage and Problem Finding

Stage theories of development were reviewed earlier in this chapter. These described periods of childhood and adolescence that had some relevance to creativity. There are also theories that describe developments of relevance during adulthood. There is, for example, a theory that describes a *postformal stage* of development. This is especially important because it exemplifies the lifespan development of creative potentials and expression. The postformal stage does not occur in childhood; if it occurs, it is in early or middle adulthood.

This perspective assumes discontinuities and describes creativity as most likely during one particular stage. This is the postformal stage, which, as the name suggests, occurs after formal operations. *Postformal operations* are most likely during adulthood, characterized by an understanding of relativity (i.e., a recognition of the importance of immediate context and a rejection of absolutes), *dialectical thinking* (i.e., the capacity to take both one extreme position or "thesis" into account as well as the "antithesis," its opposite, and to integrate them into a meaningful synthesis), and problem finding. The last of these would be most directly related to creative achievements, given how important it can be to devote one's efforts to meaningful problems. Einstein put it this way: "The formulation of a problem is often more essential than its solution. … To raise new questions, new possibilities, to regard old problems from a new angle, requires imagination and marks real advance in science" (Einstein & Infeld 1938, p. 83).

Wertheimer (1982) suggested much the same: "often in great discoveries the most important thing is that a certain question is found. Envisaging, putting the productive question is often a more important, often a greater achievement than the solution of a set question" (p. 123). Along the same lines Guilford (1950) described a "sensitivity to problems" and Torrance (1962) described "the process of *sensing gaps* or disturbing missing elements and formulating hypotheses" as part of the creative process (p. 16, emphasis added). Runco (1994d) brought together many perspectives on problem finding and related aspects of creative work. There is, then, agreement about the role of problem finding in creativity, and several suggestions (Arlin 1975; Smolucha & Smolucha 1986) that the necessary skills mature only in a postformal or fifth stage of development.

Old Age Style

A very similar view of general age trends focuses on late life and the *old age style* that often characterizes the work of artists and creative persons in their sixth, seventh, eighth, or ninth decades of life. This is not viewed as a stage of development, probably because it is not universal, even among artists, and because it may be a matter of choice rather than a maturational (genetic) tendency. Apparently highly creative artists recognize the need to avoid routine and ruts and choose to change their style, sometimes more than once, as they grow older. The changes help them to remain flexible and increase the likelihood they that will renew their originality.

Lindauer et al. (1997) found clear indications of old age style in a large group of artists who were in their 60s, 70s, and 80s. Each had been nominated as highly creative. All three groups felt that their work had improved during adulthood. Their own ratings of their work suggested that they had much more respect for work done after age 60 than in their 30s, 40s, or 50s. The work done when the artists were in their 60s was rated the highest. These were self-reports, and as such have potential biases. Interestingly, when the artists were asked to explain the changes in their work they cited increased knowledge and skill, but also increased self-acceptance and understanding, a reduction in the weight they gave to criticism or the reactions of others, the adoption of new techniques, a tendency to experiment more, and shifts in the subject matter. A full 81% felt that their creativity had changed as they moved through adulthood. Lindauer et al. (1997) concluded that artists who are creative throughout their lives, well into their 70s and 80s and perhaps beyond, continue to learn, grow, and improve. There are changes with age but these need not reflect a decline in creativity.

Other optimistic views of aging and creativity can be found in Fisher and Specht (1999) and Langer (1989). Langer's work on *mindfulness* is nothing short of fascinating. She tied both creativity and aging to mindfulness and demonstrated how very simple manipulations encourage older adults to remain active and mindful, and how these may translate directly into improved quality of life and longevity.

Note the key word "can," in the preceding quotation (i.e., "changes with age can be for the better"). Old age style and increased creative performance are probably very much a matter of choice. The clearest example of this may be Kaun's (1991) data showing that "writers die young." He compared many different careers and found just that: Writers die young. This may be because writers work in isolation and have greatly delayed gratification (e.g., publication itself, or royalties). Their work often is criticized (literary critics tending to do just that— they criticize), and writers usually write what they know. This means that they are exposing personal materials to the world! Abra (1997) quoted one writer as saying, "Sure, writing is easy: Just sit down at the typewriter and open an artery." But some of the unhealthful tendencies of writers may result from the choices they make. First, they choose the career, thus choosing the life of delayed gratification and the like. They may also choose to follow the classic stereotype of "the great writer," which, since F. Scott Fitzgerald, has meant late nights, martinis, and a bit of eccentric carelessness. Some of this is generalization, but some of aging is a matter of choice (Box 2.5). In various ways we need to battle the changes that occur naturally as we grow old.

BOX 2.5

SKINNER ON AGING AND CONTROL OF ONE'S CREATIVITY LATE IN LIFE

B. F. Skinner, at one time America's preeminent psychologist, devoted the last part of his own life to research aging. Much of what he said applies directly to creativity and its maintenance. His ideas apply to both professional creativity (Skinner was a writer of fiction as well as research reports) and nonprofessional and everyday creativity. He enjoyed music (both listening and playing the piano) and cooking, and both of these involve some creativity.

He was disappointed initially in the problems resulting from aging, especially because he had less energy and found his sensory systems were losing their sensitivity. He did not hear as well, for instance, which of course is quite common in older adults. Indeed, most older adults lack sensitivity in all five sensory systems. This is why cooking was less enjoyable for Skinner: His recipes did not have the same pizzazz. But Skinner took the same approach to aging that he did in his research: He emphasized the environment and experience. With this in mind he developed a *compensatory environment* and prostheses to insure that he could still write and enjoy his music and cooking. For the last of these he simply changed his recipes and added more spice.

(Continued)

BOX 2.5 *(Continued)*

That compensated for the loss of sensitivity in his gustatory system. (Makes you wonder if anyone else could share his meals!) Skinner rested more, and more carefully avoided stress, thus providing the energy he needed to play the piano. To enjoy listening to recorded music, he turned up the volume. Again, these are environmental compensations, which Skinner argued, allowed the individual to *Enjoy Old Age* (the title of his book, which, importantly, is printed in large print; presbyopia is also common in older adults).

Skinner (2005) wrote a novel early in his career: *Walden Two*. It described a utopian world where everyone accepted the fact that consequences (reinforcers and punishers) control our lives unless we mindfully control them. Late in life Skinner's writing was nonfiction; he was writing scientific papers. Memory was therefore very important, for scientific writing draws heavily from what others have done, from theory and previous research. Sadly, memory losses and difficulties are extremely common in older adults,

and Skinner experienced great frustration when he found that he had a wonderful idea, only to discover that it was something that he had written about already, perhaps decades earlier. He suggested "memoranda not memory," the idea again being to use the environment to compensate. Write things down; don't trust your memory. Keep a pad of paper next to the bed, a pen in your pocket. Skinner even asked his wife to help him, at least when he could not remember people's names.

The critical message is to adapt, to make adjustments, to use the environment when you grow older. In many ways you simply need to make certain choices and thereby have some control over creative activities, and for that matter, control over your life. Skinner's ideas about creativity during late life, and the enjoyment of late life, are therefore entirely consistent with one of the themes of this book, namely, that much of our lives, and much of our creativity, is under our own individual control. Much of it is a matter of choice.

The artists in the research just described reported difficulties resulting from changes in their sensory and physical capacities. These did not debilitate them, however, for they continued to work and learn and create. Still, it requires a choice, which I recommend to each of us, a choice to invest in our creative potentials throughout our entire lives.

CONCLUSIONS

Creativity takes various forms at different points in life. There are common slumps, as well as stages. These may be tied to maturation, but the research on families suggests that parents and the home environment provide experiences that may also dramatically influence creative potentials. Some of the variables reviewed in this chapter can be controlled by parents (e.g., family size). Others probably cannot be controlled by parents.

Parents will also provide experiences and therefore options. Certain experiences may be most important for the fulfillment of creative potentials, though of course here it depends on the domain of creative talent. A child with an artistic inclination may benefit the most from visits to museums and galleries, whereas a child with musical potential may benefit the most from concerts and the like. Then again, parents should provide varied experiences to their children and not rely on one kind of outing. After all, a child may have interests but the parents are not yet aware of it! It may be that it is the trip to the museum that triggers the child's interest in science or art. Along the same lines, diverse experiences seem to be beneficial. This may be because they show the individual a variety of perspectives, which in turn can be related to flexibility and the recognition of diverse options.

There are important developmental questions that have yet to be sufficiently examined in empirical research. The research on creativity in middle and late life is not adequate, especially given the graying of America. Another area of needed research involves single parents. Cornelius and Yawkey (1986) examined the imaginativeness of preschoolers in single-parent families, and Jenkins et al. (1988) looked specifically at children's divergent thinking after parental separation, but these are two fairly small-scale studies, and single parenting is enormously common.

This statement about needed research should not imply that our understanding of development is inadequate. This chapter does not give a complete picture of how potentials are fulfilled, but it does identify maturational tendencies and family influences. These tell part of the story and complement what we find in the educational, biological, and cultural research that is reviewed in the other chapters of this book.

The old age style involves change. Creative artists often make changes, and these may allow them to retain an original attitude and high levels of creativity. The old age style may not be limited to one's artwork, however. Making changes for the sake of change may characterize one's entire lifestyle. Consider in this regard the artist Katsushika Hokusai (1760–1849), who should be famous for his series of prints, "Thirty-Six Views of Mount Fuji," and especially for one print in that series, *The Great Wave*. *The Great Wave* is on bookcovers, on the Internet, on clothing, and of course on prints available at Art.com and other similar outlets. I have a print of it on the wall of my kitchen. Yet it is unlikely that most people who recognize the print will know the name of the artist. Why? Partly because he changed his name over 30 times during his career (Krull 1995).

This is remarkable in part because it shows that certain creative people are not concerned about reputation. Gardner (1993a) suggested that highly creative persons are self-promoters, which makes sense given the importance of fame and reputation (Kasof 1995; Simonton 1995), but reputation is in several important ways independent of talent (Runco 1995c), and apparently the tendency to worry about one's reputation (and the tendency to promote one's self) is not universal among creative persons. I wonder if this is also related to the interest many artists have in names and pseudonyms. The Beatles song *Rocky Raccoon* has the lyric, "Her name was McGill, and she called herself Lil but everyone knew her as Nancy," and Paul Simon and Bob Dylan also play with varied names in their songs. Perhaps it is just the flexibility and playfulness of creative individuals that leads them to this; it may not be old age style at all, just creative style. As a matter of fact that was the other commonality identified by Gardner (1993a) in his extensive study of Freud, Einstein, Picasso, Stravinsky, T. S. Eliot,

Martha Graham, and Gandhi. Not only were they frequent self-promoters, they were also childlike (and playful).

There is yet another possible explanation for the frequency with which artists play with names. Each of them could be dealing with an epistemological issue, namely (no pun intended) that concerning the meaning of a label or name. Shakespeare, and Gertrude Stein somewhat later, insisted that "a rose is a rose is a rose … a rose by any other name would still smell as sweet."

3

Biological Perspectives on Creativity

INTRODUCTION

Some of the most exciting research on creativity as of late involves the brain and biological correlates of originality, novelty, and insight. For years the biological approach to creativity was fairly stagnant, at least relative to the advances made in the cognitive sciences and various other perspectives on creativity. This stagnation reflected the difficulties involved in conducting good genetic and neuroanatomical research on creativity. Ironically, it may also have resulted from a kind of rigidity, not unlike what we have discussed in this book (as precluding creativity). It was very difficult for geneticists, neuroanatomists, and others in related fields to view creativity as a legitimate topic for empirical study. Even when their newer technologies were applied to language, depression, and other psychological concerns, creativity seemed to be too ambiguous.

Roger Sperry's seminal work on the split brain (Sperry 1964) might be viewed as an exception to that, though his own work was not really on creativity. The patients he studied, who had the two hemispheres of the brain surgically separated in surgery known as a

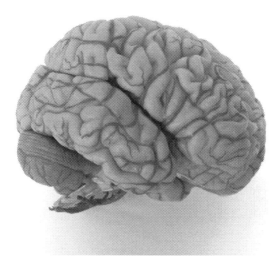

FIGURE 3.1 One view of the brain. The curious cerebellum is in the lower left of this view.

commissurotomy, were also studied by Bogen (1969), Hoppe and Kyle (1990), and TenHouten (1994); their focus was on creativity, so in the long run that split brain research was informative. Yet that was about it for neuroanatomical studies of creativity (Figure 3.1).

Genetics did not fare much better. Inferences were drawn from genealogies (see later) and from a behavioral genetic method that compared either identical (monozygotic) and fraternal (dizygotic) twins, or biological and nonbiological parents with their children. This is not controlled research, however, and the reliable information about the genetic and neuroanatomical bases for creativity accumulated only very slowly—until recently. Now it is growing as quickly as any other perspective on the topic.

A number of technologies developed in the past 20 years, including magnetic resonance imaging (MRI) and positron emission topography (PET), have led to much better research on the brain, and on creativity in particular. It is fascinating research in part because much of it focuses on the actual mechanisms and processes that underlie creativity. It is not easy going because creativity is complex; a number of factors and processes are involved, but great headway is being made. And no longer are creative studies dependent on weak inferences that for years were required (e.g., from dissected to live brains, from handedness to hemispheric specialization). Indeed, the biological research on creativity is as valid and trustworthy as anything else in this textbook or field.

This chapter covers a fairly wide area. As we implied, the biological perspective includes both brain research and genetics. There are also relevant studies of physiological processes, such as those related to stress and exercise. These both have been tied to creativity and are examined briefly later. To be comprehensive, the older research just mentioned (e.g., split brains, twin studies) is included in this review. This not only gives a more complete picture of what biological research has been done on creativity; it also shows how evidence generated using different methodologies converges on several key aspects of creativity. In fact, much of what has been learned from the so-called older studies nicely complements the newer findings from the most recent genetic, MRI, and PET studies of creativity. Put differently, many of the MRI and PET studies drew on the older studies to determine hypotheses or research targets.

This chapter addresses several important questions. Does creativity run in families? How much is genetic, and how much experiential or environmental? What parts of the brain are associated with creative work? Are specific parts of the brain related to certain kinds of creativity? What motivates the creator? Do exceptional or eminent creators have genes or brains or something that the rest of us do not?

HEMISPHERIC ASYMMETRY AND THE SPLIT BRAIN

Much has been written about hemispheric dominance, hemispheric specialization, and creativity. This is largely because of the impressive work of Sperry (1964), for which he was awarded the Nobel Prize about 20 years after his initial findings were published. This research demonstrated clearly that the two hemispheres are specialized. It also confirmed that the corpus callosum (the bundle of nerves bridging the two hemispheres) allows interhemispheric communication. When severed by commissurotomy, the two hemispheres worked much more independently. One seemed to be uninformed about the other. To be precise, in a commissurotomy, several structures are severed, including the dorsal and ventral hippocampal commissures and the anterior commissure, "and in some cases, the massa intermedia" (TenHouten 1994, p. 226).

Care must be taken with the concept of a *split brain*. This is in part because most of us have intact brains, and because creativity probably requires, or is certainly the most likely, with an intact brain. As we will see, the creativity complex is apparent on a neuroanatomical level. There is no one "seat" of creativity in the brain, one responsible location or even hemisphere. Creativity may not draw from the entire brain but it certainly draws on many different brain

---

BOX 3.1

HEMISPHERIC SPECIALIZATION

- Dominant hemisphere processes: sequential, logical, analytical, and verbal, or propositional (Bogen 1969; Katz 1997; Vartanian & Goel, 2005).
- Nondominant hemisphere processes: simultaneous, holistic, visuospatial, appropositional, pattern-recognition, synthesis (Bogen 1969; Katz 1997; Levy-Agresti & Sperry 1968).

Dominant hemisphere processes often are assigned to the left hemisphere, and non-dominant processes to the right, but if an individual is left-handed, hemisphericity (the dominance of one hemisphere and asymmetry of the cerebral cortex) is diminished or even reversed. Nebes (1977) suggested that the term *dominant hemisphere* should be avoided, given the distribution of processes across both hemispheres. He suggested that hemispheric *dominance* be replaced with hemispheric *specialization*.

structures and processes. Still, identifying the specializations of the two hemispheres does help to explain what is processed where. Various labels for typical specializations are presented in Box 3.1.

The research on the two hemispheres has frequently been misunderstood, at least in regard to creativity. After an extensive review of the research, Katz (1997) concluded that there is "a tendency to treat the functions of the cerebral hemispheres in an overly simplified fashion without recognizing that, even with a highly lateralized function such as language, one can find evidence that both hemispheres are engaged at some level." He described "the simplistic argument that the essential aspect of creativity resides in the right hemisphere. The claim that creativity is located 'in' the right hemisphere (cf. Edwards 1979; Hendron 1989) should be dispelled with at once."

Very few generalizations can be drawn from Sperry's (1964) study because the patients were epileptic. That is why they had the surgery—to minimize their proclivity for grand mal seizures. It also was a small sample (29 patients), which further precludes generalizations. As a matter of fact the specializations uncovered by Sperry—the left playing a role in language, for example—did not even characterize all the individuals in his small sample! Then there is the impressive fact that they all had a commissurotomy. This puts a complete kibosh on generalizations. In the strictest sense, generalizations should apply only to other epileptics who received the same surgery. There are additional data suggesting specialization of certain brain structures, and these have utilized other noninvasive technologies, which is one reason why the idea of hemispheric specialization is widely accepted.

It is clear, then, that we should not generalize specifically from Sperry's (1964) initial study. This point is labored here because there are a number of published recommendations and even treatment and enhancement programs (reviewed by Atchley et al. 1999) that make unwarranted generalizations. These are usually easy to identify. If they say something like "learn to use your right hemisphere," you might ask how someone who has not had a commissurotomy can disconnect the left hemisphere. (If they offer you surgery to that end, decline and beat a rapid retreat.) For that matter, why would anyone want to rely on the right hemisphere, given that creativity (and any other important function you can name, including language) requires both hemispheres?

Why was the right hemisphere labeled the creative one? It may be because often creativity is assumed to be illogical or at least nontraditional in its logic. Traditional logic or sequential processing was assigned to the left hemisphere, and left creative logic for the right (or nondominant) hemisphere. Perhaps it was also the holistic processing of the right hemisphere, for that can play a role in many of the arts (e.g., the visual arts). Yet the need for a collaborating brain is clear, even in the visual arts. In Flaherty's (2005) words, the "lateralization model applies poorly to language-based innovation. This is a significant defect, since symbolic verbal communication underlies most creative thought and its cultural transmission and may have driven the evolutionary increase in the size of the human brain" (p. 147).

Bogen and Bogen (1969), Hoppe and Kyle (1990), and TenHouten (1994) all worked with the original commissurotomy patients, and unlike Sperry (1964), each of them looked specifically at creative functioning. In several studies, Hoppe (1988; Hoppe & Kyle 1990) compared eight of the commissurotomy patients to eight matched control subjects. The matching insured that the groups were comparable in terms of linguistic and ethnic background, sex, age, and especially handedness. The method employed by Hoppe is often used to study the impact of affect and emotion on creativity and cognition. It involves an emotionally evocative film that is viewed by the research participants. Participants describe their feelings and general reactions to the film, which they view several times. Hoppe also obtained electroencephalogram (EEG) readings. Significantly, the commissurotomized individuals described their reactions in unemotional terms. They seemed to be completely deficient in affect. It was almost episodic, meaning that the focus was on the event and situations in the film rather than on the meaning of the action. This is shocking because the films were blatantly evocative. In one, a small child is in a swing, but then the swing is empty—the child is gone. The implication is that something traumatic has happened to the child. Not only did the commissurotomy patients fail to react to the disappearance of the child, they even failed to interpret fairly obvious symbolism (e.g., the empty swing). In the words of Hoppe and Kyle, the reactions of the patients was "dull, uninvolved, flat and lacking in colour and expressiveness. Commissurotomy patients tended not to fantasize about, imagine or interpret the symbols, and they also tended to describe the circumstances surrounding events, as opposed to describing their feelings about these events" (Hoppe & Kyle 1990, p. 151).

Hoppe and Kyle (1990) described the lack of emotions as a kind of *alexithemia*, which means just what is implied—that the person lacks emotionality. Alexithemic individuals probably will not get too excited about opportunities and challenges; they will thus have difficulty being creative. There was some indication that the alexithemia was associated with the language areas of the left hemisphere and the right temporal lobe. If that EEG result holds up to replication, it would be consistent with the definition of alexithemia that includes difficulty in expressing one's emotions (see *Alexithemia Defined*, below). It is not simply lack of affect but also a cognitive problem in that affect cannot be put into words. Simplifying, the person cannot find the words to express emotional reactions. Later in this chapter other EEG data are summarized. EEGs may be the exception to the rule in that it is the one method that has long been a useful technique and remains so in studies of creativity. Later in this chapter further research on the emotional neuroanatomical bases of creativity are explored. Emotions are quite important for creativity and are being examined with PET and MRI methods. First we should finish discussing the research with the commissurotomy patients.

TenHouten (1994) worked with the same patients (and researchers, for that matter) as Sperry (1964), and analyzed the transcripts of the verbal reports mentioned earlier. He went on to coauthor 10 or more papers with Bogen and Hoppe (the latest being Hoppe & Kyle 1990; see TenHouten 1994). One of his approaches involved handwriting analysis. Like Smith (1988), TenHouten concluded that there is a weak but positive relationship between various handwriting indices (which are thought to be indicative of brain function) and creative potential. Smith developed a Graphological Creativity Quotient (GCQ), graphology being the study of handwriting. It focused on intuition, autonomy, flexibility, openness, spontaneity, and two or three other tendencies with less obvious connection to creativity. Smith reported a correlation of .30 between her GCQ and divergent thinking. That is certainly positive, and it was statistically significant, but it is unimpressive, perhaps because handwriting is influenced by so many other things in addition to creative potential.

ALEXITHEMIA DEFINED

Split-brain patients tend to be alexithemic. This refers to "a cognitive-affective disturbance with ... a lack of feelings for words. The alexithemic person does not lack words for feelings in the same way that a color-blind person can say 'the sky is blue.' Although the word alexithemia, coined by Sifneos (1973), has the literal meaning, 'no words for feelings,' the meaning of this aspect of alexithemia is better conveyed by the Greek word athymoalexia, which means 'no feelings for words.' ... The alexithemic thus has difficulty describing his or her feelings to other persons" (TenHouten 1994, p. 225).

HANDEDNESS AND HEMISPHERICITY

There are other methods for investigating brain asymmetry and specialization. Dichotic listening tasks, for example, have been employed, typically with nonexceptional individuals. In dichotic listening tasks two different messages are presented, one to the right ear, one to the left ear. Memory is then assessed, the assumption being that the dominant hemisphere should remember its message better than the so-called minor hemisphere. Sometimes, images instead of verbal messages are presented to the two visual fields. Another method involves monitoring conjugate eye movement, the idea being that when reflecting on some idea, individuals shift the direction of their eyes to the right if left-hemisphere dominant and to the left when right-hemisphere dominant (Katz 1997; Kinsbourne 1974; Zenhausern & Kraemer 1991). Hines and Martindale (1974) forced subjects to look to the left, using special goggles, and reported a benefit when individuals had to look to the left (right hemisphere) while they worked on creativity tasks.

Handedness is sometimes used as an indication of hemispheric dominance or hemisphericity, with right-handed people being compared with left-handed people. Differences are not overwhelming by any means. Burke et al. (1989), for instance, found that left-handed individuals do slightly better than right-handed people on visual or figural tests of divergent thinking but are no different in verbal divergent thinking. Intriguingly, they suggested that when left-handed persons have an advantage, it may be because they have developed a kind of creative coping skill. Left-handed people often find themselves in environments that are made for right-handed people. Perhaps this contributes to their adaptability and creative thinking.

There are several reports of left-handed persons outnumbering the right-handed in creative and eminent samples. Peterson and Lansky (1977), for instance, reported that 29% of one university's architecture faculty was left-handed, and although that is far from the 50% that might be expected since there are two hands, it is well above the typical percentage of left-handed individuals in the general population. Most people are right-handed. Peterson and Lansky also found higher than expected proportions of left-handed persons in applications to schools of architecture. There was further indication that the left-handed students performed better in that same school. Annett and Kilshaw (1983) and Byrne (1974) reported similar proportions of left-handedness, the former in mathematics (students and professors) and the latter in a sample of musicians.

These reports are by and large indirect and observational, at least in the sense that the focus is on handedness or behavioral tendencies and not actual brain structure or function. Hemisphericity and dominance are inferred from particular behaviors or tendencies. Fortunately neuroanatomy and related brain sciences have advanced to a point where direct measurement is possible. Hemisphericity and other important brain structures and processes contributing to creative thinking and behavior have in recent years been studied with EEG, PET, cerebral blood flow, and MRI techniques.

BRAIN WAVES AND THE ELECTROENCEPHALOGRAM

Numerous EEG studies suggest that there are particular brain wave patterns and brain structures associated with creative problem solving, or at least specific phases within the problem-solving process (Martindale & Hasenfus 1978; Martindale & Hines 1975; Martindale et al. 1984) (Figures 3.2 and 3.3). Martindale and Hasenfus (1978), for example, obtained EEG readings from 12 undergraduates with electrodes over the right posterior temporal area of the brain. Wave activity was recorded while the students waited for the study to begin, after the experiment had begun and they were directed to think about a fantasy story they could write, and while they were actually writing the story. Findings indicated that the students who had been rated by their instructors to be highly creative did indeed exhibit higher alpha activity during the inspiration phases than during the elaboration phases of the writing project. No differences were found for the students rated as less creative.

In a second experiment students were allowed to find inspiration by free associating and then were asked to elaborate by writing a story. Half of this sample of students received explicit instructions to be original. The other half were not given explicit instructions. Two measures of creative potential were also administered: the Remote Associates Test and the Alternate Uses (divergent thinking) Test. EEG readings were taken from electrodes over Wernicke's area of the left hemisphere. As in the first experiment, EEGs were recorded three times: during waiting, free associating, and writing. Alpha activity was identified during the inspiration phase, but only in the group who received explicit instructions to be original. Baseline alpha activity was not related to any measure of creative potential. Martindale and Hines (1974) also reported that alpha levels might be enhanced. More specifically, alpha levels of subjects increased when they were asked to suppress alpha activity and when they tried to enhance it. Practitioners of biofeedback would not be surprised by the fact that alpha activity

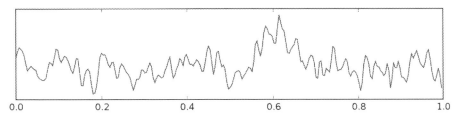

FIGURE 3.2 Example of EEG print-out. *Source: Wikimedia Commons, http://en.wikipedia.org/wiki/File:Eeg_raw.svg.*

FIGURE 3.3   It can be difficult for famous creators to find the time to do anything other than their work. Einstein generously submitted to an EEG—and later, well after his death, his brain was dissected. Now that is generous! *Source: Wikimedia Commons, http://en.wikipedia.org/wiki/File:Albert_Einstein_Head.jpg*

can be altered. Whether or not this translates into actual creative behavior is still somewhat of an open question.

Martindale et al. (1986) used EEG to compare the two hemispheres of the brain and to examine *primary process* cognition. The interest in primary process largely was justified by the theory that creativity is most likely when an individual moves from *secondary process* thinking (which is logical and reality oriented) to primary process (which allows free association, analogical cognition, and uninhibited thinking). Kris (1952) referred to this movement as regression in the service of the ego. He proposed that primary process is associated with an inspiration stage of the creative thinking process and that secondary process is associated with an elaboration stage.

Martindale et al. (1986) and Martindale and Hasenfus (1978) tested these ideas using EEGs. Because EEGs can ascertain the level of cortical activity and arousal, Martindale et al. hypothesized that low cortical arousal would be indicative of the inspirational phase of the creative process (and regression in the service of the ego) and high cortical arousal in the elaboration phase (and secondary process). They also predicted individual differences, such that creative persons would experience more primary process thinking than less creative persons, at least in an inspiration phase of problem solving. With this in mind the research subjects were asked to write stories, the content of which was then examined for predetermined indicators of primary process. It was found that the degree of *basal asymmetry* (i.e., high right-hemisphere activity and low left-hemisphere activity) was related to primary process. Primary process was not related to situational (short-term) variations in EEG activity of either hemisphere nor to hemispheric asymmetry. It was positively related only to the stable long-term measures of asymmetry.

EEGs suggest a complex kind of activity while individuals work on divergent thinking tasks (Molle et al. 1996, 1999). The complexity disappears when those same individuals work on convergent thinking tasks. As discussed in Chapter 1, divergent thinking tests provide useful estimates of the potential for creative problem solving. Convergent thinking, on the other hand, plays a much smaller role, if any, in creative problem solving. Sometimes it actually interferes with creative thinking. Molle et al. (1996) described the complex neural activity when participants were thinking divergently as similar to that which occurred when the participants were relaxed. This led them to explain their findings in terms of a possible loosening of associative bonds. This explanation is consistent with the view that creative thinking involves the exploration of remote associates (Mednick 1962) and with Martindale et al.'s (1986) work on low levels of cortical arousal. Importantly, Molle et al. (1996, 1999) found the complex neural patterns in the frontal cortex of the brain. Benedek et al. (2011) used EEGs but offered a slightly different conclusion. They felt that the frontal cortex is related to creativity, but only because it is responsible for top-down (conceptual) cognition, which includes creativity. To their credit, and in support of their view, they included tests of both divergent and convergent thinking. This research, and several other lines of investigation, suggest that we examine what has been discovered about the prefrontal cortex.

PREFRONTAL CORTEX

The prefrontal cortex has probably received more attention than any other part of the brain in the more recent studies of creativity. Even when some other part of the brain is involved—and typically other structures (e.g., limbic system, temporal lobes) are involved—they usually collaborate with the frontal lobes. The prefrontal cortex itself is thought to be primarily responsible for higher cognitive functions, including attention, perception, memory, arousal, self-reflection, and perhaps consciousness itself (Dietrich 2004; Vandervert et al. 2007). It may play a role in social decisions, temporal integration, and abstract thinking as well (Damásio 1994).

The role of the prefrontal cortex in creative thinking and behavior comes from several sources and uses different methodologies. Carlsson et al. (2000), for instance, measured the regional cerebral blood flow (rCBF) of two groups. A creative group had higher rCBF during a relaxation period, but more variability across experimental conditions as well. Changes in rCBF occurring between relaxation and work periods were bilateral and most obvious in the anterior prefrontal, frontotemporal, and superior frontal regions of the brain.

The frontal cortex has also been implicated in tasks requiring musical, visual, and verbal creativity (Petsche 1996) and, less directly, in research showing that there is increased activity in the frontal cortex when individuals are happy. Dietrich (2004) was quite precise in his prediction about the association between mood and "hyperactivity in the VMPFC region but

BOX 3.2

CORTICAL AROUSAL AND ART

Arousal plays a significant role in psychobiological theories of art. Berlyne (1971), for example, viewed art as "a complex assemblage of elements, i.e., information, in response to which the nervous system became 'aroused' by virtue of the artwork's constituent components, namely novelty, complexity, incongruity, ambiguity" (from Dudek 2012). Dudek (2012) summarized this line of work as follows:

> Arousal has been identified as the psychophysiological energy dimension mediated by activity of the reticular system. Independent measures of arousal are EEG, EKG, and EMG. Stated simply Berlyne's psychobiological theory of aesthetics postulates that the hedonic tone of the stimulus is determined by its arousal potential. The latter is a function of three (and often four) variables which are as follows: psychophysical (intensity, saturation, pitch, brightness), ecological (meaning or signal value), and collative (complexity, novelty, surprise, absurdity). The fourth is contributed by non-focal stimuli. Of the four, the collative variables were seen as contributing by far the largest share to arousal. Like Wundt, and Fechner before him, Berlyne found arousal is most pleasant in the middle ranges of stimulation.

Dudek referred specifically to the individual's *hedonic response* to art.

Martindale (1984, 1988, 1990) also stressed arousal and explained it as a result of evolutionary pressures. He held a very different perspective about the origin of the aesthetic response. He deemphasized form within art and instead emphasized meaning assigned by the individual. It is, in a sense, a difference between bottom-up information processing (which begins with the stimulus) and top-down processing (which begins with the

expectations and cognitive processes of the viewer). Martindale (1988, p. 34) concluded that "in confronting a work of art people seem primarily to search for and attend to meaning rather than to form. Thus meaning usually emerges as the primary determinant of aesthetic pleasure." His ideas have proven very useful in studies of historical changes (Martindale 1990) and style (Hasenfus et al. 1983), and are consistent with his various EEG investigations (Martindale et al. 1986).

Ramachandran and Hirstein (1999) extended Martindale's (1990) evolutionary view and his theory that the human brain reacts in predictable ways to various aspects of art. They described how the neurological reactions to art have directed artists, at least in the sense that art is created in order to experience the brain activity. They create art because art will "titillate the visual areas of the brain" (Ramachandran & Hirstein 1999, p. 15). It sounds quite a bit like physiological reinforcement for artistic activity.

Ramachandran and Hirstein (1999) also claimed that "some types of art such as cubism are activating brain mechanisms in such a way as to tap or even caricature certain innate form primitives which we do not yet fully understand. … Many artists may be unconsciously producing heightened activity in the 'form areas' in a manner that is not obvious to the conscious mind" (pp. 20–21). It follows that some people may be drawn to the arts, if they have the intuitive sensitivities and neural mechanisms described by Ramachandran and Hirstein. Specializations within the arts may be influenced by neuroanatomical differences as well (e.g., the visual arts and the visual cortex).

(Continued)

BOX 3.2 (*Continued*)

By no means is the cortex solely responsible. The postulated neurological process goes something like this: various visual centers of the brain perceive groupings and meaningful clusters in the visual field and send preliminary messages to the limbic system. It generates pleasure, leading the individual to allocate attention to those particular stimuli, and to generate hypotheses about what the gestalt (the complete and meaningful stimulus) may be. This pleasure leads to more visual processing and a recursive process, with a back-and-forth between the visual centers and the limbic system. Eventually the gestalt may be identified, and there is a notable feeling of satisfaction, which Ramachandran and Hirstein (1999) associate with the very common "a-ha" experience (Gruber 1988).

Obviously, for nonvisual stimuli (the acoustics of music), it is not the visual cortex but the other relevant sensory centers that work with the limbic system. Ramachandran and Hirstein explicitly described the reinforcing feeling, generated by the limbic system, that they believe plays a role in both the production and appreciation of art.

A final intriguing hypothesis offered by Ramachandran and Hirstein (1999) is that simple works of art, including sketches and outlines, are sometimes more aesthetically meaningful than more detailed works. This has been noted many times in the literature but is surprising only if you think about the pleasure of some line drawing that actually loses its appeal when detail is added. The hypothesis does not compare a sketch of one object with a complete figure of a second object, but instead compares a sketch of one object with a picture of the same object after more detail has been added. This is in a sense counterintuitive, but then again readers may have experiences that demonstrate it ("that is more than I wanted to know"). Attentional limits may help to explain this. Attention is quite limited (Chapter 1; Runco & Chand 1995), and it could be that the person can focus more on what is truly pleasing in something simple like a sketch, but would be spread out and inefficient when too much detail is provided. This explanation may also explain the impressive art of autistic savants (Treffert & Wallace, 2004): They may focus on the most important features of the subject rather than dilute the art with information that is not associated with those centers of the brain that provide aesthetic reinforcement (cf. Snyder & Thomas 1997).

hypoactivity in the DLPFC region." These two regions are related to different kinds of thinking and, for Dietrich, different forms of creativity. Activation of the dorsolateral prefrontal cortex is likely to support deliberate creativity rather than spontaneous creativity. The latter is more associated with activation among the temporal-occipital-parietal lobes. There is both experimental (Hirt 1999; Isen et al. 1987) and clinical (Shaw et al. 1986) evidence for the benefits of a happy mood for creative thinking. There is also evidence suggesting that negative mood states can facilitate creative thinking, depending on the specific task and measures of creativity (Kaufmann & Vosburg 1997, 2002). The studies demonstrating that a positive mood state is associated with creative thinking are consistent with the other, more direct support for the importance of the frontal lobes.

LITHIUM AND CREATIVITY

Shaw et al. (1986) reported benefits of lithium carbonate on the creativity of a group of outpatients who had been diagnosed with bipolar (mood) disorders. Shou (1979) reported specific benefits to artistic productivity, again with lithium. Lithium carbonate ($LiCO_3$) is widely used in the production of ceramics and glass, as well as in the treatment of depression and manic-depression.

Ashby et al. (1999) went so far as to specify increased dopamine levels in the prefrontal cortex and anterior cingulate and the resulting increase in flexibility of thought. Dietrich (2004) argued cogently for the flexibility that is supported by working memory, and therefore the prefrontal cortex: "Given that perseveration to old information is anathema to creative thinking, it is evident that a fully operational prefrontal cortex enables cognition that is necessary for creative ability" (p. 1014). This conclusion is consistent with studies in brain (prefrontal cortex)-damaged individuals and nonhuman species who perseverate and show obvious inflexibility.

Working memory often is discussed in neuroanatomical theories of creativity. What exactly is it? To begin with it is the cognitive basis of conscious thought. When a person actively and mindfully considers anything, that information is in working memory. It is sometimes equated with short-term memory, the idea being that we are not aware of the huge amount of information that resides there, but we can retrieve it and use it in short-term or working memory. It is sometimes useful to think of two parts to working memory: a slave component, which allows the conscious manipulation of information, and an executive component, which directs and focuses attentional resources. All of this may depend on the prefrontal cortex.

Theories emphasizing the role of working memory tend to define the creative process in terms of combinations. As Dietrich (2004) put it,

> it can be concluded that the prefrontal cortex has a search engine that can "pull" task-relevant information from long-term storage in the TOP [temporal occipital parietal] areas and temporarily represent it in the working memory buffer. Once online, the prefrontal cortex can use its capacity for cognitive flexibility to superimpose the retrieved information to form new combinations (p. 1016).

This is an entirely acceptable view of creative thinking from the cognitive psychological point of view. Rothenberg (1999) and others (Baughman & Mumford 1995; Brophy 2001; Mumford et al. 1997; Scott et al. 2005) have also identified combinatorial processes leading to creative insights and solutions.

Apparently the prefrontal cortex contributes to creative thinking in three different ways (Dietrich 2004; Vandervert et al. 2007). First, it may be necessary for *judgment* about an idea or solution. This kind of judgment in turn requires the conscious awareness of an idea, which means working memory (one function of the prefrontal cortex) is critical. Note, however, that processing that occurs before an insight, before conscious awareness of an idea, before an "a-ha," may not depend on the prefrontal cortex—something, somewhere else, thus is involved. The prefrontal cortex also assists with necessary *integrations*. These may be necessary after an insight occurs, when there is that conscious awareness of the idea. At that point, it is beneficial to have sustained attention and "buffering." Abstraction may also be useful at this point. The third contribution of the prefrontal cortex is that it assists with idea *implementation*. This relates insights to the goals and subgoals that are a part of most creative work, especially at mature and professional levels.

The rationality supported by the prefrontal cortex may be responsible for judgments about creative behavior or, as Dietrich (2004) put it, "assessing whether a particular new idea is creative as opposed to merely new." This statement actually conveys two key ideas: (a) that creativity depends on divergent and convergent processes; and (b) that various cognitive theories of creativity mesh well with discoveries of brain function and structure.

One small puzzle concerns a particular kind of judgment, namely the social judgment of appropriateness. Apparently, individuals with particular prefrontal lesions have difficulty with these judgments and rely on the wrong cues when deciding what is right and wrong. This might appear to be good for creativity. After all, creative individuals often are described as eccentrics, nonconformists, radicals, or contrarians. These may imply a tendency toward socially inappropriate behavior. Yet more often than not, the unconventional tendencies of truly creative people are intentional and discretionary. They know what they are doing. Creative individuals may be aware of social convention but simply do not give it much weight. Creative work may be more important to them than fitting in, so although they are aware of social convention, they choose to think in an original and unconventional fashion. Judgment is required for creativity—it is not lacking. Along the same lines, creative ideas are not only original, they are also fitting, valuable, or effective in some fashion. This all implies an intact and functional prefrontal cortex.

Specialization within the Prefrontal Cortex

The prefrontal cortex does not always operate as one unit. Vartanian and Goel (2005) described specialization within the prefrontal cortex:

> Rather than having a unified role, different regions of right PFC [prefrontal cortex] may have different functions in the creative process. Specifically, the ventral aspect of right PFC appears to mediate the generation of set shift hypotheses … whereas the dorsal region of right PFC appears to mediate the executive aspects … of the creative process. … A further comparison of successfully versus unsuccessfully completed Match Problems revealed activation in right ventral lateral PFC (BA 47), left middle frontal gyrus (BA 9) and left frontal pole (BA 10), thus identifying the former as a critical component of the neural mechanisms of set-shift transformation. By contrast, activation in right dorsal lateral PFC (BA 46) covaried as a function of the number of solutions generated in Match Problems, possibly due to increased working memory demands to maintain multiple solutions 'on-line,' conflict resolution, or progress monitoring. These results go beyond the patient data by identifying the ventral lateral (BA 47) aspect of right PFC as being a critical component of the neural systems underlying lateral transformations, and demonstrate a dissociation between right VLPFC and DLPFC in hypotheses generation and maintenance (p. 1170).

This research involved functional MRIs (fMRIs) of 13 patients but is in many ways consistent with earlier demonstrations of asymmetry in patients with prefrontal lesions (Goel & Grafman 2000).

Goldberg et al. (1994) tied the right prefrontal cortex to veridical decision making, with the left responsible for adaptive decision making. The left side of the prefrontal cortex may be sensitive to patterns, and the right side involved when no patterns are involved. Novel situations may not fit recognized patterns. They are, in a sense, what is known as ill-defined, and as such offer opportunities for original and creative thinking.

Flaherty (2005) also found specialization that may be viewed as frontal subsystems:

> Lesions of medial prefrontal cortex can produce amotivational, abulic states of decreased creative drive. Dorsolateral prefrontal cortex's importance for working memory and flexible problem-solving suggests a greater role in creative skill than in drive. Motor and premotor cortex are probably more necessary for performance than for conception of a creative plan. While lesions of all of these systems would be detrimental to idea generation, orbitofrontal lesions may have a partly opposing effect, as they can produce disinhibition syndromes that at least superficially resemble mania (p. 151).

WHERE IN THE HEAD?

Dorsal, on the back, top, or upper surface   *Ventral*, the lower portion.
Medial, situated on or toward the middle

Bekhtereva et al. (2000) used PET and found bilateral activity in the prefrontal cortex when participants were working on verbal creativity tasks. They later replicated this and offered additional support using both PET and EEG (Bekhtereva et al. 2001). Yet evidence also supports commonalities among verbal and nonverbal tasks. This is in some ways contrary to cognitive studies that suggest divergent thinking differs depending on the nature (e.g., verbal, figural) of the task. According to Vartanian and Goel (2005), these kinds of differences are not based on structures specifically within the prefrontal cortex:

> Our results demonstrated that solving anagrams in a relatively unconstrained way (e.g., "Can you make a word with CENFAR?") compared to a condition where solutions were restricted to particular semantic categories (e.g., "Can you make a country with CENFAR?") activated a network of areas including the right ventral lateral PFC (BA 47). The combined results from Match Problems and the anagram task demonstrated that hypothesis generation in relatively more open-ended settings activates a network that includes right ventral lateral PFC (BA 47), regardless of the spatial or linguistic nature of the stimuli.

Specialization within the prefrontal cortex is also suggested in research on conventionality and the desire to "be cool." This is not research directly on creativity, but then again, creativity is complex, and one critical part of that complexity reflects unconventional and thereby original tendencies (Runco 1996d). Consider, then, the MRI research that found that many people like to "be cool." They prefer conventional products and the things that others like as well. They are likely to care about fads and fashions. Extrapolating, they may have difficulty being creative because, again, creativity often depends on the acceptance of or even interest in the unconventional. Unconventional thinking can lead to original ideas. Conventional tendencies make that difficult. The MRI reveals that the area of the brain that seemed to be active when viewing cool images was Brodmann's area 10, which is one part of the frontal lobe.

HIERARCHIES WITHIN THE BRAIN

The brain seems to be specialized in a number of ways, with different structures sometimes having privileged roles in function and process. For our purposes the specializations and unique processes of the various functions may be less important than the systems, interconnections, and collaborations among structures. Hoppe and Kyle (1990) used Arieti's phrase, the *Magic Synthesis*, to refer to the remarkable collaborations among structures and systems that support creative work.

BOX 3.3

IS IT MAGIC OR JUST A BUTTERFLY?

Creativity is not an easy thing to define or explain. No wonder that many theories of creativity looked to magic, intuitive leaps, the muses, incubation, or some unconscious process. Each of these seem to accept that there is something inexplicable about creativity. Granted, intuition is no longer described as entirely unconscious; plenty of empirical studies are suggestive of underlying processes. Further, creativity may be called magical because it is special and surprising, not because it is inexplicable. Yet more than any other chapter in this text, and more than any other perspective on creativity, the neuroanatomical (and genetic) research suggests that we are getting close to the nuts and bolts of creativity.

It may, however, be necessary to be creative. We may need to develop new theories to explain new research results. One way to do this is to adapt theories from other fields. Chaos theory is, for example, very useful for explaining what would otherwise seem inexplicable. Perhaps the seemingly magical aspects of creativity can be understood with a creative interpretation of the *butterfly effect*. This is often used to explain the weather, the economy, and a number of other natural phenomena where a small error eventually generates a large catastrophe (Gleick 1987). Creative insights often result when we turn an idea upside down, and the butterfly effect may thus explain how small changes on a neurochemical level can lead to enormously original and grand ideas—that is, to important creative insights.

Closer to the biological perspective is the idea of *emergenesis* (Lykken 1981). This occurs when some result is not obviously or directly tied to preconditions, or at least when the result is not a simple linear or additive sum but is instead a multiplicative product. Waller et al. (1993, p. 235) applied emergenesis to "the etiology of creativity ... [and concluded that] personality and cognitive factors are likely to act in a multiplicative (synergistic) rather than additive manner." As such it explains what cannot be explained by local causal factors. Research on the genetics of creativity has already benefited from emergence (Harrington, 1990; Waller et al. 1993) in explaining how exceptional children or talents may be found in families that do not seem to lean in that direction and how creative potential may be heritable such that it is fairly equivalent in identical (MZ) twins but not fraternal (DZ) twins. Chapter 11 puts the concept of emergence into a philosophical context.

With this in mind (an apt phrase in this chapter about the brain), it is vital to recognize the systems and hierarchies among brain structures. This is necessary to accurately understand the neuroanatomy of creativity, but it is also precisely the interplay of systems that allow the flexibility and adaptability of the brain. It's a bit like a basketball team that can have five players on the court for one kind of offense or defense, but can also have five other players on the court for a completely different offense or defense. And various combinations of those two units will allow a multitude of other possible offenses and defenses. With a number of structures involved in creative neural activity, a multitude of processes and great flexibility are possible. Small wonder some theories of creativity emphasize insight, and others divergent thinking, adaptable or flexible thought, or various kinds of problem generation and problem solving. There are different ways to be creative and different neuroanatomical structures and circuits to support them.

Damásio (2001) described the entire brain hierarchy as follows:

- central nervous system (the highest level)
- macrosystems
- circuits
- neurons
- synapses
- molecules.

He emphasized that it is best to examine "the higher organization levels of the brain: the large scale systems which are made up of several macroscopic regions. At these levels, we have a better chance of making a transparent connection with the sort of mental processes studied in the cognitive sciences, and with complex phenomena, such as creativity" (p. 60).

Circuits, systems, and networks may be, in functional terms, most important for understanding creativity. Many of them, however, do connect with the prefrontal cortex. Its influence is larger than that of any other brain structure. Consider in this regard Dietrich's (2004) framework of creative thinking. He described four different types of creative thinking, each with different neuroanatomical bases. These are emotional and spontaneous, emotional and deliberate, cognitive and spontaneous, and cognitive and deliberate. He felt that each represents a specific circuit in the brain. Yet they all depend on the prefrontal cortex. Quoting Dietrich (2004, p. 1015), "Once a novel combination has been generated, to turn it into a creative idea, a value assessment by the prefrontal cortex is required. Thus, all four types of creativity share a 'final common pathway,' regardless of the circuit that generated the novelty." The stress here is clearly on pathways and circuits rather than individual structures.

THE CEREBELLUM AND CREATIVITY

The cerebellum interacts with the prefrontal cortex in a very important way. To understand how, something must be said about working memory, its evolution, and its capacity to manipulate ideas:

> It has often been remarked that an explanation is required for the threefold to fourfold increase in the size of the cerebellum that occurred in the last million years of evolution. … If the selection pressure has been

BOX 3.4

HOW BIG IS THE HUMAN BRAIN?

The brain is, in a word, humongous. Consider this (Andreasen 2005):

- The cerebral cortex contains approximately 100 billion neurons (10^{11}).
- The cortex of the cerebellum contains another trillion (10^{12}).
- Subcortical "islands" of gray matter (e.g., the thalamus) contain several more billion neurons.

- Subtotal: Well in excess of one trillion neurons.

That in turn must be multiplied by the number of synapses, for these allow each neuron to communicate with other neurons. They dramatically increase the complexity of the human brain, for each of those trillion neurons just calculated has between 1000 and 10000 synapses.

Even this grossly underestimates the potential of the brain. Recall here that creative thinking utilizes circuits and interactions of cells and regions, and the number of combinations of these is, of course, some huge mathematical result of all possible combinations of interactions. Some of these may be nonlinear, meaning that the result is not even some simple mathematical product but is instead, well, as close to infinite as anything in the universe.

Recall also that the circuits and higher systems of the brain are likely to be most important for our understanding of creativity (Damásio 2001). Creativity may not be a direct result of neural chemistry but instead may depend on interactions among systems and subsystems. No wonder creative insights sometimes seem to be unpredictable; they may depend on nonlinear interactions among a quadrillion (10^{15}) cells and synapses!

BOX 3.5

METAPHORS OF MIND

The brain is huge and as complicated as anything in the universe. Not surprisingly, it can be difficult to grasp and explain. Metaphors often are used to this end. The brain, for instance, has been described as a pony express, messages being taken from one place to another. It also has been compared to the old telephone switchboard. Sir John Eccles (1958) described the pros and cons of the "telephone exchange" metaphor, but concluded that the circuitry of the brain is much more complicated and much less predictable than this metaphor allows. More recent metaphors involve computers, yet even these fall short. No wonder the newest attempts use nonlinear and chaos theory to describe both the working of the brain and creativity (Ludwig 1998; Richards 1996; Zausner 1998).

strong for more cerebellum in the human brain as well as for more cerebral cortex, the interaction between the cerebellum and the cerebral cortex should provide some important advantages to humans. ... A detailed examination of cerebellar circuitry suggests that its phylogenetically newest parts may serve as a fast information-processing adjunct of the association cortex and could assist this cortex in the performance of a variety of manipulative skills, including the skill that is characteristic of anthropod apes and humans, the skillful manipulation of ideas (Leiner et al. 1986, p. 444, quoted by Vandervert et al. 2007).

This is a fascinating take on creativity and the cerebellum, no less because Vandervert et al. explore parallels between the way the cerebellum handles ideas and the way it handles movement and sensation. They quoted Ito (1993) on the notion that "the cerebellar manipulation of ideas is no different from its manipulation of movement." Ito (1993, 1997) also described how "in thought, ideas and concepts are manipulated just as limbs are in movements. There would be no distinction between movement and thought once encoded in the neuronal circuitry of the brain; therefore, both movement and thought can be controlled with the same neural mechanisms" (1993, p. 449). Vandervert et al. (2007) extended this and suggested that the mind solves problems much like the body solves problems. In a sense the cerebellum insures an efficient process, often with such success as to allow manipulations of limbs or ideas without attentional resources or conscious effort.

Evolutionary pressures not only enlarged the cerebellum, they also offered a selective advantage to the structures that would allow communication between it and the cerebral cortex. "This million or so years of rapid evolution of cerebro-cerebellar circuitry included, of course, operating-system control of the central executive, visuospatial sketchpad and speech loop of human working memory" (Vandervert et al. 2007). Apparently there are over 40 million nerve tracts connecting the cerebral cortex and the cerebellum. To understand that figure it is helpful to know that it is larger than the number of optic nerve tracts, which is itself quite extensive. Vandervert et al. (2007) also noted that "In addition, the cerebellum itself contains approximately 100 billion neurons; this is more than the rest of the entire brain."

Research outside creative studies supports the notion that the cerebellum is involved in the processing of language and ideas, as well as motoric information (Leiner et al. 1986). Vandervert et al. (2007) extended this line of thinking by suggesting that the cerebellum would play a role when the individual is faced with novelty. The capacity to deal with novelty seems to be analogous to anticipation and expectation, or perhaps hypothesis generation. Each of these requires that an original interpretation be constructed. Quoting Vandervert et al.:

In confronting a novel situation, the individual may need to carry out some preliminary mental processing before action can be taken, such as processing to estimate the potential consequences of the action before deciding whether to act or to refrain from acting. ... In such decision-generating processes, the prefrontal cortex is activated. ... This cortex, via its connections with the cerebellum, could utilize cerebellar preprogramming to manipulate conceptual data rapidly. As a result, a quick decision could be made.

The cerebellum plays a role in this process but depends heavily on the prefrontal cortex for the construction of meaning and decision making.

Creative thinking may also benefit from the existence of what Vandervert et al. (2007) described as neuroanatomical architectures. These architectures allow working memory to manipulate mental models and concepts. Significantly, this may involve a kind of decomposition of concepts as part of cognitive adaptations. Vandervert et al. pointed to the sketches of Thomas Edison and the anecdotal reports of Einstein to support their ideas, though, as is no doubt apparent, they also supported their view of the cerebellum with brain-imaging studies as well. An examination of Edison's sketches shows that they do indeed exemplify the process whereby concepts evolve and adapt into new ideas and perhaps inventions and discoveries.

In contrast, Brown (2007) questioned the role of the cerebellum in creative work. This does not undermine the idea of systems within the brain collaborating on creativity. Almost definitely the neuroanatomical structures contributing to emotions interact with the frontal lobes and the other relevant structures. Vandervert et al. (2007) responded to various critics, and then in 2013 marshaled yet more evidence for their view that "everyday creativity … can be best understood (and interconnected) as hybridization in working memory that takes place through the collaboration of the cerebral cortex and the cerebellum" (Vandervert in press).

Temporal Parietal Junction

Ritter et al. (in press) recently pointed to the role of the temporal parietal junction (TPJ) in creative thinking. They felt that it "boosts" flexibility of thought; again and again the importance of flexibility for creativity has been recognized in this book! Ritter et al. outlined an interesting theory whereby violations of expectations can allow an individual to avoid functional fixedness (see Chapter 1). The TPJ had been shown in previous research to function when expectations are violated and Ritter et al. applied this to creative thinking. They also drew from the research on cognitive structures (as in the Piagetian work, where structures are "schema" and lead to expectations).

THE EMOTIONAL BRAIN

Creativity does not result from cognition alone. It is complex, and as such depends on motivation, attitude, interest, and various other extracognitive processes (Albert & Runco 1989). It would be difficult to prioritize these processes, but surely emotional processes must be recognized. No wonder, then, that neuroanatomists are looking to the emotional brain in their search for creativity. Recall here the emphasis placed on affect by Hoppe and Kyle (1990) in their studies of alexithemia, and by Damásio (2001), and Vartanian and Goel (2005). Recall also the emotional vs. cognitive processes described by Dietrich (2004). Vartanian and Goel put it this way: "the emotional brain mediates the interaction between preferences and cognitive demands via orbitofrontal cortex" (also see Bechara et al. 1999, 2000). Affect has also received a great deal of attention in the nonbiological studies of creativity (e.g., Runco & Shaw 1994; Russ 1999).

The so-called emotional brain would be important to motivate, interest, intrigue, and drive creative work. It would assign value to ideas and information and recognize what is, at least personally, important. It would play a significant role as what Gazzaniga (2000) referred to as an "interpreter" within the left hemisphere, interpreting events in terms of their meaning. Ironically, although that is important, there is also a potential advantage to the right hemisphere's freedom from this interpretative process. Simplifying, the hemisphere does not need to reflect on the meaning of tasks or situations but simply deals with them. Keep in mind that it is actually dominance that is the issue, not left vs. right hemisphericity. The left is typically the dominant hemisphere, but it does not matter if it is the left or right hemisphere. It is the dominant hemisphere that likely houses the interpreter and the nondominant hemisphere that can deal with problems in a simple and uncomplicated fashion.

Flaherty (2005) referred to the important affect as a kind of drive. She argued that creativity depends on the same neuroanatomically based drive that is manifested in *hypergraphia*, as well as mania. Hypergraphia is "a compulsive drive to write [which] helps anatomically characterize creative drive. … Hypergraphia is generally proposed to reflect decreases of temporal lobe activity. It is most common when the lesion is in the right hemisphere, perhaps because the left, language-dominant side is then disinhibited" (p. 148). This is a reasonable argument given how many others have found mania (one of the bipolar disorders) to be associated with creativity. Flaherty concluded that creativity involves the frontal lobes, but also the temporal lobes and, most important for the creative drive, the limbic system. The temporal lobes are involved in their interaction with the frontal lobes; the former are involved in blocking and inhibition, which can interfere with creative associations. A relaxed or damaged temporal lobe, then, may allow wide associative horizons or other creative cognition. Flaherty (2005) also looked specifically at the amygdala, a structure the shape of a walnut found in the anterior temporal lobe: "Alterations in amygdalar function, in assigning emotional meaning or affective valence to events or ideas, may underlie the idiosyncratic passionate interests of manic patients. Although in most cases their pursuits are misguided or overly risky, in mild bipolar disorder they can be turned to creative use" (p. 149). Note that this model is at least tripartite and emphasizes systems rather than brain structures. Both Flaherty (2005) and Ramachandran and Hirstein (1999) emphasized the role of the limbic system (Box 3.6).

Bowden (1994) described how persistence and energy are useful for creative work and are possible advantages provided to creative people when they have a tendency toward mania or the bipolar disorders. They are, in this light, secondary advantages of the bipolar disorders. Bowden wrote, "bipolar disorder may be unique among the psychiatric disorders in that, in some instances, it confers advantages on persons who have it. These advantages largely show up in areas of creativity and work performances" (p. 73). Richards (1997) concluded much the same, using the term *compensatory advantage*. Nettles and Clegg (2006) were also close to this in their work on the evolutionary advantages of creative talents. (The former is explored in Chapter 4 and the latter in Chapter 13.) The persistence and energy mentioned by Bowden (1994) refer to emotional and not cognitive processes. There may also be a cognitive advantage, which he called increased rate and speed of associative concepts (p. 80). The support he marshaled was not experimental but represented various artistic and scientific domains.

Affective and other extracognitive processes are implied by Damásio's (2001) list of requirements for creativity. Indeed, courage and motivation were at the top of this list. Next came extensive experience, and perhaps an apprenticeship within the appropriate field. After that, Damásio listed "insight into the workings of the self and into the workings of other minds. This applies mostly to the arts" (p. 64). Turning to macro-level neural systems, Damásio said

the first requirement here is the strong generation of representational diversity. What I mean by this is the ability to generate to bring to mind a variety of novel combinations of entities as images. These images are prompted by a stimulus which comes either from the words outside, or from the inside world. Many of these

---

BOX 3.6

NEUROANATOMY AND THE THRESHOLD THEORY OF CREATIVITY AND INTELLIGENCE

Flaherty (2005) pointed to an interaction of the prefrontal and temporal lobes and the limbic system in her model of creativity. As an interesting aside, this model contains an explanation for the threshold theory: "Low latent inhibition can flood an organism with stimuli, and is seen in psychosis. ... But low latent inhibition is also characteristic of creative individuals with high intelligence. ... It may be that highly intelligent subjects can find patterns in what would otherwise be a disorienting barrage of sensory data" (p. 149). Latent inhibition results from repeated exposure to some stimulus. Eysenck (1997a) offered this rationale for studying latent inhibition: "non-reinforced pre-exposure to a stimulus retards subsequent conditioning to that stimulus because during such pre-exposure the subject learns not to attend to it. ...

The relevance of latent inhibition to creativity lies in the fact that it *correlates negatively with both schizophrenia and psychoticism*." For Eysenck, psychoticism and creativity both reflect an underlying overinclusive tendency. Carson et al. (2003) offered a slightly different take on the relevance of latent inhibition. They found that creative achievement increased when latent inhibition decreased. Their data came from meta-analyses, which implies very good reliability and generalizability, though no actual experimental control. Still, it makes sense, given theories of creative cognition, that low latent inhibition would be related to creative achievement. This fits with the idea that creative thinking entails a broad associative universe. It also fits with the concepts of divergent thinking and overinclusive thought, as contributions to originality.

---

representations had to be discarded because they are not relevant; but the images are there to choose from. This process is not unlike the generation of diversity that has permitted the process of natural selection and evolution (p. 65).

This indicates again that the working memory, and thus the frontal cortex, is important for creativity. Damásio actually included large memory capacity in his list of requirements. For Damásio, working memory allows an individual to generate and store representations but also allows the individual to manipulate representations and to recombine and rearrange them. He qualified this slightly when he described the capacity to recognize novel representations. As he put it, "I suspect that a marvelous prefrontal cortex generating many new items and holding them online would be of little use if we did not have the ability to execute good selections based on an aesthetic or scientific goal" (p. 65). The last requirement Damásio listed was a decision-making apparatus.

The emotional brain plays a significant role in creative efforts, but it does not work alone. Each of these descriptions of the emotional brain reinforces the idea that creativity requires systems and interactions among neuroanatomical structures.

MANIPULATIONS OF THE HUMAN BRAIN

B. F. Skinner (1956) proposed that good science should predict and control. The idea is that if you really understand some phenomenon you can predict when it will occur (and when it won't) and control it. Skinner is best known for *behaviorism*, or what should probably be called *operant theory*. Yet his ideas characterize all laboratory sciences. That is why laboratory experiments manipulate independent variables: to determine if they are causally related (and controlled) dependent variables. With this in mind, some of the most impressive work on the creative potentials of the human brain was reported by Snyder et al. (2003). They simulated neural impairment in the left temporal lobes to test the possibility that everyone has the potential to perform as artistically inclined savants perform. They hypothesized "latent savant skills" in nonartistic individuals. Savants are often artistic, though sometimes their skills are mathematical or the like and do not lead to creative or original performances. Yet their talents are remarkable—more than that, they are truly extraordinary.

Snyder et al. (2003) administered 15-minute pulses of repetitive transcranial magnetic stimulation (rTMS) to 11 adults ("local university students"), thereby creating "virtual lesions" in the fronto-temporal lobes. Their prediction sounds the most reasonable if you keep in mind that "savant skills can emerge 'spontaneously' following an accident" (p. 149). Several controls were used: one placebo stimulation, and one in the multiple baseline research design, with the experimental treatment beginning at different times for different individuals. The participants of this research were tested four times using drawing and proofreading tasks: once before rTMS treatment, once during treatment, and twice after treatment (15 and 45 minutes after). Results indicated that 4 of the 11 research participants demonstrated stylistic changes after rTMS. These changes were apparent to a committee of judges only after rTMS treatment (not after placebo treatment), and manifested in drawings that were life-like, flamboyant, and complex. Two of the participants also showed improvements in proofreading (finding errors in short proverbs). Savants are sometimes described as too literal in their use of language, which does imply that they might be accurate proofreaders. That may not sound all that relevant to creativity, but in some ways it is relevant. Many children enter a kind of literal stage in language usage, where metaphors are uncommon, and this is close to the age of the fourth-grade slump (Gardner 1982). A huge amount of research confirms the role of metaphor in creative thinking (e.g., Miller, 1996), and metaphor is exclusive of literal language. The metaphorical individual is not literal, and vice versa. Snyder et al. did not mention metaphor but felt it was significant that the impact of the rTMS led to savant-like tendencies in both art and literal language usage. They are certainly correct that the proofreading findings are more objective than those concerning the artwork. No committee judgments are necessary for proofreading.

Snyder et al. (2003) emphasized that the rTMS *inhibited* the neural processes of the fronto-temporal lobes. They suggested that this inhibition allows the individual to recognize and use "lower level neural information" (p. 157) and tap information that is otherwise subconscious. That explanation is not far from the theory of regression in the service of the ego, used earlier in this chapter (Kris 1952; Martindale et al. 1986). It is also consistent with Rothenberg's (1990) study of the novelist John Cheever. Cheever felt that his talent was in part a reflection of his capacity to access the unconscious (described further in Chapter 4). Flaherty (2005) described a different kind of manipulation, in particular, "subcortical deep

BOX 3.7

MUSIC AND THE BRAIN

Many of the more rigorous studies on the human brain have been conducted with musicians and individuals with obvious musical talent. Musicians are thought to be nearly ideal candidates for neurophysiological studies because (a) much of the training occurs early when the brain is still highly adaptable, and (b) the training is repetitive and covers a long period of time. Admittedly, it is possible that the unique findings from musicians' brains are a result of inborn tendencies. They are not necessarily entirely adaptations to practice and experience.

Schlaug (2001) reported that there are particular areas of the brain which show idiosyncrasies in musicians. These include the motor cortex, the cerebellum, and the corpus callosum. He also pointed to "neural correlates of one unique musical ability, absolute pitch" and found that one particular structure within the brain was active when musicians are using their absolute pitch. This is the planum temporale.

This line of work confirms an asymmetry of the human brain. That asymmetry is of the planum temporale, "a brain area containing auditory association cortex and previously shown to be a marker of structural and functional asymmetry" (p. 699). These findings are based primarily on fMRI neuroimaging studies. Absolute pitch is found in approximately 1 of every 10000 individuals. Limb (2006; Limb et al. 2006) conducted a series of creative studies of music and improvisation. They actually ask musicians to perform while in brain-imaging apparatus! The subjects are asked to perform music that precludes improvisation, and then to perform improvisational music. The findings were summarized as follows: "brain areas deactivated during improvisation are also at rest during dreaming and meditation, while activated areas include those controlling language and sensorimotor skills" (López-González and Limb 2012). It is also interesting that there does seem to be hemispheric specialization when rhythm and melody are played. And that certain musical interpretations (e.g., is something off key?) may involve some of the same brain structures (e.g., Broca's area) as language.

brain stimulating electrodes near the nucleus accumbens" (p. 151). This apparently also had a beneficial impact, though it certainly sounds less appealing (and more invasive) than the magnetic stimulation. Both are more attractive than dissection, the next methodology to be reviewed.

THE BRAIN OF ALBERT EINSTEIN

Diamond et al. (1985) dissected the brain of Albert Einstein, as well as 11 "control brains," and measured the ratio of neurons to glial cells. The former are responsible for the processing of information, whereas the latter physically and metabolically support the neurons. The 11 control subjects had died from nonneurologically related diseases and were between the ages of 47 and

80 years. Both right and left hemispheres were sampled (areas 9 and 39), as were the prefrontal and inferior parietal associative areas. The neurons and glial cells were differentiated through staining. Diamond et al. found that the ratio of neurons to glial cells in Einstein's brain was smaller than those of the controls. Of course generalizations from one sample, even Einstein, cannot be made across other exceptional individuals nor scientists as a whole, but Diamond et al. did offer the conclusion that the small ratio may "reflect the enhanced use of this tissue in the expression of his unusual conceptual powers in comparison with control brains" (p. 204).

ALBERT EINSTEIN

In the early 1950s a Princeton neurologist convinced Einstein to submit to an EEG. Einstein was asked to think about relativity and then let his mind go blank. The findings were reported in *Life Magazine*, February 26, 1951, p. 40, under the article "Recording Genius." *Life Magazine* presents the EEG chart (also available in Gamwell 2005, p. 297).

Postmortems have been done on various other populations. Schlaug et al. (1995a, 1995b), for example, examined the brains of individuals with perfect pitch, and Scheibel (1999) examined the auditory area of the brain of a musician with perfect pitch. Apparently neurons in that area were not so numerous but were unique in that they were "not densely packed" (Sacks 1996). Yet just as generalizations from epileptic individuals should be avoided because of their exceptionality, so too should care be taken with these special samples.

ALTERED STATES AND BRAIN FUNCTION

There is a long tradition in psychology that focuses on errors and malfunctions. Freud (1966) examined psychoses and neuroses and then developed a theory of the healthy psyche. Rock (1997) looked to illusions and developed a theory of perception. Motley (1986) examined verbal errors and slips and developed a theory of lexical organization. In the same vein, it is possible to examine atypical or altered states of consciousness to infer healthy brain function. Some of these are intentionally induced altered states of consciousness. Hypnosis, alcohol, and marijuana have all been examined in empirical research. They each have an impact on the brain and on creative performance.

Hypnosis

There may be a connection between hypnosis and creativity because they both involve the preconscious. As Krippner (1965) put it, "hypnosis … may aid the breakdown into the preverbal realm where the creative inspiration has its origin" (p. 94). The preverbal realm is the preconscious. In this light there may be a connection because creative persons and creative processes do sometimes draw from the preconscious (Rothenberg 1990; Smith & Amner 1997) and because they tend to be open to experience (McCrae 1987). Openness may allow them to consider ideas in the preconscious—and the possibility of being hypnotized—as reasonable and feasible. Note the wording, however: some creative persons, some creative processes, and some of the time. Not all creativity relies on the preconscious. Some creative acts are intentional and tactical instead. Furthermore, differences among creative persons suggest that whereas some employ certain paths in their creative efforts, others take other paths.

Bowers (1979) also reported an association between hypnotizability and creativity. It is difficult to interpret this particular study, however, because of its only moderate sample size ($N=32$) and the use of a composite index of creativity. That composite did include a divergent thinking test (i.e., consequences), but scores were combined with ratings from a measure of creative activities. She also reported moderate but statistically significant correlations between creativity and absorption, and between what she called *effortless experiencing* and creativity. Effortless experiencing would seem to parallel Langer's (1989) concept of mindfulness, as well as absorption and flow (Csikszentmihalyi 1999). Indeed, we have a set of parallel processes, with these and absorption (also see Bowers 1967, 1978).

It may be that the relationship between hypnosis and verbal creativity is different from that between hypnosis and nonverbal material (Ashton & McDonald 1985).

Manmiller et al. (2005) found certain creative styles to be related to absorption more than hypnotizability. They did not, however, administer EEG, PET, or MRIs (Ashton & McDonald 1985; Bowers 1968, 1971; Bowers & van der Meulen 1970; P. Bowers 1967; Gur & Reyher 1976).

Drugs and Creativity

Different drugs have different effects. Some of them seem to influence creativity via their effects on inhibition and attention (Goodwin 1992; Post 1996). Any drug that relaxes the individual, for example, can broaden or defocus attention. This may increase the range of available ideas. Next we examine alcohol and marijuana.

BOX 3.8

DRUGS AND CREATIVITY

A large number of individuals have taken drugs and lost their lives, or at least suffered dramatically. A few prominent examples are given below. It is still easy to misdiagnose these kinds of causes of death. Note also the wording, "taken drugs and lost their lives." The ambiguity is intentional. Sadly, the frequent use of drugs among famous samples may send a message to children or to gullible individuals in the population at large. Kaun (1991) found writers to die at a young age, and one possible contribution is the F. Scott Fitzgerald stereotype of good writers being heavy drinkers. Musicians may also have a

stereotype that includes drug use (Plucker & Dana 1999).

- John Belushi
- Richard Burton
- Edgar Allen Poe
- Janis Joplin
- Charlie Parker
- Kurt Cobain
- Jimi Hendrix
- Michael Jackson
- Amy Winehouse
- Heath Ledger
- Whitney Houston

Alcohol

Ludwig (1995), Rothenberg (1990), Noble et al. (1993), and Goodwin (1992) have all written extensively about alcohol and creativity, much of the interest being in the interaction between alcoholism and creativity. There is also research on the physiological effects of alcohol, which is of course what is most relevant to the present chapter.

Norlander and Gustafson (1998) examined the impact of alcohol on divergent thinking. Various controls were used, including placebo and control groups. Body weight was taken into account, as well. Results indicated that the experimental group (the only one that actually received alcohol) had higher originality scores than the control group but lower flexibility scores than the placebo group. In addition, alcohol seemed to have its greatest impact when a moderate dose was given—not too much nor too little. Norlander and Gustafson (1997) used poetry tasks but found a more ambiguous relationship between alcohol and creativity.

It goes without saying that our own personal impressions about the impact of alcohol are much too subjective to consider. This is especially true of alcohol and other drugs that may distort one's judgments. Someone could easily have a few drinks and think they have a wonderful idea, only to sober up and realize it is not as wonderful as it sounded when it was first conceived. It may be that ideational generation is about the same or even hindered when someone is under the influence but their judgment is distorted.

Marijuana

Much of the research on marijuana and creative potential is anecdotal or indirect. Tinklenberg et al. (1978), for example, described the effects of marijuana on associations to novel stimuli. Any work that does examine creativity directly is inconclusive (Bourassa et al. 2001). DiCyan (1971) looked specifically at poetry.

Psilocybin is the hallucinogenic compound $C_{13}H_{18(20)}N_2O_3P_2$. It is found in the mushroom *Psilocybe mexicana* and other related species.

West et al. (1983) asked 72 adult males to write stories after examining pictures from the Thematic Apperception Test (TAT). The TAT has been used for years to study personality. It is a projective measure that has been used on occasion to identify creative tendencies. West et al. used it merely as standardized stimulus for story-writing. Subjects were instructed to write during a baseline, where no manipulation was administered, and then to write another story in an experimental condition. Here control subjects received a placebo and experimental subjects received "20 mg doses of delta-9 tetrahydrocannabinol" (p. 466). All stories were transcribed and entered into a computer for analysis with the *Regressive Imagery Dictionary*. This identifies words and phrases that are indicative of primary process thinking. As expected, the experimental group did indeed write stories with higher primary process than the control subjects. The proportion of primary process was also higher in the experimental condition than the baseline.

Martindale and Fischer (1977) administered psilocybin but did so before (baseline), during, and after the "drug experience" (p. 195). They found that the stories written when the subjects were high contained more primary process content but, importantly, were also more stereotyped than those written before or after the experience.

Most recently Bourassa et al. (2001) compared novice and regular users of marijuana under three conditions: intake, placebo, and control (no marijuana). Comparisons indicated that there was no relationship between intake and divergent thinking among the novices but a reduction among the regular users.

Apparently marijuana can either enhance or inhibit creative potentials. There is some uncertainty, however, because it is surprisingly difficult to ascertain how drugs actually influence people. This is especially the case for both alcohol and marijuana because there are stereotypes and expectations associated with each. Self-reports about the effects of alcohol or marijuana, then, are extremely suspect because they would be significantly biased by expectations. Even measures of behavior may be biased by expectations. To further complicate matters, the effects may vary from individual to individual and task to task, and for any one of these there may be an optimal level of ingestion. If that is the case there may be benefits, but only up to a point, and that point may vary from individual to individual and task to task. As a matter of fact, Weckowitz et al. (1975) found this kind of complicated effect. They administered a battery of tasks to individuals. The amount of marijuana ingested varied from person to person. They found that low levels of marijuana were associated with enhanced performance, at least on certain tests of divergent thinking, but that higher doses inhibited performance. Victor et al. (1973) reported a more generally positive correlation between marijuana and creativity.

After reviewing the literature on drugs and creativity, Plucker and Dana (1999) pointed to numerous inconsistent results and methodological problems (e.g., select samples), especially when they broaden the search to include tobacco and caffeine. Perhaps we should be relieved that there is very little on the topic of drugs and creativity! Then again, consider the creative persons who took drugs and lost their lives.

Before moving to the next example of manipulation and leaving the topic of drugs and creativity, recall here the research cited earlier on lithium and creativity (Shaw et al. 1986; Shou 1979).

Exercise and Stress

Before leaving the topic of altered states of consciousness and these various manipulations, two pertinent areas of research should be mentioned, namely exercise and stress reduction. Both of these are intentional, and both are related to both physiology and creativity.

Steinberg et al. (1997) found that exercise enhances certain indicators of creativity. They also found that the benefits appear to be independent of mood. This is notable because exercise could improve mood, which could then enhance creativity. That possibility was rejected, however, with a significant independent benefit of exercise. There is, of course, the question of what kind of exercise and how much (Gondola 1986, 1987). Aerobic exercise seems to be effective, even with children (Herman-Toffler & Tuckman 1998). Curnow and Turner (1992) combined music and exercise in their work with college students.

Stress and Creativity

Stress and anxiety can inhibit thinking and distract an individual (Smith et al. 1990). Fortunately, much can be done about stress, with benefits to physical health and creativity in particular. Khasky and Smith (1999) suggest relaxation for stress reduction and creativity. Stress can also be mitigated by evaluating, monitoring, and changing one's thinking patterns and reactions (Runco 2012; Seyle 1988).

Self-disclosure may greatly benefit immune functioning, and it is often a creative act (Pennebaker et al. 1997). Disclosure refers to the individual sharing what might otherwise be private thoughts. Pennebaker et al. demonstrated that when college students have a regular opportunity to write about what is going on in their lives, their immune systems (T cells) improve. This research is discussed in more detail in Chapter 4, but for now it is relevant that self-expression, a key part of many creative efforts, is directly related to physiology, and in particular to immune functioning.

Group Differences

The research on altered states, exercise, and stress implies that certain physiological correlates of creativity are the result of particular choices and experiences. Group and individual differences in creativity and physiology therefore would be very likely. Differences, for example, might be expected between fit and sedate people, or between those who are adaptable and experience only low levels of stress, in contrast to individuals who experience a great deal of stress. There are other group differences that may not depend on an individual's choices and intentions.

Consider first the stroke victims and others who have some sort of lesion or damage to the brain. Ramachandran and Ramachandran (1996), for example, described a condition called *anosognosia*, which is found in approximately 5% of stroke patients who have damage to the right side of the brain. They may be partially paralyzed but deny it. Ramachandran and Ramachandran suggested that they are unable to accept the paralysis because they are incapable of modifying old beliefs. They are unable to move an arm or leg, but that information is ignored because it is inconsistent with old belief systems. Ramachandran and Ramachandran did not collect data about creativity, but their work suggests that rigidity and inflexibility may sometimes have biological bases. This is germane because flexibility is an important part of many creative activities (Runco 1985) and because people become more rigid and inflexible as they get older (Chown 1961). This may at least in part result from changes in the nervous system. Almost certainly those changes reflect experience as well, older adults having invested more time in a particular routine or perspective (Rubenson & Runco 1995), but this just means that both nature and nurture are involved. No surprise there. Surely not all older adults become inflexible. Some, such as the artists who employ the "old age style" discussed earlier, appear to be quite flexible. These artists are seen to have changed their work, even in their seventh, eighth, and ninth decades of life (Lindauer et al. 1997).

Some group differences would be expected based on expertise and domain-specific skills. Sergent et al. (1992) took PET and MRI readings while their subjects listened to, read, or played music. The results suggested that these last two tasks "entail processing demands that are realized by a cerebral network distributed over the four cortical lobes and the cerebellum"

(p. 108). Both left and right hemispheres were involved in sight-reading and playing music. Recall also the group differences implied by the autopsies cited earlier (Scheibel 1999; Schlaug et al. 1995a, 1995b).

Age Differences and Maturation

The predictable changes in late life, just mentioned, indicate that some group differences are related to, even determined by, age. They may be *maturational*, which implies that they reflect an unfolding or fulfillment of genetic potentials. When they are maturational there are general commonalities, much like the onset of puberty. That happens at about age 11 for girls and age 12 for boys, though there are individual differences and variations around these typical ages. Maturational tendencies influence creative potentials, such as those that set the stage for the fourth-grade slump (Runco 1999a; Torrance 1968b; see Chapter 2). The impact of maturational process on creative potential may be moderated by (and indeed, is largely a function of) neuroanatomical development. Predictable maturational changes are sometimes explained in terms of critical periods of development.

The fourth-grade slump initially was attributed to the educational system and the conformity demanded by many aspects of the educational system. More recent explanations emphasize brain development. It is quite possible, for instance, the nervous system matures to a point at age 9 or 10 years such that the individual becomes sensitive to conventions and to their utility. Given that conventional behavior is often unoriginal—it is a kind of conformity—this could explain the fourth-grade slump, although it should be emphasized that not all children show a loss of originality. The fourth-grade slump may be experienced by 50% or perhaps slightly more of the children in the United States. Note also that those data are now dated (Torrance 1968b).

The fourth-grade slump may attract as much attention as it does because it can help explain various kinds of behaviors. It is manifested in a loss of originality, but at about that same age (fourth grade, age 9 or so), children's art becomes highly representational, and therefore conventional. The language of children at this stage also becomes more conventional. Their attire and social behavior become much more—hugely more—conventional. Peer pressure acquires enormous potency. The point is that the tendency to weigh conventions heavily is apparent in many aspects of development (Runco & Charles 1997) and is seen in a large number of individuals. This can suggest maturation is at work. There is, beyond a doubt, a loss: Younger children are preconventional and more creative than children at age 9 or 10 because of it (Rosenblatt & Winner 1988).

DIFFERENT TASKS, DIFFERENT STRUCTURES, AND NETWORKS

Differences also reflect the task at hand. Different tasks require different cognitive processes, and therefore different neuroanatomical substrates, which may be why some individuals prefer to do certain things (e.g., dance) instead of others (e.g., mathematical puzzles). It is especially useful to consider different tasks because, although several different cognitive processes already have been reviewed (e.g., insight and divergent thinking), and although various brain structures have been examined (e.g., frontal lobes, cerebral hemispheres, the limbic system, and cerebellum), additional relevant research has been done on correlates of creativity. This research employed divergent thinking tasks and insight problems. There is additional research on the neurophysiology of metaphor.

Mashal et al. (2007), for example, had 15 adults read different word pairs. Some were unrelated words, but others were either conventional metaphors, novel metaphors, or literal metaphors. The novel metaphors might seem to be most indicative of creative verbiage, but it is possible that all metaphors are creative, as long as they are original, and also likely that creativity often depends on metaphoric thought (Getz & Lubart 1997; Gibbs 1999; Gruber 1996; Miller 1996). Still, the most interesting comparison was between the conventional and novel word pairs. The latter were associated with higher levels of activity in the right hemisphere, and in particular in the right posterior superior temporal gyrus, right inferior frontal gyrus, and left middle frontal gyrus.

Jung-Beeman et al. (2004) asked participants in their research to solve problems that required associative thinking, not unlike those on the Remote Associates Test. This test of associative skill does not tap quick, insightful processes, although the judgments of success used by Jung-Beeman et al. might give the feeling of an insight. (As a matter of fact, all insights may imply a sudden solution that is unrelated to the actual cognitive processing required by the task (Gruber 1988), but more on that later.) fMRI indicated that it was the right superior temporal gyrus that was most active when the individuals had a feeling of insight.

Schneider et al. (1996), on the other hand, administered anagrams, some of which were apparently unsolvable. Solvable anagrams might allow the individual to feel an insight, but surely unsolvable ones would not. PET scans indicated increased regional cerebral blood flow to the hippocampus when the individuals received the solvable anagrams, and presumably when there was a feeling of insight. Luo and Niki (2003) also compared solvable and unsolvable problems (riddles) and found similar findings about the hippocampus and insight. Standing back from these studies of metaphor and anagrams, Vartanian and Goel (2005) concluded, "The results of these three imaging studies on insight converge on the role of the right temporal lobe and in particular the hippocampus in insight solutions."

Thus insight problems differ from other kinds of problems in the underlying neural processes (Vartanian et al. 2003), as well as in the emotional reaction. Vartanian et al. (2003) described insight as a kind of shift "from one state in a problem space to a horizontally displaced state rather than a more detailed version of the same state (i.e., vertically displaced state)." Such shifts or transformations may be "necessary for overcoming set effects and facilitate widening of the problem space" (Vartanian et al. 2003). Mental sets can interfere with thinking such that creative insights are difficult to find. At times we approach our experience or a problem from one angle and have difficulty shifting to a different perspective. However it is accomplished, a shift or transformation is likely to provide the "a-ha" feeling, and perhaps satisfaction, relief, or even surprise as well (Gruber 1988; Jausovec 1989). Once again, creativity is both cognitive and affective.

GENETIC BASIS OF CREATIVE POTENTIAL

We have now covered a variety of brain structures and processes that may play a role in creative potential and performance. What of their origin? Why does the brain develop such that we have these potentials and talents? Why are there individual differences in neuroanatomy (and as a result variation in creative talent)? Each of these questions is answered

BOX 3.9

SIR FRANCIS GALTON ON HEREDITY GENIUS

Sir Francis Galton, first cousin of Charles Darwin, contributed a great deal to the social and behavioral sciences. He made many important contributions to the area of assessment and may have been the first to use the so-called *bell curve* to describe human abilities. He also uncovered several of the factors (e.g., birth order) that are still thought to contribute to exceptional ability. In *Hereditary Genius* (Galton 1869), he suggested that high ability runs in families, and this too has held up in recent empirical studies (e.g., Runco & Albert 1985). The problem arises when the biological aspects of heredity are emphasized to the exclusion of the nonbiological aspects. Heredity is not just biological. Socioeconomic status, for instance, is typically stable from generation to generation, and this allows educational level to be maintained. Intergenerational educational stability can in turn explain some of Galton's findings about exceptional performance running in families. Highly educated parents tend to have highly educated children (and this was especially true in Galton's own era). But this too can be taken too far. Education, like the other potential contributing factors reviewed in this paper, apparently contributes to creative achievement only up to a point. Some education may be vital for achievement in some domains, but beyond a certain level, education does not help. In fact, it apparently can be detrimental to achievement. It can take time away from other important (non-academic) experiences. Moreover, it can inculcate a dogmatic or even rigid manner of thinking (Simonton 1984; Torrance 1962).

in much the same way—nature and nurture are to blame. This takes us to the second major issue within the biological perspectives on creativity, namely, that involving genetic contributions. This is not much of a transition for us. In a sense we are moving from brain structure down to the neural and chemical level of genes. But these genes provide the basis for each of the neuroanatomical structures and systems discussed so far in this chapter.

The First Candidate Genes for Creativity

Reuter et al. (2005) extrapolated from genetics studies of personality and inferred that certain genes would be related to creativity. They identified personality traits (e.g., exploratory interests and eagerness to solve problems) which are both *dopaminergic* and also consistent with what is known about characteristics that support creativity.

They proposed that one particular dopamine receptor (*DRD2*) might manifest itself in creative potential. Noble (2000) previously reported that the most relevant allele (i.e., *DRD2 A1*) is found in approximately 30% of the population, at least among Caucasians. (Ethnic background is often held constant in genetic studies; variations that might result are eliminated by examining only one ethnic group. The study of Caucasians is thus merely an experimental requirement. Others have also held ethnicity constant but examined other groups besides Caucasians.) Reuter et al. proposed that the *TPH1* (tryptophan hydroxylase) gene might also be involved in creative thinking.

BOX 3.10

WHAT PART OF CREATIVE POTENTIAL IS INHERITED?

Hans Eysenck (1997a) suggested that overinclusive thinking, not creativity per se, runs in families. Overinclusive thinking is manifested as a kind of associative tendency. The overinclusive individual included atypical things in his or her conceptual categories. When asked to name square things, for example, the overinclusive individual may say "basketball." This tendency leads the individual to some bizarre, and at times psychotic (Eysenck's term) cognition, but sometimes it is beneficial. It may help certain individuals to find creative ideas. After all, creative things are atypical in their originality. When the overinclusive person is not psychotic but sometimes thinks in an original fashion, they have psychoticism instead of psychosis (Eysenck 1997a). What is more relevant here is that overinclusive thinking runs in families. That may be expressed as psychoticism, or as psychosis. This is Eysenck's explanation for the stereotype of the "mad genius."

Originally defined by Cameron (1938; Cameron & Margaret 1951) and then applied to families and creativity by Eysenck (1997a), *overinclusive thinking* refers to a conceptual disorder in which the boundaries of concepts become overextensive. Associated ideas, or even distantly related ideas, become incorporated into the concepts of schizophrenics, making them broad, vague and imprecise. A second aspect of overinclusive thinking is the 'interpretation' of irrational themes. Completely irrelevant, often personal ideas intrude themselves and become mixed up with the problem solving process (Eysenck 1997).

Overinclusive thinking may be expressed in psychosis or psychoticism. The former is psychopathological; the latter is indicative of creative potential. It does not, however, guarantee creativity. Eysenck (1997a) postulated that "the ability to weed out unsuitable and unusable associations must be the distinguishing mark between the word salad of the schizophrenic and the utterances of the poet."

This is all very relevant to the discussion of genetics because it is not creativity that runs in families, according to Eysenck, but overinclusive thinking instead. That is the potential that is inherited. Some use their overinclusive tendencies for creative thinking, others are unable to do so and are psychotic. This is discussed further in Chapter 4.

Reuter et al. (2005) extracted genetic material from 92 individuals. These same individuals took six tests of creative potential. The *DRD2* gene was associated with verbal creativity and a total creativity index. Individuals carrying the *DRD2 A1* allele had higher creativity scores, at least on one index (verbal creativity) and the composite index. The *TPH* allele was significantly related to figural creativity, numeric creativity, and the total creativity index. A third (serotonergic) gene, labeled *COMT SNP*, was unrelated to the creativity indices. None of the three gene loci were related to traditional intelligence.

Importantly, Reuter et al. (2005) implied that genes influence neural transmission. In a manner of speaking, then, their results represent the same neuroanatomical perspective as those just reviewed, though they focused on a different level of analysis (neural rather than brain structures). This research reinforces the rationale for the current chapter in that it reflects biological interactions among genes and neuroanatomy. In other words, it bridges the neuroanatomical research and the genetic research. As a matter of fact, Reuter et al. referred to the "mesocortical dopamine (DA) projections into the forebrain [which] are known to be involved in cognitive functioning and therefore can be assumed to be involved in creative thinking as well" (second page of preprint). This is actually a slippery argument, extrapolating from cognitive functioning in general to creativity in particular, but at this stage in the genetic research on creativity, that is certainly an acceptable position. Note that this logic is consistent with the neuroanatomical (nongenetic) research reviewed earlier, which assigns a privileged role to the frontal lobes.

There may also be something in the association between the *DRD2* allele and the persistence or mania of some creative persons, given its role in nicotine addiction and perhaps alcoholism (Noble 2000; Noble et al. 1993). Eysenck (2003) described how dopamine reception may explain why creativity often is related to psychopathology. He gave this simple graphic:

$$\text{DNA} \to \text{Dopamine D2} \to \text{(lack of) latent inhibition} \to \text{P}$$

where P represents a tendency toward psychoticism, that is, indicative of "a dispositional variable predisposing a person to psychotic illness if subjected to sufficient stress, and containing a combination of personality traits related to typical psychotic and pre-psychotic personalities" (Eysenck 2003). Psychoticism is also correlated with various indicators of creative potential (Eysenck 1997a, 2003).

Runco et al. (2011) criticized the "first candidate" research because the measures of creativity used by Reuter et al. were too broad and did not focus on originality. Runco et al. replicated and extended the "first candidate" research with this in mind (and better measures of creative potential) and also found associations with dopamine (both *DRD2* and *DRD4*). These correlations were much stronger for fluency than originality, however, and Runco et al. raised the possibility that dopamine only supports ideation and productivity and not originality per se. If this is the case it would be inappropriate to infer that dopamine is related to creativity. Originality is necessary but not sufficient for creativity (Runco & Jaeger 2012). Originality can be separated from creativity (see Chapter 13).

A reanalysis of the same genetic data, using multivariate analyses of variance instead of multiple regression, suggested a slightly different conclusion (Murphy et al. 2013), namely that dopamine might be more strongly related to originality than Runco et al. (2011) had found. Strong associations specifically with ideational fluency (the production of a large number of ideas) were confirmed with the MANOVA. Apparently the relevance of dopamine to creativity is still somewhat of an open question.

HERITABILITY

Heritability is the statistical index of shared genes, or variability due to genetic factors. It is much like a correlation coefficient, with a maximum possible value of 1.00 (100% genetic). Behavioral genetic research inferred it from individuals who have identical genetic make-up but dissimilar environments, such as identical twins reared apart. Significantly, heritability does not preclude environmental influence.

Twin and Adoption Studies

The genetic basis of creativity has also been studied using behavioral genetic techniques (e.g., Barron & Parsi 1977; Reznikoff et al. 1973). This technology, such as it is, was adapted from investigations of the heritability of intelligence. The premise is that the genetic contribution to some phenotype (i.e., a manifest trait or capacity) can be inferred by comparing monozygotic (MZ, identical) twins, who are 100% alike genetically, with dizygotic (DZ, fraternal) twins or with two siblings who are not twins, who are only 50% alike. Alternatively, parents and their biological children can be compared with adoptive or foster parents and children. The assumption here is that the child shares 50% of their genetic make-up with the biological parents but does not share environment with the biological parents if raised in another home. Studies using these techniques and measures of IQ have reported that as much as 80% of intelligence is genetically determined (Jensen 1980). Identical twins tend to have very similar IQs even if they are reared in different environments. The correlation between the test scores or personality traits of MZ twins reared apart is used as a direct index of heritability (Waller et al. 1993).

Nichols (1978) and Waller et al. (1993) reviewed all studies on twins and creativity and concluded that "approximately 22% of the variation in this dimension [divergent thinking] is due to the influence of genes" (Waller et al. 1993, p. 235). Waller et al. also examined indicators of creative potential among 157 pairs of twins reared apart. They calculated a heritability index of 0.54, which also supports a notable contribution to creativity, in this instance specifically to the creative personality. The correlation between DZ twins was, in contrast, – 0.06.

Care must be taken with the term "influence of genes." Genes do not translate directly into behavior. They provide potentials, or what is called a *range of reaction*. Genes set a range to which the environment and experience react. The outcome is an interaction of genes and environment—nature and nurture. Guilford (1962) referred to something like this with the idea of limits:

> Heredity probably does determine limits, both upper and lower, within which development can occur. Experience or learning may have considerable room within which to operate and produce results. The best working assumption to adopt is that education can do a great deal to promote the development of individuals in the way of preparing them to perform creatively, if not in the way of strengthening their creative abilities (p. 164).

Twin and adoption studies also make several dubious assumptions. In twin studies that compare MZ twins reared apart with siblings reared together, for instance, there is an assumption that the former do not share environments. Any similarity in their IQs, personality, or creativity is assigned to genetic similarity. Yet actually they do have similar environments, even when reared apart. They are both human, breathe air, live in houses, and are likely to speak the same language(s). They experience the same culture, which means they encounter many of the same values, expectations, and experiences. The best conclusion is that both nature and nurture play a role. In fact, the impact of the latter depends on the former. This again is the message of the range of reaction.

Kinney et al. (2000–2001) used a slightly different methodology. They compared adoptees who may have had a genetic liability toward schizotypy but who did not manifest negative schizophrenic behavior. Apparently the adoptees had a creative advantage in that they were able to think in an unconventional fashion, and thus think creatively, but they did not have such unconventional tendencies as to make them actually schizophrenic. This research is explored further in Chapter 4.

Genealogies

Genealogies are often suggestive of genetic contributions to creative potential. They are not reliable indicators, however, and at best offer hypotheses that could be tested in controlled research. Actually, that would be the case if the study of genealogies offered any coherent message about the genetics of creativity, but it does not. Some genealogies seem to confirm a genetic basis for creativity in that many family members manifest obvious talent. Yet many others (e.g., Shakespeare) offer contrary evidence. Shakespeare, arguably the leading innovator in the history of the English language, may well have had illiterate parents. But no doubt the danger of this approach is obvious: The focus is usually on individual cases, and their families. Also problematic is that we mostly have data about the families of eminent creators. Very little data exists about noneminent individuals. This creates a selection bias and undermines the value of genealogical data.

To make matters worse, the genetic contributions to creativity (or anything else) cannot be clearly inferred from talents that "run in families." That is because genes are shared by families, but so is environment, as is education, money, and various other possible influences on talent. So again, studies of genealogies are probably the least useful sources of data for genetic studies of creativity.

CONCLUSIONS

The interdisciplinary nature of creative studies is readily apparent in this chapter: social/conventional, develop/maturation, clinical, and cognitive, for example. There is especially good complementarity among neuroanatomical and cognitive psychological theories of creativity. This is clear in the parallels involving divergent and convergent thinking, for example, but also in the mutual use of the concepts of working memory, insight, hypothesis generation, imagery, and even the idea of ideation. Neuroanatomists also have found labels for their discoveries and hypotheses in the research on mood and psychopathology. Earlier we discussed biological bases for primary and secondary processes, mania, and overinclusive thinking, just to name three examples. Ardena et al. (2010) reviewed all available brain-imaging evidence on creative thinking, drawing from 45 different studies. They concluded that no one brain location is associated with all expressions of creativity. This might make sense, given the theory of creativity as a complex, but then again, creativity could be parsimoniously defined as involving only one, or a very small number, of processes (Runco 2010b), and the failure to reach consensus on brain location could easily reflect the different measures used in the 45 investigations. Too often in this research creativity was confused with insight, which, as discussed in Chapter 13 (and Chapter 1), is unfortunate given how easy it is to distinguish one from the other.

The prefrontal cortex certainly does receive a great deal of attention in the neuroanatomical research. Yet this just means that it plays a key role in the creative process. That process involves various structures and circuits, or networks. Not only is the idea of "right-brained creativity" to be rejected, the whole idea of one responsible area or locus of the brain is inaccurate. As a matter of fact there are at least two assumptions that need to be rejected. First is the assumption that creativity depends entirely on one part, structure, or location of the human brain. Second is the assumption that creativity will eventually be explained at the most microscopic level, namely, the cellular and neurochemical level.

These are not independent ideas. Both reflect a kind of reductionism that simply does not apply to human biology or to creativity. Human behavior (especially cognition) is much too varied, adaptable, and diverse to expect simple canalized neural processes. Creativity epitomizes adaptability and must be viewed as a complex. It would be enormously unreasonable to expect any one (circuit, hemisphere, lobe) brain locus to be responsible. It must be a collaborative effect and controlled by different brain structures and processes.

Genes, neurotransmitters, and other micro-physical processes are vital for creative thinking, but almost certainly it is much better to look to brain circuitry and the interplay of different brain structures than to any one gene, structure, location, or chemical for explanations. These circuits are not the most microscopic part of brain hierarchy. In one sense this is good news. It is not necessary to dig deeper and deeper, with increasingly powerful microscopes and imaging technologies to increase our understanding of creativity and the brain.

It also means that simple treatments and explanations will not suffice. There are interesting data about uric acid (Kennett & Cropley 1975) and even testosterone (Hassler 1992; Reuter et al. 2005), but these research results will probably only have explanatory power as each is related to larger neural systems and circuits. Creativity very likely depends on various anatomical structures and neurochemical processes and their interaction.

Perhaps these two assumptions can be replaced with two intriguing postulates. The first postulate is that the human brain supports different kinds of creativity; the second postulate is that different human brains lead to different kinds of creativity.

The research on domain differences and differences between various kinds of creative cognition (e.g., hypothesis generation, insight, divergent thinking) supports that first postulate. The second postulate is very clearly supported by the research on group and individual differences, as summarized at the end of the last section of this chapter.

Implicit in this material is the idea that the brain provides humans with a productive, proactive, flexible, and generative mind. No wonder the idea of divergent thinking permeates the creativity literature. Much of the research in this chapter used tests of divergent thinking to estimate the potential for creative thought. That is, of course, how these tests must be defined. They are not tests of creativity. After several reviews of the literature Runco (1991b, 1999d, 2013b) put it exactly that way: Tests of divergent thinking provide useful estimates of the potential for creative thinking. These tests were used in the research on the "first candidate gene" (a Uses test), EEG and PET research (Bekhtereva et al. 2000; Martindale 1977–78), investigations of marijuana (Weckowitz et al. 1975), and in studies of familial relationships (e.g., Runco & Albert 2005), just to name a few topics covered in this chapter.

The generative potential of the human mind is also apparent in its capacity to anticipate, predict, infer, and even interpret. In one recent study fMRIs confirmed that the auditory cortex is active when music is remembered (McCrae 1987). It is also active when music is muted; the brain seems to fill in the gaps, pulling information from memory. If lyrics are involved, a larger system of the brain is active, and if the music is associated with a particular experience (or perhaps event, even a movie's theme song), even more brain activity occurs. Of most relevance is the finding that the human brain can fill in the gaps in a constructive manner.

At least some of the time, and perhaps a great deal of it, the generative capacity of the human brain might specifically result from combinatorial processes. At least there seems to be an implicit consensus in that direction among neuroanatomical investigations. Dietrich

(2004, p. 1011) referred to this when he wrote, "the prefrontal cortex contributes highly integrative computations to the conscious experience, which enables *novel combinations* of information to be recognized as such and then appropriately applies to works of art and science (pp. 1011–1012, italics added).

Combinatorial processes have also been recognized in previous cognitive psychological research on creativity and in other observations and reports. Sir Peter Medawar, for instance, said,

> In human creativity a cognate process must be at work: human creativity must be a rapid combination and recombination and reassortment of ideas. The memory retaining the more plausible juxtapositions rather as if a computer were programmed to produce jokes of a random kind while a selective process would sort out those that were genuinely funny or really silly or meaningless (quoted by Damásio 2001, pp. 63–64).

Recall also that Damásio (2001) himself referred to "the variety of novel combinations of entities as images" and "representational diversity." This is one reason the working memory often is implicated in creative thinking. Combinations may take place within the working memory. Working memory also aids in making the important choices and decisions that are involved in creative efforts.

The mind is not just generative, however, and this is a good thing since creativity requires more than just ideation and productivity. It requires direction, decision making, editing and functions of the temporal lobe. Recall here how many theories reviewed in this chapter put emphasis on inhibition as well as production. As Brown (2007) put it, "thinking depends on the inhibition of irrelevant memories as much as the arousal of what is pertinent." These ideas are also consistent with the cognitive research on creativity, and in particular with studies of evaluative processes (Runco 1991d; Runco & Basadur 1993).

There is some indication that the cerebellum is involved in some creative work, though it must be emphasized that, relative to the other structures mentioned in this chapter (e.g., prefrontal cortex, temporal lobes), this is an untested structure (Brown 2007). Still, it is intriguing to consider the possible role of the cerebellum, especially given the possibility that some creative thinking is muscular or kinesthetic. Einstein's anecdotal descriptions of creative work are consistent with this possibility (Vandervert et al. 2007), as are observations from Sir John Eccles from his 1958 *Scientific American* paper on "The physiology of the imagination." Sir John tied imagination to sensory information processing by the brain. He also described how congealed neural patterns were created by neural signals (he called them *engrams*) and how this allows both imagery and memory. Such imagery was, for Eccles, a simple form of imagination. Quoting Eccles (1958):

> The wealth and subtlety of stored memories and critical evaluations imply that in the neuronal network there is an enormous development of complex engrams whose permanency derives from the postulated increase in synaptic efficacy. … Such are the prerequisites leading to creative insight. (p. 144) … The creative brain must first of all possess an adequate number of neurons, having a wealth of synaptic connection between them. It must have, as it were, the structural basis for an immense range of patterns of activity. … The synapses of the brain should also have a sensitive tendency to increase their function with usage, so that they may readily form and maintain memory patterns. Such a brain will accumulate an immense wealth of engrams of highly specific character. If, in addition, this brain also possesses a peculiar potency for unresting activity … the stage is set for the deliverance of a "brain child" that is sired, as we say, by creative imagination (p. 146).

More recently, Memmertt (2007) described the creative thinking of athletes, and Gardner's (1983) theory of multiple intelligences includes a bodily domain. Significantly, one of the criteria for a distinctive domain is that it is based on unique brain structures (Gardner 1983).

Gibbs (2006) also saw movement and muscular bases of thought. He looked to Einstein's description of a "muscular type" of mental entity and found references to Einstein's *embodied thought processes* in a famous experiment. Apparently Einstein "pretended to be a photon moving at the speed of light. He first imagined what he saw and how he felt, and then became a second photon and imagined what he now experienced of the first photon" (Gibbs 2006, p. 123). He went on to quote Cyril Stanley Smith, famous for his work on the structure of metals. Smith reported experiencing the feeling of the metals he studied—their "hardness and softness and conductivity and fusability and deformability and brittleness … all in a curious internal and quite literal sensuous way… [the] aesthetic feeling for a balanced structure and a muscular feeling of the interfaces pulling against one another" (Gibbs 2006, pp. 123–124).

It may not come as a surprise, then, that there is some uncertainty about the generality of creativity (Baer 1998a; Plucker 1998) and the generality of the underlying biological processes (Flaherty 2005).

Yet Katz (1997) concluded:

> There appears to be some privileged role in creativity to the cognitive functions associated with the right hemisphere. This conclusion is based on the performance of gifted youth, EEG recordings while participants are taking tasks that purportedly measure creativity, and indirect measures such as conjugate lateral eye movement data. Although based on a narrower set of converging operations than that on which the first conclusion rests, it should be emphasized that a right hemisphere superiority is found in the majority of cases where cerebral hemisphere asymmetries arise; rarely does one find evidence for left hemisphere superiority. [Also] there is some evidence that different creative tasks may differentially call upon the cognitive resources for which the two hemispheres are specialized. *That is, the cognitive processes (and hence the hemispheres subserved by these processes) necessary to be creative as an artist appear to be different than those required for math. It may well be that the highly creative are better able to make use of the cognitive resources of the hemisphere that is nondominant for the creative task at hand* (emphasis added) (p. 220).

Genes influence neuroanatomy. Any demarcation between these two perspectives on biology, the genetic and the neuroanatomical, is somewhat artificial. Simply put, genes determine which structures and processes will be available. More specifically, they provide the potential for creativity. This idea is captured in the concept of a range of reaction, which applies to every level of the brain process and structure hierarchy presented earlier—as well as to the personality traits, cognitive skills, and motivations that are reviewed elsewhere in this book. Perhaps the point to emphasize is that the traits, capacities, and abilities that are discussed throughout this chapter constitute *phenotype*, but are dependent on *genotype*. Phenotype is exactly that—the traits and abilities that are manifested because there was genetic potential that was reinforced and supported by experience and environment. Nature and nurture both play a role in the neuroanatomical bases for our creativity and in all things human.

Biological contributions are important in part because of their implications. Biology, for example, might be used to explain the skewed distribution of creative performances (Simonton 1984). A surprising number of theorists believe that creativity is limited and not widely distributed. This may be a scientific convenience, however, and reflect their thinking that we can be objective in our study about creativity only if we look at instances of individuals or products about which there is no ambiguity (Gardner 1993a). One attractive alternative is that creative potential is widely distributed, even if world-class performances are not, the implication being that each of us has potential that can be exercised and fulfilled.

There is debate regarding extraordinary creativity. Dietrich (2004) was explicit about his assumption that creative thinking is merely a reflection of the same processes that sometimes generate uncreative or routine cognition. This implies that neural circuits that support creative insights may be the same as the circuits that sometimes lead to routine and uncreative cognition. Andreasen (2005), on the other hand, implied that extraordinary creativity may depend on extraordinary cognition and an extraordinary brain.

Flaherty's (2005) model, which involves the temporal and frontal lobes and the limbic system, implies generality. In her words,

> While the correlation between manic states and creativity is strongest for language-based fields, temporal lobe changes can also produce the equivalent of hypergraphia in other creative fields. Frontotemporal dementia is the best-known example. A subset of these patients has neurodegeneration that selectively affects the temporal lobe. Up to 10% of that subset develops compulsive artistic or musical interests, even when they had no preexisting artistic tendencies (p.148).

This kind of generality is clearly contrary to the various theories of domain-specificity (Baer 1998a; Gardner 1983) but it implies generality across domains and not necessarily across individuals. Miller et al. (1998) presented data in support of the relationship between frontotemporal dementia and artistic interests.

Individual differences were suggested by several lines of neuroanatomical research. They were supported by the research comparing more and less creative groups (Carlsson 2002), for example, and of course by the research on the first candidate gene. Also consider Scheibel's (1999) argument that "we must assume that the more nimble the frontal cortex, the more capable it is of playing with new combinations of stored items" (p. 3). That both implies individual differences and pinpoints the combinatorial process discussed previously.

Dietrich (2004) was very clear about group and individual differences. He contrasted expertise with creativity, some people having more of one or the other: "Knowledge and creativity involve different neural circuits. Knowledge is largely TOP [temporal occipital parietal] but creativity (dorsolateral) prefrontal cortex. An uncreative expert would have an 'endowed' TOP but less-remarkable prefrontal cortex" (p. 1020). A highly original but not very effective individual would have the opposite constitution. The creatively intelligent person, of course, would have both. Not surprisingly, this view acknowledges domain differences. The artistically inclined person "possesses a finely honed emotional brain" (p. 1021).

Mood (Dietrich 2004, p. 1022) and age (Axelrod et al. 1993; Chown 1961; Dietrich 2004; Rubenson & Runco 1995) both may predispose certain individuals to certain thinking modes. This also follows from the maturation of the prefrontal cortex, which does not reach maturity until the early 20s. Children would not have the discretion or meta-cognitive supports, then, to be creative in the same way as adults. They will also have less of a knowledge base, but this can work for or against creative thinking. Knowledge sometimes provides a person with options, but at the same time it leads to routine, assumption, and other enemies of original and creative cognition. Children may be creative in a different way from adults, the former more spontaneous and uninhibited, the latter more tactical and deliberate (Dietrich 2004;

Runco 1996a). Age differences are also apparent in late life. At that point the problem is inflexibility (Chown 1961; Rubenson & Runco 1995).

There is also a bit of a debate about the role of consciousness, creativity, and the underlying neuroanatomical structures. Vandervert et al. (2007) and Damásio (2001) cited the working memory in their descriptions of creative processes and, as noted earlier, what a person is conscious of is in his or her working memory. It is easy to see how working memory would play a role in any creative work that requires conscious awareness, attentional focus, or sustained concentration. These are functions of working memory and in turn implicate the prefrontal lobes. Yet not all kinds of creative work are consciously done. Consider, for example, the cognition that allows overinclusive thought, primary process, the exploration of loose conceptual boundaries, or defocused attention.

Dietrich (2004) felt that "by definition, creative insights occur in consciousness" (p. 1011) but he implied that something may occur before consciousness (and the prefrontal lobe) kicks in:

> Concisely stated, creativity results from the factorial combination of four kinds of mechanisms. Neural computation that generates novelty can occur during two modes of thought (deliberate and spontaneous) and for two types of information (emotional and cognitive). Regardless of how novelty is generated initially, circuits in the prefrontal cortex perform the computation that transforms the novelty into creative behavior. *To that end, prefrontal circuits are involved in making novelty fully conscious, evaluating its appropriateness, and ultimately implementing its creative expression* (Dietrich 2004, p. 1023, italics added).

Insight and incubation are frequently involved in creative thinking, and they require preconscious activity (Gruber 1988), but there is no insight unless an idea or solution makes its way into consciousness. The "a-ha" moment is exactly that, the moment the idea makes its way into conscious awareness. That idea, however, may have been percolating for some time below the level of consciousness, and benefiting from the lack of censorship. Gruber (1981b) presented data on the process that occurs before every "a-ha" and described it as *protracted* (also see Rothenberg 1990; Wallace 1991). Dietrich (2004, p. 1016) viewed the workings of the unconscious as parallel processing.

There is debate about consciousness and the unconscious, and about extraordinary and ordinary creativity. Yet the research on the biology of creativity supports two reasonable postulates: (1) the human brain supports different kinds of creativity, but (2) different human brains lead to different kinds of creativity.

The summary of genetics and creativity helped with the question of etiology. A more general perspective on etiology involves evolutionary theory. The brain is a product of evolutionary pressures (Jerison 1974), as are its genetic bases.

Health and Clinical Perspectives

Happiness in intelligent people is the rarest thing I know.
Ernest Hemingway, **Islands in the Stream (p. 97)**

Relish the struggle, that's the way.
Dick Francis, **Bolt**

Every act of creation is first of all an act of destruction.
Pablo Picasso (quoted by Kao 1991, p. 16)

ADVANCE ORGANIZER

- The Mad Genius Controversy
- Affective Disorders
  - Emotional Creativity
- Suicide
  - "Writers Die Young"
  - "The Price of Greatness"
- Immune System Efficiency
- Stress
- Anxiety
- Aggression and Crime
- Psychosis
- Schizophrenia
- Special Populations
  - ADHD
  - Physical Impairments
- Adaptability
- Self-Actualization

INTRODUCTION

The benefits of creativity are easy to see. Creativity, for example, is responsible for much in our day-to-day lives. (Have you listened to any music today, in the car, on a stereo or computer, or in an elevator? Have you admired a graphic on your computer, or an ad in a magazine? Have you enjoyed a TV show, worn some stylish clothes, or joked with a friend?) It is also behind much of our cultural evolution and technological progress. And it is fun. It gives life authenticity and spontaneity.

There are, however, potential concerns or even costs to creativity. There may be a stigma attached to highly original behavior, for instance. ("What a weirdo!") Much more serious is the concern about creativity and health. Many famous creators have suffered from diseases of various sorts. Many suffered from psychopathology, and some from a physical ailment. This chapter discusses all the possible relationships between creativity and both psychological and physical health. As we will see, the various expressions of creative talent are related in various ways to a diverse set of illnesses and problems. Yet we will also see that creative efforts can contribute to positive health. Creativity can help the individual maintain both psychological and physical health.

This chapter addresses the following questions. Does creativity lead to positive mental health? Is it related to positive physical health? Are there differences among domains (e.g., poets, writers of fiction, performers)? What causes what?—does creativity influence health or health influence creativity? How is creativity related to stress and anxiety? The first question to be addressed is the oldest and even has a label, namely, the "mad genius controversy" (Box 4.1). Are all creative people a few bubbles off plumb?

BOX 4.1

THE MAD GENIUS

The relationship of mood disorders and creativity has long been observed (Becker 1978; Becker 2000–2001; Goertzel & Goertzel 1962). Many refer to "the mad genius controversy" because there are potential problems and ailments, but also numerous examples of healthy creative individuals. The debate is an old one, as these quotations imply.

> Those who become eminent in philosophy, politics, poetry, and the arts have all tendencies toward melancholia.
>
> Aristotle, *Problemata*

> Great wits are sure to madness near allied/ And thin partitions do their bounds divide.
>
> John Dryden, English dramatist (1831–1900)

> There is no great genius without a touch of madness
>
> Seneca (5 BC–AD 65)

> Everything great in the world comes from neurotics. They alone have founded religions and composed our masterpieces.
>
> Marcel Proust

> The lunatic, the lover, and the poet/ Are of imagination all compact.
>
> William Shakespeare, *A Midsummer Night's Dream*

The volitional excitement which accompanies the disease [mania] may under certain circumstances set free powers which otherwise are constrained by all kinds of inhibition. Artistic creativity namely may be the untroubled surrender to momentary fantasies or moods, and especially poetical activity by the facilitation of linguistic expression, experience a certain furtherance.

Emil Kraepelin (1921–1976, p. 17, quoted by Ramey & Weisberg 2004)

FIGURE 4.1   Ernest Hemingway won the Pulitzer Prize for Fiction in 1953 and the Nobel Prize for Literature in 1954. He often worked in a wonderful plantation style home, in Key West, among palms and his numerous cats. Sadly, he committed suicide in 1961. *Source: Wikimedia Commons, http://en.wikipedia.org/wiki/Hemingway.*

AFFECTIVE DISORDERS

Most of the research on creativity and psychopathology focuses on the affective disorders. Affect refers to emotionality, and the affective disorders include depression and the bipolar disorders. Bipolar disorders are characterized by mood swings, with depression at one extreme and mania at the other. The latter is defined in terms of elation and energy. There are various kinds of bipolar disorders that vary in terms of degree, directionality, and duration. These are potentially very serious disorders, in part because depression is predictive of suicide. Of course all of us experience some sort of depression from time to time, but when it is chronic and severe, there is a tendency toward suicide ideation. Suicide ideation in turn sometimes leads to a suicide attempt (Figure 4.1).

Andreasen (1997) reported especially high rates of suicide in writers, as well as a tendency toward a bipolar disorder. She found particular support for bipolar II and bipolar III, which are characterized by subclinical levels of depression, as well as mood swings. Similar results were reported by Jamison (1997), also working with a group of writers. The idea of subclinical levels is very important and will be revisited throughout this chapter (also see Schuldberg 2001).

Ludwig (1995, p. 138) compared various creative domains and found depression to be highest in poets (77%), but also quite common among writers of fiction (59%), artists (50%), writers of nonfiction (47%), and composers (46%). Individuals in the military and involved in exploration seemingly never suffered from or reported depression (Box 4.2).

How might affective processes influence creative efforts? First consider the role of physical energy. When depressed, people do not have much energy. But if there is a mood swing and an experience of mania, there is great energy, elation, and often productivity. It might even

BOX 4.2

FRACTALS AND PSYCHOLOGICAL DISTURBANCE

Ludwig (1998) used fractal geometry, and in particular the concept of *self-similarity*, to explain differences between the creativity of artists and scientists. This involves comparisons of the two domains on different levels. That is, of course, the key to fractals; they show similarity across each level of analysis. Ludwig therefore changed levels of analysis by first examining them on a very general level, but then performed more specific analyses comparing the methods used in each. His data were archival but represented over 1100 eminent individuals. Ludwig concluded that

the relation that exists is not between mental illness and creative expression per se but

between the presence or absence of mental illness and particular forms of creative expression. Employing the metaphor of the fractal, we find that as we focus on professions within professions within professions, the same patterns that exist at a macroscopic level in comparisons among professional groupings also tend to exist at more microscopic levels of analysis. The dominant pattern that seems to hold is that the more particular professions rely on mathematical, natural, formal, and objective modes of creative expression or problem solving, the lower the prevalence of mental illness in their members; the more a profession relies on emotive elements, personal revelations, and subjective forms of creative expression, the higher the prevalence (p. 100).

---

be the swing that is important and not the mood per se. It may be that a person experiencing a bipolar episode has masses of energy and produces prolifically. A writer may get 1000 pages written in a week! But then mood swings and depression set in. If this person looks back at those 1000 pages, he or she might not be very pleased. After all, it is difficult to be pleased when you are unhappy. The depressed person may throw out 999 pages. But perhaps there are a few sentences or phrases that sound good, even while depressed. And if the mood swings again, this person may have another productive phase, followed by another critical phase. After a long period of time the person may produce a poem or book-length manuscript that passes muster despite depression and personal criticism! It is as if the person is his or her own editor.

Creative efforts might also offer a relief or catharsis. It may seem less likely than decreased energy and output, but it is possible that depression (or any psychological disturbance) is alleviated by keeping busy. This is especially true if the disturbance is otherwise difficult to face (Jones et al. 1997). Creative efforts might offer the affected person some escape or repose.

Another hypothesis about the affective disorders of creative individuals focuses on their tendency to immerse themselves in their work (Gruber 1988). This is another way of saying that they are intrinsically motivated, though *immersion* is more descriptive of actual behavior instead of an internal state. Immersion might best be viewed as a manifestation of intrinsic motivation. And there are several reasons why depression and negative affect may be associated with it.

Immersion implies that the individual focuses his or her life on the topic or subject, be it playing chess, playing music, playing sports, or playing with designs. It further implies that the person is thinking about the subject for most of the day, every day, year after year. This intellectual focus means that the person has few resources for anything else, including a social life and the consideration of his or her own feelings. Carl Jung was quite clear about the problems that can come about with this kind of imbalance in a person's life (see Miller 2009). One of them is depression, or negative affect.

Immersion also implies that the individual has a huge investment in his or her work or field of interest. Using psychoeconomic logic, this further implies that the individual has a great deal at risk. Runco (1998) applied this logic and reasoning to the biographical information about the poet Sylvia Plath. He concluded that Plath's suicide might be viewed as a result of her enormous investment in writing, and some unfortunate depreciation of that work.

DOMAIN DIFFERENCES IN PSYCHOPATHOLOGY

The domain differences debated throughout the creativity literature (e.g., Baer 1998a; Plucker 1998) may be clearest in studies of psychopathology. Domain differences have certainly been noted for a long time (e.g., Plato, Aristotle). Wittkower and Wittkower (1963, chapter 5) give an especially detailed history of *Homo melancholicus*. Domain differences are also clearly and objectively delineated by Ludwig (1995) in his extensive archival study.

AFFECT AND MOOD

Other possible explanations are suggested by mood studies (e.g., Isen et al. 1985; Kaufmann & Vosburg 1997). These typically involve participants who are free of disorders, but they are suggestive of the workings of mood, and some actually manipulate mood (Hoppe & Kyle 1990; Kaufmann & Vosburg 1997). This research indicates that information processing tendencies are influenced by mood. It turns out that either negative mood or positive mood can facilitate creative problem solving, but it depends a great deal on the task at hand. Some tasks benefit from negative moods and some from positive moods. Kaufmann (2003) explained this in terms of task demands. In his words, some tasks are "mood sensitive."

It appears that there is more appreciation of positive mood (e.g., Forgas 2000; Hirt 1999; Isen 1993, 1999; Isen & Baron 1991). Hirt's (1999) review of the research is sometimes quoted: "individuals in positive mood states have been reliably shown to be more creative on a range of tasks than are individuals in other mood states … [the] effects of (positive) mood on creativity appears to be remarkably robust in terms of the mood induction procedure used and the range of possible creativity tasks that have been measured" (pp. 241–242).

Which tasks benefit from positive affect? There are several, including those measured in the Remote Associates Test (see Chapter 9), insight problems (Estrada et al. 1994; Greene & Noice 1988; Isen et al. 1987), and word association tasks (Isen & Daubman 1984; Isen et al.

BOX 4.3

EMOTIONAL CREATIVITY

Emotional creativity can be defined as one's ability to feel and express emotions honestly, and in unique ways, that are effective in meeting the demands of both intra- and inter-personal situations ... emotional creativity refers to a person's ability to be creative in the emotional domain. ... At the lowest level, emotional creativity involves the particularly effective application of an already existing emotion, one found within the culture; at a more complex level, it involves the modification ('sculpting') of a standard emotion to better meet the needs of individual or group; and at the highest level, it involves the development of a new form of emotion, based on a change in the beliefs and rules by which emotions are constituted (Averill 1999a, p. 334).

An interplay between emotional creativity and cognitive creativity is also suggested by Averill's (1999b) statement, "On the border between cognition and emotion lies creativity" (p. 765). There appear to be two possibilities: First, the creative *process* may vary with emotional variations, and second, emotions

themselves may be the *product* of a creative process (Gutbezahl & Averill, 1996).

In some ways the concept of emotional creativity was a natural outgrowth from the earlier theories of emotional intelligence (Goleman 1995; Salovey & Mayer 1990). Yet just as creativity is distinct from IQ, so too is emotional creativity distinct from *emotional intelligence*. Fuchs et al. (2007) defined the latter as "the disposition to attend to, perceive, and appraise one's own feelings as well as those of others, being able to name and differentiate various closely related feelings and emotions (e.g., loving and liking), make appropriate decisions to cope with inter- and intra-personal situations, accurately experience and express emotions, and to regulate emotions for promoting personal growth." Emotional creativity, on the other hand, refers to personal evaluations of events, judging and reacting to personally significant information.

1985; cf. Greene & Noice 1988). The supposed benefits of positive mood include overinclusive thought, loose conceptual boundaries, original word associations, broader categorization of information, and more ideational intrusions (see Bowden 1994; Jamison 1993; Schuldberg 1990, 2001), a broader range of options, and an increase in the number of ideational associations. All of this adds up to a higher probability of finding an original idea. There is also some indication that negative affect can lead to a flexibility that is apparent when the person needs to shift from one category of thought to another.

Kaufmann (2003) cited several reports of ambiguous benefits of positive mood (e.g., Jausovec 1989; Weisberg 1994) but for obvious reasons emphasized his own experimental studies. Kaufmann and Vosburg (1997), for example, reported two experiments in which positive affect failed to facilitate insight (the *two-string problem* and the *hatrack problem*). As a matter of fact individuals in a positive mood did the worst of all and were outperformed by participants in neutral, control, and negative mood experimental conditions. In a subsequent study Kaufmann and Vosburg (2002) uncovered an interaction in which the impact of mood varied depending on the time on the task. Positive mood was beneficial early on, but after the individual had produced a number of ideas negative mood seemed to be better. Kaufmann (2003) argued that

> positive mood participants scored significantly higher in early production, whereas negative and neutral mood participants significantly outperformed the positive mood participants in late production. Indeed, the positive mood condition seemed to produce a steep, noncreative, response gradient, whereas the negative and neutral conditions were closer to the flat association gradient held by Mednick (1962) to be characteristic of creative individuals (p. 133).

Affect sometimes acts as a kind of cue specifically for memory and associations, which are themselves tied to emotions. It may be quite general, according to Bower (1981), in that affective states activate everything in memory related to that general emotion. As Russ and Schafer (2006) described it, there may be emotional themes in fantasies, associations, and memory. One particular emotion therefore activates or primes a large number of possibilities.

There is a psychoanalytic basis explanation for the impact of mood. Simplifying some, if a person does not block or repress emotions, he or she is more likely to have creative associations. As Russ and Schafer (2006) put it, "the lack of repression or blockage of ideas, memories, and associations, should facilitate broad associations in a number of areas." Getz and Lubart (2000) confirmed that objects that are inherently emotional or "affect laden" tend to elicit a particular kind of divergent thinking.

Russ and Schafer (2006) investigated the impact of mood by studying the fantasy play of children from the first and second grades. Affect in play was assessed by videotaping children while they play with puppets. The children are asked to give voice to the puppets, that is to talk out loud, as if they were a character or the puppet. The videotapes are then scored for the frequency of emotion or affective expression, and the variety of affect categories. Russ and Schafer also administered the Alternate Uses divergent thinking test (see Chapter 2), with four affect-laden stimuli and four neutral stimuli. They found that fluency was significantly correlated with the amount of affect in memory. Originality was not. When IQ was statistically controlled, the affect in play was not significantly related to fluency, though it was before IQ was controlled. Negative affect and originality were significantly correlated both before and after taking IQ into account. Contrary to expectations, the relationship between affect and play and divergent thinking was not stronger when children received the affect-laden stimuli. Butcher and Niec (2005) used a similar methodology with somewhat different results. They did find a relationship between negative affect in play and parental ratings of creativity.

ALEXITHEMIA

Recall from Chapter 3 that *alexithemia* refers to low emotionality, especially a disinclination to express emotions. According to Fuchs et al. (2007), "individuals with alexithemia are usually characterized as matter-of-fact, concrete thinkers, liking of structure, less emotionally oriented, and less fantasy prone." Hoppe and Kyle (1990) suggested that the alexithemia found in their patients hindered creative thinking. These patients had commissurotomies, which is explored in Chapter 3. Certainly alexithemia would take the thrill out of creative efforts and preclude the satisfaction of an "a-ha" moment. It may also undermine the intrinsic interest that drives so many creative efforts.

SUICIDE

BOX 4.4

SUICIDE AND DEATH RATES

Suicide is one of the more common causes of death. It is more common than AIDS, homicide, and even atherosclerosis. It accounts for approximately 13 of every 100 000 deaths. Diseases of the heart are most common (approximately 296 per 100 000 deaths), followed by malignant neoplasms (200), cerebrovascular diseases (59), accidents (38), influenza and pneumonia (30), and diabetes (19). Suicide is eighth, though it does vary from age group to age group. Even though life expectancy is on the rise, the rate of suicide is also on the rise. Between 1950 and 1988, the U.S. Bureau of Census found a 100% increase.

The World Health Organization (WHO, from May 12, 2003, Reuters) put it this way: "Traffic kills four times as many people as wars and far more people commit suicide than are murdered." They noted that one-tenth of the global death toll in 2000 was injury-related (both accidental and deliberate), with 1.26 million road injuries at the top of the list. Suicide was next (815 000), and then interpersonal violence (520 000). Wars and conflict ranked sixth—between poisoning and falls—with 310 000 deaths. WHO found income level, age, sex, and geographical region each played a part in the distribution and incidence of fatal injuries. Fatalities from injury were twice as prevalent among men as women, especially in road accidents (three times as many men as women) and men were also three times as likely to be murdered. Death rates from road accidents, burns, and drowning were particularly high in Africa and Asia, and homicides were three times as frequent as suicides in Africa and the Americas. In Southeast Asia and Europe suicide rates were more than twice the murder rates. Suicide is not uncommon.

Depression does more than enervate. In fact, it can be fatal! It does not itself kill people, but there is an unfortunate association in that suicide is more likely when people are depressed than when they are not depressed. Psychologists view depression to be a predictor of suicide. (This is true of clinical depression, not everyday moodiness.)

There is some indication that suicide takes an especially heavy toll in highly creative groups. In Ludwig's (1995, p. 148) extensive archival study, suicides were most common in writers of poetry (20%), with musical performers next but at about half that rate (9%). There were no reports of suicide in Ludwig's sample of architects, explorers, composers, or social or public figures. Among the artists, suicide attempts occurred mostly before age 30. In Ludwig's entire sample of just over 1000 persons, 11% attempted suicide with 4.4% succeeding. Admittedly this was an archival study involving only high-level creators. Generalizations can only be considered carefully, if they are considered at all. Table 4.1 shows the means of suicide within Ludwig's sample. Some of the famous people who have killed themselves are listed in Box 4.5.

Suicide is associated with particular attitudes and cognitive tendencies, as well as depression. Creative individuals are typically open-minded, for example, even about suicide, at

---

BIASES DISTORTING STATISTICS ABOUT SUICIDE AND CREATIVITY

There are certain biases that may distort our statistics about suicide and creativity. First, suicides may provide salient information that is easy to remember. It may be more difficult to remember suicides among the noneminent, and of course there are numerous counter-examples—creative people who have not committed nor attempted suicide! If it is a famous creator who commits suicide, it is deemed newsworthy. Sadly, we often do not remember only objective details and representative information; we remember and reason with what is salient. Causes of death may also be slanted such that if there is any ambiguity, the coroner's report does not pinpoint suicide.

TABLE 4.1 The Price of Greatness: Methods of Suicide among 1000 Eminent Persons

Carbon monoxide	2
Poison	3
Hanging	7
Jump from bridge	1
Gas oven	1
Wrists slashed	1
Drowning	4
Gunshot	6
Drug overdose	18

BOX 4.5

SUICIDE AMONG CREATIVE SAMPLES

- John Berryman
- Truman Capote
- Hart Crane
- Ernest Hemingway
- Jimi Hendrix
- Janice Joplin
- Jack London
- Marilyn Monroe
- Dorothy Parker
- Sylvia Plath
- Phil Ochs
- Mark Rothko
- Anne Sexton
- Alan Turing
- Virginia Woolf

least in the sense that they are less judgmental than their peers (Domino 1988). Their attitudes may imply an acceptance of suicide only because they are generally open-minded. This possibility exemplifies the problem of hidden causal factors (Box 4.6).

Other research has been conducted with noneminent samples. Orbach et al. (1990), for instance, studied individuals in an outpatient clinic and psychiatric emergency room. They administered a problem-solving task to each. This task did not require originality per se, but creativity often involves problem solving. Results indicated that individuals who thought about suicide tended to solve problems with solutions that lacked versatility and tended toward avoidance. There were also signs of dependency, with those who thought about suicide more likely to look to others for solutions to their problems.

Lester (1993) found that women were more likely to attempt suicide but less likely to succeed. That is, there were fewer fatalities in the women he studied (also see Lester 1999). Lester pointed to relationship problems among creative individuals who thought about suicide. He also suggested that birth order was relevant, and in particular, that suicide ideation was least likely among youngest children in the family. His samples include both eminent creators (e.g., Dorothy Parker and Virginia Woolf) and the general populations.

A small irony is suggested by research showing depressed persons to be realistic in their thinking; it is nondepressed individuals who are unrealistic. Miller and Porter (1988) explained, "it was the depressives in these studies who displayed rationality and accuracy! Depressed people were more realistic. It was the nondepressives who exhibited an illusion of control or what can be called an *optimistic bias*" (quoted by Heinzen 1994, p. 73). Perhaps that illusion of control fails when suicide is contemplated, or perhaps the illusion of control allows for realistic thinking, but some also have a tendency to be rigid and inflexible as well. Mraz and Runco (1994) found rigidity and inflexibility to be very important in predicting suicide ideation.

BOX 4.6

THE PROBLEM OF HIDDEN CAUSAL FACTORS

Very frequently, when two things are correlated, there is a hidden cause. This is the *third variable problem* or the problem of hidden causal variables. They are called third variables when there is one predictor (or perhaps set of predictors) variable and one criterion (or set of them) variable and the research is being conducted to determine how these two are related. The predictors are sometimes called *independent variables* and the criteria *dependent variables*, but this depends on the experimental design. For our purposes what is important is the attempt to infer causality. What causes psychosis? What causes depression?

Correlations are helpful when addressing these questions, especially if a correlation is found and other requirements are met (e.g., causes must come before effects), but frequently there are hidden variables that may be causally related to our criterion of interest, be it psychopathology or creativity. Variable A can be correlated with Variable B but not cause Variable B. Variable B might depend on Variable C. The relationship between A and B may reflect the hidden relationships between Variables A and B with Variable C. It is a veritable soap opera.

Mraz and Runco (1994) took a multivariate approach and examined depression and several different problem-solving skills. They used various tests of divergent thinking (see Chapter 1) and examined six different cognitive predictors, in addition to hopelessness. The last of these was predictive of suicide ideation, but the most accurate prediction took inflexibility into account as well. More specifically, suicide ideation was most likely when the individual was fluent in problem-generation tasks (i.e., they identified a large number of problems) and inflexible in solving problems. This combination of thinking tendencies actually predicted suicide above and beyond the prediction that relied solely on measures of depression. The prediction included a statistical interaction between fluency and inflexibility, which merely implies that both of these things have to be present for an accurate depiction of suicide ideation. Inflexibility in this context implies that the individual sees very few and only very similar solutions to a problem. This is in contrast to a flexible individual who sees a wide range of very diverse solutions. It makes sense that someone might be depressed and suicidal if they think they have both a large number of problems and very few kinds of solutions.

Recall here the difference between suicide attempts and suicide ideation. The latter simply means that the person thinks about suicide. There is no guarantee that an attempt will be made. In fact, many people think about suicide. You might say it is normal to do so. What really worries clinicians is when an individual both contemplates suicide and also actually develops a plan for carrying it out.

Schotte and Clum (1987) also found rigidity and inflexibility to be related to suicide ideation. They implicated stress as well but, unlike Mraz and Runco (1994), felt that suicide ideation was more related to depression, hopelessness, and affect than to thinking tendencies (also see Schotte & Clum 1982). The different results may reflect the different analytic techniques employed. Only Mraz and Runco tested interactions among the predictors. This would seem to be an important point; interactions are more indicative of what actually goes on than are simple "main effects" and predictions based on individual emotional and cognitive tendencies. The use of problem generation as well as problem solving apparently also made a difference. More will be said about problem generation in Chapter 9. Before leaving the topic of suicide we should discuss creativity and longevity. Like suicide, longevity is by definition a very serious concern.

Longevity

Writers sometimes take their own lives. Some do it quickly and commit suicide. Others, knowingly or not, do it slowly, by sabotaging their health, which amounts to much the same thing, at least in the long run.

Evidence from yet another archival study indicates that "writers die young" (Kaun 1991). Indeed, writers had the shortest life expectancy of all career areas. The writers in Kaun's (1991) sample lived an average of 61.7 years. Cartoonists were next, at 67.9 years, followed by musicians at 68.9 years, and architects at 69.4 years at the time of death. The composers, dancers, singers, conductors, painters, and photographers in this particular data set represent the creative domains with longer life expectancies. There are several possible reasons for this. One possibility is that writing is a stressful or difficult career. It frequently has mostly delayed gratification. It also usually requires solitary work. There may be some volition in this, however, given that writing is also associated with an unhealthful stereotype. In particular, someone may think that to be viewed as a writer he or she needs to conform to the stereotype, and therefore should smoke and drink heavily. Kaun described the general lifestyle of writers as "ill suited to good health" (p. 388). Perhaps that stereotype has changed recently, but it was a prevalent one at least since the time of F. Scott Fitzgerald. Writers may also react to criticism and poor sales. Abra (1997) quoted one famous writer saying, "Sure writing is easy. Just sit down at a typewriter and open an artery." Recall here also what the author John Cheever said, namely that his anxiety was provoked by the personal uninhibited nature of his writing (Rothenberg 1990).

The different possibilities here underscore the difficulties involved in determining the directions of effect in studies of creativity and health. Could a writing career undermine health and lead to an early demise? If so, the creative work is the cause and the short life expectancy is the effect. Yet it is possible that health is the causal factor, or at least an influence. Perhaps there is something about ill-health that leads people to writing. This would be the clearest in the case of psychological disturbance, such as depression, for that could motivate someone to seek a medium in which to vent or battle their demons. Much the same could be said about physical problems as well. They too could direct the unhealthy into writing instead of, say, sports or a career involving demanding public performances.

It is important to acknowledge that although many writers die young, many creative individuals live a long time (Lindauer 1991). As a matter of fact, Simonton (1983, 1985) proposed that eminence is most likely to be achieved if the individual begins working at a young age, works on a regular basis from day to day and year to year, and lives a long time. These recommendations follow directly from Simonton's (1990a, 1999a) historiometric research, which is explored in Chapter 7. They certainly characterize many famous creators (e.g., Pablo Picasso and Jean Piaget).

Of the various directions of effect just mentioned, the most likely may be that which has creative talent as the causal agent and ill-health the effect. This makes the most sense because there is also evidence that writing contributes to positive health (Pennebaker et al. 1997), which of course allows for the same direction of effect. Why two different outcomes—positive or negative health? Perhaps it depends on the kind of writing. Pennebaker et al.'s evidence for the benefits of writing allowed entirely self-expressive writing. They referred to it as *disclosure*. Hence writing that allows the individual to express him- or herself may help the individual, whereas other kinds of writing may not have the same benefits. If this is the case, the old adage, "write about what you know" takes on great importance. Admittedly, Pennebaker et al. (1997) did not have data on life expectancy. Their indicators of positive health involved immune functioning, and in particular the efficiency of the immune system. It really is impressive research, given that the criteria were based on blood tests. You don't get much more objective than that. Earlier studies had concluded much the same thing about creativity and immunity (e.g., Eisenman 1997), but usually the latter was estimated using self-reports (e.g., "How often do you get sick?"), which are much less objective.

STRESS

Self-expression and disclosure may contribute to health in that they allow a release (Box 4.7). People can vent or get something off their chests. There are, however, other ways to deal with problems. One thing is definite: Problems should be addressed, one way or another.

BOX 4.7

SELF-EXPRESSION AND HEALTH

Several theories of creativity imply that one of the best things a person can do to maintain health is to find opportunities for self-expression. This was implied by research on disclosure and the immune system, for example, and also true of the research on self-actualization, to be discussed later. The relationship of self-expression and health also fits well with research outside the creativity literature. Eysenck (1988), for example, claimed that self-expression plays a large role in the determination of health. He described in detail the cancer-prone personality, which is essential to an individual who does not express his or her emotions. This is analogous to the coronary-prone individual, though of course the behaviors in question, both causal and health-related, differ. In the one case it is cancer and the other case it is heart disease. After referring data from a 15-year longitudinal study, and concluding that personality has a significant influence on physical health, including cancer, Eysenck cited a famous physician from 1906, Sir William Osler, who apparently claimed that "it is very often much more important what person has the disease than the disease the person has" (Eysenck 1997b, p. 277).

Health problems may arise if the organism does not cope in one way or another. In fact, a failure to cope leads to a particular kind of problem, namely stress. Stress is defined as a failure to adapt or cope (Seyle 1988). This is important because it suggests methods for improving health, and although generalizations should be avoided, it is probably safe to hypothesize that just about everyone experiences stress. Low levels may not lead to problems, but even moderate amounts can influence our social relationships, our intellectual functioning, our emotional stability, and our health. Stress may also be related to creative potential and creative performance.

In support of this view, Nicol and Long (1996) found higher levels of creativity to be associated with low levels of stress in a sample of music hobbyists. Interestingly, this was not true of their sample of music therapists. Still, Nichol and Long described creative thinking as a coping resource.

Like so much in the health and creativity literature, it seems that stress and creativity have a complicated relationship, although there are conflicting views. Scott (1985) proposed that creativity is related to stress and that creative individuals will have more stress than others. In his words, creative persons

> stand either above or outside the norm most readily accepted by society ... and dissimilar people are treated by the remainder of society as a threat to the search for saneness. Secondly, society offers all people a very patterned and structured way of life through a set of expectations and rules designed to maintain stability and minimize change. Many people opt to accept these patterned instructional ways without question because they offer stability and acceptance by others. However, this is not the option chosen by GTC [gifted talented creative] people if they are to exercise their talents (pp. 240–241).

This is entirely consistent with research on the psychic costs and stigma of being creative (Rubenson & Runco 1992a, 1992b). It is also consistent with one of the core characteristics in creativity mentioned in Chapter 9, namely their *sensitivity*. This sensitivity may make creative individuals more prone to stress reactions, along with leading them to creative experiences and interpretations of experience.

Another view conceptualizes creativity as a cognitive moderator (Carson & Runco 1999). It may, for example, moderate such that an individual's interpretation of experiences is different from the actual experience. That may sound odd, but there is a huge literature confirming that perceived stress is not the same as actual objective experience. That is, in fact, how perception is defined, as the interpretation of experience. Perceptions always differ from actual experience, though not always to a large degree. This is top-down information processing, which means that expectations and assumptions direct thought instead of thought merely being a reaction to actual experience. This is why people have varied interpretations of experiences. Two people can have the same experience but each walk away with a different interpretation of it. There are, then, no environmental stressors. Events and hassles are merely potential stressors because so much of the reaction is top-down and depends on the individual. Stress is a matter of interpretation. This line of thinking is useful when explaining how creativity can be related to certain ailments and disturbances but at the same time related to certain kinds of health. We will return to this topic later in this chapter.

Runco (2012) suggested that the cognitive processes that moderate between objective events and the interpretation of stress may be associated with the constructive cognitive processes that allow creative insights. This follows from constructivist theories of knowledge, such as Piaget's (1970, 1981). Carson and Runco (1999) tested this view by administering tests of divergent thinking and stress, the latter with measures of objective events and of "hassles."

EXAMPLES OF EVENTS: SCALE OF STRESS AND HASSLES

Stress is a reaction, a failure to cope. It sometimes is measured by examining personal histories and by asking the individual how many stressors they recently experienced. Other times it is viewed as a day-to-day occurrence and measured by asking about minor hassles. Slow traffic, noisy construction work outside the window of your office, repeated interruptions, a power outage while computing—these are hassles.

ANXIETY

Anxiety is also a signal that something isn't right with one's world (May 1996). Anxiety certainly can influence creative thinking and creative performance. Consider Saldivar's (1992) description of the poet Sylvia Plath and her "fear of her imaginative power as a solvent that might be more destructive than transforming" (p. 117). Consider next the view of Patrick White (1912–1990), Nobel laureate in literature. He put it this way: "My creative self, frozen into silence by the war years, began to thaw … [and I] started writing the novel which became *The Aunt's Story*. I can't say it poured onto the paper after the years of draught; it was more like a foreign substance torn out by handfuls" (White 1981, p. 127).

This parallels the feelings of the prize-winning author, John Cheever (Rothenberg 1990). Cheever described experiencing great anxiety because of his creative insights. In his case, the creativity caused problems rather than the problems stimulating the creativity. After extensive interviews with Cheever, Rothenberg (1990) explained how

> the creative process … involves gradual unearthing of unconscious processes … the creative person embarks on an activity leading to discovery and knowing himself or herself in a very fundamental way … such an unearthing process is fraught with a good deal of anxiety as it unfolds. Also, anxiety and strain arise from carrying on a high level performance in the especially demanding work of creative accomplishment (pp. 196–197).

Rothenberg also proposed that "creative operations derive from healthy functions [but] they generate mental conflict and tension. In addition to the mental strain induced by these translogical modes of thinking, anxiety is generated because these modes also function to unearth unconscious material during the course of the creative process" (1990, p. 187). Rothenberg was referring to Janusian and homospatial thinking as translogical.

TRANSLOGICAL THINKING AND CREATIVITY

Rothenberg (1990) described two kinds of creative thinking, both translogical. In *Janusian thinking*, opposites are brought together in new and creative ways. Light can be a wave and a particle, for example, even though both are incompatible. Existentialism describes an acceptance of mortality but also a joy in what one has here on earth.

In *homospatial thinking*, the individual brings two images together into one new and creative product. It is homospatial in a literal way: They are different images but occupy one visual space. Rothenberg actually has manipulated homospatial thinking using special projectors.

Similar ideas have been reported in less select samples. Carlsson (2002), for example, found that the more creative individuals in her group of research participants had a higher level of anxiety than the less creative individuals. Interestingly, the more highly creative individuals used more defense mechanisms than the less creative individuals. They were, however, flexible in their use of strategies, which makes perfect sense given the relationship of flexibility with creative potential. Smith et al. (1990) examined the relationship of creativity and one particular kind of anxiety, namely, test anxiety.

PSYCHIC COSTS OF CREATIVITY

Creativity sometimes has *psychic costs* (Rubenson & Runco 1992a, 1992b). Creative things are, after all, original, and they may be unusual or unconventional. Some people may view them as different or even strange. These things imply that a person can behave in a creative fashion but there may be costs, including psychic (emotional) costs.

Smith and Amner (1997) developed a method for investigating unconscious processes. They referred to it as *percept-genesis*, the idea being that interpretations of experience are personally constructed. The process is not entirely manifest, but the workings can be seen under the right conditions. Smith and Amner's method allowed them to identify individual differences in the processes involved in the construction of interpretations, that is, in percept-genesis. In brief, their hypothesis is that creative individuals may have an advantage in their facility with preconscious materials.

ALCOHOLISM AND DRUG ABUSE

Stress and anxiety are sometimes battled with alcohol or other drugs. In the large archival study mentioned earlier, Ludwig (1995, p. 133) found a full 60% of those involved in theater probably had alcoholism, with writers of fiction and musicians not far behind (41% and 40%, respectively). Alcoholism was rare in the military and in individuals in the natural sciences, social sciences, or social activism (each at or below 10%). Ludwig (1995, p. 135) also found distressing rates of drug abuse. It was most common in the musicians in the sample (36%), with persons in theater and writers of fiction and poetry next in terms of incidence (24%, 19%, and 17%, respectively). Explorers, sports figures, and persons in the military seemingly never abused drugs (or it was not reported in the biographical data). Goodwin (1988) found writers to be especially prone to alcoholism, and Noble et al. (1993) found some evidence of alcoholism having a genetic basis.

Here again experimental research complements observations and archival studies of eminent creative people. Norlander and Gustafson (1998), for example, looked at the different phases in the creative process and how each was influenced by alcohol consumption. They found alcohol consumption to be related to improved incubation (Norlander & Gustafson 1996), as well as high originality but only in the illumination phase of the creative process. Alcohol consumption seems to inhibit flexibility during illumination. It was also related to poor verification, which is the last phase of the creative process (Norlander & Gustafson 1997). Importantly, Norlander and Gustafson were extremely precise in the methods used to administer alcohol. They used 1.0 milliliter of alcohol (100% pure alcohol, not Bud Light nor even Captain Morgan Rum) for each kilogram of bodyweight.

PHASES IN THE CREATIVE PROCESS

Much of the research on the influence of alcohol relies on Wallas' (1926) conception of the creative process, which begins with preparation and then moves through incubation, illumination, and verification phases. This model, though quite old, is consistent with much of the recent research on the creative process (Runco 2001).

Svenssen et al. (2006) administered alcohol to two experimental groups in an attempt to manipulate primary and secondary process. Surprisingly, they found that the alcohol group seemed to use secondary process more than primary process. The prediction had been that alcohol would allow primary process but inhibit secondary process (Norlander & Gustafson 1996,

1997, 1998). The surprising finding may explain the common misconception that alcohol frees up our thinking and therefore improves our creativity. Thinking while intoxicated may actually be more original, but it may also be unrealistic and worthless. Truly creative insights are both original and worthwhile. Perhaps intoxicated individuals are simply very poor judges of their own thinking. They may indeed have a really bizarre and therefore original idea, and they may like it because it is original, but they fail to see that even though it is original, it is worthless.

A number of factors are actually relevant. Svenssen et al. (2006) acknowledged several:

> To sum up, primary process thinking can be associated with both high and low levels of arousal, low levels of frontal-lobe activation, and cognitive disinhibition. … Emotional states, such as aggression, can produce a high level of arousal … and an inhibition of executive functioning. … Further, high doses of alcohol have been shown to produce a lower activity in the PFC (prefrontal cortex) … leading to a reduction of executive functioning.

The connection between alcohol and blood flow has been established, and if that decrease occurs in the prefrontal cortex, it may lead directly to problems in cognitive inhibition (Martindale 1999). Problems with secondary process are not always found in the research on alcohol consumption, however. Sometimes they may be disguised by compensatory actions on the part of the individual (Svenssen et al. 2006). This kind of compensation can be seen when someone puts extra effort into concentrating on things like walking and talking just because they know they are drunk.

PRIMARY AND SECONDARY PROCESS

You probably have noticed that primary process cognition has been implicated in various studies of creativity and health, including those investigating alcohol and anxiety. What is primary process? How does it differ from secondary process, and what role does each play in creativity?

PRIMARY AND SECONDARY PROCESSES

Primary process cognition is "dream life experience characterized by a drifting unorganized succession of images that may be fused or displaced from their usual context, also thought with affect-laden content, especially sexual or aggressive" (Helson 1999, p. 361).

Primary process reflects impulse, libido, and uncensored thoughts and feelings.

Secondary process cognition is "purposeful, rational, and guided by conventional restraints" (Helson 1999, p. 361). It is realistic, practical, reality-oriented.

Primary process is associative and uninhibited. It is impulsive, libidinal, and free of censorship. Secondary process, in contrast, is realistic, practical, and reality-oriented. Each of these might contribute to creative efforts, and in fact there is some evidence that creative individuals are able to shift from one to the other. Some tasks require more of one than the other. Think back to the idea of phases used in the research on alcohol discussed above (Svenssen et al. 2006). The idea was that each uses a unique ratio of primary and secondary processes. Inspiration, for example, might be more primary, and process and verification

BOX 4.8

FREUDIAN CONCEPTS USED IN STUDIES OF CREATIVITY

There is small irony in Freud's confession that "the nature of artistic attainment is psychoanalytically inaccessible to us," and even more pointedly, "before creativity, the psychoanalyst must lay down his arms" (both from Gardner 1993a, p. 24). Freud rarely wrote about creativity, though he did devote time to art, wit, and humor. The irony is that many of his ideas, in addition to primary and secondary process, are used in studies of creativity.

Freud did write about poetry and art. He concluded that sublimation was often a motivation for creative work. Sublimation occurs when an individual finds socially acceptable expression for unconscious needs and desires.

Catharsis may assist in the relief of psychic tension. Csikszentmihalyi (1988a), for example, distinguished between *cathartic originality*, which is artwork motivated by current discomforts, and *abreactive originality*, which uses symbolism and perhaps a rearrangement of repressed traumatic experience to successfully relieve tension.

Freudian theory is apparent in Kris' (1950) hypothesis of *regression in the service of the ego*.

Simplifying some, this occurs when a creator taps his or her instinctual and unconscious drives and uses them as a source of information. Because this kind of information is not directed at reality it can offer a very spontaneous and unique perspective. This in turn can lead an individual to creative insights. Of course it is a double-edged sword in that an individual might have easy access to such information, but at the same time that information can elicit anxiety and disturbance (Rothenberg 1990).

Diaz de Chumaceiro (1996) related Freud's theory to poetry, which is of course an unambiguously creative domain.

Many others have tied psychoanalytic theory to the arts (e.g., Fine 1990, chapter 10), and of course the same argument applies here that art is unambiguously creative.

Niederland (1973) applied the psychoanalytic perspective on creativity specifically to human aging. This may be one of the more timely applications of the psychoanalytic perspective, given the demographic trends in the United States and the so-called "graying of America" (e.g., Preston 1984).

---

more secondary (Katz 1997). Studies by Arieti (1976) and Hoppe and Kyle (1990) both described truly creative work as a result of a "magic synthesis." This occurs when primary and secondary processes blend and collaborate, the result being a creative insight. It is possible that both processes can be used in an alternating manner, first one and then the other, but creativity is thought to involve both in a synthesis and simultaneous fashion.

Martindale and Dailey (1996) reported that primary process was related to word association remoteness, as well as judges' ratings of the creativity of these same stories. It was also related to scores on a divergent thinking test and to artwork and essays written to describe that artwork (Martindale et al. 1985). Less creative individuals seem to rely primarily on secondary process (Martindale 1999). They may actively suppress primary process because it is too libidinal and uncensored. For this reason they may miss many creative ideas. Yet the alternative is probably worse. It is potentially psychopathological. Psychosis is, for instance,

BOX 4.9

REGRESSION IN THE SERVICE OF THE EGO

One of the most cited examples of psycho-analytic thought is the theory that creativity involves the regression in the service of the ego (Kris 1952). There are two phases in this regression: one of inspiration and one of elaboration. The first phase involves the ego turning to the unconscious for fantasy and creative ideas, and the second involves the ego's modification of these thoughts. (The inspirational phase seems to parallel the concept of incubation, and may be responsible for "a-ha" experiences.) Regression in the service of the ego is thought to have an adaptive function, but is temporary. As you may guess due to the unconscious nature of this process, there is little empirical support for regression in the service of the ego.

Noppe (1996) viewed regression in the service of the ego as a kind of cognitive style. He felt that creative people tap the unconscious, interrupting rational constraints on new ideas. Noppe also contrasted this with progression in the service of the ego, which can be defined as movement "thru irrational and organized set of strategies for communicating the breakthrough" (p. 679).

very generally defined in terms of the individual being out of touch with reality. They do not employ secondary process.

Primary process is not limited to special populations. We all have access to primary process. Sometimes it is elicited in research in order to study the impact on creative thinking. Svenssen et al. (2006), for instance, asked one group of individuals to watch an action film, and another group to watch a neutral film. Both were asked to write down their own endings for the films. The contents were then examined with a revision of the Regressive Imagery Dictionary (RID). This allowed the researchers to identify the primary and secondary process content in the written endings of the films. As you might expect, the action film elicited more primary process endings.

Dudek and Verreault (1989) examined the primary process ideation and creativity of children. They were especially interested in the transformation of primary material, such as that which may result from regression in the service of the ego (Kris 1952). Dudak and Verreault describe this process as occurring when

> the sources, or raw material, of creative production are crude untransformed drive affects. The contents of these affects are coated central nervous system representations of lived and felt experiences. They emerge symbolically in the form of primary process ideation. This is a drive laden, pleasure oriented, analogical mode of thinking. It is characterized by condensation, symbolization, contradiction, and so on—forms of thinking that have no concern for reality. In order to transform primitive feelings into symbolic forms which are socially acceptable, the ego must call upon an array of mechanisms and thought forms that impose reality oriented, secondary processed thought (p. 65).

Dudak and Verreault found that children with high scores on the Torrance Test of Creative Thinking expressed more primary process ideation, as well as more regression. It was, however, effective regression, which is precisely what is described by "regression and the service of the ego."

Methods have been devised to assess shifts between primary and secondary processes. They employ projective measures, such as word association tests. Wild (1965) used word association along with an object-sorting task and found a high number of shifts (primary to secondary and back) among a sample of art students.

Taft (1971) referred to much the same, although he used the term *ego-permissiveness*. This occurs when an individual is capable of letting go and allowing primary process material to influence thought and action. Taft also described "hot creativity," which involves the "preconscious rather than unconscious, since it is partially in contact with and accessible to the conscious activity of the ego. The primary processes involve the entertainment of unusual ideas, the neglect of logical principles, and the expression of material which is usually kept under control because of its association with repressed impulses, such as aggression and sex, or even just strong emotions" (pp. 345–346). Cold creativity, on the other hand, involves "secondary process thinking [which] adheres closely to conventional and familiar material … is based on the reality of the environment and marked by controlled logic" (p. 346). This is very helpful, especially in tying secondary processes to conventions. As noted in Chapter 2, conventions play a large role in socialization and are antithetical to some creative thinking.

Yet another take on the role of primary and secondary process involves a gradual shift from one to the other. Some forms of artwork may start with primary process but gradually employ more and more secondary process (Noy 1969). The artwork thus may start with very personal and libidinal issues but gradually become more realistic and widely interpretable. This view is compatible with the ideas just presented that different phases employ different proportions of primary and secondary process (Katz 1997; Svenssen et al. 2006).

Martindale (1999) described how primary and secondary processes may be influenced by the individual's level of arousal. An optimal level of arousal (not unlike the typical wakeful state of mind we experience in our day-to-day lives) will usually support secondary process. Primary process is more often associated with either very low levels of arousal, or sometimes with very high levels. This explains why there is a tendency to fantasize with elevated physical activity (Ewing et al. 1982). That might increase arousal levels, making primary process more likely. Eysenck (1997a) argued that stereotyped thinking (which is certainly uncreative) is associated with high arousal and that creative thinking results from low arousal.

Certain physical conditions, such as the activity just mentioned, may determine arousal levels, but there are more basic and causal explanations. Martindale (1999) pointed to cortical activation, the idea being that the status of the nervous system underlies arousal levels and creative thinking. He described how low levels of cortical activity could facilitate creative inspiration. Note again that generalizations across all creative activities (and phases of the creative process) are avoided. Importantly, Martindale further pointed to frontal lobe activation (p. 149). This is important because research and theory lately has shifted such that the frontal lobes are most closely tied to creative work (and has shifted away from an emphasis on so-called right-brain activity).

Martindale's (1999) theory is that the frontal lobes monitor and can suppress threatening or unacceptable thoughts. They are responsible for the cognitive inhibition that can filter out divergent, bizarre, or creative insights. Thus lower frontal lobe activity would be indicative of lower inhibition and higher creativity. Martindale used EEGs to support this hypothesis. This research and others using EEG and exploring arousal and cortical activation are described in Chapter 3.

COGNITIVE INHIBITION

Cognitive inhibition can be defined as a reduction of executive functioning (Svenssen et al. 2006). This implies that the individual is less actively monitoring his or her thoughts and less likely to make decisions about the appropriateness of those thoughts. Whatever the label, this individual would think in a less constrained fashion and in a more creative manner.

Much of the research on primary process is inferential. Some of it is quite convincing (e.g., Martindale 1975), but the existence of primary process must be inferred. It is manifested in language and action, but it is not something that can itself be observed. We only see its effects. Further, even if primary process is strongly related to originality and uninhibited thoughts, we should keep in mind that creativity involves more than just originality. Creative things are original and effective. This implies that both primary and secondary processes are useful for creativity. Creativity is a result of that magic synthesis, or at least of an efficient shunting from primary to secondary process, and back again. This efficient shunting may be indicative of the balance among processes that actually characterizes nearly every aspect of creativity (Runco 2001a; Runco & Sakamoto 1996).

BALANCE AND OPTIMAL FUNCTIONING FOR CREATIVITY

It is remarkable how many aspects of creativity require optimization. There is a balance of divergent and convergent thinking, primary and secondary processes, nonconformity but conformity, conventionality but unconventionality, independence but collaboration, just to name a few examples (see Runco 2001a; Runco & Gaynor 1993; Runco & Sakamoto 1996).

Prentky (2000–2001) presented a neurocognitive model that predicts that an *optimal degree of deviation* from normal patterns of information processing is necessary for creative work. This deviation can be either in the direction of expansion of awareness via extensive scanning and hyperalertness or in the direction of constriction of the field of awareness and hyperfocus on details.

PSYCHOSIS AND PSYCHOTICISM

Although the most common health issue in the creativity literature is probably that involving the affective disorders, there is also a growing interest in relationships with psychosis and schizophrenia. These disorders are explored next. First I must emphasize that it is unrealistic to entirely separate the various disorders. There is significant overlap. Not too long ago they

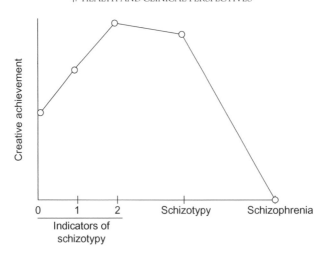

FIGURE 4.2 Creative achievement may be most likely with 1 to 2 indicators of schizotypy, but not extreme schizophrenia (Kinney et al. 2000–2001; Sass & Schulberg 2000–2001).

were viewed as distinct. At that time "schizophrenia was viewed as a 'primitive' disorder involving fixation at or regression to early instinct- and affect-dominated modes of experience that are relatively devoid of the capacity for self-consciousness or of a sense of differentiation between self and the world" (Sass & Schuldberg 2000–2001, p. 1). Now it seems to be most accurate to acknowledge some overlap. This is suggested by the ideas of a *schizophrenia spectrum* (Sass & Schuldberg 2000–2001) and by the dimensional model of schizo-affective disorders (Cox & Leon 1999). Schizophrenic tendencies (*schizotypy*), psychosis-proneness, and the so-called mood disorders (e.g., bipolar disorders) have each been associated with creativity (Figure 4.2). Cox and Leon (1999) described the dimensional model within which

> psychosis encompasses a continuum that connects schizophrenia to depression, and which includes bipolar disorders. … Proneness to psychosis can be thought of as a set of schizotypal symptoms or personality traits. The concept of proneness to psychosis, therefore, is interchangeable with the concept of schizotypy, which represents subclinical manifestations of psychosis (p. 26).

Once again we must also acknowledge domain differences. In his archival study, Ludwig (1995, p. 141) found "schizoid-like psychoses" (which includes "florid mania") in individuals involved in theater (17%), architecture and writers of poetry (each 13%), and writers of fiction (11%). Sports figures and explorers were at the other end of the spectrum; in those groups schizoid-like psychoses were unheard of. These figures do not really capture the problems of Ludwig's sample. That is because many of them suffered from multiple problems. Indeed, 59% of the sample who had one disorder actually had more than one.

Perhaps most important is the difference between manifest disorders and the genetic potential for them (i.e., between genotype and phenotype). Consider in this regard Kinney et al.'s (2000–2001) investigation of adoptees who had schizotypy, and therefore a genetic liability for schizophrenia. They had higher "overall peak creative accomplishment in their jobs or hobbies" than did a group of control subjects. Kinney et al. suggested that recurrent illusions, "magical thinking," and unusual speech patterns were the most likely to indicate schizotypy and creative potential. They concluded that the genes that confer increased liability for major psychiatric disorders such as schizophrenia may also have a positive side, as appears to be the case for bipolar disorders. ... That is, given a favorable environment, these genes may also be associated with personally and socially beneficial phenotypes, such as enhanced creative functioning. It is possible that—by analogy with the heterozygote advantage conferred on carriers of the sickle-cell gene—there may be some kind of compensatory advantage for a major gene or genes for schizophrenia, which helps to maintain the putative gene or genes in the population, despite the low fertility of schizophrenics themselves. ... Enhanced creativity may represent one type of compensatory advantage (p. 23).

Interestingly, the creative advantage stemming from schizotypy seemed to be most obvious in avocational activities and accomplishments. This is in direct contrast to the creative advantage of the bipolar disorders, which is manifested in actual vocational accomplishment. Kinney et al. (2000–2001) explained this in terms of temperament, and in particular the possibility that individuals suffering from bipolar disorders may be "more gregarious, competitive, driven, and occupationally ambitious, whereas the schizophrenia-spectrum individuals may tend to have more social anxiety and to be better able to realize their creative potential in less competitive, avocational, spheres" (p. 24).

Ludwig (1995) also reported advantages of certain disorders:

From examination of the various biographical materials, I found evidence that at least 16% of those persons who suffered from an emotional disorder showed an improvement in their creative activity at some point in their lives in response to emotional disturbance. This improvement involved greater productivity, overcoming writing blocks, the generation of new ideas, inspirations, or better performances (p. 166).

Ludwig pointed specifically to alcoholism and mania as having occasional advantages.

Eysenck (2003), like Kinney et al. (2000–2001), emphasized the biological basis of psychopathology. He explained how particular genetic potentials gave certain individuals a tendency toward idiosyncratic cognitive inhibition known as *overinclusive thought.* This can lead to psychosis, but often the individual has the benefits of overinclusive thought without the psychosis. This is manifested as psychoticism. Psychosis is a form of psychopathology, whereas psychoticism is not. The individual does have a tendency toward overinclusive thinking, but not to a degree that he or she is psychotic. In fact, that overinclusive tendency may facilitate creative ideation. Eysenck (2003, p. 109) also hypothesized that the neurotransmitter dopamine played a key role, a prediction that is gaining support. This view is discussed in detail in Chapter 3.

Research by Carson et al. (2003) supports this theory of psychosis. They specified that the nervous systems of creative individuals are more open to environmental stimuli than those of less creative individuals. This kind of openness would provide the creative person with more information, and perhaps provide a wide range of options and associations. It would give them richer subjective experiences. Rich experience, sensitivity, and openness to experience each have been tied to creative thinking in personality and operant research (Epstein, 1990; McCrae 1987; Wallace 1991). The biologically based openness to experience is also consistent with low levels of latent inhibition found in numerous studies of creative persons (Eysenck 1997b, 2003). Eysenck himself supported the possibility of a genetic basis with genealogies that do indeed show that families of creative persons often also contain psychotic relatives. He also cited experimental work with psychotic individuals in support of this theory. Psychotics do display quite original thinking, but it is so original that it is unrealistic, and therefore uncreative.

ZEN, OVERINCLUSIVE THINKING, AND CREATIVITY

Overinclusive thinking allows the individual to relegate cognitive structures and think without classifying. In this light there is an interesting parallel with Zen in that it recommends that individuals accept experiences as they are, without attempting to classify them. This surely would allow a broad associative net and divergent ideation. Langer's (1989) demonstrations of mindfulness are also relevant; she describes methods for enhancing the desired mental state and creativity. Zen is reviewed in Chapter 12 (see also Pritzker 2011).

Interestingly, Eisenman (1992) worked with incarcerated persons for quite some time and found that psychotic prisoners had lower creativity than conduct disorder prisoners. So much for the idea that criminals are creative, but in socially unacceptable ways. Still, it is interesting that many famous creative people have spent time in jail. Box 4.10 presents a list of examples (Figure 4.3).

Recall here the possibility that hidden variables are involved in creative processes. That applies to the relationship of crime and creativity and to psychosis. Psychopathology might appear to be related to creativity, but only because both depend on overinclusive thinking. Box 4.11 discusses another possible hidden variable, namely *self-rumination*.

DEPRESSED CREATIVE PEOPLE WIN PRIZES

Prizes often are given to serious works. Does that mean that only serious works are creative? Comedy is not creative? More likely, it is a cultural bias, the assumption being that playfulness and humor are not serious, not important (Adams 1974). This might explain why prizes are often awarded to individuals who have bipolar disorders or other indications of psychopathology. The rate of depression, for example, in creative samples may reflect the fact that awards are given only to serious works, more than the actual incidence of mood disorder in creative people.

Support for the association between psychoticism and creativity was presented by Merten (1995) and Eysenck's own measure of psychoticism which is often associated with divergent thinking test scores. Several studies also have failed to support the relationship (reviewed by Reuter et al. 2005), perhaps because of different sampling and levels of ability represented in the participants.

ADHD AND CREATIVITY

Attention deficit hyperactive disorder (ADHD) is defined in terms of impulsivity, inattention, and perhaps hyperactivity. Recently the intersection of ADHD and creativity has been explored. Healy (2005), for example, argued that there are two types of creative children,

BOX 4.10

CRIME AND CREATIVITY

A large number of famous creative persons have spent time in jail or were forced to relocate after being accused of a crime (list adapted from Brower 1999).

James Baldwin
Brendan Behan
Stephen Biko
Nikolai Bukharin
John Bunyon
Roger Casement
Miguel de Cervantes
Eldridge Cleaver
John Clelland
Thomas Cranmer
Edouard Daladier
Daniel Defoe
Thomas De Quincey
Eamon De Valera
Robert Devereux
Milovan Djilas
John Donne
Fyodor Dostoyevsky
Giuseppe Garibaldi
Emma Goldman
Władysław Gomulka
Maxim Gorky
Antonio Gramsci
Dashiell Hammett
Václav Havel
Alger Hiss
Benjamin Jonson
Jomo Kenyatta
Arthur Koestler
Thomas Kyd
Osip Mandelstam
Herman Melville
Thomas More
Oswald Mosley

Marco Polo
Ezra Pound
Pierre Joseph Proudhon
Walter Raleigh
Bertrand Russell
Marquis de Sade
Henry David Thoreau
Leon Trotsky
Françoise Voltaire
Paul Verlaine
Lech Walesa
Oscar Wilde
Ludwig Wittgenstein
Thomas Wyatt

Moral Innovators

Jesus Christ
Martin Luther King, Jr.
Mahatma Gandhi
Rosa Parks

**Painters and Musical
    Composers**

Honoré Daumier
Egon Schiele
Gustav Courbet
George Grosz
Paul Gauguin
Michael Tippet
Scientists
Galileo
Vavilov
Lavoisier

Stage Performers

Lenny Bruce
Leadbelly
Robert Mitchum
Mae West

(Continued)

BOX 4.10   (*Continued*)

Other

Alfred Krupp
Napoleon Bonaparte
Joan of Arc
Socrates
Alfred Dreyfus
Frank Lloyd Wright

Work Banned, Fled Homeland, Fled Country, or Ostracized

Paul Tillich
Walter Gropius
John Calvin
George Grosz
Victor Hugo
Hannibal
Oskar Kokoschka
Paul Hindemith
Roman Polanski
Melina Mercoun
Marie Stopes
Fritz Lang
Richard Strauss
Thomas Mann
Cicero
Salman Rushdie
Dante
Baruch Spinoza
Enrico Fermi
Herrmann Hesse
Richard Wagner
Emile Zola
Albert Einstein

Individuals Who Were Executed

Socrates

Earl of Surrey
Thomas More
Thomas Cranmer
Jesus Christ
Claus von Stauffenberg
Roger Casement
Antoine Lavoisier
Lady Jane Gray

Individuals Assigned to a Lunatic Asylum

Vincent van Gogh
Paul Gauguin
Emma Goldman
Friedrich Nietzsche
Henry David Thoreau
Camille Claude
Mahatma Gandhi
Ezra Pound
Edward Dmytryk
Gustav Courbet
O. Henry
Thomas More

There is some variation among the preceding examples in the sense that some were unambiguously creative and perhaps working in unambiguously creative fields, whereas others may have been famous for other reasons. There is a difference between fame and creativity, which is an extremely important point in historical analyses (see Chapter 7). Often their fame has nothing to do with creativity. It is also uncertain how crime and the like could be related to creativity. Perhaps they each rely on unconventional tendencies. Original ideas may result from unconventional tendencies, and laws are conventions and might thus be questioned or ignored.

namely those who display characteristics that are a part of ADHD and those who do not. Healy proposed that it is the creative children with ADHD who are less socially accepted in the classroom and elsewhere. She also felt that they would have lower self-esteem than

"A world of disorderly notions, picked out of his books, crowded into his imagination." p. 2

FIGURE 4.3   Don Quixote, by Miguel de Cervantes, was written while the author was in prison. The image presented here is from the engraving of Gustave Doré, its caption being, "A world of disorderly notions, picked out of his books, crowded into his imagination." *Source: Wikimedia Commons, http://en.wikipedia.org/wiki/File:Gustave_Dor%C3%A9_-_Miguel_de_Cervantes_-_Don_Quixote_-_Part_1_-_Chapter_1_-_Plate_1_%22A_world_of_disorderly_notions,_picked_out_of_his_books,_crowded_into_his_imagination%22.jpg.*

creative children who do not have ADHD tendencies. Finally, she felt that part of the reason for an overlap would be that the two populations have similar executive functioning deficits.

Cramond (1994) also reported an overlap between ADHD and creative potential. She administered the Torrance Test of Creative Thinking (TTCT) to a group of ADHD children and found that nearly one-third had scores that were high enough to qualify for creativity programs in the schools. Cramond then administered the TTCT to creative children and found that 26% had ADHD tendencies.

BOX 4.11

WHY WE SING THE BLUES

Verhaeghen et al. (2005) suggested that self-rumination underlies both depression and creative talent. Their data, from college students, confirmed that self-rumination was associated with past and present depressive tendencies. Self-rumination was also related to creative interests and the fluency, originality, and elaboration scores form a test of divergent thinking. Importantly, the direct relationship between creative interest and depressive tendencies was not significant. This of course suggests that self-rumination explains observed covariation of depression and creativity.

Shaw and Brown (1991) examined 32 children, half of whom had ADHD tendencies according to teachers' ratings. They found the ADHD children had higher figural creativity test scores than did the control group. Importantly, all children in the research had a relatively high IQ score of 115 or higher.

In the most extensive study yet on ADHD and creativity, Healy (2005) began by testing 67 children between the ages of 10 and 12 years. Approximately half were diagnosed with ADHD and the others were not. Diagnoses of ADHD were provided by licensed psychologists or psychiatrists using the DSM-IV. Healy administered the TTCT to all children, as well as a classic test of insight, namely the two-string problem. Importantly, the two groups did not differ significantly in their IQs. There was a difference (the mean of the ADHD children being 110 and the mean of the control group being 116) but this was not statistically significant. Analyses indicated that the two groups did not differ in terms of the total score from the TTCT nor in terms of success on the two-string problem. When specific scores from the TTCT were examined, only one of five indices showed a significant difference: control subjects had higher scores than ADHD children on the elaboration index. The groups did not differ in terms of fluency, originality, abstractness of titles, nor resistance to premature closure. Healy suggested that these results support the idea that ADHD children may not be any more creative than children without ADHD tendencies.

In a second study, Healy (2005, chapter 3) examined 89 children between the ages of 10 and 12, 29 of whom had ADHD tendencies but no manifest creative talents. Twelve had manifest creative talents as well as ADHD symptomology, 18 with manifest creative talents and no ADHD symptomology, and 30 control participants. Healy expanded her assessment by including reaction time and cognitive measures of working memory and inhibition control. Perhaps most important was that 40% of the children with manifest creativity "displayed clinically elevated levels of ADHD symptomology, but none had full criteria for ADHD" (2005, p. 40). Healy also reported that creativity and ADHD were related to deficits in a reaction time and the speed at which individuals could name objects. She also concluded that 40% of the creative children "displayed significant levels of ADHD symptomology that were within a clinical range on standardized scales of ADHD" (p. 60). Healy felt these findings supported the idea that some creative children may have ADHD tendencies and some creative children may lack ADHD symptoms. Healy pointed to "significantly more difficulty filtering out possibly irrelevant information" as one reason why there might be a connection between ADHD and creativity. This may not sound like an efficient mode of thought, but creativity may benefit from a wide range of options and a broad associative horizon.

PHYSICAL IMPAIRMENTS

John Lennon, Helen Keller, George Patton, Norman Rockefeller, J. Seward Johnson, Woodrow Wilson, and perhaps even Albert Einstein all had dyslexia (Ludwig 1995, p. 233). Many other famous creative people had speech problems, visual problems, or were otherwise physically challenged. Dyslexia actually represents the least frequent category in Ludwig's (1995) extensive analysis of handicaps (also see Cravats 1990). Physical impairments may motivate certain individuals, and some try to compensate using creative work. Then again, Ludwig's sample was chosen for their eminence, and although many were architects, composers, and writers, others worked in areas that were not necessarily creative.

ADAPTABILITY AND MALADAPTATIONS

One way of viewing the complicated relationships that exist between creativity and psychopathology used a continuum of adaptive and maladaptive expressions of creative potential. From this perspective, psychopathology is a maladaptive result of genes and experience. Genetic potentials and experiences that lead to creative accomplishment are, on the other hand, adaptive.

There are a large number of reports of creativity providing an individual with the capacity to adapt and cope. As a matter of fact, Cohen (1989) suggested that adaptability is the life-long indicator of creative potential. In other words, she believed that you can see some form of adaptability in all ages, and at every age this capacity is indicative of the potential for creative work. She referred to it as a continuum of adaptive behaviors. Smith and Van der Meer (1997) referred to creativity as "a high level defense, or if one prefers not to stretch the concept too far, a coping strategy" (p. 25). They also referred to the benefits of "emotionally distancing oneself from an unalterably bad situation" (p. 607). Recall here that regression in the service of the ego (Dudek & Verreault 1989; Kris 1952) is an effective form of regression. It is adaptive.

Adaptations are apparent at all ages. Lindauer (1991) described how art can compensate for sensory, physical, and emotional disadvantages that may arise as the artist ages. Interestingly, he found evidence that aging artists often alter their artistic style as a "result of personal conflicts in late life" (p. 219). He contrasted Wordsworth and Shakespeare, for the former was "unable to shift from the spontaneousness of his youth … to philosophical and contemplative reactions more appropriate to later life. … Shakespeare, on the other hand, met aging's new requirements by shifting from works of history and comedy to tragedy" (p. 219). This might be called adaptation or accommodation.

Adaptations are also useful during youth. Albert and Elliot (1973) described how "pre-adolescent creative children are less likely to use repressive defense in recognizing a personal conflict, and, along with this, appear to have greater cognitive facility with and access to cognitive resources at different levels of consciousness than less creative people" (p. 177).

Reynold (2003) found creativity to be a resource for textile artists who were suffering from serious illness. He concluded that "the experience of biographical disruption, stemming from the crisis of illness, dissatisfaction with unproductive time, and a growing need for self-fulfillment, appeared to create a search for a meaningful occupation" (p. 393). The textile art gave them the opportunity to find meaning.

Pine and Holt (1960) reported that creative college students (males) had more effective control and more adaptive regression. They differed significantly from noncreative normals in primary process functioning. Very similar results were reported by Cohen (1961): Twenty art students nominated as creative by their professors had more adaptive regression and higher creativity than randomly selected art students (also see Dudek & Cote 1994).

THE ADAPTABLE MIND IN DESIGN

Meneely and Portillo (2005) found a kind of adaptability within design styles. In particular, they discovered that adaptability in design reflected a "flexibility within styles." Significantly, design is one of those unambiguously creative domains. Their investigation showed a significant correlation between measures of creative personality and that flexibility within styles. There is no one creative style in design, then, but instead creative design students were able to move from one style of thought to another. Adaptability is frequently defined in this fashion—as a kind of flexibility.

The logic connecting creativity and adaptability hinges on the concept of flexibility. A huge amount of empirical work shows that creative people are flexible (Guilford 1968; Runco 1991b) as does another body of research that shows that adaptability reflects flexibility. As Runco (2012) put it, "a flexible individual … will have alternatives and choices when solving problems, and therefore solutions are likely and frustration and distress are unlikely. Inflexible individuals, on the other hand, follow routines, make assumptions, and have difficulty when problems lead to fixedness (i.e., a perspective of the problem that precludes a solution, but that is difficult to circumvent)." Recall here Carlsson's (2002) recent suggestion that creativity provides a flexible use of strategies for dealing with anxiety.

Culture, Creativity, and Adaptability

The concept of adaptability seems to vary across cultures. Consider the Asian concept *wa*, which refers to something like "balance" (Figure 4.4). In particular, an individual is said to have, or be in, *wa* when they are comfortable with their environment. Logically, there are two ways to maintain this kind of balance: you can either avoid conflict and traumas or you can control your thinking such that, when conflicts are encountered, you are not disturbed. This second option implies a kind of adaptability. It may also help a great deal if you are creative and flexible. Suppose, for example, you have a plan for your day's activities. Suppose there are certain priorities in that plan; but something happens (e.g., flat tire, check does not clear, someone lets you down, it rains, etc.). These keep you from sticking with and fulfilling your plans. If you are inflexible, you may be disappointed or angry. But if you are flexible, you may see alternative routes and options, and you may get done what you wanted to get done, or you may at least be productive and not feel like you have wasted your day.

Many things are out of our control. The trick is to know which things can be controlled and which cannot. The *Serenity Prayer* captures this idea extremely well.

SERENITY PRAYER

Grant me the serenity to accept the things I cannot change, the courage to change the things I can, and the wisdom to know the difference. (The *Serenity Prayer* is generally thought to have been written by Reinhold Niebuhr.)

People from Asian cultures are sometimes quite explicit about the need to adapt and maintain one's balance, or *wa*. Although there is a premium put on harmony in many Asian countries (Kwang 2002), *wa* does not necessarily require conforming adaptations, bending, or giving in. Adaptations may be creative instead. Harmony is not necessarily a matter of conformity; it can be found in a creative fashion.

This emphasis on *wa* and adaptability may explain why Bruce Lee, for example, was said to prefer the metaphor of water to describe a creative life. Water flows and adjusts to obstacles; it changes as is required. Yet it is remarkably strong. It can wear down rocks and push heavy objects.

FIGURE 4.4   Balance is important for health, and creativity can help a person maintain balance, or *wa*. That is because creativity supports adaptability, and given that we cannot avoid all stress and challenges, it is best to be able to adapt to them. *Source: Wikimedia commons, http://en.wikipedia.org/wiki/File:Balance_scale_IMGP9755.jpg.*

Creativity and adaptability are often highly related, but distinct. They are far from synony-mous. Creative skills can greatly assist an individual, which is one of the advantages of creativity and one of the reasons why creative individuals may sometimes maintain psychological health. They have problems but adapt to them. It may even be that some creative skills develop as the individual adapts. In *Cradles of Eminence,* Goertzel and Goertzel (1962) reported that many cre-ative persons had had troubling and difficult childhoods. They adapted to the troubles, however, and the resulting skills served them well later in life. Runco (1994b) reviewed the large literature on creativity as it results from trauma, tension, and discomfort. He emphasized that practical implications should only very carefully be drawn from that research. Under no circumstances should the adaptability that may result from difficult circumstances justify imposing trauma on others! That would be unethical and unjustified. After all, that which does not kill you might make you stronger—or it may wear you out.

Creativity and adaptability may go hand in hand some of the time, but they also differ dramatically other times. This may be clearest in situations where it is most adaptable to con-form, in which case the individual is not being creative. The separation of creativity and adaptability is also supported by the occasional maladaptive behaviors of creative individu-als (e.g., criminality and incarceration). As Valliant and Valliant (1990) put it, "creativity is most surely a form of play, a means of having fun and not just a means of resolving conflict" (p. 615). In other words, creativity is sometimes related to adaptability, but is sometimes inde-pendent of it and related to play and spontaneous self-expression.

Creativity also has been conceived as an adaptive process on a cultural level (Lumsden & Findlay 1988; Mumford & Mobley 1989). Adaptability is also discussed in Chapters 3 and 7. It has been used to describe the cognitive bases for creativity and as a developmental force (Cohen 1989). It is, then, one of the most powerful concepts in the creativity literature.

ENCOURAGING CREATIVITY

Flaherty (2005) noted the two sides (good and bad) to depression:

> Although creative subjects paradoxically more often have a history of depression than the average, their creative work is not done during their depressions, but in rebound periods of increased energy between depressions … (Jamison 1989). When depression is treated, frontal lobe function normalizes on functional imaging (Goldapple et al. 2004). Creative block usually improves as normal levels of motivation return with the caveat that side effects such as mood flattening or agitation from antidepressants can be counterproduc-tive. Stimulants can help depression, as well as creativity. … Nonpharmacologic treatments of depression such as exercise and phototherapy may help creativity and productivity even in blocked subjects with no signs of depression (Steinberg et al. 1997) (p. 151).

There are several ethical issues that must be considered when considering treatment. For example, should an artist be treated for an affective disorder, if he or she depends on creative output? This might be an easy decision if severe depression is involved, given the relationship between depression and creativity. Perhaps at lower levels of disturbance treatment with drugs such as sertraline should be avoided, but at severe levels it should be seriously considered.

The benefits to alcohol are easy to misunderstand. It is quite possible that alcohol interferes with judgment, and when drunk an individual may conclude that he or she is having a huge number of good ideas. The ideas may not be so hot, however—it could just be the poor judgment. For some, alcohol is a means of escape (from anxiety or depression) rather than a means of finding inspiration (Rothenberg 1990).

There seems to be a consensus about the value of self-expression. Recall here the ideas of Eysenck, Pennebaker, and Maslow; each felt that self-expression would lead to sound health. Self-expression is, for example, a large part of self-actualization, and Pennebaker et al. (1997) found that disclosure actually improved the efficiency of the immune system. Surely these reports indicate that self-expression should be encouraged, and many forms of self-expression are quite creative.

Humor may also help. It is strongly correlated with creativity (O'Quin and Derks 1997) and has also been connected to positive health (Cousins 1990). As O'Quin and Derks (1997) put it, "using humor to cope with adversity should be a very creative way to live" (p. 25). There are data that do not support the impact of humor. Friedman et al. (1995) reported that longevity was unrelated to humor, and Rotton (1992) found that comedians do not live a long time.

SELF-ACTUALIZATION AND THE COURAGE TO CREATE

Never regret a genuine show of feelings. Archie Goodwin, in *The Bloodied Ivy* **(Robert Goldsborough, 1988, p. 41)**

Creativity may be encouraged (and blocks to creativity removed) through actual therapy. This may be clearest in the case of Maslow's (1971) humanistic therapy. It may help the individual develop and strengthen "the courage to create" (Rogers 1995). Courage may be necessary because creative things are often unconventional and misunderstood. Many people will shy away from them for that reason. Humanistic therapy is intended to convince the individual that they are unique and worthwhile, even if unconventional. For Rogers (1995), "The mainspring of creativity appears to be the same tendency which we discover so clearly as the creative force in psychotherapy—man's tendency to actualize himself, to become his potentialities … the individual creates primarily because it is satisfying … because this behavior is felt to be self-actualization" (pp. 351–352).

Both Rogers (1995) and Maslow (1971) explicitly tied creativity to self-actualization. Maslow suggested that creativity may be inextricable from psychological health. Rogers wrote that, "the concept of creativeness and the concept of the healthy, self-actualizing, fully human person seem to be coming closer and closer together, and may perhaps turn out to be the same thing" (1995, p. 57). Maslow (1968) also claimed that "SA [self-actualized] creativeness is 'emitted,' or radiated, and hits all of life, regardless of problems, just as a cheerful person 'emits' cheerfulness without purpose or design or even consciousness" (p. 145).

Several empirical efforts support the connection of self-actualization and creativity (Runco et al. 1991a).

May (1975/1994) saw creativity as constructive and not compensatory. He defined creativity as "the process of bringing something new into being" (p. 37). In explaining the courage to be creative, May emphasized intensity, absorption, engagement, passion, and commitment. Furthermore, he was very clear that creativity is a sign of psychological health. He wrote that creativity is "the expression of the normal people in the act of actualizing themselves" (1975, p. 38). Maslow described self-actualized individuals as having an accurate understanding of themselves and their world. They are spontaneous, independent, and creative.

Maslow's (1971) theory includes a hierarchy of needs, with humans having physiological and safety requirements at the lowest level; psycho-emotional (e.g., esteem) requirements at the next level; and at the highest level, a need for self-actualization. Put simply, this is the need to fulfill one's potential—to understand and accept one's self. Any progress toward self-actualization should also benefit the expression of creative potentials. Chapter 2 discussed a variety of other techniques for the enhancement of creativity.

CREATIVITY AS DESTRUCTION

This chapter started with several quotations about creativity, one of them being Picasso's "Every act of creation is first of all an act of destruction." Because scholarship requires one to do one's homework, I did just that and (thanks to the energetic assistance of Rainer Holm-Hadulla), found the following: "Take for instance, a twig and a pillar, or the ugly person and the great beauty, and all the strange and monstrous transformations. These are all leveled together by Tao. Division is the same as creation; creation is the same as destruction" (Chuang-tzu, 369–286 BC, quoted by Yutang, 1942).

So there was a precedent to Picasso's idea about destruction. This is of interest because there is a controversy about who first feels the need for paradigm shifts and changes in worldviews. Shlain (1991) argued in detail that artists see the need for changes, and capture new paradigms, well before scientists

realize that there is a need for change. Miller (2009), on the other hand, offers many examples of scientists who foresaw paradigm shifts, with artists eventually following along.

Interestingly, it is not at all clear that Picasso even said that about destruction. Attempting to find the exact date, we found nothing—no evidence that he actually said it. Several Picasso scholars indicated that he probably did not actually make the claim about destruction and creativity. Still, historical records are fallible, as are searches of them, but it is also possible that this idea was incorrectly attributed to Picasso. He might not have minded so much. Apparently he was unconcerned that people sold things with his name on them, even if he had not painted them. He may not have minded if he was famous for an intriguing and oft-quoted idea about creativity (as well as for Cubism and so many other artistic breakthroughs).

CONCLUSIONS

The relationship between health and creativity has been debated for hundreds of years. Often the debate is one-sided: It is easy to see how creativity may be related to "madness" and psychopathology. Aristotle noted the melancholy of poets, as have many philosophers and scientists since his era.

The relationship between creativity and health is, however, surprisingly complicated. Creative potential is sometimes tied to indicators of health, but sometimes also, in other samples, tied to indicators of ill-health. Ludwig (1995) demonstrated that the relationship varies from domain to domain, which complicates things further.

Creativity is related to depression and the affective disorders schizophrenia, criminality, suicide, stress, and short life-span. As for health, creativity has been related to self-actualization (Maslow 1970), which is the epitome of psychological health. Creativity is also associated with coping and adaptability. Very impressively, but somewhat less directly, self-expression during activities—such as free writing—is associated with approved immune functioning. There are self-reports and anecdotal suggestions that creative efforts are associated with a decrease in the frequency of illness, but the impressive work comes from blood tests of the efficiency of the immune system (Pennebaker & Seagal 1999).

More recently, evidence has been accumulating for a bidirectional relationship, for example, and in actuality this might be expanded beyond two variables. Health status can certainly influence creative work. Creative work can also influence health, which is why more and more recognition is given to bidirectionality. The third possibility is that both health and creativity reflect some third variable. In this light, creativity and health might not influence one another in any direct fashion but instead may be correlated only because they are both related to self-expressive tendencies, sensitivity, or perhaps a cognitive or associative tendency. At this point we simply do not know if creativity is the cause, or health is the cause, but we do know that both psychological and physical health is related to creativity.

There is controversy in this area. Some debate the role of consciousness and the unconscious. The classic Freudian view acknowledges an interplay of conscious and preconscious material—usually it is conflict. A very different view of creativity and the psyche was presented by Kubie (1958) in his fascinating work, *The Neurotic Distortion of the Creative Process*. Like Freud, Kubie felt creativity involved the interplay of unconscious, preconscious, and conscious systems. However, unlike Freud, he suggested that creativity and mental disturbance were in opposition to one another. The optimal condition for creativity was therefore a minimum amount of conflict, coupled with the ability to access the preconscious voluntarily. Flexibility is, for Kubie, a measure of health and creativity.

Kubie (1958) also questioned the cultural stereotype of a creative person as a healthy and adaptable one. This stereotype may not be as common now as it was when he prepared his argument; these days creative individuals are often viewed as more eccentric than typical and healthy, and many of the common disturbances, especially the affective bipolar disorders, are widely recognized. Kubie focused on neurosis rather than the affective or mood disorders. Kubie's concern, echoed by Kavaler-Adler (1993), is that creative individuals will not find happiness or fulfill their potential if they believe that by merely doing creative or artistic work, reparation will occur. Incidentally, Kavaler-Adler's analysis was applied only to Charlotte Bronte, Emily Bronte, Emily Dickinson, and Edith Sitwell.

This chapter opened with the controversial notion of the "mad genius." Not only are there indications that creativity has benefits for health, but there are a number of possible flaws and biases in the research on the psychological problems associated with "madness." Perhaps this area receives so much study because it is newsworthy and surprising. The good news is that it continues to receive a great deal of attention. It is a rich area of research, and a rich source for ideas about our health and well-being.

CHAPTER

5

Social, Attributional, and Organizational Perspectives

Doesn't mean that much to me, to mean that much to you. **Neil Young, "Old Man"**
They knew he had never been on their TV, so they passed his music by … He was playin' real good, for free. **Joni Mitchell, "For Free"**
No matter what you think, you can always get somebody else to go along with you. **Dashiell Hammett, The Thin Man**
No man is an island. **John Donne**
The things you think are useless, I can't understand. **Steely Dan, "Reeling in the Years"**

ADVANCE ORGANIZER

- Social Theories
- Attributional Theory
- Collaboration
- Competition
- Organizational Theories

- Innovation
- Teams
- Leadership
- Marginality
- Brainstorming and Social Judgment

INTRODUCTION

Social influences on creativity have received a huge amount of attention in the scholarly research, especially of late. This is because social processes and structures represent such dramatic influences on creativity. Very likely, no creative potentials would be fulfilled without social support of some kind. Moreover, creative efforts often would go unrecognized without social attributions and recognition. Some creative people work for that recognition. Many are influenced along the way by competition and other social situations. Industries and organizations attempting to stay competitive, diversify, and innovate look to situational influences in order to insure that the creativity of their employees is supported.

Creativity, Second Edition
http://dx.doi.org/10.1016/B978-0-12-410512-6.00005-9

For those reasons the second part of this chapter examines the organization, teams, and the like. Yet "social influence" is a broad concept and covers more than organizational issues. Many influences on development and growth, for example, including those presented by parents and teachers, reflect social processes. In that light this chapter presents one perspective on social processes, with complementary perspectives given in the chapters covering the developmental, cultural, and historical perspectives.

The various social perspectives are quite practical. Indeed, the developmental, educational, and social/organizational research demonstrates very well that creativity is a practical concern and not just an academic topic of study. This practicality will be particularly obvious in the discussion of organizational theories, for these tie innovation and productivity to different aspects of the creative process. Late in this chapter additional practical implications are explored. Some may operate on the most general level, namely within society at large. The effects are apparent in indicators of *aggregate creativity*.

The social perspective has spawned various focused theories, including the *attributional* theory of creativity (Kasof 1995), a theory of the creative class (Florida 2002, 2005), and the *communitarian* theory (Seitz 2003). Each is described after we address the general question: How do social factors influence creativity? The discussion then shifts to questions about organizations and pinpoints how teams, brainstorming, and other organizational arrangements can influence both creativity and innovation. At the end of the chapter we step back further, to a macro-social level and examine society at large. It may be that cities in the United States, and even countries around the world, differ in their creative talents. Why is that, and what determines it? In the conclusion to this chapter we address the question: Can anything be done to direct social influences toward the fulfillment of creative potential?

SOCIAL INFLUENCES ON ENVIRONMENTS AND SETTINGS

On the most general level the social perspective on creativity posits that social factors can support, undermine, or neither support nor undermine each others' creativity. Most of the time there is some influence; the third option (neither support nor undermine) is rare.

Seitz (2003) identified a wide a range of social influences:

> The individual is seen as situated within a social matrix and it is the influence of the ladder that shapes citizen's unique preferences, personal choices, and individual creative pursuits. Creativity is not posited to be merely the result of intra individual factors ... but the consequence of the confluence of cultural domains at social and political institutions that directly and indirectly influence the development of individual creative expression. Under this view, liberal democracies, predicated on individual choice, fail to uncouple individuals from the view points of existing ideologies and practices in a similar manner to the way the cultural marketplace of ideas fails to unite individuals to communal practice.... Human creative identity is thus shaped by "recognition, misrecognition, or its absence" in recognition from others.... That is to say, creativity is distributed. For instance, in terms of formal educational institutions, it resides not exclusively in the individual student but is dispersed among ones classmates, the teacher and pair of professionals that oversee the classroom, the cultural prosthetics that augment creative and intellectual growth ... and the larger school and community.

Social influences are both interpersonal and environmental. This is not an easy distinction to maintain, however, given that many environments depend on people. Teachers and managers, for example, create environments that are sometimes supportive of creativity. They can themselves model and reinforce creativity, in which case we might isolate interpersonal influence, but teachers and managers may also support creativity indirectly by demonstrating that creativity is a valuable thing. Teachers might accomplish this by displaying the work of famous creators on the walls of the classroom, managers with incentives. They may also provide (or withhold) the resources that support creative efforts. Resources are very important for creative efforts, as we shall see throughout this chapter.

Consider a classroom, home, or organization that provides *unconditional positive regard* (Rogers 1995). This should give individuals (children or employees) a sense of psychological safety, and allow them to express themselves in spontaneous and creative ways. Some feel that it will lead naturally to creative self-expression. Harrington et al. (1983) found it to be very useful in the home, and Bennis et al. (2000) described something very similar within organizations. It might be more difficult in organizations than in the home, or in schools or a clinical setting for that matter. Managers may need to direct their employees more than a parent or teacher directs a child, more than a clinician directs a patient. Parents, teachers, and counselors may be more concerned about growth and development than productivity. They can afford to act as moderators rather than managers or directors.

There is a small debate about unconditional positive regard and settings that provide it. Operant theory, for example, suggests that individuals receiving unconditional positive regard are being reinforced for just about anything. They need not grow or create; it doesn't matter; whatever happens they will receive unconditional positive regard. It is, in this light, a kind of reinforcement that is not contingent on any appropriate behaviors. Then there is the view that some sort of tension is necessary for creative efforts. Many case studies support this idea (reviewed by Runco 1994c), as does Ryhammar and Smith's (1999) study of organizational climates and a recent meta-analysis of organizational influences on creativity (Hunter et al. 2007). This debate may be resolved if *person–environment interactions* are recognized. That concept will be discussed in detail later in this chapter. First a key premise of the social perspective must be explored, the premise of social judgments.

SOCIAL JUDGMENT

The social perspective on creativity suggests that interpersonal judgments are involved in all creative work. This assumption can be seen in many definitions of creative products and accomplishments (which require recognition of some sort) in systems theories of creativity (Csikszentmihalyi 1990a), and even in measurement methods (e.g., the consensual assessment technique; Amabile 1990). Weisberg (1986) conveyed this idea as follows: "It is a mistake to look for genius either in the individual or in an individual's work. Rather, genius is a characteristic that society bestows upon an individual in response to his or her work" (Weisberg 1986, p. 88). Simonton (1990a) suggested much the same and proposed that creativity implies persuasion in that creative people change the way that others think. Consider also the systems theory of Csikszentmihalyi (1990a), which describes creativity as something that begins with the individual who has an idea or product that influences the field (a group of appropriate judges), and eventually changes a domain (e.g., art, music, science).

Social judgment is all-important in Kasof's (1995) attributional theory of creativity. As you might guess, from this perspective creativity is not inherent in any idea or product but is instead attributed by some social group. Kasof went so far as to suggest that if the theory holds up, individuals interested in earning a reputation as creative should develop impression management skills. These can then be used to positively manipulate the attributions given by some social group.

This social psychological view is entirely consistent with the sociological perspective of talent. There "the concept of a 'great philosopher' is a social construction, reflecting the needs of intellectual networks fixated on a competition for attention more than on the intrinsic quality of ideas or on a disinterested search for truth" (McLaughlin 2000, p. 171). Along the same lines, there is a clear need for sociologists to view creativity as "a product of networks, not individuals [which] … cannot be understood outside an analysis of the efforts of thinkers to gain attention, fame, and influence in the constant struggle for eminence that creates innovation within intellectual life" (McLaughlin 2000, p. 172). In this view, creative ideas are embedded in networks and organizations, some of which are intergenerational (Collins 2000).

The sociological perspective even explains fame and eminence. This is implied by the *law of small numbers*. It

> ensures that there is only a limited attention span available at any historical moment for unique schools of thought or intellectual contributions. Intellectuals then struggle to create 'coalitions in the mind' as they recombine old positions, attack orthodoxies, place themselves in noble genealogies, position themselves as loyal followers of more established scholars and traditions, or branch out on their own to try to build disciples and a unique theoretical position. Few succeed in this brutal competition for attention, as the law of small numbers makes almost all of even the most energetic and accomplished thinkers forgotten intellectuals, at least in the long run. Sociological networks are central to this process (McLaughlin 2000, p. 173).

Most dramatic, however, is the claim that "the content of new ideas flash into the minds of intellectuals in their creative moments," determined not by individual genius but by historical dynamics, organizational realities and the "flux of interaction ritual chains" (McLaughlin 2000, p. 173). Perhaps the social psychology of creativity will help sociologists with their desire to "see through the personalities" (McLaughlin 2000, p. 174) of creative individuals in order to identify the important social influences.

CONCERNS WITH SOCIAL AND ATTRIBUTIONAL PERSPECTIVES

> The very essence of the creative is its novelty, and hence we have no standard by which to judge it.
> *Rogers (1995, p. 351)*

Assumptions about social judgments raise quite a few questions. First, as Murray (1959) put it long ago, "who is to judge the judges, and who is to judge the judges of the judges?" Second, and along the same lines, experts often have unique perspectives, and they are sometimes quite inflexible in their thinking (Rubenson & Runco 1995). Their judgments may very well disagree with one another! So again, who do you trust? Third, there are a huge number of famous cases of misjudgment. These indicate that either judgments are biased and sometimes simply incorrect, or that something can be uncreative, then creative, and then uncreative again. It all depends on who you ask. That does not do much credit to social judgments.

Box 7.11 in Chapter 7 lists some of the more notable misjudgments. It includes the Beatles, Rudyard Kipling, William Faulkner, Picasso, the Wright brothers, Lewis Carroll, Rembrandt, Leonardo da Vinci, and many others.

The suggestion about impression management is especially disturbing. It may lead to *displaced investments* (Runco 1995c). These occur when someone devotes their time and energy to impression management, or for that matter to any other activity that is not really involved with the creative work at hand. If someone is taking photographs for publicity, for example, that is time away from writing the novel or song or painting the landscape. Additionally, creativity is often intrinsically motivated, and sometimes it needs to be just that. If the individual is thinking about impressions or reputation, he or she may very well be distracted. Attention will not be focused on the topic at hand and original insights are therefore unlikely. Gruber (1988) described the necessary process as a kind of *immersion*. He even saw it in children; there he referred to the *binges* that reflect intrinsic motivation and focus. These may be necessary for the person to develop the knowledge base and deep understanding of nuances within a domain that are required for detailed work. It is difficult to be immersed in the information or problem if you are thinking about how other people might react to you or your work.

There are much better ways to invest one's time than in impression management. Rubenson and Runco (1992a, 1995) actually listed the kinds of active investments in creative potential that might have reasonable payoffs (especially in contrast to what might be a displaced investment in impression management skills). These included the study of creativity (read this book!), or perhaps the study of a particular creative area, such as art, or computer science, or design. It can even help to study creative individuals. These are *remote models.* Inspiration might be found by attending concerts or visiting museums. Spending time with creative people is also beneficial. Such investments in creative potential are analogous to financial investments. Talent may accumulate with such investments, and there may be appreciation as well—and hopefully a payoff in terms of success, enjoyment, and satisfaction. There are even benefits to one's health (see Chapter 4).

DISPLACED INVESTMENTS

In "While I waltz off on a book tour," the novelist Alice Hoffman described how a writer might be touring *or* writing. Each takes time; time invested in one is time away from the other. This is how she concluded as she left for a visit to a bookstore during her tour: "As I look out the window of the limo, I think about how it is true not only that my characters do not exist without me, but also that I do not exist without them. Without them, I am simply a woman in a hotel room. With them, I am a writer, one in a desperate hurry to get home to whoever's waiting." (Hoffman 1994)

It is true that some creative efforts are improved when the individual considers the audience. This may be especially true of performing creators, but it may also be true of anyone who works best under that kind of pressure. It is also true that many creators are interested primarily in the social impact of their end products. One of Gardner's (1993a) conclusions about famous creators was, in fact, that they sometimes tend toward self-promotion. Still, it seems most reasonable for creative people to leave most impression management to an agent and devote themselves to developing their talent for original and creative work.

As a matter of fact, impressions are difficult to predict, and therefore difficult to manipulate. How often have performing artists focused their efforts on an audience only to receive bad reviews? And how often have creators seemingly ignored or even insulted the public, all the while being praised for their work? This last case is clearly exemplified by the numerous contrarians throughout history. Chapter 7 lists a few examples of contrarianism, including Walt Disney and Bob Dylan. Contrarians may not care too much about reputation or popularity. Grammy award winner Bob Dylan may be of this nature.

> Dylan has often said that he never set out to change pop songwriting or society, but it's clear he was filled with the high purpose of living up to the ideals he saw in [Woody] Guthrie's work. Unlike rock stars before him, his chief goal wasn't just making the charts. "I always admired true artists who were dedicated, so I learned from them," Dylan says, rocking slowly in the hotel room chair. "Popular culture usually comes to an end very quickly. It gets thrown into the grave." (Hilburn 2004)

Noel Coward apparently focused on amusing others and did not give a hoot about enduring work. An interview he gave in 1931 was recently quoted in the *Los Angeles Times*:

> As far as I am concerned, posterity isn't of any frightful significance; I think if it were I'd become self-conscious and wouldn't be able to work at all. I could no more sit down and say "Now I'll write an Immortal Drama" than I could fly, and anyway I don't want to. I have no great or beautiful thoughts. More than anything else I hate this pretentious, highbrow approach to things dramatic. The primary and dominant function of the theater is to amuse people, not to reform or edify them (Herman 1993, p. F17).

BIAS IN SOCIAL JUDGMENT

In addition to being difficult to predict, social judgments are often just plain biased. Some of this can be explained in terms of *zeitgeist*, and in the United States as of late, in terms of a kind of romanticism (Sass & Schuldberg 2000–2001). These have led to a view that creativity is often indicative of insanity and the "mad genius" (see Chapter 4). Creative talent is often now only expected of "weirdos" and eccentrics.

One kind of bias results from the fact that creators and those doing the judging (e.g., an audience) always hold different perspectives. This leads to the fundamental attribution error, which occurs when one person is doing something, and someone else is observing. The latter, not surprisingly, is called "an observer," but the former is assumed to be involved in some act or action and is thus called (less intuitively) the "actor." In general, an actor's attention is directed to the act, whereas an observer's attention will tend to be on the actor him- or herself. This makes perfect sense, for even the eyes are directed in different places, and it is unlikely that an actor will be watching him- or herself. Attentional resources are limited, so they will be concentrating on the setting. So when asked to explain the action, the actor considers what he or she saw—namely, the immediate environment, the setting, the context. The observer, on the other hand, tends to explain the very same action in terms of the actor's ability or personality. This is a fairly predictable bias, which applies to many situations where the creative person is misjudged or overlooked.

COLLABORATION AND CREATIVITY

Evidence for social influences on creative efforts can be found in the various investigations of collaboration. This may take the form of what Chadwick and de Courtivron (1993) called "intimate partnership." They identified 13 famous creators, each of whom was greatly influenced by a significant other. Rodin, for example, was influenced by Camille Claudel. André Malraux was influenced by Clara Malraux. Virginia Woolf was influenced by Vita Sackville-West. Max Ernst was influenced by Leonora Carrington. Henry Miller was influenced by Anaïs Nin. Dashiell Hammett, author of *The Big Sleep* and various other murder mysteries, was influenced by Lillian Hellmann. Perhaps best known in this volume is the relationship between Frida Kahlo and Diego Rivera. Note the various domains sampled here, including sculpture, painting, and writing.

John-Steiner (1997) also examined the role of collaboration in creativity. She examined a number of famous collaborations, including Albert Einstein and Neils Bohr, Martha Graham and Erick Hawkins, Marie and Pierre Curie, Georgia O'Keeffe and Alfred Stieglitz, Jean-Paul Sartre and Simone de Beauvoir, Pablo Picasso and Georges Braque, Igor Stravinsky and George Balanchine, Anaïs Nin and Henry Miller, Ariel and Will Durant, Sylvia Plath and Ted Hughes, Margaret Mead and M. C. Bateson, and Aaron Copeland and Leonard Bernstein. Note that there is competition as well as collaboration implied there. One of the most interesting and important examples of collaboration involves that of the Wright brothers. Consider their work strategy, which involved arguing. They would often argue, but apparently it was intended to test ideas and not because they were in fact angry. That is suggested by the fact that they would yell and scream about what they believed, Orville arguing for one thing, Wilbur for another, and then, very quickly, they would change sides and continue arguing. Wilbur would now yell and scream in favor of the other point of view, which Orville supported just moments before, but Orville now was yelling and screaming in favor of the view that Wilbur held just moments before. They created quite a scene.

Stillinger (1991) took the extreme view of social influence. He mentioned friends, spouses, ghostwriters, agents, editors, translators, publishers, censors, transcribers, printers, and a combination of these as influencing individuals.

MULTIPLE AUTHORSHIP

According to Stillinger (1991), no literary work is entirely individual. His idea of multiple authorship is based on analysis of social influences on a long list of creators, including those given below.

William Wordsworth
Samuel Taylor Coleridge
Lord Byron
Mary Shelley

John Keats
John Stuart Mill
Charles Dickens
Thomas Hardy
Oscar Wilde
George Bernard Shaw
Joseph Conrad
James Joyce
David Lodge
Samuel Beckett

(Continued)

George Orwell

D. H. Lawrence

Washington Irving

Nathaniel Hawthorne

Herman Melville

Mark Twain

Henry Adams

Sherwood Anderson

Upton Sinclair

Pearl S. Buck

T. S. Eliot

Eugene O'Neill

e.e. cummings

F. Scott Fitzgerald

William Faulkner

Ernest Hemingway

Thomas Wolfe

Nathaniel West

Irving Stone

James Michener

Robert Lowell

Kurt Vonnegut Jr.

Joseph Heller

Truman Capote

Malcolm X

John Updike

Sylvia Plath

Stephen King

and others.

Some collaboration was less than mutual—and occasionally not acknowledged (e.g., Coleridge). It is instead what Stillinger (1991) called *creative plagiarism*.

COMPETITION AND CREATIVITY

Not everyone enjoys collaboration. Some prefer to work alone, and some work independently but are driven by competition (Figure 5.1).

The relationship between creativity and competition is not a simple and direct one. As was the case with collaboration, sometimes competition stimulates creativity, and sometimes it does not. James Watson, who shared a Nobel Prize for his work on the structure of DNA, apparently was quite competitive (Watson 1968). Collaboration and competition are both apparent in the story of his research on the structure of genetic material, *The Double Helix*. He and his collaborator, Francis Crick, monitored carefully the work of Linus Pauling, who was also working on DNA. Another example is given by The Beatles, who were also competitive, at least some of the time. This was not so much competition between Lennon and McCartney as between the Beatles and other top performing bands (Clydesdale 2006). In their studies, Torrance (1965) and Raina (1968) provided additional data showing improved creativity with rewards and competition.

Competitive situations can be either informative or controlling (Shalley & Oldham 1997). It is much like motivation in this sense, for extrinsic factors can also be informative or controlling. The differences are quite important for creativity because the former may not inhibit creative efforts the way the latter seems to do just that. Only certain extrinsic factors may hinder creative effort. Shalley and Oldham's empirical results were only partly supportive of their hypotheses about the two kinds of competition.

Very importantly, competition, like so many social and environmental influences on creative work, influences individuals only after they are interpreted by the individual. In other words, there are significant individual differences and what may be stimulating for some individuals is inhibitory for others. This is the premise of person–environment interactions.

FIGURE 5.1   Many things in life are competitive, including sports. Competition spurs the creative spirit in some people, but in others, competition is a distraction or a situation to be avoided. Some people are more creative in competitive situations, while others are less creative. *Source: Wikimedia Commons, http://en.wikipedia.org/wiki/File:Citi_Field_Day.jpg.*

PERSON–ENVIRONMENT INTERACTIONS

Very possibly, one of the most important lessons to be learned from the social perspective on creativity is that different social influences and settings have different results on different people. The impact of any social or organizational factor can only really be understood by taking the individual into account. There is, in other words, always an important *person–environment interaction*. This applies to collaboration, competition, and almost definitely all social influences on creative work (Box 5.1). It explains how certain factors, even the unconditional positive regard described earlier, can stimulate the creative efforts of some people and some organizations, but cause other individuals to freeze.

Without a doubt, many individuals are disturbed by tension of any sort, or at least inhibited by it. Just as beauty is in the eyes of the beholder, so too is the interpretation of conflict and tension. This is a very important point because without it we may have very unfortunate recommendations for enhancing creativity. Someone might inappropriately create tension to stimulate creativity, assuming that it works for everyone, but they would very likely be inhibiting the creativity of the more sensitive individuals. To make matters worse, there is some indication that creative people as a group are especially sensitive to

BOX 5.1

COMPETITION FOR SOME BUT NOT OTHERS

The idiosyncratic effects of competition are apparent in biographies of Brian Wilson of the Beach Boys. He was both depressed and intimidated by the competition (Clydesdale 2006). The Beatles, on the other hand, may have benefited from competition. As Clydesdale (2006, p. 17) put it, "their dream was to be bigger than Elvis." Apparently the Beatles also watched the record charts and compared their ranking in sales with the Beach Boys and other contemporary groups.

Braque and Picasso had an interesting blend of competition and collaboration, not unlike that of John Lennon and Paul McCartney. Gardner described it as "good natured as well as cooperation" (quoted by Clydesdale 2006, p. 19). Spurling (1998, p. 405) referred to this same competition as "a rivalry that proved one of the richest and most productive in Western art."

social factors. After conducting a meta-analysis of organizational factors Hunter et al. (2007, p. 69) concluded that "creative people, people evidencing the individual attributes related to creative achievement, appear especially reactive to climate variables." This makes perfect sense, given personality research showing that one characteristic shared by many (but not all) creative people is that they are in some ways sensitive (Greenacre 1957; Wallace 1991).

The key factor is perception: individuals perceive environmental and situational variables idiosyncratically. Perception is a top-down process; it is not entirely dependent on objective information but instead is based on expectation and interpretation (Carson & Runco 1999; Millward & Freeman 2002; Nicol & Long 1996; Runco 2012). The objective environment is therefore not all-important for creativity, or just about anything else. This might even apply to the permissive environments (Wallach & Kogan 1965), which are generally conducive to creative efforts, as was the case for the environment that provides unconditional positive regard (Rogers 1995). Those would be best for the creative efforts of many people, whereas others may prefer some drama, conflict, or challenge.

Some of the clearest evidence for individual interpretations of experience can be found in the research on stress. What really matters is how the individual interprets a situation. This makes sense because that is how we react to any event: We all react in different ways. One person may experience stress given a particular experience, whereas the same experience is actually enjoyable to other people. This is why many people studying stress do not believe that there is any such thing as a stressor. A *stressor* would be something in the environment that *always* elicits stress, which is not possible. Stress depends on an individual's interpretation. Newer measures of stress assess perceived stress rather than stressors, just as newer measures of social influences focus on perceptions. Examples of these measures are discussed later.

It is likely that the impact of social and situational factors will also vary from time to time, as well as from person to person. Low and Abrahamson (1977) suggested exactly this after finding that entrepreneurs are motivated in different ways as they move through the innovation process. They are likely to be motivated by technical innovation early in the process, or perhaps social goals. As they move through the process, however, they are motivated by action and progress, and perhaps even the risk involved. Eventually, their motivation becomes financial as they near the end of the process.

These claimed person–environment interactions apply to both social and physical features of environments (Stokols et al. 2002). Fortunately the top-down nature of these effects can be taken into account when assessing a specific setting or organization. Amabile and Gryskiewicz (1989), for instance, assessed expected (rather than actual objective) evaluation as a potential inhibition on creative work. Employees may all experience the same evaluations from the same supervisor or manager, but the effects will vary with each individual's interpretation. This is of course only one important organizational influence on creative efforts.

PROFESSIONAL MARGINALITY

Marginality has been mentioned throughout this volume (see Box 9.1) and is a counterexample to the idea of "fit." Marginality may take various forms (e.g., cultural, professional) but always implies that the individual is outside of a group (Dogan & Pahre 1990). That is what leads to the original perspective: The individual is outside, looking in.

A sociological perspective of marginality uses different terminology but nonetheless recognizes the benefits of alternative perspectives. Burt (2004), for example, focused on groups, networks, and "holes" within networks. He described how "opinion and behavior are more homogeneous within than between groups, so people connected across groups are more familiar with alternative ways of thinking and behaving" (p. 349). Connections across groups would suggest a kind of intergroup marginality. Burt went on,

> people who stand near the holes in a social structure are at higher risk of having good ideas … opinion and behavior are more homogeneous within than between groups, so people connected across groups are more familiar with alternative ways of thinking and behaving, which gives them more options to select from and synthesize. New ideas emerge from selection and synthesis across the structural holes between groups. Some fraction of those new ideas are good … a good idea broadly will be understood to be one that people praise and value (pp. 349–350),

Burt tied this line of thought to classic theories from Adam Smith and John Stuart Mill. The former was quoted as saying (in 1766) "when the mind is employed about a variety of objects it is some how expanded and enlarged" (from Burt 2004, p. 350). The latter was quoted as well (in 1848): "it is hardly possible to overrate the value … of placing human beings in contact with persons dissimilar to themselves, and with modes of thought and action unlike those with which they are familiar."

These ideas lead us to organizational theories of creativity. Quoting Burt (2004) one last time,

> Brokerage across the structural holes between groups provides a vision of options otherwise unseen, which is the mechanism by which brokerage becomes social capital…. The organization is rife with structural holes, and brokerage has its expected correlates. Compensation, positive performance evaluations, promotions, and good ideas are disproportionately in the hands of people whose networks span structural holes. The between-group brokers are more likely to express ideas, less likely to have ideas dismissed, and more likely to have ideas evaluated as valuable (p. 349).

ORGANIZATIONAL THEORIES

Social influences are a major concern within organizations that target innovation and creativity. Consider this description of creativity in organizations:

> In Western culture creativity has been described as one of the essential resources in the development and renewal of society. Along these lines, many experts consider it to be one of the most important characteristics that the CEO of a corporation can possess. A firm's success often depends on the creative vision of its leadership.... Furthermore, 70% of the cost of a product is determined by its design.... Therefore, creative designs can lead to substantial cost savings for manufacturers. As a result, creativity training for employees has become widespread (Clapham 1997; Thackray 1995). According to the 1995 US Industry Report, corporations have budgeted billions of U.S. dollars for developing creativity in employees (Hequet 1995) (Zha et al. 2006).

Ryhammar and Smith (1999) identified the following as critical organizational influences on creativity: organizational structure, culture, climate, resources, workload pressure, and leadership style. Ryhammar and Smith wisely recognized the relevance of the individual personality and the likelihood of person–environment interactions. Their data suggested that the most relevant personality characteristic was openness. That parallels the openness-to-experience trait reviewed in Chapter 9, but for Ryhammar and Smith, it also reflects a kind of tolerance for diversity.

ORGANIZATIONAL CLIMATE

One way to operationalize the social supports and inhibitions within a business is in terms of an organizational climate. Isaksen et al. (2000–2001) offered the following: "Climate is defined as the recurring patterns of behavior, attitudes, and feelings that characterize life in the organization. At the individual level of analysis, the concept is called psychological climate. At this level, the concept of climate refers to the individual perceptions of the patterns of behavior. When aggregated, the concept is called organizational climate" (p. 172).

Ekvall and Ryhammar (1999) defined organizational climate in terms of the interplay of institutional policies, goals, strategies, tasks, workload, resources, technology, and, of course, staff. They suggested that creative outcomes are the most likely if the following conditions are met:

- The organizational climate challenges individuals with tasks, goals, and institutional operations. Work must be meaningful. "The development and survival of the organization is important" to employees.
- Employees have opportunities and initiative. This may be apparent in how communication within and outside the organization and in the methods available obtain information. Communication rules are important.
- There is support for new ideas. They are encouraged and rewarded.
- Employees are trusted and feel that trust. This will support their initiative. Risk is minimal because employees know they are trusted and in turn trust the organization (e.g., leaders, managers).
- There is a permissive environment with frequent discussion and debate but no actual animosity.

• Risk taking is supported. Experiments and the accompanying risks are tolerated. Risk is viewed as a part of the creative process.

The third item in this list is especially intriguing. It says something about organizational values. These values do need to be verbally or formally expressed to employees, but that can be communicated and reinforced in many ways. Basadur (1994) offered an interesting example of how creativity is valued in organizations in Japan: There, new ideas for improvement were encouraged with prizes and ever-ready suggestion boxes. Good ideas actually were called "Golden eggs."

Ekvall and Ryhammar (1999) described a measure of organization climate that covers 10 areas: (1) support for ideas, (2) challenge, (3) time for ideas, (4) freedom, (5) trust and openness, (6) dynamism/liveliness, (7) risk taking, (8) playfulness and humor, (9) debates, and (10) conflicts and impediments. Given the importance of innovation and creativity for organizations, and therefore the importance of good objective research on the same, it will come as no surprise that there are a number of similar measures.

MEASURING THE CLIMATE FOR CREATIVITY AND INNOVATION

Mathisen and Einarsen (2004) presented a careful review of several of the measures available for assessing organizational support for innovation and creativity. These measures were the *Creative Climate Questionnaire*, *KEYS: Assessing the Climate for Creativity*, the *Team Climate Inventory, Situational Outlook Questionnaire*, and the *Siegel Scale of Support for Innovation* (also see Witt & Beorkrem 1989).

Amabile (1990) presented a model of creative organizational climates that specifies eight measurable climate dimensions: organizational encouragement, encouragement by supervisors, freedom within the organization, pressure and workload, resources, organizational hurdles and impediments, challenging work and assignments, and support for work groups.

There is some indication that important organizational outcomes can in fact be predicted from the available measures. The outcomes in the research usually include some combination of the following: (1) return on organizational investment; (2) entrepreneurship; (3) innovation and innovation adoption; (4) publications; (5) expert judgment, usually of innovations or products; and (6) supervisory or even self-ratings by the employees and participants (Hunter et al. 2007).

To really understand (and accurately assess) how organizational factors influence team work, job satisfaction, innovation, and creativity, it is important to consider moderators. A *moderator* is a kind of variable that determines how strongly a particular dimension will influence organizational and individual behavior. Project demands and the type of innovation are examples of moderators; the need for various organizational supports will vary depending upon each of these. Various individual factors may also moderate the impact of climate, including an individual's satisfaction with his or her work, the individual's perception, and perhaps even the individual's mood.

When teamwork is involved, team factors also moderate the impact of organizational climate. Team factors include the size of a team, the cohesion and personality of its members, its tenure (i.e., how long it has been together), and its heterogeneity or homogeneity (Katz 1982; Rubenson & Runco 1995). Teams can be difficult to form because there are so many influences. There are also different potential outcomes. Kurtzberg (2005) demonstrated that diversity within teams may contribute positively to the ideation and problem-solving efficacy of a team, but at the same time lowers satisfaction.

Optimal Teams

Groups might be composed such that creative solutions are likely. Simply put, optimal groups should be fairly heterogeneous and not too large. This is because individuals who have made large investments in their own field of expertise have large knowledge bases, which they can bring to the group in a very useful fashion, but they also have a tendency toward inflexibility. This inflexibility has been recognized in the psychological literature (Chown 1961), and may be a natural part of aging, but it also can be explained in terms of the huge investments made by anyone with expertise. Whenever there is a large investment, even in one's skills and knowledge base, there is something to protect and a great deal at stake. Suppose someone invests 30 years in a particular line of thought, but then an alternative perspective is made available. This alternative would devalue the individual's expertise much like depreciation can occur with real world assets. An individual will resist such depreciation and devaluation to the extent of cognitively rejecting alternatives and alternative perspectives. This resistance may stimulate a healthy discussion within a group. Indeed, it would be wise in a brainstorming group to have two or perhaps three individuals with a great deal of expertise. They would bring large knowledge bases, but would also be very likely to debate subtleties of the problem at hand.

The group should be heterogeneous, however, meaning that it should also contain two or three novices. They are the most likely to be open-minded and flexible, since they have little to lose. A new idea may attract or intrigue them. The novices would benefit from the knowledge bases and the debating but would be open to new possibilities and syntheses. Two novices might be best because group size is very important. This follows from the likelihood that, in a group, the costs are high, at least in the sense that every idea is shared with other people. Consider what happens when an individual is working alone: He or she is not taking a risk by thinking about or even recording bizarre and unconventional ideas. Original ideas are, in fact, likely to be unconventional, and perhaps even a little bit strange. But these are difficult to share with other individuals for precisely the reason that they are unconventional. Thus there is a general tendency for larger groups to inhibit creative thinking more than smaller groups or what are sometimes called *nominal* groups. This is a bit of a misnomer because a nominal group is the smallest possible case—someone working alone. Importantly, teams with long tenure may become more homogeneous (Katz 1982).

Brainstorming in Teams and Organizations

Teams often use brainstorming. Brainstorming is based on three guidelines: Team members should (1) avoid judgment, (2) focus on the quantity of ideas and not their quality—produce as many ideas as possible, and (3) try finding ideas via *piggybacking* or *hitchhiking*. This means working in a team and using other people's ideas as a springboard for one's own thinking.

The first of these is sometimes worded "postpone judgment," which is different from avoiding judgment. If it is postponed, you can return to it later. And that is very likely necessary. At some point ideas and solutions do need to be evaluated. Otherwise they may be of very low quality. Both divergent thinking and convergent thinking are necessary for truly creative thought (Basadur 1994; Runco 1999d). Postponed judgment may be useful at first, for divergence, but at some point convergence and judgment are necessary. This is actually where problems often arise when brainstorming. It is so difficult to truly postpone judgment. Team members can read each other and infer reactions and judgments, even if they do not explicitly criticize.

That is one reason why brainstorming is typically ineffective. Admittedly, if the intent is to strengthen cooperation among a group of individuals (*team building*), brainstorming might be useful. If, on the other hand, there is a real need for original solutions and ideas, a great deal of research suggests that brainstorming is not the best method. The problems with brainstorming are varied. Some can be dealt with by the careful composition of teams. These problems and team composition options are discussed next.

There is a large amount of research demonstrating that group problem solving is not as effective as individuals working alone, at least when creativity is desired (for reviews, see Paulus & Nijstad 2003, or Rickards & De Cock, 2012). Groups can contribute to collaboration and cooperation and perhaps team building and organizations, just as teamwork might benefit school children in the sense that they will learn to cooperate and consider other perspectives. But in a real world setting where actual creative solutions are needed, groups are not as likely as individuals to succeed. In addition to the increased risk in groups there is also the possibility of *social loafing*, where individuals do not put as much effort into a job when they are sharing responsibilities, and a productivity loss, where individuals simply do not contribute as much individually as they would if they were working alone or in a dyad (Diehl & Stroebe 1987, 1991).

The inhibition of creative thinking in groups may be greater than it first appears. This is because what is inhibited is not only one creative idea, but any time one creative idea is ignored or dismissed because of the social pressures, it is actually an associative chain of possibilities that is lost. The individual does not even begin to pursue a line of thought if the initial idea is risky and dismissed. The assumption here is that creative thought is associative,

---

PSYCHIC COSTS

Brainstorming may not lead to the best ideas. There is a tendency toward *productivity loss*, for example, and another toward *social loafing*. Part of the problem is that when in a group, there are potential psychic costs to being original. After all, original ideas are always unusual, and therefore the person thinking in an original fashion is unusual. They may be respected for it, but instead are sometimes labeled eccentric, difficult, unconventional, weird, or "a few bubbles off plumb."

BOX 5.2

ARTISTS IN ORGANIZATIONS

Different organizations have different climates. They also have different objectives and missions. Runco (1995a) investigated an unambiguously creative organization involved in the commercial arts. The employees were, then, commercial artists. One of the measures just cited (developed by Witt & Beorkrem 1989) was administered to the artists, along with measures of personality and job satisfaction.

Easily the most significant finding was that individuals in the organization with the lowest level of job satisfaction were the most creative. Creative potential was estimated with psychological tests rather than their artwork, but there is a logic to the finding. It makes sense that artists may prefer individualized work and autonomy, and therefore are dissatisfied with the social climate of an organization.

---

but of course there is a great deal of evidence supporting the value of remote associates (Mednick 1962; Runco 1985) (Box 5.2).

Runco (2003c) suggested that these kinds of psychic costs can help us understand why there is a fourth-grade slump in creativity. Many children are highly creative before the fourth grade, but then seem to lose some of their creative potential. This may be a reflection of our biological wiring, with the preadolescent becoming more sensitive to conventions and therefore less likely to behave in an unconventional fashion. It may also be educational because by the fourth grade, individuals have had quite a bit of pressure placed on them to follow the rules in school and to learn what teachers deem to be important. Part of it may also involve the child's peers, because at that age children like to fit in and peer pressure is extremely intense, but a creative child may feel the stress of being unusual. Runco et al. (2012) summarized the impact of costs this way:

> There are also costs to creative work. These include pecuniary costs (time and resources expended during work), and psychic costs such as emotional wear and tear of overcoming the obstacles often encountered in creative work. The initial negative reaction which often accompanies creative work may affect one's self confidence or task motivation. Psychic costs may furthermore include social isolation for one's deviant ideas. Peers, whose work is devalued by the appearance of the new creative ideas, may seek to punish or ostracize the person who upsets the apple cart.

Virtual Teams

The idea of psychic costs implies that there may be a benefit to working in virtual teams, or that electronic brainstorming might be more effective than face-to-face brainstorming. These might provide some degree of anonymity, and thereby lower the potential costs to original ideas. Sosik et al. (1998) found exactly this—anonymous groups had higher originality scores and were more flexible than control groups without anonymity.

Nemiro (2002) defined *virtual teams* as "groups of geographically dispersed organizational members who carry out the majority of their activities through information technology"

(p. 69). In a qualitative study she inferred the presence of four stages in their work: idea generation, development, finalization/closure, and evaluation. These are extremely close to other models of the creative process (e.g., Runco 1994e; Wallas 1926), though for obvious reasons Nemiro emphasized the role and impact of communication among virtual team members. Apparently communication varied within each of the four stages.

LEADERS AND LEADERSHIP

Leaders are important in many ways. Isaksen et al. (2000–2001) described it this way:

> Acts of leadership occur whenever strategic problems are solved, decisions are made, or information exchanges result in actions. Leadership behavior is very visible to individuals in the organization, especially during times of change. Leaders may be senior managers, supervisors, and others who hold formal positions of influence or those who demonstrate an informal influence on others. Leadership behavior has a major influence on the perceptions people have about the climate for creativity and change (p. 173).

Leaders also control resources and define the roles of the organization, team, or group (Redmond et al. 1993).

Different leadership styles may significantly influence creative work. With this in mind, Jung (2000–2001) compared transformational and transactional leadership styles within brainstorming groups. One of the so-called groups was the nominal group, each of which contained only one person. He found that these nominal groups outperformed the brainstorming groups and that, when in groups, *transformational* leadership was significantly more effective than *transactional* leadership. Transformational leaders "actively encourage followers to take innovative and creative approaches rather than conventional and traditional ones" (Jung 2000–2001, p. 186). Transactional leadership, in contrast, "tends to be based on an exchange process whereby followers are rewarded for accomplishing specified goals" (p. 187).

Sosik et al. (1998) also found a benefit to transformational leadership. They felt that this may result from the tendency of transformational leaders to "use intellectual stimulation, promote consideration of different viewpoints, and inspire collective action to promote group creativity" (p. 112).

ORGANIZATIONAL ATTITUDE

Another significant potential moderator reflects the attitudes of employees within an organization (Runco & Basadur 1993). Basadur (1994) identified two very relevant attitudes, one reflecting openness to new ideas, and a second scale related to a tendency toward premature closure. Basadur and Hausdorf (1996) identified three additional organizational attitudes, which they labeled "valuing new ideas," "creative individual stereotypes," and "too busy for new ideas."

Attitudes probably should be given a great deal of attention in any social setting, including organizations, because they do influence actual behavior (Basadur 1994; Basadur et al. 2000) and because they are quite easy to change. Attitudes by definition are short-term, temporary states of mind. They are not like traits, for example, which are thought to be quite stable.

Meta-Analysis of Organizational Factors

As noted elsewhere in this volume, one of the most powerful methods for examining the impact of any influence on creative effort is that of *meta-analysis*. Hunter et al. (2007) conducted such a meta-analysis using results from 42 previously published studies. The results suggested a 14-dimension model of organizational climate, as presented in Table 5.1. Importantly, each of these should probably be prefaced with "perception of... ." This would acknowledge the subjective top-down perceptions of the climate, which are much more important than any objective index of the climate.

Results of the meta-analysis also indicated that the most important factors may be those reflecting positive interpersonal exchanges, intellectual stimulation, and challenge. Recognition and resources were not very important, at least in the meta-analysis. The significance of moderators was suggested by the fact that individual perceptions were strongly related to the various criteria of organizational creativity.

The same meta-analysis supported the earlier ideas about costs influencing organizational climate and teamwork. In particular, Hunter et al. (2007) found that *capital intensity* mitigated the impact of climate on creative performance. They define capital intensity in terms of prior investments and concluded that these "may limit the feasibility of pursuing new ideas and thus restrict ... the effect of a creative climate" (p. 83). Psychoeconomic theory predicts precisely this: When you have a huge investment, you may be less open to new ideas. This applies on both the organizational and individual level.

TABLE 5.1 Dimensions in and Definitions from Hunter et al.'s Meta-Analysis of Climate Factors

Dimension	Definition
1. Positive peer group	Peers and teammates are perceived to be stimulating and trustworthy. Good communication
2. Supervisor	Supervisor allows autonomy and supports original ideas
3. Resources	Resources are available and organization is willing to allocate them
4. Challenge	Assignments are challenging but not overwhelming
5. Mission clarity	Expectations and goals include creative work
6. Autonomy	Individuals are given independence
7. Cohesion	Little conflict and a sense of working together as a unit
8. Intellectual stimulation	Ideas are encouraged and discussed in a useful fashion
9. Top management	Creativity is encouraged by top management
10. Rewards	Creativity is appropriately rewarded
11. Flexibility & risk-taking	The ambiguity and uncertainty of creative work is tolerated
12. Product emphasis	Results of the work are expected to be original and of high quality
13. Participation	Supervisors and employees work together. Communication is honest and open
14. Organizational integration	Internal (teams) and external (outsourcing) resources are well coordinated

Hunter et al. (2007) found that conditions of high turbulence and high competitive pressure and high production pressure were associated with a climate that could in turn stimulate creativity. The impact of competition and pressure was not uniform, however; it varied across dimensions of creativity. Firms and individuals are apparently likely to be less productive, and thereby conserve resources, but also more selective. They will therefore be expected to produce higher quality, and perhaps more original and creative products, when experiencing pressure, even though they produce fewer products overall.

Finally, this meta-analysis indicated that the impact of organizational climate was similar in individualistic and collectivist cultures. The relationships between climate and creativity were, on the other hand, stronger in nonindustrialized than industrialized countries. These results are impressive in that they reflect a meta-analysis; yet the number of relevant studies used in the comparison of culture and industrialization were small. Hunter et al., however, were not studying the cultures directly but instead analyzing previous studies of culture. As you might expect, these results about culture were based on much less data than those summarized in Table 5.1. Still, they are consistent with much of the cross-cultural research summarized in Chapter 8. Basadur et al. (2001) also examined the impact of culture on organizational climate and attitudes.

COMMUNITARIANISM AND CREATIVITY

This finding from the meta-analysis was presented last because it is a good reminder that organizations are embedded within cultures. They share the values of the culture that houses them. They cannot be understood without also taking culture and historical and political conditions into account. Of course the same thing can be said about all creativity.

This is the premise of *communitarianism*, which Seitz (2003) described in this fashion:

> Historical, political, and social influences greatly constrict creative activity and creative self-expression in the arts, sciences, and entrepreneurship. Moreover, the differential distribution of power and resources among individuals and groups in society, as well as the impact of the norm of self-interest in Western capitalist cultures, deeply constrain creative self-expression. This includes political and religious censorship, corporate control and influence, copyright restrictions, as well as cultural and economic constraints. Communitarianism—the school of political thought that holds that individual self-expression is best nurtured within communities of association—proposes that creative activity emerges from a shared sense of community whose lingua franca is social capital, not merely human capital. Any creative product, therefore, emerges from a unique coincidence of individual intellective abilities; the social and cultural organization of a scientific, artistic, or entrepreneurial domain; the structure and complexity of the field of legitimization; and the distribution of power and resources within a group, community, or society.

AGGREGATE CREATIVITY AND SOCIETY AT LARGE

Something should be said at this point about the most general social influence on creative talent, namely society at large. This would explain why Florida (2002, 2005) has found differences among countries and cities in terms of their proportions of a creative class (Figure 5.2, Tables 5.2 and 5.3). The United States was ranked 11th in this listing.

FIGURE 5.2   Map of Europe. Some countries are more creative than others, at least if you rely on particular, professional indices of "creativity." Some countries, and some cities for that matter, seem to attract "the creative class." *Source: Wikimedia Commons, "This image is in the public domain because it contains materials that originally came from the United States Central Intelligence Agency's World Factbook." http://commons.wikimedia.org/wiki/File:Physical_Map_of_ Europe.jpg.*

TABLE 5.2   Countries Ranked in 2002 According to Proportion of the Creative Class

Ireland

Belgium

Australia

Netherlands

New Zealand

Estonia

United Kingdom

Canada

Finland

Iceland

United States

TABLE 5.3 US Cities Ranked According to Proportion of the Creative Class

Austin, TX

San Francisco

Seattle

Boston

Raleigh-Durham

Portland, OR

Minneapolis

Washington-Baltimore

Sacramento

Denver

At the bottom of the list is Detroit, Norfolk, Cleveland, Milwaukee, Grand Rapids, Memphis, Jacksonville, Greensborough, New Orleans, Buffalo, and Louisville.

The creative class is the segment of a population that is involved in creative work. Florida (2002) defined a class as "a cluster of people who have common interests and tend to think, feel, and behave similarly, but these similarities are fundamentally determined by economic function—by the kind of work they do for a living" (p. 8). The creative class includes artists, musicians, designers, engineers, scientists, and others who produce knowledge and ideas. This class of people is, of course, critical in today's society. It has replaced farmers, manufacturers, service workers, and even the knowledge worker at the top of the list of valuable groups.

The United States was ranked 11th in the world in 2002 (Florida 2002) but is moving down the list. In 2011, for example, the United States was 27th. The top 10 had changed as well. Updated figures from Florida (2011) show the following countries in the top 10:

1. Singapore (47.3% of the population in the "creative class")
2. The Netherlands (46.3%)
3. Switzerland (44.8%)
4. Australia (44.5%)
5. Sweden (43.9%)
6. Belgium (43.8%)
7. Denmark (43.7%)
8. Finland (43.4%)
9. Norway (42.1%)
10. Germany (41.7%)

Other notables include the United States (ranked 27th), Russia (ranked 20th, with 38.6%), Brazil (ranked 57th, with 18.5%), and China (ranked 75th, with 7.4%).

Two points should be underscored. First, Florida (2011) pointed out that these rankings and percentages cover entire countries–and do not apply uniformly within any one country. In his words, "America is a big country and my own research shows that the distribution of Creative Class jobs is geographically concentrated, with certain regions like Silicon Valley, greater Washington, D.C. and college towns like Boulder, Colorado scoring as high as the leading nations."

The second point to underscore is that creative talent, as represented by membership in the "creative class," is not dependent on education. Again quoting Florida (2011), "In the U.S. … nearly three-quarters of adults with college degrees are members of the Creative Class, but less than 60 percent of the members of the Creative Class have college degrees: In other words, 4 in 10 members of the Creative Class—16.6 million workers—do not have college degrees." Either creativity is not strongly associated with traditional and academic intelligence, or the education offered by colleges does not lead directly to creative talent. The rankings and percentages above and the quotations are from:http://www.theatlanticcities.com/jobs-and-economy/2011/10/worlds-leading-creative-class-countries/228/#slide1 (accessed October 2013).

Florida's (2002, 2005) explanation for differences among countries and cities involves three Ts: technology, talent, and tolerance. The last of these is entirely social; it is tolerance by a society (or group of citizens, in the case of a specific city) for diversity. Tolerance also has been emphasized by Richards (1997) and Runco in their discussions of educational influences on creativity in the schools. There, too, creative individuals may be a bit different and require tolerance. It is one of those things that is inherent in creative people. They are original, which means that they are different, and this can cause problems in many social situations. That is especially true when the creative person suggests a change, as they often do. Along the same lines, Dacey et al. (1998) noted that, "increased tolerance provides more opportunities for creative output, because an appreciation of diversity allows a greater number of creative products to be produced and accepted" (p. 251).

BOX 5.3

THE BOHEMIAN INDEX

Theories of social influence suggest that the costs of being creative need to be decreased (Rubenson & Runco 1992b, 1995). One way of doing this is to better tolerate diversity. This will allow creative people to more easily express themselves and share ideas. It will have other results as well. As a matter of fact, one index of tolerance is based in part on the number of gay individuals living in a community. (This, of course, is standardized to take overall population size into account.) Tolerance will also support writers, musicians, artists, and other creative groups. Florida (2002) uses the proportions of such creative careers in his *Bohemian Index*.

HUMAN CAPITAL AND THE CREATIVE CLASS

Long ago Guilford (1950) argued that creativity is a natural resource. Forty years later Rubenson and Runco (1992b, 1995) described creativity as a form of *human capital*. They put it this way:

> Our theory is based on the concept of creative potential as an element in the human capital of individuals, and leads to an economic model of the markets for creative activity.... Applying the economic theory of human capital, this model postulates the existence of a creative potential for each individual as the product of some initial endowments (based on both genotype and environment) and on investments the individual may make in learning creative modes of thinking. The model describes the process by which individuals decide the quantity and form of such investments, and shows how this decision depends on a number of extrinsic and intrinsic factors. The investment by individuals in their creative potential is in many important ways analogous to investment in formal education, and as such is based on considerations of the costs of the investment (including psychic and time costs) and the expected benefits of increased creative potential to that individual. Interestingly, distinctions between creative potential and formal education lead the model to predict some significant differences in the extent to which individuals will invest in these two forms of human capital.... Human capital refers to the specific skills and knowledge which also enter into the productive process. As such, human capital as a general category can include many different specific attributes. The discussion of human capital typically focuses on formal education and job skills, but creative potential should also be considered one component of an individual's human capital.

They go on to describe how supply and demand both influence investments in creative talents. What is most relevant to the idea of social influences is their idea about the market for creativity and the impact of demand. Both lead to investments, specifically in creative potential and increases in the supply of creative people.

Along the same lines, Florida (2002) described how

> human creativity is the ultimate economic resource. The ability to come up with new ideas and better ways of doing things is ultimately what raises productivity and thus living standards. The great transition from the agricultural to the industrial age was of course based on natural resources and physical labor power, and ultimately gave rise to giant factory complexes.... The transformation now in progress is potentially bigger and more powerful.... The current one is based fundamentally on human intelligence, knowledge, and creativity. (p. xiii)

Florida (2002) found that fewer than 10% of the American population was involved in one of these areas in 1990, but today the United States has approximately 20% in these groups. Ireland has over 30%. The United States leads the world in gross economic production of the creative class with an estimated $1.7 trillion, which is equal to or in excess of the other two major divisions of workers (service and manufacturing).

Obviously, the creative class depends very much upon other groups and individuals, especially the groups Florida (2002) labeled as belonging in the service sector. Indeed, he seemed to think that much of what we should be doing to fulfill creative potential is to allow individuals who are currently not in the creative class to use their creativity. Just to mention a few examples, Florida describes how office cleaners, delivery people, and many others in the service economy, or sector of our population, represent the "infrastructure of the creative age" (p. xv). Florida also mentions areas that are creative but not necessarily in the sense of idea and knowledge production. He refers to construction, landscaping, and work in the hair salon or spa as creative. And as was the case with his suggestions about the service economy, he believes that we need to further reward and appreciate the creativity of these groups.

These ideas have numerous practical implications. As you might expect, Rubenson and Runco (1992b, 1995) described how the costs for being creative (e.g., stigma) need to be lowered and the benefits need to be raised. Along the same lines, Florida (2002) pointed to increased tolerance. This is much the same as decreasing the stigma and costs for being creative.

Human capital may be a result of what was described earlier as *brokerage* (Burt 2004). This particular kind of brokerage is the control exerted by someone working between groups.

A broker can control what each group shares with the other, and given that creative insights may be the most likely when the groups intersect (or their knowledge is integrated), the broker has great leverage and "capital." He or she has something no one else has. Burt (2004) applied this logic to organizations that may be divided into teams or groups. He described teams or groups as part of an organizational structure and places the broker on the edge of a structural "hole." He wrote, "social capital exists where people have an advantage because of their location in a social structure" (p. 356).

This is consistent with theories of marginality as beneficial to creativity. The difference would seem to be that the marginal individual has moved from one context to another, while the broker bridges two contexts at the same time. Additionally, the marginal individual is the creative one, while the broker facilitates creativity by bridging groups or contexts.

Burt (2004) went into detail about the benefits of working between groups (and near structural holes):

> People with connections across structural holes have early access to diverse, often contradictory, information and interpretations, which gives them a competitive advantage in seeing and developing good ideas. People connected to groups beyond their own can expect to find themselves delivering valuable ideas, seeming to be gifted with creativity. This is not creativity born of genius; it is creativity as an import-export business. An idea mundane in one group can be a valuable insight in another (p. 389).

This assumes a particular view of creativity. For Burt (2004), creativity is

> a diffusion process of repeated discovery in which a good idea is carried across structural holes to be discovered in one cluster of people, rediscovered in another, then rediscovered in still others—and each discovery is no less an experience of creativity for people encountering the good idea. Thus, value accumulates as an idea moves through the social structure; each transmission from one group to another has the potential to add value. In this light, there is an incentive to define work situations such that people are forced to engage diverse ideas (pp. 388–389).

One implication of this view is that good ideas are those with value, and value is not really inherent in the idea. So once again, social judgment takes on a huge role. As Burt (2004) described it, this

> is the shift in focus from the production of ideas to the value produced. The brokerage value of an idea resides in a situation, in the transaction through which an idea is delivered to an audience; not in the source of the idea, nor in the idea itself…. what matters is the value produced by the idea, whatever its source…. an idea is as valuable as an audience is willing to credit it with being. An idea is no less valuable to its recipients because there are people elsewhere who do not value it. The certain path to feeling creative is to find a constituency more ignorant than you and poised to benefit from your idea (pp. 388–389).

This perspective meshes with attributional theories of creativity (Kasof 1995). They too relegate the idea, process, or creative individual and focus on the impact of the idea and the attributions (of value, or novelty, or whatever) provided by some audience.

CONCLUSIONS

This chapter discussed the many ways that social processes and structures influence creative potential and creative performance. Much less was said about the other direction of effect, with creativity influencing social processes and structures. This was implied by some of the discussion of organizations, but to be most accurate we should actually acknowledge bidirectional influences, with social factors influencing creativity and creativity influencing social settings. Bidirectional influence is implied by the fact that organizations must be structured to support creative work. They are, in a sense, responding to the unique needs of creative people and the creative process. Also consider the concept of the creative class, just described. It, too, will influence society in many ways, but is also a result of societal opportunities and markets (Florida 2002; Rubenson & Runco 1992a, 1992b, 1995). Other examples of creativity as a causal agent are given in Chapter 7. Many eminent creators are discussed therein, and most are well known precisely because of their influence.

BOX 5.4

COGNITIVE RESTRUCTURING

Cognitive restructuring may explain how people have insights. Insights seem to be very sudden (Gruber 1988), and as such there may be an underlying reorganization of thought. This is often called a "restructuring" because the changes actually are occurring in our cognitive structures (e.g., schema, concepts, scripts, stereotypes). Cognitive restructuring of another type allows individuals to intentionally change their perspectives. This allows a reduction of stress, for stress is a matter of interpretation. It is not a direct result of our experience; our experience influences our behavior only after we interpret the experience. Stress reduction through restructuring requires that the individual intentionally monitors and alters his or her interpretations such that what was stressful before is perceived to be less dramatic and harmful. Of course other stress reduction techniques are available. It is a good idea to relax and play, as well as monitoring your interpretations.

The idea of intentional cognitive restructuring applies broadly to social influences on our creative behavior. It may be that we can minimize the impact of inhibitions by changing the way we think. You might even say that creative thinking about these inhibitions will insure that they do not undermine our creative thinking.

Early in this chapter I proposed that the social and organizational perspectives were very practical. There is a bit of a paradox here, for social factors are often extrinsic. They may be interpersonal, for instance, or environmental, and as such they may appear to be out of the individual's control. Yet each is actually controllable. This is in part because of what was said earlier about person–environment interactions and, more specifically, top-down processing. Very few behaviors, cognitive or otherwise, are reflexive. Very few are involuntary. Most are mediated by our interpretive and perceptual tendencies. This implies that each of us does indeed have a great deal of control, even over the influence of other people and the environment.

Society at large should evaluate how we are investing our resources. Consider, for example, investments (or lack thereof) in creative potential and how those differ from investments directed toward formal education. Formal education has fairly clear benefits, including literacy, mathematical skills, and critical thinking skills. These are typical of graduates of a formal educational institution. An employer can assume that he or she will have a literate and cognitively capable individual if he or she invests organizational resources in high school or college graduates. But what if the individual being considered for a job has invested the same amount of time into creative potential rather than formal education? The benefits are much less clear and certain, and therefore the prospective employer is taking a much larger risk by investing in that potential employee. Very frequently people are averse to such risk and do not make investments in people (or anything) that has a risky benefit. For this reason it is likely that much more investment is made into formal education than into creative potentials.

There is a need to decrease the costs associated with creativity, with a parallel increase in the benefits given to creative behaviors. These benefits may take the form of incentives of various sorts. Perhaps that prospective employer needs to take the long view and consider the long-term benefits of creative ideas. Frequently investments do not pay off for quite some time, and therefore are not recognized with a short-term perspective. This may be a political problem, as well, because often decisions are made by the government in response to immediate needs. Simplifying a great deal, an individual who holds office for only four years may use that time frame in making decisions, and therefore devalues potential long-term benefits of investments in creative potential.

Numerous procedures are available for the short term. There are tactics to solve immediate problems in a creative fashion, for example, many of which are outlined in Chapter 6. There are programs for the schools as well (see Chapter 6). Simply put, educators can create opportunities for creative work, model creative behaviors, and support creative efforts. Long-term goals are also needed. If we nurture creativity in young students now, in 15 or 20 years those same individuals will be highly creative members of the workforce.

It isn't enough to have creativity as one part of programs for gifted and talented children. As Walberg and Stariha (1992) pointed out, it is very important to make decisions that allocate resources and support the creativity of all children. The bigger payoff (and perhaps necessary benefit) will result from efforts to nurture the creative potential of everyone.

6

Educational Perspectives

When I look back at all the crap I learned in high school, it's a wonder I can think at all.
Paul Simon, "Kodachrome"
We learned more from a three minute record, baby, than we ever learned in school.
Bruce Springsteen, "No Surrender"

ADVANCE ORGANIZER

- Enhancing Imagery and Artistic Skills
- Meta-analyses
- Implicit Theories of Teachers
- Experience in Teaching as Investment
- Classroom Environment
  - Permissive vs. Test-like
  - Performance-oriented
- Learning Theories
  - Personalized Instruction
  - Self-Efficacy Tolerance
  - Exceptional Students
    - Disadvantaged
    - Gifted

- The Classroom Environment
- Teachers
  - Modeling Creativity in the Classroom
    - The Ideal Student
- Information and Creativity
- Mentors and Informal Education
- Enhancement
- Tactics
- Squelchers
- Education of Older Adults
- The Humanistic View of Enhancement

INTRODUCTION

The first part of this chapter summarizes the educational perspective on creativity. The second part focuses on learning theories and their recommendations for teaching and enhancing creativity. In a sense, the first part focuses on general features of education, including the classroom environment and, of course, the teacher. The second part focuses more on the learning process, which, of course, might be used in the classroom. Learning, however, often does occur informally, outside of the classroom.

There is a pessimistic tone to much of the educational research. This is unfortunate, and in many ways unfair. It is, however, somewhat understandable. The United States, for example, has fallen behind in many creative fields (Florida 2002). Yet it is unfair in that creativity is a difficult educational objective (Rubenson & Runco 1995). It is much easier to build a curriculum for, say, mathematics than art. More generally, creativity is inherently individualistic, and most educational systems involve groups. Where is there room for self-expression in a classroom with 40 students?

Traditional education often stifles the creativity of students. Creativity may require unconventional thinking, for example, and autonomy, and these and other correlates of creativity can make life difficult for a teacher. They are not a part of what is known as *the ideal student* profile (described in detail later). Simplifying some, teachers seem to believe that the ideal student is polite, punctual, conventional, and anything but nonconforming (Raina 1975; Raina & Raina 1971; Torrance 1963a). This is true even though they claim to have great respect for creativity (Dawson et al. 1999; Westby & Dawson 1995)! No doubt they do respect creativity, in the abstract, but not when faced with a classroom with 30 energetic children!

To make matters worse, creativity is somewhat unpredictable. After all, not all unconventional people do highly creative things; you can be unconventional and not be creative. This unpredictability is a huge problem for educators. With the current emphasis on accountability, educators simply do not have the time to invest in curriculum that may not pay off. This problem may be easiest to see if you consider it exactly this way—as a matter of investment in students' potentials (Box 6.1).

BOX 6.1

ECONOMICS OF EDUCATION

One of the more recent theories of creativity is *psychoeconomics*. This may not sound like it applies directly to education, but actually it does help to clarify what needs to be done in the classroom and why there are problems designing education that supports creativity. Consider, for example, the idea of educational objectives. Educators have only so much time in the school day, and just so many resources, and there is a great deal of accountability in today's schools, at least in the United States. This all means that the curriculum must have a clear payoff. Creativity does not. It is often dependent on a student's intrinsic motivation and the self-expression of an individual student. Additionally, creative thinking is original, so by definition an educator will not know what the result will

be if he or she presents an open-ended task that in fact does allow creative thinking. One problem, then, is that the benefits are uncertain and it is difficult to justify the costs (i.e., the investment of time).

Think about it this way: If you were an employer and had to choose between two applicants, who would you choose? One of them had a degree from a good college and had invested four years of his or her life to developing (e.g., verbal and mathematical) traditional skills. The other applicant had invested the same amount of time into his or her creative potential. In the first case you know what you will get. But in the case of the creative applicant, it is hard to say. Creativity is like that; it is an unpredictable commodity.

Then there is the stigma that is sometimes attached to creativity. At the extreme is the "mad genius controversy" (see Chapter 4), which implies that geniuses (or at least creative geniuses) have a tendency toward insanity. Less extreme is the stereotype of creative persons as eccentric and weird. At the very least there is the discrepancy between the creative personality and that "ideal student" (Torrance 1995) just mentioned. If there is any sort of stigma attached to creativity, it is difficult for educators (or parents) to do what it takes to encourage it. In fact, educators need to do at least three things if they wish to support creativity in their students (Runco 1991b):

1. Provide opportunities for children to practice creative thinking.
2. Value and appreciate those efforts.
3. Model creative behaviors themselves.

How likely is it that any of these will be done if there is a stigma attached to creativity?

The same thing can be said about parents and their impact on children. They, too, need to present opportunities, reinforce, and model creativity. Much of what is reviewed in this chapter applies to good parenting and informal education as well as formal education. In fact, a number of topics in this chapter apply better outside the classroom rather than inside. This is true of the idea of optimal experience, for example.

Formal and informal education can support creative talents. More specifically, parents and teachers can insure that children (and adults) fulfill their potential. Of course the message about potentials from Chapters 3 and 9 applies here; there are genetic boundaries. Those boundaries are essentially fixed (at least until genetic engineering advances, and the ethical issues concerning it are resolved), but most important is the range provided by the genetic boundaries. They should be viewed in that way, as potentials for fulfillment and growth and not limits. Each student has the potential for creative expression. What, then, should education do about it?

THE IDEAL STUDENT

One of the problems just mentioned was that of the *ideal student*. What exactly is the ideal student? Do teachers really prefer uncreative students?

Torrance (1972) found that teachers prefer students who are punctual and courteous. They also prefer students who follow assignments. Nonconformity is a problem. Indeed, many of the characteristics associated with creativity (see Chapter 9), including autonomy, unconventionality, and nonconformity, are exactly contrary to the stereotype of the ideal student. Looking across cultures, Cropley (1992) and Raina and Raina (1971) found evidence that teachers view the behaviors and personality traits of creative children unfavorably. Similar views have been found for parents (Raina 1975; Singh 1987).

Getzels and Jackson (1962) compared high IQ and highly creative students and concluded that:

> The data are quite clear-cut. The high IQ groups stands out as being more desirable than the average student, the high creativity group does not. It is more apparent that an adolescent's desirability as a student is not a function only of his academic achievement. Even though the scholastic performance is the same, the high IQ students are preferred over the average students by their teachers, the creativity students are not. This result is quite striking, for if anything, the reverse should be true. Here is a student—the high IQ one—who is doing scholastically only what can be expected of him. Here is another student—the high creativity one—who is

doing scholastically better than can be expected of him. Yet it is the former rather than the latter who is enjoyed more than the average student by his teachers! (Cattell & Butcher 1968, pp. 267–268).

The situation may not be as bad as these findings suggest. There are more positive results in an investigation by Thomas and Burke (1981), who tested the possibility that teachers prefer academic skills over creative talents when working with students. They were also interested in the issue of openness and the possibility that unstructured classrooms are more conducive to creative thinking than highly structured and traditional classrooms. They were well aware of the fact that openness and creativity are each difficult to operationalize and study, and particularly interested in avoiding overly simplistic dichotomies between open and closed groups. In fact, their prediction was that an intermediate level of openness would be conducive to creativity. This certainly makes sense given the available evidence for optima in influences in creativity (Runco & Sakamoto 1996). Cropley (1992) also went into some detail about problems with both overly structured and entirely unstructured classrooms. As Thomas and Burke described it, classrooms should have "a dual emphasis on both fact acquisition and leeway for self-expression … (to) provide the optimal environment for growth and creative ability" (p. 1154). In this sense it may not be so much a matter of optimization but more a matter of allowing structure on certain tasks and informality in other tasks.

Thomas and Burke (1981) studied several hundred children from six schools representing nine school environments. Both six- and seven-year-old children were involved, and data were collected from the children as well as from their teachers and parents. Four raters judged the schools along 10 dimensions (which were identified in earlier research). Schools then were classified as informal, intermediate, or formal, based on composite rankings. The creative thinking potential of the children was assessed with the Torrance figural tests. These were scored for five indices, including fluency, flexibility, originality, elaboration ("the number of ideas added to complete a basic idea"), and a verbal score based on the children's titles for their own drawings. Teachers evaluated the children using the Wallach and Kogan (1965) behavior rating scale. This apparently asks for nine judgments about each individual child and concerns primarily the classroom adjustment. The parents also completed a divergent thinking test and furthermore evaluated their own children with the Ideal Child Checklist.

The 10 dimensions used in the ratings of these schools focused on the acquisition of facts, the distinctiveness or integration of subject matters, academic achievement, methods of evaluation, allowance and recognition of artistic and verbal expression, priority given to self-awareness, evaluation of peer relationships, the system of decision making and rule implementation, the range of behaviors allowed in the classroom, and the range of group behaviors allowed in the classroom.

Results were surprising in that the teachers involved in the study did not seem to view creative children as poorly adjusted. There were significant sex differences, which are not all that common in the research on creative thinking. The hypothesis about intermediate levels of structure and formality in the classroom was only partially supported. In particular, Thomas and Burke felt that increases in divergent thinking were found in both informal and intermediate classrooms.

Thomas and Burke (1981) suggested that discrepancies between their findings, such as those showing teachers to appreciate creative students, might reflect the reliance on nonverbal tests of divergent thinking. This is relevant both to a discussion of school assignments ("What task allows creative thinking?") but also for cognitive theories of creative thinking.

BOX 6.2

SEX DIFFERENCES IN CREATIVITY

Thomas and Burke (1981) found that certain classrooms were better than others in terms of supporting divergent thinking skills. Not surprisingly, the sex of the students moderated the impact of school environment. Thomas and Burke suggested that the girls in their sample may have been more sensitive to school influences than boys.

Sayed and Mohamed (2013) recently summarized the research on gender that has relied on tests of divergent thinking:

> About 100 studies compared the divergent thinking scores between males and females. Nearly 50% of these studies reported no gender differences (Baer 1998b). No gender differences have been reported in the studies of divergent thinking using Wallach and Kogan battery in 5th–8th graders (Runco 1986a), divergent thinking test in 114 4th–6th grade students (Gaynor & Runco 1992), Wallach-Kogan creativity test in 1418 students ranging from 1st–9th grade (Cheung, Lau, Chan, & Wu 2004), and Divergent Movement Ability Test in preschool and elementary school children (Zachapoulou & Makri 2005). Males scored higher than females in the studies of Tegano and Moran (1989) using multidimensional stimulus fluency measure with a sample of preschool, 1st, and 3rd graders. Mixed results were obtained by He and Wong (2011) using the Test of Creative Thinking-Drawing Production (TCT-DP) in a sample of 985 school children, Dudek, Strobel, and Runco (1993) using the verbal and figural forms of the TTCT with 1445 5th and 6th graders, and Chan et al. (2001) using Wallach-Kogan ideational fluency test with 462 elementary students. Cheung and Lau (2010) concluded that females in junior high grades excelled boys in verbal flexibility, figural flexibility, figural uniqueness, and figural unusualness using the electronic Wallach-Kogan creativity tests in a sample of 2476 4th- to 9th- graders and Misra (2003) found female superiority using Openness to experience task with 156 Indian students."

Sayed and Mohamed's (2013) own findings, from 901 students (kindergarten through sixth grade) in Egypt indicated no sex differences, at least in terms of main effects. Sayed and Mohamed did find grade effects, as well as an interaction between grade and sex. The latter was only apparent in three subscales of the nine used. Two of these are clearly related to creativity (both tied to unconventionality) but one is not as clearly tied (i.e., completing incomplete fragments when drawing).

Another extensive review (Runco et al. 2010) looked more broadly at sex differences instead of focusing on divergent thinking. The conclusion was that reports of sex differences in creative thinking are somewhat mixed. Some research has found sex differences, some has not (see Baer 2012). Historically there were clear sex differences, but these certainly reflected the opportunities given to boys and men. Perhaps most important is that although some sex differences have been reported, both boys and girls have a range of potentials. If we focused on average performance, it is possible that differences would be found, but if we look at the entire range of potentials, across all students, we will find mostly overlap. What seems to be best for creative thinking is psychological androgyny (see Chapter 9). This is characteristic of both boys and girls (and men and women) and supports creative thinking much better than stereotypically male or female behaviors (Harrington et al. 1983).

BOX 6.3

NEUROANATOMY OF SEX DIFFERENCES

Many sex differences reflect the opportunities given and expectations directed to boys and girls. There may be biological and neuroanatomic bases as well. The corpus callosum, for example, matures dramatically at puberty, which suggests that interhemispheric communication improves as well. Puberty occurs about one year earlier in girls than boys. This might influence mathematical performance in particular, though it may also influence creative thinking, given the role of the corpus callosum in creative processes (see Chapter 3). Hassler (1992) reported there is an optimal testosterone level for creative musical performance. It is near the lowest level of the range for males and near the highest level of normal female testosterone levels.

BOX 6.4

CREATIVITY TASKS AND ASSIGNMENTS

What kind of assignments are best for creative thinking? Thomas and Burke (1981) suggested that "it is possible that non-verbal expressions of creativity in the classroom may be more acceptable to teachers than verbal creativity and that personality attributes that go along with figural creativity may be more congruent with teacher values and classroom expectations" (p. 1161). Richardson (1986) and Runco and Albert (1985) supported the distinction between verbal and nonverbal tasks, the former referring to the two-factor theory. One factor is verbal, one nonverbal. This is important because some students may be more comfortable with one or the other. In addition, for many students nonverbal tasks are less familiar and thus less likely to elicit rote associates and original ideas. If this is true, nonverbal, visual, and figural assignments would be best for exercising creative thinking.

This is complicated by individual differences. Some students may be less familiar with nonverbal tasks, but that does not mean they are more comfortable with them! Older students in particular might be less familiar with all open-ended tasks, and as a result might not apply themselves. In this case it might be best to employ a fading technique, from learning theory. The student might be given a familiar task that is only slightly open-ended, such as a Similarities task ("How are a potato and carrot alike?"). This should not intimidate them, but it is open-ended. After they develop some comfort with slightly open-ended tasks, they can be given a slightly more open-ended task, such as Uses (e.g., "List uses for a shoe"). In this fashion even students who are accustomed to and uncomfortable with the structure of academic assignments can gradually learn to think divergently and deal with open-ended tasks, be they verbal or nonverbal. This is especially important if we want students to take what they learn in the school setting and apply it to the natural environment. After all, in the natural environment, most problems and tasks are not clearly presented. They are instead ill-defined and open-ended. More will be said about these issues of generalization and fading in the last part of this chapter.

IMPLICIT THEORIES OF TEACHERS

Teachers hold idiosyncratic views about creativity. These have been empirically studied and the specifics of their unique implicit theories of creativity identified.

Implicit theories, including those held by teachers, are best understood by contrasting them with the *explicit* theories, which are held by scientists and researchers. These are explicit in the sense that they must be articulated so they can be shared (via presentations and publications) and tested (via hypotheses and research). For these reasons they must be made explicit. Implicit theories, on the other hand, need not be articulated, shared, nor tested. They are personal, though stable. The implicit theories about children's creativity held by teachers are extremely important because they lead directly to expectations, and expectations are very powerful influences on students' behavior. This reflects the well-known Rosenthal effect (Rosenthal 1991), also called the Pygmalion effect (see Figure 6.1).

PYGMALION IN THE CLASSROOM

The Rosenthal effect is also known as the Pygmalion effect, after a Greek myth. In that myth the King of Cyprus carved a statue of a woman who was so beautiful that he fell in love with her. She was later brought to life by Aphrodite. That is the metamorphosis that implies great potential and great change. Rosenthal's 1991 book was titled, *Pygmalion in the Classroom*. If you do not care for Greek myths, there is a contemporary version, namely, George Bernard Shaw's play, with the metamorphosis of Eliza, which was even more recently made in the movie, *My Fair Lady*. Each of these suggests that great changes are possible.

FIGURE 6.1   1857 painting of Pygmalion. In myth, the statue came to life.

Rosenthal (1991) demonstrated that great changes in students may result from expectations. He did not measure creativity in his own research, but the implications are clear. In his sample, students who were expected to develop quickly and learn a great deal did just that. Students who were expected to have more difficulties and learn more slowly did just that. What was the difference between the two groups? What their teachers expected of them.

Implicit theories (and the expectations they imply) can be identified and defined using the social validation method. This method demonstrated its usefulness in research on exceptional populations. Runco and Schriebman (1983), for example, conducted a social validation in which school-aged children judged the behavior of a group of autistic children. Runco (1984) used social validation techniques to examine the expectations and standards of teachers for creative children. Runco (1989a; Runco et al. 1993) compared the implicit theories of parents and teachers concerning creativity.

Social validation requires two phases. First an open-ended questionnaire is given, and later the contents of it are placed on a checklist, which is then used to collect Likert-scale (quantitative) data. Runco (1984) developed the Teachers' Evaluation of Students' Creativity (TESC) with this method and then asked a sample of school teachers to use it to describe their students. The teacher ratings were correlated with other measures of creative potential, including scores from a test of divergent thinking. The TESC ratings were unrelated to children's IQs. Hence the teachers were identifying creative potential and not just looking for general intelligence. Subsequent studies used the social validation method to examine the implicit theories of parents. Runco et al. (1993), for example, compared parents and teachers, and found that parents and teachers held similar ideas about children's creative traits. The parents and teachers agreed that creative children are often Adaptable, Adventurous, Clever, Curious, Daring, Dreamy, Imaginative, and Inventive. The parents and teachers did not agree very much when asked to describe uncreative children. There was some consensus about uncreative children as Aloof, Cautious, Conventional, Fault-finding, and Unambitious.

Johnson et al. (2003) extended this line of work by comparing teachers and parents in the United States and India. They also collected data about the social desirability of creativity, which is, of course, germane to the question of creativity and the ideal student. Contrary to what might be expected based on the earlier research on ideal students, Johnson et al. found

---

EXPLICIT AND IMPLICIT THEORIES

Explicit theories are scientific. They are held by researchers, scientists, and anyone who must articulate ideas. *Implicit* theories, on the other hand, need not be shared nor tested. They are held by parents and teachers. The implicit theories of parents and teachers have been identified, as have the implicit theories about intelligence, creativity, and wisdom (Sternberg 1985), and about artistic, scientific, and everyday creativity (Runco & Bahleda 1987b). The implicit theories within different cultures have been explored by Chan and Chan (1999), in Hong Kong, and Johnson et al. (2003) in India and the United States. Spiel and von Korff (1998) studied the implicit theories held by politicians, teachers, artists, and scientists.

that their teachers and parents did distinguish between indicative and contraindicative aspects of creativity, and by and large they also viewed creative traits desirably. There were significant differences between the United States and India for attitudinal and intellectual traits, but for the most part parents and teachers agreed with one another about creativity.

TEACHING EXPERIENCE

Interestingly, Lee and Seo (2006) found that teachers with more experience held biased views about creativity. Fortunately bias was apparent only in the recognition that creativity involves cognitive, personal, and environmental components. It is not, then, a bias such that teachers treat creative students poorly. Still, this kind of bias is unfortunate and may lead to inappropriate treatments and expectations. It is troubling that more experienced teachers developed a stronger bias. It is also slightly disturbing that Lee and Seo found that teachers emphasized the cognitive components of creativity and tended to relegate the personal and environmental components. Personal components in this research included motivational and emotional components. These would be very important because they include intrinsic motivation and wide interests, and other commonly recognized critical traits and aspects of the creativity complex.

It makes some sense that the teachers would emphasize the cognitive components of creativity, given that their job is to educate children. This may lead them to assume that they should be increasing the vocabulary of their charges and facilitating problem solving and other intellectual skills. But in terms of creativity, intrinsic interest and other personal characteristics should be recognized. If the environmental components are relegated it may be that teachers do not do enough with the physical environment or even the atmosphere of the classroom. Atmosphere and physical setting of course can exert strong influence on the expression of creativity. People tend to be the most creative when they are in a safe and permissive environment, for instance. This finding about environmental influences being relegated is particularly intriguing because other research on mathematics and achievement test scores has indicated that Asian parents and teachers tend to be more optimistic about the possibility of fulfilling potentials. Apparently it is fairly common in the United States to assume that if a child performs at a particular level, it is because of their innate talents. When a parent or teacher takes this perspective, he or she may not do much to fulfill potentials because performance is presumed to be a given. Asian parents and teachers, on the other hand, apparently tend to view performance as more a reflection of motivation and effort than innate talents. This perspective leads them to encourage hard work and increased efforts.

Another disconcerting finding in Lee and Seo's (2006) research is that the teachers seemed to define creativity in terms of actual products and productivity. That is an objective perspective on creativity because you may be able to count products. A similar finding supports the use of portfolios where students can compile their accomplishments. This is a concern, however, because it may penalize the students who need assistance the most. These are the students with clear potential for creativity but who may be lacking the skills necessary to complete a finished product. They may have huge potential that goes unrecognized because they do not know how to complete the products and projects that will earn attention. It is easy to see that this should be a top priority for educators—to identify and encourage students who are not yet productive but have the potential to be so.

BOX 6.5

INVESTING IN CREATIVE POTENTIAL

Students often are surprised to learn that grades in college can be dramatically improved. Research suggests that most any C student could be a B student, and most any B student could be an A student. Virtually every student can improve one full grade point. All they need to do is invest approximately 20 more hours to their studies each week! So far, none of my own students has reacted well to this news. Instead, they tend to respond with a highly technical explanation for why it will not work, something along the lines of, "Get real Professor Runco."

Yet both academic performance and creative behavior respond well to good hard work. In fact, one of the commonalities among successful creators is their work ethic and persistence. It may be apparent early in life, for prodigies share the same capacity for hard work. Prodigies vary from domain to domain (e.g., chess, music, mathematics), but they share a drive and a willingness to invest time into the subject matter. While most children are jumping rope, prodigies may be reading chess strategies, practicing their instrument, or otherwise investing time into their skills.

The differences between the experienced and less experienced teachers, reported earlier, is not altogether a surprise. Most older adults become less flexible in their thinking (Chown 1961; Rubenson & Runco 1992a, 1995) and tend to follow routines more and more. It is as if they have more knowledge to draw from but rely on it rather than mindfully developing new understandings (Langer 1989; Runco 1990e). Biases and inflexibility are not uncommon among older adults and seem to occur in many fields, not just education. Perhaps the recognition of this tendency to become less flexible as each of us grows older will allow us to avoid bias and remain flexible. Many enhancement techniques are available to anyone who wishes to utilize them (see Chapter 12).

CLASSROOM ENVIRONMENT AND SETTING

It is unfortunate that environmental influences on creativity were not fully appreciated in the social validation research just reviewed. This is because a great deal can be done within the classroom setting to encourage the creativity of students (Figure 6.2). In fact, some of the earliest empirical research on divergent thinking confirmed that the environment plays a critical role. Unless it is permissive and supportive, creative skills will remain hidden.

In the 1950s and 1960s, many people were unconvinced that creativity was distinct from intelligence. This view was supported by early research. Getzels and Jackson (1962), for example, found strong correlations between their measures of creative potential and scores from traditional tests of academic achievement and intelligence. They concluded that creativity was just one kind of intelligence. That conclusion was quickly questioned, however, in part because Getzels and Jackson employed measures of creativity that did not encourage creative thinking. Of most relevance here is that Getzels and Jackson administered their tests of creative

FIGURE 6.2   Much like the home or the organizational setting, the classroom may influence the fulfillment of creative potentials and the expression of creative talents. *Source: Wikimedia Commons, http://commons.wikimedia.org/ wiki/File:W-classroom.jpg.*

potential just as if they were traditional educational tests. The students in that research easily could have fallen into their test-taking mode and not realized that there was an opportunity to think divergently and creatively. (When you take a test in school, did you think about your grade and what was expected of you? If so, you probably were not developing and exploring original ideas, but were instead thinking about correct or conventional responses that would lead to a good grade.) Wallach and Kogan (1965) found that when tests were sufficiently open-ended (and allowed originality and divergent thinking), and when the tasks were administered in such a way as to allow or even encourage independent thinking, there was a difference between creativity and intelligence. Wallach and Kogan gave the creativity tests in a permissive, game-like atmosphere (not a test-like classroom atmosphere). The tests were not called tests; the students were told "These are games … spelling doesn't matter … there are no grades nor incorrect responses … tests are not tests … have fun … take your time." Every effort was put into informing the students that the creativity tasks were not school tests. And it paid off: Students who had performed at a moderate level on the test of traditional intelligence or academic achievement sometimes did exceptionally well on the test of creative potential.

A somewhat different approach to environmental support for creativity is suggested by Carl Rogers' theory of *unconditional positive regard* (Harrington et al. 1983; Rogers 1995). This ties creativity to spontaneity and self-actualization. It also indicates that if an individual is certain that he or she is truly and sincerely respected and appreciated, that individual will be spontaneous and creative. Harrington et al.'s data suggest that this applies to the home, and a large body of research suggests much the same about organizational settings. It could very well apply to the classroom as well. Unconditional positive regard, given by teachers, parents, and friends, will likely contribute to creative expression.

CLASSROOM AS ORGANIZATIONAL SETTING

Many ideas in the industrial and organizational research on creativity support the conclusion that environment and setting influence creative thinking and behavior; much of this can be adapted to the school setting. There are clear parallels between the supervisor in an organization and a teacher, for example, and both should respect an individual's autonomy if creativity is to be encouraged. Both settings involve resources, as well, such as time; and both supervisors and teachers should provide sufficient time if they want their charges to be creative.

TEACHERS AND MENTORS

Teachers can support creative talents in various ways. They can provide unconditional positive regard, for example, but they can do much more than that. They can, for instance, support creativity with particular attitudes and actions. The teacher is, after all, a model for students.

Teachers can model creativity in various ways (Belcher 1975; Runco 1991b). Many students will simply imitate the teacher, which means that teachers should think divergently, solve problems in an original fashion, display flexibility, all with an appropriate amount of discretion (i.e., sometimes unconventional, sometimes conventional). It is not, however, just overt behavior that is important, but also the values that are communicated through those overt behaviors. Teachers may discuss alternatives and thinking divergently when they demonstrate or introduce a topic, and in doing so they will present children with actual divergent ideas but also suggest to them, even without putting it into words, that creativity is a valuable thing, a worthy thing. This is the process of *valuation.* The opposite of valuation is evaluation or criticism. Evaluation should be offered very carefully. Very clearly, evaluation in the form of "squelchers" should be entirely avoided.

MENTORING CREATIVITY

Mentors, like teachers, can encourage creativity. Many famous creators have emphasized the role played by their own mentors (Simonton 1984; Zuckerman 1977). Interestingly, Simonton suggested that mentors and their students should be (only) optimally similar in interests and approaches. If they are too similar, the student merely follows in the footsteps of the mentor. If they are too different, the student probably will not benefit from the expertise and connections of the mentor. This characterization may only apply directly to mentor relationships during adulthood (e.g., college, graduate school, postdoctoral positions). Very likely there is a need for a closer relationship between mentors and younger students.

Squelchers

Educators need to do certain things and avoid doing certain things. As we will see in Chapter 12, creativity is supported by removing blocks and inhibitions as well as by finding supports and encouragement.

Educators certainly should avoid *squelchers*. These are the things we say to ourselves and to others that squelch or inhibit creative thinking (Davis 1999), such as:

- You've got to be serious!
- That's a waste of time!
- That's not my job!
- Too risky!
- It will never work!
- It'll mean more work!
- It will never fly!
- It will cost too much
- Be practical!
- Can't be done.
- Too expensive.

These are just examples—different people have their own idiosyncratic squelchers. If a person is close to his or her parents, for example, the most influential squelcher might be, "What will your parents think?"

Davis (1999) also described the possible inhibition of rules, traditions, policies, procedures, and regulations. He concluded, "like habit, such predetermined guides tend not to promote creativity" (p. 167). This is very true, but is a reminder of the trick to educating for creativity. Educators need to allow creativity but also support socially acceptable behavior. Students should think for themselves but also know when to follow the rules. With this in mind you might think that one of the most important things for creativity is discretion. Not only is "discretion the better part of valor," it is also a big part of the kind of creativity we should encourage in our students—not wild abandonment, but discretionary self-expression.

Immunizing Students

Educators also should avoid emphasizing grades, gold stars, incentives, and other extrinsic motivation. This is because creativity often depends on *intrinsic* motivation. Of course both *extrinsic* motivation and intrinsic motivation can be involved in creative efforts, but intrinsic motivation may allow a student to follow his or her own interests without worrying about pleasing the teacher. The student may be self-expressive instead of conforming. Additionally, extrinsic factors sometimes direct one's thinking. A student may be thinking more about "What does the teacher expect here?" instead of thinking in a self-expressive manner.

The biggest concern is that students will overjustify their actions. Overjustification occurs when a behavior is initially intrinsically motivated, but the individual begins to earn rewards for it as well. Sadly, the intrinsic interests are sometimes lost! It is as if the student sees the rewards and forgets about his or her own interests. After all, if you have one reason for doing something, why worry about other reasons? Rewards may be enough justification by themselves (hence the term, overjustification).

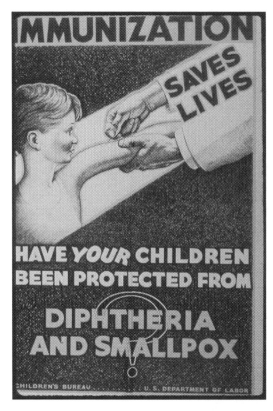

FIGURE 6.3 Just as people can be immunized against disease, so too might they be immunized against the things which inhibit creative thinking. *Source: Wikimedia Commons, http://commons.wikimedia.org/wiki/File:%22Immunization_-_Saves_Lives%22_-_NARA_-_514611.jpg.*

Fortunately students can be immunized such that they will not lose their intrinsic interests (Hennessey et al. 1989; Hennessey & Zbikowski 1993) (Figure 6.3). Apparently role-playing is an effective method for this kind of immunization.

EGO STRENGTH AND SELF-EFFICACY

Runco (2004) also emphasized extracognitive educational objectives. He even suggested that ego strength needs more attention than the cognitive skills used in creative thinking. Ego strength will support a student's self-confidence and allow him or her to follow intrinsic interests. Of course there is an optimal level of confidence, and discretion is also necessary so the student will know when to follow intrinsic interests and when to listen to extrinsic feedback. Ego strength is important because for creative expression "the individual needs to resist pressures to conform his or her thinking, to stand up for his or her own ideas. This will sometimes be contrary to socialization pressures and it may be especially difficult around age 9–10.

This is when children in the USA enter Grade 4 and apparently there is a tendency (around the world) for children to become the most conventional and conforming at that age."

A similar perspective is suggested by research on self-efficacy. Beghetto (2006), for instance, demonstrated that teachers and the classroom environment both influence students' creative self-efficacy. This gives them confidence. It indicates that creative talents are a part of their self-image. In addition to believing in themselves and their own creativity, Beghetto found that students above the mean creative self-efficacy score were more likely to believe that they would attend college than students below the mean. Those above the mean also reported spending more time on homework and reported being more involved in science or language arts activities outside of school. They were similarly more active in after-school art, band, drama, sports, and scouts. This is a very important point given Milgram's (1990) ideas about extracurricular involvements being more predictive of talent than curricular achievements. Very likely such extracurricular involvement is indicative of both self-efficacy and intrinsic motivation.

Students with high levels of creative self-efficacy respond to the ability-related feedback given by teachers. In fact, Beghetto (2006) discovered that "of all the variables included in the model, students' reports of teachers providing feedback on their creativity (i.e., teachers telling them that they were creative) served as the strongest unique predictor of students' creative self-efficacy." Incidentally, Beghetto reported that high- and low-self efficacy groups were not different in the frequency with which they reported watching TV, playing video games, or playing with their friends.

CREATIVE ATTITUDES

Educators need to take various aspects of the creativity complex into account. Creativity results from particular cognitive processes, attitudes, values, motivation, and affect. It has been said that attitudes represent the most malleable part of the creativity complex. Attitudes are very different from personality traits. Personality traits are relatively stable, some even life-long. Attitudes, on the other hand, may shift from day to day, or even hour to hour. A student might think creative people are weird, for example, because they do such unconventional things. Yet if they see someone they admire acting in a creative fashion, or read about one of their favorite musicians and his or her creativity, the underlying attitudes can change very quickly.

Attitudes about creative people are important, but educators should also consider attitudes about creative ideas and about assignments intended to exercise creative skills. After all, if you tell students that "this is just a game, spelling does not matter, and no grades will be given," you could easily lose some students. They may think, "okay, this is not important." That is a reaction that can be changed if students develop good attitudes.

We can again look to psychometric work to identify attitudes that support creativity. One such attitude is openness to ideation, which simply means that the student (and teacher) appreciates divergent thinking and original ideas and solutions. Runco and Basadur (1993; Basadur et al. 2000) assessed this attitude with a short questionnaire (e.g., "original ideas are fun"). Of course, it is equally important to battle the attitudes that can interfere with creative thinking. This includes the attitude labeled *premature closure* (Basadur 1994). For students in the elementary grades, attitudes about people and behavior are probably most important.

That is because students at those ages are extremely sensitive to peer-pressure and "what my friends think." In other words they are highly conventional (Runco & Charles 1997). Davis (1999) described a range of relevant attitudes, and his measure, the *How Do You Think Test*, contains many good examples of both supportive and inhibitive attitudes.

ENHANCING IMAGERY AND ARTISTIC SKILLS

Imagery skills may seem like tangential skills but they do play a significant role in many creative efforts. Imagery is often useful in the arts. It can also facilitate problem solving when transpositions are important (Finke 1990; Houtz & Frankel 1992; Rothenberg 1996, 1999). It is also useful for the comparison of objects and for encoding and storage. After all, "a picture tells a thousand words." Rothenberg (1996, 1999) has demonstrated the benefits of imagery (in particular, homospatial thinking). Admittedly there are other reports of small or nonexistent relationships between imagery and creative works (e.g., Campos et al. 1997; Khatena 1971; Morrison & Wallace 2001). There is also a meta-analysis showing that enhancement efforts focused on imagery were less effective than those focused on ideation (Scott et al. 2004a, 2004b). Still, this may be because it is easier to communicate about (and therefore enhance) ideation. It is not necessarily the case that imagery is inherently less trainable.

Perez-Fabello and Campos (2007) reported that "training in artistic skills considerably enhanced mental imaging capacity." This implies a particular direction of effect, with artistic skill leading to imagery, but of course it can go both ways. Imagery may contribute to artistic skills. Most likely there is a bidirectionality where each contributes to the other. Perez-Fabello and Campos referred to something like this as a "mutual reinforcement." Campos and González (1994, 1995) and Khatena (1971) also reported correlations between imagery and artistic skills.

PROBLEM FINDING AND EDUCATION

Another quite specific educational objective is suggested by the growing literature on *problem finding*. This is a general umbrella label for various processes that precede any problem solving. Quite some time ago Wallas (1926) described the creative process as following four steps: preparation, incubation, illumination, and verification. Newer models are fairly similar, especially in the idea of preparation, which may involve problem identification, problem discovery, problem generation, or problem construction (Csikszentmihalyi & Getzels 1971; Reiter-Palmon et al. 1997; Runco 1994a). A two-tiered model of the creative process is presented in Figure 6.4. There may be some recursion through the steps such that the individual revisits the preparation or incubation stage after attempting to verify an idea. Recursion means just that—it is a kind of recycling back through earlier stages.

Educators may be tempted to present problems to students. They may feel like it is part of the job, to give assignments. Yet problem discovery is an important skill, especially for creative work, and it should also be included in a curriculum, in addition to problem solving. Students need the opportunity to develop questions for themselves, not just answer them. This supports the idea about open-ended assignments, which allow students to follow their

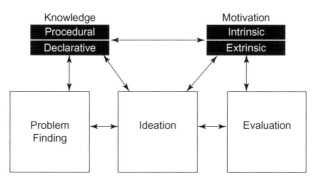

FIGURE 6.4 Two-tier model of creative thinking. The three boxes on the primary tier each represent sets of skills. Problem finding represents problem identification, problem definition, and so on. Ideation represents ideational fluency, originality, and flexibility. Evaluation represents valuation and critical evaluation. Additional components and details are given in the text. *Adapted from Chand and Runco (1992).*

intrinsic interests and define the problem(s) for themselves. Here again there is an important caveat in that education should be balanced. It should not contain only closed- or open-ended tasks, nor only extrinsically or completely intrinsically motivated topics.

REMOTE MODELS

Recall here that educators should consider:

- giving students opportunities for creative thought;
- encouragement for creative thought; and
- modeling of creative behavior.

The last of these can be embedded into the curriculum. Teachers need not be the only models for students' creativity. Students can also experience remote models. These are simply people they do not actually meet. They might experience them via a podcast, a video interview, or in a book. Remote models actually have at least one advantage over other models. They might be famous people, eminent creators. After all, you can read about Einstein.

Educators should, of course, be selective. Not all biographies and autobiographies are of the same quality; and they do not all emphasize creativity. There is one series of biographies that works well with younger students. This is Krull's (1993, 1994, 1995) series of books, *Lives of the Musicians, Lives of the Writers,* and *Lives of the Artists.* These are especially useful both because they discuss creative people, not just any famous person, and because they treat famous people as real people—just plain folks. It would be unfortunate if a book or podcast about a famous person gave the impression that there is a difference between famous people and the rest of us. They are just people, and look at how amazingly creative they were! Krull's books convey this idea that anyone can be creative. It is even in the subtitles—*And what the neighbors thought.* The neighbors had far from favorable impressions of some of the creators. Beethoven's neighbors must have thought he lost his hearing, he plays music so loud! (Actually, he did lose his hearing.)

BRAINSTORMING

The word "brainstorming" is in *Webster's Dictionary*. This may not surprise you, but it should. After all, it was originally technical jargon, a word from the social and behavioral sciences. Not many words make the transition from the sciences to everyday vocabulary. Then again, brainstorming procedures are so popular that it probably is not much of a shock to find it in *Webster's Dictionary*. Still, its lack of effectiveness may surprise you. Hundreds of studies have examined the effectiveness of brainstorming, and it is clear that, as a technique for improving creative thinking, it does not work.

IQ AND WEBSTER'S DICTIONARY

Not many words make the transition from the technical parlance to *Webster's Dictionary*. Yet "brainstorming" did, as did "IQ." The second of these is quite a surprise because there are so many criticisms of it, and because it is just an abbreviation (for Intelligence Quotient). But what wonderful news! Now you can use your Q tile in the game of Scrabble without a U! Ten points! And with a little luck the person competing with you will question it and demand that you consult *Webster's*. Don't forget your victory dance.

Brainstorming relies on three principles and these are essentially guidelines for what a brainstorming group should do:

- Postpone judgment.
- Produce as many ideas as possible. ("Quantity not quality.")
- Work as a group. Piggyback or hitchhike—use someone else's ideas to stimulate your own thinking.

I admit it: I tried to surprise readers with the extreme claim about the ineffectiveness of brainstorming; actually brainstorming has some advantages. It may assist with team building, for example, and students may learn to share ideas and consider other perspectives if they practice working in groups and brainstorming. Furthermore, the very fact that a teacher encourages brainstorming and works it into the curriculum should support the appropriate attitudes we discussed above.

Brainstorming is not the best way to solve problems. If people work alone and then pool their ideas they are more likely to generate larger numbers of more original solutions (Rickards & De Cock, 2012). Actually, brainstorming probably inhibits divergent thinking, because people have a tendency toward *social loafing*. If responsibilities are shared, it is easy to put less effort into the assignment. Most important may be the fact that we are social animals (Aronson 1980), and as such, are very good at reading other people. We can, for example, easily judge the authenticity of someone's smile. (We look to small wrinkles around the eyes, not the amount of teeth showing.) We can also easily determine if someone likes our ideas. They may not say, "What a lousy idea" or actively squelch us (see "Squelchers" above), but they also are unlikely to show the same reaction to ideas that they like as ideas that they do not like.

Evaluations may keep a person from following intrinsic interests and may shift focus to what has been done before or what others think and expect. All of this would be contrary to creative thinking, which is easier when the individual is intrinsically motivated and thinking about new possibilities rather than old solutions. Evaluations that are critical (rather than informational or supportive) are also troublesome because they keep teams and groups from sharing in a way that allows true collaboration. No wonder Rickards (1975) found that organizational members stopped freely speculating when they were assigned to formal brainstorming sessions.

Part of the problem is in the evaluation of ideas. Creative problem solving requires that new ideas are generated, but also that there is some evaluation and selection to insure that the solutions pursued are original. During brainstorming, team members have a tendency to evaluate ideas for practicality and feasibility rather than originality (Rietzschel et al. 2010). One hypothesis is that this is because, in some settings, there is a bias against originality (Mueller et al. 2012). That may be most apparent in organizations, where people are trying to keep their jobs or earn a raise! Yet it may be that it is not a bias as much as it is skill at evaluating ideas. After all, Runco and Smith (1992) found that people are not particularly good at recognizing their most creative ideas, and evaluation is easier than producing all-new ideas. Another hypothesis is that if the teams tend to select the wrong (unoriginal) ideas, explicit instructions (Runco 1986a; Runco et al. 2005a, 2005b) might be able to shift performance towards creativity and away from practicality and feasibility criteria.

Yet another problem with brainstorming is suggested by the tendency of people to follow the "path of least resistance" (Finke et al. 1992; Ward 1994; Ward et al. 2002), only generating ideas that come to mind relatively easily. This is probably related to *satisficing* (using the first solution that comes to mind instead of taking into account all options).

The big problem is risk. If one student works alone and simply writes down ideas, where is the risk? Who is to know if an idea is weird? This is an important question because the most original ideas are the most likely to be misunderstood by others. After all, they are original precisely in the sense that no one else thinks of them! Original ideas, then, are risky. If a student is working alone, there is no problem, at least if the teacher assures students that their ideas need not be shared with the entire class. But put students in *dyads* (a brainstorming group with two members) or, worse yet, a larger group, and the risk increases. And the originality of the ideas decreases.

There are ways to improve on brainstorming. It may help to share examples of good ideas with team members, for example (Dugosh & Paulus 2005), and apparently it is a good idea to break a problem down for a team such that they focus on small problems, within the larger task (Rietzschel et al. 2007). Along the same lines, there is some indication that it helps to require that problem solving in the team is sequential (moving from subproblem to subproblem) rather than all-at-once and simultaneously dealing with all aspects of the big problem.

One especially interesting approach to increasing original thinking involves narrowing, rather than broadening, ideational possibilities. As Rietzschel et al. (in press) put it,

> when people generate ideas about a broad topic, there are many highly accessible and uncreative ideas available; getting 'past' these ideas may be very difficult.... When people generate ideas about a narrow brainstorming problem, it requires less effort to deplete the pool of noncreative ideas, because there are, by definition, fewer noncreative ideas to be found in a narrow problem than in a broad problem. When people continue brainstorming after the most accessible and least creative ideas have been generated, their later ideas will be more original. Thus, expending the same amount of cognitive effort, people are more likely to generate creative ideas about a narrow topic than about a broad one.

Although narrowing might seem, at first, to be contrary to the concept of divergent thinking, it does follow logically from the work of Finke et al. (1992). They found that "restricting domains of interpretation" in a creative task can stimulate creative performance, because this "reduces the likelihood that a person will fall back on conventional lines of thought" (p. 32).

INFORMATION AND CREATIVITY

Next is an issue that cuts across all educational objectives. In particular, how much information should be given to students? This may be an ambiguous question, but that is in part because it applies across so much of the curriculum. It is relevant to all assignments, regardless of topic of subject matter, and all lectures and discussions as well. It is a very important question because creative thinking requires that teachers do not provide too much information, nor too little.

Simply put, excessive information can be detrimental because that can stifle originality. Students can be creative only if they are original, and originality in turn assumes that they are thinking for themselves. Originality requires independent thought; it is by definition novel, unique, or unusual. Thus, if students are given too much information they may have little opportunity to think for themselves.

Consider, in this regard, the television. Television broadcasts preclude active involvement on the part of the viewer. Every program provides sound, action, video, everything. There are 60 frames each second in TV broadcasts, and each frame "tells a thousand words," to borrow that cliché. To make matters worse, the pace is often so fast in TV shows that there simply is not enough opportunity for independent thought, and little if any resulting creativity. Not surprisingly, there are many other things a child can do that will be more likely to be optimally stimulating for creative thought. Sadly, the TV displaces the child and keeps him or her from those other things (Sneed & Runco 1992) (see Figure 6.5).

What about formal education? Does it currently provide the right amount of opportunity and information, or are educators too heavy of hand and providing too much information?

HOW MUCH EDUCATION IS BEST?

Another way of asking "How much information is best?" is to look at education as a whole. Simonton (1984) did just this and asked, "How much education is best?" Historiometric analyses of eminent individuals indicated that you can have too much education! Simonton found optimal levels of education in various fields, with scientific achievement the most likely if a student quits before earning his or her PhD, and politicians better off with only a year or two of college. At the time Simonton published his findings, only one U.S. President had earned a doctorate.

There are empirical demonstrations of how different levels of information influence creative thinking. Runco et al. (2006), for example, demonstrated that basic factual knowledge is correlated with performance on certain kinds of divergent thinking tests, but only if the factual knowledge was in the same domain as the divergent thinking test. Runco et al. (2006)

FIGURE 6.5 Child watching TV. Not much opportunity for creativity.

TABLE 6.1 Questions Used in the Study of how Levels of Information Influence Creative Thinking (Runco et al. 2006)

Subtest A	1. List things that move on wheels
	2. List transportation that might be available in the future
	3. List ways to improve your commute to work or school
Subtest B	1. List names of streets from Orange County
	2. List as many car parts as you can
	3. List different types or names of cars
Subtest C	1. List uses for a shoe
	2. List uses for a brick
	3. List uses for a newspaper
Subtest D	1. List different types or names of plants
	2. List things found in a classroom
	3. List possible careers
	4. List book titles

Subtest C was based on the Uses Test from Wallach and Kogan (1965). Question 1 was from their Instances test. Their figural (visual) test was also given.

worked with college students at a commuter university, and hence used "transportation" as one realistic domain of knowledge. Some of the questions they used are listed in Table 6.1. Subtest A represents divergent thinking test questions that might draw on knowledge about transportation but would also allow originality. Scores on it were correlated with those from

Subtest B, which draws on transportation knowledge but has much less opportunity for originality. It is much more factual. Scores from these two tests were correlated, indicating that factual knowledge is relevant to divergent thinking. Scores from Subtests C and D were not related to one another, indicating that factual knowledge does not always play a role in divergent thinking. It only helps when there is a common domain (e.g., transportation). The scores from the figural test were also unrelated to factual knowledge.

These results imply that students might benefit, to some degree, by learning facts, but that there is probably more to thinking in an original fashion than just knowing the facts. It seems that divergent thinking might also be better exercised if tasks are not dependent on factual knowledge. Runco et al. (2006) concluded that certain exercises and tests of divergent thinking might actually be slanted, much like the experimental bias that plagues some of the older tests of IQ.

Recall here that a great deal depends on what is conveyed in the instructions or directions given by educators. Creative expression can be encouraged or discouraged even before students actually begin their work! Consider in this regard the research summarized earlier about permissive environments. Wallach and Kogan (1965) encouraged divergent thinking in part by being certain that the students approached the assigned tasks as games rather than tests. Students were told to play and not worry about time, grades, spelling, and the like. The result: good separation of divergent from convergent thinking and more originality from the students. It is relatively easy to introduce creativity exercises with "Now we have some games—time to be original!" but later introduce academic tests with something like "Now it is time to show me what you have learned from your reading assignment—watch your spelling!" This is a big part of creative potential: knowing when to be original and when to draw from memory. Educators can help with original thinking, with memorization, and with the decisions involved in knowing the difference.

EXPLICIT INSTRUCTIONS

Instructions and directions are a critical part of academic work and have a significant impact on creativity exercises. For those reasons, they have been examined many times in the creativity research. A multitude of task and test directions have been examined and the methods for encouraging creative thinking greatly refined. This research suggests that several aspects of directions are important. Directions, for example, might convey a process to students ("Here is how you should think about this task") or they may convey standards and criteria ("Here is the kind of idea or solution you should attempt to find"). The former are *procedural* instructions and the latter *conceptual* instructions (Runco et al. 2005). The research also suggests that different processes can be targeted. The originality of ideas can be encouraged with one kind of instruction (e.g., "Think of ideas that no one else will think of") and flexibility with another (e.g., "Think of a variety of ideas … tap different categories or themes"). Fluency can also be encouraged ("Give as many ideas as you can … the more, the better"). There are a number of different explicit instructions that can be used.

Educators must provide opportunities for creative thinking. Open-ended tasks allow divergent thinking, and questions often can be worded such that there is room for originality. Suppose an elementary school student raises his or her hand and asks, "Why is Sacramento the capital of California?" The teacher could respond, "Because of the Gold Rush. Do you know other state capitals?" A better response might be, "In part because of the Gold Rush and what was going on in California when they chose a capital. Can you think of other reasons besides the Gold Rush that could explain it?" This is a bit more open-ended. It does convey the important facts and suggest that it is good to know them. But it also allows for divergent thinking.

Note that it also treats information as conditional rather than absolute. Langer (1989) demonstrated that when people deal with absolutes they are relatively mindless, meaning that they just remember a fact and do not really invest any thought into it. They rely on existing knowledge structures and are not very original. But when knowledge is conditional instead of absolute, there is room for creativity. The individual can think in new ways and perhaps develop new insights and conceptual understandings. There is room for creativity.

Incidentally, the benefits of explicit instructions in part might reflect the fact that they are given before students start working and thereby provide a kind of advance organizer. The advantage of an advance organizer is that individuals understand that structure of knowledge right up front. They know how to think about and organize the information and do not need to devote resources to that, but instead can concentrate on what is to come. Advance organizers now are found in most text books, such as this one, because they facilitate learning. Explicit instructions are probably also effective because they inform students about the criteria for success (e.g., "Give only original ideas") and sometimes about the processes that will lead to success (e.g., "Give only ideas that no one else will think of").

TO UNDERSTAND IS TO INVENT

"Instructions" denote teaching, whereas "directions" may merely guide the individual and may not instruct in a strict sense of the word. What are often called instructions are frequently merely directions. This is an important point for educators, and parallels a debate concerning education as a whole. Piaget (1976), for example, suggested that one kind of education leads only to memorization and superficial learning (and often would have a teacher directing rather than instructing), but actual understanding is more likely to result from education (and "instructions") that allows students to think about and use the information. The title of his monograph, *To Understand is to Invent*, shows how relevant this is to studies of creativity.

LEARNING THEORIES

The heading of this section is plural because there is more than one learning theory. The different learning theories all focus on changes in behavior resulting from experience, but they differ in terms of the kinds of behaviors that change, and the kinds of experiences that lead to those changes.

Operant theory focuses on consequences: behavior changes when the individual has an experience that has led to either reinforcement or punishment. All *reinforcers*, even negative reinforcement, increase the probability that the behavior will be emitted again in the future. All *punishers* do the opposite: lower the probability that behavior will be emitted again in the future.

Operant Theory

It may come as a surprise to hear that learning theories deal with creativity. That is because "creativity" is not necessarily observable, and learning theories, especially operant theory, prefer overt behaviors.

It will not come as a surprise to hear that operant theories of creativity emphasize reinforcement and experience and deemphasize internal states and motives. Skinner (1972) expressed discontent over the view that an artist could be understood without taking the environment into account:

> Why, indeed, do artists paint pictures? The traditional answers are not very helpful. They refer to events supposedly taking place inside the artist himself.... They represent the artist as a complex person living a dramatic life, and they give him exclusive credit for the beautiful things he creates.... Nor does the traditional view help us in furthering the production and enjoyment of art.

Skinner used the idea of reinforcement history to explain art and creativity. Artists, for example, even when not immediately rewarded for their creativity, still behave in a fashion that reflects what reinforcement they previously have experienced. He felt that in their pasts, they must have been reinforced for creative behaviors, and for that reason continue to display

---

BOX 6.6

OPERANT TERMINOLOGY

- *Operant*—A voluntary behavior that is emitted to earn a reinforcer or avoid a punisher.
- *Positive reinforcement*—A consequence that, when given to a person, increases the likelihood of behavior being emitted in the future.
- *Negative reinforcement*—A consequence that, when taken away, increases the likelihood of behavior being emitted in the future.

- *Punishment through withdrawal*—A consequence that, when taken away, decreases the likelihood of behavior being emitted in the future.
- *Punishment through application*—A consequence that, when given to the person, decreases the likelihood of behavior occurring again.
- *Extinction*—behavior disappears because it is not reinforced. "Time out" can be viewed as a kind of extinction.

them. In this way Skinner was able to explain the production and the appreciation of artwork as controlled by the consequences given to the discrete behaviors involved in each. Though it is an extreme view and seems to relegate the emotions and motives of the artist, the concept of reinforcement histories is useful. It suggests that educators can provide a sound foundation for creative thinking while students are in the classrooms, and if the reinforcement is given correctly, those students may continue to behave in a creative fashion long after they complete their education.

Epstein (1990) circumvented the problem of creativity by looking to a more observable and operational behavior, namely *insight*. This is defined as a sudden solution to a problem. It may seem to come out of nowhere, but most researchers agree that insights have histories and the process is actually protracted (Gruber 1988). Epstein preferred the concept of insight over creativity because in the former, the solution resulting from an insight can be seen. The individual may not know initially how to solve a problem, but given the right experiences (and reinforcement), he or she may have an insight and can then solve the problem.

Insights, for Epstein (1990), result from spontaneous integration of previously learned responses. Such an integration was demonstrated in several projects with pigeons, and later with college sophomores. In both cases subjects learned specific discrete behaviors, and then at a later time spontaneously integrated these in what appears to be an insightful solution to a problem. In actuality the insight is merely a new combination of those discrete skills that were reinforced and learned at an earlier time. This research is impressive in its experimental control. It is limited, however, by its assumption that creativity is dependent upon insight and thus one kind of problem solving. Creativity might very well be more than problem solving and reflect a kind of self-expression where there is no clear-cut problem.

The insight problems given to the pigeons in Epstein's (1990) research were adapted from much earlier investigations (Kohler 1925) of the insightful problem-solving skills of chimpanzees. One of these involved placing a chimpanzee in a cage with a banana slightly out of reach. A stick is placed in the cage, and chimpanzees typically demonstrate insight and solve the problem of reaching the banana by using the stick. Another problem involves a banana hanging out of reach from the ceiling of the cage. Boxes are placed in the cage, and after the chimpanzee's initial difficulty, it solves the problem in what appears to be a sudden flash of insight.

Epstein's (1990) view was that problem solving can be controlled by consequences given to behaviors. These consequences were administered as part of special training. Epstein administered Kohler's insight problems to pigeons, but first he conditioned them. "Conditioning" in this context refers to training. It involves breaking down the solution into discrete steps, and then using operant principles to reinforce each of these discrete behaviors. One discrete behavior might be pushing a small box; another might be pecking a banana (disguised pigeon chow) on a string. Insight is then demonstrated by putting the pigeons in the cage and showing that they spontaneously integrate the distinct responses into one appropriate chain—that is, into a solution. Epstein demonstrated that four and even five discrete steps can be integrated by a pigeon.

Epstein thus demonstrated that pigeons can solve insightful problems, even though their cognitive abilities are no match for those of the chimpanzee. The implication is that this type of problem solving can be explained without reference to cognitive processes. All that is necessary, in Epstein's view, is the right conditioning and experience. Even a pigeon can do it.

THE CREATIVE PORPOISE

Operant procedures have been used to teach porpoises to emit novel behaviors (Figure 6.6). The porpoises were conditioned with a reinforcement procedure called *shaping*, and the target behavior—novelty—defined in terms of behavior that had never before been emitted (Pryor et al. 1969). This may be relevant to creativity because creative behavior is novel, just as it is original.

FIGURE 6.6   The creative porpoise can be trained. *Source: Wikimedia Commons, "This work is in the public domain in that it was published in the United States between 1923 and "1977 and without a copyright notice." http://commons.wikimedia. org/wiki/File:Marineland_of_Florida_porpoise_1963.JPG.*

Behavioral research with pigeons, porpoises, and other species certainly gives us one explanation of how some behaviors can be controlled. This information is useful for the operant technology, and may be utilized in particular educational settings. Furthermore, it is a very objective technique. There is little judgment involved in determining what is novel. Granted, there is the question of whether or not all insightful and creative behaviors can be related to previous experiences. Some insight problems may be related to experience; but where is the connection between Einstein's theories of relativity and his previous experience? Truly revolutionary ideas may have their impact and be deemed "creative" because they offer a break from the past. Revolutions may result from paradigm shifts more than a gradual accumulation of knowledge and skill (Kuhn 1962).

A final question concerns what actually is being explained by conditioning insight and novel behavior. Overt and discrete behaviors are reinforced, but where does the actual interconnection of repertoires take place? Where is the spontaneous integration? We have no direct data on the actual connections, only on the novel behavior supported by them. This makes little difference to operant theorists. What is important is actual performance.

That idea may appeal to educators as well. Certainly, the operant perspective is extremely useful. It suggests, for example, that insights may be influenced by previous experiences, and that reinforcement does not necessarily undermine the relevant behaviors. It suggests further that educators should provide students with small, manageable, discrete objectives and information rather than huge and grand lessons and projects. Discrete lessons may later be integrated spontaneously in useful and creative ways.

GOODBYE TEACHER

Many of the same ideas about reinforcement, discrete behaviors, and gradual progress are used in the Personalized System of Instruction (PSI). PSI is personalized in that students work alone. For this reason, Keller's (1968) description of the PSI was titled, "Goodbye teacher." In his article he argued that operant techniques can be used in the classroom (also see Skinner 1985). In particular, he proposed that

- Each student works at his or her own pace.
- There is a "clear specification of terminal skills" (p. 79).
- Students receive immediate feedback.
- Students master the assigned material.

This is very different from most courses, where every student does the work according to one syllabus and on one schedule; where grades are sometimes not given to students immediately (days may pass before exams or papers are returned); and where students must accept whatever grade they receive on a test, paper, or quiz. They usually do not retake exams—except in PSI. There they must retake examinations (alternative forms, of course, not the exact same examination) until they achieve unit mastery. This means that a student focuses on one unit, one topic, one assignment, until he or she fully understands it. Keller's own students did not move on until they had earned a 95% or better on the examination or quiz in question. It was likely to be a quiz rather than an extensive exam, given the principle of operant theories that well-defined discrete behaviors are learned most easily. Research testing PSI has supported its usefulness.

Reese and Parnes (1970) tested something very similar to PSI, known as programmed instruction, and targeted several of Guilford's (1968) divergent production tests (e.g., Alternate Uses and Consequences), one of Torrance's (1974) tests (Product Improvement), and a creativity scale from the California Psychological Inventory (CPI). The design of this investigation required three groups: a programmed instruction group, an instructor-trained group, and a control group (all high school seniors). The programmed instruction and instructor-led groups received two 40-minute sessions each week for one semester (13 weeks). The former worked individually using booklets, with proctors available for answering administrative questions. The latter used the same booklets, but as implied by the name of their group, they worked in a "conventional classroom fashion," complete with instructors. This group was encouraged to discuss the material with one another and with the instructors. In general, posttest evaluations indicated that the instructor-led group was significantly more creative than the programmed instruction group, and both experimental groups were more creative than the control group. This was true of three of four divergent thinking fluency measures and the one elaboration measure. No differences were found on the creative personality index of the CPI.

Reese et al. (1976) used programmed techniques in a two-year (four-semester) college course. Like Reese and Parnes (1970), Reese et al. used several of Guilford's (1968) tests to evaluate the efficiency of the program. They also examined "idea-finding," "knowledge and recognition of ideas," and "judging ideas." Thus the divergent and convergent facets of Guilford's structure-of-intellect (SOI) model were represented. In fact, because different facets of Guilford's model were emphasized in each semester of the experiment, 45 measures were used in this study. This is an impressive array of tests, and probably representative of the SOI model, but it also may have contributed to the rate of attrition: 70% of the original 150 experimental subjects completed the course, and only 37% of the original 182 control subjects. As Reese et al. pointed out, these figures bring the external validity of the findings into question. For this reason, after the program and measures were completed, the researchers compared those who completed the course with those who did not. Because of the limited data, these comparisons included only pretreatment scores, but there was very little indication that those who completed the program differed from those who did not. Additional comparisons indicated that the students who received the program performed better than the control subjects in the SOI tests of cognition, convergent production, and divergent production. There were no significant differences in memory, nor in the tests of evaluations. Those familiar with the SOI model will be interested to know that the experimental group had higher scores than the control subjects in the semantic and behavioral contents, but there were no differences in the figural or symbolic contents. The experimental group also exceeded the control group in most of the SOI "products" (e.g., units, classes, systems).

Glover and Gary (1976) evaluated the effects of reinforcement, practice, and instructions on various facets of divergent thinking, including fluency, flexibility, originality, and elaboration. They had eight fourth- and fifth-grade children practice a type of Alternative Uses divergent thinking task. Each day a teacher printed a noun on the blackboard, and students had 10 minutes to "list all possible uses for that object." During the five-day baseline, reinforcement was given to each student for fitting ideation. The experimental or treatment condition was started on the sixth day of the study. It involved a discussion (and definitions) of fluency, flexibility, elaboration, and originality, and competition between two groups (each half of the class) for the best ideas. The team that scored the most points was reinforced with early recess, and milk and cookies. On days 7 through 25, one of the four indices was chosen, and the groups competing again focused on that one dimension of divergent thinking.

The Torrance Tests of Creative Thinking (TTCT) was administered to the children as a pretest and as a posttest. The results indicated that three of the indices increased in response to reinforcement. This was especially true of the fluency and flexibility scores. Elaboration scores did not increase significantly. Unfortunately, the treatment used in this study was tripartite. It involved reinforcement, instructions, and practice. Reese et al. seemed to be interested primarily in whether or not these standardized indices of creativity were susceptible to treatment, rather than what part of treatment was most effective, and this experimental design did not allow the unique contribution of each treatment to be assessed. Nonetheless the findings are convincing, especially because it is entirely consistent with research reported by Campbell and Willis (1978). Campbell and Willis used tokens for reinforcing the creative ideation of fifth-grade children and found that each of their measures showed the improvements expected by their multiple baseline research design.

This line of research is important because it confirms that operant procedures can be applied to behaviors that are traditionally recognized as indicative of creativity. It is disappointing that so few investigations have assessed the critical and evaluative components of creativity. Reese et al. (1976) did assess "judging ideas," but apparently did not find any instructional effects. Also, they defined judgment in terms of the SOI model, where evaluation is somewhat convergent and not the kind of evaluative thinking that is better used with divergent thinking (Chand & Runco 1992; Runco 1994a).

It is also disappointing that the efficacy of displaced practice with measures of creative potential has yet to be studied (e.g., Mumford et al. 1994). Displaced practice may be the most powerful form of learning. The idea is simple: Students learn best when they practice material, and the impact of practice is best when it is spread over several periods of time. It would be best, then, to work on divergent thinking, or some other creativity task, for 30–60 minutes, and then put that aside for the remainder of the day, and then invest another 30–60 minutes on another day. If four hours are invested all at once and the results compared with those of four one-hour sessions, the latter is likely to be much more effective.

GENERALIZATION AND MAINTENANCE

The downside of many operant techniques is that what a student receives or hears in the classroom may not carry over to the natural environment. This is true of most formal education; the effects may not generalize. Fortunately there is a technology of generalization and maintenance (Stokes & Baer 1977). Maintenance is most likely if the reinforcement is given intermittently. If it is predictable, and students depend on it, extinction will occur as soon as three or four behaviors are displayed without reinforcement. Here again it is important to move in a gradual way. It is often best to start with plenty of reinforcement but gradually thin the schedule such that students work for quite some time for even one reinforcer. Intermittent reinforcement also can be used but only if the schedule gradually moves from a fixed one to the less predictable and intermittent one.

Generalization occurs when a skill or lesson is applied across settings (e.g., the classroom and the natural environment), and maintenance occurs when it endures (from one time to another). Generalization is the most likely if students realize the value of what is being taught. They will attend more to the lesson or exercise and are more likely to think about it later, in other settings. Generalization is also most likely if the practice is varied. If an educator works only with Alternative Uses questions as exercises, for example, students may not recognize that ideational fluency, flexibility, and originality will help them in other kinds of open-ended tasks. If an educator practices Alternative Uses tasks, but also Instances, Similarities, Pattern Meanings, and perhaps some other forms of divergent thinking tasks that are discussed in Chapter 9, the student is more likely to realize that the various ideational skills apply across tasks and environments. Generalization is likely.

Realistic tasks are especially likely to encourage generalization. Several of these are described in Chapter 9. They often ask students or the respondent to solve problems that they themselves have encountered, or could encounter. The task should allow creative thinking, and thus will probably be open-ended, but this is easily done. Runco and Chand (1994), for example, used realistic divergent thinking tasks in their investigation of the impact of explicit instructions. They confirmed that performance on realistic tasks is more predictive of creative accomplishment in the natural environment than is performance on unrealistic tasks. Incidentally, they included problem generation tasks, much like those described earlier.

The operant procedure known as *fading* could be used as well. In fading, students are given a great deal of assistance with the creativity tasks. The tasks used should also be fairly easy and intuitive. When those tasks are mastered and the student is comfortable with them, slightly more challenging tasks are presented. When these are mastered, even more challenging tasks are presented. The tasks do not need to be challenging in the sense of difficulty but might increasingly resemble the kinds of problems found in the natural environment. Generalization may also be most likely if assignments contain instructions about the natural environment.

Many parents and teachers use a kind of fading without thinking much about it. Suppose a parent is teaching a child to hit a baseball. At first the parent teaching the child may provide a huge but lightweight bat, a big inflatable ball ("you can't miss!"), and simply hold the ball until the child strikes it. Later, the parent may lob the ball gently. The parent is fading, gradually removing the assistance and slightly later may change to a real bat, a tee for the ball, and a softball. Eventually the parent is throwing a hardball to the child's strike zone at 90 miles per hour … well, perhaps that is exaggerating the final stage of fading, but it makes the point that fading gradually changes the task. Teachers might give explicit instructions about tactics with simple divergent thinking tasks (e.g., "Name all of the square things you can think of") and prompt the individual at first, but then gradually change the practice tasks, making them more and more realistic, and finally the student is practicing the tactic with problems that resemble the challenges of the natural environment. Generalization is, at that point, the most likely.

META-COGNITION

Something should be said about lifelong creativity. After all, much of what is done in the educational setting is intended to help students in the natural environment, and ideally it will also help them throughout their lives. This is no easy task, given how quickly things are changing. Yet creativity is particularly useful in this regard. As Bruner (1962a) said, "we must prepare our students for the unforeseeable future." They will be able to deal with the future if they develop creative skills.

In this light the most important creative skill may be meta-cognitive. This is literally "cognition about cognition," and includes self-reflection, self-monitoring, and conscious decisions about how to react to experience. Recall here the need for students to make choices and to exercise discretion about when to be original and when to conform. Meta-cognitive skills will be useful in the natural environment through the life span, and allow individuals to invest in their creativity, battle routine, and choose mindfully, tactics for creative action.

BOX 6.7

WRITING POETRY IN THE CLASSROOM

When was the last time you wrote poetry? Do you know how to write poetry? I often use a poetry task along with fading in the classroom (adapted from Hennessey et al. 1989). I use a short, well-structured poem, much like haiku. This allows me to begin with an easy task, it is so well structured. I might, for example, ask my students to write a poem with the following requirements:

- It must contain five lines.
- The first line contains only one noun (I give them the noun, something like "insect").
- The last line contains only one noun— and it is the same one as in line 1!
- The second line of the poem contains two words, both of which are adjectives that apply to the noun in line 1.
- The third line contains only three words, but each is an action word that could be applied to the noun.
- The fourth line contains any number of words, and any kinds of words.

That may not sound like it allows much self-expression, but you'd be surprised. The results are often impressive, given that students just learned the technique and write for only a few minutes. But what is more important is the fading. We do the same task a second time, but with some fading. I usually allow them to pick their own noun. Everything else remains the same. We write a third poem, usually on a different day, which has even less structure, because of the fading procedure, and so on, until students make all the decisions themselves. This exercise demonstrates fading, with results that are unambiguously creative.

The nouns used are somewhat important. They should be evocative and widely meaningful (e.g., sunshine, hope, children, butterfly). Osgood et al. (1975, p. 72) presented a list of words with universal meanings, which might be very useful for poetry writing.

Then again, the best poems result from the least structure, when students choose their own nouns. I will never forget one of my students, a university senior, who was given the last assignment and chose as her noun, "my ex-boyfriend." The fourth line of her poem was, "What was I thinking?"

DISADVANTAGED CHILDREN AND REINFORCEMENT

As you might expect, given the corpus of research on the perspective of creativity, educators might employ reinforcement. They might, for example, selectively reinforce convergent or divergent thinking, or a combination of the two, and do so selectively, depending on task demands. As a matter of fact, reinforcement would be quite important because educators may need to combat and compensate for children's tendencies to conform to peer pressure and their general conventionality, especially in the fourth grade. There is a potential problem in that reinforcement can undermine the intrinsic interests of students (Amabile 1990; see Chapter 9), but this kind of overjustification can be avoided. Epstein (1990), Glover and Gary (1976), Moran and Liou (1982), and Milgram and Feingold (1977) each describe the role of reinforcement in creativity. Apparently it is particularly useful with exceptional students. Moran and Liou, Milgram and Feingold, and Ward et al. (1972) each described the benefits of concrete reinforcement for the creative efforts of disadvantaged students. Moran and Liou actually uncovered a differential effect of reinforcement, with the concrete reinforcers enhancing the performance of children with below-average verbal skills but inhibiting the performance of average students. This may be a general tendency, given that Milgram and Feingold found something very similar in their research with disadvantaged Israeli students. They found benefits to both concrete (i.e., candy) and verbal (i.e., praise) on tests of divergent thinking.

Eisen (1989) and Runco (1992a) also described the creativity of disadvantaged children. Bruch (1975) explored the creativity of "culturally different children." Fortner (1986) concluded that learning disabled students could benefit from a program of "productive thinking," and Gold and Houtz (1984) felt much the same about "educable mentally retarded" students. Holguin and Sherrill (1990) took a reasonable approach with "learning disabled boys" and focused on their motor (nonverbal) creativity. As they pointed out, it is often useful to take confidence and attitude into account when studying disadvantaged populations, rather than focusing on cognitive potentials alone. Johnson (1990) described the creative thinking potentials of "mentally retarded deaf adolescents," and Marschark and Clark (1987), the verbal and nonverbal creative potentials of children with hearing impairments. Platt and Janeczko (1991) demonstrated how art activities can be adapted to the needs and talents of disabled students. (Many labels for special populations are no longer used, some because of their connotations about learning and implied value judgments. A few of the original labels are retained here for specificity. The more recent labels, such as disadvantaged, are indeed much better and avoid unfortunate connotations. They are, of course, still labels, and often still generalizations.)

It is vital to recognize the diverse forms creativity may take in disadvantaged populations (Runco 1992a; Solomon 1974; Swensen 1978; Torrance 1968a, 1971). It may be, as just noted, for example, nonverbal. An appreciation of diversity should be the norm in our educational system (and indeed, around the world, in all aspects of life), but it is especially critical for creativity. Creativity assumes diversity; it requires individuality, and that individuality may be tied to the special backgrounds and potentials of disadvantaged populations.

GIFTED STUDENTS

The discussion of disadvantaged students suggests that educational procedures should be adjusted for different individuals and different populations. As a matter of fact there is strong reason to think about educational programs specifically for the enhancement of creativity of gifted children.

The separation of traditional intelligence and creativity does not imply that intellectually gifted children are never creative. Far from it! Although most gifted and talented programs in the United States still rely entirely on the IQ to select participants (usually based on an IQ of 130, which puts them in the 99th percentile), there does seem to be a trend toward the more reasonable view that giftedness includes creative talents. Renzulli (1978), for example, defined giftedness in terms of general ability (e.g., the IQ), creative potential, and task motivation. Milgram (1990) and Albert (1980) also have lobbied convincingly for recognition of creative potentials within gifted and talented programs.

BOX 6.8

INDIVIDUALIZED EDUCATION

Virtually every major theorist (e.g., Piaget, Skinner, Vygotsky) has pointed to individualized instruction. Skinner (1972) found reinforcement to be effective only for certain individuals, or at least certain individuals to react to particular reinforcers. Very frequently, when fading or any other operant procedure fails it is simply because the consequence was not powerful enough, and what worked with others does not work with everyone.

Yet not all highly intelligent children behave in a creative fashion, nor do they fulfill their creative potentials. In fact, some time ago Hollingworth (1942) found that children with IQs of 180 (which puts them in the 99.99999% percentile) have difficulty being original. They also experience anxiety when there is no one correct answer for some problem or task. That puts them at a serious disadvantage in the natural environment, since so few problems in the natural environment are so clear-cut. It implies that it may be that individuals will be best prepared to deal with life (i.e., the natural environment, such as after graduation) if they develop their creative skills. These may be more important than the memorization and convergent thinking that is all too common in many schools.

None of this suggests that creativity is unrelated to intelligence or to academic aptitude. The threshold theory suggests that creativity and intelligence may be moderately related, at least at certain levels of ability, and research summarized immediately following shows how creativity may help students even while they are in school.

CONCLUSIONS

Education can influence the creativity of students in various ways. One general perspective focuses on opportunities to practice creative thinking, support for creative behavior, and modeling and valuation of creative thinking and creative behavior. Educators should also inculcate values that appreciate creative things. They must be careful to balance intrinsic and extrinsic motives and avoid overjustification. Ideally all of this will complement what the student experiences in the home and in society as a whole. A child will have the greatest chance of fulfilling creative potentials if he or she has both a challenging and supportive home life and a challenging and supportive educational experience.

Various specific educational objectives and techniques were described in this chapter. Ideation was targeted in much of the research, but attitudes, values, and motives must also be considered. The entire creativity complex should be recognized by the educational system, not just specific cognitive skills. In fact, although we can target specific educational objectives, these should not distract us from the broad view. Just over 40 years ago Getzels and Jackson (1962, p. 124) called for a general improvement in the support given to creativity:

Boldness in thinking, free rein to the imagination, and creativity in performance will not be easily forth-coming through piecemeal lessons and artificial stimulants. What is needed is a change in the entire intellectual climate in which we the parents and the teachers as well as the children function. We need alteration in parental attitudes towards giftedness and towards success, change in the attitudes of teachers towards highly creative students and in the attitudes the children themselves acquire probably even before they come to school. It is the general climate … that needs transformation.

Anyone working with students should keep in mind that there are things you can do for children to effectively stimulate their intelligence and character, but that do nothing for creativity. Creative talents are distinct from other talents, and you might do something that benefits a child (say, practice a particular academic skill) that does nothing for the child's creative talents. This is implied by most of the work in this text, and in the field of creativity studies. Recall here that there is some overlap between creativity and traditional intelligence, but the two are far from synonymous. Moreover, the skills underlying traditional intelligence (and things like high grades in school) are very different from those that support original and creative thinking. This is especially clear in the dichotomy of convergent and divergent. It is also apparent in many educational and IQ tests, where the individual finds the one correct answer by searching his or her long-term memory. There isn't much room for original thought there! That can be contrasted with tasks that are open-ended and allow an individual to spontaneously construct or otherwise develop something new (e.g., an idea, solution, insight, or direction for further thought). With this in mind you can probably walk into a bookstore, looking for a gift, and buy books that would be very good for a child but would do nothing for the skills necessary for creative thinking. The same holds for a toy store, or for the development of curriculum. If you want creativity, you should target creativity. Recall also that some studies show that some children with very high IQs actually have difficulty thinking creatively (Hollingworth 1942).

In many ways this chapter complements Chapter 2, with its developmental perspective on creativity, but also Chapter 1 and the cognitive perspective. Given what was said about metacognition, Chapter 12 will be useful, and given the earlier proposal about the parallels between the organizational setting and the classroom, it is also quite possible that additional tactics and strategies could be adapted from the industrial and management literature, which is quite extensive. As a matter of fact, one very useful tactic for creative thinking involves "borrow or adapt." Often good ideas are found by looking "outside the box," so to speak, and in areas that overlap but are not identical with one's own field. In the present case educators might find a creative idea for the classroom by looking outside the educational literature (and in the industrial and organizational literature).

7

History and Historiometry

We are entering an Age of Unreason … a time … for thinking the unlikely and doing the unreasonable. **Charles Handy, The Age of Unreason (1991, p. 4)**
Perhaps our posterity will find today's truth tomorrow's error. **Boring (1971, p. 64)**
The dead make up the majority. **Boring (1971, p. 56)**

ADVANCE ORGANIZER

- The Historical Perspective
- *Zeitgeist*
- Multiples
- The Dark Side
- Matthew Effects

- Planck's Principle
- Trigger Effects
- Historiometry
- Marginality

INTRODUCTION

The invention of the airplane is surely one of the most important achievements of the twentieth century. It is a fascinating example of creativity, in part because the inventors (Orville and Wilbur Wright) surprised most everyone with their achievement. They were bicycle mechanics, not engineers, and apparently no one really expected them to develop the first flying machine. Yet in 1903, in Kitty Hawk, North Carolina, Orville Wright flew their airplane into history. That airplane is currently on display in the Smithsonian Museum of Space and Aeronautics in Washington, DC.

The Wright brothers employed a variety of tactics to insure their success. They broke the overarching problem of flight down into small workable problems, for example, and they collected a huge amount of data, even building their own wind tunnel. They studied birds in flight, which suggests that they used what is now called a "look to nature" tactic for finding ideas. More will be said about these tactics in Chapter 12.

What is most critical for the present chapter is that the Wright brothers were working in a time and place that was ripe for invention. It is impossible to understand their creativity

Creativity, Second Edition
http://dx.doi.org/10.1016/B978-0-12-410512-6.00007-2

205

without taking into account the historical and cultural context of that time. Indeed, a full understanding of creative work must always acknowledge historical and cultural contexts.

There was a particular *zeitgeist* in 1903 (*zeitgeist* is the German word for the "spirit of the times"). *Zeitgeist* imposes a value system and provides prerequisites for specific kinds of creativity. The Renaissance is sometimes explained in this fashion. After all, some general creative values must have been shared in Italy at that point in time; why else would so many individuals and groups, across all domains for performance, all direct their efforts to original works? Looking again at the first airplane, it certainly helped that bicycles were enormously popular around the turn of the century. The Wrights, then, could support themselves in a shop that allowed them to tinker with mechanical inventions. New modes of transportation were in the public eye, including the bicycle and hot air balloons. The word *zeitgeist* is somewhat difficult to define in a precise manner, but hopefully it is clear that the airplane was possible in part because there was a general appreciation for new inventions and new modes of travel. Admittedly, to be accurate, we must acknowledge various renaissances rather than just one (Boorstin 1992), but the explanatory power of *zeitgeist* applies to each of them.

There are other perspectives on renaissances and on the macro-level influences on creative work. This chapter discusses all of these influences, starting with the more historical and then covering cultural variables. Various interesting controversies are discussed, including the occurrence of multiple discoveries (i.e., inventions or discoveries that are found and presented by different individuals very close to the same date) and the "Great Person" theory (the idea here being that *zeitgeist* only contributes so much and that extraordinary creative achievements require an extraordinary individual as well (Boring 1950, see notes)). It is best to say a few things about the historical approach and methods before we turn to the specific phenomena, cases, and controversies.

HISTORICAL ANALYSES

The unique characteristic of the historical perspective is its focus on change and time. Often the conclusions offered by historians apply to certain peoples, cultures, processes, or domains, but in every case the evidence used to draw these inferences is from times past. Granted it is impossible to investigate an era or event without taking the location into account. This is why much of what historians have to say applies to different cultures and different settings. But unlike the work that focuses on culture and ecology, the historical perspective always emphasizes change through time.

The historical analysis is itself a creative process. Historians must draw on records and artifacts, but they do not have complete information at their disposal. It is not simply a matter of reading the facts. An interpretation must be constructed. This is a daunting task. The information historians have may easily be biased by previous historians, biographers, and autobiographers. It is likely to be slanted precisely because it was prepared in another era. Some of this is unavoidable. Consider the limitations of our recorded history. That is a reflection only of those cultures and individuals who could record information. This suggests that much of the recorded history, and certainly all of that which is written, was prepared by literate individuals. There is more to historical data than written history, and other ways besides writing to record history, but still, what we know of the past is based on the individuals who left us

BOX 7.1

CREATIVITY IS NOT CONTINUOUS

You might think that creativity increases in a gradual fashion—More people, more opportunities, more technology, more creativity. Not so. The idea of a renaissance is contrary to the notion of continuous increases, and apparently there have been several renaissances (Boorstin 1992). Also consider Thomas Kuhn's (1962) famous distinction between normal science, where most everyone shares assumptions and findings accumulate in a gradual manner, with a paradigm shift, where assumptions are questioned and an entirely new perspective and world view appears (also see Nickles 1999). Kroeber (1944) described something like this in his theory of *configurations*. These are clusters or groupings of creative individuals within certain periods of time (decades or even longer). He explained such clusters in terms of role models and similar social processes. Simonton (1984) presents a detailed evaluation of these various perspectives. The conclusion is clear: Creativity is not a constant across historical eras.

As a matter of fact, the United States may be on the downswing. Florida (2002) has data

suggesting that we are not in the top 10 in the world, though at one point, after World War II, many people considered the United States to be the most innovative nation in the world. Why the downswing? There are many influences, but one was identified some time ago by Toynbee (1964):

> In present-day America, it looks to me, the affluent majority is striving desperately to arrest the irresistible tide of change. It is attempting this impossible task because it is bent on conserving the social and economic system under which this comfortable affluence has been acquired.... American public opinion today is putting an enormously high premium on social conformity; and this attempt to standardize people's behavior in adult life is as discouraging of creative ability and initiative as the educational policy of egalitarianism in childhood (p. 8).

Toynbee saw creativity in a minority rather than in everyone; the title of his article was, "Is America neglecting her creative minority?" Hence egalitarianism ignores the creative talents of the gifted.

---

clues. They were often literate, and often the winners rather than the losers of battles (both natural and within the species).

Historians offer a picture of the past, a description of creative persons during earlier eras, and even predictions for the future. The last of these must be based on inferences drawn about the past; here the historian fills the gaps in those incomplete records, and hopefully does so objectively and logically. That is where the creativity is the most obvious. The historian reconstructs the past and creates it anew.

This is a creative process. It is not, however, always accurate. Sometimes it is fairly accurate, with only a few gaps or uncertainties, but sometimes there is huge ambiguity and very little certainty. And sometimes the interpretation is simply wrong. This can be said without hesitation because it has been discovered again and again: It is not uncommon to discover that an historical "fact" is actually incorrect. This is why there is such attention to *revisionist history*. That too is merely a part of the creative process. New meanings are created, often from new data. They may also be created because of a new interpretation rather than the discovery of new data. Hopefully such new interpretations are more objective and accurate than the previous ones, but that is not always the case. The reconstruction could be biased, or distorted by what Butterfield (1931) called an historical bias.

HISTORICAL AND WHIGGIST BIASES

In 1931, Lord Butterfield described difficulties in conducting historical analyses. He referred to these as *historical bias*. Gould (1991) described much the same but found many examples specifically in Whiggist interpretations of the past; he therefore referred to the *Whiggist bias*. Both of these are biases in the sense that the historian (or whoever) is judging the past using his or her own values. Errors are systematically slanted in favor of contemporaries.

Historical actions can only really be understood by taking the *zeitgeist* and context of those times into account. Historical interpretations that are creative (in their originality and constructive nature) may be biased or inaccurate, but that is actually how creativity works. It leads to things that have some value, but value varies from group to group and era to era. Cropley et al. (2008) explored this idea in great detail in a recent discussion of malevolent creativity. McLaren (1993) went into much the same territory in his discussion of the dark side of creativity.

We have, then, two important messages about historical analyses. First, judgments about historical creativity must be made very carefully, if they are made at all. Unless we can reflect on our own values and biases, and see their place in the context of historical change, we cannot be good judges of the past.

More generally, the second message is that context, historical and otherwise, must be taken into account when studying the creative works of the past.

It is especially easy to make mistakes when judging and comparing eras. This is, however, precisely where the biases of Whiggist history are the most likely, especially if the comparison is between the past and the present. We need to behave objectively. But think of the benefits of an historical analysis: Those influences on a renaissance might be identified and targeted in the present! To paraphrase the scholar Howard Gruber, "Where will we hang all of the paintings?" And where will we house all of the inventions? How will we find the time to enjoy all of the new technologies and creative works?

This is one reason to examine the history of creativity. It is also interesting to examine how creativity has changed through history, and how creativity has actively contributed to changes in history. Creativity does not simply respond to environments and settings, it contributes to their evolution. So again, history is a creative process. It is creativity unfolding.

PREHISTORY

Humans seem to have always been creative. There is debate about when humans appeared in the evolution of *Homo sapiens*, yet it is clear that creativity is not a recent development. It is much older, for example, than written language. Andreasen (2005) put it this way:

We do know, even without written records, that some of these prehistoric people possessed the gift of creativity—the capacity to see something new that others did not. Someone picked up a stone and saw a tool. Someone realized that it could be made sharp and pointed by chipping away at it. Someone recognized that a group of people could join together and hunt large food-rich animals, using their collective intellect and strength. Someone suspected that seeds could be planted and crops grown … that circular wheels could facilitate moving heavy objects… . Some of these early creative people must have become storytellers…. Some became artists, as attested by the magnificent drawings in the 17,000 BC Cave of Lascaux in the Dordogne in France… . We have so many amazing examples of human creativity from human prehistory and history, such as the pyramids of Egypt and the Mayan ruins at Chichin Itza, the statues of Nemrut Dag in Western Turkey, the Acropolis in Athens … the Roman roads and aqueducts (pp. 2–3).

Andreasen (2005) mentioned many artifacts, such as paintings and statues, but very importantly, she also mentioned intangibles and creativity that is not immediately tied to a concrete product:

Even during their early history, human beings have had the spark of creativity. They could see things that did not exist. They could imagine. They could yearn for beauty … search the skies … study animals and plants…. They could imagine beings and forces, greater than themselves, which were guiding and shaping their world. They could even create moral codes that minimized the importance of individual survival and sublimated it to some higher cause (pp. 3–4).

This underscores the idea that history analyses are not always based only on products. Creativity through history is also apparent in morals, ethics, and similar abstract innovations. It is especially notable that the creative process may lead directly to morality (Gruber 1993; Runco 1993a; Wallace 1991). This of course is an alternative to the possibility of malevolent creativity, as just mentioned.

GANDHI AND CREATIVITY

Gandhi is probably much better known for his principles than any tangible product he left behind. He developed a means for passive resistance, for example, and for convincing the British that he was sincere and that his cause was significant. These innovations are not hanging in any museum, but they are creative, valuable, and enormously important. Gandhi was creative.

ZEITGEIST AS HISTORICAL PROCESS

In one of the seminal papers for creative studies, Boring (1971) defined *zeitgeist* as "the climate of opinion as it affects thinking" (p. 54) and "the total body of knowledge and opinion available at any time to a person living within a given culture" (p. 63). He traced the term to what may be the original use by Goethe in 1827. Goethe apparently used the concept of *zeitgeist* to describe Homer's broad influence on thought, emphasizing the "unconscious, covert, and implicit effects of the climate of opinion" (Boring 1971, p. 54).

Boring (1971) and more contemporary scholars do not limit themselves to unconscious processes. In fact, Boring felt that *zeitgeist* can be monitored and controlled, but only if it is a conscious, overt, and explicit process. It is a process in the sense that it is ongoing and not a

BOX 7.2

ZEITGEIST AND PRODIGIOUSNESS

Feldman (1994) explored the role of the *zeitgeist* in society's appreciation of talent and prodigies. He asked,

> How do these broader contextual forces affect the development and expression of potential? As we have noted the prodigy exists within sociocultural, historical and evolutionary contexts that each affect the expression of potential. By virtue of the point in time and the place in which the prodigy is born, he lives within a context of a certain *Zeitgeist* or spirit of the times, a political atmosphere of stability or unrest, war or peace, and a cultural milieu in which role models either do or do not exist in various fields. Certain philosophies, myths and belief systems characterize the ideological atmosphere in which the child is raised (p. 179).

Feldman added, "All in all it is not so much a matter of whether one is simply in the right place at the right time. It may instead be a matter of being the right person in the right place at the right time. A certain type of talent may have a higher probability of accomplishment when the spirit of the times favors that particular form, whereas another may have an advantage when the *zeitgeist* shifts to another emphasis" (p. 181).

The role of chance in our appreciation of giftedness and prodigiousness has been debated by Albert (1988), Gruber (1988), and Simonton (1988).

static state. More accurately, it is a historical process. He tied *zeitgeist* to culture and to communication. *Zeitgeist* is, then, "the total sum of social interaction as it is common to a particular period and particular locale. One can say it is thought being affected by culture" (p. 56). *Zeitgeist* is not, therefore, universal and worldwide. Different cultures have different *zeitgeist*, as do different eras and geographic locations.

Sometimes *zeitgeist* inhibits creativity. Boring (1971) captured this with, "the Zeitgeist acts as inertia in human thinking. It makes thought slow but also surer" (p. 61). The certainty is good for the sciences, and in fact the ideal case for all creativity may be where there is both some freedom of thought but also some inertia, or at least some quality control. Again thinking of the sciences, *zeitgeist* has been "a conservative force that demanded that originality remain responsible, that it be grounded on evidence and available knowledge" (p. 62). Without some grounding, you have only originality or, in Boring's terms, *cranks* and *paranoid enthusiasts*. Boring defined these as highly original people whose work is worthless, albeit original. Note the implication being that originality is not inherently good and valuable. It can be quite good, but it also can be worthless. The same claim is made in Chapter 13, when creativity is defined. There originality is described as necessary but not sufficient for creativity. It is not sufficient because some originality is worthless. This is the difference between the cranks identified by Boring (1971) and malevolent creativity. The latter has some value, albeit value only for violent or dishonest groups. Boring also described a total lack of originality. This is *plagiarism*, which of course indicates that one individual merely copies another.

A GENIUS AHEAD OF HIS OR HER TIME?

Anticipated discoveries may be taken as evidence of the impact of *zeitgeist*. Again quoting Boring's (1971) influential paper, "Not only is a new discovery seldom made until the times are ready for it, but again and again it turns out to have been anticipated, inadequately perhaps but nevertheless explicitly, as the times were beginning to be ready for it" (p. 55). It was for this reason that Albert (1975), in another seminal paper, concluded that "there is no such thing as genius before its time." A highly creative idea or invention may reflect genius but no one recognizes it unless it is a part of *zeitgeist* and something that people will appreciate. This view of creativity depends on attributions of creativity by judges or groups. There are concerns about this line of thought, as we saw in Chapter 5.

Csikszentmihalyi (1990a) held a similar view about attributions and for that reason rephrased the common question, "Who is creative?" to "Where is creativity?" His description is a systems theory of creativity, because it describes how creative efforts may begin with an individual but are not recognized unless they eventually influence a *field* (people working in that area) and then a *domain* (the discipline or area, such as physics, art, mathematics, or design). As a domain changes, individuals change as well, and they will think in a fashion that is consistent with the new ideas in the domain. The information within a domain can be seen as a part of *zeitgeist*.

MULTIPLE DISCOVERIES AND SIMULTANEITIES

Zeitgeist is also apparent in shared insights and multiple discoveries. Boring (1971) described these as *near-simultaneities* and *near-synchronisms*. Whatever the label, these occur when two or more individuals or teams discover something at nearly the same time without working together. These imply that discoveries are a part of the *zeitgeist* and therefore available to anyone working in a particular area. This idea is contrary to the Great Person theory, which gives credit for discoveries to the talents of some extremely talented individual. Simultaneous discoveries are quite numerous. Sometimes they are called "multiples," for multiple discoveries, and sometimes they are called simultaneities. As early as 1922 Ogburn and Thomas identified 148 "contemporaneous but independent discoveries or inventions" (Boring 1971, p. 55). More recently Lamb and Easton (1984) provided a huge number of examples. Table 7.1 lists a few of the more notable discoveries.

One of the more interesting cases of multiple discovery is that of black holes. One key player was Subraimanyan Chandrasekhar (Miller 2005; Singh 2005). "Chandra" exemplified contrarianism as well as *zeitgeist*. Singh (2005) described Chandra's background and behavior:

> Chandrasekhar was born in Lahore in 1910, when the British Raj still ruled India. Although he grew up among intellectual nobility (his uncle C.V. Raman won the 1930 Nobel Prize in physics), he still faced prejudice, as demonstrated by one particular journey. His father worked for the railway, so Chandra was always allowed to travel first class, much to the chagrin of an English couple who shared his carriage on a trip to Madras. They began complaining and asked that the young Indian gentleman be moved to a different carriage, although they expressed relief that Chandra at least was wearing Western clothes. This prompted Chandra to leave, but only so he could change and return in his traditional attire. He defiantly stood his ground; eventually the English couple was moved to a different carriage (p. R8).

BOX 7.3

SYSTEMS THEORY ANSWERS, "WHERE IS CREATIVITY?"

Boring (1971) described the "single scientist as an organic system ... a discovery machine, with a certain input from the literature and from other forms of social communication and also ... from nature" (p. 57). Boring felt that *zeitgeist* was like a stream, flowing such that "Zeitgeist, of course, inevitably influences the conception of the Zeitgeist" (p. 57).

Several others also have used the analogy of a system to describe the creative process. For Csikszentmihalyi (1990a), the system has the individual working within a *field* and a *domain*. Ideas and values may be proposed by an individual but are not creative, in this theory, unless they influence a field and eventually a domain, in which case they may, in turn, influence other individuals working in that area. The deemphasis on the individual led Csikszentmihalyi to propose that "where

is creativity?" is more important than "who is creative?"

Gruber (1988) described an evolving systems theory of creativity. It is developmental, systematic, pluralistic, interactive, constructionistic, and experientially sensitive. It describes work developing over a long period of time and is pluralistic in that the creator may have a number of insights and projects. Most important for the present chapter may be that this approach is interactive: "The creative person works within some historical, social, and institutional framework" (pp. 28–29). Also very important is the constructionistic nature of the work. That implies that the creator is not a passive recipient of experience but chooses and shapes his or her world. The creator is proactive and in fact may contribute to the events and works, which in turn, shape history.

TABLE 7.1   Multiple Discoveries

Discovery	Discoverers
Calculus	Leibnitz and Newton
Logarithms	Briggs and Napier
Electricity	Franklin and D'Alibard
Evolutionary theory	Spencer and Darwin
Light bulb	Edison and Joseph Swan
Mouse trap	William Hooker and James Henry Atkinson
Safety pin	Walter Hurt and Charles Rowley
Black holes	Chandrasekhar and Lev Landau

You can see how easy it is to focus on people rather than on historical context and *zeitgeist*. Yet Merton (1961) examined the data and concluded that "the pattern of independent multiple discoveries is ... the dominant pattern rather than a subsidiary one" (p. 110). There are other reasons to question the Great Person approach to creative work, in addition to the frequency of multiple discoveries (see Ione 1999; Lamb & Easton 1984). The Great Person approach tends to deemphasize social influence. Even Sir Isaac Newton acknowledged those working before him with his famous admission of "standing on the shoulders of giants."

Stillinger (1991) went so far as to claim that there are no solitary geniuses, no "great persons" who work alone and deserve all credit for their creative accomplishments. He detailed the collaborations and lines of influence in the work of John Keats, John Stuart Mill, William Wordsworth, Samuel Coleridge, Ezra Pound, and dozens of others. Influence can be extremely difficult to determine, especially because some of it may not be entirely conscious to the creator, and some of it may be intentionally suppressed in an effort to suggest originality. Some of it simply is not a part of the historical record.

One provocative implication of these ideas about *zeitgeist*, multiple discovery, and social influence was raised by Ogburn and Thomas (1922). It is the question they used as the title to their paper, "Are inventions inevitable?" This may be the case, at least if *zeitgeist* is all-important. If Darwin had not proposed evolutionary theory, Spencer would have (and did). Of course, simultaneous discoveries are not always identical, which is no doubt why Boring (1971) labeled them near-simultaneities. Also, at least in the case of Spencer and Darwin, there was a huge difference in the amount of support provided by the creator. Darwin had been working with his data for approximately 20 years and had evidence that Spencer did not (Gruber 1981a). Additionally, it is probably not an all-or-nothing proposition. Very likely *zeitgeist* provides information and values, but the "prepared mind" and creative individual must come along to develop the insight. Just because the *zeitgeist* is ripe does not guarantee that someone will make the discovery. Inventions are not, in this light, inevitable—at least not if you consider the impact of personality and the various motivational, attitudinal, biological, and cognitive factors reviewed throughout this volume!

Is it Chance or is it Inevitable?

Chance favors the prepared mind. *Louis Pasteur*

The origin of the great man is natural; and immediately this is recognized, he must be classed with all other phenomena in the society that gave him birth as a product of his antecedents. Along with the whole generation of which he forms a minute part, along with its institutions, language, knowledge, manners, and its multitudinous arts and appliances, he is a resultant…. You must admit that the genesis of the great man depends on the long series of complex influences which has produced the race in which he appears, and the social state into which that race has slowly grown…. Before he can remake his society, his society must remake him. All those changes of which he is the proximate initiator have their chief causes in the generations he descended from. If there is to be anything like a real explanation of those changes, it must be sought in that aggregate of conditions out of which both he and they have arisen. *William James (1880)*

Zeitgeist may either facilitate creative work and discovery or inhibit them. Zeitgeist favors certain domains at certain times. What is valued is apparent in conventions (Boring 1971). These in turn are good when they provide individuals (and a field) with the knowledge that allows them to recognize the worth of truly creative discoveries and insights. They may be bad when they pressure potentially original individuals into conventional—and therefore unoriginal—lines of work and thought. *Zeitgeist* is intimately tied to cultural values, which operate on a larger level but are also potentially facilitative or inhibitive.

Significantly, Boring (1971) felt that the bad side of *zeitgeist* can be avoided if an individual can "remain ignorant of bad knowledge" (p. 57). This may be one reason Piaget and Skinner read extensively outside their own fields of study (Gruber 1996; Skinner 1956). They seemed to be aware of the potential *cost of expertise* (Minsky 1988; Rubenson & Runco 1995). The individual might also "resist the zeitgeist" (Boring 1950, p. 57). That is not easy—far from it. It is impossible unless the individual is extremely self-aware. The individual needs to know how he or she is influenced by very general values and expectations, and these are amorphous and typically implicit. They are for most of us invisible, much as the water is invisible to the fish. You can't battle an invisible enemy.

TOOLS AND CREATIVITY

Tools and instruments frequently change the *zeitgeist* in a dramatic way (Boring 1971). It may seem to complicate things, given that tools may result from creative work, but then subsequently influence it. Yet that is exactly what happens. Tools are both causes and effects of the creative process.

Tools often accelerate the rate of change. Consider in this regard the fact that lenses had been available for hundreds of years, but only in 1608 was the telescope invented. It was invented by six or more people independently, all within approximately one year, shortly after Galileo discovered Jupiter. This in turn caused a shift in the *zeitgeist* such that there was a keen interest in astronomy and quite a bit of discussion about where humans fit in the universe. Similar changes quickly followed: "the invention of the simple microscope, the compound microscope, the Voltaic pile, the galvanic battery, the galvanometer, the electromagnet, and recently the electron tube—the possibilities opened up by the availability of a new important instrument change the atmosphere within a field of science and lead quickly to a mass of valid research" (Boring 1971, pp. 60–61).

New tools and the work they allow are often resisted. In 1863, Manet's *Le Déjeuner Sur L'Herbe* was rejected by a jury of the *Paris Salon*, in part because of the style. Manet relied on his palette knife rather than his brush. A more recent example of art styles changing after new tools develop is the emergence of "nano art." In the musical domain, the tools are instruments. Consider Bob Dylan, who was initially a folk artist. He heard others play his songs with electric guitars, however, and then shocked his fans with an electric concert. Noted rock critic Robert Hilburn (2004) put it this way:

> Dylan's career path hasn't been smooth. During an unprecedented creative spree that resulted in three landmark albums ("Bringing It All Back Home," "Highway 61 Revisited" and "Blonde on Blonde") being released in 15 months, Dylan reconnected with the rock 'n' roll of his youth. Impressed by the energy he felt in the Beatles and desiring to speak in the musical language of his generation, he declared his independence from folk by going electric at the Newport Folk Festival in 1965. His music soon became a new standard of rock achievement, influencing not only his contemporaries, including the Beatles, but almost everyone to follow.

<hr>

BOX 7.4

COSTS AND BENEFITS OF EXPERTISE

Experts have extensive knowledge bases. Not only do they have a great deal of information at their fingertips, but the knowledge is richly interconnected, so to speak, with numerous useful associations. This provides them with certain cognitive skills, such as *automaticity*. They can, then, deal quickly with information, at least "givens" from within their specializations. The knowledge of experts is also extremely well organized. It may be hierarchical, with more abstract information at the top of the hierarchy and concrete information toward the bottom. Note that the expertise is domain-specific. Experts far exceed others (novices) in their domain of specialization but not outside that specialization (Welling 2007).

Simon and Chase (1977) proposed that approximately 10 000 hours were needed for most experts to develop this kind of long-term working memory and expertise. In their words,

> there are no instant experts in chess—certainly no instant masters or grandmasters. There appears not to be on record any case (including Bobby Fischer) where a person has reached grandmaster level with less than about a decade's intense participation with the game. We would estimate, very roughly, that a master might spend perhaps 10,000 to 50,000 hours staring at chess positions, and a class a player, 1,000 to 5,000 hours. For the master, these times are comparable to the times highly literate people have spent in reading by the time they reach adulthood. Such people may have reading vocabularies of 50,000 words or more.

If a chunk is a chunk as to learning time … then we would expect a chess master to have a comparable chess vocabulary.

Ericsson (2003b) described modifiable representations, which should support certain kinds of creative thinking. These represent information and reality but do so in a fashion that can be modified. They are adaptable rather than fixed, rigid, or static, and they allow a kind of flexibility, which of course is quite useful for creative problem solving. Ericsson (2002, p. 41) described how "the essence of expert performance is a generalized skill at successfully meeting the demands of new situations and rapidly adapting to changing conditions." That adaptability could support creative thinking.

Yet there are potential costs. These result from the intricate knowledge bases. Experts know a field so well that they sometimes stop considering the details. They make assumptions that no one else would make—but assumptions can be costly. This is why professional marginality is not uncommon. Then a novice, someone from outside one field, moves into a new field. They have the advantage of a fresh perspective and they do not make the same assumptions as the experts. Darwin, Piaget, Freud, and many others seem to have benefited from a lack of expertise in the fields where they contributed most creatively (evolutionary biology, developmental psychology, and psychoanalysis, respectively). There seem to be costs and benefits to expertise.

In addition to the suggestion that instruments may be tools of creative work, Dylan demonstrates contrarianism in his work. As a matter of fact, in the same interview Dylan described the influence of folk artist Woody Guthrie, but emphasized "you can't just copy somebody. If you like someone's work, the important thing is to be exposed to everything that person has been exposed to." More will be said about contrarianism in Chapter 12.

THE INVENTION OF THE ZERO

In the domain of mathematics, numbers are tools. Even the zero is a tool. According to Lau (2005): "To create, in some way, can mean to come up with something from nothing. When we think of nothing, we think of zero." Most important was Lau's short history of the zero. Apparently, long ago, at least in golden ages, there was no need for a zero, in part because people saw no need to represent something that did not exist. Numbers were used, often by traders, but if they had no sheep, they said they had no sheep. The zero was not needed. The Greeks adopted various mathematical concepts of the Babylonians and Egyptians, and added to geometry, but they had difficulty with the zero, especially in the sense of adding nothing to something or measuring something that had zero length, width, or volume. Most problematic was division, given the undefined result, but multiplication was not much better. You actually erase a number if you multiply it by zero! Lau felt this was both mathematically and philosophically difficult. This is because the zero is tied to concepts of nothingness, emptiness, and the like, but those things were not compatible with that era's *zeitgeist*. "As a result, they decided not to accept zero." In India, the story was quite different. They were philosophically comfortable with the concept of the zero, as well as emptiness, nothingness, and infinity. Lau felt that allowed them to move from geometry to algebra. In addition to showing cultural differences in acceptance of the zero and illustrating the function of the zero (as a tool), Lau reminded his audience to consider how the Greeks may have failed by not altering their mindset. In addition to the idea that the zero is a tool, there are lessons in Lau's brief history about *zeitgeist* apparent in the influence of philosophy on mathematics.

Burke (1995) implied that tools and instruments provide a new and deeper perspective on our lives. He looked carefully at the recent past and described how

> during that time we have carried with us and cherished beliefs that are pre-technological in nature. These faiths place art and philosophy at the center of man's existence, and science and technology on the periphery. According to this view, the former lead and the latter follow. Yet … the reverse is true. Without instruments, how could the Copernican Revolution have taken place? Why are we taught we gain insight and the experience of beauty only through art, when this is but a limited and secondhand representation of the infinitely deeper experience to be gained by a direct observation of the world around us? (p. 295).

In a moment we will explore Burke's (1995) ideas about *trigger effects*. Tools may trigger dramatic changes. But first we should consider the downside of tools. Weapons have been mentioned already, and they exemplify the potential downside of new inventions. Yet as Tenner (1996) noted, a large number of actual tools (and many aspects of technology) often create more problems than they solve. Tenner's book is titled, *Why Things Bite Back: Technology and the Revenge of Unintended Consequences*. If anyone has experienced a computer crash and loss of data, they have experienced one of the common examples of this. The computer HAL in the book and movie *2001: A Space Odyssey* is another example, albeit as yet a hypothetical one. The numerous examples of information overload can also be cited at this point, for it, too, is a product of modern society and can stifle our creativity and undermine our health (Elkind 1981). No wonder some societies do not believe in linear progress (Hann 1994)!

INFORMATION OVERLOAD

People of all ages are overloaded with responsibilities, options, and information. Wurman (1989) reported that

> More new information has been produced in the last 30 years than in the previous 5,000.... The total of all printed knowledge doubles every 8 years.... Inundated with technical data, some scientists claim that it takes less time to do an experiment than to find out whether or not it has been done before .... About half of the U.S. workforce has a job that is information related.... The number of components that can be contained on a computer chip is doubling every 18 months.

If these things do not impress you, consider the fact that the average American newspaper has more than doubled in number of pages in the past 20 years. There are well over 125 long-distance telephone companies—in California alone. There are approximately 1500 television stations available as well. Remote controls for your VCR or DVD player often have 40 or 50 buttons—that is just the remote control. The instruction manual for them is also typically over 50 pages. And how many remote controls and owner's manuals do you have? Dozens no doubt.

LAMARCKIAN EVOLUTION AND CHANGE

Historical and cultural changes are occurring at a faster and faster rate. Tools may contribute to this, but that is only part of the story. Acceleration is unavoidable, at least for cultural evolution. Biological changes may be mostly gradual and slow (Wilson 1975).

Charles Darwin described biological evolution and noted that great expanses of time were necessary. This was in part because changes ("adaptations") are not retained as soon as they appear. It takes long, long periods of time for "the survival of the fittest" to select those species that have best adapted. But that view applies only to biological change; social, cultural, and technological change does not require the same huge expanses of time. Once a technology is introduced into society, for example, it is maintained. Computer chips did not need to be invented again and again; once was enough. (Actually, twice was enough, given that two people invented them at nearly the same time. Chips were included on our list of simultaneous discoveries.) Further, many inventions and innovations are generative. Again consider the computer chip, which led to the subsequent invention of hundreds of other advances. That is Lamarckian evolution and advance (as described by Jean Baptiste de Lamarck, an immediate predecessor to Darwin).

THE ACCELERATION METAPHOR

The metaphor of acceleration has been challenged by some ... and rightly so.... It is not grounded in fin-de-siecle nostalgic imaginings, nor in post-modernist "space-time compression," nor in alarmist futurology. It refers rather to the very concrete, rapid, and dramatic changes that have

(Continued)

affected the lives of ever-greater numbers of people in the course of the twentieth century.... These changes can be approached in any number of ways, all of them controversial. The imminence of demographic catastrophe has been preached since Malthus. Environmental concerns have also become an important preoccupation (Hann 1994, pp. 1–2).

Gleick (2000) went into great detail about the impact of acceleration. He described the process simply as *Faster*, which is the title of his book. He is quite thorough, as the subtitle implies: "The acceleration of just about everything."

This description of historical change shows how difficult it is to extricate the historical perspective on creativity from discussions of culture. As a matter of fact, in some ways that is an undesirable thing to do. If historical factors are separated from cultural factors, the resulting models and theories are not very realistic. In this chapter these factors are often separated, but that is only for clarity, so the discussion can focus on one thing at a time. It is important to keep their interplay in mind.

DOMAIN DIFFERENCES AND DOMAIN-SPECIFIC *MICROGEISTER*

Changes are even apparent in the breadth and function of a *zeitgeist*. Each *zeitgeist* probably had broader influence in history compared to the present. Yet that is no longer the case. Even that has changed! Now there are clear domain differences, even within an era or culture. These are *microgeister*.

No longer do scientists all share the same particular concerns and values (the "spirit" in *zeitgeist*) as artists, as they did in previous centuries. Historically, the various domains and fields were smaller, more contiguous, and more similar. Science did not at that point rely so heavily on technology—just to name one obvious example of how current science differs from historical science, and from most forms of contemporary art. Now it appears that artists may have their own concerns, and scientists their concerns. These are far from identical as you would expect if there was one overarching *zeitgeist*. Perhaps the best evidence of the difference is the fact that art and science are "out of sync." Artists seem to concern themselves with particular issues, and only later do scientists develop the same interests. Manet's art anticipated Niels Bohr's and Einstein's ideas about physics and relativity by 40 years. Many examples of art foreseeing scientific concerns were identified by Shlain (1991) and Boorstin (1992). The former wrote, "Literature, like her sisters, music and the visual arts, also anticipated the major revolutions in the physicist's world view" (p. 290).

The media (TV, radio, Internet, news services) probably change the current *zeitgeist*. Although I do not have any evidence for this, if you think about *zeitgeist* being spirit of the times, which was alive and well before the advent of the Internet, television, and other forms of mass media, the spirit must have been communicated in conversation and shared values. These days, however, communication is so quick and broad that someone in one part of the world can actually observe what is going on in other parts of the world. You might think that this would just quicken the pace or spread the values of a particular *zeitgeist*, but actually it could change them. No wonder, then, many artists, or at least novelists, believe that because of movies and television, reality now imitates fiction rather than the other way around (Pérez Reverte 2002, p. 270)!

CREATING OUR SENSE OF SELF

Surely one of the most important creations of history involves our sense of self. Boorstin (1992) cited the invention of the essay, various confessions (e.g., Rousseau's from 1766) and apologia and autobiographies (e.g., Benjamin Franklin's, from about the same time), poems, and even political statements (e.g., the Declaration of Independence) as examples.

Florida (2002) also described the creation of our sense of self. In his words,

> Modern life is increasingly defined by contingent commitments. We progress from job to job with amazingly little concern or effort. Where people once found themselves bound together by social institutions and formed their identities in groups, a fundamental characteristic today is that we *strive to create our own identities*. It is this creation and recreation of the self, often in ways that reflect our creativity, that is the key feature of creative effort. In this new world, it is no longer the organizations we work for, churches, neighborhoods, or even family ties that define us. Instead, we do this ourselves, defining our identity along the dimensions of our creativity (p. 7, emphasis added).

This "creation of our sense of self" is a dramatic example of everyday creativity. Creativity often can be categorized as artistic, mathematical, musical, verbal, or as fitting neatly into a well-recognized domain, but sometimes it is much broader and more workaday (Runco & Richards 1997).

ECONOMIC CHANGES INFLUENCING CULTURE AND HISTORY

Florida's (2002) perspective on creativity is largely economic, but his findings describe cultural and historical changes. Consider, for example, his description of the means by which the United States became a world power:

> it built the most powerful and dynamic economy in the world, and it did so largely by building creative strength: by eagerly fostering the birth of new industries, by maintaining a free and open society, by making massive investments in creativity (such as higher education, scientific research, and culture), and most of all, by drawing waves of energetic, intelligent people from all over the world to its shores (p. xxiii).

Note the interplay of societal values, economics, and historical forces.

Economic factors of various sorts influence historical change. Florida (2002), for instance, believes that

> as nations' economies advance, the values favored by their people tend to shift along two scales. They move from "traditional" values (marked, for instance, by respect for civil and religious authority) toward more "secular-rationale" (freethinking) values, and from "survival" values (favoring financial and social stability) to "self-expression" values favoring individuals' right to express themselves (pp. xxiv–xxv).

This is entirely consistent with Boorstin's (1992) division of history into three phases: "creative man," moving to "creation of the world," and then to "creation of self."

Murphy (1958) referred to the spasms of creativeness, which were found when society had surplus resources, leisure time, and "a social class that cares more about discovery of the new than about conquest" (pp. 144–145). This ties economics with attitudes and *zeitgeist*.

The Clockwork Muse

The economic perspective implies that creativity is predictable. Simplifying, the premise is that there are specific influences on creativity (e.g., affluence), and when these all come together or point in the same direction, creativity is likely. A second perspective also assumes creativity is predictable. This is Martindale's (1990) theory of the clockwork muse.

Martindale (1990) examined data from a variety of domains, including French poetry, American short stories, classic Greek work, operas, cathedrals, prints, so on, and concluded that in order to maintain a level of arousal and to fulfill basic needs, artists tend to rely on two complementary processes. First, individuals explore style, changing the rules and structure of their domain, and the specifics of how ideas are expressed. After a time stylistic opportunities are exhausted, and there's a need for a change in content. Martindale describes this as a matter of an increase in primordial content. This parallels the idea of primary process in its lack of inhibition and primitive nature. Primordial thought is dedifferentiated, associationistic, and undirected.

Catastrophe and Opportunity

Then there are unpredictable influences on creativity. Catastrophes, for example, are largely unforeseen and definitely precede many creative changes in history. Daniel Boorstin (1992), retired Librarian of Congress, reviewed a huge number of creative events and found each to follow a catastrophe. The destruction of cities by fire, for example, allows new and creative architecture. Boorstin also identified opportunity and technology as historical conditions for creativity. There is, then, a parallel on the micro- and macro-levels of analysis in that catastrophes frequently influence the creativity of individuals as well as societies. Creative individuals often speak of the trauma or tension in their lives that motivated their creative efforts.

The same can be said about opportunities. They, too, operate on micro- and macro-levels. This may be why renaissances are localized. They not only occur at one point in time, they also occur in one location. The renaissance city or state may not only share values and appreciate creative work, but it may operate such that creative people have the opportunities to use their talents.

This in turn reinforces the economic perspective, for opportunities are sometimes financial. A creative individual may move to a particular city because they feel comfortable there (there is high tolerance), but also because they can do their intrinsically motivated work and be paid for it! But it is also not just about money. Again quoting Florida (2002), "creative people … don't just cluster where the jobs are. They cluster in places that are the centers of creativity and also where they want to live. From classical Athens and Rome, to Florence of the Medici and Elizabethan England, to Greenwich Village and the San Francisco Bay Area, creativity has always graduated to specific locations" (p. 7). Interestingly, he emphasized the three Ts: technology, tolerance, and talent. Creative people may indeed prefer or even require a tolerant *zeitgeist* and society. They are, after all, unconventional and sometimes even rebellious. Clearly there are implications of these ideas about tolerance and opportunity for organizations, schools, and the family. Some of these are described in Box 7.5.

BOX 7.5

ECONOMIC THEORIES OF CREATIVITY

Economic concepts are very useful for explaining some of the fluctuations that occur from era to era, in creative activity and many other domains. Even the most basic economic concepts, cost and benefit and supply and demand, have good explanatory power. Take a renaissance: At that point in history many segments of a given population were creative and innovative. Why? Because there was an obvious benefit, and the demand was high. Society appreciated and rewarded creative efforts. Moreover, the costs were low. The result is an increase in the supply of creativity. Although this may sound simplistic, keep in mind that this is an attractive feature in theories: they have explanatory power but are parsimonious. Also keep in mind that these economic concepts do not just apply to the exchange or flow of cash. They also explain psychological tendencies. Indeed, Rubenson and Runco (1992b, 1995) developed a psychoeconomic theory of creativity with exactly this in mind. It relies on economic concepts, including those given earlier, but is applied to tolerance and social stigma, divergent thinking, and ideation. The notion that "the cost of creativity is low" during a renaissance implies that there is little social stigma to being unconventional and creative. There is, then, a high tolerance for creativity. That is not always the case: frequently creative behaviors are costly. An individual can be alienated for them, in which case there is a cost for being creative. Consider in this regard a highly creative child in the elementary grades. If he or she is too unconventional and creative, classmates may not be all that comfortable. Worse, the teacher may not be appreciative. After all, creative behaviors are not always a part of what teachers consider to be "the ideal child" (Dawson et al. 1999; Runco 1984; Torrance 1995). Perhaps in a renaissance a creative child is appreciated and even placed in an apprenticeship with great promise of a productive and lucrative career. In that way the costs are low and benefits are high for creativity.

CREATIVITY IN PORTLAND, OREGON

Portland, Oregon is supporting its artists and other "creatives." Perhaps the *zeitgeist* is changing. Certainly the costs are diminishing and the benefits are improving. Here is how Bulick (2005) put it:

In Portland, as in developing cities around the world, artists have played a vital role in animating neighborhoods in their search for inexpensive, flexible space to live and work in. In the now-familiar cycle, shops, restaurants and residents soon follow, more upscale development occurs and artists are forced out by escalating rental rates…. In New York City, where the "Soho syndrome" was coined, artists have migrated to the outer boroughs and to places such as Newark, which initiated live/work space development specifically to attract artists. In Portland … the buzz on the street is that some young creatives are deciding to leave. Portland needs more—and more affordable—spaces for creativity to flourish as a vital resource for our economy and livability…. The city should become a pro-active partner with private developers, the philanthropic community and the nonprofit cultural sector to develop live/work spaces, studios and cultural facilities while property values and available building stock still permit it…. What's at stake? Well, The Oregonian has provided ample coverage of Portland's recent success in attracting the so-called creative class—the young designers, software engineers, artists and other knowledge workers who are creating new enterprises and sustaining the most potent sectors of our economy. This influx has helped fuel an explosion of energetic, artist-run organizations that are putting Portland on the international map as a Mecca for creativity.

Note his suggestions about economics. This makes perfect sense, but may come as a surprise to anyone who believes that creative efforts are always intrinsically motivated. And apparently it is a two-way street, or what is described elsewhere in this book as bidirectional. Creative individuals are drawn to cities and places where they can afford to work (they receive support), and in turn contribute to the city and local economy. Bulick (2005) was very clear on these points:

> And what makes Portland attractive to these young creatives? The answer is a tolerant, progressive civic culture and a user-friendly, dense urban core close to nature—and the presence of other talent. But anyone who has asked young creatives what is most important to them has heard resoundingly: "Cheap, flexible space!" Other communities have developed strategies to attract and retain creative talent. A cultural planning process I facilitated in Santa Cruz, Calif., in 1999 cited the urgent need to develop cultural space before it became unavailable and unaffordable. The city is now leading a major effort to redevelop an old tannery into artist studios, housing, performance halls and galleries .... Similar projects include the Torpedo Factory in Arlington, Va., and—surprisingly—one that is on the drawing board in Vancouver, right next door. Prince Georges County in Maryland formed a public/private partnership to develop the Gateway Arts District to include artist housing, studios, an African American museum, office space and galleries. Minneapolis has used its redevelopment tools to provide support for a variety of cultural facilities, including more than two dozen smaller, neighborhood-based projects focusing on economic development and revitalization. St. Paul, Minn., founded Artspace, a nonprofit cultural space development entity, to address the need for artist live/work spaces there—and to leverage private philanthropy into the equation .... Portland is lucky to have some developers with long-standing commitments to providing inexpensive space for artists. Some are eager to ramp up adaptive reuse of Portland's remaining warehouse stock to meet the growing need if zoning and financing can be expedited. Public officials also are beginning to recognize the critical need to develop cultural space .... So why the fuss? Because, as this issue emerges into civic consciousness, it must be fully understood and vigorously debated. Accelerated development of creative space is an economic development and livability issue paramount to the future of our community—and even our ability to retain the jobs and tax base needed to address other critical urban issues such as education and social welfare .... Portland needs to assure that it can continue to attract and retain the creative talent needed to shape our future prosperity and quality of life.

Creativity is tied to quality of life, and in a general way. Communities that attract and support creative individuals will benefit. The benefits are not just for the creative persons themselves; they are larger than that. There are social and cultural benefits to creativity.

SERENDIPITY

Creative works and attitudes are not always predictable. They may sometimes be quite unpredictable. Creativity may sometimes be significantly influenced by serendipity, chance, and accidents.

Creative inventions and ideas often are found by accident, or at least with some unintentionality. Table 7.2 lists some examples (also see Foltz 1999).

Burke (1995) emphasized serendipity and accidents in his theory of connections. He noted, for example, that "a self-educated Scottish mechanic once made a minor adjustment to a steam pump and triggered the whole Industrial Revolution" and "thanks to a guy working on hydraulic pressure in Italian Renaissance water gardens we have the combustion engine" (p. vii).

TABLE 7.2 Accidental Discoveries

Bread	Cellophane
Corn and wheat flakes	Dry cleaning
Wheaties	Dyes for fabrics
Coffee	Masonite
Cracker jack	Matches
Crepes suzette	Microwave cooking
Ice cream soda	Rayon
Peanut brittle	Stainless steel
Raisins	Liquid paper
Vinegar	Modern paper
Worcestershire sauce	Qwerty
Kites	Arc welding
Crack in the Liberty Bell	Bakelite
Microwave oven	Fingerprinting
Licorice Allsorts	Gravity
Ether and nitrous oxide	Photography
Quinine	Telephone
Saccharin	Celluloid
Sucaryl	Guncotton (nitrocellulose)
Nutrasweet	Nitroglycerin
Avon cosmetics	Dynamite

Burke also described how varied influences may be. As he put it "one thing leads to the discovery of another" (p. 289). He gave quinine, dye, and the electromagnet as examples of this kind of convergence. It is almost a cumulative thing, but it is not linear. The contributions are sometimes quite diverse. The key word is connections, for Burke's analysis uncovered fairly remote influences, as they connect one after another, often leading to dramatic innovations and results.

Burke (1995) acknowledged that people sometimes intend to change the world and innovate. Thomas Edison is an excellent example of this. Edison very intentionally focused on invention and innovation.

WAR AND RELIGION

War and religion are also "major stimulants to innovation" (Burke 1995, p. 290). Every extensive analysis of creativity through history has had something to say about both (Boorstin 1992; Burke 1995; Simonton 1983). Burke (1995) described how "the use of the cannon in the 14th and 15th centuries led to defensive architectural developments which made use of astronomical instruments that became the basic tools of mapmaking. The introduction of the stirrup, and through it, the medieval shock troop, helped to change the social and economic structure of Europe" (p. 290). The military still has an enormous R&D budget, and the results are apparent outside the battlefield.

One implication of Burke's (1995) observations about connections, convergence, religion, and war is that there is no one path to creativity. Various creative works have resulted from diverse historical pathways; no one pathway characterizes all creative insights and inventions. Some of these connections and influences may seem to be fairly linear, especially if they follow a nice neat chronology, but more often than not the influence is nonlinear. In either case many creative products reflect a progression of inventions that eventually culminates in some *über* invention. Burke described the telephone, for example, as an integration of previous inventions, reflecting the contributions of Leon Scott, Michael Faraday, H. C. Oested, André Ampère, William Sturgeon, Hermann von Hemholtz, and of course Alexander Graham Bell (Burke 1995, pp. 78–79).

For Burke (1995), the steps in a connective progression may involve everyday creativity. He is quite explicit that history is influenced dramatically by each of us. For Burke, history is about everyman (or everyperson, to use the modern and non-sexist label). He put it this way: "In some way or another, each of us affects the course of history … ordinary people have often made the difference" (p. vii). This separates Burke's approach from the historiometric approach, described later.

Porter and Suefeld (1981) described how war might lower creativity but civil unrest might increase it. The impact of war, according to Porter and Suefeld, resulted from "fear for those involved or one's own life, a threat to one's values, and economic hardship" (p. 327). Civil unrest, on the other hand, supposedly allowed information to flow within the society and is generally a more flexible *zeitgeist*. There is more sharing, which can be conducive to creative work. Individuals are not afraid to express themselves.

TRIGGER EFFECTS AND EMERGENESIS

The path among connections is clearly nonlinear when it contains "triggers." These are inventions that lead to a diverse set of subsequent insights and inventions. Burke (1995) referred to the Trigger Effect because he felt it was relatively common throughout history, and a very important part of the process. In Burke's (1995, p. 45) words, "When Enrico Fermi, an Italian immigrant to the United States, and his colleagues triggered the world's first atomic pile in Chicago in 1941, science opened Pandora's Box. Out of it came new ways to healing, new tools with which to study the structure of the universe, the potential for virtually free electric power—and the atomic bomb."

Recall here what was said earlier about historical records and inferences. Sometimes there are large gaps in the connective pathway. These gaps are artifacts of the historical method; our knowledge of history is limited and biased (Runco 1993b). In addition, just as there seems to be a jump in an individual's thinking when he or she has an "a-ha" insight, so too are there moments when inventions and innovations seem to be emergent. Emergenesis occurs when something is not directly tied to previous conditions, at least in a simple linear manner. It is as if the creative result is more than the sum of the preexisting contributions.

Perhaps we could explain emergent creativity if we had complete and unbiased historical information. This, too, would parallel what we know about the insights produced by individuals; they tend to be explicable and protracted rather than sudden and truly out-of-the-blue (Gruber 1981b). For now, our historical analyses must accept gaps and unknowns. Hindsight is not always 20–20, nor can we go back and collect more historical data from the past.

MATTHEW, PYGMALION, AND FOUNDER EFFECTS

Religions have had dramatic impact on history and apparently can influence creativity, both for the good or the bad (Box 7.6). The material in Box 7.6 allows us to segue to an important phenomenon (or what behavioral scientists prefer to call an "effect"), observed through history but with a Biblical moniker. Did you ever hear the expression, "the rich get richer"? It is true through history, including the creative domains, and is called the Matthew Effect, after that book in the Bible.

Merton (1968) took that term from the Bible's book of Matthew and used it to explain why "the rich get richer" in scientific research, with individuals who produce a large quantity of work tending to continue producing at a high rate, and those who have some impact on their field tending to have continued impact. This effect has empirical support in research on citations and publications. It is important in part because it reminds us that part of the creative process is subjective and dependent on the judgments and attributions given by one's audience.

It might sound like a description of investment trends—and it is, for that matter—but it is also true of those who perform in a creative fashion. Individuals who achieve a little bit in a creative field tend to continue to achieve throughout their careers. The rich get richer. It is also important in educational settings. Walberg and Stariha (1992) described Matthew Effects wherein students who start their educations with successes are likely to continue achieving academically. This makes great sense because a child who stands out will attract the attention of his or her teacher, and that individual will no doubt look to that child for continued

---

BOX 7.6

CREATIVITY AND RELIGION

Religion is often mentioned along with war as an example of very general historical influence on creativity. Religious beliefs may operate like *zeitgeist*, influencing the thinking of large groups. Interestingly, many religious leaders of the past have been contrarians (e.g., Jesus, Gandhi). Yet the effects are not always beneficial. Dacey et al. (1998, pp. 18–19), for example, suggested that the Greeks were more innovative than the Romans, even though they preceded them, because of the constraints and restrictive thinking of Christianity.

achievement. In this light it is consistent with the so-called Pygmalion Effect, which shows how expectations of teachers can lead to actual changes in behavior of students. (Pygmalion, the king in a Greek myth, fell in love with a statue, which Aphrodite then brought to life.)

This might be explained in terms of talent. After all, it takes a talented individual to accomplish that first small thing, and it takes talent to continue to accomplish similar or grander things. Yet the Matthew Effect may also reflect attributional tendencies and the power of expectations. Artists who suggest a new perspective, for example, often attract a great deal of attention for that suggestion, and then may just keep on attracting attention even if they do very little from that point forward. Scientists who win important prizes may be widely read, regardless of the quality of their subsequent work. It may be that a creator's name has a significant impact on the reception of their work, and someone can make a name for themselves with one great creative production.

For this reason Nicholls (1983) described the Founder Effect (also called the Historical Priority Effect). This is apparent when an individual who initiated a line of work continues to gain credit, even if they did not have much of a reputation before and even if they "discovered" or proposed only one influential idea. Frederick Banting, discoverer of insulin, is a clear example.

THE INDIVIDUAL IN HISTORY

Creativity is complex, and for that reason accurate explanations of it are also complex. There is no one causal agent or determining factor. This was apparent in Chapter 3: There, both nature and nurture together determined creative potentials and performances. History is also multivariate. There are general pressures, like *zeitgeist*, but also influential figures. Indeed, many historical pressures operate specifically through individuals. Historical changes, especially the paradigm shifts, sometimes begin when an individual offers an original idea. That may reflect *zeitgeist* and context, and it may not go very far without subsequent social, cultural, and historical conduits. But the individual is involved in the process.

So far in this chapter we have examined a variety of historical factors, and now we turn to the study of individuals as they have influenced history. Much can be learned about historical factors from the study of individuals. As May (1975/1994) described it, creativity and imagination "reveal the underlying psychological and spiritual conditions of their relationship to their world; *thus in the works of great [creators] we have a reflection of the emotional and spiritual condition of human beings in that period of history*" (p. 52, italics added).

There is a rich literature on creative historical figures. A huge number of biographies, autobiographies, and psychohistories (e.g., Erikson 1958; Freud 1989; Gedo 1980) have been published about famous creative people. They may provide the most telling information about historical phenomena which are difficult to examine directly. After all, how do you measure *zeitgeist*? It may be that the qualitative perspective of many biographical sorts of studies is particularly useful for historical phenomena, which are difficult to measure in an objective fashion. These biographies and case studies are also useful for hypothesis generation. They may suggest predictions that could then be examined in empirical investigations with larger groups. This is not to say that a qualitative study is valuable only for hypothesis generation. Generalizations should await studies with larger groups and controls, but generalizations are not the only objective of empirical science.

To the degree that these are qualitative rather than quantitative, case studies suffer from the methodological pitfalls of other qualitative studies. They also are by definition single-subject research designs, although typically they are not really designed research in the sense that you would see it in experimental psychology textbooks. They do typically involve single cases. Sometimes patterns can be found among single cases, which is one justification for qualitative research and inductive science. Another was noted earlier: Qualitative studies allow the study of qualitative phenomena.

Psychohistory is not mere biography. Biographies prepared by historians—where the emphasis is on the individual's actual behavior and historical context—sometimes refer to psychological processes and interpret behavior from a psychological perspective. Psychohistories are prepared by individuals whose primary interest is in psychology, or perhaps psychiatry. Freud himself presented biographical studies of Leonardo da Vinci, and Erik Erikson did much the same for Martin Luther. Of course most biographical and autobiographical investigations fall somewhere between these two extremes, the purely historical and purely psychoanalytic, but again it would be difficult to attempt to classify every investigation with absolute certainty. Fortunately, it is not necessary to classify the various investigations.

The biographical investigations that are of the most use to creative studies are probably those that have been prepared by individuals with a strong background in the existing creativity literature. They are the most likely to note and interpret the variables that other research has deemed to be pertinent. This not only insures that the biography is of interest to individuals who study creativity; it also offers an indirect validation because the variables discussed have been demonstrated to be relevant in other research or by other individuals. Table 7.3 gives a list of this kind of case study.

Howard Gruber refined the case study technique (Davis et al., 2012). Not surprisingly, then, two of the best examples of this methodology are Gruber's book on Charles Darwin (Gruber 1981a) and his work on Jean Piaget (Gruber 1996). Wallace has used this theoretical perspective in her work on the novelist Dorothy Richardson (Wallace 1991). (Richardson was a primary figure in developing the stream of consciousness technique for literature.) Wallace and Gruber (1989) presented 12 case studies in one edited volume. This all adds up to a very good picture of Gruber's (1988) evolving systems theory of creativity.

This approach also was used in a detailed case study of the Indian Mathematician Tagore, winner of the 1913 Nobel Prize for Literature (Raina 1997). Raina was explicit about the constructive perspective, which is sensitive to phenomenological details as well as objective productivity. His case study truly does take sociohistorical context into account, as any biographical study should. It is especially good reading because it represents one of the few case studies that focuses on the creativity of a non-Western polymath.

Gardner (1993a) has also taken a biographical approach in his studies of Freud, Einstein, Picasso, Stravinsky, T. S. Eliot, Martha Graham, and Gandhi. Each individual represented a distinct domain of talent (Table 7.4). Gardner also collaborated on a detailed case study of Georg Cantor (Gardner & Nemirovksy 1991). In addition to drawing from the creativity literature, these case studies highlight the neuropsychology, cognition, and developmental underpinnings of Gardner's (1983) theory of multiple intelligences. The domains are verbal-symbolic, mathematical, bodily kinesthetic, spatial, musical, intrapersonal, and interpersonal. Gardner concluded that each of these relies on a somewhat different part of the nervous system and brain, and that each has an idiosyncratic developmental history. Reviewers of

TABLE 7.3　Biographies and Case Studies

Martha Graham	Root-Bernstein et al. 1993, 1995
Emily Dickenson	Ramey & Weisberg 2004
Karl Popper	Kurz 1996
Jean Piaget	Gruber 1996; Vidal 1989
John Cheever	Rothenberg 1990
Paul Klee	Pariser 1991
Pablo Picasso	Gardner 1993; Pariser 1991; Simonton 2007
Henri de Toulouse-Lautrec	Pariser 1991
Dorothy Richardson	Wallace 1991
Benjamin Franklin	Mumford 2002
Rabindranath Tagore	Raina 1997
William Shakespeare	Simonton 1999b
Anne Sexton	Sanguinetti & Kavaler-Adler 1999
George Bernard Shaw	Tahir 1999
Beethoven	Hershman & Lieb 1998
William James	Osowski 1989
Albert Einstein	Gardner 1993; Miller 1992
Anais Nin	John-Steiner 1997
T. S. Eliot	Gardner 1993
Sylvia Plath	Lester 1999
Wright brothers	Jakobs 1999
Brontë sisters	Albert 1996; VanTassel-Baska 1999
Lewis Carroll	Morrison 1999
Hans Adolf Krebs	Holmes 1999
Charles Darwin	Gruber 1981a; Keegan 1999
Georgia O'Keeffe (Figure 7.1)	Zausner 1999
William Wordsworth	Jeffrey 1999
Robert Schumann	Weisberg 1994
Vincent Van Gogh	Brower 2003
Michael Faraday	Tweney 1996
Benjamin Franklin	Mumford 2002
George Eliot, George Meredith, Arnold Benedict, Virginia Woolf, and Charles Dickens	Porter & Suefeld 1981
John Irving	Amabile 2001
E. H. Gombrich	Kozbelt 2008
Thomas Edison	Carlson (2000)
Kekulé	Wotiz & Rudofsky (1954)
Marie Curie	Thurston (1999)
Sigmund Freud	Elms (1999)
Sigmund Freud	Ippolito (1999)
Cezanne	Machotka (1999)

TABLE 7.4 Domains of Talent and Exceptional Examples

Domains	Exceptional Examples
Verbal symbolic	T. S. Eliot
Spatial	Picasso
Interpersonal	Gandhi
Bodily kinesthetic	Martha Graham
Mathematical	Einstein
Intrapersonal	Freud
Musical	Stravinsky

From Gardner (1993).

Gardner's work have reacted mostly to his conclusion that famous creators are sometimes childlike, and often self-promoters.

There is plenty of respect and appreciation for Gardner's theory, even with one or two criticisms, such as that directed to the childlike behavior in the case studies. Gardner drew from several fields, including the neurosciences, and marshaled a great deal of data and support. Although domain differences have been recognized at least since Patrick (1935), or even Galton (1869), Gardner's is the most comprehensive theory of domain differences. And it has the most empirical support.

FIGURE 7.1 Georgia O'Keeffe at an exhibition of her work "Life and Death." *Copyright UPI/CORBIS/Bettmann.*

BOX 7.7

WHAT'S IN A NAME?

Some individuals (e.g., Michelangelo) are known primarily by a first name, others known by their last, and some recognized only with both first and last names. This is not really a problem. It is problematic, however, when creative persons change their names. According to one popular source, Katsushika Hokusai, known in part for his painting of *The Great Wave*, changed his name over 30 times (Krull 1995)! Apparently that was the thing to do, then, and consistent with the *zeitgeist*. Interestingly, *The Great Wave* is just one work in Hokusai's *Thirty-Six Views of Mount Fuji*. This may exemplify "deviation amplification," the exploratory strategy often used by artists and creative persons.

Another individual who frequently changed his name was Fernando Pessoa, also known as Alberto Caeiro, Alvar de Campos, Bernardo Soares, Ricardo Reis, and so on. Pessoa was "Portugal's major 20th century writer" (Esgalhado 1999, p. 377). Apparently he developed at least 72 personas, each with its own name, and each with a perspective that was captured in Pessoa's works. This change in the *nom de plume* was in this fashion a large part of his creative process. Pessoa has 72 personas, and wrote as if he was able to experience each. Each seems to have had its own imaginary world. This parallels what Root-Bernstein and Root-Bernstein (2006) said about paracosms and the advantages of them for creative work.

BOX 7.8

OTHER DOMAINS

The idea of a spiritual domain did not pass muster. Nor did an emotional domain, though that is not to say that there is no such thing as emotional intelligence. And certainly, affect plays a large role in creative work. One domain does seem to be tenable, and it may be the most important domain of all. It is the everyday creativity domain (e.g., Runco & Richards 1997). Runco (2013a) describes ideation (just having ideas) as everyday creativity, which makes good sense if you see value in the theory of personal creativity and if you see this as distinct from social creativity (and the requirement of judges and attributions). Rollo May (1975/1994) described things like household chores and flower arranging as examples of everyday creativity. What about getting dressed (in an original and yet fashionable way), dealing with interpersonal situations, and copying with day-to-day hassles? How about adapting your budget to your income, and arranging the furniture in your home? Surely these can be original and useful and thus fit the definition of creativity.

New domains (or at least areas in which an individual can be original and effective) arise as history unfolds. Technology has introduced a large number of new areas in which creative work is possible. Even "gaming" allows creativity and now often draws on technology. The business of games and gaming may surprise you:

In spite of the current economic downturn, in 2010 the video game software industry was worth around $56 billion, thus doubling the size of the recorded music industry, exceeding by nearly 25% the magazine business, and equating to about 60% the size of the film industry, counting DVD sales as well as box-office receipts .... To date, over 424 million next-generation gaming consoles have been sold worldwide ..., and approximately 190 million western households are expected to own next-generation consoles by the end of 2012.... One of the main factors that have influenced the enormous growth of this industry has been the great amount of creative ideas that underpin successful products. Thus, as game development requires high levels of creativity and large numbers of creative people ... the game industry is a giant that feeds on creativity (Fabricatore & Lopez in press).

Still, most research on creativity focuses on a small set of domains which have stood the test of time (and meet Gardner's (1993a) stringent criteria for what constitutes a domain). One of these is the symbolic domain, which includes language and writing.

Rothenberg (1990) presented a fascinating biographical study of prize-winning author John Cheever. Rothenberg's perspective is more psychoanalytic, or at least clinical, than the previous examples, but especially fascinating in part for that reason. He reported, for example, that Cheever seemed to have access to a primitive, uninhibited, preconscious material. This is important specifically for creativity because it may have provided Cheever with especially creative insights, options, and ideas. This access to the unconscious is consistent with earlier research. Interestingly, the same tendency to look to the unconscious had another significant effect: It scared Cheever. This is what a psychoanalyst would expect; the ideas and feelings we have below consciousness are often uncensored and frightening. One reason we have defense mechanisms is to protect ourselves from these fears. The individual who has access to the material that is below or outside consciousness may have access to uninhibited and creative ideas, but at the same time is going to experience these uncensored and potentially frightening ideas. This is one explanation for the disturbances that are not uncommon in the creative population.

It also can explain the frequency with which we see alcoholism in creative persons (Ludwig 1995; Noble et al. 1993). Cheever discussed the possibility that he drank because of the fears just described. Standing back, what is also important is that Cheever's creative skill led to a psychological problem. This is a very clear causal pathway, and the direction of causality between creativity and psychological health is often debated. Some individuals think that certain unhealthful tendencies, including depression or bipolar disorders, contribute to or lead to creative potential and creative efforts. Other individuals believe exactly the opposite. A third possibility is that there is a factor, perhaps an overinclusive tendency in one's thinking, which leads to both ill-health and creative work. In this case, health and creativity are related only because they are individually associated with some underlying characteristic or tendency. In statistical terms it would be a "hidden variable" sometimes also known as the "third variable problem." Rothenberg's work with Cheever supports the view that certain emotional and cognitive tendencies come first and lead to creative work rather than the other way around. Of course, the causality may be bidirectional. There is no reason to assume that only one direction of affect is in operation. Many of these ideas, including the role of the unconscious, depression and the affective disorders, overinclusive thought, and health, are discussed elsewhere in this book.

Keep in mind that not all biographical studies are reliable and useful. Like all historical analyses, a great deal depends on the quality of the information and the interpretations of the biographer.

There is a more objective alternative. This is *historiometry*, which is "the application of quantitative methods to archival data about historic personalities and events to test nomothetic hypotheses about human thought, feeling, and action" (Simonton 1999a, p. 815). Nomothetic hypotheses deal with groups and universals. They can be contrasted with idiographic hypotheses about individual differences. This approach is among the most promising in all creative studies, given its perspective, breadth of application, and objectivity. Simonton (1984, 1990a) has demonstrated how useful historiometry is for the study of various historical, political, social, and cultural influences on genius and talent. It works on several levels. In one report, Simonton (1997c) examined how war, political instability, political fragmentation, and civil disturbances each influence "societal health." Historiometry can also be applied to individuals, as is evidenced by Simonton's (1999a) studies of Ludwig von Beethoven (Simonton 1987b), Napoleon (Simonton 1979), and William Shakespeare (Simonton 1999b).

Shakespeare is an excellent case for historiometry because it uses objective data rather than biographical details. Very little is known about Shakespeare himself (Simonton (1999b) summarized it in 20 lines of an encyclopedia), but the playwright left a corpus of works that can be examined with highly objective historiometric techniques. Take Shakespeare's 154 sonnets. They are formatted in a similar Elizabethan fashion (14 lines of iambic pentameter) but vary in their "aesthetic success" (Simonton 1999b, p. 560). This is evident by the variation with which the sonnets are quoted or included in anthologies. Note the objectivity there: These things can be counted. That is the advantage of historiometric techniques. Simonton also describes the "variety of themes," "richer vocabulary," and "primary process" imagery of the more successful sonnets, success again being defined in terms of quotations and anthology counts.

Simonton (1999b) had even more objective data from Shakespeare's 37 plays. He used frequency of their being recorded, performed, or quoted, along with film, operatic, and print editions and versions. Again note the objectivity; these things can be counted. Standardizing and then ranking the plays, *Hamlet* represents the most successful play, with *Henry VI Part 3* the least. Intriguingly, Shakespeare's more successful plays seem to have been written when he was in his late 30s or perhaps late 40s. This is a typical finding in historiometric research. Not only are objective indicators of success and popularity derived; they can be used to determine optimal ages and to empirically test the Matthew Effect and other historical tendencies.

That Shakespeare did his best work in midlife is consistent with findings from Hull et al. (1978) and the Planck Hypothesis. This posits that younger scientists are more open and receptive to new ideas, and therefore more flexible. Yet youth is not all-important, or creative success would start at its peak and diminish through the life span! Youth and flexibility are beneficial but expertise also contributes to success, and it takes time to develop that. No wonder, then, that there is an optimal age for creative achievement (Simonton 1984, 1999b). Additional support for these ideas was presented by Dietrich (2004). After reviewing neuroanatomical research Dietrich concluded that "It seems that, as we age, a certain version of reality becomes so 'hardwired' through decades of reinforcement that the continuously diminishing ability for cognitive flexibility is overpowered. Or in Nietzsche's words, 'convictions are greater enemies of the truth than lies'" (p. 1022).

Simonton concluded that historiometry supports three important factors that contribute to eminence: (1) being precocious and beginning to produce early, (2) generating a relatively large number of products on a regular basis, and (3) longevity. One may think that precocity is *the* vital component, for an individual who starts early must have a cumulative advantage, whereas a creator starting later may be discouraged by the reinforcements being directed to the precocious. However, this assumes that feedback (e.g., reinforcement) is all-important, and it is thus incongruent with the view that creative individuals have personality traits that lead to their productivity. Perhaps those with the traits leading to creative and productive performance are apparent early in one's life. This explanation is the most realistic, for it is probable that most real-world behaviors are overdetermined.

Crozier (1999) found that in many domains it is career length that is the critical factor. This is an especially interesting finding because it is directly contrary to the idea of marginality. Many famous creators have studied one field early on and then shifted to another. This kind of professional marginality gives them an advantage, as evidenced by Darwin (who borrowed ideas from geology in his theories of biological evolution), Piaget (who started by studying biology and used many of the key concepts in his studies of cognitive development), and Freud (who studied physiology and applied key concepts to his theory of psychoanalysis). Different paths may all lead to creative accomplishment. Some invest long periods in their careers (Crozier 1999), others benefit from a change, from one career to another. It may be that the individual does not need to give up one career and move completely into another. Piaget and Skinner both suggested reading outside one's own field, and Lindauer's (1999; Lindauer, et al. 1997) studies of the old-age style suggest that there are benefits to changing styles rather than changing careers.

Historiometric studies of eminence and genius frequently use productivity. This often works well. Without a doubt productivity is a useful index of fame, and it is highly correlated with certain indicators of quality as well (Table 7.5).

TABLE 7.5   Productive Creators

Creator	Works
Johann Sebastian Bach	46 volumes of compositions
Alfred Binet	277 publications
Charles Darwin	119 publications
Albert Einstein	248 publications
Sigmund Freud	330 publications
Sir Francis Galton	227 publications
Abraham Maslow	165 publications
William James	307 publications
Henri Poincaré	500 papers, 30 books
Arthur Cayley	995 papers
Nobel laureates	3.9 papers per year

From Albert (1975).

Corbin Sicoli (1995) studied the background of a small group of women, each of whom had written best-selling popular songs between 1960 and 1990. She reported many commonalities in their backgrounds: Most had been first- or second-born children and had experienced parental loss at an early age (also see Albert 1980). They had shown signs of early talent and lived near a "cultural mecca." Few had earned college degrees, and most had relationship difficulties (often after achieving financial success). They tended to leave home before age 19, had fewer children than average for women in their cohort, collaborated frequently, and had a tendency toward anxiety or a depressive disorder. Many had abused drugs, and few expressed strong feminism. They demonstrated a capacity to leave their work only to return in a successful manner. Cole and Zuckerman (1987) offer a parallel report on successful women in science.

Popularity can be operationalized, as can productivity. Simonton (1990a) related both to the idea of creativity as a kind of persuasion. He proposed that talented and creative individuals can be identified because their works are so outstanding and important that they persuade others of their worth. This may follow from productivity. That is because of a constant probability of success (Simonton 1999c). In this view, each composition, artwork, or creative product has an equal chance of influencing the field and being deemed original; hence, the more the creator produces, the higher the overall probability that he or she will achieve eminence.

Eminence is rare. In fact, many historiometric studies have confirmed Lotka's Law, which holds that the majority of creative things are produced by a minority of individuals (Albert 1975; Simonton 1984). This law describes the distribution of wealth as well as talent.

HISTORICAL EFFECTS AND LAWS

Lotka's Law. "The number of individuals making a certain income, Q, is inversely proportional to some power of Q" (Simonton 1999d, p. 185).

Price Law. "The number of individuals who have made contributions to a given field, square root of k is the number of individuals who were responsible for half of all those contributions" (Simonton 1999d, p. 195).

Matthew Effect. The rich get rich, the poor get poorer (Merton 1968).

Trigger Effect. One invention may lead to a variety of new ideas and subsequent inventions.

Pygmalion Effect. Expectations have a dramatic impact on the expression of behavior, including creative behavior.

Planck Hypothesis. There is an optimal age for creative work, though it may vary from domain to domain.

LIMITATIONS AND DISADVANTAGES OF THE HISTORICAL APPROACH

Historical analyses are difficult. Data are incomplete and may be slanted. There are even problems with the objective approaches to history, such as historiometry. Objective indicators of creative talent may be slanted toward products, for example, and although something is popular at one point in time, reputations change. Misjudgment about creative people and creative contributions to society are nothing short of rampant.

PRODUCTIVITY

Every measure of productivity and popularity must be interpreted with care. Each is useful and objective, but it is not a direct measure of creativity per se. Popularity, influence, and persuasiveness are also useful, but they do limit the score of our historical analysis. They can be used in studies of eminent persons but may not help forward theories about children's creativity, everyday creativity, or the creative process (Runco & Richards 1997).

PERSUASION, PRODUCTIVITY, CREATIVE PLACES AND PEOPLE

Creativity is studied from many angles. These are sometimes categorized as one of the following:

- **Person:** Traits and characteristics of the creative individual (e.g., open-mindedness)
- **Product:** Inventions, patents, works of art, publications

- **Process:** Either stages of thinking, or perhaps phases with individual and societal inputs
- **Place:** Situational pressures on creativity
- **Persuasion:** Creativity is associated with ideas that are so good that they change the way others think

---

REPUTATIONAL PATHS

The English scientist Henry Cavendish invented and discovered many important things. In Bryson's (2003) words,

> In the course of a long life, Cavendish made a string of singular discoveries—among much else, he was the first person to isolate hydrogen and the first to combine hydrogen and oxygen to form water—but almost nothing he did was entirely divorced from strangeness. To the continuing exasperation of his fellow scientists, he often alluded in published works to results of contingent experiments that he had not yet told anyone about. In his secretness he did not merely resemble Newton, but actively exceeded him. His experiments with electrical conductivity were a century ahead of his time, but unfortunately remained undiscovered until that century had passed. Indeed, the greater part of what he did was not known until the late 19th century when the Cambridge physicist James Clerk Maxwell took on the task of editing Cavendish's papers, by which times credit had nearly always been given to others (p. 60).

Cavendish may have been the most brilliant man of his time. He discovered or anticipated Ohm's law, Dalton's law of partial pressures, Charles' law of gases, the law of the conservation of energy, Richter's law of reciprocal proportions, and much about electrical conductivity. He foresaw the work of tidal friction as it slowed the rotation of the earth, some of Kelvin's work, and much else. He apparently set the table for the so-called noble gases, many of which were not actually fully identified until 1962—200 years after Cavendish did his research. In

---

BOX 7.9

WHO WAS COPERNICUS?

An excellent example of the problems with historical analyses is Polish astronomer Nicolaus Copernicus, from the sixteenth century. As Wertheim (2006, p. R2), described it,

> more so than any other giant of the scientific revolution, Copernicus remains shrouded in mystery. We know his work through his epochal book, *On the Revolution of the Heavenly Spheres*, but of the man himself we have only fragments. Unlike Galileo Galilei, whose life was laid bare in the long, drawn-out process that culminated in his trial, or Johannes Kepler, whose ecstatic personality leaps from the pages of his books and letters, or Isaac Newton, who wrote millions of words of bad theology and left thousands of pages of notebooks with his thoughts on everything from the nature of light to his moral turpitude, we have very little with which to interpret the private nature of the man to whom the word 'revolution' has become indelibly affixed. Newton, Galileo, and Kepler all have their great biographers, while Copernicus has languished in the shadows of literary imagination.

Historical analyses are often plagued by a lack of information.

---

the late 1790s, with a small piece of equipment, Cavendish calculated that the weight of the earth was slightly in excess of 6 billion trillion metric tons. This is approximately 13 000 000 0 00 000 000 000 000 000 pounds. Today's much more sophisticated estimates give us a number which is within 1% of Cavendish's estimate.

Cavendish did not have the reputation he deserved, at least not until late in the twentieth century. This often happens; reputations change. It is one reason reputations may not be good indicators of creative talent. After all, how can a person's creative talent vary, just because other people's opinions vary?

Runco and Kaufman (2006) calculated that of 1100 individuals described in *Encyclopedia Britannica*, the majority had reputations that changed significantly between the 1910 and the 2000 editions. Other examples of significant changes in reputation include William Blake and Rembrandt. If reputations change so much, can we use them to study history? Perhaps, but it is also likely that the people we study (and write about in our contemporary biographies) will be demoted in the future, and individuals we do not recognize at this point in time later turn out to have the most significant impact on society.

Reputations change, but as a matter of fact it is also easy to misjudge creative people and inventions during our own eras. This may be because they are original, and therefore different. For whatever the reason, a huge number of creative people and inventions have been misjudged during their own time.

Misjudgment

The Wright brothers probably benefited enormously from the *zeitgeist* of the early 1900s. Their invention of the airplane also demonstrates another important historical phenomenon, namely misjudgment. In their case it was delayed recognition. True, the first *"Flyer"*

BOX 7.10

WHO WAS SAMUEL MORSE?

Historical analyses are sometimes biased. Even if there is sufficient information about a creative person, it is sometimes distorted. Consider in this regard Samuel F. B. Morse. He is often credited with the invention of the telegraph (Figure 7.2), but his interest was in art. Early on he aspired to make a career (and income) from painting history, in the tradition(s) of Michelangelo, Raphael, and Titian (Petroski 2003; Silverman 2003). He tried once to capture the Grand Gallery of the Louvre on one canvas (yes, with dozens of miniature renditions of the original artworks), apparently assuming that crowds would pay a great deal to view one canvas if it was big enough and contained enough. He also attempted to paint a large canvas specifically to hang under the dome of the Capitol in Washington DC, but not surprisingly that commission never materialized. It is interesting that he had original ideas about art and painting, not about the subject matter about which he earned his fame. Looking back we see Morse as an inventor, not an artist. It is furthermore noteworthy that he was motivated by income (an extrinsic influence), given common lore about intrinsic motivation (see Chapter 9). The point here, however, is that contemporaries of Morse (and Morse himself, for that matter) probably held a different view of his creativity than we do today.

Morse's actual accomplishment is somewhat mundane, at least in the sense that he merely extended existing technologies rather than creating the telegraph out of the blue, on his own. In fact, we cannot be certain who had the key ideas first, and the telegraph is probably another example of a "multiple discovery." As this term denotes, these are discoveries made by more than one person at nearly or precisely the same time. Morse was working on long-distance communication for several years when he heard about the work of a Frenchman on the same process. Morse apparently displayed the self-promotion that is sometimes seen in ambitious people (Gardner 1993a): He criticized the French invention, suggesting that it was more optical and thus analogous to existing techniques than his own electrical telegraph. Incidentally, the first public demonstration of this electric telegraph, or "lightning line," was in September of 1837. It covered 1700 feet, following a complex wire array inside one single building of New York University. In 1844 Morse sent a message much farther, namely from Washington DC to Baltimore. The daughter of the U.S. Patent Commissioner chose the now-famous message: "What hath God wrought?"

is currently in the Smithsonian Museum of Space and Aeronautics, but it took over 40 years to get there. It seems that the Smithsonian tried to push the credit for air flight on a man by the name of Langley. His flying inventions were, to use the trite but useful phrase, "fairly complete failures." The Wrights' *Flyer* was stored under a tarp in Dayton, Ohio for years (Dayton being the hometown of the Wrights), but eventually was shipped to London and put on display. The Smithsonian did not credit the Wright brothers nor obtain the first *Flyer* until 45 years after the historic flight.

PONY EXPRESS STABLES MUSEUM, ST. JOSEPH, MISSOURI (BOTH)

Standing (Left to Right): J.W. (Billy) Richardson; Johnny Fry.
Seated (Left to Right): Charlie Cliff; Gus Cliff.

FIGURE 7.2   This photo shows riders who worked the Pony Express. Apparently it inspired Samuel Morse when he conceived of the relays for the telegraph. *Source: Wikimedia Commons, http://commons.wikimedia.org/wiki/File:Riders_Pony_Express.jpg*

Misjudgments are at least as common outside the sciences and, for example, within the arts. The highly creative art in the East, for example, and specifically that of Indian artists, was greatly misjudged by the English who first traveled there. According to Ramachandran and Hirstein (1999), Indian artists were exploring nonrepresentational art long before Picasso, but it was not recognized because the English were "unconsciously comparing Indian art with the ideals of Western representational art—Renaissance art in particular" (p. 16).

There are even biases *about* science. Eysenck (1997b) described how

> science ... from its beginning, had to battle with the tradition of quackery. Astronomy had to rid itself of its connections with astrology. Chemistry had to cut out its connection with alchemy. The battle was bitter and protracted. Newton was devoted to alchemy, and did much work in that field... . Needless to say it did not produce any new knowledge. Kepler was employed as a court astrologer ... and his astronomical labors were secondary. Not until the time of Dalton did chemistry rid itself of this incubus... . In psychology ... there is such a battle between science and quackery, with such doctrines as existentialism, humanistic psychology, hermeneutics, and above all psychoanalysis constituting the mind's non-scientific part (p. 273).

Creative people and works, such as the Wright brothers and those Indian artists, may have been misjudged in their own time, but it is also common to misjudge earlier creative efforts. Recall here the idea of Whiggist and historical bias, described early in this chapter. Runco (1999c) lists a large number of classic misjudgments about creative people and creative works (Box 7.11).

Judgments by Famous Creative People

It can be difficult to judge creativity. Contemporaries seem to make mistakes with some regularity, as do historians. Creative people also have difficulty judging their own talents. Take Benjamin Franklin. He certainly qualifies as an unambiguously creative individual. Franklin's impact was enormous, especially in his earlier work toward understanding electricity. He characterizes an inventor in the sense that he not only developed an idea, but also developed techniques and applied his ideas in very practical ways. Again, electricity best exemplifies this for not only did Franklin study the process but he also applied his findings. This is especially true in his invention of the lightning rod, which has since prevented an enormous number of fires and deaths, saved a huge amount of money, and is still used frequently today. Franklin is also well known for the Franklin stove, "double spectacles" (bifocals) (Figure 7.4), and his innovations for libraries and the postal service. Apparently Franklin's own preferred invention was his "armonica." This was an instrument he developed by aligning 37 crystal bowls in such a way that they could be rotated. He played music on the armonica in much the same way that playful individuals sometimes wet their finger and twirl it on top of a wine glass. Franklin had 37 crystal glasses in a range of frequencies available to him when playing the armonica. This invention is interesting in that it may have resulted from analogical thinking, or an analogical tactic. But it is also interesting because Franklin is probably more famous for his work on electricity or the other inventions mentioned previously, yet his own preference was for the armonica. This does not necessarily reflect any misjudgment on Franklin's part, though it does demonstrate once again that creators sometimes have judgments that differ from those of their audiences.

Misjudgment on Franklin's part may be more apparent in his work on the "phonetic alphabet." Franklin attempted to modify the English alphabet such that there were six additional letters. These captured common sounds in the English language, hence the term a phonetic

BOX 7.11

FAMOUS MISJUDGMENTS (ADAPTED FROM RUNCO 1999C)

- The first successful powered flight took place just after the turn of the century in 1903, but it was not formally acknowledged for decades. The Wright brothers' *Flyer* aircraft was in storage in a small shed in Dayton, Ohio, hometown of the Wrights, for 25 years. It was eventually put on display in London, but was not appreciated or showcased by the Smithsonian Museum until 1942— 38 years after the first flight at Kitty Hawk, North Carolina.

- The Beatles changed rock 'n' roll. Yet in 1963 the Decca Recording Company stated, "We don't like their sound. Groups of guitars are on the way out." Capitol Records also failed to recognize the appeal of the Beatles, at least in 1964. They decided, "We don't think they'll do anything in this market."

- Writers often are misjudged. The publisher of the Popular Library, for example, was certain that Richard Bach's *"Jonathan Livingston Seagull* would never make it as a paperback."

- A review of Lewis Carroll's *Alice in Wonderland* pointed out that "We fancy that any real child might be more puzzled than enchanted by this stiff, overwrought story."

- The editor of the *San Francisco Examiner* told Rudyard Kipling, "I'm sorry, Mr. Kipling, but you just don't know how to use the English language."

- Henri Matisse, Gertrude Stein, George Braque, and several others artists reportedly visited Picasso while he painted *Les Demoiselles d'Avignon* in 1906 and 1907. They did not like it. It was

indeed a dramatic shift, but very soon it was very positively judged. Alfred Barr, Director of the Museum of Modern Art in New York, referred to it in 1937 as "the most important painting of the 20th century" (Rubin, Seckel, & Cousins 2004). Some say this painting initiated Cubism.

- Alfred Harcourt told William Faulkner's publisher, "You are the only damn fool in New York who would publish it." He was referring to *The Sound and the Fury.*

- Sometimes misjudgment is directed at media or technologies. In 1910 the publication, *The Independent* felt that the cinema is a "fad [that] will die out in the next few years."

- Rembrandt was an unambiguously creative artist. He was not, however, well-respected in his own time. Other artists (e.g., Jan Lievens, Adrien van der Werff) were much more respected.

- Picasso's work was described as "the work of a madman" by the art dealer Vollard in 1907.

- Leonardo da Vinci epitomizes a Renaissance man. But in his own time he was often seen as more of an eccentric than anything in secret, because of the possible public reactions. This says something about what may be required to do creative work. The creator may need to take a risk or relegate public reaction and rely on intrinsic values and motives. No wonder intrinsic motivation and an openness to risk-taking are widely recognized correlates of creative work.

- Many of Leonardo's inventions (e.g., the helicopter) were not appreciated during

(Continued)

BOX 7.11 *(Continued)*

his own time but were eventually revisited and completed.

- The monk Gregor Mendel discovered some basic genetic tendencies in his research on peas. His work was completely overlooked for nearly 50 years.
- Benjamin Franklin is often regarded as a brilliant inventor and statesman. Apparently his talents were not as well respected in his own lifetime. According to Bill Bryson, author of *Made in America*, many of Franklin's contemporaries had difficulty tolerating Franklin's involvement in the politics of the time. Consider next the Gettysburg Address, now widely accepted as one of the greatest of the speeches by U.S.

presidents. It was not always widely respected. Immediately after the speech reactions were quite critical. The *Chicago Times* referred to Lincoln's "flat and dishwatery utterances." Yet throughout most of the latter part of this century school children are asked to memorize the words (Figure 7.3).

- Margaret Thatcher once stated, "No woman in my time will be Prime Minister or Chancellor or Foreign Secretary—not the top jobs. Anyway, I wouldn't want to be Prime Minister; you have to give yourself 100 percent."
- Finally, as Martindale (1990, p. 220) noted, "few people liked Beethoven's Moonlight Sonata when it was first played: it broke too many rules."

alphabet. There was a letter representing the "th" phoneme, and another representing the "ing" phoneme. Franklin also deleted a few letters, including j, q, w, x, and y. Many others have explored alternative alphabets. Indeed, Noah Webster, of *Webster's Dictionary* fame, favored Franklin's phonetic alphabet and continued to work with it even after Franklin had given up.

ART HISTORY

Before concluding the discussion on historical perspectives on creativity, we should consider one other area of study, namely art history. This is directly relevant to the discussion because art is such an unambiguously creative domain. Also, art often functions as a window into society, and that window shows *zeitgeist*, attitudes, and values about creativity extremely well. Art may be especially accurate at capturing the *zeitgeist*. After all, artists did foresee the work of Einstein and Niels Bohr (Shlain 1991).

HEIDEGGER AND BEUYS ON ART AND HISTORY

Truth does not exist in itself beforehand, somewhere among the stars ... it is after all only the openness of beings that first affords the possibility of a somewhere and of a place filled by present beings... . The happening of truth ... is historical in many ways... . Art is historical, and as historical it is the creative preserving of truth in the work.

Heidegger (quoted by Jones 1997, pp. 61, 77)

(Continued)

> I have come to the conclusion that there is no other possibility to do something for man other than through art ... only the creative man can change history, can use his creativity in a revolutionary way ... art equals creativity equals human freedom.
>
> *Beuys (quoted by Jones 1997, p. 212)*

A number of texts offer comprehensive overviews of art history, but Dudek's (2012) review is especially useful for students of creative studies. Here are some of the key events (and styles) described by Dudek:

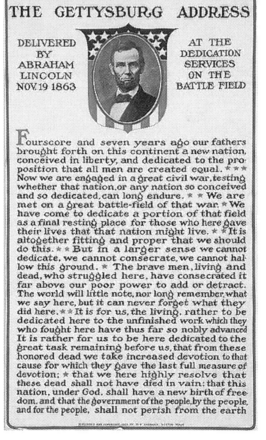

FIGURE 7.3   Many school children memorize the Gettysburg Address, but even it was misjudged when it was first given. *Source: Wikimedia Commons, This media file is in the public domain in the United States. This applies to U.S. works where the copyright has expired, often because its first publication occurred prior to January 1, 1923. http://commons.wikimedia. org/wiki/File:Gettysburg_Address_(poster).jpg*

FIGURE 7.4 Bifocals.

Dudek (2012) continued:

Aristotelian and Kantian theories of aesthetics laid great stress on the category of the transcendent object; that is, on a category of objects beyond the limits of possible experience and knowledge.

The Greeks regarded the arts as handicrafts to serve purposes that were approved by society. The criteria with which to judge such products were concreteness and craftsmanship. The artists' goal was to produce a representation of the ideal in the context of Plato's theory of Ideas. The Greek artist's purpose was to improve on and perfect nature by eliminating imperfections in order to arrive at an ideally beautiful figure according to the "idea" of the beautiful in the mind's eye. With this purpose in mind Greek sculptors and Renaissance artists worked out the canons of proportion for the most perfect human figure…. Interestingly, the Greeks had no term for artist and no concept of the artist as conceived today. The artist was regarded as a craftsman or artisan.

The Romantic focus on the individual as source of artistic inspiration and style was rapidly undermining the Aristotelian system of aesthetics that characterized Western art since the Renaissance. Impressionism was already on solid ground, despite fierce attacks by the Parisian critics. The criteria that had defined good art for two millennia, namely beauty, order, proportion, unity, symmetry, and concinnity were seriously in question. Over the next 100 years they were to become completely obsolete.

The concept of beauty as an intellectual idea … came into prominence during the Renaissance and it was not until the end of the 17th century that the notion of beauty as feeling and emotion rather than as idea began to emerge.

The concept of art as an object of beauty and value for purposes of sheer contemplation did not emerge until the 18th century and it was not until the first half of the 20th century that the idea of art as novel and original creation with autonomous criteria specific to art itself became established. This view emancipated the work from subjugation to all forms of instrumental purposes. And by mid 20th century the Greek and Renaissance ideals were no longer relevant. The success of the revolution in the arts was fully realized in the Cubist, Dadaist, Constructivist and Surrealist movements in the first three decades of the 20th century. Further developments led to Abstract Expressionism (1940s) and Pop, Op, Minimal and Conceptual Art (1960s and 1970s) …. They were all expressions of a totally different spirit and a totally different concept of aesthetics. In the 1980s, with the demise of modernism and the ascendance of Postmodernism, a pluralist philosophy relegated aesthetics to a no-man's land of greater proportions than ever.

The most relevant criterion for the evaluation of works of art became significance, that is, the work's novelty and capacity to offer a new perception of reality.

The succeeding developments in 20th century art were unprecedented with a progressive emergence of new modes of inspiration, execution, and presentation. The spearhead for these changes was the avant-garde and its evolution was greatly assisted by rapid developments in electronic media.

The avant-garde is by definition art that is ahead of its time, that is shocking, disturbing and therefore viewed as socially objectionable. Its specific aim is to undermine the existing order and to replace it by another. It attempts to do this by contradiction, challenge, confrontation and self-assertion. The avant-garde first defines its distance from the establishment and tries with all its resources to make itself felt as an oppositional force aiming to redefine the limits of art.

PROPORTION IN ART

Proportion is still studied today. There is, for example, research on the *golden section* (Konecni 2003). This "is a proportion that has in its various geometric, arithmetic, biological, architectural, and artistic contexts fascinated, for over 2000 years, some of the finest minds in philosophy, the sciences, and the arts. It has been considered the epitome of beauty by aestheticians and used in many different fields. In the twentieth century, Huntley (1970) used it as a major example of aesthetics in mathematics, Bouleau (1963) identified it in major Western paintings, and Le Corbusier (1954) made it the building block of his *Modulor*—the proposal for a fusion of the functional and the aesthetic in architecture" (Konecni 2003, p. 267). The golden section is known as ϕ, or phi, after the Greek architect and sculptor Phidias. It is roughly equivalent to 0.618.

As a matter of fact, rebellion and contrarianism play an enormous role in much of our modern creativity. Two examples from music (rock 'n roll and jazz) both exemplify this. Runco (1999c) listed a long list of contrarian creators, some outside of music and the arts.

ROCK 'N' ROLL

The avant-garde is rebellious. Apparently all of rock 'n' roll is, then, a reflection of the avant-garde, at least according to the *Los Angeles Times*. In a 1998 book review, rock is called "a disagreement with established power—a refutation of authority's influence" (Linfield 1998, p. E6). It may be even more general, at least in music. I say that because Duke Ellington, no rock star, was also contrarian. Ludwig (1995) described how knowingly or not, Ellington exploited traditional musical rules as inspiration for his jazz. If he learned that he was not supposed to use parallel fifths, he immediately would find a way to do so; if told that major sevenths must always rise, he would write a tune in which the line descended from the major seventh; and if the tritone was forbidden, he would find the earliest opportunity to use it and, to emphasize the point, would let it stand alone and exposed (pp. 7–8).

ROMANTICISM

Many changes in attitudes about creativity reflect the Romantic tradition. Sass and Schuldberg (2000–2001), for example, described how

> the romantics borrowed various ideas from Greek antiquity, the Italian Renaissance, and the Enlightenment and then developed a perspective that implies that madness or mental anguish is a necessary condition for serious creative activity, at least in the arts. As a result ... many modern writers have actually courted madness in a willful fashion or have sought to appear mad as a way of ensuring their own creative worth (p. 2).

Becker (2000–2001) contrasted the Enlightenment attitudes with those of the eighteenth- and nineteenth-century Romantics:

> The dominant Enlightenment view of the genius as an educated individual whose abundant imagination was properly tempered by good taste, training in the classics, and an appreciation for the masters proved unacceptable to the romantic spirit. To create a new independence, genius could no longer be seen in the Enlightenment terms of balance, proportion, and a synthesis of mental powers. The romantics, therefore, granted the imagination a clear predominance over those faculties traditionally seen as the rational counterweights to the imagination (p. 49).

The Romantics wanted a unique identity. They needed to break from that past. This led them away from the view that imagination and talent were to be used in moderation and controlled. Again quoting Becker, "The need of the romantics, then, for a sense of identity and for their own intellectual and artistic independence led them to adopt a system of premises that left them defenseless against the label of madness. Trapped by their own logic, they came to see their madness as inevitable" (p. 49). Hence the idea of an eccentric, outlandish, or even mad genius. This attitude is alive and well, as it were. Just look at the creative stereotypes in the media.

This also explains why we so often look for psychopathology among creative persons. Becker (2000–2001) wrote, "although the Enlightenment tended to reward creative individuals who were healthy and rational with the distinction of genius, the 19th and 20th centuries (since the time of romanticism, that is) have shown a distinct preference for those creative individuals who are diseased and, specifically, schizophrenic" (p. 52).

Cubbs (1994) implies that the romantic view of the artist as an outsider and rebel has redefined creativity such that it becomes something special, magical, and non-universally distributed. She described this as a significant change, for "while in the past much art may have overtly served collective values and shared traditions of the established social order, often reinforcing the dominant powers of church and state, it now claimed an allegiance only to the spectors of the imagination, to the ideals of self expression, and to a mythical realm of subjectivity held to be the magical province of creativity and genius" (p. 79). She hypothesized that Romanticism was a reaction to the "crumbling social order and modern alienation brought about by the industrial revolution" (p. 79) and a reaction to materialistic values and empiricism.

The romantic perspective may explain some of the admiration oft-given to rebels, contrarians, eccentrics, and even unconventional and marginal individuals. "Marginal," in this case, refers to individuals who are outside a domain. Various kinds of marginality have been identified, including cultural and professional marginalities (Gardner & Wolf 1988;

Lasswell 1959; Simonton 1988). McLaughlin (2000) suggested that each is an expression of romanticism, and given how often product brands and pop groups are given rebellious names (e.g., "The Outlaws"), this seems to make sense. This may be more true of the United States than anywhere else—after all, our Founding Fathers were revolutionaries! And without a doubt there is an optimal level of marginality (McLaughlin 2000). Too much makes a person entirely intolerable. We will not even understand them enough to be interested. Within that optimal boundary, however, they are intriguing and offer fresh, uninhibited ideas.

Romanticism, with its emphasis on individuality and subjective and irrational processes, may be most obvious in recent history, but it may have been brewing, so to speak, for quite some time. At least that is implied by Dudek and Marchand's (1983) uncovering long-standing difficulties in individualism: "Each epic is inevitably characterized by a variety of idiosyncratic styles; but its unique style results from the fact that these are generally subordinate to a broader underlying principle—a core principle which dominates the times until a new paradigm releases it. It is in this sense that Classicism in its broad outlines was dominant for some 1000 years, without preventing strongly individualized (personalized) variants." Perhaps individualism is inextricable from original and creative work.

CREATIVITY IN SOCIAL CONTEXT

Individuality has also been very recently questioned. Consider the postmodernistic emphasis on context and audiences (Jones 1997). Jones put it this way: "the artwork finds its creative completion in the spectator's interpretation" (p. 209). This is very significant, in part because it relegates the creator, or at least makes the creative person one part of the process. Recall here the systems view, which begins with the individual, leads to the field, and eventually influences the domain (Csikszentmihalyi 1990a). In the chapter on the social perspective on creativity we will find this a reflection of the attributional view of creativity, with social judgments as important as the product itself (Kasof 1995; Runco 1995c).

> No individual is responsible for producing an invention ex nihlo. The elevation of the single inventor to the position of sole creator best exaggerates his influence over events, and at worst denies the involvement of those humbler members of society without whose work his task might have been impossible (Burke 1995, p. 288).

Nietzsche seemed to think in this fashion, for he emphasized "the aesthetic activity of the audience" which "involves creation in that 'we fabricate the greater part of the experience and can hardly be compelled not to contemplate some event as its "inventor" ... one is much more of an artist then one realizes'" (Nietzsche 1886/1973, quoted by Jones 1997, p. 209). Heidegger can again be quoted as well: "The 'world is never an object' but is the consciousness of the subject conditioned by culture and history" (Jones 1997, p. 211). Art thus tells us about culture, as well as history. It tells us about ourselves—and about the efficacy of creative efforts. Surely this is one of the most important lessons from history (and this chapter).

CONCLUSIONS

Various historical events and situations seem to influence creativity, among them war, civil unrest, and economic ups and downs. Yet one of the most significant influences on creativity is *zeitgeist*, the spirit of the times. This is manifested in attitudes, expectations, and assumptions about creative things and creative people. This is what draws people into creative endeavor—or scares some of them away from it. The important lesson from history may be that different eras have different ways of thinking. They don't just have different environments and resources, though that is also true. The world you see around you is in many ways (e.g., tall buildings, fast cars, large cities) very different from what was present for much of human history, and previous generations did not have the Internet, mass media, TiVo, and huge libraries. They may also have had less discretionary time, though apparently that is debatable. Each of these things can influence creativity. *Zeitgeist*, attitudes, expectations, and assumptions certainly do. *Zeitgeist* is an overarching and hugely powerful force.

The discussion of Romanticism demonstrated one dramatic change in assumptions about creativity. It led to the view that individuals should be individuals. In a word, they should be unique. This view can be seen in aesthetic expression and the rapid changes in artistic style; the intent there is to change, to stay new, to be original. This view is also apparent in the social and behavioral sciences. Humanists, including Maslow (1971) and Rogers (1995), tied uniqueness to self-actualization and health.

The interesting thing is that current *zeitgeist* has brought creativity and several undesirable traits together. Now that creativity is tied to independence and unconventional tendencies, we must admit that creativity also is associated with certain forms of psychopathology. They, too, led to unconventional behaviors, and in certain instances, creativity. The association of creativity and health is explored in more detail in Chapter 4, but we should remember that *zeitgeist* plays a role in all of this. It was the change in attitudes about creativity that led to the recognition that creative people may have unconventional tendencies. Lachmann (2005) makes this very clear in his description of Richard Wagner, Marc Chagall, and Igor Stravinsky. Each of them "violated expectations" in their work, and each was creative but also, at least temporarily, disrespected because of it. Lachmann (2005, p. 162) described how "Stravinsky's ballet *Sacre du Printemps* so shocked its audience when it was first performed in Paris in 1914 that it was called 'perverted' by music critics. The audience at its performance broke into a near riot." He concluded that "What is judged to be 'perverted' is defined by context, by place and by time" (p. 162; also see Benedict 1989; Szasz 1984). So, too, for creativity. That was the point of the misjudgments listed in Box 7.11.

There is a practical side to *zeitgeist* and these ideas about their impact on creativity. That is because the attitudes and assumptions about creativity from any one era will not only influence reactions to artists (and the labels used to describe them and their work), they will also affect who does what. Psychoeconomic theory is relevant here with its prediction that certain eras will allow a creative child to explore his or her potential, perhaps with an apprenticeship (as in the case of da Vinci) within the domain of talent. In psychoeconomic terms, these opportunities allow individuals to make active investments in their potentials (Rubenson & Runco 1992, 1995). They can explore the arts, or some chosen creative endeavor, knowing that it is acceptable. It may even be rewarded! But those rewards depend on the *zeitgeist*. In a *zeitgeist* that favors creativity, individuals with obvious talents will easily find careers and perhaps economic stability. Contrast that with a *zeitgeist* that favors conventions and conformity. Who will an employer think is the most desirable prospective employee? Not the creative individual—too risky. The point is that *zeitgeist* is a useful concept that allows us to understand the past, but it is more practical than that because it helps us to consider what investments and behaviors will be appreciated and rewarded.

BOX 7.12

DIFFERENT BUT INCOMPARABLE: THE GREAT HISTORICAL IRONY

It may come as a surprise that specific historical eras are rarely compared with one another. Exceptions include Bullough et al. (1980), Gray (1966), Kroeber (1944), Lamb and Easton (1984), and Naroll, Benjamin, Fohl, Hildreth, and Shaefer (1971). Bullough et al., for instance, compared eighteenth-century Scotland with fifteenth-century Italy. Then there are comparisons of configurations (Kroeber 1944) and phases in the scientific process (Kuhn 1962). Yet direct comparisons are surprisingly uncommon. This is because it is not really fair to compare historical eras, nor

cultures. They are different but incomparable. That is the irony of the historical approach: Changes and differences can be easily identified but these suggest that comparisons are not reasonable.

It is also unfair to compare people working in different eras. Recall here the impact of tools on the creative process and how they sometimes triggered significant changes. Consider this: Sigmund Freud published an impressive 330 books and articles, but what would he or another luminary have done with electronic dictation or a word processor?

The most important consideration in studies of famous figures, and in fact in all historical analyses, is objectivity. This is more difficult than it may sound because all our efforts reflect our own assumptions, expectations, and values. Of course this is one benefit of historical analyses: They highlight the biases of the present. They show us how others thought and felt, and when these differ from our own thoughts and feelings, it is only reasonable to question the objectivity and universality of our ways. So much in life makes sense only within a particular historical and cultural context. With this in mind we must be very careful interpreting history. Our interpretations will color our conclusions.

Without a doubt creativity can be understood only by taking both historical context and the influence of individuals into account. Davis et al. (2012) suggested exactly this:

> To understand the creative individual we are interested in recreating the fullest possible context. We try to reconstruct the cultural and intellectual environment of the individual who produced the creative work. The nature of our subject matter compels us to take an historical, developmental perspective. What intellectual, artistic, literary movements were occurring at the time which made this person's achievement possible? What prevailing currents made the work difficult? At the same time how do we understand the special achievements of this particular individual? Is it continuous with ideas that were influential at that time? If so, why was it this individual who achieved a significant advance? And how did he or she differ from others who

approached but did not solve the same problem? Creative work is, in this light, a function of *zeitgeist* and the individual's talents.

The historical approach has many advantages, and a few disadvantages. The latter were reviewed earlier, and include the difficulties in being objective, concerns about what objective indicators are used (e.g., productivity and reputations), and historical relativity. One limitation was not explored in any detail—ideas that are culture-specific. They do not apply direction to the Asian emphasis on universals and harmony (Kwang 2002). The next chapter addresses this.

CHAPTER

8

Culture and Creativity

No one ever looks at the world with pristine eyes.
Ruth Benedict, Patterns of Culture (1989, p. 2)

ADVANCE ORGANIZER

- Cultural Values
- Stop Rule
- Squelchers

- Tolerance
- Individualism vs. Collectivism
- Global Creativity Index

INTRODUCTION

Orville and Wilbur Wright seemed to be in the right place at the right time. Not many people believed that they would be the first to fly. Even within the United States, the Smithsonian had predicted and even supported one of the Wrights' competitors. Apparently the Wrights also were considered to be extreme long shots in France. The French had invented the hot-air balloon, and many reportedly thought that their inventors naturally would fly first. The French had an attitude about flying and invention. Horace Walpole, fourth Earl of Oxford, went so far as to say, "If something foreign arrives at Paris, they either think they have invented it, or that it was always there" (quoted by Schiff 2005, p. 7). This of course says something about *zeitgeist*. It reflects the spirit of the times, but we should perhaps say "of the times within a particular place." There are numerous examples of cultural and geographic differences in attitudes about creativity.

COLLECTIVISM AND CREATIVITY

One of the most widely recognized differences between cultures is that of individualism vs. collectivism. Hofstede (1991) presented an especially clear definition of them:

> Individualism pertains to societies in which the ties between individuals are loose: everyone is expected to look after himself or herself and his or her immediate family. Collectivism, as its opposite, pertains to societies

in which people from birth onward are integrated into strong, cohesive in-groups, which throughout people's lifetimes continue to protect them in exchange for unquestioning loyalty (p. 51).

Collectivism is most typical of Asia and the East. There it is a reflection of Confucianism (Cheung & Scherling 1999) and is manifested in an emphasis on harmony, sociocentric thinking, self-sacrifice, a strong work ethic, and respect for elders and those in authority positions. Simplifying some, harmony may lead individuals to conventional behavior, whereas independence might more easily lead to unconventional and creative behavior. As Burke (1995) described it,

> The medieval Chinese were without a doubt the most fruitfully inventive people on Earth. However, the fact that the technology of the modern world is Western shows to what extent the two cultures were different

BOX 8.1

CHINESE INVENTIONS

Gunpowder, silk weaving, paper, clockwork, the waterwheel, the horizontal loom, and various astronomical instruments are all Chinese innovations (Burke 1995). Without a doubt, cultural values are important for creativity, innovation, and invention. In fact, certain cultural values seem to lead specifically to invention and others specifically to innovation. At least this was the premise of Evans' (2005) comparison of the United States and Great Britain. He proposed that Britain nurtures invention and inventors. Alexander Fleming, known for his discovery of penicillin in 1928, Robert Watson Watt, inventor of a system of radar in 1935, and Frank Whittle, designer of a jet engine in 1930, exemplify this. They were all British. Yet according to Evans their inventions and discoveries were little known and underutilized until American innovators marketed them. Evans suggested that America became a technological and scientific giant, truly leading the world, because it valued practicality and innovation. He further tied the interest in marketing and commercial production of inventions to the "anti-elitist" attitude that is common in the United States, and indeed

which was instrumental in the founding of the United States in 1776.

Evans (2005) also cited Henry Ford (the Model T automobile and assembly line), Orville and Wilbur Wright (the airplane), George Eastman (photographic materials and apparatus), Garret Augustus Morgan (the gas mask and traffic signal), Sara Breedlove Walker (hair care products), and Levi Strauss (blue jeans). Evans was very careful with the selections of these cases and described the specific criteria he used to identify innovators. He actually had a board of judges that included representatives from MIT and Yale University to aid in his selection of cases. Henry Ford may be the best example. After all, cars were invented in Europe, but they were initially toys for the extreme upper class. Then Ford designed the Model T and developed the mass production techniques so almost everyone in the United States with an income could drive a car. Strauss is another good example. He patented his jeans in 1873. These were innovations in the sense that Strauss used rivets (an existing technology) to hold the jeans together.

at time vital in the history of the effects of innovation on society. In the stable, civilized East the innovations were not permitted to bring about radical social change as they were in the brawling, dynamic West. The chief reason for this may have been the stultifying effects of Chinese bureaucracy .... There was no drive for the individual to use technology to improve his lot and so rise in the world, because rising in the world was out of the question (p. 68).

Bureaucracy can certainly undermine the creative attitude, but values and the resulting expectations are at the heart of the collectivism–individualism continuum. Indeed, values are central in whatever cultural differences are found. Values allow certain personalities and inhibit others. Values dictate developmental experiences and parenting practices, as well as educational emphases. Rudowicz (2003) supported this with her observation that

> the Chinese notion of a person, consequently the educational goals and practices, differ significantly from the western concepts. The traditional Chinese social system was rather rigid, defensive, discouraging independence and stressing the importance of social harmony which could be achieved through compromise, moderation, and conformity…. People were required to look for guidance either upwards towards authority or backwards to the traditions of the past. Therefore Chinese parents and teachers have put much emphasis on obedience, self-discipline, moral conduct, and responsibility.

There are several indications that much of what Burke (1995) identified in the preceding quotation is still operating, just as it was in medieval China (Kwang 2002; Runco 2001a). It could be weaker and less influential at this point, but the values have been remarkably stable.

FAMILIES, EDUCATION, AND VALUES

What is honored in a culture will be cultivated there. Attributed to Aristotle by Torrance (2003, p. 277)

Values are communicated via various institutions, including the family and the school. Albert (1994, 1996), for example, described how "families pool in and interpret for all members the culture. This means that one of the first things that a child is placed in is a culture, without being asked, 'do you want to be part of this or not?'" Stein (1953, p. 319) noted that "a culture [also] fosters creativity to the extent that its parent–child relationships and child-rearing techniques do not result in the setting up of rigid boundaries in the inner personal regions." Cropley (1973) described how cultural pressure can "reduce range of variety of behavior." This is an important part of socialization and conveys the idea of a stereotypical ideal student (Raina & Raina 1971). When the emphasis is on harmony, socialization is homogenizing and does not encourage the child to explore unconventional options nor behave creatively (Cropley 1973).

Of course, as is the case in virtually every comparison of group differences—be they sex differences, cultural differences, or anything along those lines—there is a great deal of within-group variation. This is a vital point to keep in mind because it means that although group averages and tendencies may differ dramatically, there are individuals within each group who are more typical of the other group. There are many Americans, for example, who have collectivist tendencies, just as there are Chinese who are quite individualistic. With this in mind it is inappropriate to refer to "the East" and "the West," or to Eastern and Western cultures. At the very least it is a generalization.

CROSS-CULTURAL COMPARISON ERROR

In addition to pointing to socialization and the family, the emphasis on cultural values also underscores the fact that cultures, like historical eras, should not be compared. Such comparisons are simply unfair. Any comparison will require criteria, and those criteria will reflect one culture or another. It is analogous to the historical and Whiggist biases described earlier; there it was deemed unfair to compare different eras, especially if the individual doing the comparing relies on present-day criteria and values.

In my Foreword to Kwang's (2002) book, I singled out his argument that the East and the West both have something to offer creative efforts. Here is the summary statement from that Foreword:

> [Kwang] captures what may be the key idea in cross cultural studies, namely that cultures differ but cannot and should not be directly compared. Any such comparison is unfair, much like the common expression (in the West) about comparing apples and oranges. Just to name one example, the West might seem to have an advantage for fulfilling creative potentials in that it allows the individual more liberty. Individuality is encouraged, rewarded, expected. There is probably more autonomy in the West, less pressure for conformity and harmony. On the other hand, human emotions are treated in different ways in the East and the West, with the East typically more open to and in control of emotions. This is especially significant when it comes to creativity because emotions have such weight in creative work.

Different cultures express creativity in different domains and behaviors. They cannot be directly compared, at least in the sense that they are ranked. They differ, but any ranking assumes criteria and standards that probably do not apply to all cultures.

STOP RULES, CONVENTIONS, AND CULTURAL INHIBITION

Justice has two arms, one for punishing, the other for rewarding. Culture has two arms as well. It can reward behaviors that are valuable or punish behaviors that are taboo. The behaviors that are rewarded are those deemed to be valuable within that culture. The behaviors punished are deemed inappropriate. Values determine what is rewarded or punished. Cultural influences cannot be understood by simply examining what is valuable and what is encouraged. We must also take note of what is extinguished. Magyari-Beck (1991) claimed, "individuals can successfully practice their creativity if and only if there are no substantial obstacles in the society preventing them from their creative work" (p. 419).

Individuals within a culture internalize what have been called *stop rules* or *filters* (Anderson & Cropley 1966). In some cultures, individuality and originality are acceptable and allowable, and perhaps even rewarded. The more they are rewarded, and the less they are punished or ignored, the more creativity will flourish. Other behaviors may be considered, especially by children (who have yet to fully grasp cultural values), but even then they are not expressed if the stop rules have their effect.

A third option, in addition to rewarding or punishing creativity, is to ignore it. In the case of creative behavior, this implies tolerance. Hence in a family (or classroom, or business), certain expressions of originality may be allowed. They are neither punished, nor reinforced. If this occurs, it is likely that individual differences in motivation and temperament will determine how much originality is expressed. Its expression will not be solely determined by

BOX 8.2

SQUELCHERS

Chapter 6 defined squelchers as the things we say to ourselves and to others that tend to inhibit creative thinking and behavior (Davis 1999). Squelchers often reflect cultural values. Others may reflect family values, though of course these tend to assume cultural values as well. Here are examples of inter-personal squelchers:

- What would your mother think?
- That's not my job
- Don't rock the boat
- We've always done it the other way.
- We've always done it that way!
- Don't make waves!
- You can't fight city hall (Figure 8.1).

FIGURE 8.1 City halls can be aesthetically appealing, as this photo of London's City Hall shows quite clearly. But there may be something to the idea that, too often, "You can't fight City Hall" squelches creative thinking. This is just one type of squelcher. *Source: Wikimedia Commons, This work has been released into the public domain by its author, Arpingstone. This applies worldwide. In some countries this may not be legally possible; if so: Arpingstone grants anyone the right to use this work for any purpose, without any conditions, unless such conditions are required by law. http://commons. wikimedia.org/wiki/File:City.hall.london.arp.jpg.*

the contingencies. Tolerance is especially important for creativity because sometimes it is unconventional and surprising. It often reflects nonconformity. But if that is tolerated, the benefits may be apparent: Creativity may occur if the individual is so inclined. There are cultural differences in the acceptable latitude for behavior and in tolerance levels. There are, then, two different contexts in which creativity may be found: that which rewards it and that which merely tolerates it.

Adams (1974) named a variety of cultural taboos that can inhibit the expression of creative behavior. In much of Western culture, playfulness and humor may be acceptable only in certain groups (e.g., children) and places (e.g., during play time). They may be taboo when any actual work needs to be done. That of course is a problem if the "work" requires creative thinking. Imagine going into a meeting with your boss, and after he or she says, "This is a serious problem for us—how would you handle it?" you reply, "Let's try telling some jokes, playing around with it for a while!" You are likely to hear what Davis (1999) called a *squelcher*: a phrase like "get serious," "that will never work," or "the boss won't like it" (Box 8.2).

TOLERANCE, TALENT, AND TECHNOLOGY

Many cultural differences reflect varying degrees of tolerance. Indeed, Florida (2005) pointed to the three Ts—tolerance, talent, and technology—to explain global differences in creativity. He then identified members of the creative class and calculated population proportions to rank cities and countries in terms of their support for those individuals. Different cities and countries have different amounts of the three Ts, which supposedly translates directly into creativity.

The creative class represents a group of people, around the world, who supposedly represent a new and distinct social class. This class is made up of individuals who work in creative ways or in creative fields. This includes engineers, scientists, architects, educators, artists, writers, and entertainers. These groups share an economic role or function, which is to produce new ideas. These ideas may be expressed in original technologies or other products with a creative form or content. Interestingly, people in the creative class supposedly share certain traits, including diversity, merit, and individuality. This, of course, is one of the controversial aspects of Florida's thesis, for a great deal of research has demonstrated differences among creative groups, especially those representing different domains (e.g., architecture vs. the arts).

Florida (2005) estimated that the creative class presently comprises 38 million people. He further estimated this class to account for more than 30% of the workforce in the United States, but this figure is decreasing. He does not agree with Gruber (quoted by Runco 2003d) that creativity is on the rise, at least in the United States. China and India are now ostensibly supporting creative talent better than the United States, and Ireland (Dublin) and Australia (Sydney) are already well ahead of the United States, proportionally speaking (Florida 2005).

Although this approach to culture and national differences is intriguing, obviously it assumes that creativity is a mature skill and tied to professional activities. It does not apply well to everyday creativity. Recall here his ideas about merit as an important characteristic. The three Ts perspective is useful, however, in pinpointing differences that may result from varying levels of tolerance. It applies very broadly and can be applied in educational or everyday settings to encourage creativity. Tolerance is among the most important capacities a parent, teacher, or boss can possess if he or she wishes to encourage creativity. Creative people are often unconventional, and sometimes downright eccentric or nonconformist, but if we want their creativity, we should tolerate their unconventional ways.

This is especially true because of the benefits they may bring to our lives. Elsewhere I proposed that cultural marginality stimulates creativity. Lasswell (1959, p. 213) said much the same: "A well-known occasion of innovation is when peoples of diverse cultures intermingle, as when the Roman Empire expanded its domain. Biologists speak of 'hybrid vigor'; and presumably some innovations that occur must be attributed to whatever increase of basic capability results therefrom. More obvious is the effect of intermingling upon maps of knowledge."

Campbell (1960) also supported this view: "persons who have been uprooted from traditional cultures, or who have been thoroughly exposed to two or more cultures, seem to have the advantage in the range of hypotheses they are apt to consider, and through this means, in the frequency of creative innovation" (p. 391).

EMPIRICAL STUDIES

A number of empirical investigations have explored cultural differences. Jellen and Urban (1989), for example, administered their own Test for Creative Thinking-Drawing Production to children in 11 different countries. Scores from England, Germany, and the United States were higher than those for children from Indonesia, India, and China. Jellen and Urban had expected high scores from children in the Philippines, but that did not occur. Nevertheless, they concluded that Western culture is more conducive to divergent thinking than is Eastern culture.

Jaquish and Ripple (1984) reported contrasts of various age groups sampled from Hong Kong and the United States. The youngest age group consisted of 9-year-old children, the oldest, 60-year-old adults. Jaquish and Ripple relied on an acoustic test where one word is presented and examinees write down their reactions. Then another word is presented, and again examinees write down their reactions. There are four such test items (words). They found that the adults produced more original reactions than the children, with groups from the United States outperforming their counterparts from Hong Kong.

Rudowicz et al. (1995) reported higher scores in Chinese children in Hong Kong, in contrast to children in the United States, at least in terms of the Torrance figural tests of divergent thinking. This test is a bit different from the figural tests of Wallach and Kogan (1965) in that the children were required to use a set of circles to create a figure. (In the Wallach and Kogan figural tests, an abstract line drawing is presented and examinees write down what the drawing could represent. There, only the stimulus is figural but the response is verbal.) Rudowicz suggested that it might have been the experience with Chinese characters that gave the children from Hong Kong the advantage. This explanation deemphasizes cultural values (e.g., individualism vs. collectivism of thought), but of course differences could result from a combination of those values and specific experiences.

Pornrungroj (1992) also used the Torrance figural tests in a comparison of Thai children who were born and raised in Thailand with Thai-American children who were born and raised in the United States. Comparisons indicated that the children born in Thailand had higher divergent thinking scores, across the board (fluency, flexibility, originality, and elaboration).

In the most recent examination of such differences, Zha et al. (2006) administered the Creativity Assessment Packet (Williams 1991) to 56 Chinese graduate students and 55 graduate students native to the United States. This is, of course, a select sample, all individuals being highly educated. Every individual was in a doctoral program at the time of the investigation. In fact, Zha et al. looked at Graduate Record Examination test scores, in addition to the divergent thinking test scores from the Creativity Assessment Packet.

Not surprisingly, tendencies toward individualism and collectivism were assessed with the Individualism–Collectivism Test (Triandis 1995). Put briefly, this focuses on the examinee's perception of his or her responsibilities and obligations, which may be toward their culture or society. There are three subtests, one for attitudes, one for self-concept, and one for values.

Zha et al. (2006) reported that graduate students from the United States performed at higher levels than Chinese graduate students on four of the five indicators of creative potential. The exception was flexibility, which was not significantly different in the two groups. The largest effect size (and therefore difference) was in the originality scores. The U.S. students also had the expected individualistic tendencies and the Chinese students the expected collectivistic tendencies. They also earned higher scores on the quantitative section of the Graduate Record Examination. Surprisingly, correlations with the two cultural groups failed to find strong associations between individualism and divergent thinking. Only two of the 30 correlations that might have supported this association were statistically significant.

Zha et al. (2006) wrote:

> Independent sample t-tests revealed that American graduate students were more individualistic than Chinese graduate students.... The stereotypes that Chinese, as a whole, seek conformity and the approval of others and from society, whereas Americans, as a whole, seek personal happiness and self-actualization with less regard for the needs of society received some confirmation herein.... Asian countries tend to be more collectivistic compared to the United States, emphasizing conformity and obedience, whereas American culture emphasizes the achievement of personal goals.

Some time earlier, Avarim and Milgram (1977) reported that individuals in the Soviet Union tended to have lower scores on tests of divergent thinking than individuals in the United States and individuals in Israel. They suggested that there was more dogma in the Soviet Union, and that this led to more conformity and less originality.

Research in Norway and India found that aesthetic and theoretical values predicted divergent thinking measures among high school students (Paramesh 1971; Sen & Hagtvet 1993), but not all of the evidence supports these findings (Kumar 1978).

Of course not all cultural research is psychometric. Mead (1959) compared Samoans, Arapesh, Bali, and the Manus and found that creativity was viewed and encouraged differently in each. For the Samoans, creativity involves making only slight changes in traditional forms of creativity. For the Arapesh, creativity lacks form and "flounders in the helpless ineffectuality in the present." For the Manus, creativity lacks traditional form but "a restless seeking, a reaching-out for the new" is developed in these people so that they become "not the inheritors of tradition but the willing originators of forms of which they are virtually ignorant" (p. 231). Mead hypothesized a link between mental health and creativity, which is of course compatible with the views of Lachmann (2005) and others from Chapter 7. Mental health, for Mead (1959), is the absence of mental illness and the presence of "active fulfillment of individual potentialities" (p. 222). For her there are two key questions concerning creativity and culture: "How is the problem of individual creativity handled? Which individuals, under what circumstances, have an opportunity to experience creativity?" (p. 223).

Cultural Rankings

Torrance (2003) threw a broader net by using indicators of what he called creativity level, creativity characteristics, and creative occupational aspiration. He used these to rank locations around the world. Some are states, some countries. His rankings are as follows.

1. Minnesota
2. California
3. West Germany
4. Norway
5. China, Singapore
6. Tamil, Singapore
7. Western Australia
8. Malay
9. Singapore
10. Georgia, Black
11. India, New Delhi
12. Western Samoa

Age Differences Within Culture

Torrance (2003) also reported cultural differences in what he had previously labeled the fourth-grade slump. The United States generally shows the slump in fourth grade, but India and Germany show it one or two years later, at least in Torrance's figural test of divergent thinking. Some cultures apparently show little discontinuity and slump. In Western Samoa, apparently there were significant differences between different schools. These particular investigations support the idea of overlap among cultures. That is because the fourth-grade slump probably characterizes only about 50–60% of the student body; it does not happen to everyone, even within one culture. Hence you might have a slumping fourth grader in a highly creative culture who behaves more creatively than a particular student who is in a less creative culture but is not slumping. The high in the low groups might be higher than the low in the high group, if that makes it clearer.

Interestingly, Raina (1989) reported that Indian children did not experience the slump. He described a continuous growth rather than discontinuity. Other within-culture investigations are:

- Baldwin (2003) on African Americans
- Garcia (2003) on Chicano populations
- Oral (2003) and Guencer & Oral (1993) on Turks
- Niu (2003) on Ancient China
- Hallman (1970) on Hindu theories of creativity
- Chein (1983) on Taiwan.

FAMILY AND EDUCATION

Many aspects of culture, including cultural values, are communicated to children through the family. This is true, for instance, of values of what is appropriate and what is inappropriate. Socialization is pretty much just that—communication (by parents and teachers) of what is appropriate and acceptable for children and students. Cropley (1967a) described this as follows:

> Whatever levels of [creative] potential are present in a child, the direction in which they are developed (towards convergence or divergence), will be … guided by the kinds of interactions the children have with their parents. In turn, the parents' thinking about how children should be treated is related to the way in which they themselves were reared, in fact, to the prevailing cultural notions about what is right and what [is] wrong behavior in children. If a culture imposes severe negative sanctions against certain behaviors, most parents will try to suppress them in their children, while they will try to foster those behaviors of which the culture approves (p. 62).

CULTURAL TRADITIONS AND CREATIVITY

Values sometimes are tied to geographical and cultural traditions. Skills may be nurtured out of necessity, or because they were once useful. Mistry and Rogoff (1985), for example, found that the Eskimos have developed keen figural abilities to meet the demands of hunting. They extended this line of thought to the development of talent. Talents develop in specific domains. Further, different cultures value and foster varying skills, thus different talents are encouraged in different cultural contexts. The individual development of specific talents occurs, then, in cultural contexts in which the value of a particular talent is stressed, and that talent is then selectively developed. Different cultural groups may foster different cognitive skills that are adaptive to a particular environment.

CREATIVITY IN ORGANIZATIONS AND BUSINESS

Basadur (1994) found the organizational climate in Japan to encourage creativity. He described mean incentives, and even a language that supported originality. In one organization there was a suggestion box and new ideas were treated as "golden eggs."

Walberg and Stariha (1992) wrote about a kind of underinvestment by various cultures, which was the theme discussed by Rubenson and Runco (1992a), though they focused on underinvestments in the United States.

CULTURAL PRODUCTS AND PROCESSES

Raina et al. (2001) suggested that one idiosyncrasy of the West is the emphasis on products, and the use of novelty and appropriateness as criteria and indicators of creativity. They felt that the East was more process-oriented and focused on "the experience of personal fulfillment" (p. 148). This claim about cultural differences was supported in an investigation of literary creativity. Unfortunately their conclusion about cultural differences is weakened somewhat by the fact that they present data from case studies, with the individuals studied being winners of the prestigious Jnanpith Award ("the highest literary award in India").

This is slightly problematic because it means that the evidence used to support the conclusion about cultural differences is itself slanted toward products. Individuals who won this award had been productive in the sense of writing award-winning literature. It would also be unfair to conclude that all creativity in the West is product-oriented. There are dozens if not hundreds of descriptions of the creative process, especially among artists in the West. Admittedly, most individuals doing research on creativity appreciate creative products because they can be studied using highly objective techniques; but this does not mean that it is the only perspective of creativity in the West. It is merely a bias that characterizes the scientific research that is done in the West.

Perhaps more convincing, then, was Raina et al.'s (2001) observations about similarities between India and the West. They found, for example, "frustrations and sufferings" (p. 151) among the eminent award winners and cited the work of Albert (1971) and others on the frequency of similar earlier experiences among creative individuals raised in the West. There is also a similarity in the sense that "defiance of tradition has been a feature common to many Jnanpith laureates" (p. 153). Creative individuals in the West are also typically nonconforming and unconventional. Very likely, creativity is inherently original and as such requires some kind of unconventional behavior. A final similarity noted by Raina et al. was that the authors in their study tended to be involved in networks of enterprise. This often holds true of creative individuals in the West as well (Davis et al. 2012; Gruber 1988).

IMPLICIT THEORIES

Culture communicates to individuals via standards, norms, values, and *zeitgeist*. The last of these, as explained in Chapter 7, refers to "the spirit of the time" and the attitudes and values that are shared at a particular time in a particular place. This definition suggests that a fruitful method for the study of culture and creativity involves implicit theories. These are the views held by parents, teachers, and other nonscientists.

Spiel and von Korff (1998) examined the implicit theories of scientists, artists, school teachers, and politicians. They studied the implicit theories of "individuals who are assumed to influence others views on creativity" (p. 43). More specifically, they examined the implicit theories of artists, scientists, teachers, and politicians from Germany and Austria. Very importantly, they found extreme variability in the implicit theories. In fact, they found more variability among the various professional groups (teachers, politicians, and so on) than between the German and Austrian participants, and more among the professional groups than was found between males and females, especially among artists in the West. Admittedly, most individuals doing research on creativity appreciate creative products because they can be studied using highly objective techniques, but this does not mean that it is the only perspective of creativity in the West. It is merely a bias that characterizes the scientific research done in the West.

Johnson et al. (2003) uncovered differences between India and the United States in the implicit theories of creativity that were held by teachers. They used the same methodology that was described in Chapter 6 to identify the traits that teachers felt were most strongly related to creativity (and traits that were unrelated, or contraindicative). They concluded,

> Indian parents and teachers viewed traits commonly considered to be creative or uncreative by U.S. parents and teachers in very similar ways, with few exceptions…. Comparisons were made within and across cultures between the creativity and desirability ratings of each item. The findings support the previous results … in that parents and teachers in the U.S. view creative traits in children favorably. They do not support the conclusions of the Indian studies regarding the undesirability of creative children (Raina 1975; Raina & Raina 1971; Singh 1987). In fact, in the present study parents and teachers in both countries viewed, for the most part, creative traits as desirable and uncreative traits as undesirable. These observations were qualified, however, by the adjectives which received creativity and desirability ratings in opposite directions. These, as mentioned earlier, gave some reassurance that measures derived from parent and teacher implicit theories, and ratings collected using them, are not merely the influence of social desirability. These observations suggest that the adults not only recognize the indicative and contraindicative aspects of creativity, but they understand that some of the traits associated with creativity in children may be undesirable.

CULTURAL METAPHORS FOR CREATIVITY

Cultural differences in attitudes about creativity can often be inferred from language and metaphor. This is perhaps most obvious in the Eastern metaphors for creativity. Sundararajan (2004), for instance, described how "Chi'i [the vital breath] is intimately related to the Taoist notions of spirit and creativity" and is strongly connected with nature and natural phenomena (Goleman et al. 1992; see Figure 8.2).

FIGURE 8.2 E. Paul Torrance wrote about the relationship between Zen and creativity. Later, Pritzker (1999) elaborated on this relationship. *Source: Wikimedia Commons, Statement from Wikimedia: "I, the copyright holder of this work, release this work into the public domain. This applies worldwide. In some countries this may not be legally possible; if so: I grant anyone the right to use this work for any purpose, without any conditions, unless such conditions are required by law." That is from the website. http://commons.wikimedia.org/wiki/File:Kanji_zen.jpg.*

SATORI AND ZEN

Torrance (1979a) looked to Japanese culture in his search for an understanding of creativity. He spent some time living in Japan and emphasized parallels between the Japanese concept of *satori* and creativity. *Satori* apparently can be defined in various ways, and it may be one of those Zen concepts that must be discovered for oneself. Torrance did point out that *satori* is a kind of enlightenment and understanding, a kind of "a-ha," which results from devotion, being in love with something, constant practice, concentration, "absorption to the exclusion of other things" (p. ix), and most of all, persistence. Clearly, it is possible that the experience of *satori* parallels and may overlap with Csikszentmihalyi's (1990) concept of flow.

CONCLUSIONS

At one point in time, the people designing tests of intelligence felt they could refine the administration and format of a test such that it would be "culture free." The intent was to minimize or avoid an experiential bias. This kind of bias systematically favors individuals who have had certain experiences and penalizes individuals who have not. Efforts along these lines did not last long, however, for it quickly became apparent that each of us is a product of our culture. Culture always influences our development, values, thinking, and behavior. The people designing tests gave up on their efforts to develop a "culture-free test" and turned to "culture-fair tests."

Each of us is indeed a product of culture. Sometimes is it more than one culture, but nonetheless we are each tied to our background and our upbringing, and these in turn are determined partly by our cultural background. Creativity is influenced by culture in various ways.

It is certainly true that cultural differences tend to reflect differences in values. If something is valued in a culture, it will be noticed, appreciated, and rewarded. Most cultural differences can be best understood by examining values.

Generalizations about everyone in any one culture are usually inappropriate, but there is a unique risk in studies of creativity and culture. This is because several dimensions of culture have been shown to differ among cultures and may inhibit creative persons—yet creativity is sometimes a reaction to inhibition! This is a distinct problem, and to convey that, the two issues with generalizations about culture can be summarized:

- Any one aspect of a culture (e.g., harmony, individualism) may not characterize every individual within that culture.
- Even if one of those aspects of culture does characterize a particular individual, he or she may not have the predicted reaction to it.

It is thus inappropriate to assume that any cultural factor (or any potential influence of any sort) is necessarily effective. This is especially true of those factors that are described as inhibitive. Every individual interprets the environment in an idiosyncratic fashion. Two individuals can have the exact same experience but have entirely different interpretations of it. This is especially clear in the research on stress (Runco 2012) and in the research on creativity. Hence the factors identified within any one culture might be labeled inhibitive, but they are really only "potentially inhibitive," and we should expect some creative persons to be immune.

In fact, some creative persons may thrive! Many creative persons are challenged by things that would debilitate or inhibit most other persons. Consider the research on handedness and creativity. Burke et al. (1989) suggested that left-handed individuals are sometimes creative precisely because their handedness puts them in situations where they must cope, and their reactions are sometimes creative precisely for that reason. This conclusion is, however, based on a small sample of subjects; more data should be collected before any conclusions about the impact of a right-handed world on left-handed persons are warranted.

Other support for the view that potential inhibitors challenge creative persons is biographical and autobiographical. There are notable problems with both biographies and autobiographies, mostly involving subjectivity and potential biases, yet there is quite a bit of commonality among them. Data should be collected using experimental methods, but at the very least the biographical studies do suggest that some persons are untroubled by problems, and in fact challenged by them. It may be useful to view it this way: creativity can be a kind of problem solving, and some individuals employ creative problem-solving tactics and procedures when they are faced with problems. Some even prefer problems and ambiguity, they sometimes seek them out! Along the same lines, some creative persons have described the disappearance of problems (Runco 1994e). The problems do not really vanish, of course; they just stop being problems. It becomes a joy, and when it does, the situation that was once a problem has become something completely different, namely, an opportunity or challenge.

9

Personality and Motivation

When you're strange, no one remembers your name.
The Doors, *"People Are Strange"*
No man clearly understands the sources of his own creativity, and it is only since Freud that we have begun to have an inkling of how general this lack of understanding of one's own motives and of the sources of one's own ideas. **Boring (1971, p. 55)**

ADVANCE ORGANIZER

- Introduction
  - Advantages and Disadvantages of the Personality Perspective
  - IPAR Studies
  - Longitudinal Studies of Personality
  - Deviance, Controlled Weirdness, Contrarianism
- Parental Personalities
- Paradoxical Personalities
- Motivation
  - Necessity as the Mother of Invention
  - Intrinsic and Extrinsic Motives
- Values
- Conclusions

INTRODUCTION

People change as they get older. They also display different behaviors when situations change. They may act one way in certain situations but another way in different situations. There is, then, some stability, consistency, and continuity in our behavior, but also some variation. Personality is made up of those characteristics that show some stability. Indeed, much of the research on personality is designed to identify stable traits. Traits are characteristics that show stability.

DEFINING PERSONALITY

What is personality? Personality can be defined as "that pattern of characteristic thoughts, feelings, and behaviors, that distinguishes one person from another and that persists over time and situations" (Phares 1986, p. 4). Note that this does not rely entirely on traits. Also important is that "the critical feature is the unique way in which each person combines these traits" (Phares 1986, p. 6). This may explain why not every creative person shows exactly the same traits.

Do creative individuals have particular traits and tendencies? Very likely they do. In fact, in a meta-analysis of personality and creativity, Feist (1998) concluded that,

> Empirical research over the past 45 years makes a rather convincing case that creative people behave consistently over time and situation and in ways that distinguish them from others. It is safe to say that in general a "creative personality" does exist and personality dispositions do regularly and predictably relate to creative achievement (p. 304).

The flip side is also true. Quoting Mumford and Gustafson (1988), "many reasons exist for an individual's failure to develop ideas or to translate ideas into action, but one of the more important influences appears to be the individual's unique personality" (p. 34).

This chapter examines theories and research on the creative personality. There is an extensive body of research to review; some of the first empirical investigations of creativity looked to personality and attempted to identify the core characteristics of the creative individual.

The personality approach to creative individuals offers a unique perspective on creativity, with both advantages and disadvantages. It has an advantage over many other approaches in that standardized assessment techniques are available. These allow an assessment of the reliability and validity of the empirical findings. The California Psychological Inventory (CPI), for example, has a Creative Personality Scale, as does the Adjective Check List (ACL). Admittedly the predictive validity of these scales is not overwhelming. In other words, an individual with usually high levels of autonomy may not be particularly creative. In fact, an individual with the creative personality profile—high levels of the traits just mentioned, and low levels of competing traits—may not behave in a creative fashion.

This lack of predictive validity may be due to the uncertainty about whether or not the traits manifested by creative individuals actually led to their creative performance. This is the problem of causality. The personality traits in question may have facilitated the creativity of artists and scientists involved in the development of the measures, but personality is only part of the story. Additionally, personality assessments often specify individual traits and tendencies, but what is most important is the constellation of traits. Creativity is a complex, after all, and no one predictor, cognitive, affective, or personological, tells the whole story. Research indicates that the traits do not guarantee creativity, and many individuals have the traits mentioned earlier, but do not perform creatively.

A second problem with the personality approach is that of situational influences. Most psychologists recognize that human behavior is a function of both stable traits *and* environmental, situational variables. Think of a school-aged child, for instance, who is shy and slightly introverted. She may not be too eager to sing, dance, or draw while in her classroom and around her classmates; but in the comfort of home, she may sing, dance, *and* draw in a spontaneous and creative manner. Her creative potential and personality is the same in the home and in class, but the situations vary in many ways, and these can facilitate or inhibit creative expression. Personality traits are relatively stable but not absolutely constant.

This chapter addresses the question given earlier, "Do creative individuals have particular traits?" The answer seems to be affirmative, and interestingly, these represent both positive and negative traits. Each is discussed later, as are certain contraindicative traits, which are characteristics that are not found in creative individuals. As you might expect, there are traits that allow creativity but also some that hinder it. Domain differences are identified in this chapter, as they were in just about every chapter of this book. How do artists differ from scientists? How do musicians differ from painters?

PERSONALITY ASSESSMENT AND RESEARCH

Everyone studying creativity owes a great deal to the seminal studies conducted at the Institute of Personality Assessment and Research (IPAR). Many of these investigations were conducted nearly 50 years ago. This may seem like a long time, but that apparently does not matter. Many of the findings and interpretations from IPAR (e.g., Barron 1972; Gough 1975; Helson 1999; MacKinnon 1965) still hold true.

IPAR was established at University of California, Berkeley in 1949. It was originally funded by the Rockefeller Foundation. The staff included Eric Erikson, Richard Crutchfeld, and Harrison Gough. At that point Frank Barron was a graduate student affiliated with the IPAR. Donald MacKinnon was the first director. Early studies at IPAR involved architects, writers, mathematicians, and space specialists. Both Helson (1999) and MacKinnon (1975) released histories of IPAR.

In one seminal study MacKinnon (1963) examined the personality, regulations of the ego, and images of the self of architects (Figure 9.1). "Images of the self" were "conceived of as an individual system of perceptions, conceptions, and images of himself as a person" (MacKinnon 1963, p. 253). It follows that he would collect data from self-reports and include questions about the ideal self.

There were three groups of architects. The first (Architects 1) was composed of highly talented architects who had been identified by professors of architecture in the University of California system. A second group of architects (Architects 2) was matched with the first group in terms of geographic location (where they did their professional work) as well as age. Each in fact had worked with one of the architects in the first group for at least two years. A third sample (yes, Architects 3) also was matched on geographic location and age but had never worked with any of the Architects 1 group. The idea here was a wide representation, with Architects 1 representing a very high level of professional creativity, Architects 2 a moderate level, and Architects 3 a lower level of creativity. Keep in mind that there was a restricted range. Talent levels varied, but all participants were professional

FIGURE 9.1   Architecture is an unambiguously creative domain. Not surprisingly, the creativity of architects has long been studied. *This is a photo of the Sydney Opera House.*

architects and presumably all at least somewhat talented. MacKinnon compared the three groups in terms of personality, ego, function, and images of the self, but he also correlated his various measures with a creativity rating. This was obtained from a large group of architectural experts, including professors from around the nation and editors of architectural journals.

Looking at the self-reports from the Adjective Check List, MacKinnon found the most commonly given descriptor by Architects 1 was *imaginative*. For the other groups it was *civilized* and *conscientious* (Architects 2 and 3, respectively). MacKinnon (1965) wrote: "Architects 1 [most creative], more often than either architects 2 or 3, see themselves as inventive, determined, independent, individualistic, enthusiastic, and industrious…. A strikingly different image of the self is held by both architects 2 and 3, who more often check as self descriptive the adjectives responsible, sincere, reliable, dependable, clear-thinking, tolerant, and understanding" (p. 255). MacKinnon also found less creative architects to be defensive, an idea that is consistent with the research on the self-actualization of creative individuals (Maslow 1968; Rogers 1954/1959; Runco et al. 1993). As we will see later in this chapter, self-actualization is indicative of self-acceptance and honesty about one's self. As a matter of fact, creativity ratings of the architects were positively correlated with the number of unfavorable adjectives checked, meaning that more creative individuals saw themselves in a less favorable light. This also could indicate that they were honest about themselves and tended less toward socially desirable responding. More creative individuals are more likely to admit that they have unfavorable tendencies. The most creative group of architects also had the lowest self-control scores.

ISSUES IN METHODOLOGY

- *Restricted range*: A homogeneous sample of subjects, or perhaps set of scores, that does not show much variation and therefore may not represent the population at large.
- *Socially desirable responding*: The tendency of most people to describe themselves in a favorable light, or at least respond in a manner that is consistent with expectations and cultural values. Creative individuals may not do this as much as others.

Of additional interest is MacKinnon's measure of *lability*. Harrison Gough developed the ACL and described lability in the following way:

> Though there is a facet of high ego strength in this scale [lability], an adventurous delighting in the new and different and a sensitivity to all that is unusual and challenging, the main emphasis seems to be on an inner restlessness and an inability to tolerate consistency and routine. The high scoring subject is seen favorably as spontaneous, but unfavorably as excitable, temperamental, restless, nervous, and high strung. The psychological equilibrium, the balance of forces, is an uneasy one in this person and he seems impelled towards change and new experience in an endless flight from his perplexities. The low scorer is more routinized, more planful, and conventional. He reports stricter opinions on right and wrong practices, and a greater need for order and regularity. He is described by observers as thorough, organized, steady, and unemotional (quoted by MacKinnon 1963, pp. 259–260).

Not surprisingly, lability was indeed correlated with the creativity scale ratings.

Note the comment about an uneasy equilibrium. Something along these lines has been found many times over in studies of creative personalities. Late in this chapter this will be related to observations of the "paradoxical character" associated with creativity. Note also the negative relationship with routine and conventions, and the suggestion that less creative people are less emotional. This very likely relates to the sensitivity and the emotional drive that often characterize creative people. Some of this implies a lower level of what MacKinnon called *personal adjustment*. You will see similar reports throughout this chapter: Creativity is associated with both favorable and unfavorable traits. In fact, you can probably see why it is useful to begin this chapter with a review of the IPAR studies: They covered a great deal of ground, much of which we are still exploring in the field of creative studies.

MacKinnon (1965) reported a correlation between the creativity scale scores and autonomy, but a negative correlation with the endurance scale from the adjective checklist. He was very careful to interpret the second of these because he felt that the endurance on this scale might be short term and that creative individuals may have their own kind. As he put it, the endurance tapped by the Adjective Check List

> involves working uninterruptedly at a task until it is finished, sticking to a problem even though one is not making progress, and working steadily at a single job before undertaking others. Endurance of this short range type is not so characteristic of the highly creative person as is endurance over a long period of time, even a lifetime, with much more flexibility and behavior and variation and specific means and goals. In the life history interview, for example, the more creative architects, more often than the less creative, point turning to another activity when seriously blocked at a task and returning later to it when refreshed, whereas less creative architects more often report working stubbornly at a problem when blocked in their attempts at solutions (p. 262).

MacKinnon may have been thinking of what more recently has been called a "network of enterprise": the tendency of creative individuals to have several things going on at once and to be able to move back and forth among them (Gruber 1988). This gives them an advantage, noted by MacKinnon, in that someone can habituate or encounter some sort of block, and put the task aside but continue to work in a relative area, only to come back refreshed and probably taking advantage of incubation and those kinds of benefits.

MacKinnon also reported that the more creative individuals preferred "the challenge of disorder to the barrenness of simplicity" (p. 263). This, too, was later confirmed by Barron (1995) among others. It is sometimes tested with various preferences for complexity measures (Barron 1955, 1963b).

Turning to the description of ideal selves, MacKinnon found that the most creative architects, unlike the other groups, would have liked to improve their interpersonal reactions and social relationships. They wanted to be more considerate, forgiving, sociable, sympathetic, kind, generous, tactful, warm, and patient. They also would prefer having a higher level of energy, as was indicated by the terms "energetic" and "enterprising" in their reports of ideal selves.

Many of these findings from MacKinnon suggest that the more creative architects are the least conventional. In fact, at one point MacKinnon concluded that "it is at once apparent that creative architects feel their primary responsibility is to their own high standards of what is right and proper in architectural design" (p. 273). They are independent and autonomous in more ways than one. MacKinnon added,

> their less creative colleagues report more often being able to take other people's ideas and concepts and fashion them into practical architectural designs and programs.... The independence with which creative architects work is revealed in their expressed dislike and avoidance of administrative work ... and in the frequency with which they assert that they are not team men and prefer to work alone.... indeed, they see themselves as much less interested than their colleagues in making a serious effort to keep up with current publications in the literature and architecture (p. 274).

They were, then, autonomous and independent and perhaps intentionally marginal, at least in a professional sense. Dudek and Hall (1991) reported a follow-up of the creative architects first identified by MacKinnon. The average age of the architects at the time of the follow-up was 71 years. The oldest was 88, the youngest 62. Interviews indicated that many of the architects were still productive. This was especially true of those with clear drive and commitment. Dudek and Hall also identified overlearned architectural skills, salesmanship, aesthetic sensitivity, and the willingness to delegate responsibility to be critical for lifelong productivity.

Various investigations have confirmed that personality is predictive of career choice and performance (Holland 1997; Kelly & Kneipp 2009). Holland, for example, claimed that people choose careers based in large part on their personalities. This claim was supported by his own data, as well as that of Kelly and Kneipp (2009). Much of the work on this topic uses Holland's own measures of interests. It has been used in various studies of creativity (e.g., Ludwig 1995; Runco et al. 2012a) and is summarized in Table 9.1.

Interestingly, the artistic type seems to be the easiest to predict. Kelly and Kneipp (2009), for example, found it to be most strongly related to attitudes and creative behaviors ($R = .51$).

TABLE 9.1 Holland Interest Types

Type	Examples
Artistic	Values aesthetic activity
Social	Thinks about helping others, welfare, teaching
Investigative	Thinks about abstractions, science
Realistic	Enjoys practical matters, working with mechanical devices
Enterprising	Tends to organize and lead or direct
Conventional	Values structured activity

BOX 9.1

MARGINALITY

Piaget, Freud, Darwin, and many other creative individuals discussed in Chapter 7 were professionally marginal. They each worked outside their fields, Piaget drawing from biology in his work on cognitive development, Freud studying physiology before developing psychoanalytic theory, and Darwin looking to several other fields, including geology, in his writing about biological evolution. Skinner and Piaget both explicitly recommended intentional marginality, at least in the form of reading outside one's own area of expertise. Gardner (1993) argued that famous creators actually desire marginality. He referred to *asynchrony* as one form of a desirable tension, in this case, between the individual and the field or the domain. In his words, "I maintain that each of our individuals stands out in the extent to which he or she *sought* conditions of asynchrony, receiving a kind of thrill or flow experience from being at the edge and eventually finding it difficult to understand why anyone would not wish to experience the fruits asynchrony" (p. 382). Much of this complements the contrarianism of creative individuals, which is discussed later in this chapter. It is also entirely consistent with a theme of creative studies, namely that many parts of creative accomplishment (and the fulfillment of creative potentials) are a function of choice and intentions.

LONGITUDINAL STUDIES

Longitudinal studies are especially interesting and useful. There is some issue about the stability of personality (Rubin 1982) and the possibility that personality changes through the life span must be acknowledged. Still, this does not weaken associations found between specific traits and creative potential or performance.

Several other longitudinal studies were initiated just about the time IPAR was started, and MacKinnon was observing the architects for the first time. In one of these longitudinal studies, started in 1950, 80 graduate students, all male, were observed and received various measures of intelligence and creative potential. Forty-four years later these were assessed again, when the individuals were 72 years old. Comparisons indicated stability over the years. Most important may have been that personality variables, including tolerance and "psychological mindedness," explained 20% of the variability in the measures of creative potential. Some traits (e.g., psychological mindedness) were more stable than others (e.g., dominance). Feist and Barron (2003) saw indications of "norm-doubting," self-acceptance, and openness to experience related to creativity. They refuted earlier suggestions that creative scientists were hostile and arrogant.

Yet another longitudinal study, the Mills Longitudinal Study (Helson 1996), began in the late 1950s. Women at Mills College were invited to participate in 1958–1959 and again one year later. They received various measures of personality (e.g., the California Psychological Inventory, the ACL, and the Minnesota Multiphasic Personality Inventory). Creative potential was estimated from faculty nominations. Actual creative performance was based on career success (when the women had reached their 50s). Helson (1996) admitted that "Although our emphasis has been on career productivity as the realization of creative potential, we have kept in mind that creative potential may be actualized in other ways, such as insight into and development of one's own personality" (p. 90). Data were collected from the parents of the longitudinal participants, as well as from the women themselves.

A measure of validity was demonstrated by the fact that the IPAR staff identified the same women as the Mills faculty; they agreed on creativity ratings. Additionally, various measures showed the more creative women to be less conforming and more original, at least on measures of divergent thinking (but not the Thematic Apperception Test). The creative women also displayed social poise and assurance, achievement through independence, and persistence. You can no doubt see the profile emerging from these various studies. They seem to agree, for example, that creative individuals are autonomous and persistent.

Helson (1999) described an interesting aspect of this particular longitudinal study: The women in this sample experienced the Feminist Movement early in their adulthood. One message of that movement concerned personal independence. This means that the participants in the Mills study may have had an experience (the Feminist Movement) that other women will not have. This kind of *cohort effect* plagues many longitudinal studies. Frequently a group being followed has an experience that other cohorts will not. This implies that they may be a unique sample, and of course generalizations to other cohorts (who have not had the same experience) are therefore questionable. The benefits of longitudinal research outweigh the drawbacks, but of course limitations must be acknowledged, just as Helson (1999) so carefully did. In the Mills study, the particular experience may have been especially germane because independence plays such a key role in creativity. Importantly, correlations between originality, complexity, and creative temperament administered at different points in the longitudinal study (e.g., ages 21 and 27) indicated fairly impressive stability ($r_s < .44$, and some above .70).

DOMAIN DIFFERENCES

Even early on it was clear that there are differences between various domains of creativity. Studies at IPAR, for example, focused on and compared creative talents within particular domains (e.g., architecture, writing). Even work in the 1930s assumed domain specificity (e.g., Patrick 1935, 1937, 1938, 1941). Still, the most convincing evidence for such differences was presented by Howard Gardner (1983). He marshaled developmental, cognitive, and experimental research in his description of what were eventually eight domains. The eight domains in Gardner's theory are musical, mathematical, verbal, bodily-kinesthetic, spatial, interpersonal, intrapersonal, and naturalistic. The architects in the IPAR studies represented an interesting blend of skills. No doubt they were strong in spatial skills, but there is more to architecture than spatial skills. Several other groups (e.g., writers) were involved in IPAR studies as well as architects.

PERSONALITY OF ART STUDENTS

Art may represent the most unambiguously creative domain of all. No wonder, then, that artists often participate in studies of the creative personality. Getzels and Csikszentmihalyi (1976), for example, worked extensively with art students from the Chicago Institute of Art. The art students were observed and received various measures, including the Allport-Vernon-Lindzey Study of Values, the Thematic Apperception Test, and a sentence completion test. The observations were very informative, especially in the finding that the more creative students spent more time preparing to work than did the other students. Getzels and Csikszentmihalyi described this preparation as a kind of problem finding. That meshes well with the cognitive literature on problem discovery and problem generation (Runco 1994e) and, according to follow-up assessments done years later, was very important for the success of the artists. Those students who spent more time thinking and preparing before they painted (while in the studio when data were first collected) turned out to be the most successful artists 18 years later (Csikszentmihalyi 1990a). They had a distinctive pattern of traits as well, with high scores on introspection, imaginativeness, self-sufficiency, aloofness, and sensitivity. Contraindicative traits included ego-strength, cheerfulness, conformity to social norms, and conscientiousness.

Artists also have been studied by Simon (1979), Jung (1962), Bachtold (1973), and Gridley (2006). Simon (1979) administered the Myers-Briggs Type Indicator (MBTI) to members of an art guild and found them to be oriented toward intuition (over sensation). This is indicative of the preference for hidden patterns and hidden meanings and a preference for facts over ideas. Jung (1962), whose theory was used in developing the MBTI, reported a preference toward turning inward (toward oneself), and an idea orientation in his work with artists. Bachtold (1973) administered the 16 Factor test to both established writers (authors) and artists, and then later to a large sample of writers, scientists, psychologists, and artists. The more creative individuals in these various samples were less conservative and more adventurous than the general population. Gridley (2006) reported that the artists in his sample of approximately 120 full- and part-time professionals were more liberal and not conservative.

AUTONOMY, INDEPENDENCE, AND NONCONFORMITY

Autonomy in its various manifestations may play a pivotal role in all creative work. This may be because autonomy is functionally related to creativity. It is functional and necessary for all creativity. That is quite a grand claim, especially given how difficult it is to define creativity, yet there is one thing on which everyone agrees. Creative things are always original. There is more to creativity than originality, but originality is absolutely necessary. Moreover, originality may require some sort of autonomy. Originality implies that the person is doing something that is different from what others are doing, and that is probably easiest if he or she is independent and autonomous.

Autonomy may also underlie and explain a range of other correlates of creativity. Creativity has been related to nonconformity, rebelliousness, and unconventionality (Crutchfield 1962; Griffin & McDermott 1998; Sulloway 1996), for example, and it is easy to see how these each might depend on autonomy. Surely people can most easily rebel if they are autonomous. Just as surely, it would be difficult to rebel if you depended on other people (low autonomy). This implies that contraindicative indicators may reflect a kind of conformity.

Traits and Creativity

Indicative traits (e.g., autonomy) are positively related to creativity. *Contraindicative* traits (e.g., conformity) are negatively related to creativity. The presence of these traits may inhibit the expression of creative talents (i.e., actual creative performance) or the fulfillment of creative potentials.

It also explains why creative individuals are not always universally admired. Take the classroom, for example, where creativity is less admired than more conventional tendencies, such as courtesy and punctuality. Westby and Dawson (1995) described how many teachers may even state that they value and encourage creativity in their classrooms, but when asked to describe ideal students list mostly contraindicative traits. Educators prefer dependability, reliability, and "good-natured" children to those who are "nonconforming," and "individualistic." Educators do usually deal with large groups, so no wonder they prefer children who are easy to instruct and direct.

Independence is sometimes encouraged. Runco and Albert (1985) discovered that the parents of many gifted children expected reasonable autonomy. This was evidenced by the things they allowed their children to do and the ages at which the children were allowed to do them. Parental estimates of the appropriate ages for each of the activities were negatively correlated with the divergent thinking of the children.

This is not to say that parents should give complete freedom to their children! Parents should provide their children with some freedom, but also show that the children must make good decisions. Parents should be authoritative but not overly authoritarian nor entirely permissive. Children need some independence, but if they have too little, they will not develop the self-control and discretion that are also necessary for creative thinking.

SELF-CONTROL

Dacey et al. (1998, p. 116) emphasized self-control in their profile of creativity. In their words, "An almost symbiotic relationship exists between creativity and self-control, in that one needs creativity in order to envision a plan or visualize a desired outcome, two elements that are essential to self-control." Dacey and Lennon differentiated two kinds of self-control: The first type is "the immediate control that we use in our everyday lives at any given moment, such as conforming to appropriate forms of behavior, sticking to a routine, or following a schedule to meet a deadline…. The second type of self-control requires insight, faith, and a vision of the future…. [It] is motivated by passion, self-confidence, and a sense of self-worth" (pp. 120–121).

Runco (1996d) referred to something similar and labeled it *discretion*. He suggested that all children are creative, though the degree of potential may vary from person to person. What is shared, in this view, is the capacity to assimilate and construct original interpretations of experience. We all have the capacity to be original, then, but of course creativity requires more than that. Creative things are also fitting. This is where control and discretion come in. They insure that originality is used to appropriate ends. Importantly, discretion may explain why some people are creative some of the time but conform at other times. Personality theory describes something like this as a trait × state interaction, the idea being that we have stable traits but they are expressed in different ways in different environments or settings.

CONTROLLED WEIRDNESS

The view just described, with originality and appropriateness both involved in creativity, and autonomy but discretion also involved, is probably what led Frank Barron (one of our IPAR heroes) to suggest, "dare to be a radical, but don't be a damn fool." He also wrote about *controlled weirdness* (Barron 1993). That label says it all! The person has the potential to be weird but controls it. They are imaginative, but also realistic. Carlsson (2002) used the term *controlled imagination*.

DEVIANCE

Several traits associated with creativity can lead to deviance. In this case the individual is too original, too autonomous, and the discretion or control is lacking.

What is deviance? It depends who you ask. As Eisenman (1994–1995, 1997) noted, both psychologists and sociologists look at deviance, but they do so from different perspectives. Eisenman felt that "there has been a terrible flaw in the sociological approach…. With few exceptions sociologists have seen deviance as something bad, while deviance should simply mean different. Thus creativity is deviance because it involves statistically infrequent behavior. The person who is independent in a conforming group is deviant, but perhaps in a good way" (p. 55). Eisenman's own empirical studies of deviance sampled prisoners who were either psychotic or had a conduct disorder. He found both groups to be relatively uncreative. His findings thus did not support the theory that "delinquency may develop as a creative enterprise for many adolescents" (Eisenman 1994–1995, p. 1). He did admit that many creative persons may have difficulty responding to authority. (Think back to MacKinnon's (1965) more creative architects, with their avoidance of administrative work.) The autonomy and independence of creative individuals could easily lead to a questioning of authority. Of course it may not be so dramatic and lead to incarceration! Runco (1994c) found a milder case in research within businesses: The most creative individuals were the least satisfied. One explanation of this is that organization is a kind of authority and has authority figures, such as supervisors, managers, and bosses.

Eisenman (1994–1995) estimated the creative potential of incarcerated subjects with two standard measures. The first was a preference for complexity. Barron (1995) had used this measure with great success in IPAR studies, and Eisenman felt it most appropriate for his study because it is a nonverbal test and is probably independent of intelligence and educational level. Eisenman also used the Thematic Apperception Test (TAT), in which examinees are shown pictures (on small cards) and asked for an explanation of the scene on the card. Essentially, the individual is asked to tell a story about what is implied by the scene on the card. This is a highly verbal projective task, the idea being that creativity is projected onto the unique way that individuals interpret their world. In addition to the finding that both groups of incarcerated individuals were relatively uncreative in both their TAT interpretations and their preferences, Eisenman found that the psychotic prisoners performed at lower levels on the creativity tests than did the conduct disordered prisoners.

PSYCHOTICISM

Some definitions of psychopathology emphasize deviance (Benedict 1989; Szasz 1984). This can create problems, given that deviance is just a kind of difference (Eisenman 1994–1995). Think of it this way: If you put an aborigine from some nontechnological area in Manhattan, they will be deviant (maybe not in Los Angeles or Venice, but Manhattan, definitely). But they are not sick; they are just different. That being said, certain forms of psychopathology, such as psychosis, are sometimes associated with creative talent. In fact, clinical studies of creative individuals have identified a number of characteristics that also could be listed in this chapter as well. They are in the other chapters because they often are associated with psychopathology. Various forms of deviance are included in the present chapter, but they each reflect some control or discretion as well. Look at it this way: Many of the traits listed here reflect the controlled weirdness of creative people, while the traits in the clinical research on creativity reflect just plain weirdness.

IMPULSIVITY AND ADVENTUROUSNESS

Eisenman also worked with art students who, when encouraged to be impulsive, produced more creative works (Grossman et al. 1974). The study found that individuals who smoked marijuana had relatively high scores on tests of creativity and adventurousness and relatively low scores on authoritarianism. At one point Eisenman admitted that

I previously mentioned that prisoners tend to be low on creativity … there are occasional exceptions, but, unfortunately the exceptions tend to be in the area of crime: Some prisoners have creative skills when it comes to being a criminal. One kind who uses their creative and impulsive tendencies for horrible purposes is the anti-social personality disorder. This is the proper term … for what used to be called psychopaths, and then later, sociopaths. The anti-social personality is impulsive, without conscience, has little or no anxiety, and no empathy for others, although they may be clever in sizing up others in order to manipulate them (p. 63).

There are debates about the "dark side of creativity" (McLaren 1993) and malevolent creativity (Cropley et al., 2008), and the creative antisocial personality would surely fit into one or both of those.

CONTRARIANISM

In moderation, originality, the questioning of authority, and autonomy are good things. In fact, it may be that there is a certain attraction to people who do just that. That would explain why so many products are given names implying rebellion and independence, and why so many musical groups have names implying the same. How many groups have been named "The Outlaws" for goodness sake?

CONTRARIAN ARTISTS

I've got friends in low places. *Garth Brooks*

You may be right, I may be crazy, but it just might be a lunatic you're looking for. *Billy Joel*

Happiness is a warm gun. *The Beatles (Figure 9.2)*

The fact about contemporaries … is that they're doing the same thing on another railway line; one resents their distracting one, flashing past, the wrong way … One keeps one's eyes on one's own road. *Virginia Woolf, 1931 (from Ippolito & Tweney 2003)*

FIGURE 9.2 The Beatles were contrarian. They wrote thought-provoking lyrics ("happiness is a warm gun"), cut their hair and dresses in new styles, and did many new and different things in their music. They often broke with tradition. *Source: Photo by Taylor Ray Runco, 2013.*

Controlled weirdness can lead to *contrarianism*. A contrarian is someone who does something different from what others are doing. The term seems to have been used first in the field of economics (Malkiel 1990), but now is used widely in studies of creativity (Rubenson & Runco 1992a; Sternberg & Lubart 1996). What is important for creativity is that the contrarian thinks in a fashion that differs from how others think. Creative ideas may result, in part, because contrarian cognition leads the individual to original ideas and original directions. Contrarianism deserves special attention because it can be abused and confused so easily. It is intentional, sometimes tactical. If it is unintentional it is best to call it oppositional thinking, defined by Ludwig (1995) as "the almost automatic tendency to adopt a contrary or opposite response" (pp. 7–8).

By no means does being a contrarian guarantee creativity. There are many uncreative contrarians. Some are contrarians for contrarian's sake, or more likely because it can attract attention (Runco 1995c). But if it leads only to original ideas and has no aesthetic appeal, I would call it uncreative contrarianism. Then again, your opinion about aesthetic appeal may differ from mine. We might appeal to social norms and obtain a consensus, and then I would end up in jail just like Cervantes and Lenny Bruce. It is sometimes difficult to determine what is appropriate. For this reason we will turn to values and intentions later in this chapter.

Crutchfield (1962) had quite a bit to say about contrarianism and creativity. He referred to some contrarians as *counterformists,* and he claimed that "some individuals are driven to react negatively to the group, to rebel against it, to repudiate its standards. They are actively countersuggestable. We may call them counterformists in order to distinguish them both from conformists and those nonconformists who we have termed true independents" (p. 137).

Violations of Expectations

Some contrarianism involves "violations of expectations" (Lachmann 2005, p. 162). Lachmann described how these lead to surprise and shock, and as such they are attention-getters. So that attention could very well motivate perversion. Lachmann gave Marc Chagall and Richard Wagner as examples of how violations of expectations may be related to creativity. As Lachmann put it, "Violations of expectations provide a motive for both creativity and perversion." His ideas relate easily to contrarianism, because that may be used for creativity, or for uncreative but unusual actions. Runco (1999d) referred to the latter as "contrarianism for contrary's sake," the idea being that the individual is not working toward creativity but instead his or her original actions are used to gain attention. Clearly, contrarianism can be a good thing, but this is clearest when it leads to truly creative efforts. It may not be a good thing when it is used to other ends.

A biological and cognitive explanation for the role of expectation violation can be found in Ritter et al. (in press) and is summarized in Chapter 4.

A true independent is more likely to be truly creative than a counterformist, who has "manifestly ego-involved motivations" (Crutchfield, 1962, p. 137). These ego-involved motivations would supposedly greatly impair creative work. Crutchfield (1962) added, the "counterformist strives for difference for difference's sake" (p. 137). This is exactly what we meant when we said that the contrarian is working toward the wrong ends. He or she would be expected to be original only to be original and not because originality is useful toward the solving of a worthwhile problem. Crutchfield correctly predicted that any societal reward given for counterformists and deviation "are eventually to corrupt whatever creative impulses the individual possesses" (p. 138). He even suggested that society can "decontaminate the deviate" by bringing the counterformist under control of those societal rewards. Of course it may be a gradual process.

Crutchfield (1962) also correctly worried about the judgment of the counterformist. Clearly the individual who is working to be different for difference's sake will judge anything that is in any way deviant to be good and anything that is conventional to be bad. A truly creative individual, on the other hand, will tend to judge efforts in terms of contributions toward solving of worthwhile and creative problems.

Note again that traits can be worded such that they are indicative (e.g., nonconformity and independence) or contraindicative (conformity, counterformity).

CHILDLIKE TENDENCIES, PLAYFULNESS, DAYDREAMING, AND PARACOSMS

Creative persons may have a tendency toward playfulness. This may be a reflection of their spontaneity and self-actualization. Whatever its origin, it no doubt helps them to find divergent and original ideas. In fact, recommendations for enhancing creativity often include a suggestion about "being more playful," and many businesses have recently attempted to bring playfulness into the workplace (e.g., Berg 1995; Starbuck & Webster 1991; Tang & Baumeister 1984). March (1987) really brought this point home with a *technology of foolishness.*

DEFINING PLAY

It is surprisingly difficult to define play (see Dansky 1999; Lieberman 1977; Piaget 1962). Mark Twain's (1876/1999) definition, from his novel *Tom Sawyer*, is as good as any: "Work is what a body is obliged to do, and play is what a body is not obliged to do" (pp. 25–26). This ties play to intrinsic motivation, which suggests yet another connection between creativity and playfulness (Figure 9.3).

Play apparently is frowned upon in certain cultures and circles, at least if it is an adult who is playful. Adams (1974) listed it as a cultural block, his thinking being that in the United States, if an adult has a problem, they should be serious about solving it. He criticizes that view since it may preclude original thinking. Fortunately there is evidence that adults can be playful. Gardner (1993a), for example, found the creators in his detailed study to be childlike, and this implies a kind of playfulness. Then again, he was studying high-level "Big C" creativity.

The childlike tendencies of some creative people lead them in a useful direction. Consider in this regard the *paracosms* and *worldplay* of certain creative adults (Root-Bernstein and Root-Bernstein 2006). Worldplay may involve a kind of fantasy life and daydreaming, which could be manifested in the construction of futuristic or other imaginary worlds and imaginary companions. Apparently worldplay occurs in a moderate proportion of certain creative groups,

FIGURE 9.3   Play often involves toys, such as these toys. Play is difficult to define but without a doubt is good for the fulfillment of creative potentials.

across domains, and is sometimes connected to actual professional endeavors (Root-Bernstein & Root-Bernstein 2006).

PERSEVERANCE AND PERSISTENCE

The perseverance and persistence of creative individuals have been recorded again and again. Csikszentmihalyi (1996) found it to be a common theme in his interviews with over 90 established artists, for example, and many others have emphasized it (e.g., Torrance 1988). Persistence might be viewed as a prerequisite for creative accomplishment simply because important insights often demand a large investment of time. Insights may seem to be sudden and quick, but actually there is likely to be a protracted development to each (Gruber 1988). They feel sudden because they pop into consciousness, but they have been germinating below the level of consciousness for some time. That germination usually involves searches, and perhaps even restructuring of one's knowledge base, and the acquisition of the necessary knowledge, like the incubation and insight process, can take quite some time. We are, however, talking about high-level accomplishment, and everyday insights might be much faster. For high-level accomplishment, Hayes (1989) and Simon (1988) estimated a 10-year rule. A decade may be necessary for the person to master the knowledge necessary to understand the gaps and nuances of a field. Domain differences are apparent of course simply because some domains have more knowledge to master than others. Persistence would be especially important in the larger domains. It is possible that creative individuals are not so much persistent as they are intrinsically motivated, but they appear to be persistent because they are so motivated. Intrinsic motivation is discussed next. For Cropley (1997b, p. 236), "In addition to possessing certain personal traits, creative individuals are characterized by their willingness to expend effort." That is a good definition of persistence: The willingness to expend effort.

Persistence would explain why creative individuals are able to battle with adversity (Chambers 1964; Cox 1983). They keep at it until they adjust or cope. This could work the other way around: Adversity may help them to develop persistence. Nietzsche said, "that which does not kill me makes me stronger." It may be that adversity teaches the individual to persist. Adversity may be overcome if the person is persistent, so persistence becomes an operant, a tactic that is employed whenever difficulties are encountered in the future.

Perseverance was clearly important to the seven "exemplary" creators studied by Gardner (1993a). They were each hardworking and almost obsessive in their commitment to their work. This gave others the impression that the creative person was focused on him- or herself. Gardner described how the famous creators frequently ignored or even misused others in efforts to complete their work. Perhaps this also was a reflection of their intrinsic motivation and persistence more than antisocial tendencies.

OPENNESS TO EXPERIENCE

The field of personality is rather large. There are dozens, perhaps hundreds of theories and models. Of all the models of personality currently available, the Big Five model (McCrae & Costa 1987) is certainly one of the most widely studied and respected. It has been used in various studies of creativity and personality (John & Srivastava 1999; King et al 1996; Kwang & Rodrigues 2002; McCrae 1987; Wolfradt & Pretz 2001). Its "openness to experience" dimension seems to be the most strongly tied to creativity (Dollinger et al. 2004; George & Zhou 2001; MacKinnon 1960; McCrae 1987; Pruhbu et al. 2008). Helson (1999) labeled *openness* a "cardinal characteristic" for creativity, and the only other cardinal characteristic she listed was *originality*.

Interestingly, Feist's (1998) meta-analysis suggested that scientists and artists varied in the degree to which they were extraverted and conscientious, but they shared a high level of openness. Recent empirical studies within particular domains include that of Greengross and Miller (2009). They studied comedians, administering a measure of Big Five traits to 31 professional comedians, 9 amateurs, and 10 comedy writers. Compared with a control group, all comedians scored higher on openness. Comedy writers in particular scored highest on this trait, implying that openness might be especially important for creative writing.

DEFINING OPENNESS

McCrae (1987) describes *openness to experience* in detail, relying on the NEO personality inventory. Openness in this perspective involves a sensitivity to fantasy, feelings, aesthetics, ideas, actions, and values. McCrae and Sutin (2009) added that openness is characterized by an imagination and curiosity when considering new ideas, sensations, and feelings.

Once again it is easy to see an interaction among creative characteristics. Just as persistence and intrinsic motivation may interact, and may sometimes lead to what appears to be self-promotion and asocial tendencies, so too could openness to experience interact with a range of behaviors and tendencies, including autonomy, unconventionality, and sensitivity. As a matter of fact, Amabile et al. (1993) administered the NEO Five Factor Inventory to a small group of professional artists and found a strong tendency toward openness, and openness to be related to a preference toward intrinsic motivation as measured by the Work Preference Inventory.

THE BIG FIVE PERSONALITY TRAITS

The Big Five Personality Traits are neuroticism, extraversion, openness, agreeableness, and conscientiousness.

Openness to experience may be directed outward or inward. It sometimes has a downside. Rothenberg (1990), for example, described the author John Cheever and the pros and cons of his openness to the subjective experiences. Cheever won a Nobel Prize for literature—and he was an alcoholic. In interviews with Rothenberg he described in detail how his openness to preconscious material gave him original ideas but scared the daylight out of him. The implication is that it can cause someone to drink.

Experimental support for this kind of openness to one's subjective world was supplied by Gudmund Smith (Smith & Amner 1997; Smith & van der Meer 1997). Similarly, Carlsson (2002) concluded that "the strong subjectivity in a highly creative person most likely entails disadvantages as well as advantages—the openness and attraction towards complexity also puts a strain on the individual."

The newest report has extended the Big Five model such that now it has a hierarchical structure (Digman 1997). This points to two higher order factors (alpha and beta), which also seem to be related to *stability* and *plasticity* (DeYoung et al. 2002). The former is loaded on *agreeableness*, *conscientiousness*, and *emotional stability*. High levels indicate that the individual is likely to maintain goals, relationships, and emotional states—hence stability. Beta is loaded on *extraversion* and *openness*. Individuals with high beta are likely to explore and seek novelty (DeYoung et al. 2002). Importantly, it may be easier to relate the hierarchical structure, and especially stability and plasticity, to biological contributions to personality and creativity. DeYoung (2006) has gone as far as to do just this, pointing to particular unique neural networks and neurotransmitters. Dopamine, for example, may be key for plasticity. It is related to certain forms of sensitivity and to responsiveness to novelty (DeYoung et al. 2005).

Conscientiousness

Furnham et al. (2006) and King et al. (1996) found that conscientiousness was positively related to creativity, though the latter only found it among individuals with the highest creativity test scores. McCrae (1987) used a personality measure of creativity and also reported a positive relationship with conscientiousness. Other researchers have proposed that conscientiousness is too broad a trait and should be broken down (e.g., Hough 1992; Mount & Barrick 1995; Tett 1998). They point to "order" and "dutifulness" as things that can be treated separately from the other facets of conscientiousness. Even more critical was the work by Necka and Hlawacz (2013), who argued that "relationships between creativity and psychometric personality traits are scarce and weak, suggesting lack of anything like creative personality." Necka and Hlawacz argued that it is more useful to look to temperament than to personality when explaining creativity. In their words,

> another possible explanation of the scarcity of links between creativity and personality pertains to the notion of temperament .... This term refers to basic individual traits that exhibit themselves quite early in onto-genesis and serve as the foundations for further development of personality. Temperamental traits, such as activity and reactivity ... or need for stimulation ... are sometimes referred to as one's "real nature," whereas personality involves not only basic inborn tendencies but also effects of long individual history of external influences, such as education, training, or life circumstances.

ANXIETY

The strain just mentioned may sometimes create anxiety. There is a small complication, in fact, because although creative talents often give a person an advantage in the form of coping skills, creative efforts and processes can at other times frighten or disturb.

Anxiety is one example of disturbance. It can undermine just about any performance, and indeed has been related to various measures of creative talent. There are clear individual differences or tolerances. Sometimes the individual has too little challenge and effort is not required. There may even be boredom (Csikszentmihalyi 2000)—too much and anxiety results. Alternatively, a difficult situation may challenge and even energize the individual, but if that person experiences anxiety, the difficulty is too extreme or coping is not adequate. Simply put, anxiety is a signal that something is wrong.

Two very good experimental studies of anxiety as related to creativity have been reported in the *Creativity Research Journal* (Carlsson 2002; Smith et al. 1990).

TOLERANCE OF AMBIGUITY

Vernon (1970) seemed to think that tolerance of ambiguity was the most important trait for creative work (cf. Golann 1962; Stoycheva 2003a, 2003b). Tolerance of ambiguity may allow the person to deal with the ill-defined nature of problems that have creative potential. It may also allow them to tolerate the range of options that should be considered. Some people may be more comfortable with closure (Basadur 1994; Runco & Basadur 1993). They are uncomfortable with the uncertainty that is a part of not having a solution ready at hand. This may lead them to *satisficing*, which is the tendency to take the first adequate solution that comes to mind (rather than postponing judgments and considering a wider range of options). Tegano (1990) offered evidence that the Tolerance of Ambiguity Scale was positively correlated with a creativity-style index.

The most recent analysis of tolerance of ambiguity (Merrotsy 2013) seemed to be comprehensive and concluded that evidence is lacking and that tolerance of ambiguity may not be well defined nor functionally tied to creativity.

Tolerance of ambiguity may be especially useful when working on problems in groups. This of course would include brainstorming, but other group work as well. Comadena (1984) demonstrated empirically that a tolerance of ambiguity was predictive of ideational fluency (i.e., the tendency to produce a large number of ideas) when brainstorming.

Interestingly, Furnham and Avison (1997) found tolerance of ambiguity to be associated with aesthetic preferences. In particular, individuals with a high tolerance of ambiguity preferred surrealistic paintings.

Such tolerances may reflect the openness mentioned earlier. It is easy to see that if someone is open to different possibilities, that person by definition will be tolerant of a wide range of options. He or she may even tolerate the stigma that is sometimes attached to being a creative eccentric or unconventional person (Rubenson & Runco 1992a). From another angle tolerance may be of great value when working with unconventional people! This kind of interpersonal tolerance is frequently necessary in educational settings, when a creative child has original ideas that are not in line with the curriculum or lesson plan (Runco 1991f), and also on a larger scale in society where diversity is necessary for cultural evolution and creativity (Florida 2002; Richards 1999).

Tolerance may also be required for creative persons to tolerate themselves! You may have noticed that the constellation of characteristics and traits that describes creative people is an odd mix. Of course not all creative people have all the traits mentioned in this chapter, but still they may have what have been called *paradoxical personalities* or *antinomies* (Barron & Harrington 1981; Csikszentmihalyi 1996). People sometimes have problems with such personal paradoxes. Many of the Freudian defense mechanisms were intended to hide or resolve such things, and fascinating research on cognitive dissonance (Festinger 1962) demonstrated how we might change the way we think to avoid certain kinds of intrapersonal conflicts. The tolerance that characterizes creative people may allow them to accept their own paradoxical personalities. In their list of the characteristics of creative people, Barron and Harrington (1981) referred to the "ability to resolve antinomies or to accommodate apparently opposite or conflicting traits in one's self concept, and finally, a firm sense of self as "creative" (p. 453). More will be said about these paradoxes and antinomies as we move through the remainder of this chapter. The very next characteristic to be discussed may seem incompatible with tolerance itself.

SENSITIVITY

Greenacre (1957) suggested that artists have a biological tendency toward unusual levels of sensitivity. Sundararajan (2004) claimed that poetry in particular requires sensitivity. She meant both the writing and the reading of poetry and quoted Owen (1992, p. 302) on how "poems teach attention to … subtle differences." She also tied sensitivity, which is often noted in artists and other creative individuals, to openness, which is also thought to be a common personality correlate of creativity. She also suggested a connection to the Chinese concept of *Chi*. (This is not the same thing as *Ch'i*, which is a kind of energy and is sometimes spelled *Qi*.)

Various individuals, including Ezra Pound and psychologist Rollo May, have referred to artists as "the antennae of the race" (see Abra 1997, p. 60). This idea was echoed in Shlain's

(1991) demonstration that artists often capture key ideas before scientists. They may do this because they are antennae, they are sensitive to gaps, changes, *zeitgeist*.

Sensitivity may direct our perception. This was implied by the quotation earlier, but is also quite apparent in what Stein called physiognomic sensitivity (also see Wallach & Kogan 1965). "When an individual sees a stimulus in terms of human (or human-like) actions or feelings, his perception is physiognomic" (Stein 1975, p. 5). Stein cited three empirical studies suggesting a connection between creativity and physiognomic sensitivity. He also described connections to empathy, affect, and artistic style.

An intrapersonal sensitivity is suggested by the psychological mindedness uncovered by MacKinnon (1962) in the IPAR studies, and by Smith and van der Meer's (1997) study of older adults. They noted, "creativity is an attitude toward living, which may or may not be associated with artistic talent, scientific originality, or other typically creative endeavors.... The creative person is driven by an urge to look deeper than the surface of everyday living, to find the historical roots of his or her existence, and to let this insight form one's future prospects" (p. 335).

The paradox here concerns how creative people can be sensitive but at the same time resilient and stand up to pressures to conform and be conventional. Very likely their sensitivity is such that they feel and see details and nuances but not the kind that leads them to give in to norms and conventions. Alternatively, we can use the idea of a constellation again such that creative people must be both sensitive and adaptable in order to see those nuances but also resist pressures to conform. For reasons like this, Runco (2005) suggested that the most important thing parents and teachers can do to protect the creativity of their children and students is to reinforce ego strength. That will allow even sensitive children to deal with pressures to conform. If the term ego strength is too psychodynamic for you, think of it as a kind of courage. As May (1975/1994) said, we each need the "courage to create."

CONFIDENCE

The ego strength would be manifested as confidence. Confidence may be particularly useful in some of the more performance-oriented domains. Perhaps it is useful in all creative domains, but to varying degrees. Consider what it will take to perform the highest (world class) levels. Talent, of course, but also confidence. Without confidence the individual may not even try to maximize his or her skills. The individual may need to believe "I am the greatest" before he or she puts the effort into demonstrating it.

Athletic domains probably require extraordinary levels of confidence. Without extreme confidence, the athlete may not put 100% into the effort. Consider in this regard the sprinter named Justin Gatlin. He won the 100-meter sprint in the World Track and Field Championships in 2005 and was the Olympic Champion in 2004. His margin of victory in the former was the largest in history, the winning time being 9.88 seconds and second place being 10.05 seconds. Gatlan was interviewed after the race and said "So I did get some kind of record, huh? It is great to show how dominant I am this year, running fast times consistently and winning every race. I prayed before the season to be dominant, and it has all come together" (*USA Today*, Sports, Section C, Monday August 8, 2005, p. C1). Dominance was also frequent in interviews with Shaquille O'Neal, world champion center for the Los Angeles Lakers, and

BOX 9.2

PARENTAL PERSONALITIES

Certain personality traits seem to reflect genetic background. This does not mean that a parent's personality will be readily apparent in a child's personality, but there may be traits that are shared, and thus if the environment supports them, parent–child correlations would be found. It is also probable that certain parents are likely to encourage the key characteristics of their children, such as the ego strength we just discussed. Also think back on our discussion in autonomy and the correlations between parental expectations for independence and children's creative potentials.

More recent research found parental influences on achievement motives. This is very relevant to the discussion of autonomy because it was a particular kind of achievement motive, namely, achievement through independence. Runco and Albert (2005)

found that the gifted boys in their sample, and the parents of these boys, had much higher scores than is usual on the achievement through independence scale of the CPI. They also had significantly lower scores than the normative groups in terms of achievement though conformity. This fits extremely well with the creativity literature, for creative persons are usually independent. It is difficult to be creative without being independent. The reason given earlier in this chapter was that creativity requires originality, and originality can be found through independent thoughts and actions. Originality cannot be found through conformity. As a matter of fact, originality is just about the opposite from normative. Additional support for this was given by Gough et al. (1996), who found Ai scores to be correlated with Barron-Welsh Art Scale scores.

BOX 9.3

ZEITGEIST AND PERSONALITY

The concept of *zeitgeist* ("the spirit of the times") was very useful in Chapter 7 and the historical perspective therein. *Zeitgeist* is also relevant here. Consider the example *zeitgeist* of the 1950s. Mount Everest and the four-minute barrier to the one-mile footrace were both conquered (1953 and 1954), and a recent biography of Roger Bannister, the first person to break the four-minute barrier, indicates that both were related, at least in the optimism and *zeitgeist*. Apparently Bannister and his coaches were very familiar with the news coverage of Edmund Hillary and Sherpa

Tenzing, who had just recently conquered Mount Everest (Figure 9.4). They felt that Everest was one of the last natural remaining challenges and hoped that an Englishman would accomplish the feat. Hillary (a New Zealander) and Tenzing (a native Sherpa) did indeed conquer Everest, not too long before Bannister conquered the mile.

See Figure 9.4.

Bannister may have been confident in part because the other challenge had been met. Additionally, this was not long after World War II. The individuals involved, and their

(Continued)

BOX 9.3 *(Continued)*

countries, survived it. They heard about the optimism of the post-war United States. The United States was, at that time, growing into the scientific and industrial power, and apparently all over the world the attitude of the Americans was well recognized. Americans were optimistic and confident. The *zeitgeist* of the times, then, was filled with optimism about what could be accomplished. Of course, the biographer of Bannister makes it clear that he had a natural talent, an incredible work ethic, an exercise regimen that worked extremely well (Bannister was studying medicine at the time) and a good deal of "cheek." The last of these says something about Bannister's personality, and in particular his persistence and confidence. Apparently he was also a bit of a contrarian, almost always insisting on training in his own fashion and often resisting the strong suggestion to work with a coach.

FIGURE 9.4 Mount Everest.

with Muhammad Ali, who often claimed "I am the greatest." Perhaps this is what it takes, in some areas, to be a world champion. In more cooperative domains it is unlikely that an overly confident individual will get far. Social attributions are so important and reputations are essentially social constructions (Kasof 1995; McLaughlin 2000).

Self-confidence was one of the key characteristics identified by Feist (1998) using meta-analytic techniques. He also found openness to experience, as well as low conventionality. Domain differences (e.g., artists vs. nonartists, scientists vs. nonscientists) were apparent.

META-ANALYSIS OF PERSONALITY

Meta-analysis is one of the most powerful techniques in the social and behavioral sciences. Scott et al. (2004a, 2004b) used it twice to examine the impact of creativity training (also see Ma 2006). The power comes from the robust statistics used as well as the data. The data represent individual studies (i.e., the effect size reported in each study), so in a sense each data point represents a sample.

In most domains, a modicum of confidence is probably appropriate. Potentials probably are fulfilled only when there is a fit between the individual and the requirements of the domain (Albert & Runco 1989; Runco & Albert 2005). An athlete with too little confidence may never reach his or her top performance. An overconfident writer may not put the time into his or her novel and thus fail to refine it so it is the best literature it can be.

SELF-PROMOTION

Recall here Gardner's (1993a) finding creative people to be self-promoters. This was undoubtedly the case for the individuals he studied. Picasso, Stravinsky, Gandhi, Freud, Graham, Einstein, Eliot—they were eminently creative. This might suggest that the ideas of fit and domain-specificity are incorrect, but then again there is some question over the generalizability of any case study result. Counterexamples of self-promotion are not difficult to find. Richard Feyman was well-known for disregarding honors and "doing his own thing." Charles Darwin avoided debates over evolutionary theory. (Thank goodness for Thomas Huxley, "Darwin's bulldog.") Bob Dylan frequently shuns publicity. It is a complicated issue. Someone might even promote him- or herself by saying self-defacing things and presenting a modest persona. Many creative people do this kind of impression management (Kasof 1995; Runco 1995c).

Mozart exemplifies this. He had a reputation for composing without rough drafts and only in final form, but evidence suggests that he actually went through many early versions of his compositions (Cropley et al. 2008). This seems like impression management; Mozart may have been manipulating his public persona.

INTROVERSION

A tendency toward self-promotion might suggest that creative people are extraverted rather than introverted. There is conflicting information about this. Introversion, for example, is sometimes a part of the stereotype of the creative person. Feist and Barron (2003) included it in their profile of the creative personality, and Cheek and Stahl (1986) found shyness to be significantly related to the creative potential of children. Yet a great deal of research has reported negligible correlations between introversion and creativity. It very likely depends on the domain in which the individual is working or interested.

Another possibility is that what sometimes appears to be introversion is actually just focus or task commitment. After all, creative people are often persistent and highly motivated about their work and projects. For that reason they put a great deal of time into creative efforts. This is time away from other activities, which for some may include time away from socializing. You might say there is displacement, or a "cost."

OPPORTUNITY COSTS

"There is no such thing as a free lunch." If someone invests time in one thing (e.g., creative work), he or she has less time for other things. Economists refer to *opportunity costs* to describe this sort of thing (Rubenson & Runco 1992a). Much the same is found in developmental psychology where children who watch enormous amounts of television (the national average is nearly 30 hours/week!) do not have time for imaginary play, reading, and socializing. This is *displacement theory* (Runco 1984).

Beghetto (2006) found that students high in creative self-efficacy spend as much time with their friends as other students and are, if anything, more active in bands, drama, and similar social groups. This is certainly inconsistent with the idea of introversion as a core characteristic for creativity.

PARADOXICAL PERSONALITIES AND ANTINOMIES

Although this chapter lists many different characteristics, it is best to describe the creative personality as a constellation and complex. No one trait leads directly to creativity—they interact. It is a complicated interaction. This is most obvious in the paradoxical personalities and antinomies mentioned earlier.

MacKinnon (1962), Barron (1964; Barron & Harrington 1981), and Csikszentmihalyi (1996) each described these paradoxes. Csikszentmihalyi (1996, p. 47) described how creative people have "tendencies of thought and action that in most people are segregated." Bledow et al. (2009) referred to something like this but used the label, *dynamic shifting* (p. 365). Martindale (1989) used the label *osillation* (p. 228), and Koberg and Bagnall (1991, p. 38) preferred *alternating psycho-behavioral waves*. Kuhn (1963) is famous for his idea of the *essential tension*.

Practically speaking, if teachers want to support creative development, they may need to tolerate such paradoxes. If parents want their children to fulfill creative potentials, they too may need to tolerate, or even support, paradoxes. If businesses want innovation, they must hire and reward paradoxical personalities (Cropley & Cropley, in press).

Cropley and Cropley (in press) took this a step further and saw tension for creativity in things like simultaneously disagreeing and agreeing within a work group (also see Haner 2005). An example they offered from the business setting strikes me as very common in university work: simultaneously supporting departmental goals but at the same time pursuing one's own scholarship. This may be related to a third example, namely the situation where input and the needs of others are balanced along with one's own feelings and needs (see Hulsheger et al. 2009). Maital and Seshadri (2007, p. 27) offered a general description of "the need for free, unfettered creativity, together with the need for focused, systematic discipline– and the overriding imperative to make these two qualities not only co-exist" (quoted by Cropley & Cropley in press).

Cropley and Cropley (in press) themselves used the 4P theory of creativity and focused on the process paradox, the personal factors paradox, the motivation paradox, the mood paradox, the product paradox, and the press paradox. Examples of each are as follows: divergent vs. convergent thinking (process), innovative personality vs. adaptive personality (personal properties), proactive motivation vs. reactive motivation (personal motivation), generative vs. conserving feelings (personal feelings), radical product vs. routine product (product), and freedom-oriented management press vs. necessity-oriented management press (press).

It is possible that it is the creative work itself that allows incompatible traits to coexist. MacKinnon (1962, p. 490) may have felt this way when he wrote, "it would appear that the creative person has the capacity to tolerate the tension that strong opposing values create in him, and in his creative striving he effects some reconciliation of them." Or it could simply be that contradictions constitute one of the costs of doing creative work. Artists have been known to accept their own mood swings and depression because they know these things can contribute to their creativity. Intrapsychic tension may represent a similar necessary sacrifice.

MacKinnon (1962) also reported one of the more interesting examples of a personality paradox. He found creative architects to be open to emotions and self-aware and to express a wide range of interests. At the same time, although his sample was male and data collected when sex-role stereotypes were fairly polarized, the architects were open to feminine options in thought and behavior.

The tendency toward paradoxical combinations of personality traits is not limited to architecture. Csikszentmihalyi (1996) uncovered a number of paradoxes in his interviews with highly successful individuals representing a range of domains and careers. His sample seemed to be both logical and naive, disciplined yet playful, introverted and extraverted, realistic but imaginative, objective but passionate, and feminine and masculine. Gardner (1993a) found that his seven exceptionally creative people exhibited unusual combinations of personality and intelligence, and this, too, cut across domain. Gardner described how the cases differed from one another in terms of their dominant intelligences (such as linguistic, personal, logical, spatial, musical, scholastic, bodily, mathematical), as well as in the breadth and combination of their intelligences, but how they shared self-confidence, alertness, childlike curiosity, unconventionality, dedication, and obsessive commitment to their work.

The paradoxes are not indicative of some recent trend, either. Einstein was born in 1879, for example, George Eliot in 1819, and Gandhi in 1869. Each was studied by Gardner (1993a). In fact, over 40 years ago, Barron (1964) wrote that

> individuals who distinguish themselves in artistic, scientific, and entrepreneurial creation exemplify vividly in their persons the incessant dialectic between integration and diffusion, convergence and divergence, thesis and antithesis.... I have attempted ... to understand the specifics of this essential tension.... I have come to the following most general conclusion: In the sequence of related acts which taken together as a process result in the creation of something new, there occur consistently a rhythmic alteration and occasionally a genuine resolution or synthesis of certain common antinomies (p. 81).

As a matter of fact, it really is remarkable how well early studies of the creative personality (e.g., Barron 1955; Drevdahl & Cattell 1958; Gough & Woodworth 1960; MacKinnon 1960; Maslow 1971; Rogers 1954/1959; Taylor & Barron 1963) have held up to empirical scrutiny. On that topic of endurance I should also turn to self-actualization. Its relationship with creativity has been recognized for over 50 years.

SELF-ACTUALIZATION

Maslow (1968) defined "self-actualizing (SA) creativity" as springing from the ordinary events of our lives. He believed that the drive toward self-actualization is innate in all humans and will seek to unfold naturally as long as a person lives. SA creativity is an important part of that process of unfolding:

> SA creativeness stresses first the personality rather than its achievements, considering these achievements to be epiphenomena emitted by the personality and therefore secondary to it. It stresses characterological qualities like boldness, courage, freedom, spontaneity, perspicuity, integration, self-acceptance, all of which make possible the kind of generalized SA creativeness, which expresses itself in the creative life, or the creative attitude, or the creative person. I have also stressed the expressive or Being quality of SA creativeness…. SA creativeness is "emitted," or radiated, and hits all of life, regardless of problems, just as a cheerful person "emits" cheerfulness without purpose or design or even consciousness (p. 145).

Self-actualization is a reflection of an individual's character and personality. It is therefore apparent in everything the person does. It exemplifies everyday creativity and the creative process. Rogers (1995) recognized this: "The action of the child inventing a new game with his playmates; Einstein formulating a theory of relativity; the housewife devising a new sauce for the meat; a young author writing his first novel; all of these are, in terms of our definition, creative, and there is no attempt to set them in some order of more or less creative" (p. 350). Maslow agreed "that a first-rate soup is more creative than a second-rate painting, and that, generally, cooking or parenthood or making a home [can] be creative" (p. 136).

Self-actualizing tendencies may be one reason why creative people are sometimes seen to be playful and childlike (Gardner 1993a). Children are spontaneous, uninhibited, and authentic, much to the advantage of their creativity. Self-actualized individuals are also spontaneous, uninhibited, and authentic, with the same benefit. The benefits apply across the life span. Vaillant (2002) listed creativity as one of four basic activities that make retirement rewarding. (The other three are replacing workmates with a new social network, rediscovering how to play, and continuing lifelong learning.)

Self-actualization is not only involved in actually creating, it is also involved in viewing and appreciating creative things. Consider Rollo May's (1975/1994, p. 22) position that "in our appreciation of the created work … we also are performing a creative act … we are experiencing some new moment of sensibility. Some new vision is triggered in us by our contact" with the work of art.

Rogers (1995), too, located the primary motivation for creativity in the individual's innate need to actualize him- or herself, to become his or her potentialities. This brings us to the topic of motivation.

MOTIVATION

It is difficult to discuss personality without talking about motivation. A number of the characteristics and tendencies listed previously are inextricable from certain motives. Some may be a direct expression of motivation (e.g., persistence). Very likely, most of our motives have a basis in our genetic make-up (some of which we share with others, and some of which may reflect individual differences) and our experience.

You might say that intrinsic motivation is most important for creativity and that extrinsic factors (incentives, rewards, grades, or even surveillance) sometimes inhibit creative efforts. There is much more to it than that, however. There are different paths to creative performance, different reasons to fulfill creative potentials. Consider the adage, "necessity is the mother of invention."

NECESSITY AS THE MOTHER OF INVENTION: REACTIVE MOTIVATION

One perspective on the motivation for invention and perhaps creativity assumes that they are the result of some need and therefore a response to a problem of some sort. One of the more interesting demonstrations of this was in the research of Finke (1990), who found that undergraduates tended to be the most inventive when they were unable to choose the category in which they were presented a problem. Some undergraduates were forced to focus on furniture, and others were forced to focus on toys. Similarly, some were forced to focus on a part of the furniture or toys such as a handle or a wheel, but others were allowed to choose the part or even category in which to work.

Sometimes creative efforts are motivated by a desire for immortality. As May (1975/1994) put it, "Creativity is a yearning for immortality. We human beings know that we must die. We have, strangely enough, a word for death. We know that each of us must develop the courage to confront death. Yet we also must rebel and struggle against it. Creativity comes from this struggle out of the rebellion the creative act is born [expressing] a passion to live beyond one's death" (p. 31). Lifton (1973, p. 5) suggested that this kind of motivation reflects the desire for "an inner sense of continuous symbolic relationship, over time and space, with the various elements of life." Lifton thus felt that the goal was a symbolic immortality. Along the same lines, Yalom (1980) referred to the role of leaving behind an imperishable legacy in assuaging death concerns. Rank (1989) and Becker (1973) both looked to creative efforts as the best route to individuation. Maslow (1970) and Rogers (1980) described how terror of death was mitigated by self-actualization and openness to experience, which are both in turn associated with creativity.

Intrinsic motivation has been associated with talent at least since the time of Sir Francis Galton's (1869) *Hereditary Genius*. He pinpointed intrinsic motivation as one of the most important "qualities of intellect and disposition," and went on to explain its function as an "inherent stimulus." Approximately 100 years later Nicholls (1983) argued, "First ... it

BOX 9.4

INTRINSIC MOTIVATION IN HISTORY AND ART

Galton (1869) described the importance of intrinsic motivation for talent, but even before that it was a recognized influence on artwork. Woodmansee (1994) referred to a little known essay by Karl Philipp Moritz (1756–1793), written in German, with a title that translates to something like "Toward a Unification of all of the fine arts and letters under the concept of self sufficiency." In it, Moritz defined art as "self-sufficient totalities" (from Woodmansee 1994, p. 11). Artworks in this view are produced and consumed "for their own sake." Moritz also suggested that a work of art is produced and consumed "disinterestedly," which may be interpreted as "purely for the enjoyment of their internal attributes and relationships, independently of any external relationships or effects they may have" (Woodmansee 1994, p. 11). Dudek (2012) more recently described something like "art for arts' sake." Moritz's essay was written in 1785.

Interestingly, Woodmansee went on to quote Jacques Derrida from an essay titled "Economimesis," in which "free art" is distinguished from "mercenary art." Derrida referred to the potential "salary" that might influence someone as they produce or consume art. These same ideas are being rediscovered in modern-day psychoeconomic theories of creativity (Rubenson & Runco 1992a; 1992b; 1995; Sternberg & Lubart 1995).

maintains the activity needed to establish the necessary skills or information and to generate the necessary possible solutions.... Second, it brings an attitude of mind that allows task requirements to come to the fore" (p. 270). Recall also the IPAR research and the seminal research of MacKinnon (1962), Crutchfield (1962), and Golann (1963).

MacKinnon (1962) described intrinsic motivation as more of a trait, and expression of personality as more than a temporary state. More recently Csikszentmihalyi (1996) explained how temporary states and personality traits both support creative work, and he pointed to the flow state (not a trait) and the autotelic personality, where "auto" refers to oneself, and "telos" to a goal. This points toward intrinsic motivation. In a series of impressive investigations Amabile (1990) demonstrated that creativity most often is associated with intrinsic motivation and that extrinsic motivations can interfere with creative work, but that both can sometimes energize the creative person.

Hennessey (1989) demonstrated that people can be immunized so that extrinsic factors will not entirely undermine creative efforts. Hennessey used a videotape that showed a child of the same age as the viewers, discussing academic work. The children in the videotape were modeling intrinsic motivation. Children being immunized also received direct training (storytelling emphasizing the value of intrinsic motivation, and paper-and-pencil exercises). Apparently the immunization was successful. The children were resistant to extrinsic pressures. Hennessey and Zbikowski (1993) reported similar positive results of immunization procedures, but a number of questions were raised about the same by Gerrard et al. (1996).

Rubenson and Runco (1992a, 1995) took a different approach in their explanation of how extrinsic factors can influence creativity. They used the psychoeconomic model, and especially the idea of a costs:benefit ratio. Costs and benefits can both be extrinsic. In psychoeconomic terms, high costs or low benefits are both likely to inhibit creative efforts. Low costs and high benefits, of course, have the opposite effect. There are implications of this at every level, from the child to society as a whole. If we want a creative society, we need to minimize the costs and increase the benefits such that creative potentials are fulfilled. Importantly, costs may be financial or psychic. The latter result from a stigma attached to creativity if it is aligned with the "mad genius" or any form of deviance.

Heinzen (1994) described a useful continuum of motivation, with intrinsic motivation on one end of the continuum and extrinsic motivation on the other. This does imply that a person is motivated by one or the other, which may not be the case (e.g., artists who love their work and earn an income with it). More useful, then, may be Heinzen's description of a continuum with proactive creativity at one end and reactive creativity on the other. The former is associated with intrinsic motivation and the latter with extrinsic. The idea of proactive creativity is very important for our society and might help us to most effectively deal with global and environmental problems (Gruber 1997; Richards 1997).

PROACTIVE CREATIVITY

Creativity can be adaptive and assist with coping and life adjustments. Many adaptations are reactive; the individual is responding to some need. Creativity can be *proactive* as well as *reactive*. It is associated with problem finding as well as problem solving. Proactive creativity may be of utmost importance for contemporary society, if we are to avoid serious environmental, political, and social problems (Gruber 1997; McLaren 1993; Richards 1997).

The impact of extrinsic factors will depend on the individual and the nature of the contingency. Shy individuals, for example, may be especially sensitive to evaluative feedback (Cheek & Stahl 1986). At least as significant is the nature of the extrinsic factor. Feedback that is informative rather than evaluative, for instance, though still extrinsic, does not inhibit creative efforts (Amabile 1990; Deci & Ryan 1985).

Inspiration may motivate. Wilber (1996) described art in this way: "Great art grabs you, against your will, and then suspends your will. You are ushered into a quiet clearing, free of desire, free of grasping, free of ego; through that opening or clearing in your own awareness may come flashing higher truths, subtler revelations, profound connections. For a moment you might even touch eternity; who can say otherwise, when time itself is suspended in the clearing that great art created in your awareness?" (p. 90). Maslow described religion as a result of creative insight.

Then there are motives that are reactions to adversity or discomfort. These are quite numerous and include catharsis as an attempt to relieve psychic tension. Runco (1994a) attempted to review all such motives in his chapter, "Creativity and its discontents." In the vernacular of motivational psychology, these are probably "avoidance goals" (Elliot & Dweck 2005), creativity is a kind of competency, and intrinsic motivation in general "an inherent psychological need of the human being."

Before turning to the role of values in motivation and creativity, something should be said about a small controversy. This has *engagement* on one side and *boredom* on the other. The former is a very popular concept. Grants are being given for studies of engagement, and schools now seem to ask about targeting it as much as anything else. Although such fads always get me thinking that there is a new label for an old concept, there is no doubt that engagement is a good thing and is probably directly related to creative performances. The reasons for this parallel the bridges between creativity and (a) mindfulness (Langer 1989; Runco 1990e) and (b) intrinsic motivation (Amabile et al. 1990). An individual engaged in a task is the most likely to care about the quality of the work. He or she is likely to be focused on the work and free of distraction—and possible evaluation or extrinsic evaluations. An engaged individual is likely to put effort into the task at hand and thereby explore associations and alternatives. Theories of student engagement break it down into factors labeled *absorption*, *challenge*, *thrill*, and *interest*. It seems to be both emotional and cognitive.

There is empirical work on engagement, intrinsic motivation, and creativity. Gilson and Shally (2004), for example, suggested that engagement, at least in organizations, depends on risk tolerance and the right attitude. Zhang and Bartol (2010a, 2010b) reported that creative process engagement mediated between creativity and intrinsic motivation. Hu et al. (in press) found that engagement and intrinsic motivation were only moderately correlated. This relationship was found in an Asian sample, however, and although there is no obvious reason to think of idiosyncrasies in this relationship, generalizations are probably not warranted without future research. Significantly, only 9% of variability in students' creativity was shared with (and explained by) engagement.

The other side of the controversy looks to boredom. As Mann and Cadman (in press) put it,

> Contrary to popular wisdom, boredom is not the result of having nothing to do. It is very hard to come up with a situation where a person's options are so limited that he or she literally can do nothing. Rather, boredom stems from a situation where none of the possible things that a person can realistically do appeal to the person in question. This renders the person inactive, and generally unhappy. Thus, boredom is the result of having nothing to do that one likes rather than nothing to do per se. (p. 1 of their ms)

They went on to tie boredom to neural activity, emotions, affect, concentration, and creativity. They cited earlier work that described how boredom "can lead to a search for variety." This is interesting, given the role of variety (usually labeled flexibility) in creative thinking (Runco 1985).

VALUES

Values play a significant role in creative behavior. Frankly, this would seem to go without saying! That is because people do not do things unless they are important—unless they value them. Values of course can be subtle, implicit, or tacit rather than obvious and explicit, but still they underlie our motives and behavior. Rarely if ever is creativity displayed unless it is motivated.

Values have been tied to creative behavior for a long, long time. In fact, it is probably crystal clear why this chapter began with an overview of the research conducted at IPAR. So much of it influences research and thinking even today. MacKinnon (1962), for instance, used a technique called the Allport-Vernon-Lindzey Study of Values in his work with architects, writers, and other highly creative individuals. Similarly, Hall and MacKinnon (1969) found that certain values were positively correlated with creativity, whereas others were significantly and negatively correlated with creativity. Values are manifested as interests, motives, and commitments. Helson (1990) demonstrated that values contribute to a person's identity.

AVOID CLICHÉS LIKE THE PLAGUE

The expression, "crystal clear" (used in this last paragraph), goes back a long way. It is trite, and trite expressions are uncreative. Each of us should find new metaphors and avoid clichés. To quote Safire (1990), "Avoid clichés like the plague." Am I making myself lucid?

Values are manifested in particular behaviors, including self-direction (Dollinger et al., 2007). The connection is very clear in Dollinger's definition of self-direction as having as its goal "independence in thought and action expressed in exploration and free choice to follow one's own interests which would seem to be the core values for the creative person." Along the same lines, Sagiv (2002) reported that individuals who worked in or had a preference for artistic occupations tended to describe themselves in terms of self-direction and universalism values. They strongly leaned away from conformity, tradition, and security (also see Helson 1990).

Dollinger et al. (2007) found that self-transcendence and openness to change were significantly correlated with creativity (measured with the photo essay procedure and Adjective Check List). Tradition and security values were negatively related to the two measures of creativity. Individuals who valued creativity and aesthetics, the second defined in terms of "a world of beauty," had higher scores on the two measures as well. Importantly, social recognition was not correlated with the measures of creativity.

These ideas about openness to change are consistent with the personality research connecting openness to experience with creativity (McCrae 1987). Importantly, Dollinger felt that the value "openness" was more important than the analogous personality trait. In his eyes values are at least partly consciously controlled and can therefore be enhanced. In other words, creativity can be encouraged by supporting the value of openness. In fact, Dollinger offered several concrete suggestions along these lines, including travel through different cultures, the idea being that different values are appreciated in different ways and different cultures and an individual could move to a culture that values independence and therefore would be most likely to improve their creative behavior.

Values that tend to be positively correlated with creativity include independence and autonomy. Values that tend to be negatively correlated with creativity include harmony and conventionality. One interesting value that has been positively correlated to creativity in some research but negatively in other research is power motivation (cf. Dollinger et al., 2007; Helson 1990). This is especially interesting because that might suggest the self-promotion we just discussed. Elsewhere I suggested that self-promotion actually would hinder creative achievement because it would take time away from creative work (Runco 1995c). Self-promotion and impression management are, in this light, displaced investments.

BOX 9.5

VALUES AND PSYCHOECONOMIC THEORY

Creative things are always original. They are, however, more than just original. Originality is necessary but not sufficient for creativity. Creative things must also have value or utility. They may solve a problem or be effective, but they cannot be only original. Psychoeconomic theory has provided an operational and objective means to define and examine this second aspect of creativity, which is exactly why it was called utility rather than the more common descriptor, "appropriate" or "aesthetic appeal."

Economists have long studied value and utility, for obvious reasons, and similarly one can examine the relationships that exist among creativity, originality, and value. Incidentally, psychoeconomic theory has also conceptualized creativity in terms of investments (and displaced investments), cost and benefit, and contrarianism, and in the idea to "buy low and sell high." Runco et al. (2006) presented an overview of the economic and psychoeconomic perspectives on creativity (also see Rubenson & Runco 1992a, 1992b, 1995; Sternbert & Lubart 1996). The economic perspective has been very useful in recent creative studies.

BOX 9.6

VALUES IN CREATIVE REASONING

Values should be included in models of the creative process. Runco (2006b) used simple cognitive models to demonstrate how creative decisions and behavior might result when the individual uses this kind of reasoning process:

$$\text{Choice} = (I_1 * V_1) + (I_2 * V_2) + (I_3 * V_3)$$

The I terms reflect information, which interacts with the value terms (V). This is a simple additive model and the thresholds and optima discussed earlier, concerning confidence (and all creative things for that matter), could be included easily with exponents, just as in a multiple regression testing curvilinear trends. Of course, the person need not be aware of how choices are made, but those choices do depend a great deal on what information is at hand and the values the person assigns to that information and the options. A creative person will likely value unconventional things and devalue conformity and conventionality. The choices made will reflect that.

Jay and Perkins (1997) suggested that values play a significant role in problem finding. They stated, "as to the how of problem finding, these values are some of the most important criteria, serving to bias the generation and selective filtering of problems." This "selective filtering" is an example of how choice is involved in creativity (see also Schwebel 1993). Jay and Perkins (1997) also suggested that creativity emerges because the person in question is trying to produce things that satisfy the values he or she embraces. Similarly, values can promote problem finding in that values, too, may be causes of problem finding. For example, the desire to push at the limits of one's understanding and to break boundaries is a strong impetus for initiating problems. These values directly promote problem finding by instigating the process; moreover, they help to explain why people make the effort to problem find. Similarly, individuals who value originality are likely to generate and select problems with a bias toward the criterion of originality, thereby promoting the quality of problem finding.

Values are at least as obvious in the preferences that characterize creative people. Earlier we discussed the preference for complexity (Barron 1972; Eisenman 1999).

CREATIVE PERSONAL IDENTITY AND CREATIVE PERSONAL EFFICACY

Jaussi et al. (2007) related values to the creative personal identity. She put it this way: "Creative personal identity will be positively related to creativity at work because individuals will engage in behaviors that reaffirm identities that are important to them." Jaussi and coworkers were very interested in the workplace and reported that

> because of the desire to maintain positive self-regard … individuals for whom creativity is part of their self-definition will seek out opportunities to be creative at work in order to maintain positive self-regard and affirm a key part of their self-concept…. individuals who see creativity as an important part of who they are (i.e., have a strong creative personal identity) will engage in creative efforts both inside and outside of work to reaffirm this important identity.

Creative personal identity is distinct from creative personal efficacy (Tierney & Famer 2002). Self-efficacy refers to a general tendency to monitor and control oneself and thereby insure personal effectiveness (Bandura 1997). Creative self-efficacy is, of course, more specific. Tierney and Farmer (2002) defined it as "the belief one has the ability to produce creative outcomes" (p. 1138). Tierney and Farmer (2002), Schack (1989), and Beghetto (2006) all demonstrated that creative self-efficacy is strongly related to actual creative performances.

Noted psychologist Albert Bandura (1997) emphasized self-efficacy in his definition of creativity. He claimed that "above all, innovativeness requires an unshakeable sense of efficacy to persist in creative endeavors" (p. 239). Creative self-efficacy thus leads individuals to expend the effort it takes to be creative. They believe in themselves, which is important given how often creative ideas are original and unconventional and how often there is a risk involved (Rubenson & Runco 1995). Recall here the role persistence seems to play in creative accomplishments.

Jaussi et al. (2007) distinguished creative self-identity from creative self-efficacy as follows:

> While creative self-efficacy is the capacity to do a job creatively, an individual with a high creative personal identity will be driven to do everything creatively, not just the job, because creativity is fundamental to his or her self-definition. For example, a somewhat creative person in his or her formal job may well know that he or she has the ability to deliver a creative presentation (high creative self-efficacy). Yet, he or she may not do so all the time. Even if this individual delivers creative presentations consistently, creativity may not be demonstrated in everything he or she does at work (e.g., when participating in hallway discussions or generating ideas at lunch).

> The capacity judgment to be creative does not imply constant accessing and utilization of that capacity, and thus the relationship between creative self-efficacy and resultant creativity at work, while positive and strong, may still leave variance yet to be explained (Jaussi et al., 2007, p. 249).

Jaussi et al.'s empirical results supported this view. Indeed, a measure of personal identity contributed to the prediction of rated creativity above and beyond that of a measure of creative personal efficacy. Personal identity and personal efficacy did not interact with one another. There is, then, clear independence between the two.

Certain aspects of a creative personal identity interact with process variables and tactics, including one that parallels the idea of professional marginality. In particular, Jaussi et al. (2007) found that a worker's benefiting from nonwork experiences and knowledge (e.g., about hobbies) depends on his or her creative identity. What may be most important is that workers who did bring nonwork skills and experiences to bear on work projects were more creative. Perhaps it is indicative of flexibility and wide interests (both of which have been tied to creativity). Jaussi et al. felt that the benefits resulted from the fact that the individual's creative personal identity would be reinforced more frequently and thoroughly by the creative success that occurs at work. Restated, the individual would have evidence of his or her own creativity both outside of work and while at work. Additional evidence on avocational bridges to creativity work were presented by Root-Bernstein et al. (1995).

VALUES, RISK TOLERANCE, AND PSYCHOLOGICAL ANDROGYNY

Values can help us to understand two other tendencies of creative persons: risk tolerance (or risk taking), and psychological androgyny. Simply put, creative ideas are sometimes risky (Rubenson & Runco 1992a, 1992b, 1995). They are untested, after all, because they are original. They are also unconventional, for the same reason. There is, then, a risk involved in considering or sharing ideas, and the more original the idea, the larger the risk. Someone with a low level of risk tolerance is unlikely to consider, explore, and share original ideas.

Psychological androgyny is defined as a kind of eclectic combination of both masculine and feminine behaviors. Highly stereotyped and conventional people shy away from androgynous behaviors and instead stick with conventional sex roles. Flexible people, on the other hand, and especially those who are open to experience and who do not value conventional behaviors to the extreme, do not use stereotypes to make decisions. They use their own authentic feelings and intrinsic motives instead. They may value authenticity or even creativity itself more than fitting in and public opinion. As a result, they have a wider range of options available to them when faced with a problem and a wider range of perspectives with which to view experience. These lead naturally to creative thinking and creative behavior. Think back to MacKinnon's (1962) findings about the male architects being open to stereotypically feminine options, and Csikszentmihalyi's (1996) findings about the paradoxical balance of masculinity and femininity of his interviewees. Certainly these ideas fit well with the idea of marginality as well. Importantly, the psychologically androgynous person also tends to be psychologically healthy, as well as creative (Bem 1986; Harrington et al. 1983).

CONCLUSIONS

The creative personality can be described with some combination of the following traits, tendencies, and characteristics:

- Autonomy
- Flexibility
- Preference for complexity
- Openness to experience
- Sensitivity
- Playfulness
- Tolerance of ambiguity
- Risk taking or risk tolerance
- Intrinsic motivation
- Psychological androgyny
- Self-efficacy
- Wide interests and curiosity.

In addition, the creative person also values creativity and intentionally invests time and effort in creativity. They choose to fulfill their creative potentials and choose unconventional and original ideas and careers.

Some of these traits stand out because they fit so nicely with what we know about creative cognition. Flexibility, for example, helps to explain divergent thinking, and the childlike and unconventional tendencies of some creative types meshes with the tendency of some creative persons to build paracosms. Autonomy could easily support original thinking. There is an openness value as well as an open-to-experience trait. The list goes on, and each gives a kind of validity to what was proposed about the creativity complex.

Not all of the things listed above are actual "traits" in the strict sense of the word (Phares 1986). Even so, they are consistent with the idea that creativity is a complex, and the notion that interactions among traits, attitudes, abilities, and values best capture that complex.

Three points should be emphasized:

- The creative personality varies from domain to domain, and perhaps even from person to person. There is no one creative personality. Those interactions are more important than individual traits. The creative constellation recognize combinations and interactions among traits. Recall here how persistence was associated with intrinsic motivation, confidence with self-promotion.
- There are indicative traits and contraindicative traits. Autonomy is an indicative trait; autonomy should be supported if creative performances are desired. Conformity is contraindicative; it should not be encouraged. Of course the idea of optima applies here. Moderation in all things.
- Some of the traits that are indicative of creativity are admirable, respectable, and socially desirable. Yet some of them are often unattractive and low in social desirability. This applies to the contraindicative traits as well: some are admirable, some are not.

THE CREATIVITY FRACTAL (FIGURE 9.5)

Creativity represents a complex or syndrome. In fact, now that we have covered the personality perspective on creativity, it seems we might use the "borrow or adapt" tactic for creative thinking (see Chapter 12) and adapt the concept of fractals (Gleick 1987; Ludwig 1998; Mandelbrot 1982). Most important may be the self-similarity of fractals. This indicates that many features of the natural world show the same patterns regardless of the level of analysis. Creativity is a complex, with personality playing a large role. The creative personality is also a complex (or constellation). There is no one key trait for creativity. What works on the most general levels may work on specific levels (e.g., personality, cognition, affect, attitudinal) as well.

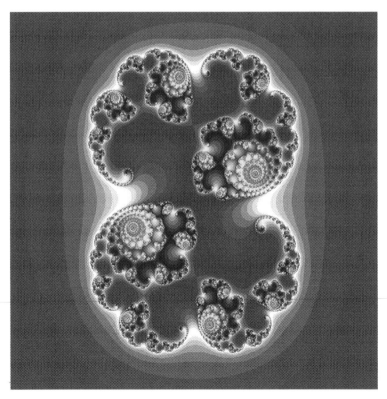

FIGURE 9.5   Fractal Julia set. *Source: Wikimedia Commons, the free media repository. This work has been released into the public domain by its author, Solkoll. This applies worldwide. In some countries this may not be legally possible; if so: Solkoll grants anyone the right to use this work for any purpose, without any conditions, unless such conditions are required by law. http://commons.wikimedia.org/wiki/File:Julia_set_(highres_01).jpg*

Next, no prediction of creative performance would be accurate without taking the immediate environment into account. This is the state × trait theory, with introverts only introverted in particular environments, and unconventional people sometimes only unconventional in certain situations. The idea of "fit" is also relevant here, though that usually is applied to a compatibility between the person and a domain or career (Albert & Runco 1989).

Finally, many of the characteristics described herein depend on values, intentions, and choice. Individuals can decide to be proactive, for example, and they can direct energy and resources toward self-efficacy. They can control weirdness. This is not to say that all our behavior is under our control. No one fulfills their creative potential without putting some effort into it, either. Intentionality has great generality as well—it applies to most everything in this chapter. Just as certain is that every trait listed in this chapter is dependent on an individual's potential. Individuals have the potential to be contrarian, weird, autonomous, and so on, and those potentials are not unlimited. At the very least they have genetically based boundaries. Potentials can be fulfilled if the right choices are made, but they cannot be exceeded, choice or no choice.

This last point allows us to distinguish between creative behavior and what Cattell and Butcher (1968) called pseudocreative behavior. Contrarianism, for example, might lead to unusual behavior, but it is only sometimes useful for truly creative work. Other times it is essentially a publicity stunt. The difference is in the underlying intentions. Values are no doubt relevant as well. One contrarian values publicity, the other creativity.

Admittedly some creative persons do appreciate attention and acclaim. That was apparently true of the eminent creators examined by Gardner (1993a). Then again, his was an extremely select sample (Picasso, Gandhi, and Einstein included), and each was in fact famous! No wonder, then, that a desire for fame was involved. Self-promotion might not be valued by other creative people (e.g., Feynman, Darwin) nor valued by noneminent people. It can actually be a distraction and lead to misplaced investments. The person may be trying to attract attention instead of developing the skills and knowledge base that would allow authentic creativity.

Intentionality and choice should be emphasized in any enhancement efforts. But can they be measured and studied? Piaget seemed to think so, though he relied on observations and empathic inference rather than numeric measurement, and he did not address creativity. Piaget did distinguish between subjective moral reasoning and objective moral reasoning in that the former took intentions into account.

Enhancement efforts should also look to unconventional behaviors of various sorts. Yet clearly this is a prime example of the need for moderation. Runco (1996a) suggested that parents and teachers target unconventional behaviors (and the correlates, such as autonomy, and even contrarianism) but only while also teaching discretion. Creative thinking may require some unconventionality, but Frank Barron was right on target when he said, "dare to be a radical, but don't be a damn fool."

10

Creativity and Politics

ADVANCE ORGANIZER

- Creative Political Products
- Political Rhetoric and Speeches
- "Spin"
- Hidden Variables
- Resources and Constraints
- Bridges with Economics
- Costs and Benefits

- Political Philosophy
- Liberalism
- Personality
- Freedom and Independence
- Conservatism
- Authoritarianism

There may be no better place to begin a chapter on creativity and politics than with Sir Winston Churchill. Sir Winston was prolific and creative in both his writing and his politics. Consider this statement from a speech in August 1940: "Never in the field of human conflict was so much owed by so many to so few." This was part of a speech that described the bravery and valor of the British military, and in particular the Royal Air Force pilots who were fighting the Luftwaffe as part of the "Battle of Britain."

This particular quotation came to mind as I pondered the topic of creativity and politics. That is because what is painfully obvious is that politics is so important, in so many ways, to everyone, and yet it is so often overlooked, at least in creativity studies. That disparity between level of importance and amount of research may be larger for politics than for any other topic in the field of creativity studies. Perhaps it is the "fish not seeing the water" phenomenon.

This chapter examines the few studies of creativity that have acknowledged politics. It also discusses several theories of creativity that, with a bit of reading between the lines, imply that political conditions influence the expression of creativity and the fulfillment of creative potentials. The first few sections of this chapter will focus on the theories and findings that show the clearest connection of creativity with politics. The last few sections will explore connections which are not as obvious, perhaps because some theoretical context is required or where the connections are implied but perhaps have not yet been empirically investigated.

CREATIVE POLITICAL PRODUCTS

As is the case with all macro-level influences on creativity, there is a bidirectionality, with creativity both being an influence on history, politics, economics (or whatever macro influence is being examined) and influenced by that same macro factor. The political situation of any one time and place thus influences creative behavior and the fulfillment (or lack thereof) of creative potentials, and at the same time creativity is also a contributor to that political situation. In a manner of speaking it is another example of how creativity is best viewed as a process (Box 10.1).

What are the best examples of creative political products? It would be interesting to examine elections to identify the "spin" offered by campaigns, perhaps using a modified version of the speech-analysis method described by Katz-Buonincontro (2012), but apparently this kind of investigation has yet to be done. If that spin puts a new perspective on a candidate or issue, and it is effective (e.g., swaying voters), it would be creative! The creativity of political spin is probably strongly related to the "impression management" efforts of certain wannabe creators (Kasof 1995; Runco 1995c).

BOX 10.1

CREATIVITY AS POLITICAL–ECONOMIC–HISTORICAL PROCESS

Creativity can be examined from various perspectives, including "person," "place," "product," or "process" (Rhodes 1961; Richards 1999; Runco & Kim 2011). The process perspective is often especially useful. This is true when considering the role of creativity in history, politics, and economics, and when considering the impact of those same things on creativity. The following equation captures the idea of process in a simple manner.

$$(PHE1 \times CB1CP1) \Rightarrow (PHE2 \times CB2CP2) \Rightarrow (PHE3 \times CB3CP3) \text{ etc.}$$

PHE is the abbreviation for political, historical, and economic context, which is really just "what's going on at one time and place." CBCP represents creative behavior and creative potentials. This includes both the immediate expression of creative talents (e.g., what mature creators are producing and changing) and the creative potentials of individuals who are not at that time productive but are instead developing the constellation of drives and skills that may eventually allow them to behave in a creative fashion. In the equation CBCP includes numbers (e.g., CB1CP1) because the creative behaviors in any one era and in any one culture tend to differ from what is considered creative at another point in time and in other cultures (Csikszentmihalyi 1990a; Simonton 1995). Also, the potentials of one political–historical–economic context, if fulfilled, will lead to different creative behaviors in later and different political–historical–economic contexts. So CB1 is going to be different from CB2. The important conclusion is that things change. Creativity is influenced by context and in turn changes subsequent contexts.

The clearest examples of creative political products include actual artifacts, such as the Declaration of Independence, the Magna Carta, and the U.S. Constitution. This is why Schiff (2005) titled her historical examination of the founding of America *A Great Improvisation*. Along the same lines, Ellis (2007) titled his historical analysis of the birth of the United States *American Creation*. The democratic republic was a new idea, as were many of the rights, laws, and amendments proposed by the individuals who argued and fought for independence. Read any of the documents listed above; the creativity is obvious in each. They were political documents, or artifacts, and they resulted from creative efforts.

Political speeches have been treated as potentially creative political products. Speeches frequently target creativity (and innovation), as exemplified by President Barack Obama's statement, offered at the Export Import Bank's Annual Conference on March 11, 2010: "Our single greatest asset is the innovation and the ingenuity and creativity of the American people. It is essential to our prosperity and it will only become more so in this century" (Obama 2010).

Another example can be found in Bill Clinton's speech from September 2012, in which he nominated President Barack Obama for a second term of office. Clinton described the President as "a man who believes we can build a new American Dream economy driven by innovation and creativity, education and cooperation" (para 3).

Katz-Buonincontro (2012) examined recent speeches and concluded that there are

two types of rhetorical appeals to long-held educational values.... pragmatic claims about student creativity focus on economic recovery, which implies a need to teach and research the link between creativity, academic success and workforce preparation. In contrast, humanist claims about student creativity emphasize a teaching and research agenda of promoting self-realization, cultural identity formation, and aesthetic learning principles, which include empathy and emotional awareness in addition to cognitive aspects of creative thinking and problem solving (p. 257).

The speech by Bill Clinton quoted above illustrates the pragmatic focus. Clinton stated,

It turns out that advancing equal opportunity and economic empowerment is both morally right and good economics. Why? Because poverty, discrimination, and ignorance restrict growth. When you stifle human potential, when you don't invest in new ideas, it doesn't just cut off the people who are affected. It hurts us all. We know that investments in education and infrastructure and scientific and technological research increase growth. They increase good jobs, and they create new wealth for all the rest of us (Clinton 2012).

A speech or other political product can be creative even if it does not mention creativity. This same thing can be said about language outside of public speeches. Be it oral or written, language is very often creative. People often say things that they have not heard or said before. They are creating new sentences and new meaning. This is the generative aspect of language identified by Chomsky (1965) and it was the rationale used in Chapter 1 to support the position that language may be the best example there is of *everyday creativity*. But keep in mind the difference between political influences on creativity and political results of creativity. A politician can say something about creativity and innovation without doing anything to support them!

WHICH SPECIFIC POLITICAL FACTORS INFLUENCE CREATIVITY?

Seitz (2003) felt that political context often constrains entrepreneurship, self-expression, and creativity. He pointed specifically to "the differential distribution of power and resources among individuals and groups in society, as well as the impact of the norm of self-interest …

political and religious censorship, corporate control and influence, copyright restrictions" (p. 385) as key influences on creativity and its correlates, such as entrepreneurship. Seitz also described how these influences vary from era to era. He concluded that there is a periodization of political influence, with tradition-bound periods and occasional revolutions. Gray (1966), Martindale (1990), and Kuhn (1962) all described similar historical cycles, with renaissances and then periods without manifest creativity. Kuhn's (1962) ideas on cycles are especially well known. He described scientific revolutions occurring only after periods of rich but stable tradition. Kuhn described tradition-bound periods as *normal science* and revolutions as *paradigm shifts*.

Interestingly, Seitz (2003, p. 385) cited "Karl Marx's view that art and politics are the surface manifestations of the same underlying social order." This is interesting because it implies that there is yet another possible relationship between politics and creativity. This chapter started with a description of two relationships, one with political context influencing creativity and the second with political ideas being the result of creative efforts. Marx (and later, Seitz 2003) implied that there may be a third variable at work which actually leads to both creativity (e.g., art) and politics. This is a reasonable view and is entirely consistent with what is often called a third or "hidden" variable in correlational studies. Two things can be correlated, not because one causes the other, but instead because there is a third variable, probably hidden, that is the actual causal agent.

Brockman (1993) also referred to political and religious censorship in his description of possible influences on creative efforts. In addition, he described (a) a lack of grants and funding, (b) corporate control over the exchange of information and other resources, (c) the impact of oligopolies, monopolies, (d) copyright restrictions, and (e) awards from corporations that are given, not to revolutionaries, but to individuals who support the status quo. Some of this is clearly economic, but it would be very difficult to extricate political influence from economic. That is why the political–historical–economic (PHE) composite was used in Box 10.1 rather than just one political, economic, or historical factor. Note also that in the lists of influences, creativity is influenced by both constraint and support. Translating, both *costs* and *benefits* are involved (Rubenson & Runco 1992a) (Box 10.2).

The situation is even more complicated than the PHE composite implies. Philosophy is also involved. Chapter 11 goes into more detail about the impact of different philosophies on creativity, but a political context always assumes a philosophy, so something must be said here as well. Seitz (2003) was well aware of this when he described

A theory of government and society that became increasingly influential in the 17th century, liberalism, created the conditions for individualism. These conditions are currently demarcated in contemporary Western democracies according to three premises. The first premise requires that all citizens receive equal treatment and consideration, independent of any particular conception of what is an acceptable lifestyle—that is, one either advocated by state ideology or formal government intervention. Similarly, the second and third premises set the conditions for individualism by endorsing both representative democracy and a market economy, as these promote the economic and ethnic equality of all citizens.... Thus, by institutionalizing fair and equal consideration of the needs of all citizens within a system of market relations and political representation of the people's will, liberalism fosters creative production by encouraging individual creative expression (pp. 389–390).

This goes a long way to explaining how political context influences creativity.

It is easy to see how the political orientation towards individualism can influence creativity. Without a doubt it directly influences the individuality and autonomy that are always

BOX 10.2

CENSORSHIP INHIBITS CREATIVITY

Censorship is sometimes a political decision. History includes too many examples where it has inhibited creative efforts. Books are, for example, occasionally banned for political reasons. *Huckleberry Finn* (Figure 10.2), *The Grapes of Wrath*, *1984*, *The DaVinci Code*, and several of Ernest Hemingway's novels have all been banned. Other banned books:

Alice's Adventures in Wonderland (1865)
All the King's Men
All Quiet on the Western Front (1929)
Animal Farm (1945)
As I Lay Dying
Brave New World (1932)
The Call of the Wild
Candide (1759)
The Canterbury Tales (1300s)
Cat's Cradle
Catch 22 (1961)
The Catcher in the Rye
A Clockwork Orange
The Color Purple
The da Vinci Code (2003)
Diary of Anne Frank (1947)
Fanny Hill (1748)
A Farewell to Arms
For Whom the Bell Tolls
Frankenstein (1818)
Gone with the Wind
The Great Gatsby

The Grapes of Wrath (1939)
Green Eggs and Ham (1960)
The Gulag Archipelago (1973)
Howl (1955)
In Cold Blood
Invisible Man
The Jungle (1906)
Lady Chatterley's Lover (1928)
Lolita (1955)
The Lord of the Flies
Of Mice and Men
One Flew Over the Cuckoo's Nest
Madame Bovary (1856)
Mein Kampf (1925)
1984 (1949)
The Naked and the Dead (1948)
Peyton Place (1956)
Rabbit, Run
The Satanic Verses
A Separate Piece
Slaughterhouse Five
Sophie's Choice
The Sun Also Rises
To Kill a Mockingbird
Tropic of Cancer (1934)
Uncle Tom's Cabin (1852)
Ulysses (1922)

Note. For additional information go to the American Library Association Website (www.ala.org/advocacy/banned)

included in lists of core characteristics for creativity. Several other traits (e.g., conservatism) are also clearly tied to particular political orientations. These are discussed towards the end of this chapter.

The origins of individualism go back at least as far as Jean-Jacques Rousseau and Thomas Hobbes (Kwang 2002). Kwang tied in individualism to Kant's ideas about freedom, or what he called "self imposed tutelage" (p. 2). Kwang's interest in individualism, like many of those studying creativity, was related to culture and cultural differences. Chapter 11 goes into detail about cultures varying along an individuality–collectivistic continuum.

In a sense individualism implies that an individual is free to use his or her intellect. It further implies that there is no one correct lifestyle or government for supporting creative potentials and creative behavior. Kwang (2002) tied individualism to moral relativism, as well as to the *Closing of the American Mind* (the title of Allen Bloom's famous book about higher education).

INDIVIDUALISM AND FREEDOM

In Western society, the broadest politically determined influence on creativity is "freedom" and its corollary, independence. Both played a central role in the formation of the United States, as is obvious by examination of the U.S. Constitution and Declaration of Independence. The latter refers to certain "unalienable Rights, that among these are Life, Liberty and the pursuit of Happiness." Liberty is synonymous with freedom. Later the Declaration gives freedom as reason to reject the King's rule, the rationale being that "a Tyrant … is unfit to be the ruler of a free people." The connection between this political freedom and some of the other things listed above (e.g., resources) is implied by one of the last sections of the Declaration. There it states that the intent is to

> solemnly publish and declare, That these United Colonies are, and of Right ought to be Free and Independent States; that they are Absolved from all Allegiance to the British Crown, and that all political connection between them and the State of Great Britain, is and ought to be totally dissolved; and that as Free and Independent States, they have full Power to levy War, conclude Peace, contract Alliances, establish Commerce, and to do all other Acts and Things which Independent States may of right do.

The list of signatories can be found, along with the remainder of the Declaration, at http://www.archives.gov/exhibits/charters/declaration_transcript.html.

All U.S. citizens should probably have a copy of the Declaration hanging on their walls. It is an impressive document which influences all Americans' lives, every day. It does so in part by guaranteeing various freedoms, several of which (or perhaps all) support creativity.

The U.S. Constitution (Figure 10.1) similarly provides and emphasizes freedom and liberty. The stated purpose of its authors was to "secure the Blessings of Liberty to ourselves and our Posterity, do ordain and establish this Constitution for the United States of America."

The concept of freedom is no doubt a part of *zeitgeist* in the United States (and hopefully elsewhere) and may be a part of the implicit theories of citizens when they think about what is allowable and appropriate behavior. Because there is an overarching freedom, provided by the political system, individuals are free to express themselves, and this includes creative self-expression. In fact, it could be that if self-expression is truly and literally an expression of oneself, then all self-expression is creative.

Before changing the topic, it is worth noting that freedom has a role in creativity, not just on the social and political level, but also in education and in the home. Chapter 2 describes how creative behavior tends to thrive in environments that are characterized by *psychological freedom* (Harringon 1980). Certain kinds of freedom are also apparent in the research on organizational factors that support creativity. Even before psychological freedom was studied in education, the home, and business, it was recognized as a critical influence on creative self-expression in Humanistic theories (Maslow 1968; Rogers 1954/1959). The idea here is that

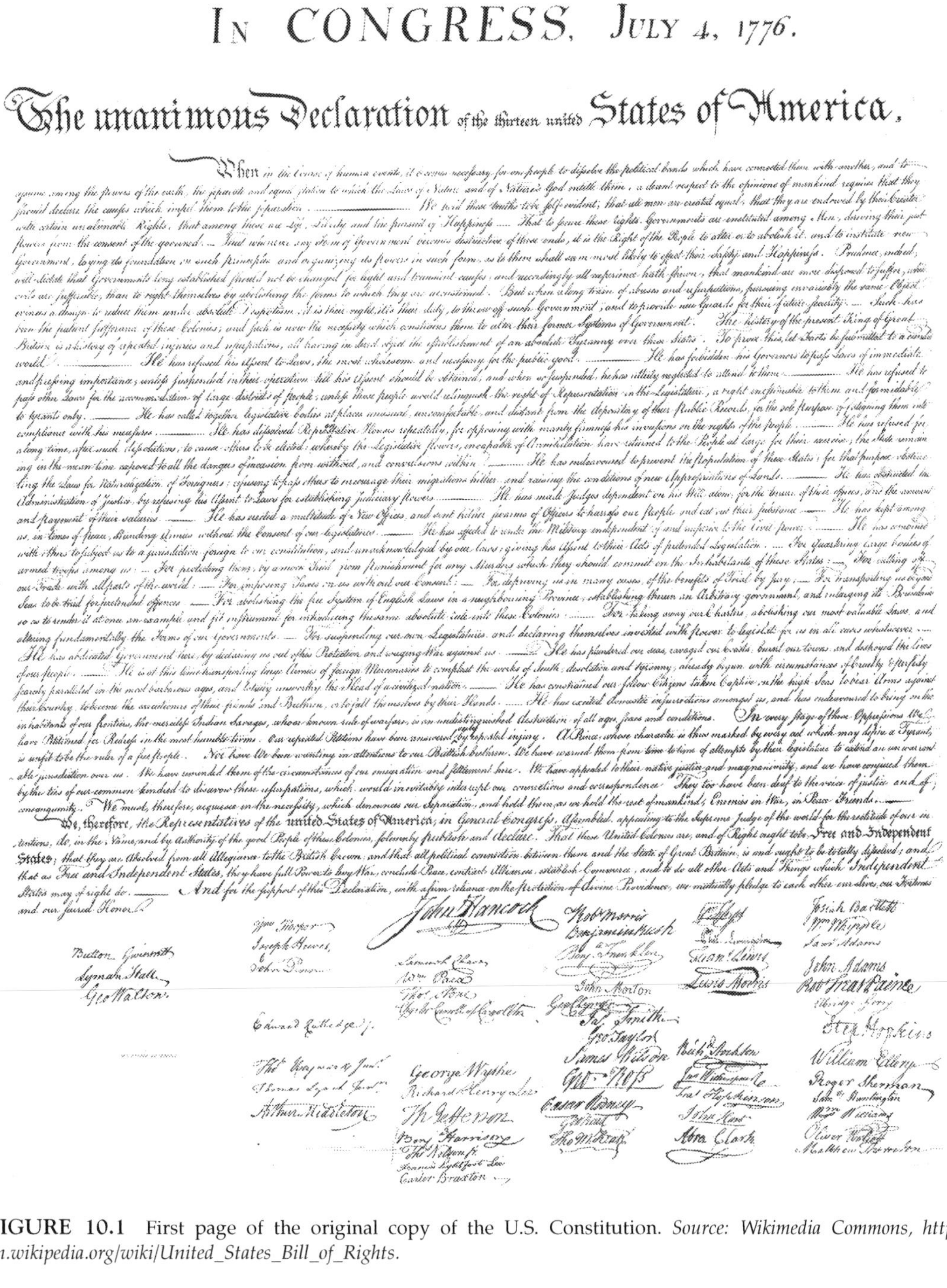

IN CONGRESS, JULY 4, 1776.

The unanimous Declaration of the thirteen united States of America,

When in the Course of human events, it becomes necessary for one people to dissolve the political bands which have connected them with another, and to assume among the powers of the earth, the separate and equal station to which the Laws of Nature and of Nature's God entitle them, a decent respect to the opinions of mankind requires that they should declare the causes which impel them to the separation. — We hold these truths to be self-evident, that all men are created equal, that they are endowed by their Creator with certain unalienable Rights, that among these are Life, Liberty and the pursuit of Happiness. — That to secure these rights, Governments are instituted among Men, deriving their just powers from the consent of the governed, — That whenever any Form of Government becomes destructive of these ends, it is the Right of the People to alter or to abolish it, and to institute new Government, laying its foundation on such principles and organizing its powers in such form, as to them shall seem most likely to effect their Safety and Happiness. Prudence, indeed, will dictate that Governments long established should not be changed for light and transient causes; and accordingly all experience hath shewn, that mankind are more disposed to suffer, while evils are sufferable, than to right themselves by abolishing the forms to which they are accustomed. But when a long train of abuses and usurpations, pursuing invariably the same Object evinces a design to reduce them under absolute Despotism, it is their right, it is their duty, to throw off such Government, and to provide new Guards for their future security. — Such has been the patient sufferance of these Colonies; and such is now the necessity which constrains them to alter their former Systems of Government. The history of the present King of Great Britain is a history of repeated injuries and usurpations, all having in direct object the establishment of an absolute Tyranny over these States. To prove this, let Facts be submitted to a candid world. — He has refused his Assent to Laws, the most wholesome and necessary for the public good. — He has forbidden his Governors to pass Laws of immediate and pressing importance, unless suspended in their operation till his Assent should be obtained; and when so suspended, he has utterly neglected to attend to them. — He has refused to pass other Laws for the accommodation of large districts of people, unless those people would relinquish the right of Representation in the Legislature, a right inestimable to them and formidable to tyrants only. — He has called together legislative bodies at places unusual, uncomfortable, and distant from the depository of their public Records, for the sole purpose of fatiguing them into compliance with his measures. — He has dissolved Representative Houses repeatedly, for opposing with manly firmness his invasions on the rights of the people. — He has refused for a long time, after such dissolutions, to cause others to be elected; whereby the Legislative powers, incapable of Annihilation, have returned to the People at large for their exercise; the State remaining in the mean time exposed to all the dangers of invasion from without, and convulsions within. — He has endeavoured to prevent the population of these States; for that purpose obstructing the Laws for Naturalization of Foreigners; refusing to pass others to encourage their migrations hither, and raising the conditions of new Appropriations of Lands. — He has obstructed the Administration of Justice, by refusing his Assent to Laws for establishing Judiciary powers. — He has made Judges dependent on his Will alone, for the tenure of their offices, and the amount and payment of their salaries. — He has erected a multitude of New Offices, and sent hither swarms of Officers to harrass our people, and eat out their substance. — He has kept among us, in times of peace, Standing Armies without the Consent of our legislatures. — He has affected to render the Military independent of and superior to the Civil power. — He has combined with others to subject us to a jurisdiction foreign to our constitution, and unacknowledged by our laws; giving his Assent to their Acts of pretended Legislation: — For Quartering large bodies of armed troops among us: — For protecting them, by a mock Trial, from punishment for any Murders which they should commit on the Inhabitants of these States: — For cutting off our Trade with all parts of the world: — For imposing Taxes on us without our Consent: — For depriving us in many cases, of the benefits of Trial by Jury: — For transporting us beyond Seas to be tried for pretended offences — For abolishing the free System of English Laws in a neighbouring Province, establishing therein an Arbitrary government, and enlarging its Boundaries so as to render it at once an example and fit instrument for introducing the same absolute rule into these Colonies: — For taking away our Charters, abolishing our most valuable Laws, and altering fundamentally the Forms of our Governments: — For suspending our own Legislatures, and declaring themselves invested with power to legislate for us in all cases whatsoever. — He has abdicated Government here, by declaring us out of his Protection and waging War against us. — He has plundered our seas, ravaged our Coasts, burnt our towns, and destroyed the lives of our people. — He is at this time transporting large Armies of foreign Mercenaries to compleat the works of death, desolation and tyranny, already begun with circumstances of Cruelty & perfidy scarcely paralleled in the most barbarous ages, and totally unworthy the Head of a civilized nation. — He has constrained our fellow Citizens taken Captive on the high Seas to bear Arms against their Country, to become the executioners of their friends and Brethren, or to fall themselves by their Hands. — He has excited domestic insurrections amongst us, and has endeavoured to bring on the inhabitants of our frontiers, the merciless Indian Savages, whose known rule of warfare, is an undistinguished destruction of all ages, sexes and conditions. In every stage of these Oppressions We have Petitioned for Redress in the most humble terms: Our repeated Petitions have been answered only by repeated injury. A Prince, whose character is thus marked by every act which may define a Tyrant, is unfit to be the ruler of a free people. Nor have We been wanting in attentions to our Brittish brethren. We have warned them from time to time of attempts by their legislature to extend an unwarrantable jurisdiction over us. We have reminded them of the circumstances of our emigration and settlement here. We have appealed to their native justice and magnanimity, and we have conjured them by the ties of our common kindred to disavow these usurpations, which, would inevitably interrupt our connections and correspondence. They too have been deaf to the voice of justice and of consanguinity. We must, therefore, acquiesce in the necessity, which denounces our Separation, and hold them, as we hold the rest of mankind, Enemies in War, in Peace Friends. —

We, therefore, the Representatives of the united States of America, in General Congress, Assembled, appealing to the Supreme Judge of the world for the rectitude of our intentions, do, in the Name, and by Authority of the good People of these Colonies, solemnly publish and declare, That these United Colonies are, and of Right ought to be Free and Independent States; that they are Absolved from all Allegiance to the British Crown, and that all political connection between them and the State of Great Britain, is and ought to be totally dissolved; and that as Free and Independent States, they have full Power to levy War, conclude Peace, contract Alliances, establish Commerce, and to do all other Acts and Things which Independent States may of right do. — And for the support of this Declaration, with a firm reliance on the protection of divine Providence, we mutually pledge to each other our Lives, our Fortunes and our sacred Honor.

FIGURE 10.1 First page of the original copy of the U.S. Constitution. *Source: Wikimedia Commons, http://en.wikipedia.org/wiki/United_States_Bill_of_Rights.*

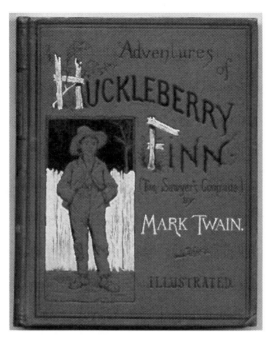

FIGURE 10.2 Mark Twain's *Adventures of Huckleberry Finn* is often labeled The Great American Novel. Yet 100 years ago it was banned in the United States. The image here is from the cover of the 1884 edition. *Source: Wikimedia Commons, http://en.wikipedia.org/wiki/File:Huckleberry_Finn_book.JPG.*

individuals can be spontaneous and authentic when there is psychological freedom. Chapter 11 describes the Humanistic view in detail and underscores that spontaneity and authenticity are parts of self-actualization, and that self-actualization is in turn inextricable from creativity.

Independence, like freedom, seems to be tied to creativity on multiple levels of analysis. Independence is provided by certain political situations, but it is also cited throughout the creativity literature, often in studies of individuals and their personalities or their cognitive tendencies (e.g., Albert & Runco 1989; Barron 1995; Barron & Bradley 1990). It is the disposition towards independence and the capacity to think in an autonomous fashion that leads to ideas and solutions that are different, contrarian, and original.

POLITICAL EVENTS

Political orientation (e.g., liberalism or conservatism) can influence creative behavior and potentials, as can specific freedoms provided by political context. Particular events that reflect political situations also seem to have an impact. Simonton (1990b) described how civil disturbances, international war, external threats, and political instability may each have an impact on societal creativity. Simonton's argument was quite precise and bridged political events to both the form and the quality of societal creativity. He was also able to describe why certain

TABLE 10.1 Examples of Items from Barron's Nuclear Arms Reduction Scale

1. I think a nuclear exchange could easily be precipitated by accident.

2. The policy of "deterrence" through "balance of terror" is the best solution in the forseeable future.

3. I wish we had more opportunity to participate in fallout shelter drills and other civil defense.

4. I would push the button if I had to.

5. I favor a nuclear freeze now.

6. We should spend a lot less money for armaments if we want a strong economy.

The entire NAR can be found in Barron and Bradley (1990). A Likert scale is used for the responses.

events have an immediate impact, while others have impact only after a delay. Still others have a transient impact, while some have lasting impact.

Interestingly, it is not just war, but certain kinds of wars (i.e., what Simonton 1990 called defensive wars and balance-of-power wars) that influence creativity, or at least invention and discovery. Other kinds of wars (imperialistic and civil) have no impact. Contrary to common lore, medical knowledge does not benefit from war.

Art, not just science and invention, is influenced by war. Simonton (1983), for instance, found "prudence" to be a common theme in plays written when the dramatist's country was losing a war, and Martindale (1975) found discussions of morality and the secondary process content of poems to vary with war casualties. Porter and Suedfeld (1981) reported that the integrative complexity of English novelists changed when the author's country was at war. Simonton (1990b) cited research on changes in music (melodic structure) and fashion (including the length of the skirt and the neckline) changing when there was a war.

Barron and Bradley (1990) also investigated war, or at least attitudes about war, and in particular nuclear war. They developed the Nuclear Arms Reduction (NAR) Scale, a 10-item self-report with indicated pro-freeze or pro-build-up (of arms). Barron and Bradley found that scores on the NAR scale were related to independence of judgment, complexity of outlook, and the disposition towards originality. All three of these are in turn associated with creative potential (see Chapter 9). Examples from the NAR are presented in Table 10.1.

So far, most of the discussion in this chapter has examined political influences on creativity. The results of that influence were mentioned, but the review of Barron and Bradley's (1990) empirical study with the NAR and the disposition towards originality makes for a nice segue to a review of the few empirical studies in this area. They tend to assess the personality traits that are both functionally associated with creativity and also sensitive to political situations.

CONSERVATISM

Political analyses often contrast conservative and liberal political views. There is a sizable literature on conservatism and personality traits. Indeed, there is a large enough literature that Jost et al. (2003) were able to conduct a meta-analysis that included previous empirical research on relationships between conservative thought and its correlates. Results indicated that conservatism was related to the need for structure, cognitive closure, the avoidance of uncertainty and intolerance of ambiguity, and a tendency to follow rules. The last of these implies that it would be difficult to be highly conservative and creative, given that creativity often benefits from a bending or breaking of rules or even contrarianism (Runco 2011). In fact, creativity also benefits from a tolerance of ambiguity and uncertainty (Barron 1968, 1995), so there are several reasons to think that creativity and conservatism would be inversely related to one another. Political conservative tendencies probably make it difficult to think in a creative fashion.

Additional support for this line of thought can be found in the empirical research on the artistic preferences of conservative individuals. A number of studies suggest that conservative individuals usually prefer simple rather than complex paintings and representational rather than abstract paintings (Wilson et al. 1973), simple over complex poetry (Gillies & Campbell 1985), unambiguous rather than ambiguous literature (McAllister & Anderson 1991), and music that is familiar rather than unfamiliar (Glasgow & Cartier 1985).

McCann (2011) reported an empirical study of conservatism, openness, and creativity. He examined patents, as a quantitative measure of creative talent, and compared 46 of the 50 United States. (Adequate data were simply not available for four of the States.) McCann estimated conservatism from voting tendencies. (Casting a vote for George W. Bush in 2004 was taken to indicate a conservative tendency.) He also used a telephone survey of 141 000 households in which respondents were asked to rate their own conservative tendencies. Openness was estimated from a standard measure of the Big Five personality traits (openness, neuroticism, agreeableness, extraversion, and conscientiousness). Correlations indicated that conservatism was strongly but negatively related to the number of patents awarded and was highly but positively related to openness. These relationships (both coefficients < .50) remained significant even when IQ, degree of urbanization, and socioeconomic status were statistically controlled.

Zysberg and Schenk (2013) used self-reports to assess the association between political orientation and creativity. They used the How Do You Think Test for creativity and developed their own short self-report for political orientation. The latter provided a rating of where each individual was on a left–right continuum (left being liberal, right being conservative). Zysberg and Schenk sampled Israeli students, and for that reason also felt that a rating for "willingness to trade the occupied territories in Israel in return for peace" was useful. They used correlational analyses and structural equation modeling to analyze the data and found that the self-ratings of social and political attitudes were indeed associated with creative potential. Creativity was also related to parental educational levels, and political attitudes with religion. More religious individuals tended to be more conservative. The relationship with religion makes a great deal of sense, as does the correlation with parental education. Indeed, it is likely that political attitudes (and religion) have developmental histories. They are both probably developed during childhood and reflect, to a large degree, family values. Box 10.3 goes into some detail about the family, as does Chapter 2.

CONCLUSIONS

Creativity is frequently described in theory and in research as a complex or syndrome (MacKinnon 1965; Mumford & Gustafson 1988). Granted, it is vital to distinguish creative potential from creative performance (Runco 2007), for these two things may bear almost no relationship to one another! Creative potential may be suggested by the capacity to produce

BOX 10.3

VALUES AND FAMILY AND MODERATOR

Importantly, all political (and cultural) influences on creativity influence creative behavior (that is, the actual expression of creativity) as well as the possible fulfillment of creative potentials, including that of children, as they mature. Yet the actual impact of political regimes, and systems depends on the family. As Albert (1978, 1980) states, the transformation of basic skills into actual talents depends on family—family values, family models, experiences chosen by the family. The family filters what the political and cultural situation provides. The family may not be able to eliminate political or cultural conditions (short of emigration), but it does moderate and filter.

ideas, for example, while creative performance may be manifested as an award, an invention or patent or publication, or some other product. I have said many times that it is probably best to avoid the word "creativity" and only use the adjective, "creative." This would lead to useful specificity: Someone writing about creativity would need to specify, "creative product," or "creative personality," or "creative potential," or "creative process," and to specify what is under consideration.

That being said, it does appear that things are not quite as complicated as is sometimes assumed. This book suggests that there is in fact quite a bit of convergence. Sure, there is research on the creative personality, and it points to all kinds of relevant traits, and there is work on creative cognition which identifies various intellectual processes that may support original solutions and ideas. The present chapter shows that there is a critical mass of theories on the politics of creativity, and quite a few political orientations and events that influence creative behavior can be identified. Things are not quite as complicated as the idea of a complex may suggest, however, because there is convergence among the literature on personality, cognition, and politics. Recall here what was said (in this chapter) about politics and philosophy. Recall also the conclusions about freedom and independence. These are constituents of personality and cognition and politics![1]

The bridge between politics and personality is not a new discovery. Adorno et al. (1950) opened the classic volume, *The Authoritarian Personality*, with this statement about the origins of personality:

> the political, economic, and social convictions of an individual often form a broad and coherent pattern, as if bound together by a mentality or spirit, and that this pattern is an expression of deep-lying trends in his [or her] personality. The major concern was with the potentially fascistic individual, one whose structure is such as to render him [or her] particularly susceptible to anti-democratic propaganda (p. 1, quoted by Merrotsy, 2013).

---

[1] Some of my most recent work on creativity has questioned the details of the creativity complex (Runco 2007, 2010b, 2010c). I have outlined a theory of parsimonious creativity which goes to the opposite extreme and focuses on what is vital and universal. Parsimony is, of course, a vital part of the scientific method, so this line of work helps to make creativity studies as scientific as possible.

BOX 10.4

THE DARK SIDE OF CREATIVITY—LEONARDO DA VINCI

The dark side of creativity is often difficult to determine. Consider in this regard Leonardo da Vinci (Figure 10.3). A huge number of his creations, inventions, and designs, and much of his artwork involve military devices and weapons. Many others that do not seem military were applied by da Vinci to military action. He was, in fact, at least as well known in his own lifetime as a military engineer as an artist.

Leonardo designed bombs, some of which exploded into smaller bombs like today's scatter bomb. He designed catapults, tanks, knight-robots, and armored boats, ladders, and bridges. He designed a leather underwater suit that he suggested be used for sneak attacks. He developed his own recipe for gunpowder and then designed a weapon that could shoot 33 times without reloading. (It had 11 barrels on each of three panels; one side would shoot 11 times and the next panel would rotate into place and shoot its 11 shots, followed by the last panel of 11 barrels.)

Historians think Leonardo was interested in patronage, which may have attracted him to weaponry, but then again, he chose to move to the military hot-spot of Renaissance Italy. As Bert Hall (2002), author of *Weapons and Warfare in Renaissance Europe*, noted, "One of the things that shocked his [Leonardo's] contemporaries and even some modern people today is that he moved from Florence, the cultural capital of Northern Italy, to Milan, which was clearly the political and military bad boy of all Italian city-states" (Hall 2002).

Leonardo had great success in Milan, mostly because of his artwork. Florence was his hometown, or close to it: Even his name, da Vinci, was taken from the small village just

outside of Florence, Vinci. Leonardo was an illegitimate child and may have taken da Vinci as appellation instead of the name of his biological father. This is also interesting because it suggests that Leonardo was a risk-taker and a nonconformist. He was extremely tactical in his career and creative efforts. More will be said about the various tactics used by Leonardo (e.g., look to nature, change perspective by enlarging, put a problem aside and come back to it later, adapt existing ideas and inventions) in Chapter 12.

Leonardo was probably not vicious or cold-blooded. He was interested in weapons, but it may have been more because of the opportunities to support his work and integrate art with science (into military engineering) than an authentic interest in warfare. Historians explain his military interests in terms of a fascination with physics and the mechanics of movement (e.g., throwing an object, such as a bomb or arrow). If the dark side of creativity is taken as an evil motivation to create, or a motivation to create evil devices, Leonardo is not dark. If the dark side is an unintended result of harmless creative activities, such as gunpowder being first used for fireworks but then later employed in weapons, then Leonardo is a good example. And of course there are creative insights that initially are intended to be inhumane, such as atomic fission used in nuclear bombs, but with non-military implications (e.g., atomic energy). The three alternatives reflect different "directions of effect" (what is first, the evil or the humane?) and different intentions. This should come as no surprise, given that psychologists studying morality also emphasize intentions. Indeed, the morality of a particular

(Continued)

BOX 10.4 (*Continued*)

act might best be determined by taking intentions into account. A child may break an expensive dish, but if that child was trying to help his or her parents, it is not "wrong." But if that child breaks the same dish intentionally, perhaps in a tantrum or to get even with his or her parents, it very likely is "wrong." The only difference is the intentionality.

Political attitudes have been associated with creativity, with specific correlations with authoritarianism, core values, and religiosity (Barron 1963a; Rubinstein 2003). Authoritarian individuals tend to be more willing to accept religious opinions and attitudes, and tend to present right-wing political views and attitudes. Recent personality studies of creativity and political orientation point to the correlation between *self-reliance* and creativity, and *openness* and creativity (Dollinger et al. 2010). Recall here the findings of McCann (2011) and Zysberg and Schenk (2013), which also uncovered a negative correlation between creativity and conservatism, and a positive correlation with openness to experience.

The dark side of creativity should be mentioned while we are on the topic of connections. After all, one of the political events covered in this chapter was war, and that is certainly an example of the dark side! But is the dark side of creativity not just human nature? This question is addressed in Box 10.4, which goes into some detail about Leonardo da Vinci's extensive work on bombs, tanks, and other military material. Leonardo actually moved from city to city in order to obtain patronage for his work, and this took him to Milan, where there was great interest in new military inventions. Other examples of the dark side of creativity are

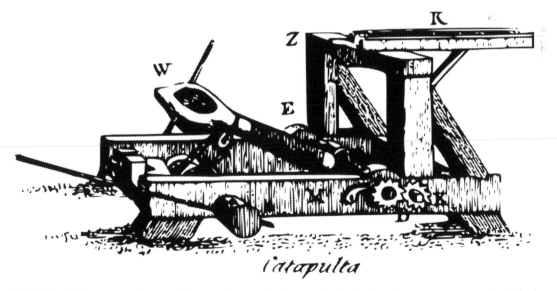

FIGURE 10.3 A catapult, not unlike one designed by Leonardo. He designed many weapons, each of which might fall under the category of "the dark side of creativity." *Source: Wikimedia Commons, This file is from the Open Clip Art Library, which released it explicitly into the public domain, using the Creative Commons CC0 1.0 Universal Public Domain Dedication. http://commons.wikimedia.org/wiki/File:Catapult.svg.*

BOX 10.5

MALEVOLENT AND BENEVOLENT CREATIVITY

Cropley et al. (2008) also looked to the dark side, and in particular to malevolent creativity. They contrast this with benevolent creativity, the former being intentionally evil (e.g., terrorism, crime) and the latter socially beneficial. Malevolent creativity "involves effective novelty that is beneficial to one side in some conflict of interests, but is bad for the other." Cropley et al. delineated malevolent creativity and offered a number of interesting hypotheses using the components of it. Novelty, they predict, can add value to a solution, for example. They also predicted a decay of novelty, especially for solutions that are widely recognized and effective.

Very importantly, Cropley et al. (2008) offered a number of "principles of malevolent creativity:"

1. People whose intentions are antisocial can, and do, exhibit creativity in their actions irrespective of whether the majority social environment approves of their aims.
2. Creativity, whether benevolent or malevolent, is a competitive lever that does not respect societal conventions. Its benefits are available to all who choose to use it.
3. Creative products (solutions) are characterized by a hierarchy of four parameters: relevance and effectiveness, novelty, elegance, and generalizability. We must analyze terrorist products, as well as our own counterterrorist solutions, against these criteria.
4. The more creative a solution (i.e., the more novel, elegant, and generalizable), the more effective it becomes.
5. The more creative a solution, the more it reduces the effectiveness of competing solutions.
6. A solution's novelty will decay over time.
7. Exposure of a solution will accelerate the decay of its novelty.
8. As a solution's novelty decays, so does its effectiveness (provided that countermeasures are put in place or activated).
9. Competing solutions, especially creative competition, will accelerate the decay of novelty and effectiveness.
10. Proactive, preemptive counterterrorist solutions are also highly creative solutions. They exhibit the characteristics of functional creativity.
11. Highly creative, preemptive counterterrorist solutions must be deliberately engineered. They will not happen of their own accord.

---

explored by Cropley et al. (2010). For what it is worth, my own chapter in that volume argues that there is no dark side (Runco 2010a).

One recent conception of the dark side of creativity points to benevolent creativity (Box 10.5) (Cropley et al. 2008; Eisenman 2008; Lee & Dow 2011). The socially beneficial side of creativity is also implied by the careful study of Gandhi (Gardner 1993a, 1993b). Talk about an important consideration for parents, teachers, and governments! It may be that benevolent creativity is the most important of all potentials in need of fulfillment.

Creativity and Philosophy

ADVANCE ORGANIZER

- Bidirectionality
- Existentialism
- Transcendence
- Philosophy of Science

- Determinism
- Nondeterminism
- Realism
- Emergence

The creativity literature contains surprisingly few discussions of philosophy. There are exceptions (e.g., Hausman & Anderson 2012), but these are rare and not often cited. If they are not often cited, they are rarely acknowledged. This may be because philosophy is usually aligned with the humanities rather than the sciences, while creativity studies have been working toward scientific respectability for at least 60 years. Still, philosophy is relevant to science, and to creativity studies, in several ways. For example:

- The philosophy of scientists influences which questions are asked, which topics are studied, and which methods are used to study creativity—or study anything, for that matter.
- Philosophical assumptions underlie everyone's assumptions and expectations about the role of creativity in life, development, aging, work, society, culture, and so on.
- All approaches to creativity (e.g., political, behavioral, economic) make assumptions about what it means to be human and what it means to be creative.

This chapter reviews philosophical perspectives on creativity. It includes summaries of key philosophers, some ancient (Plato, Aristotle), some dated but still relevant (Kant, Nietzsche), and some contemporary, or close to it (e.g., Wittgenstein), each having something to say about creative behavior. It might be most accurate to say that this chapter reviews philosophies rather than the views of philosophers. It is of course never a good thing to categorize people in terms of career (or to categorize them in any way!), and as a matter of fact the views summarized in this chapter have often been proposed by people who are not typically viewed as philosophers. Some of the philosophies outlined herein were proposed by artists or scientists, not philosophers.

BOX 11.1

BIDIRECTIONALITY IN CREATIVITY STUDIES

Most of the time, human behavior is *overdetermined*. In other words, it is influenced by more than one factor. Human behavior is not, for example, just an expression of genetic make-up but instead a function of nature and nurture, genes and experience (see Chapter 2). The concept of bidirectionality applies to the influences on human behavior, including those that contribute to creative potential and creative behavior. There is even bidirectionality with nature and nurture: Experience may be necessary to trigger genetic tendencies, and genetically inherited tendencies sometimes lead to certain experiences (Scarr & McCartney 1983). Bidirectionality is also apparent on the more abstract and philosophical level of worldviews: A person's worldview can lead to certain expectations for creative capacities, and creative capacities can contribute to the construction of one's own philosophy. Put more concisely, philosophy both influences, and is influenced by, creativity.

Different philosophies address different aspects of creativity; some describe how a person could be creative, or why, whereas others describe what constitutes creativity. This chapter summarizes how each of these questions is answered and defines the terms and processes used in doing so. Clearly, the questions covered are of extreme importance. "How can a person be creative?" leads to an explanation of the creative process, for example, and "Why are people creative?" is clearly tied to explanations of motivation and creative intentions. Very likely, all of the important questions addressed in the creativity research make assumptions that can only be explored via a philosophical discussion.

As is the case in many chapters of this book, there is *bidirectionality* (Box 11.1): Creativity is defined by various philosophies (P→C), but, in addition, creative thinking has influenced philosophers and philosophies themselves (C→P). The best philosophies are the creative ones.

PHILOSOPHY IN EVERYDAY DECISION MAKING

Philosophy is about life. The "-logy" suffice implies "the study of," which sounds academic and formal, but in actuality, philosophy is very commonly far from formal. In a manner of speaking, personal philosophy guides life each and every day. It may be that an individual has not articulated or formalized a personal philosophy, perhaps because much of the meaning only operates on a preconscious level (much like *implicit theories*, which are discussed below), or because it is the kind of knowledge that is beyond one's own awareness (Nisbett & Wilson 1977). Still, philosophy is about "the living of one's life" and contains the assumptions and expectations that lead directly to the decisions one makes while doing just that.

Making Courageous Decisions

Paul Torrance is one of the most frequently cited theorists in the field of creativity studies. Torrance is best known for his tests of creative thinking (see Chapter 1), but before those were published he worked for the U.S. Military (see Millar 1995). This was from 1951 to 1957, during the Korean War. One of the concerns of the brass in the Air Force was about survival when an officer was in enemy territory. In particular, they wanted to know why so many bomber crews failed to survive once on the ground. This was particularly puzzling because the crews were highly trained, and they often survived the crash (usually by parachuting unharmed to the ground); but once on the ground, many of them were unable to survive for even short periods of time. Torrance was asked to design a program that would increase the probability of survival. After careful analysis, he identified a set of key characteristics that were to be targeted and supported by the Air Force to increase the survival of its personnel in enemy territory. These characteristics were:

- Inventiveness
- Creativity
- Imagination
- Originality
- Flexibility
- Courage
- Decision-making skills.

Torrance was certain that creativity (and imagination, inventiveness, originality, and flexibility—all strong correlates of creativity) played an important role in survival, even when enemies are looking for you! One thesis of this book is that the same characteristics are useful for a person's day-to-day survival, even if not in a military situation. In fact, the last characteristic listed—decision making—is almost definitely also critical for all types of creative behavior (Runco et al. 1999), and it may be that a good philosophy for all of us is to make decisions such that we are utilizing our creativity every day. That certainly will make us more adaptable, and probably lead to a higher quality of life, even if we are not in battle. Creative action may require mindful decisions, given how easy it is to fall into habit and follow routine. It may also require courage (also on the list above), given how much pressure there is to conform and fit in. It is a good thing to fit in some of the time, but it is often a good thing to be creative, and that often means being unconventional rather than conventional. No wonder May (1975/1994) titled his well-known book, *The Courage to Create.*

Torrance was describing a set of behaviors that reflect an effective and useful approach to life. They are part of a philosophy: be mindful, express yourself, invest in originality, even if mindful decisions are required, and be courageous. In this light, creativity can be a part of philosophy, or what might be called a person's *worldview.*

Philosophy as Worldview

A worldview is a broad perspective on life and the universe. It is indicative of a person's philosophy. Although the distinction between *philosophy* and *worldview* is a bit fuzzy, it may be easier to relate the latter to your own life. You may not think that you hold some formal philosophy, but very likely, if asked, you could say a few things about your worldview—what you expect out of life and your assumptions about the world. In fact, the most important thing about this chapter is not the review of philosophies or the philosophers. What is most important is the idea that philosophy plays a role in all our lives.

In a manner of speaking, the philosophies covered herein are a special breed of *explicit theories* that are studied by social scientists. Explicit theories are academically solid and shared among the academy. They are often quite different from the *implicit theories* held by nonscientists, but the implicit theories have *ecological validity* (Runco 1984; Sternberg 1985). Similarly, formal philosophy may be logical and rigorous, but somewhat removed from the concerns of everyday behavior. That being said, philosophy does an excellent job of describing alternative worldviews and assumptions about life and our world, and these worldviews and assumptions are a part of what goes on in the natural environment. This chapter does review formal, academic philosophy, but when possible, connections are made with day-to-day situations and ideas that influence creativity. Each of our worldviews directly influences our decisions and creative efforts.

A second reason to recognize that philosophy is implied by worldview is that there are discussions of worldviews in the creativity literature, and a summary of them will take us one step closer to grasping the relationship between philosophy and creativity.

Goswami (1996) described three worldviews with relevance to understanding creativity. First is the *mechanistic* worldview. It could also be labeled materialistic, given that it parallels the Newtonian view of the universe, with absolutes (rather than relativity) governing how things work. Goswami described it as if there is "only one domain of reality in the worldview … matter moving in space-time" (p. 47). Thus the universe is much like a machine. The important implication is that things (including creative behavior) are predicable and reality is discovered rather than interpreted or created from naught.

Next is the *organismic* worldview. This emphasizes change, growth, or (using a word that fits nicely with humanistic views of the creative process), *becoming* (Maslow 1968; Rogers 1954/1959). Goswami (1996) is fairly specific and, when describing the organismic worldview, pointed to "a creative unfolding of purposiveness of the universe and of the individual" (pp. 47–48).

The third worldview is *idealist*. The emphasis here is on consciousness, and in particular on *transcendence*. The physical world is relegated, as is all matter, at least if one can in fact transcend and live only in one's consciousness. Goswami wrote, "there is transcendence in creativity because consciousness is transcendent" (p. 48). More broadly speaking, a theory of creativity that recognizes that ideas are independent of the physical world would be idealist. The idea is everything.

SUBJECTIVITY AND OBJECTIVITY

One of the fundamental issues underlying many of the key questions of philosophy concerns the relationship of the objective world with subjective experience. This is both a key question for philosophy, and is also crucial when thinking about philosophy and creativity. After all, if you are creative, you create, and that may bring something from your own subjective world (e.g., imagination) into existence in the objective world. Note that a distinct relationship of the objective and subjective worlds is apparent in each of the three worldviews outlined by Goswami (1996) and summarized above.

A person who feels that the objective and the subjective are independent of one another may not put much effort into creating or inventing or the like. After all, nothing can or will have an impact on the objective world. Behaving or performing creatively is often thought to give life meaning, but why invest in creativity if the subjective and objective are completely independent? If an individual's worldview assumes that they are independent, creating may not give meaning to life.

There is an alternative, whereby the individual attempts to discover the truth. Even if the person cannot have an impact on the objective world, via creativity, it might be worthwhile to explore the objective world, and perhaps find out what it's all about. Plato described something like this in *The Symposium* and *the Republic*. He explained how artists may imitate what they observe in the objective world. Good artists are supposedly better at imitating and representing "forms" and "ideals."

Significantly, the originality requirement of creativity (Runco & Jaeger 2012) was not imposed throughout most of history. Artists were imitators, not originators. Even during the Italian Renaissance, as Becker (2000–2001, p. 46) put it, "Unlike the modern conception of the genius, one that stresses originality as the distinguishing feature of the creative individual, the standard of the humanistic tradition involved the *imitatio-ideal*."

Perhaps as significant, Plato felt that the creative process was beyond the understanding of the artist. The Muses were goddesses who inspired artists to create. The belief was, since the artist does not understand where such good ideas originate, they must originate elsewhere, outside of the mind of the artist. They are given to the artist by a Muse. There were particular Muses for particular domains of creative expression. Originally there were three of them, but later four, and later still seven. Depending on who you talked to (or more accurately, which era you consider), there were Muses for music, art, drama, science, geography, mathematics, and philosophy. There was little agreement about the Muses (even how many there were) until the Renaissance.

Aristotle held a very different view. He saw artists as craftsmen, working toward an aesthetic goal, or *telos*, and understanding what steps would lead toward fulfillment of that goal. Whereas Plato appreciated divine inspiration, and in particular gifts from the Muses, Aristotle emphasized the creator him- or herself as finding a *telos* and the means to attain it. Aristotle did propose that melancholia played a large role in creative achievement, but he did not mean depression or illness (Wittkower 1973). He meant that the artist or creator has a particular balance of "humors" and these instigated creative thinking (Wittkower & Wittkower 1963, p. 102). This is not far from the view that creativity depends on a particular personality (see Chapter 9).

EXISTENTIALISM AND THE CREATIVE SYNTHESIS OF OPPOSITES

A very different worldview that allows an individual to assume an independence of the subjective and objective worlds and yet allows the personal construction of meaning was proposed many years later. This is the *existential* worldview. It requires the capacity to accept two diametric premises (one being that the objective world is in complete control, and the other that the individual him- or herself is in the driver's seat), but as a matter of fact creative thinking allows exactly that kind of synthesis and resolution (Rothenberg 1999)! An existential

BOX 11.2

SYNTHESIZING OPPOSITES

The existential worldview requires the individual to tolerate opposites. It is much like the thinking that led to the idea of *complementarity*, then, for it too accepts two ideas that are not, at face value, actually compatible. Such tolerance of opposites is often described as a creative process. Rothenberg (1999), for example, described it in his work on Janusian and homospatial thinking, as did Arieti (1976), who called it "the magic synthesis"

(also see Hoppe & Kyle 1990). Koestler's (1964) theory of bisociation also allows for the tolerance of discrepant information. It really should be no surprise that a creative thinking process—the tolerance of opposites—plays a role in creative existentialism, however. After all, existentialism may suggest that creativity is possible and valuable, so a person with that worldview is likely to understand and invest in creative effort.

worldview puts the ball back into the individual's court and makes it possible, and compelling, to create meaning in life by living a creative life.

The existential view could easily be confused with a perspective outlined by Rank (1989) and Abra (1988). They described people who are motivated to create so they can leave something behind after they die. That is a product-oriented view. The existential view, in contrast, is process-oriented. The individual does not cheat death by leaving something behind but instead finds meaning in life, even if it is finite. A word of warning: the existential view is difficult. It may require a personal crisis and an acceptance of death as final. That is precisely what gives life its meaning. It is all we've got! (Box 11.2).

TRANSCENDENCE

The notion of transcendence was introduced above, under the discussion of *idealism*. Some sort of transcendence is also implied by various other philosophies (Box 11.3). It is also implied by the existential view, for example, at least in the sense that an individual is able to transcend what the objective world tries to impose. Transcendence is also an important part of many of the philosophical ideas that originated in the East. Raina (in press) looked into Indian philosophy as related to creativity. His latest case study focused on the physicist George Sudarshan. Sudarshan was a very influential physicist. He was one of the co-authors of the Law of Weak Interactions, for example, which was later extended and applied by Nobel laureates Richard Feynman and Murray Gell-Mann.

Noted Israeli physicist Yuval Ne'eman described the Law of Weak Interactions as one of the turning points of twentieth-century physics. Sudarshan also hypothesized that certain particles ("tachyons") could travel faster than the speed of light, so obviously he was capable of thinking in a contrarian fashion. Raina (in press) included the Quantum Mechanical Theory of Optical Coherence, the Theory of Instability, Decay and Quantum Zeno Effect, Quantum Mechanics of Open Systems and Stochastic Maps in his list of Sudarshan's achievements.

BOX 11.3

METAPHYSICS AND THE CREATIVE PROCESS

The concept of *transcendence* is implied by metaphysical theories, including that of Nobel Prize winner Henri Bergson. In fact, Bergson's (2007) last book was titled, *The Creative Mind*. Chapter IV is devoted to metaphysics. In it, Bergson describes how "Philosophers agree in making a deep distinction between two ways of knowing a thing. The first implies going all around it, the second entering into it. The first depends on the viewpoint chosen and the symbols employed, while the second is taken from no viewpoint and rests on no symbol" (p. 133).

Bergson relates "going around a thing" to analysis, and "entering into it" to intuition. Transcendence is implied by "the sympathy by which one is transported into the interior of an object" (p. 135). There is no interest in reducing that thing to components, no need to describe it with symbols. In fact, Bergson defines metaphysics as "the science which claims to dispense with symbols" (p. 136). This view gets especially interesting when Bergson relates it to the writing of a novel.

Sudarshan was also a philosopher. He clearly (though not concisely) defined transcendence in this quotation:

> Timelessness is the quintessential experience that characterizes the most complex and advanced stages of the flow state. According to Sudarshan, this is the time of our dreams and poetry and fine arts. This is the transcendent time, the creative time of contemplative awareness, times of quietness (santi) when we are lost to ourselves and the time tends to lose its directionality and we see no difference of the outside world from the inside world. There is characteristic change in the perception of time during the enchanting events. "Normally time flows past to future, causation is from past to future, and each moment is transient. But at the time of discovery, or any spiritual peak experience, time has duration but no sense of being transient. The topology of time itself changes" (from Raina, in press).

Raina's own wording is also on target:

> Creativity in its finest form … contains something that we cannot explain by the normal algorithmic process of discovery. It contains a non-algorithmic process, a non-algorithmic operation and a nonlinear dynamic. Being a free, non-rule activity, by which we achieve new structures in our experience and remold existing patterns to generate novel meaning, creativity has occurred spontaneously at random moments requiring the mind to wander unfettered by the rigidities of accepted knowledge or conventional rules (Raina, in press).

Raina's (in press) use of the case study method is entirely consistent with accepted methodologies (see Davis et al. 2012; Gruber 1981a, 1988, 1996). Raina seems to feel that physicists offer especially clear ideas about philosophy, as it relates to creativity, which is interesting in that physics is probably the science that is the most concerned with subjectivity and objectivity. Consider relativity, for example, and what is says about a universal reality or absolutes, or consider the fascination with the God particle. Miller (1992, 2009) also pointed to physicists as fruitful case studies for philosophy and creativity. Not surprisingly, both Raina (in press) and Miller (1992) included Albert Einstein in their investigations. Raina was fairly conservative in his citing Einstein, however. He pointed out that Einstein "says precious little about the creative process itself nor did he indicate how the creative process fits within epistemology. Einstein was nevertheless to be given credit for anticipating, by at least 20 years, the revolutionary philosophies of Thomas Kuhn and Paul Feyerabend, which are also so amenable to discussion of creativity and discovery."

The philosophy of Sudarshan holds creativity to result from *sattva guna* (serene goodness) and *sattvika bhava*, which predisposes a person to creative action. Horan (2007, 2009) has also explored Eastern conceptions of creativity and described how transcendence and creativity may result from meditation and intuition.

Pritzker (2011) described how Zen applies to creativity. Zen is quite old. It goes back at least to the Bodhidharma, around AD 520. Of most relevance to the present discussion is Priztker's expose of Zen in calligraphy, art, architecture and design, gardening, and of course *haiku*. Pritzker (2011, p. 540) explained that "the purpose of Zen painting is to penetrate beyond the perceptions of the rational mind, to show nature's essence." Also, "the Zen garden was designed, like a painting, for viewing with the hope the emotional reaction of the viewer would inspire greater awareness" (p. 540). "Haikus represent Zen thinking in their absolute absorption in the moment, offering a direct clear unmistakable experience without reference to anything else" (p. 541). In Chapter 1 the theory of mindfulness (Langer 1989) seemed to focus on many of these same objectives.

PHILOSOPHY OF SCIENCE

Case studies, like Raina's (in press) and the other examples given in Table 11.1, have both strengths and weaknesses. The research on creativity uses many other methodologies, and most are more rigorous than case studies. One position is that case studies are best for understanding particular individuals but that they offer no generalizations. They are often suggestive of hypotheses that can be tested later, with more rigorous and experimental methods. The more rigorous methods have been used for years and are part of the traditional or orthodox scientific method. This relies on the philosophy of science, which in turn assumes determinism, rationalism, and, depending on the particular scientist, various other "isms" (Box 11.4). Occasionally things like intuition are used in scientific work (Einstein & Infeld 1938), but more often than not you need a reputation like Einstein's to get away with explaining your work in that fashion!

Determinism posits that the universe is well-structured, orderly, and thus predictable. It assumes that there are regularities, which scientists tend to call "laws," which always apply. The assumption that there are universal laws is sometimes called *mechanistic*. This line of

TABLE 11.1   Examples of Case Studies Involving Creative Scientists

George Sudarshan	Raina (in press)
Jean Piaget	Gruber (1996), Voneche (2003)
Charles Darwin	Gruber (1981a)
Neils Bohr	Miller (2009)
Carl Jung	Miller (2009)

BOX 11.4

PHILOSOPHICAL "-ISMS" WITH RELEVANCE TO CREATIVITY STUDIES

Determinism

This plays a large role in all sciences. It is, however, more general than that may imply; it also plays a role in many religions. Determinism is really a set of assumptions and expectations, and many of these apply very broadly, to religion or science. One way of summarizing the key assumption of determinism is as follows: Certain conditions lead to certain events, and whenever those conditions are found, the events always follow. Clearly this is a useful assumption if you do scientific research, at least if you are interested in cause-and-effect. Because the conditions recognized in the key assumption above tend to be a part of the objective world, determinism relegates free will. This can be a problem for creativity, given its tie to spontaneity and novelty.

Positivism

Positivism is usually viewed as a philosophy because it is quite general. There are several key assumptions. These include the idea that only knowledge obtained via scientific methods is valid. Also, mathematical and logical analyses are vital, and sensory data are objective and valid. Sensory data are obtained via the sensory capacities. Subjective experiences, in contrast, including intuition, are rejected. Positivism respects laws that govern the world and all things in it, and originally it recognized only absolute laws that are universally applicable.

Rationalism

In rationalism, reasoning is all-important. Knowledge is actually obtained via logic and reasoning (rather than through sensory data). The emphasis on knowledge implies that rationalism is an epistemology. Of most importance is probably the assumption that validation via experimentation and objective data is unnecessary for rationalism. It is, then, in direct contrast with empiricism, which puts the emphasis on data and hypothesis testing with data.

thought does not apply well to some facets of creativity. Spontaneity, for example, does not fit well with a predictable, deterministic universe. Much the same can be said about the freedom of thought that is supposedly allowed by creative ability. Hausman and Anderson (2012) tied anti-determinism to existential thought, which of course also assumes complete freedom, and thereby creative thought. Collingwood (1938), Croce (1909), Hegel, Kant, Bergson, and Pierce each dealt with these issues of freedom and spontaneity and the incompatibility with deterministic laws. Hausman (1979) seemed to think that determinism worked fairly well, early on, when the sciences were being developed. It led to a thorough understanding of many basic features of the objective world. For Hausman (1979, 1980), determinism reached its limits when it was applied to the study of human creativity.

Romanticism deserves special treatment (Box 11.5). The "-isms" in Box 11.4 all relate to the philosophy of science, and, less directly, to creativity or creativity studies. Romanticism is

BOX 11.5

ROMANTICISM

Romanticism emphasizes the individual over social and contextual explanations for achievement and eminence. The creator is described as a "lone genius" who is all-responsible for his or her outstanding performances (Nickles 1994). Romanticism also influences thinking about the forms of psychopathology that have the highest rates among creativity samples. Sass (2000–2001) and Abrams (1953) went into great detail about how romanticism influences expectations about creativity. Sass detailed how

> concepts of creativity that have prevailed in Western culture at large, at least until fairly recently, and ... have been dominant as well in psychology and psychiatry. Far from being universal or inevitable, these concepts actually have a fairly specific lineage in the history of European thought. The prevailing view is one that came to dominance with the romantic movement of the late 18th and early 19th centuries. It is a view that understands creativity in organicist, holistic, and emotivist terms, as a spontaneous rather than deliberative or mechanical process, a process that operates under the impulse of feeling and that seeks to heighten the vital sentiment of being by overcoming the felt separation between person and world, mind and body, thought and emotion. (Sass 2000–2001, pp. 56).

Sass also detailed the connection of *modernism* ("formally innovative, often avant-gardist, art and literature of approximately the first half of the 20th century," p. 56) and *postmodernism* (cultural and artistic developments largely

occurring after World War II," p. 56) to creativity and psychopathology.

Becker (2000–2001) described the advent of and impetus for romanticism:

> The relation between creativity and mental illness has been a subject of controversy in Western society from about the 1830s to the present. Although speculations regarding the mental state of creative individuals predate this period by centuries, they typically fell short of the verdict of clinical insanity. It was the romantic movement in literature that provided the single most powerful impetus for the judgment of clinical madness. By selectively adopting and redefining certain cultural axioms from the past, the romantics produced not only a logical connection between creativity and madness but also one in which madness was simultaneously a piteous and exalted condition that stood in sharp contrast to what they regarded as dreaded normality (p. 45).

Thus, the expectations of romanticism would be expected to bias observations and reports about the association between psychopathology and creativity. Elsewhere I have described a similar bias involving suicide. When celebrities commit suicide, it is newsworthy, and as such the data on suicide and fame are salient, easy to obtain, but perhaps not representative of the actual, objective correlation. Thank goodness the scientific method is available! It should minimize the impact of biased data and lead to objective and accurate conclusions.

directly relevant to creativity, and especially to discussions of "the lone genius" (who may or may not be creative) and the relationship of psychopathology with creativity.

Like Hausman (1979, 1980), De Cock (1996; Rickards & De Cock 2012) pointed to novelty as especially difficult for the traditional sciences, with their assumptions of determinism and regularity. All creative ideas and behaviors are novel. They are original. They are difficult to predict and may follow from free will and spontaneity instead of the accepted laws or expectations. Novelty creates many problems for scientific determinism.

The relativistic nature of creativity is also problematical for strict determinism. Consider in this regard the fact that many creative achievements have been ignored for years, only to be valued as unambiguously creative much later. Mendel, Rembrandt, and many others have been ignored in their own time. Van Gogh did not sell any paintings in his own lifetime. There is, then, a kind of *historical relativity*. Cross-cultural work suggests that there is also a cultural relativity, at least in the sense that accepted domains of creative performance vary from country to country. In fact, it may be that originality is not the key to creativity in Iranian cultures (Kharkhurin & Samadpour Motalleebi 2008).

Clear examples of *non-determinism* are easy to find and apply well to certain parts of the creative process. Hausman and Anderson (2012) described the work of Tomas (1958) and how he "emphasized that human creators do not know what their aims are prior to completion of the creative act, arguing that the creator does not have a target at which to aim…. With respect to his absence of an appeal to a divine source, … spontaneity seems to be implied if creative acts are not predetermined. Yet his insistence that only antecedent conditions function in creativity turns him in the direction of naturalism."

Hausman and Anderson (2012) also cited Collingwood (1938) and Croce (1909), who described the artistic process as beginning without preconceived ideas of what is to be done. Hausman and Anderson (2012) argued that much of this thinking was consistent with the views of Kant (1781/2008), for he gave artists a kind of self-determinism that would be independent of some universal, all-encompassing determinism. Kant also acknowledged the role of spontaneity in the arts, which further distances his philosophy from strict determinism.

De Cock (1996) proposed that *realism* applies better to creativity than does determinism. This is because robust empirical data are not the only important concern in realism, so the highly personal aspects of the creative process, including those reflecting imagination and affect, are tolerable. The most useful part of realism is no doubt that the concept known as *emergence*. De Cock (1996) contrasted it with the atomism of the orthodox scientific method: "The principle of atomism, one of the foundations of the old orthodoxy, expresses a commitment to the belief that phenomena can be individuated and exist independently of other phenomena to which they may be related. But in the realist perspective the social world is inherently relational and characterized by emergence."

De Cock quoted Tsoukas (1989, p. 553) to define *emergence*: "Emergent powers are created when some objects or individuals are internally related to each other to form a structure (e.g., the relationship between a superior and a subordinate). Objects or individuals are internally linked when their identity depends on their being in a relationship with the rest of the components of the structure." He also showed how these ideas fit well with the newer social and systems theories of creativity (Albert & Runco 1990; Csikszentmihalyi 1990a). Social theories look to interpersonal relationships, and systems theories look to relationships between an individual and his or her culture, or perhaps an individual and a domain and field. Emergence has become an important concept in creativity studies (e.g., Curşeu 2006; Finke 1996; Waller et al. 1993; Ward et al. 1999).

One last point should be made about the philosophy of science. Recall here that one of the critical starting points for this chapter was that philosophy (like creativity) is a part of each of our lives, every day. This is true, even for the philosophy of science. The focus on science does not remove philosophy from everyday life; in fact science is often drawn to the curious aspects of life, the intent being to provide a better understanding (which is a subjective thing) about the world (the objective reality). These ideas about philosophy and life were apparent in the thinking of Niels Bohr. His biographer summarized it this way:

> Bohr was convinced that complementarity was relevant not only to physics but also to psychology and to life itself. Its basic idea, he wrote, "bears a deep-going analogy to the general difficulty in the formation of human idea, inherent in the distinction between subject and object." As in the Chinese concept of yin and yang, complementary pairs of concepts defined reality. There is nothing paradoxical about an electron having the characteristics of both a wave and a particle until an experiment is performed on it. It dawned on Bohr that in the weird quantum world there need not be only yes and no, and an electron need not actually be either particle or wave. There could be in-betweens as well as ambiguities. An electron's wave and particle aspects complement each other, and their totality makes up what the electron is. Thus the electron is made up of complementary pairs—wave and particle, the position and momentum. Similarly it is the tension between complementary pairs—love and hate, life and death, light and darkness—that shapes our everyday existence (Miller 2009, p. 102).

Miller also listed East vs. West, consciousness and the unconscious, rationality and the irrational as complementary aspects of the world. Note in the quotation above the reference to subject and object. It is an important part of life as well as philosophy.

PHILOSOPHY AND ART

A very famous distinction could be added to the list above, to go along with East vs. West and the other dichotomies. I am referring to Snow's (1963) "two cultures." One culture is science, the other art. Feist (1991) described how these fit into creativity studies:

> Snow (1963) argued that in Western society there is an ever widening rift between those who practice art and humanities, and those who practice science and mathematics. He referred to these two camps as "two cultures," and suggested that feelings of hostility and dislike divide them .... Many psychologists have accepted Snow's argument. According to Gardner (1973), for instance, "the artist is interested in the subjective world," whereas "the scientist more typically investigates the world of objects or treats individuals as objects (p. 145).

Feist went on to extend the art–science distinction such that it applied to the creative process, and not just to personalities. He summarized this: "In global terms, artistic creativity is believed to be a nonrational, intuitive, subjective, emotional, and impulsive process, whereas scientific creativity is considered to be a rational, analytical, objective, non-emotional, and controlled experience" (pp. 145–146).

Although art and science might be seen as two cultures, it is probably best to view them as complementary rather than antagonistic. This fits well with evidence about scientists benefitting from their artwork (Root-Bernstein et al. 1995).

That being said, for the present discussion the complementary nature of art and science can be recognized and put aside momentarily so we can shift from the philosophy of science to art. Without a doubt, a great deal can be learned about the relationship between philosophy and creativity by looking to art and art history. Art is not a science and has no aspirations to be scientific, which may explain why there is more research (or at least theorizing) about art

BOX 11.6

BE THE BALL. PHYSICAL WORLD HAS ITS WAY

Samuel Taylor Coleridge (1772–1834), friend of William Wordsworth and a noted poet (e.g., "Rime of the Ancient Mariner," "Kubla Khan") and philosopher in his own right, described how he senses the "organic form" whenever he works. His work "shapes as it develops itself from within" (*Lectures on Shakespeare*, quoted by McIntyre 2008).

Michelangelo was famous for something very similar. He felt that "If a sculptor should remove little by little, with knowing skill, everything that is too much, there would emerge from it, there would be freed from it, a marvelous statue. It is not with the hands … that we paint or sculpt, but with the intellect" (from Nardini 1999, p. 17) "Michelangelo applied this idea to a block of marble that had been spoiled and abandoned by an earlier artist. When a council of experts first gazed on the results, … rivalry and jealousy had to yield to admiration. Knowing all about the spoiled block of marble, the committee unanimously declared that Michelangelo had overcome difficulties thought to be insuperable, and in creating such a beautiful statue had worked a greater miracle than if he had brought a dead man back to life" (Nardini 1999, pp. 56–57).

Harpist Derek Bell put it this way: "The less you are thinking about it, the better it comes" (quoted by Paine-Clemes 2008, p. 9).

Barbara McClintock, Nobel laureate in Medicine, seemed to believe the same thing: "As you look at these things, they become part of you. And you forget yourself. The main thing about it is you forget yourself" (quoted by Paine-Clemes 2008).

Consider next Wittgenstein's (1965) idea about the "disappearance of the problem." His idea was that creative people often start by noting a problem or gap, but they become so interested by the problem, and immersed in it, that what started as a problem becomes something else entirely. It becomes a challenge, an opportunity, a pleasant experience rather than a problem per se. The creator has become one with the problem. The subject and the object are no longer separate.

"Be the ball" was the widely useful advice from Ty Webb (played by Chevy Chase) to the caddie Danny in the movie *Caddy Shack*. What a wonderful way to transcend the objective world.

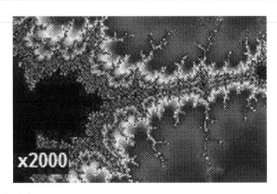

FIGURE 11.1   Fractals. The Julia set.

and philosophy than creativity and philosophy. This disproportionality probably also reflects the fact that the arts have been around for thousands of years. The study of art predates creativity studies by a long shot (Dudek 2012).

Interestingly, some branches of science have been connected to art more frequently than others. Physics may be the branch of science that is most often associated with the arts (Capra 1975; Shlain 1991). A recent area of science, perhaps qualifying as a branch of science, has also been tied to the arts. This is chaos theory (Gleick 1987). Much of chaos theory is easy to put into representations, including *fractals* (Figure 11.1), and it could be that the association between them is in part due to the aesthetic appeal of those representations. Fractals are found in nature. They are discovered, not created. What does that say about the subject–object interplay? The ideas and quotations in Box 11.6 also have something to say about art, philosophy, and the subjective and objective worlds. Also see Figure 11.1.

The Mandelbrot set is a kind of fractal. It, too, is not an invention of the human brain but is instead discovered. It illustrates the subject–object relationship, as captured by Paine-Clemes (2008):

> The set is just objectively there in the mathematics itself. If it has meaning to assign an actual existence to the Mandelbrot Set, then that existence is not within our minds, for no one can fully comprehend the set's endless variety and unlimited complication. Nor can its existence lie within the multitude of computer printouts that begin to capture some of its incredible sophistication and detail, for at best these printouts capture but a shadow of an approximation to the set itself. Yet it has a robustness that is beyond any doubt; for the same structure is revealed in all its perceivable details, to greater and greater fineness the more closely it is examined independently of the mathematician or computer that examines it. Its existence can only be within the Platonic world of mathematical form (pp. 16–17).

PRAGMATISM

Before closing, one more "-ism" should be acknowledged. This is *pragmatism*, which was founded by William James. Thought to be America's first psychologist, James had quite a bit to say about the discrepancy between the objective and subjective worlds. A biography by McLemee (2006, p. R5) described James' view in the following fashion:

> On the one hand, he said, there were "tender-minded" thinkers, prone to regarding the universe as one big, rational system whose principles we can (in principle at least) comprehend. On the other, there were the "tough-minded," who emphasized the reality of physical sensation and the limitations of human understanding before the world's swarming complexity.

It should come as no surprise that James noted this distinction. As McLemee put it,

> James became one of the first American professors of the new discipline known as "psychology." In 1890, at age 48, he published a two-volume synthesis of laboratory research and systematic theory called "Principles of Psychology" that soon became one of the definitive works in the field. His descriptions of how we experience the process of thought—how individual awareness does not simply reflect the outside world but also seems to move under its own inner pressure—anticipated the European philosophical school later called phenomenology (p. R5).

Before 1900, psychology and philosophy were not at all well distinguished from one another. Certainly, phenomenologists such as Jean-Paul Sartre and Edmund Husserl had much to say about consciousness, which is one way of describing the subjective world.

BOX 11.7

ANTICIPATING EXPECTANCY EFFECTS AND
SELF-FULFILLING PROPHECIES

William James had volumes of ideas about the subject–object distinction. His thinking on the subject emphasized the subjective and the power of the human mind, and as such anticipated what later were to become known as *expectancy effects* (including the Pygmalion effect) and *self-fulfilling prophecies*. Here are his descriptions:

"Human beings, by changing the inner attitudes of their minds, can change the outer aspects of their lives."

"The art of being wise is the art of knowing what to overlook."

"The greatest discovery of my generation is that a human being can alter his life by altering his attitudes of mind."

"Be not afraid of life. Believe that life is worth living, and your belief will help create the fact."

James did as well, and indeed is credited with coining the concept *stream of consciousness*. That concept is now used in literature, and in classics such as *Ulysses* by James Joyce, and *The Pilgrimage* by Dorothy Richardson (Wallace 1991). Those are in turn noteworthy in that they exemplify the interplay between science and art.

James developed a school of thought known as *pragmatism* (Box 11.7). It was in many ways a direct reaction to Hegel's ideas of *absolute knowledge*. As the name implies, absolute knowledge is diametric to the limited knowledge inherent in any psychology which distinguishes the subjective world from the objective world. In the case of absolute knowledge, the subjective would be aware of the objective. James vehemently disagreed with this. For Hegel it was a kind of journey, or perhaps a goal: An individual might evolve and eventually attain absolute knowledge.

CONCLUSIONS

This chapter sampled ancient as well as contemporary philosophy. The relevance of the former for the latter, and for many of the current expectations about creativity (and life) should be obvious. Many contemporary artists seem to be following Plato's philosophy. They are looking for ideals and ideas in the objective world. They are hoping to discover rather than create. They are not bringing something new into being but are instead trying to find what is important in the world. Consider attempts to find and use the *golden ratio*, also known as the golden mean or golden section. Konecni (2003) found a tendency among professional artists toward the golden ratio: "The golden section … is a proportion that has in its various geometric, arithmetic, biological, architectural, and artistic contexts fascinated, for over 2000 years, some of the finest minds in philosophy, the sciences, and the arts. It has been considered the epitome of beauty by aestheticians" (p. 267). He also described its role in aesthetics in mathematics and Western paintings, "a fusion of the functional and the aesthetic

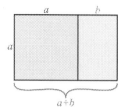

FIGURE 11.2 The golden ratio. In mathematical terms, for quantities a and b, given $a > b$, $\frac{a+b}{a} = \frac{a}{b} \overset{\text{def}}{=} \varphi$, where the Greek letter phi (φ) represents the golden ratio. Its value is $(1 + \sqrt{5})/2 = 1.6180339887\ldots$ *Source: This file is made available under the Creative Commons CC0 1.0 Universal Public Domain Dedication. http://en.wikipedia.org/wiki/ File:SimilarGoldenRectangles.svg.*

in architecture" (p. 267). It was cited in ancient Greece as "the most pleasing proportions of human anatomy," and can still be seen in Greek architecture. It is equal to 0.618 (Figure 11.2).

The golden mean is not the only number that has been targeted through history. Many other numbers have been sought and thought to have universal and enduring importance. Miller (2009) wrote

> Could there be a single number at the root of the universe …. Physicists, psychologists, and mystics have pondered this question. Some have proposed the number three—as in the Trinity and the three dimensions of length, breadth, and depth. Some have argued for four—after all, we have four seasons, four directions (north, south, east, and west), and four limbs. Some have been convinced that the answer might be the very weird number 137, which on the one hand very precisely describes the DNA of light and on the other is the sum of the Hebrew letters of the word "Kabbalah" (p. xvii).

Miller described in his book, *Deciphering the Cosmic Number*, "two mavericks," Wolfgang Pauli and Carl Jung, both of whom believed in the number 137. The point is that, just as Plato described the value of searching for ideal forms (often by creating art), many others since that time, including scientists, have devoted their lives, not really to bringing something entirely new into being, but instead to discovering something of universal importance, be it a number, a golden mean, or a scientific law. All of this fits well with the distinction between *discovery* and *creativity* presented in Chapter 13.

The distinction between discovery and creativity is also related to the subject–object issue that was introduced in the opening of this chapter and is apparent in virtually all philosophical discussions reviewed herein. There are other implications of the subject–object dichotomy, in addition to definitions of discovery and creativity. Consider in this regard the debate about "the lone genius," as it was called in the section on romanticism. The "subject–object" distinction translated into "the individual or social explanation" for creative achievement. The question is, who is responsible for creativity? The creator, the Muses, or society and culture? The Muses are no longer given serious consideration. They did help when creative people reported not knowing how they found creative ideas, but the scientific method has provided much better cause-and-effect explanations, including some that suggest that the individual has a temperament and skills that allow him or her to construct creative ideas, or, alternatively, that society and culture contain creative materials and certain individuals find, refine, and share creative insights. The social–cultural view allows for luck and being in the right place at the right time (Albert 1988).

Csikszentmihalyi's (1988a) systems theory exemplifies the social–cultural perspective. He described how the ingredients for creativity "existed long before the creative person arrived on the scene. It had been stored in the symbol system of the culture, in the customary practices, the languages the specific notation of the "domain"" (p. 325). My own theory of personal creativity (Runco 2006a) exemplifies the other extreme, emphasizing the individual. In fact, the individual is given responsibility, at least implicitly, in most investigations of the creative personality and creative cognition.

A fascinating debate reflecting the subject–object (and individual–society) distinction involves "the death of the author." That is of course a metaphorical death, the idea being that the individual author is not all-important when interpreting literature. The author is unimportant compared with "the text," which may have meaning that was not intended when the writing was done but is apparent when viewed from particular sociocultural contexts (i.e., the time and place of the person reading the text). This debate is ongoing in various branches of literature but there is no reason that the same arguments—some saying the author/individual is vital, others saying that sociocultural context is all-important—cannot be applied to all of the arts.

Another significant issue that is clearly tied to the philosophical perspectives covered in this chapter involves originality. Is it a vital part of creativity or not? It was not vital through most of history. Recall here the idea of *imitatio-ideal*, which is the label given to good art that imitates rather than originates. But the key question may not be "Is originality vital?" but instead, "Is originality possible?" Certainly an answer can be found in each chapter in this book. They are not, however, all the same answers. That is your cue, dear reader, to be creative and construct your own meaningful interpretation, drawing from the material reviewed herein.

CHAPTER

12

Enhancement and the Fulfillment of Potential

Dare to be a radical, but don't be a damn fool. **Frank Barron**

ADVANCE ORGANIZER

- Reasons to Consider Enhancement
- What Can Be Enhanced?
- Tactics, Strategies, Heuristics
  - Look to Nature
  - Turn Something Upside Down
  - Change Perspective
  - Travel
  - Question Assumptions
  - Use an Analogy
- Let It Happen Tactics

- Programs and Multiple Step Methods for Creative Thinking
- Enhancement in Organizations
- Enhancement in Educational Settings
  - Education and Enhancement for Older Adults
- Tactics for Discovery
- Tactics for Invention
- Evidence for Training Effectiveness
- Conclusions

INTRODUCTION

There are many reasons to consider the possibility that creativity can be enhanced. Most obvious may be that there are clear benefits in applied settings, such as schools and any organization that is concerned about innovation. There is, however, much more to enhancement than this. There is, for example, the idea that each of us has creative potential that can be fulfilled. If creative potentials are fulfilled, or at least maximized, the benefits of creativity (e.g., for psychological and physical health) are the most likely to be realized. The benefits will be apparent on both societal and individual levels (Florida 2002; Rubenson &

Runco 1992b; Simonton 1998). You might even say that there is a clear need for creativity on both social and individual levels, and thus a need to invest in techniques and programs that are designed to enhance creative skills.

The first question to address is suggested by the fact that creativity is a complex or syndrome. As this book attests, creativity is a reflection of cognition, metacognition, attitude, motivation, affect, disposition, and temperament. Which of these will react to enhancement? Which will provide the greatest return on the invested time and resources?

As a matter of fact, here more than any other place the word "creativity" probably should be avoided. It is a very general and abstract noun, after all, and this leads to many ambiguities. Several years ago I suggested that the word "creativity" be stricken from the scholarly research literature. That may sound fairly dramatic (and pretentious) but the suggestion was actually that the ambiguity be avoided. It can be avoided very easily by using adjectives instead. Although "creativity" is ambiguous, it is useful to refer to creative potential, creative performance, creative tendencies, and even creative personalities. This reliance on the adjective is especially useful when addressing the question, "Can creativity be enhanced?" Good answers include, "Yes, creative potential can be fulfilled" and "Yes, creative performances can be made more likely."

As is implied by the earlier question about the creativity complex, many of the topics from the previous chapters of this book must be acknowledged in any attempt to enhance creative potential. Certainly there are several specific cognitive skills that can and should be targeted (e.g., divergent thinking, flexibility), but attitude and mood should also be considered. As a matter of fact, the research on mood is very useful in that it indicates what kinds of moods are the most likely to lead to what kinds of thinking. A positive mood, for example, might be good if there is divergent thinking to be done, for positive moods seem to be conducive to wide associations and risk-taking (Friedman et al. 2003; Wallach & Kogan 1965). The mood research also indicates that individuals need to know why they are in a good mood; just stimulating a particular mood is not enough.

Recall also the idea that there are traits and capacities that are indicative of creative potential (e.g., autonomy, flexibility, openness to experience) but also traits and tendencies that are contraindicative (e.g., conformity, rigidity). Enhancement is, then, an attempt to encourage certain things and to discourage others. The same dichotomy applies to the description of environments that are conducive to creative performance: They contain or present certain things (e.g., resources) but also lack certain things (e.g., distraction, and in some cases extrinsic demands).

Long-term experiences may not be all that systematic. They may be a part of development, education, and day-to-day experience. Potential is often fulfilled in this manner, simply by having supportive or inspiring experiences. This is not really enhancement per se, though it does explain the process by which potential is fulfilled, and it does lead to suggestions for what can be done to fulfill potential. It is, for example, important to have opportunities for creative work (Zuckerman 1977), and models and mentors who support creative thinking (Albert 1988; Zuckerman 1977). Interestingly, these experiences often are sought out. They may not just happen fortuitously; many highly creative individuals put great effort into finding the right places, settings, and collaborators or mentors. Development is bidirectional, with the individual having an impact on (and selecting) experience as well as experience having an impact on the individual (Albert & Runco 1989; Scarr & McCartney 1983). (This chapter is not titled "Enhancement"; it also includes "the Fulfillment of Potential." That is because enhancement can assist with the fulfillment of potential, but potentials are also fulfilled as a part of general experience.)

Another important distinction is between short- and long-term enhancement efforts. How much training is necessary for enhancement? If the concern is general potential, surely more is better. Studies of older adults confirm that there is a need to encourage creative behaviors throughout the life span (Langer 1989), but there could be a period when enhancement is the most effective. There may also be a time early in life when certain kinds of enhancement work well but others do not work at all. There are also age-specific needs. Artists often benefit from an old age style (Lindauer 1991), but this is probably only really helpful when they have worked within one style for quite some time and they need a change—or their creativity suffers. Scientists often benefit from periodic changes in research foci (Root-Bernstein et al. 1993, 1995), but again, this is probably beneficial only at a certain point in life. Early on it is probably best if expertise is developed. Changes in research foci probably are beneficial in much the same way as the old age style, in the middle or later stages of a career.

Systematic enhancement efforts often emphasize tactics, strategies, and heuristics. These are essentially procedures for solving problems. Though specific, these easily can be included

BOX 12.1

A FORTUNATE CONFOUNDING

Scientific experiments usually involve the control of *confounding variables*. These are sometimes called *nuisance variables*, but whatever the label, they interfere with inferences about the relationship between independent (predictor) and dependent (criterion) variables.

When attempting to enhance creativity, the inextricable influences turn into a positive thing. That is because enhancement often involves a suggestion about tactics for creative thinking. Many of these tactics are outlined in the present chapter. When facilitators, teachers, or mentors suggest a tactic for creative thinking, they are not only communicating a method for thinking creatively but are also suggesting that creative thinking is a good thing. In this way tactics are often inextricable from the values and attitudes that also support creative efforts.

Still, this confounding of tactics with values and attitudes should be recognized. Otherwise, misunderstandings are likely. Consider, for example, research attempting to train right-brain thinking. Students may be asked to draw pictures upside down or do something similar to exercise the right hemisphere of their brains. There may even be clear results, with increased originality after the exercises. But this does not mean that they have learned how to use their right hemispheres. The right hemisphere is connected to the left (unless you had a commissurotomy, as described in Chapter 3!), and more likely any improvements reflect changes in the attitudes and values that are communicated by the right-brain exercises. Again, it is a confounding of procedure with attitude and value—a confounding that can work in our favor but must be recognized for an accurate understanding of creative potential.

in long-term efforts at enhancement. Indeed, there is no need to choose between long- and short-term enhancement. If the person invests in both, he or she is the most likely to reap the benefits. Individuals, then, might choose environments and careers that support their creative fortes and efforts, and seek out other long-term facilitators of creativity, but they should also learn to use specific tactics, as needed. Much of this chapter is devoted to tactical creativity, the idea being that these can be used individually or integrated into a larger program. Suggestions for mood, attitude, affect, and motivation are also described in this chapter, but mostly within the context of tactical creativity.

TACTICAL CREATIVITY AND METACOGNITION

Tactical creativity requires a certain level of metacognitive capacity. This generally matures in preadolescence. Literally *metacognition* is cognition about cognition, but it is manifested in self-awareness and self-control. These may inform an individual that there is a problem, and instead of dealing with it in some reflexive or habitual fashion, the metacognitively aware individual may mindfully approach it, and perhaps use a tactic. Tactics are only intentionally deployed, which further evidences their dependence on metacognition. Of course children may learn tactics, but they probably will not develop any on their own, nor recognize when they should be employed. It is very much the same situation as with memory and mnemonics. There, children have production deficiencies in memory usage, which means that they may be capable of using a mnemonic but do not spontaneously recognize the need nor produce the mnemonic by themselves. Both the use of mnemonics and the use of tactics depend on metacognition.

PROBLEM SOLVING WITH TACTICS, STRATEGIES, AND HEURISTICS

A *tactic* is a kind of guideline or procedure for solving a problem. Tactics are sometimes confused with strategies, but a strategy is an overall plan, usually conceived before any effort is expended. Chandler (1962) described it this way: "strategy can be defined as the determination of the basic long-term goals and objectives of an enterprise, and the adoption of courses of action and the allocation of resources necessary for carrying out these goals" (pp. 15–16). A tactic, on the other hand, is used while in process. It is essentially a trick or technique that is used when faced with a particular hurdle. Unlike strategies, which are based on long-term goals, tactics tend to be immediate reactions to hurdles that arise while working. Then there are *heuristics*, which are shortcuts. These can be contrasted with *algorithms*, which are precise processes for solving a problem or obtaining some goal. Algorithms are often like equations: If you put the effort in, you will get the correct answer. Heuristics lead to best guesses, or estimates. They are often sufficient, and frequently used in the natural environment (Nisbett and Ross 1980). Many tactics have been identified and defined specifically to facilitate creative problem solving.

Tactics are a kind of procedural knowledge. This should be a fairly obvious point because procedural knowledge is defined as "know-how," and that is exactly what a tactic is—knowledge about how to solve a problem. Procedural knowledge is contrasted with declarative or conceptual and factual knowledge in Chapter 1. The latter is in some ways also useful for certain kinds of creative problem solving (Runco et al. 2005a). Chapter 3 tied tactics to working memory, and working memory in turn to the prefrontal lobes of the brain. The maturation of the nervous system therefore also supports the idea that tactics and similar intentions are unlikely in very young children. This takes us to the question of universals. Do we all share the same potential for creative thinking?

Very likely individuals do not share the same potentials. We each have a phenotype that reflects boundaries. Just as someone with the genes that would allow his or her adult and maximum height to be somewhere between 5′6″ and 5′10″ (depending on vitamins, exercise, and so on), so too are there boundaries for creative potential. That is the beauty of the concept of potential. It implies that there is a range within which we can each operate. The boundaries differ from person to person, but it is probably unfair and misleading to suggest that one person has more potential than another person. Sure, one person may have more potential in a particular domain, or on particular tasks, or even in particular careers, but any general reference to "more potential" must be qualified to have any real meaning. Moreover, what is important is that every individual fulfill his or her potential.

Something might be learned from Public Law. This states that every individual in the United States has the legal right to be assessed in a manner that is appropriate to his or her needs and skills. Individuals differ in terms of creative potentials (e.g., domains, areas in need of improvement), and enhancement should be designed with that in mind: Find the right circumstances and environment and experiences for each person. Borrowing a concept from Chapter 5, there is a need for person–environment fit. Just as performances within an organization are most likely to be optimal when the individual's needs, interests, and strengths are taken into account, so too are potentials the most likely to be fulfilled if the individual's needs and interests match his or her experiences. A significant part of this fit is interpretive, as was implied by the discussion within Chapter 5 (also see Runco 2012; Stokols et al. 2002). Not only must objective experiences fit the needs of the individual; his or her interpretations of those experiences are also critical.

TACTICS AND EXPLICIT INSTRUCTIONS

Tactics can be communicated with *explicit instructions*. These have been used many times in enhancement studies and have been proven to be quite effective. They are explicit in that they inform individuals exactly what is expected of them. That might be accomplished quite simply, with explicit instructions directing individuals to "be creative" (Harrington 1975). They might, on the other hand, specifically direct the individuals to particular standards or criteria, such as originality (Runco et al. 2005b), or they might convey more procedural or operational information (e.g., "give ideas that no one else will think of," "give a variety of ideas," "try approaching the problem by questioning your assumptions or changing your perspective of the problem").

FIGURE 12.1   One tactic for finding new ideas is to turn the situation upside down. This can help to shift perspectives and see things in a new light. Original ideas may result. *Source: Wikimedia Commons, This file is ineligible for copyright and therefore in the public domain, because it consists entirely of information that is common property and contains no original authorship. http://commons.wikimedia.org/wiki/File:Inverted_question_mark_alternate.png.*

SHIFT PERSPECTIVES

> We are part of the universe that has developed a remarkable ability … we can hold an image of the universe in our minds. We are matter contemplating itself. **Sean Carroll (quoted by Ulin 2012, para 15)**

One of the most powerful and broadly applicable tactics for creative thinking involves a shift of perspective. This can be accomplished either literally and physically, or in some abstract manner. A tactic called *turn the situation upside down* exemplifies the former, as does another called *deviation amplification*. Even actual travel can help shift one's perspective. Each of these can be considered separately, although you will see the commonality in that they each suggest a shift of perspectives. That shift often makes it easy to break routine and find original ideas and solutions.

TURN THE SITUATION UPSIDE DOWN

A shift of perspective can be obtained by changing one's own point of view (Figure 12.1). Sometimes it is not you that needs to change but it is the problem instead. Very frequently problems can be changed such that the individual will be more interested or more able to bring his or her strengths to bear. Sometimes a problem can be changed such that conventional or routine solutions are forgotten and original solutions are easier to find.

Two examples from the Beatles exemplify the upside-down tactic. One is implied by their song, "Happiness Is a Warm Gun." Most people do not find much joy in guns, and in fact there are many reasons to be concerned about weapons and violence. Yet the Beatles went the exact opposite direction. Similarly, the lyrics to "Back in the U.S.S.R." suggest that it is "great to be back home" (in the U.S.S.R.), which was pretty much the opposite of what most people felt in the United Kingdom when that song was written. These examples might also be described as contrarian.

The dark side of creativity sometimes benefits from a kind of "turn it upside down" tactic. Consider in this regard Eastman's early cameras. These were quite simple; the photographer had no control over exposure, focus, or the like. But Eastman made a virtue of a camera's shortcomings in his advertising. He said things like "press the button, we do the rest" (Bryson 1994, pp. 235–236). You might be able to find the same tactic being used in contemporary advertising.

Another example of the benefits of "turning the situation upside down" involves marginality. No wonder marginality comes up again and again in more than one chapter of this book. There are clear benefits for creative thinking. Yet, if we are tactical, we might consider the opposite. This means thinking about marginality and related situations, where someone from one field contributes creatively to another. That may actually simplify and distort what really occurs. It certainly would be convenient if creative breakthroughs followed regularly from marginality, or from the simple movement from one field to another. But what may not be obvious is that, when a novice moves into a new field and starts throwing ideas around, very likely the experts in that field know that those ideas are bunk. Admittedly, once in a while an idea from a novice is both original and valuable; but what do you suppose the ratio is, new ideas from a novice that are (a) unoriginal or (b) low in value, relative to truly creative breakthroughs? It would not be surprising if 99.999% of the time, ideas from novices are (a) or (b). This is an other example of a historical bias. Looking back, the 99.999% of the ideas are forgotten, not recorded, not remembered, but the exceedingly rare instance where a truly creative breakthrough came from a novice is noteworthy and recorded. Historical records are selective, and they thereby can distort the actual workings of the creative process.

Is it a good idea to suggest to someone that they should change fields? Is there a more reliable method? Perhaps you should keep your day job but read outside your field for new and original ideas.

FIND OR APPLY AN ANALOGY

Roll-on deodorants are essentially giant ball point pens. *Harrison (2004, p. 44)*

A huge number of creative discoveries have resulted from analogical thinking. Eli Whitney is said to have designed the cotton gin after watching a cat trying to catch a chicken through a fence; Samuel Morse added stations to the telegraph system after pondering how stagecoaches changed their horses at each stop; Louis Pasteur drew from his knowledge of grapes in his ideas about human skin; August Kekulé said that he came to understand the structure of the benzene ring through having had a daydream about a snake biting its own tail; George Bissel designed the oil pump after studying the brine pump; James Watt developed the steam engine after hearing a tea kettle; Sir Marc Brunel drew ideas from worm tunnels in his design of underwater tunnels; and Velcro was designed after George de Mestral studied how cockleburs stuck to his dog's fur and his own clothing. Admittedly, these are historical cases, and as such are not evidence of the value of analogical thinking; they are merely illustrations. There are, however, a number of empirical demonstrations of the role of analogies in creative process (e.g., Gick and Holyoak 1980; Harrington 1981; Jausovec 1989) and a parallel literature on the role of metaphor (Hausman 1989).

Root-Bernstein and Root-Bernstein (1999, p. 142) defined analogizing as finding a "correspondence of inner relationship or function between two (or more) different phenomena or complex sets of phenomena." Sometimes, "it is the inexact, imperfect nature of the analogy that allows it to bridge the gap between the known and the unknown" (p. 143). Root-Bernstein and Root-Bernstein described analogizing as a tool of thought that can be learned for creative thinking. Similarly, Harrington (1980) was confident about "the possibility that creative problem-solving skills might be incremented by teaching the conscious use of analogy-encouraging representational modes" (p. 21). Analogical thinking is also at the heart of *synectics* (Gordon 1961), which is reviewed in detail later. What is relevant here is its use of personal analogies, direct analogies, and symbolic analogies. The first of these is a kind of empathy or identification with some external object. The second requires a comparison of two external things, such as geological changes and biological changes (á la Darwin). The third sometimes takes the form of oxymorons or other dissimilar objects or concepts (e.g., jumbo shrimp).

Some analogical thinking may depend on bodily intelligence. Here the physical feeling or action is one part of the analogy. It is a kind of proprioception, which is visceral or kinesthetic (Root-Bernstein and Root-Bernstein 1999). Harrington (1980) explained how "kinesthetic modes of representation tend to facilitate creative thinking by encouraging or demanding analogical/metaphorical transformations of information" (p. 21). Bodily analogies and representations may work better for some people but not everyone, given Gardner's (1983) ideas about multiple intelligences.

ANALOGIES AS BORROWING OR STEALING

Analogies are sometimes found by looking to nature, and sometimes by looking at your competitors' work or your own earlier work. In business and advertising, borrowed ideas are called "spin-offs." Look around and you will see a huge number of ads and business names that are analogies in a way, mostly just borrowed from common knowledge or an existing name. Here are some examples:

- "52 ways to leave your blubber" (title of article on fitness in *Los Angeles Times*)

- Deja Blue (the soft drink served on AirTrans flights)
- "Give us your best shot" (photography competition, Costco)
- Seas the Day (boating expedition)
- Hard Core Pawn (TV show, not X-rated)
- Keep an open mouth (restaurant commercial)
- Artland of America (slogan for Watkinsville, GA)
- Prepare for twist off (beverage slogan)
- Love at first bite (this tastes good!).

BORROW, ADAPT, OR STEAL TACTICS

Many famous insights have resulted from a more direct borrowing strategy. Darwin did indeed draw from geology in his theory of evolution. Freud borrowed heavily from neurology and the medical model when describing the psyche. Piaget borrowed from biology in his

BOX 12.2

THE CONTROVERSY OF ORIGINALITY

Are creative things actually original if they are analogies? Perhaps not, since they are not truly unique; they are similar to something that already existed. This is a serious issue, given that originality is the only characteristic that is included in all definitions of creativity. Creative things must be original. It will be more than simply original, but it must be original. Take a look at Warhol's *Campbell Soup can*. Is it creative? Is it original?

The creativity of new but analogous ideas may be in their interpretation. After all, if original interpretations are not creative, think how many TV shows, movies, and plays are unoriginal and uncreative! How many times has Hamlet been performed? If interpretation is unimportant, only the first was truly creative. The same argument also applies to all those TV shows and recent movies. There are a huge number of remakes, and one common technique used by movie makers is to take an old TV show and make a movie out of it (e.g., *Charlie's Angels*, *Dukes of Hazard*, *I Spy*, etc.). The concern over originality may also apply to sequels. Is only the first in a series truly original? This issue is explored further in the concluding chapter of this book.

theory of cognitive development. Musicians often borrow from various styles, the result being an original integration. Elvis Presley, for instance, apparently borrowed from gospel and country music; Shakespeare seems to have adapted many plots from his predecessors; and Benjamin Franklin may have merely reworded many of his famous clichés (a penny saved is a penny earned, early to bed, early to rise, makes a person healthy, wealthy, and wise, an apple a day …) (Bryson 1994). Consider also contemporary advertisements that ask that you to "Think outside the bun" (hotdogs) or "Think outside the bar" (find a date), or even assure you that "You are now free to move about the country" (airline). These are catchy precisely because they are adaptations of earlier sayings.

Rich and Weisberg (2004) described how the famous situation comedy *All in the Family* was in fact an "extension" of an earlier situation comedy on British TV, *Till Death Us Do Part*. Rich and Weisberg claimed that "in many cases, the new work can be seen as an extension and synthesis of works known to the creator at that time…. The novel aspects of creative work are often the result of importation of components of other work. This does not mean that there is no novelty in creative products but it does mean that novelty can be firmly based in the past" (p. 1). Rich and Weisberg also described the connections of the double-helix model of Watson and Crick to Linus Pauling's work on the structure of the alpha-keratin protein, Edison's lightbulb and earlier work on the same project, the electric light, and Picasso's painting *Guernica* to Picasso's own earlier paintings. Apparently Picasso even included specific characters that in some way correspond with those found in his earlier works, and of his contemporaries.

Not surprisingly, given these examples from TV, advertising, and even the sciences, there is some debate about the originality of adaptations and analogies (see Box 12.2).

Tactics are often used, sometimes for creativity, sometimes to make money, sometimes for both. Howkins (2001) tries to do both. He is quite explicit, and tactical, about turning your creative potential and ideas into cash. His data indicate that creative talents translate into U.S.$2.2 trillion each year! Howkins' suggestions are a bit vague but not bad as tactics:

- Own your ideas. Understand copyright and patents
- Invent yourself. Be unique
- Know when to work alone, and when in a group
- Learn endlessly. Borrow, reinvent and recycle
- Exploit fame and celebrity
- Know when to break the rules.

Whether in film or fashion, software or shoes, by focusing on our individual talents we can all make creativity pay.

The Beatles also used a borrow-and-adapt strategy early in their careers, before they were masterful song writers. As Clydesdale (2006) put it, "the Beatles' early compositions showed no sign of their later genius. 'Love me Do' was very simple. They cannot fill an album with marketable compositions. Six of the songs on their first album were covers of American songs. Similarly, their second album *With the Beatles* needed six cover songs, such as 'Roll Over Beethoven' to bring up the numbers" (p. 9). The borrow-and-adapt strategy of the Beatles was acknowledged by Paul McCartney when describing the impact of Brian Wilson and the Beach Boys' album, *Pet Sounds*. McCartney said "I think Brian Wilson was a great genius…. It is actually very clever, on any level…. It is really a very clever album [Pet Sounds]. So we were inspired, you know, and nicked a few ideas" (Clydesdale 2006, p. 13).

Sadly, some borrowing is more like stealing. According to Bryson (1994), Thomas Edison actually bought the technology for projecting for movies in 1895—and then claimed to have invented it.

CONSIDER THE NATURAL WORLD

Nature is a wonderful thing. It is inspiring, for example, and suggestive. In fact, there are several tactics that suggest that we look to the natural world. We might find inspiration there, or good analogies or find ideas that can be borrowed or adapted (see Figure 12.2).

Leonardo da Vinci and Alfred Hitchcock both used this tactic. Leonardo's armored vehicle, for example, said to be a precursor to the modern tank, contained 10 people protected by a strong, smooth, round shell. It is thought that he got the idea from looking at the tortoise. Hitchcock, describing his classic film *The Birds*, said,

> Basically, in The Birds, what you have is a kind of overall sketchy theme of everyone taking nature for granted. Everyone took the birds for granted, until the birds one day turned on them. The birds had been shot at, eaten, put in cages. They suffered everything from the humans and was time they turned on them. Don't

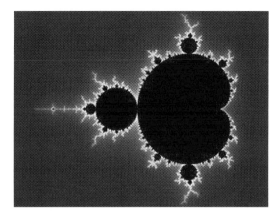

FIGURE 12.2 Art is often inspired by nature. This is true of fractals, including the Mandlebrot set. *Source: Wikimedia Commons, http://en.wikipedia.org/wiki/File:Mandel_zoom_00_mandelbrot_set.jpg.*

mess about or tamper with nature…. Man has fooled around with Uranium 235, out of the ground, and look where its brought us. It is just taking Uranium 235 for granted. It's nothing but it is plenty…. Who knows, it's feasible in the year 3000 or 4000 for all of the animals to have taken over (Schickel 1973).

Hitchcock was also in a sense using the "on its head" tactic. In the movie *The Birds* there are many examples of how birds are abused, and yet it is also the birds who do the abusing. In one scene several people are at a store counter talking about birds becoming aggressive, while in the background a customer orders fried chicken.

An article in *Science News* (April 14, 2001) described a number of energy-generating devices inspired by water and waves. These included the oscillating water column: "waves push air through turbine, then suck it back, as they advance and recede. Devices operate on shore … or offshore" (p. 235) and the Pelamis, in which the "serpentine device flexes in oncoming waves. Pivoting of segments drives pistons that pressurize oil, which runs generators". In a third example, called the McCabe wave pump, "bobbing of outer barges, hinge to central barge stabilized by underwater plate, runs pumps" (p. 235), whereas in the Archimedes wave swing, "air tank infixed, submerged tower rises and falls with passing waves. The oscillations turn a generator shaft" (p. 235). In the fifth example, with the title I like best, the Nodding Duck, "Waves tip beak of floating device…. beak's rotation relative to central shaft pumps oil, which drives generator" (p. 235). In the sixth and last example, the IPS buoy, "sea water inside open-ended tube stabilizes piston. Motion of bobbing buoy relative to piston shaft drives generator" (p. 235).

There are thus several potential benefits to looking to the natural world. Something happening in nature may suggest an analogous solution for a human problem. The devices utilizing waves (e.g., the Nodding Duck) suggest that not all solutions are analogies but instead may be direct solutions. If you look to nature you might find a solution, or you might find something that (by analogy) suggests a solution. Or you might simply find inspiration.

NATURE WARS

If people were highly creative in the *naturalistic domain*, there would be a balance such that humans cohabitated well with the natural environment. The natural environment would thrive, as would humans, who would also be comfortable and able to utilize necessary natural resources without causing damage. As it is, humans often abuse the environment—as is evidenced by the huge number of endangered species and loss of biodiversity—and the environment sometimes "abuses" humanity. The latter may not be as newsworthy as the former, but there are examples of such abuse. Serba (2012, quoted by Tobar, 2012) recently noted that "in some of the more densely populated corners of New England, trees have been filling up abandoned farms since the 1850s. Now armies of cute and cuddly creatures are filling up those forests too, including white-tailed deer. So many deer, in fact, as to become odious and obnoxious."

Deer can be quite territorial and aggressive. Then there is the beaver. Again quoting Serba (2012):

> Beavers were wiped out in Massachusetts by frontiersmen and Indian trappers and traders in the early 18th century—they never coexisted with European settlers. But in 1928 they returned to western Massachusetts as the descendants of 34 beavers from Canada released in the Adirondacks a few decades earlier.... Beavers soon thrived in resurgent forests now largely free of their old predators—including humans, no longer interested in slaughtering them en masse for the fur

trade. By 1996, the state's beaver population was estimated at 24,000. Those beavers now live amid strip malls and golf courses. People and beavers were sharing the same habitat as never before.... They had similar tastes in waterfront real estate. Both like to live along brooks, streams, rivers, ponds and lakes with lots of nice trees nearby.

Apparently there is also conflict between geese and humans:

> Canada geese disappear across the U.S. as their habitat perishes thanks to human development. But they come back thanks to human restoration efforts and to hunters who breed them as live decoys to shoot other birds. Soon much of America from the Great Plains to the Eastern Seaboard is filled with geese. Unlike their ancestors, however, many of these modern-day geese refuse to migrate. Why should they? In the ensuing century, Serba writes, humans had created a goose paradise filled with "... soccer fields, playgrounds, and parks, all planted in what happened to be the favorite food of Canada geese: grass. The geese are pretty to look at and defended by geese lovers—who face off with geese detractors fed up with the birds' disgusting droppings and by their annoying tendency to clog jet engines and cause planes to crash" (Tobar 2012).

Serba (2012) concluded with the critical point, namely that "Americans have forgotten how to be stewards of the natural world." Surely there are some people who are creative in the naturalistic domain and are, even now, good stewards. Hopefully this kind of reasoning, and an appreciation for the natural world, will increase in the future.

SIMPLIFY

The man who has begun to live more seriously within begins to live more simply without.
Ernest Hemingway

A new perspective may be found by simplifying the situation at hand. The problem may be difficult to understand if it is complex, and furthermore the problem may actually involve one small part of a given situation. If you have a problem with your car, for example, instead of just thinking "my car is on the fritz," it is almost certainly more helpful to identify the specific mechanical or electrical failure. It may be a fuse or something equally as specific and easy.

Gardner (1993a) suggested that eminent creators in various domains often simplify their thinking. He gave Einstein as example, for he apparently returned to "the conceptual world of his childhood" (Gardner 1993a, p. 10) to insure that his thinking was simple and uninhibited. Gardner concluded that "I find a noteworthy similarity … in the search for the most elementary, the most elemental forms within a domain" (p. 18). In some instances simplification avoids the confusion of complexity, but it may also allow the individual to identify the essence of a problem, the truly critical idea or issue.

EXPERIMENT

Experimenting can help identify the essence or critical issue. It is a useful tactic. It can also suggest new options. Leonardo da Vinci benefited from experimentation, as did the Wright brothers, the Beatles, and Brian Wilson of the Beach Boys. Da Vinci often experimented with water, and of course he performed a number of autopsies to explore the human body. The Wrights had a huge amount of technical data, much of it generated by experiments with a wind tunnel. The Beatles experimented in many ways. This is especially clear in the song "Yesterday," with the use of the accompaniment of a single acoustic guitar and a string quartet. In the album *Rubber Soul*, George Harrison used a sitar in the song "Norwegian Wood." This album also included a ballad, "Michelle," and this, too, was new ground for the Beatles. The next album, *Revolver*, had other ballads, and according to Clydesdale (2006), here you see the Beatles experimenting with new ideas and breaking with the past. Apparently, the song "Tomorrow Never Knows" drew lyrics from *The Tibetan Book of the Dead,* and was written with only the C chord. Perhaps most dramatic experiments were technological, but to many ears it will be obvious that the Beatles were experimenting with Indian instruments. When Brian Wilson heard the Beatles succeeding with "I Want to Hold Your Hand," he felt "I had to look beyond what I had already done, beyond the horizon, and find something new and better than anything I had ever done before" (quoted by Clydesdale 2006, p. 11). It was, it appears, a kind of personal contrarianism. More will be said about contrarianism later.

Experimentation (Figure 12.3) can contribute to creative efforts because the person may find new and original ideas or options. They also develop an expertise, though admittedly this can work both for and against the person. (Sometimes experts rely on routine and assumption and are for that reason uncreative.) Of course, a great deal depends on what it is the person is experimenting. Creative results are the most likely if the experiments focus on new and unconventional things. That is the most likely to lead to originality and creative insight. These new and unconventional things sometimes take the form of contradictions, oxymorons, or givens. These can be quite fruitful directions of thought. You can find many examples of this in music. Bob Dylan, for example, wrote "the sun isn't yellow, it's chicken," and the Beatles sang, "he's got feet down below his knees."

FIGURE 12.3 This photo shows Thomas Edison in his laboratory. You do not need a lab to experiment and find new ideas. *Source: Wikimedia Commons, http://commons.wikimedia.org/wiki/File:Edison_in_his_NJ_laboratory_1901.jpg.*

There is a bit of a paradox regarding experimentation. This follows from the fact that experiments may test various options; they may not lead directly to one solution. In that light they may not appear to be very efficient. Consider, for example, Simonton's (1990a) description of Picasso's artistic process as "inefficient." This assumes one kind of efficiency—a kind of linear progress straight from the problem state to the solution. Picasso did not work that way. He experimented and produced many sketches and figures within sketches, which eventually were omitted and do not appear in the final product. Simonton felt that this was a waste of time and effort, a kind of inefficiency. Yet in a manner of speaking, Picasso was efficient. Admittedly it required extra time and energy for Picasso to produce things he would not use, which in fact led him away from the final product, but creativity may sometimes require that. Perhaps Picasso was confident only about the final product because he had explored and rejected alternatives. He may not have found the final product without considering the breadth of options.

Biological evolution offers some justification for this reasoning. It is efficient in that it produces adaptive species, but the process requires variations, many of which do not survive. The variations (within Picasso's artistic experiments and within biological evolution) serve a purpose and make the respective processes highly efficient, even though many of the options are variations and not in direct line toward the "final product." It is a teleological fallacy that the final product can be used to judge the process. Reasoning from the product back to the process is post hoc.

Chapter 8 describes a similar reasoning when describing the value of play and foolishness in business. There the fallacy is that creative businesses are inefficient businesses because they devote resources to experiments and R&D that may eventually lead nowhere. Linus

Pauling may have been thinking of the value of experimentation and variation when he said, "Just have lots of ideas and throw away the bad ones."

DEVIATION AMPLIFICATION

A related tactic is known as *deviation amplification* (Gruber 1988). This involves the exploration of minor changes to a theme, or even a product, such as a work of art. Alternatives and variations (the deviations) are considered, though the basic concept remains the same. It is possible that this can work along with the simplifying tactic. Simplifying may help to identify the key underlying concept and deviation amplification, and then takes over to explore options and alternatives.

Consider in this regard the artwork of Katsushika Hokusai (1760–1849). Hokusai may be most famous for his painting titled *The Great Wave*, but actually that painting was one of a series of views of Mount Fuji. There are, in fact, several dozen different prints in this series, each of which includes the mountain in some way. Each print or painting had a very different perspective of Fuji, but clearly Hokusai was experimenting with one subject matter (Box 12.3).

BOX 12.3

KATSUSHIKA HOKUSAI (1760–1849)

Hokusai exemplifies various aspects of creativity. He was, for example, considered to be eccentric and intrinsically motivated. His efforts were directed to art—to the exclusion of material gain. He actually changed his name and, although it was customary in Japan in the eighteenth and nineteenth century to do so, he apparently did it much more frequently than others, more than 30 times. These days that kind of thing would make it difficult to earn and maintain a reputation.

Apparently Hokusai never cleaned his lodgings or apartment; when they got dirty he moved. According to Krull (1995), he moved over 90 times. He seemed to realize that eccentricity often led to fame, and he did many things specifically for the public and showmanship. He sometimes painted with an enormous brush, said to be the size of a broom, and did so in public and only when a large public was in attendance. Other times he painted with his feet, the brush held between his toes, or with his mouth, the brush held in his teeth (this may remind some readers of Jimi Hendrix playing his guitar with his teeth). Hokusai also sometimes painted upside down for the public or worked on a grain of rice.

Yet he was intrinsically motivated, at least in the sense that he sometimes did not even open the letters containing payments to him for his work. He apparently did not mind going bankrupt. He did, however, escape those seeking payment, namely his creditors, by moving, sometimes outside the city limits. Like Picasso, he was enormously productive—perhaps even more productive than Picasso. By some reports Picasso created 20000 works of art in his lifetime. Hokusai is said to have created over 30000. No wonder many people view motivation and productivity as the key to creative success (Figure 12.4).

FIGURE 12.4 Hokusai was creative in many ways. He may be most famous for this painting, *The Great Wave*, one image from "Thirty-six Views of Mount Fuji." *Source: Wikimedia Commons, This is a faithful photographic reproduction of an original two-dimensional work of art. The work of art itself is in the public domain for the following reason: Public domain This image (or other media file) is in the public domain because its copyright has expired. http://commons.wikimedia.org/wiki/ File:Hokusai-_Kanagawa.jpg.*

PERSISTENCE

These ideas above about experimenting and exploring deviations imply that effort must be expended. This is why Torrance (1995) suggested that creativity follows naturally when the individual is intrinsically motivated. They will, if that is the case, work hard on it. They will also care about it. They are likely to experiment and investigate about it. No wonder personality research on creative individuals finds them to be persistent. The work-hard tactic is demonstrated by the Beatles. They were not master musicians early on, but they invested a great amount of time into becoming better musicians and song-writers (Clydesdale 2006). Ringo Starr described Paul McCartney as a workaholic. That may be taking things too far—and shouldn't the word be *workic?*—but there are benefits of hard work specifically for creative performance. Persistence can be encouraged. It may be that following one's intrinsic interest is what should be encouraged rather than hard work. That should lead to persistence and may avert the stress sometimes experienced by workics. (A person addicted to alcohol may become an alcoholic. That label is formed by adding -ic to alcohol. So a person who works too much should be a *workic*, not a workaholic.)

TRAVEL

Many famous creators have recommended travel as a stimulus for creative thinking. This may be because many of them have found stimulating or comfortable places away from home. Hemingway, for example, seemed to enjoy Cuba. He had a favorite room, a favorite desk (and perhaps a favorite cigar). It may also be because the traveling itself is stimulating. This would be easy to understand given that traveling can facilitate a shift of perspective. As noted earlier, such shifts can be useful for creative thinking because they suggest new ideas and options and allow an individual to avoid fixity and routine.

The idea of travel should remind us that different tactics work with different kinds of problems, or within different domains, or simply with different individuals. Dr. Johnson, for instance, once wrote that "the use of traveling is to regulate imagination by reality, and instead of thinking of how things might be, to see them how they are" (quoted by Middlekauff 1982, p. 3). This is surely contrary to the idea of travel as a stimulus to the imagination and creativity. Apparently Johnson's view is typical of that historical period, at least in the United Kingdom. Middlekauff (1982) suggested that "Johnson spoke for the age in his desire to see things as they are and to avoid the dangerous imaginings of how they might be." His England and much of prerevolutionary America shared a suspicion of what he called "eerie notions"— the illusion of dreams and fancies. Travel will certainly have different impacts on different people. For some, travel facilitates creativity. For others, travel brings them down to earth. It can even be, for some, a stressful distraction.

Middlekauff (1982) felt there was a historical irony here. He pointed to the revolutionary thinking of Benjamin Franklin and others who developed a new and original political system, but at the same time were extremely practical and realistic. Middlekauff says:

> Franklin was a practical man. Practical men do not make revolutions; dreamers do. Yet Benjamin Franklin became a revolutionary with several million others in America. His actions suggest one of the ironies of the American Revolution: its sources in a culture of men devoted to the hard realities of life—practical men, down to earth men like Franklin himself, men who in 1776 threw off their allegiance to the empire in the name of "common sense," a phrase Thomas Paine had chosen as the title of his great tract on behalf of American Independence. That brings us to another irony: what seemed to have been common sense to Thomas Paine and to most Americans in 1776, would have struck them as uncommon madness a dozen years before (p. 3).

Actually Middlekauff's (1982) view of this second irony might be questioned, at least from a psychological perspective. What he seems to be getting at is merely *zeitgeist*. And indeed the American Revolution is a good example of *zeitgeist* and how innovations are likely within certain periods of time.

The other irony—concerning the practicality of revolutionary individuals—is actually quite consistent with what we know about creativity. Creative things are typically both original and practical. They are sometimes viewed as divergent and convergent, or as novel and yet appropriate and fitting. What Franklin and the other revolutionaries did, then, does exemplify a creative act and it is not surprising that the usefulness of the Democratic Republic that they created was both original and yet enormously useful.

The controversy about travel should come as no surprise. Again and again in this book (and in the corresponding creative studies), there have been individual differences, and many of these reflect individual interpretations. Recall here the person–environment requirement in Chapter 5, the idea being that no one environment is conducive or inhibitive of creativity; it all depends on the individual. The same thing of course applies to travel. In fact, this same idea applies to tactics in general. Some work for some people some of the time.

QUESTION ASSUMPTIONS

At the risk of being oxymoronic, although some tactics work for some people some of the time, there is a tendency that is universal, namely the tendency to make assumptions. Each of us does this every day, and usually many times each day. You might assume that the sun will come up again tomorrow, though actually the only way to be certain about that would be to see into the future. It is highly probable and a safe assumption, but uncertain. You might also make an assumption that the car stereo has not moved as you reach for the button for your favorite station (without even looking at the stereo). You might further assume that since you have a green light and can proceed through an intersection, other drivers have a red light and will stop. (It is best to give them a quick look rather than assuming that they are paying attention to the lights.)

Assumptions are both good and bad. They are good because they free cognitive resources; we do not need to think through every little detail every time we have an experience. The downside is that assumptions are sometimes wrong and, when we make assumptions, we do not consider new and original options. That can really hurt our creative thinking. Perspectives can be shifted and original ideas often found by questioning one's own assumptions.

The manager of the Beatles, George Martin, had a major breakthrough that reflected a change in his assumptions. The Beatles had a great deal of trouble finding a recording company, having been turned down by many of them, including Decca Records and Capitol Records. They eventually signed with a record company known only for comedy records. This turned out to be very fortunate because this allowed George Martin to hear them; he was soon to become their manager. At first he did not realize he had a superstar group on his hands, but this was in part because he was not looking for a group. He assumed he needed an individual. In his words, "I was looking for a new Buddy Holly and the Crickets, for a new Cliff Richard and Shadows. I did not see them as a group. Would it be Paul McCartney and the Beatles, or John Lennon and the Beatles ... then they played 'Love me Do' ... and it suddenly hit me, right between the eyes, this was a group I was listening to. I should take them as a group and make them as a group. That distinctive harmony, that unique blend of sound was the selling point" (quoted by Clydesdale 2006, pp. 8–9).

The economist Richard Florida (whose research on the "creative class" is cited many times in this book) seems to have developed his ideas after questioning assumptions in the field of economics. As he described it,

> one of the oldest pieces of conventional wisdom in this field says that the key to economic growth is attracting and retaining companies. Frustrated by the limits of conventional wisdom and even more by how economic development was actually being practiced, I began asking people how they chose where to live and work. My conclusion was that rather than being driven exclusively by companies, economic growth was occurring in places that were tolerant, diverse, and open to creativity (pp. xxvii–xxviii).

The value of tolerance is widely recognized (Richards 1997; Runco 2003b) and might even be listed as a kind of interpersonal tactic, something parents, teachers, and managers can do to support the creativity of their charges.

REDEFINE THE PROBLEM OR SITUATION

Clearly some of the most important assumptions to question involve the problem, situation, or task at hand. Too often we assume that a problem must be solved as given, but most of the time this is not true. Recall here the role played by problem finding (see Chapter 1) and the idea earlier in this chapter about shifting one's perspective. By questioning assumption the individual may redefine the problem such that original solutions are very likely.

Change the Representation

Problems can often be changed by altering the way they are represented. An obvious example of the benefits of changing the medium is that of drawing a map. Surely many of us have had difficulty following verbal directions, perhaps given as part of a dialogue, and we only understand and succeed in finding our objective once a map is drawn. The medium is at first verbal and then visual. Problems in scheduling can also be made easier with a visual aid. You probably know this, or at least have a calendar. You might compare that with a simple list of things "to do" as a means for effective scheduling. Sometimes it is a matter of finding the best medium, and other times it is the change in the medium or representation that leads to new ideas.

Change the Level of Analysis

Problems can be redefined (and assumptions questioned) by changing the "level of analysis." Root-Bernstein (1989) gave Thomas Edison's laboratory as an example of this, for Edison did not invent all the things for which he holds patents (1093 patents!), but instead developed the idea of a laboratory that would produce "work for hire" and provide him with all those inventions. Much the same can be said about Henry Ford. He did not invent the automobile; instead he invented the means to mass produce it. He was working on the level of mass production and not the level of an individual Model T.

> You can have any color [car] you want as long as it is black. *Henry Ford*

Zoom In, or Zoom Out

Not only can we move back to a more general level of analysis, we can also zoom in. Frequently we encounter a problem and interpret it on a large scale, but sometimes, if we think about it, there is really just one particular issue embedded in some ill-defined situation. It might be, as suggested earlier, a matter of simplifying and finding the essential idea, problem, or issue.

The benefits of zooming in and zooming out are especially obvious in some visual problems, including the nine-dot problem. Do you remember the solution? Yes, this is a test! Solutions can be found by zooming in to a point where the dots can be large enough to allow three lines to angle through them all (see Figure 1.5). Similarly, if you zoom out, the dots become very small and *one* line can actually connect all of them. The dots should be very small, and it helps if you have a large pencil.

THE RENAISSANCE CREATOR

Leonardo da Vinci was a highly prolific creator. He is a counter-example to the idea of domain-specific talent. He invented hundreds of things, in addition to his sculptures, paintings, and sketches (see Box 12.4). He invented a knight robot, hydro saw, ornithopter, aerial screw, air conditioner, assault boat, mobile bridges, covered ladders, mortars, tanks, and multiple-firing guns, which were precursors to the machine gun. He also had his own recipe for gunpowder and is often considered the Father of Kinesiology, with 30 autopsies to his credit.

Da Vinci wrote approximately 15 000 pages in his notebooks, much of which is still available. (Bill Gates purchased one of da Vinci's notebooks at Christie's auction house in 1994 for U.S.$28 000 000.)

BOX 12.4

LEONARDO LIVING LARGE

Leonardo da Vinci zoomed in and out in his work. He sometimes imagined that things were larger than life, and sometimes stepped back and saw them smaller than they were in reality. One of his most famous and favorite projects was a huge bronze statue of a horse. It was to weigh 18 tons and stand 24 feet tall. It was not finished during his lifetime, however, and apparently Leonardo's last words expressed regret that he did not finish it. He had devoted 10 years to this project, working on metallurgy, molding, and physics—and a variety of other issues related to the construction of such a large and heavy project.

An equally good example of his changing scale was his giant crossbow. It was an impressive weapon and invention, with laminated components to increase its flexibility, a worm-gear to allow the bow to be drawn, and silent firing. It was approximately 50 feet across (yes, 50 feet). The crossbow was not Leonardo's invention—the basic idea was not original. He changed the scale such that it became a unique weapon, but the originality was in the size of the project (the scale) rather than the conception of the crossbow itself. Creativity is often like this: it is a result of adaptations, extensions, changes in scale. If Leonardo only had changed the crossbow in some subtle manner, we might not think him all that creative. He might be viewed as merely an engineer who had adapted existing ideas. But we have other evidence of Leonardo's creative mind (e.g., his helicopter, and his art, including the *Mona Lisa*). Furthermore, his giant crossbow is original, though mostly only in its scaling. It also required that Leonardo work out a number of prerequisite details, such as the worm-gear, and it was quite a feat to design a crossbow of this size that would actually work.

KEEP AN OPEN MIND

Several kinds of openness were identified in the chapter on the creative personality. There is in fact a trait, "openness to experience," which characterizes many unambiguously creative individuals. Openness is not, however, something you have or do not have. Although it may be easier for some people and seems to come naturally to some, all of us can direct our attention such that we are open to experience and keep an open mind.

One benefit of this is that we see things we would not otherwise see. This in turn may explain why so many creative insights and discoveries seem to have resulted from *serendipity* or chance discovery. Earlier we quoted Pasteur and the famous idea that "chance favors the prepared mind." This is a critical idea because it implies that serendipitous insights and findings are most likely if the individual is open-minded. If individuals are open-minded, they are the most likely to recognize a valuable idea, even if they are not looking for it. If they are not open-minded, they may focus on the task at hand, and their expectations, and overlook a serendipitous discovery.

> If you find something that is interesting, drop everything and follow it. *B.F. Skinner, A Case Study in the Scientific Method*

CONTRARIANISM

The contrarian tactic is a good way to be original. It seems to be used with great regularity among proven creative people, but then again, there is so much overlap among tactics that it can be difficult to isolate. Contrarianism in particular is intimately tied to originality, and originality is the one aspect of creativity on which everyone agrees. If you are a contrarian, and doing what other people are not, you are likely to be unusual, unique, novel, or one of those others things that indicates originality. That is the value of contrarianism: It leads to the heart of creativity, to originality. Contrarianism is also intimately tied to a role in a large number of other tactics and more general creative behavior (e.g., marginality).

Bob Dylan has been a lifelong contrarian, at least during his professional career. He made a name for himself as a poet and folk musician, and then shocked his fans by playing an electric guitar at the 1965 Newport Folk Festival! Just about 30 years later (in 1994) he did very much the same thing, giving a "rock concert" on Music Television ("MTV Unplugged") with acoustic instruments.

Contrarianism can also be seen in comedians. Many use it tactically, to find creative ideas for their humor. This is most obvious when the humor is "off color." Lenny Bruce, a famous comedian of the 1950s and early 1960s, was jailed more than once for using profanity on stage in his jokes. George Carlin, famous for his list of "seven words you can never say on television" and performing an "unnatural act," recently discussed profanity and comedy (see Zoglin 2004, p. 8). Carlin came right out and said that "there is no question that the repressive, Christian, right-wing, business, criminal, Republican section of our country has gained the upper hand. I think the Patriot Act has been exploited to put more severe controls on our behavior into place than they ever dreamed they would have a chance to implement" (Zoglin 2004, p. 8). Carlin uses his humor to "bother people's sacred values," which is contrarian. He was explicit about being different: "I don't like easy targets [e.g., the President of the United States], and I don't like sounding like everyone else" (p. 8). That is what contrarians do: find ways to be different.

Day (2002) recently described the contrarianism of writers. As she described it, the individuals in her study

> each experienced social isolation from peers during childhood and adolescence and had a sense of being odd. As outsiders, they developed an observer's eye which became part of their personality. They all managed

to elevate oddity to a virtue by their middle school years. Being odd themselves, they also became fascinated with oddity in the outside world, creating a libido for the bizarre which is integrated into their identities and their writing.

One of Day's writers noted, "the idea of being normal, whatever that means, just horrifies me."

Day's writers were apparently flexible in their strategy use and tactics. As Day (2002) described it, "their strategy had to do with maintaining a flexible awareness of the many types of writing they do. When creative passion ebbs, all four writers turn to tasks that require technical skill instead, or different projects that reinvigorate them." This helped minimize the effects of writer's block. (As an aside, I should note that this idea of shifting one's work seems to parallel what creators with bipolar disorders often do: When they are on the depressed end of the mood continuum, they edit and criticize their own work. After all, when depressed they feel like criticizing! But when they are on the other end of the continuum, and feeling energetic and elated, they are incredibly productive (but not very critical). They may even recognize that the elation and productivity will not last, so they take advantage of it and focus on quantity over quality. I use this last term to relate the shift in work style to brainstorming, which focuses on productivity and quantity over quality, but only with the recognition that judgment is merely postponed, not eliminated.)

Recall here that tactics result from intentional decisions. Sometimes these decisions lead to certain investments of time and energy. Sternberg and Lubart (1996) used the metaphor "buy low and sell high" to describe creative contrarianism. This idea is well known in economic circles, and often used by investors (Dreman 1982; Malkiel 1990; Rubenson and Runco 1992b). Malkiel (1990) described the economic perspective on contrarianism by suggesting

> a contrarian investment strategy that is buying those stocks that have had a relatively poor recent performance might be expected to outperform a strategy of buying those stocks that recently produce superior returns. Implicit advice to investors is to shun recently fashionable stocks and concentrate on those stocks that are currently not in favor.... Of all the anomalies that have been uncovered or alleged, this one strikes me not only as one of the most believable, but also potentially the most beneficial for investors (p. 190).

He supported this with data showing that "while stock returns over short horizons, such as a week or month, may be positively correlated, stock returns over long horizons, such as a year or more, display negative serial correlation" (p. 190). This simply means that over the long run what a stock does at one period is unrelated to what it does at another period.

Sternberg and Lubart applied this to creative efforts and suggested that an individual will be most likely to earn respect for his or her creative work if he or she does the same thing, though perhaps in a particular field. In the sciences, for example, an individual might do a large amount of work in one area before others discover it, and indeed may work on it for years before other people see its value. If other people eventually do see the value of that area and line of work, there is a greater interest and demand, and it may be that the individual who has been plugging away for years earns a great reputation precisely at that point. Sternberg and Lubart were very clear in describing why some people do not earn reputations for their creativity. Of course the most likely reason is that they "buy high" and invest their time in fields or styles that other people are already using. Failure to earn a creative reputation may also occur when individuals sell too early (i.e., when the demand is low), or perhaps when the individual makes a poor choice and buys when demand is low, but into something that does not have actual potential. Sometimes an individual will fail by holding onto a line of thought for too long, in which case they just become one of the many people who are working in an area—they have not sold, so to speak. Note that this buy low, sell high metaphor applies specifically to creative reputation and social judgment. The assumption, then, is that creativity is an attribution, Kasof (1995), which is not a very realistic assumption (Runco 1995c). This line of thought also ignores the possibility that creative reputations can be earned by doing the best possible work on a particular topic. Sometimes creativity is earned by refining existing ideas or extending existing lines of thought.

The contrarian tactic is a good thing if it is a means to an end—the end being creative work. This may occur if being a contrarian opens new options. Contrarianism is not a good thing if it is an end in itself. This occurs if an individual intends to be different, and earns a reputation simply by being different. This kind of contrarianism has the same limitations as originality that is void of value or usefulness. This kind of originality leads only to bizarre behavior and ideas—they are only original, or perhaps even original for good reason (e.g., they are worthless so no one bothers with them).

DON'T BE A DAMN FOOL

Mark Twain is among the most quotable of the creative geniuses. His distinction between work ("what a body is obliged to do") and play ("what a body is not obliged to do") is as good as any you will find in the psychological literature. He also said, "I don't give a damn about a man who can spell a word only one way" (quoted by Sela 1994, p. 339). A similar sentiment was communicated by Frank Barron when he quoted one of the U.S. presidents on being a radical (see the first page of this chapter). These quotations imply that contrarian tactics might be taken too far. It is good to be original but not so original that no one understands.

Barron (1993) extended this line of thought in a theory of *controlled weirdness*. The basic idea seemed to be that (1) weird things are original things, and all creativity is original, and (2) too much weirdness makes a person just plain weird. If weirdness can be controlled, creativity is quite possible. Recall here the idea of metacognition and the weight given to intentions and decision making throughout this volume. A creative person may be intentionally weird, but only at times when weird is good—it may be creative. A creative person may decide to be weird, to be original, but other times will decide not to be weird. It is not out of control.

There are other ways of describing the weirdness. If it is intentional, it might be contrarianism. It might also be *marginality*, especially if it is unintentional.

Marginality might be professional or cultural (Gardner & Nemorovsky 1991; Root-Bernstein et al. 1993, 1995). In each case the individual is outside the norm. That seems to provide several benefits. In the case of cultural marginality, differences and nuances are highlighted. Consider in this regard de Toqueville's refreshing study of the United States. His observations are potent and fascinating, in part because of his perspective as a Frenchman. In the case of professional marginality, the benefit may be that the individual must think on an abstract level to be able to actually compare and integrate the disparate fields. Studies of analogical thinking suggest something like this, namely, that thinking about disparate fields or concepts leads to deeper schematic representations (Gentner et al. 2003). Gruber (1996) and

BOX 12.5

THE ARTIST OUTSIDER

William Blake was a contrarian. As Cubbs (1994) described him,

> included among art history's favorite outsiders is the late 18th century painter and poet William Blake. According to the popular Romantic text, Blake shunned the official patronage and academic standard of his time. Reportedly a misfit even among other artists, he entered the later years of his life unknown to the general public and facing extreme poverty. And in the end, his intense apocalyptic fantasies and fiery emotions earned him the accolades of troubled prophet, eccentric, and mad man (p. 78).

He was a contrarian although obviously it is not certain whether it was intentional or unintentional.

Jackson Pollock was also given as an example of an artist outsider and contrarian. As Cubbs (1994) described him, "in the mid 20th century, the archetypical image of the outsider was relocated in the popular legend of abstract expressionist painter Jackson Pollock, who forged a new outsider model combining his identity as an alienated artist outcast with a rugged individuality, frontier machismo, and romantic pathos of the American cowboy" (p. 79).

Cubbs (1994) also described Vincent Van Gogh as an outsider and rebel, or what I would call a contrarian. She put it this way: "The most famous reincarnation of the romantic artist outsider was Vincent Van Gogh, whose notorious artist passions ended in the suicidal madness so often associated with the anguished creative spirit" (p. 79). Cubbs was especially interested in artists who were "contemptuous of social conventions, past aesthetic tradition, and cultural orthodoxies of any kind ... this image as the artist outside who challenged the authority of the status quo. It was a role that would be best realized in the early 20th century by the modern avant-garde, who challenged their dissatisfaction with the state of Western civilization into a succession of artistic movements and manifestos charged with the rhetoric of revolution" (p. 78).

Cubbs (1994) argued that artists "inspired individuals who transcend the boundaries of culture" (p. 77). In her view,

> although rooted in countless myths and legends of earlier times, the view of artists as outsiders, was first established in Western culture, during the Romantic period. Major intellectual and popular movement of the late 18th and 19th centuries, Romanticism embraced an artistic philosophy of escape, fantasy, reverie, and revolt. It also preached a dissatisfaction with the mundane everyday world which it believed could only be redeemed through transforming through the artist's individual imagination. Exiled from common social life by the myth of their unique creative vision, artists came to be viewed as isolates, rebels, a necessary outcast from society (p. 77).

This line of thought is largely consistent with the Romantic perspective of creativity outlined in Chapter 4 (see Dudek 2012; Sass & Schuldberg 2000–2001). There the Romantic view led to an association of creativity with mental illness and the mad genius controversy.

Of course, contrarians are not all artists. Consider the work of Gandhi, Martin Luther King, Henry David Thoreau, and Gertrude Stein. Also recall Cavendish, described in Chapter 7.

Runco (2001b) implied that there was another benefit, namely access to different perspectives (e.g., one from each field). There is also the flexibility that allows shifts from one perspective to another. A third benefit is that working in different domains or areas increases the likelihood that the assumptions of one of them will be recognized and perhaps questioned. The fish may not be aware of the water—unless the fish leaves it.

Dogan (1999) pointed out that the concept of *marginality* has very different meanings in different domains. She found it first in work from 1928 by R.E. Park, a sociologist who described cultural hybrids. Marginality is also used in theories of societal pluralism, as well as economics and ethnology. Sometimes it indicates some sort of maladjustment; in certain circles it refers to an inferior portion of society. In creative studies, where a number of advances have been facilitated by marginality, it has a very different meaning, and a very positive one. Dogan gave Pasteur as an example, because early on, he apparently was a crystallographer, an experience that later gave him a useful perspective on microbes.

Each of these ideas is consistent with Jaussi et al.'s (2007) findings on the benefits of "cross-applying experiences" (e.g., hobbies used somehow in one's career), and with the creativity of heterogeneous work groups (Rubenson & Runco 1995). There might be some benefit to reading materials that are outside one's own field and talking to others outside the field as well. Indeed, Nakamura and Csikszentmihalyi (2002) felt that an individual does not need to be marginal; he or she can instead work with people who are in different (but complementary) fields. Recall here the idea of heterogeneous groups for brainstorming. If there is a dramatic need for marginality, a career change, or at least a change in one's style or focus, may be in order. The critical idea is to recognize perspectives that are different from those you typically hold.

LET IT HAPPEN

All of these suggestions, which assume that some effort is expended, can be categorized as "make it happen" tactics (Parnes 1967). Creative thinking sometimes is facilitated by simply putting oneself in the right situation. Of course what is right will depend on the individual. The point, however, is that people are often naturally creative. They may not need to be encouraged so much and simply allowed to use existing skills. As Parnes (1967) described it, often all that needs to be done is to "let it happen."

A good example of a "let it happen" tactic is incubation. An individual might put a problem aside and take a walk or exercise. They may find ideas while they are doing something else! Incubation is probably occurring while they walk, exercise, or play. Singer (1975) and Epstein (1996) suggested that there are benefits to daydreaming (pp. 67, 163), and here again all that might need to be done is find a spot where daydreaming is likely.

Play may offer similar benefits. As a matter of fact there are situations where play may be necessary! Wallach and Kogan (1965), for instance, suggested that test-like classrooms do not allow much divergent and original thinking, whereas game-like and permissive environments support divergent and original thinking. Later in this chapter a technology of foolishness will be discussed (March 1978), with implications for creativity within organizations.

Sadly, it can be quite difficult to play. Root-Bernstein and Root-Bernstein (2006) concluded that "given the general tendency of modern society to undervalue and marginalize play of all kinds, particularly in educational settings, these data [about *worldplay*] must cause concern that critical creative facilities and our children and adolescents are being short changed" (p. 421). Adams (1974) mentioned playfulness as one of the things that is difficult to do in Western culture, when you have a "serious problem." Yet it may be that playfulness will lead to original solutions.

Granted, incubation is not always useful. Smith and Blankenship (1991) described how "problems that are solved immediately require no incubation, and intractable problems which cannot be solved even with unlimited time will not be influenced by incubation time" (p. 63). Thus time is important, but only for some problems, especially because incubation often contributes to the creativity of the solution.

Original thinking may also come easily when the person exercises (Curnow and Turner 1992; Gondola 1986, 1987; Gondola & Tuckman 1985; Herman-Toffler & Tuckman 1998). When exercising there is increased blood flow, incubation, and perhaps even a bit of short-distance travel. In my case, exercise takes me anywhere from three to five miles.

AVOIDANCE TACTICS

Runco (1999d) described something like "let it happen" tactics in terms of avoidance. As he put it, sometimes certain things need to be done, and sometimes certain things need to be avoided. He pointed to a number of *barriers* and *squelchers* as specific things to avoid. The former are environmental or social situations that tend to inhibit or constrain our thinking and should therefore be avoided. Von Oech (1983) listed 10 barriers to creative thought. These reflect a tendency to (1) look to the right answer, (2) focus on what is logical, (3) follow the rules, (4) consider what is practical, (5) avoid ambiguity, (6) avoid mistakes, (7) avoid play, (8) stay within our own areas of experience, (9) avoid the possibility of appearing to be foolish, and (10) think of oneself as uncreative. Squelchers are things that we say to ourselves or to other people that imply that routine is good and original behavior is bad (e.g., "it will never work," "too risky"). See Box 8.2 (also see Davis 1999).

FLEXIBLE USE OF TACTICS

At this point it is probably obvious that there is a benefit to being flexible with creative tactics. It is unreasonable to assume that one tactic would apply to all problems and all domains, so the individual who can employ different tactics at different times will have a huge advantage. Leonardo da Vinci can again be cited: He was very flexible with his thinking and tactics. He changed the scale of his huge horse statue, for example, and for his giant crossbow. He also knew to put problems aside. This is exactly what he did with his studies of flight. His initial studies of flight were extensive, but at one point he put flight aside, only to come back to it much later in his life. This is a very useful tactic, in part because the individual might take advantage of incubation if he or she puts a problem aside. Additionally, more information might become available if completion is postponed.

Leonardo da Vinci designed what we would today call a helicopter, as well as a parachute and wings for a human. Much of his work reflected a "look to the natural world" tactic, "borrowing and adapting" from nature. His ornithopter, for example, was based on his extensive observations of birds, and the tactic was also apparent in his crossbow and his armored vehicle.

Da Vinci also gathered data for some of his designs. He knew that air flowed like water, for example, and thus experimented with wings and aerodynamics by placing different shaped paddles at different angles in streams. What he learned from this helped him design the wings for his flying machines.

The Wright brothers were also extremely flexible with their tactics and problem solving. Like da Vinci, they collected huge amounts of data, even building their own wind tunnel. They also collected information by contacting everyone else who was studying flight at that time. The Wrights also looked to nature and identified useful analogies (e.g., the wing of a bird and the wing of their "flier"). They broke large problems down into small ones. Instead of working on flight, they worked on problems of power, weight, and control of the aircraft, and they collected plenty of data. Perhaps most novel was the tactic that appeared to be nothing but arguing. While working in their bike shop, or later in the tents in Kitty Hawk, Orville would argue for one side of some technical problem and Wilbur would defend the other side. They would yell and argue—and then switch who was arguing what and argue again. The fact that they took turns with each side of each technical problem suggests that they were using this as a kind of tactic.

Other people have argued and debated for their work. Silverman (1995), for example, described how Lita Hollingworth, one of the pioneers of gifted education, "carried on arguments in her head with Galton in the same way that Wollstonecraft argued with Rousseau." Jean Piaget felt that he best defended his theories when he did the same kind of thing (Gruber 1996). What is most important here, however, is that it is best to be flexible and to use alternative strategies. At least that seemed to have worked very well for Leonardo da Vinci and the Wright brothers. Jausovec (1991), Kaizer and Shore (1995), and Carlsson (2002) each described the benefits of flexible strategy use.

PROGRAMS AND MULTIPLE STEP METHODS FOR CREATIVE THINKING

These tactics can sometimes be used singly. They can also be combined into larger programs. Many programs have been proposed. Some of the better known are reviewed next. Some of these are not extensive, but they are not focused tactics either. Each is multifaceted, or involves more than one step. In that sense these suggestions are more than just focused tactics.

Synectics

Developed as a concept in the 1960s, synectics denotes a bringing together of diverse elements in new combinations (Gordon 1961). The word is derived from two Greek roots, *syn* and *ectics*. As you may recall from earlier in this chapter, the emphasis is on analogical thinking. The intention of synectics is "making the strange familiar, and making the familiar strange" (Gendrop 1996, p. 1). The first part of this, making the strange familiar, is a kind of critical thinking. In her study of the effectiveness of synectics, Gendrop (1996) pointed to "data gathering, analysis, synthesis, and evaluation" to this end. She associated "making the strange familiar" with previous learning. The second step, making the familiar strange, is more obviously creative. To this end synectics emphasizes analogy. There is, however, a recognized need to "break old associative connections, provide a new perceptual framework, and apply this new context to the issue at hand" (Gendrop 1996, p. 1). Gordon (1972) and Gordon and Poze (1981) found improvements in the creative thinking of elementary and junior high school students, and Gendrop (1996) reported much the same (at least for originality scores) in a sample of nurses.

Creative Problem Solving

Creative problem solving usually involves the following:

1. Objective finding
2. Fact finding
3. Problem finding
4. Idea finding
5. Solution finding
6. Acceptance finding.

Alternative models have been presented by Firestien and McCowan (1988) and Treffinger et al. (1994). Firestien and McCowan (1988), for example, described creative problem solving as comprising the following:

1. Mess finding
2. Data finding
3. Problem finding
4. Idea finding
5. Solution finding
6. Acceptance finding.

Van Gundy (1992) described these as stages. He focused on facilitators and "a systematic problem solving model that employees can use everyday. CPS [creative problem solving] guides the doer through a series of divergent and convergent problem solving activities. Each activity is designed to help with one of six problem solving stages" (p. 13).

Van Gundy suggested that the facilitator has the following qualities: accurate self-knowledge, patience, an understanding of the specific task at hand, an ability to coordinate different thinking processes (e.g., convergent and divergent), good verbal skills, good human relations skills, sensitivity to nonverbal communication, good communication skills, a tendency toward positive thinking, an open mind, tolerance of ambiguity, prudence when taking risks, a tendency toward playfulness, confidence, and basic creative thinking skills. When actually facilitating, the facilitator should be well prepared, with materials and three-dimensional displays. The facilitator should start by communicating the ground rules, the most important of which is to distinguish during the meeting between criticism and evaluation and idea generation.

In this sense the facilitator is helping the group to brainstorm (see later). Indeed, the facilitator may use brainstorming techniques such as hitchhiking, piggy-backing, and emphasizing the quantity of ideas over their quality. The facilitator should create an informal atmosphere and model creative behavior him- or herself, putting a great deal of effort into listening carefully, and be prepared for periods of silence. The group may be silent when thinking. The facilitator should also monitor the time constraints and never assume that the members of the group fully understand brainstorming or the various techniques. He or she may need to remind them why they are doing what they are doing and further remind them of the procedures, such as postponing judgment. Van Gundy believes that walking around is helpful in longer sessions; the facilitator may encourage that, and should avoid subgroups and voting within the group. Very important, the facilitator is not to take the position of the expert but instead is there to allow the group to use their expertise concerning the subject matter. The facilitator is just that: someone who facilitates the process but does not necessarily lead in a particular direction or toward a particular outcome.

Lateral Thinking

Another program for enhancing creativity involves lateral thinking (De Bono 1992). The key idea is captured with the following metaphor: When faced with a problem or obstacle, do not dig deeper, dig elsewhere. De Bono also uses a metaphor of "six thinking hats." These hats refer to modes of thought. The white hat represents a neutral perspective that allows the individual to collect and use data and information. The red hat represents an individual's emotions, affect, feelings, intuition, and hunches. The black hat represents judgmental modes of thought and criticism. The yellow hat represents an optimistic perspective and emphasizes the benefits of an approach or solution. The green hat is for a kind of fertility, at least fertility of alternatives and ideas. De Bono suggests that "the green hat is for creative thinking … for new ideas … additional alternatives … [and] for putting forward possibilities and hypotheses" (p. 80). Finally, the blue hat controls the thinking process. It monitors and summarizes. De Bono suggests that the blue hat usually is worn by a chairperson if the creative work is being done in a group. He suggests that the blue hat is "for thinking about thinking" (p. 80), which, in the cognitive sciences, is labeled metacognition.

De Bono (1992) suggested that his method and the use of six thinking hats will allow groups and organizations to avoid argument and adversarial situations. Supposedly the six hats can be used for cooperative exploration and thereby more productive efforts. Obviously, the benefit of De Bono's technique is that the individual or group will cover all the bases, or at least approach problems from various perspectives. In this sense De Bono's technique is a little bit like brainstorming, at least in the sense that both ensure that alternatives are considered and criticism is postponed. De Bono does suggest that groups might agree on an agenda and a particular sequence of hats. In other words, right up front the group will decide which hats will be worn by everyone in the group and at what point they will switch from hat to hat. He even suggests that groups might benefit from devoting about four minutes to each hat.

De Bono's techniques are based on several decades of applied work in a variety of organizations. They have not been adequately tested with scientific techniques. This may be because many of the ideas are metaphorical, which are not all that easily tested, or it may be because De Bono's concerns are more applied than basic. Several of his ideas are consistent with sound empirical research, and in this sense have some indirect support. There is, for instance, clear support for the benefits of postponed judgment and shifting from one mode of thought to another, and of course for the usefulness of divergent thinking.

Bed, Bath, and the Bus

Epstein (1996) suggested that individuals have their best ideas while in bed, the bath, or on a bus. He was really suggesting that daydreaming was useful. He described the need to "capture the fleeting," by which he meant that ideas are very quick and ephemeral and the individual must therefore be ready to record them when he or she has them. Epstein specially suggested recording an idea and evaluating it at some later point. Epstein also recommended seeking out challenges.

Here Epstein is drawing from his empirical research, and in particular the idea of *resurgence* (Epstein 1990). Essentially, this has to do with interconnections between behaviors. To facilitate resurgence he suggests interacting with a variety of people or from persons with a variety of backgrounds, either careerwise or in terms of age. He also suggests keeping provocative items, such as toys, on one's desk or to simply do different things, like turn pictures upside down. A related strategy involves expanding one's world. Here he again looks to learning theory and argues for transference or transfer (from one situation or experience to new situations or experiences).

IDEAL

Bransford and Stein (1993) suggested that problem solving is most effective if the following steps are carefully followed:

1. Identify problems and opportunities.
2. Define alternative goals.
3. Explore possible strategies.
4. Anticipate and act.
5. Look and learn.

They encouraged entering the "IDEAL" cycle at any point and recycling through the steps as needed.

Dreaming and Imagery

Harman and Rheingold (1984) identified four methods that can assist individuals in both developing their creativity-enhancing personality traits, as well as helping them become more proficient at the process of creativity. These methods are guided imagery, affirmation, alert relaxation, and dreaming.

Guided imagery is an ability we all possess that allows us to conjure up images or visions of things different from our ordinary reality. According to Jung (1962) images are the form in which messages are carried to and from our unconscious, and by tapping into our unconscious we can access insights and creative solutions to life's presenting problems. Psychosynthesis is one system that uses guided imagery to assist individuals in deliberately evoking answers from their unconscious. One method used in psychosynthesis to connect with one's unconscious (or to connect with something greater) is dialogue with an inner advisor. In this imaginary dialogue, questions and problems can be presented to one's inner guide, and answers and often creative guidance is received. "If the sages are to be believed, inner teachers, helpers, and guides are available to all of us, ready to respond to our requests for assistance" (Harman & Rheingold 1984).

Affirmations are a method of combining intense inner resolve, fixed purpose, imagery, emotion, and will into a mantra that helps individuals reprogram their unconscious, allowing them to manifest the positive future outcomes they are intending. This process can be used in facilitating creativity by using affirmations such as "I have breakthrough creative insights."

Many creative insights occur when individuals experience a state of calm, relaxed openness (the incubation and illumination stages proposed by Wallas 1926). The physiological benefits of the relaxation response were apparently first found in cardiology patients (Harman & Rheingold 1984). As a result of his research he also found that the relaxation response produces a state of alertness that is conducive to creative insight. By sitting in a quiet environment, consciously relaxing one's muscles, focusing on a specific object or mantra, and assuming a passive attitude, individuals can facilitate states of consciousness that are gateways to states usually associated with breakthroughs and creative experiences. *Alert relaxation* can be seen as a means of slipping past the internal censors at the portals to the unconscious (Harman & Rheingold 1984).

Dreams are replete with images and symbols that can provide the dreamer with powerful creative insights. Since we spend a third of our lives asleep, it seems like a worthy endeavor to cultivate this mostly untapped resource. Jung (1962) claimed that by writing down our dreams and reflecting on the meanings behind the images and symbols that are evoked, we can learn a great deal about our unconscious motives, resistances, and creative urges. Once we become proficient at examining our dreams we can begin to intentionally use them to tap into our unconscious problem-solving mechanism, facilitating our creative abilities.

Brainstorming

Brainstorming is almost definitely the most often employed enhancement technique. It is not just one tactic but instead a method for divergent thinking in groups. Osborn (1963) described four brainstorming rules: "(1) Criticism is ruled out. Adverse judgment of ideas must be withheld until later. (2) 'Freewheeling' is welcomed. The wilder the idea, the better; it is easier to tame down than to think up. (3) Quantity is wanted. The greater the number of ideas, the more the likelihood of useful ideas. (4) Combinations and improvements are sought. In addition to contributing ideas of their own, participants should suggest how ideas of others can be turned into better ideas; or how two or more ideas can be joined into still another idea" (p. 156).

Firestien and McCowan (1988) found that training in creative problem solving led to greater communication among group members. They also found improvement in the resulting ideas. There is, however, some controversy. Torrance and Presbury (1984) reviewed over 100 studies and found that brainstorming was effective, at least with his own Torrance Tests of Creative Thinking as the criterion measure. Many others, however, have criticized brainstorming.

Still, as noted in Chapter 5, brainstorming has many detractors. In fact, it is a bit surprising that it is still used; questions have been raised almost from the beginning. Taylor et al. (1958), for example, compared the creative problem solving of individuals working in groups of four with individuals working alone. The tasks were fairly realistic: The Tourist Problem asked "How can the number of European tourists coming to the U.S. be increased?" The Thumb Problem asked for a list of pros and cons that would arise if people had an additional thumb. The Teacher Problem asked how to insure continued educational efficacy, given population increases. Fluency, originality, and feasibility of ideas were each inferior in the groups, compared with the individuals working alone. Dozens or even hundreds of other studies have found much the same (see Mullen et al. (1991) for a meta-analysis, and Rickards and De Cock (2012) for a recent review).

Brainstorming may not work in part because there are tendencies toward production loss (Diehl & Strobe 1987, 1991; Mullen et al. 1991; Paulus 1999). Similarly, Paulus described performance matching, which occurs when individuals align their performance with the less productive group members. Another significant problem with brainstorming is evaluation apprehension (Parloff & Handlon 1964; Paulus 1999). This occurs when group members avoid original ideas because they fear the reactions of the other members of the group. Then there is social loafing.

BOX 12.6

LEARNING THEORY AND CREATIVE THINKING

Several operant principles can be used to insure that training and enhancement efforts are maximally effective. Displaced practice is, for example, quite effective. Hence individuals should work on creative thinking exercises, but then turn to something else, and later again return to creative thinking exercises. In that fashion the practice is displaced and highly effective. Tasks should be varied to insure that the skills learned generalize to other tasks and other settings. Reinforcement must be given judiciously. Too much, and overjustification is likely. This occurs when extrinsic rewards and incentives undermine preexisting intrinsic interests.

Fading might also be used, especially if individuals are unaccustomed to divergent thinking. More structured tasks might be given at first, along with highly explicit instructions. After the individuals are accustomed to these, more open-ended tasks might be given, perhaps with less explicit instructions. Eventually, after gradual fading, the individuals will learn to think divergently and originally on their own, even with entirely ill-defined tasks and without explicit instructions. Stokes and Baer (1977) presented an outline of the "technology of generalization and maintenance," which can be adapted to enhancement efforts.

These drawbacks influence creative thinking, and there are other reasons to consider brainstorming. Such group work may contribute to team-building processes, for example. In the classroom brainstorming might help children learn to cooperate and collaborate, even if the number and originality of the ideas is lower than might be obtained if students worked alone.

Brainstorming might be used along with other individualized tasks and exercises. Indeed, learning theory suggests that students have extremely varied experiences and displaced practice. Varied experiences will contribute to the likelihood that the skills learned (e.g., divergent thinking) will generalize across tasks and settings. Displaced practice (working on open-ended tasks, then shifting to another task, and then returning to open-ended tasks) is especially effective with students. Thus there would be a benefit to brainstorming at one point and working in nominal groups (i.e., individually) at other times. Learning theory also offers suggestions for appropriate reinforcement of creative thinking (Box 12.6).

Varied experiences should include working with different kinds of groups; homogeneous groups should be avoided (Rubenson & Runco 1995). Of course there is an optimal level of group heterogeneity. Too much and it will be difficult for group members to communicate with one another. Too little and there may be a consensus bias, which is related to what others call *groupthink* (Paulus 1999).

TACTICS FOR ORGANIZATIONS

Many tactics and programs have been developed specifically for organizations (e.g., Amabile & Gryskiewicz 1989; Basadur 1994; Runco & Basadur 1993; Witt & Boerkrem 1989). With the need for accountability, most of these have been developed along with assessments and measures. These are very interesting because they pinpoint the specific things that need to be done and things that need to be avoided. They tend to capture the idea of "the creativity complex," at least in that they cover more than just cognitive skill. They cover interpersonal behaviors, the physical environment, resources, and social situations.

Amabile and Gryskiewicz (1989) pointed to freedom (freedom in deciding what to do and how to do it), challenge (a sense of having to work hard on challenging tasks), resources (access to appropriate resources, including people, materials, facilities, and information), supervision (appropriate goals, values, individual contributions, enthusiastic modeling), coworkers (a diversely skilled group, with trust and commitment), recognition (fair, constructive feedback), unity and cooperation (cooperation, flow of ideas), and specific creativity supports. They also felt that creative environments lack the following: time pressure, evaluation, status quo, and political problems. Witt and Beorkrem (1989) developed a somewhat similar measure that contains scales for time and resources, challenge, interpersonal evaluation and feedback, and autonomy.

Rickards and Jones (1991) presented a detailed inventory of barriers. They also developed the Jones Inventory of Barriers to Effective Problem-Solving to assess the presence of these blocks (Table 12.1). Rickards and Jones summarized research with architects, accountants, sales people, managers, and engineers. Their results indicate that the Jones inventory is reliable and in some ways valid. They also described the content and concurrent validity of the measure, for example, the latter being supported by the fact that scores on the Jones measure were negatively correlated with divergent thinking fluency and originality scores, a

TABLE12.1   Example Questions from the Jones Inventory of Barriers to Effective Problem-Solving

Strategy Questions (12 items)

3. I like to keep strictly to time schedules	vs.	I am easygoing about time-keeping
7. I am keen to try new ideas	vs.	I prefer ideas that have been tried and tested
8. I like sorting out complex problems	vs.	I like problems that are clearly defined
11. I like to finish a task once I have started it	vs.	I don't mind leaving jobs half done

Values Questions (6 items)

7. Rigid moral standards are unreasonable	vs.	Modern moral standards are too slack
12. He who is not for me is against me	vs.	There are good and bad aspects to most views
17. Principles should act as a guide not a rule book	vs.	One should never depart from one's principles
22. Traditions are essential in maintaining a stable society	vs.	Traditions are interesting but irrelevant to modern society

Perceptual Questions (6 items)

4. I never forget a face	vs.	I have a poor memory for faces
14. I am always conscious of people around me	vs.	I am often unaware of people
19. I cannot distinguish the sounds of musical instruments	vs.	I usually can identify a musical instrument by its sound
24. I am very conscious of noise	vs.	I am rarely aware of background noise when I am working

Self-Image Questions (6 items)

15. I try to avoid competition	vs.	I like to win
20. I often ask for help	vs.	I like to solve my own problems
25. I keep my personal feelings to myself	vs.	People usually know how I feel about things
30. Conflict should be brought into the open	vs.	I try to avoid conflict

Some questions are worded to indicate the presence of a barrier, and others are worded to indicate the absence of a barrier. The numbers in the left margin are the original question numbers (so "I am keen to try new ideas" is the first question on the Inventory, and "I like to keep strictly to time schedules," a contraindicative item, is the third question on the Inventory. From Rickards and Jones (1991, p. 307).

right-hemisphere thinking style, and an originality score from the Kirton Adaptation Innovation Inventory. These negative correlations support the theory that situational barriers inhibit creative thinking.

CREATIVITY AND COGNITIVE STYLE

Kirton (1980) described two styles: adaptive and innovative. Both can support creative thinking and each is ostensibly independent of intellectual ability. Simplifying a great deal, *adaptors* use what is given, whereas *innovators* make changes. Another very useful measure of style was described by Martinsen (1995) and Kaufmann (1979). It suggests *explorer* and *assimilator* styles.

Some elaboration might be useful. Quoting Rickards and Jones (1991),

> strategic barriers affect the approaches taken to solve problems. Examples include (a) the tendency to rely heavily on past experience or particular technique without challenging their appropriateness; (b) focusing on a narrow range of options for either problem definition or solving; and (c) adapting an over-serious approach to problems which prevents the emergence of a playful, imaginative, and humorous climate. Values barriers occur when personal beliefs and values restrict the range of ideas contemplated (p. 306).

March (1987) suggested that organizations might use a *technology of foolishness*. This requires a balance of play and reason. That balance in turn requires that managers view (a) goals as hypotheses, (b) intuition as real, (c) hypocrisy as a transition, (d) memory as an enemy, and (e) experience as a theory. It is also important, according to March, that these five methods be used alternatively, with a temporary suspension of "reasoned intelligence."

This may sound, well, reasonable, but keep in mind that there are blocks to such thinking, especially in industry. The whole idea of "work" tends to preclude any "play." That is probably a bad thing for creativity and innovation.

Blocks in the Natural Environment

Barriers are not only problems for organizations, they plague each of our day-to-day lives. In one of the best books ever written about creative problem solving, Adams (1974) identified specific cultural, perceptual, intellectual, emotional, and social blocks to creativity. His focus was on problem solving, and there is some controversy about the relationship of creativity and problem solving (Runco 1994e). Creativity may be a kind of problem solving; or problem solving may sometimes (but not always) involve creativity; or creativity may involve self-expression, play, and experimentation instead of problem solving. At the very least the blocks identified by Adams apply to the kind of creativity that is involved in problem solving.

Perceptual blocks occur when a problem is misperceived. The problem may be poorly isolated from a distracting context, or it may be too narrowly or too generally defined. The individual may be saturated and too immersed in a field to see a problem (as is the case when experts make assumptions and do not recognize some detail that they should) or have preconceptions or stereotypes that preclude a recognition of a problem. Adams suggests avoiding these blocks by employing a variety of viewpoints and perspectives, and perhaps using various (rather than one) modalities or means of representing the situation (and potential problem).

Cultural blocks often keep us from thinking in a fashion that will allow creative insight. Cultural values or traditions may keep an adult from playing, for example, or from employing humor and play to solve problems. (Anyone ever told you to "get serious" because "this is serious!"?) Culture leads us to avoid taboos and to act only in proscribed ways. Adults may be questioned if they fantasize, for example, or break stereotypes. A good example of the latter involves sex roles. Men are supposed to act like men, and women like women, but this can constrain thought such that a man cannot see solutions to problems if they involve a stereotypically feminine perspective or behavior. Supposedly men are independent (Bem 1986), but what if a problem requires a social solution? Women are often caring and relational, but what if a problem can be solved easily with an autonomous or competitive route? The point here is that sex roles are defined by culture and can actually block our thinking about problems and solutions.

Environmental blocks may involve the physical environment (McCoy and Evans 2002) or people we encounter. Our coworkers and peers, for example, may distract us or lead us astray (i.e., away from a fruitful line of thought). Our supervisors may be autocratic, and this can be a big problem for creativity because it often involves an independence of thought. A great deal of work within organizations and businesses has confirmed the possible inhibitive effects of people, their expectations, and the context. Any kind of distraction, or pressure communicated via expectations, can inhibit our creative thinking.

Emotional blocks may result from risk aversion, lack of confidence, fear of making mistakes, an intolerance of ambiguity, or impatience. Sometimes it is risky to invest one's time into an original idea or subject, or risky to share it with others. They may think you are a few bubbles off plumb! Sometimes creative things develop from ambiguous situations, and sometimes they take time to incubate. Time and a willingness to incubate can be quite important. In each of these cases, the problem is that an emotional reaction occurs (e.g., discomfort, aversion, or fear), and this in turn keeps the individual from pursuing creative work. It is for reasons like these that at least one theory emphasizes the ego strength that is necessary for creative thinking (i.e., "personal creativity," Chapter 9). Ego strength represents the wherewithal and confidence that allows the individual to take risks, tolerate ambiguity, and stand up to pressures to conform.

Intellectual and expressive blocks often occur because the individual approaches a problem from only one perspective. Cognitive flexibility would be a great help, especially if the problem is represented in one medium (e.g., it is written, or drawn), but in actuality it is more easily or more creatively solved when represented in a different domain. Everyone probably has had experiences where they needed to change how a problem was represented. Perhaps it was a word problem in mathematics that needed to be represented in numbers to be solved. Perhaps you may have found the benefits of sketching, for it can take a problem represented in one form (e.g., words or numbers) and put it all into one holistic representation. Some of the benefit may actually be in the shift itself. Shifting perspectives or representations sometimes seems to dislodge thought or suggest alternatives. Tactics are especially useful when faced with an intellectual or expressive block (Adams 1974). It is also useful to insure that you have correct information for the problem at hand (avoid "garbage in, garbage out"), and that you retain (i.e., record) what you might need as you do your research or prepare. No wonder Epstein (1996), Skinner (1985), and others have recommended carrying a notebook or tape recorder. As Epstein put it, ideas are "fleeting," and even if you have plenty of them, you must be sure to record them so they will be available when you need them.

Most of these blocks lead directly to tactics for creative problem solving. It is sometimes just a matter of avoiding the blocks! Adams (1974) did also suggest that individuals hold a "questioning attitude." Very likely, assumptions are among the most important things to question. They often lead us away from original insights and toward routine. Adams (1974) suggests that the individual should always double-check that he or she is working on the right problem, perhaps postponing judgment until there is a sufficient number of ideas (read about brainstorming in Chapter 5), and considers directed fantasy or a playful stance. Try approaching problems using more than one sensory modality and more than one medium. Next time you have a problem, try to sketch it out, or sing a song about it.

COMPETITION

Organizations are often competitive. They often compete with one another (for a "market share") or reward employees in such a manner as to create internal competition. Is competition good for creativity? There are two opposing views about competition and creativity. It is easy to guess what they are: for some individuals, competition stimulates creativity (Micklus and Micklus 1994), and for others competition can inhibit creativity.

The Beatles seemed to have benefited from competition. They competed both among themselves, and with other groups, most notably the Beach Boys. John Lennon acknowledged this when he said "there was a little competition between Paul and me as to who got the A side, who got the hit singles. If you notice, in the early days, the majority of singles in the movies and everything were mine" (quoted by Clydesdale 2006 p. 10). Paul McCartney also recognized this when he said "he'd write 'Strawberry Fields,' I'd go away and write 'Pennylane.' If I would write 'I'm Down,' he'd go away and write something similar to that, you know, to compete with each other…. It was very friendly competition because we were both going to share the rewards anyway" (Clydesdale 2006, p. 10). The manager of the Beatles, George Martin, felt that competition within the group was, as he put it, "the essential thing that made them work so well" (Clydesdale 2006, p. 11).

Competition can inhibit creativity because it is extrinsic. It can, in this sense, distract the potential creator. The likelihood of distraction is probably dependent upon the individual's personality, and in particular his or her introversion and achievement motivation.

Micklus and Micklus (1994) describe a sizable program called the Odyssey of the Mind, which is a competition specifically for creative problem solving. The Odyssey of the Mind program is well attended so obviously many people believe that competition does indeed stimulate creativity. Micklus and Micklus pointed out that competition is a part of the natural world. Many businesses, including those emphasizing innovation, and many other organizations that are inherently creative (Micklus and Micklus name NASA, for example) compete in many ways. Grants are often competitive and positions within the hierarchy of an organization

BOX 12.7

A GENERAL CLIMATE FOR CREATIVITY

One of the best examples of the interdisciplinary nature of creative studies involves the concept of a general climate for creative efforts. This climate is general (and interdisciplinary) in that it contributes to creativity in organizations, schools, clinical settings, and even the home.

Harrington et al. (1987), for example, drew from Carl Rogers' theory of creativity and pointed to the following key features of a creative climate: psychological safety, psychological freedom, openness to experience, an internal locus of evaluation, and the toying with elements and concepts. They demonstrated that child-rearing, which respected these, was associated with adolescent creative potential. Dacey (1989a) found much the same: Parents in his study did not prescribe rules but instead discussed and modeled creative problem solving. These parents almost never used conventional punishment and their own reactions seemed to have an impact on the children. They enjoyed "fooling around" and there were many opportunities for actual creative action.

tend to be competitive. In some ways the dictum "necessity is the mother of invention" is consistent with the idea that competition stimulates creativity.

Individual cases should be treated only as illustrations, and never as hard evidence, but there is a case that nicely illustrates the possibility that competition will stimulate creativity. I am referring to the story of the double helix, told by the Nobel laureate James Watson. His work with Francis Crick on the discovery of the structure of DNA was clearly motivated by competition. In particular, Watson and Crick competed with Linus Pauling. This case does bring up the possibility that competition may be the label given for motives, whereas in fact, the motivation does not result from the desire to beat out other individuals so much as it does for the kind of achievement motivation that is tied to success. In other words, someone may be motivated to achieve and accomplish something, and the only way they can accomplish it is to beat out others who are trying to do the same thing. In Watson's case, the prize was the Nobel award. Zuckermann (1977) described a large number of Nobel laureates. What may be clearest in her work is the role of mentoring. Creative individuals tended to seek out the best mentors.

ENHANCEMENT IN THE CLASSROOM

Just as there are techniques and programs that are specifically designed for organizational settings, so too can specific things be done in the classroom. Runco (1991d) listed the following:

- Be explicit. Tell students that creativity is a good thing, and tell them how to find creative ideas. Explicit instructions are just that—explicit directions about the task at hand, the best strategy to use with the task at hand, and perhaps some clue as to the criteria used to judge success on the task. Explicit instructions have been used with many different kinds of creativity tests, including tests of divergent thinking and insight, and tend to elicit more ideas and more original ideas than inexplicit instructions. Moreover, they work well with gifted and nongifted children alike.
- Target both originality and flexibility. Creative things are always original, and originality can be easily explained, even to young children ("what your friends are not doing"). Flexibility seems to be the least frequently recognized index of creative thinking, but it is very important, especially for creative problem solving, because it precludes rigidity and functional fixity (the tendency to remain in a rut and see a problem from only one perspective). Explicit instructions can target flexibility, as well as originality or fluency.
- Do not rely on tasks or assignments for which there are clearly defined solutions. It is easy to plan a curriculum when the teacher knows all the correct answers, and this kind of convergent thinking has its place, strengthening problem solving and the like. Open-ended, divergent thinking kinds of tasks also should be used. There is more fun, more surprise, and more creativity in divergent thinking than in predictable problem solving. This may seem extremely obvious, but educators should take a close look at their curricula: How much of it is truly open-ended?
- Consider beginning with tasks that have the fewest demands and constraints, and only later move to more realistic but more constrained tasks. The so-called standard divergent thinking task, which asks questions like "name square things" and "list uses for a brick," are artificial but extremely open-ended. Only gradually should the more demanding tasks (e.g., those concerning work or school) be used. This allows for a kind of *fading*, or gradual and smooth learning. This progression should contribute to the generalization of the learning across tasks and settings.
- Target transformational thinking. Michael (1999), citing Guilford's views, pointed to transformations as most critical for creativity. Children need to make changes, consider alternatives. Metaphors, similes, and analogies are useful in this regard.
- Challenge students, but only optimally. This follows from the research on optima (e.g., Runco and Sakamoto 1996; Toplyn & Maguire 1991) as well as theories of development (Piaget 1976; Vygotsky 1997).
- Use intrinsic interests. Students may not be all that thrilled by presented problems. They should be allowed to identify, define, and redefine assignments and tasks for themselves. Educators should devote attention specifically to presolution planning and attempt to convey the idea that problem identification and problem definition are as important as problem solving.
- Do not rush. Time is needed for creative work. Educators should give sufficient time for students to find original insights.
- Educators need to be creative themselves. They are models for their children. They need to think divergently, keep an open mind, experiment, and so on.

- Educators should also consider immunizing children against the potentially harmful effects of extrinsic motivation and incentives (Hennessey 1994). This is an important possibility, given the role of intrinsic motivation in many creative performances. Other suggestions are provided in Chapters 5 and 9.

CREATIVITY AND EDUCATION OF OLDER ADULTS

Torrance et al. (1989) focused on strategies for older adults. Their view was that "retirement provides a wonderful opportunity to discover or rediscover … creative abilities and talents" (p. 124). They further suggested that "the older adult has many of the necessary qualities for creativity: Time, accumulated experience, knowledge, skills, and wisdom" (p. 124). They suggested, first, "don't be afraid to fall in love with something." Here they were acknowledging that creativity often results when an individual is intensely and passionately involved with some activity. They specifically noted the motivational benefits that may be involved when someone is in love with something. Second, they suggested a whole category of cognitive activities, including "know, understand, take pride in, practice, develop, use, exploit, and enjoy your greatest strength" (p. 124). Next, they suggested "Learn to free yourself from expectations of others and walk away from the games they impose upon you" (p. 124). This is almost a contrarian strategy, but may best be viewed as simply healthy nonconformity. Fourth, and finally, Torrance et al. suggested "don't waste a lot of expensive, unproductive energy trying to be well rounded." Here again they were suggesting that an individual utilize his or her own strengths. This last idea is contrary to the explicit suggestion of Root-Bernstein (1999) and his polymath approach, whereby individuals do indeed study various areas and thereby find analogies and useful contradictions.

Torrance et al. (1989) offered suggestions specifically for older adults because creativity is conducive to health. This notion is well supported in Chapter 4 (see also Langer 1989; Pennebaker 1997; Runco and Richards 1997). Langer's (1989) suggestions for encouraging mindfulness also lead directly to improved creativity and health.

Many of these ideas are consistent with Skinner's (1983) ideas for "intellectual self-management in old age" and for enjoying old age. The key here is in one's choice of environments. Skinner suggested that as individuals grow older they are less sensitive to environmental cues, support, and information (including sensory information) and they should therefore exaggerate certain aspects of the environment to compensate. This is consistent with all the Operant philosophy, at least in the sense that the environment supports behavior. Skinner gave very simple examples, such as turning up the volume of a stereo when one's hearing begins to fail and writing things down when one's memory appears to work less efficiently. Torrance et al. (1989) suggested much the same for the elderly and proposed "to facilitate healthy growth, it is necessary that the environment somehow encourage the communication of ideas and discoveries. While a stimulating environment may be important, a responsive environment is equally or more important" (p. 125). It may boil down to having the optimal environment— one that is stimulating, but not so stimulating that it is stressful or impossible to cope. Vygotsky's concept of the zone of proximal development captures this idea of optimal environments, though he was thinking of development during childhood and the issue here is late adulthood.

Note that this discussion of how best to use environments is a reminder of the need both to do certain things but also to avoid certain things (blocks, barriers, or nonsupportive environments).

TACTICS SPECIFICALLY FOR DISCOVERY

Discovery is sometimes creative. It may be best to view creativity as one kind of discovery, or perhaps one part of the discovery process. The distinction between discovery and creativity is explored further in the concluding chapter to this textbook. What is useful here is the idea that there are tactics that are particularly useful for discovery. Root-Bernstein's (1989) extensive studies suggested that the following tactics are used by successful discoverers:

1. Train oneself widely.
2. Obtain direct experience rather than vicariously.
3. "Be different but not so different that no one takes you seriously."
4. Court serendipity.
5. Emulate the masters.
6. Utilize trial and error. Recall here what Linus Pauling said: "Just have lots of ideas and throw away the bad ones."
7. Do what makes your heart leap. That, of course, parallels Torrance's idea of falling in love with something, the idea being that you need to invest a great deal of time in something in order to do a good job with it, and in order to invest a great deal of time and give something your full attention, you must really like doing it.
8. Think big. Root-Bernstein believes that something must have "sufficient facets and ramifications." He also ties in to problem finding and quoted Peter Medarwar, who argued that "any scientist of any age who wants to make important discoveries must study important problems."
9. Keep in mind that importance of problem and solution are not dependent on the difficulty.
10. Recognize the importance of good problems, and the idea that you should take care with problem finding and problem definition.
11. "Dare to explore where there is no light."
12. Recognize that novelty is a rich source of creativity. This, of course, is a contrarian idea.
13. Renew old knowledge. This is interesting because it is contrary to contrarian strategies.
14. Challenge expectation.
15. Find a contradiction between theory and data.
16. Utilize error but not confusion. The utilization of errors was also suggested by Skinner and his case study of the scientific method.
17. "Be sloppy enough that something unexpected happens, but not so sloppy that you can't tell what happened."
18. Pay attention to things that don't make sense, especially paradoxes.
19. As Rudberstein summarized, "embrace contradiction." All data are valid, so if you find something that you don't understand but it is based on data, look carefully to make sure you understand it.
20. Create paradoxes, in part by going to the opposite extreme.

21. Ignore the obvious and check assumptions.
22. Recognize anomalies.
23. Never try to solve a problem until you can guess the answer.
24. Speculate.
25. Utilize self-criticism.
26. Consider things that are thought to be impossible.
27. Consider things that are thought to be crazy.
28. Use precision to stimulate imagination. As Root-Bernstein (1989) put it, "the wilder the ideas you wish to propose, the better they must be anchored by the accepted techniques of science" (p. 415).
29. Try to expose the existence of new phenomena rather than confirming already proposed phenomena.
30. Vary conditions over a very wide range. This seems like another way of saying experiment to the extreme.
31. Turn it on its head.
32. Synthesize by diverse research.
33. Recognize what Root-Bernstein called the novice effect: Ignorance is bliss. This makes sense in that someone lacking experience may very well lack assumptions; at the same time, they may reinvent the wheel.
34. Do your own experience with your own hands.
35. Convince yourself and then attempt to convince others.
36. Seek simplicity. This, of course, is just a matter of parsimony.
37. Explore combinations rather than looking for individual items, factors, or variables.
38. Work for a thorough understanding of relevant principles.
39. Seek beauty and appreciate aesthetics.
40. "If the data don't fit the theory, ignore the data."
41. "Not all data supporting the theory are to be believed."
42. Use theories that account for all data, but also recognize "boundary conditions" for deciding which data are relevant.

These show how creativity sometimes plays a role in discovery, and how they also may differ. Root-Bernstein (1989) suggested that an individual be widely trained, for example, whereas Torrance (1995) said exactly the opposite (don't try to be well rounded). Then there is the novice effect. Is it good to be a novice, or should you have a great deal of expertise and collect plenty of data? The third suggestion is very much like Barron's "Dare to be a radical but don't be a damn fool." "Emulate the masters" but not entirely. There is an optimal level of similarity in mentor relationships. Students should not be exactly like a mentor or they may not do original things (Simonton 1984).

Hated Inventions

Less seriously, but perhaps more typical of everyday creativity, is the list of the Most Hated Inventions of All Time. "We hate them. But we need them. They drive us nuts. But we can't live without them. We are talking about the top three most hated inventions." (Aol, 2004). These are:

1. Cell phones
2. Alarm clocks
3. Television.

This list is based on an annual survey from no less than the Massachusetts Institute of Technology. It uses something called the Lemelson-MIT Invention Index. In 2004 the survey was administered to 1023 adults and 500 adolescents. More than 30% listed the cell phone as "the most hated, must-have invention." Yes, it is a "must have." The alarm clock was cited by 25% and the TV by 23%. These figures might have changed if the survey asked merely about "most hated" and did not require "must have." Perhaps one of these others from the MIT survey would have topped the list:

- Shaving razors
- Microwave ovens
- Coffee pots
- Computers
- Vacuum cleaners.

Ninety-five percent of the same sample agreed that inventions made all our lives easier. Adolescents pointed to voicemail and e-mail in this regard, whereas adults cited credit and debit cards.

TECHNIQUES FOR INVENTION

Invention involves some creativity, but these two concepts are not synonymous. Their relationship is explored in the last chapter of this book. For the present purposes it is adequate to view invention as one kind of creative process, with some product (rather than simply self-expression or day-to-day problem solving) as the result.

Weber and Perkins (1992) focused on the invention of the Swiss Army knife. Their analysis suggests that the following tactics were relevant and may have been used: assemble components or parts for complexity; repeat or duplicate a feature (e.g., blades); add, rearrange, or delete a feature; bring independent inventions together; change the scale of the parts or whole; and find ideas in the natural world. They also described how similar tactics might have been used with the invention of the chair. Both the Swiss Army knife and the chair are interesting to consider because they are not frequently viewed as world-changing inventions. We take them for granted—especially the chair. But everyday objects must also be invented! There is creativity in the paperclip, the pencil, and dental floss.

The idea of modifying components is compatible with an older method called attribute listing (Crawford 1954) and with Osborn's (1963) 73 "idea-spurring questions." Attribute listing requires that the critical components of some product are identified and then systematically altered. The attribute might, for example, be softened, hardened, colored, or its shape changed. Things can be added or taken away. Davis (1973) and Mayer (1983) both explored attribute in some detail. Osborn's idea-spurring questions include the following: What can be added? Can it be used in a new way? How can these be combined?

BOX 12.8

WHEN TECHNOLOGY BITES BACK

Many creative insights have resulted from technological improvement. After the lens was invented, for example, theories of astronomy and physiology flourished. Technology does not always help; tools and technologies can facilitate creativity in many ways, but they sometimes backfire. Tenner (1996) outlined many examples where inventions had detrimental effects. McLaren (1993) and Stein (1993) did much the same, citing atomics and genetics. As a matter of fact, an invention does not need to have an undesirable feature to cause problems. This is because stress can be a reaction to good or bad events (Holmes and Rahe 1967). Measures of stress ("events" measures) recognize that people tend to experience stress when they have money problems or interpersonal problems (e.g., divorce), but they also recognize stress with seemingly pleasant events (e.g., weddings, vacations, holidays). Stress is a failure to adapt, and both good and bad things require adaptation. As we shall see in the discussion on health (see Chapter 4), creative skills help people to adapt, but the point here is that all technological advance is potentially stressful. Harm does not result only from evil inventions and things that "bite back" (Tenner's 1996 book is titled, *Why Things Bite Back*).

New technologies do not always improve the creativity of artworks and other products. Consider the digitizing and colorizing of movies. It has been said that certain reformatting has diminished the creativity of movies such as Peter O'Toole's *Lawrence of Arabia*. When it was reformatted much of the desert, and therefore visual appeal, was lost. CDs make it much easier to store and listen to music, but they do not have the dynamic range of good old vinyl (albums). Something is lost, something is gained.

Weber and Perkins (1992) focused on search strategies for creative invention. These are used to find useful information and identify good options. Perkins and Weber listed these search strategies:

- Sheer chance ("an active searcher poking into all sorts of matters")
- Cultivating chance ("searcher deliberately exposes him- or herself to wide semirandom input")
- Systematized chance ("systematic survey of a sizable number of possibilities within a defined set")
- Fair bet ("prototypes a possibility with reasonable expectations that it will serve with modifications")
- Good bet ("prototypes from principle and experience")
- Safe bet ("derives by formal methods something that almost certainly will work") (pp. 321–322).

Logsdon (1993), an aerospace engineer, pointed to six specific strategies: taking a fresh look at interactions, restating the problem, visualizing fruitful analogies, searching for useful order-of-magnitude changes, staying alert to happy serendipity, and breaking your problem apart and putting it back together. For the first strategy, which focuses on interactions, Logsdon gave the example of lunar astronauts who were in groups of three but then broke into a dyad for the actual lunar landing. In a sense, this is a kind of questioning of assumptions. Logsdon pointed to prisons and the penal system as containing problems that might be solved with his fresh interaction strategies. He notes, for example, how the labor intensity might be minimized by delivering meals and the like through conveyor belts. Here again you see his engineering background. The order-of-magnitude changes are similar to what was labeled "level of analysis" earlier, with Thomas Edison given as an example. Instead of inventing specific things, like the lightbulb, Edison decided to invent a mechanism by which things could be invented. The mechanism was the invention laboratory, which was indeed incredibly successful.

THE TACTICS OF THOMAS EDISON

Thomas Edison was very strategic in his work. Burke (1995) identified the six rules that Edison used: define the need, set a clear goal and stick to it, analyze the process and stages involved, assess objectively the progress, keep each team member on task, and record the work for possible examination at a later time. This is interesting because it suggests that there were tactics involved, and it also helps to distinguish between Edison's focus, which was innovation and invention, and not creativity.

TRIZ

There is also a model called *TRIZ* (taken from a Russian phrase), which details an even larger number of tactics for invention. Tate and Domb (1997a, 1997b) summarized 40 of these "principles" (see also Altshuller 1986; Savransky 2000):

1. *Segmentation*: Divide an object into separate parts. Examples include: personal computers instead of a mainframe, divided window blinds instead of one large window covering, and small delivery trucks instead of a large fuel-inefficient truck (Tate & Domb, 1997).
2. *Removal*: Remove any part that interferes or single out the one vital part. For example, the important part of a watchdog may be the bark, and this can be reproduced electronically.
3. *Local quality*: Restructure from uniform to nonuniform. Insure that each part of an object fulfills a unique function. Examples include: erasers on pencils and nail pullers on hammers.
4. *Asymmetry*: Alter the shape of objects (e.g., symmetrical to asymmetrical). Asymmetrical objects may improve if the degree of asymmetry is increased.
5. *Merge*: Bring similar or identical objects together. Bring operations together in time, or make them parallel or contiguous. Examples: Lawnmowers that cut and mulch, parallel processing computers, computer chips mounted on each side of a circuit board.

6. *Universality*: Design things that have several functions; other objects thus become unnecessary and can be eliminated. A toothbrush handle may contain the toothpaste, for example, or a child's stroller can also be used as a car safety seat.

7. *Nesting*: Put small things inside larger things. Luggage sets, for instance, are often sold or stored this way, as are measuring cups and of course Russian dolls. Jets often have retractable landing gear.

8. *Antiweight*: Merge objects to compensate or better distribute weight. A foaming agent can be injected into logs to insure that they float, for example, and helium balloons can be used to lift advertising posters.

9. *Preliminary antiaction*: Any motion or action that has both useful and harmful results might be replaced with "antiactions" which control the harm. Buffers in medicine and high pH substances exemplify this. An object can be prepared or pre-stressed such that it will oppose later unwanted stress. The rebar used in concrete does this sort of thing. Also consider the lead aprons used to protect humans from X-rays, or even masking before painting.

10. *Preliminary action*: Prepare an object, apply something when it is still easy to do. Wallpaper is sometimes pre-pasted, for instance, and surgical instruments are always sterilized. Objects can also be arranged before the work to make that work more efficient (e.g., Kanban arrangements in a just-in-time factory).

11. *Cushion beforehand*: If actions or objects are unreliable, prepare for their unwanted results before doing or using them. A reserve or "back-up" parachute is a good idea, especially given the potential results of an unreliable primary parachute.

12. *Equipotentiality*: Limit changes of position to make actions or objects more efficient. The locks in the Panama Canal show this, as do many springloaded deliveries in some factories.

13. *Invert*: Start with the inside instead of the outside, or the top instead of the bottom. Instead of rotating a tool, rotate the object to which it is connected. Move the sidewalk, not the pedestrians.

14. *Curvature and spheroidality*: Use curvilinear tools, forms, or parts instead of rectilinear ones. Arches and domes are often used in architecture. Weightlifting may be more effective with a spiral gear, for this provides continuous resistance. There is also often a benefit to the use of rotary motion instead of linear (e.g., the rotary engine, a ball point pen, and even the punch or block of martial artists), or sometimes centrifugal forces are best (e.g., spin cycle in a clothes washer).

15. *Dynamics*: Environments or objects may find their own optimal shape and motion if allowed to do so. Consider a seat with adjustable back support, for example. It may help along these lines to alter a rigid object so it is flexible (e.g., the boroscope for examinations of engines or the sigmoidoscope for medical examinations).

16. *Partial or exaggerated action*: It is difficult to accomplish 100% of an action in one attempt; break it down into several attempts. Alternatively, exaggerate, as is done with overspraying when painting (then removing the excess afterwards).

17. *Consider other dimensions*: Cutting tools sometimes now have five axes and thereby position easily, as needed. Computer chips can be mounted on both sides of a circuit board.

18. *Mechanical vibration*: Vibration or oscillation sometimes has benefits and should be applied. The electric carving knife is a very clear example of this, and induction furnaces are sometimes used to mix alloys. Sometimes the trick is to increase the frequency of the movement.

19. *Periodic action*: Pulsating action sometimes works better than continuous action. Don't force it—use a hammer! Sirens are best when they pulsate, and CPR requires a particular ratio of chest compressions to breaths. Again, sometimes the trick is to change the period or frequency of the pulsation.

20. *Continuity of useful action*: Continuous action might be best. All parts in an instrument might best work simultaneously. Think about the printing of certain computer printers (e.g., dot matrix); they print in both directions. Another example: The flywheel in some vehicles stores energy even when the vehicle is not moving.

21. *Skip something*: Avoid unwanted effects. Plastic might be deformed by heat while cutting, so it must be cut fast, before the heat builds. Similarly, a dentist's drill is super fast and this precludes burning tissue.

22. *Look at the "blessing in disguise"*: If you have lemons, make lemonade. Waste might be used to generate electric power. Recycle scraps or waste, or fertilize with it. Firefighters sometimes build fires to keep existing fires from spreading.

23. *Feedback*: Use feedback or crosscheck. Audio circuits now often include an automatic control for volume, and jet autopilots use signals from gyrocompasses.

24. *Intermediary objects or actions*: The nailset used by carpenters (between a hammer and nail) is an intermediary object. A pot holder is used between a hot dish and sensitive hands.

25. *Self-Service*: Utilize the process itself, or its side effects, to make the process more efficient. Animal waste can be used as fertilizer, for example, which then stimulates the growth of the plants the animals can eat. Compost uses old plants to grow new ones.

26. *Copies or variations*: Find an inexpensive or easier alternative. Virtual tours are often less expensive than real ones, for example, and sometimes you can measure an object from its photograph or computer image instead of buying the object or visiting the site. Sonograms exemplify this principle as well.

27. *Inexpensive or short-lived alternatives*: Many paper products, such as paper plates, or plastic products, such as plastic cups, are ideal because there is no need for longevity. Medical supplies are sometimes disposable, as are diapers.

28. *Physical or mechanical substitution*: Physical or mechanical objects are often unnecessary. Instead of an actual fence, for example, a dog may be kept in a yard with an acoustic boundary. Odors are added to gas so leaks are obvious; no mechanical or electronic sensory equipment is needed. In both cases, physical or mechanical objects are replaced with sensory ones.

29. *Hydraulics and pneumatics*: Liquids and gases can sometimes be used more easily or efficiently than solids. Shoes, for example, now sometimes rely on soft gel inserts or soles.

30. *Thin films or flexible shells*: Three-dimensional objects may be cumbersome and replaced with thin films or flexible shells. Reservoirs, for instance, can be protected from weather by floating a film on them. Same for athletic courts of various kinds.

31. *Porous materials*: Solids may also be replaced with porous material. In fact, some objects can be made less expensively if they are porous (less material is used), and objects are usually lighter if they have holes in them. Drill holes!

32. *Change color or lighting*: Lighting and color changes can improve many things for efficiency or other ends. Consider in this regard how darkrooms and submarines use special lights.

33. *Homogeneity*: There are occasional benefits to maintaining substances or bases. Certain containers, for instance, have been made out of the same materials they contain, thereby minimizing unwanted chemical reactions. Diamond cutters are sometimes made of diamonds, as well.

34. *Recover and discard*: Once an object or material has fulfilled its function, it might be best to discard it, as is the case with capsules which dissolve for the ingestion of medicine. A temporary dam can be made of ice, and then allowed to melt when the dam is no longer necessary. Alternatively, there may be a need for recovery of function or structure, as implied by lawnmower blades that sharpen themselves or cars that are "tuned up" any time they operate. No wonder these vehicles can go 100 000 miles or more without a professional tune-up.

35. *Change parameters*: There are frequent benefits to physical or chemical changes, gas to liquid, liquid to solid, and so on. Gases transported in liquid form, for example, require less volume. The consistency or concentration of substances can also lead to benefits. Rubber is more durable and flexible after vulcanization.

36. *Phase transitions*: Phase transitions can generate energy or cause useful physical changes. Pumps may run on the energy of condensation or vaporization, for instance.

37. *Thermal contraction or expansion*: Parts might fit better after thermal contraction or expansion. They might be heated or cooled, then inserted or placed, and then allowed to contract or expand for a good fit.

38. *Oxidation and oxidants*: Some SCUBA divers use certain mixtures for diving at certain depths or extended periods. Pure oxygen is used with acetylene torches, and many medical situations benefit from the administration of oxygen. Some air cleaners collect pollutants with ionized air.

39. *Inert atmospheres*: Work is sometimes easier if substances contain both active ingredients and inert ingredients. They may be easier to handle, measure, or manipulate. Consider detergents or medicines.

40. *Composite materials*: Composites improve golf scores immensely (except those of the author). Jets and airplanes are stronger and yet lighter with composites, as are surfboards (which are now very rarely wooden).

ANALYSES OF ENHANCEMENT EFFORTS

There have been a very large number of attempts to train or enhance creativity. There have been so many studies that a number of review papers have been published that do not report any new data but merely summarize and compile findings from the large number of earlier studies. These are very important because so many of the tactics identified and suggested earlier are based almost entirely on biographical reports and case studies. They might, then, not have much generality but only work for some people, some of the time. That is not such a bad thing, as long as everyone has tactics they can employ when they need to do so.

Nearly 35 years ago, Torrance (1972) found 103 studies designed to enhance creativity, which used his own Torrance Tests of Creative Thinking. His analyses indicated that, of the nine different enhancement programs, the Osborn–Parnes problem-solving approach (which emphasizes brainstorming) was the most effective. A few years later, Mansfield et al. (1978) compared six different approaches to enhancement: (1) the Osborn–Parnes techniques (e.g., brainstorming), (2) the Productive Thinking Program, which emphasizes both convergent and divergent thinking, (3) an audiotape and print program called the Purdue Creative Thinking Program, (4) a perceptual approach, presented in workbooks that were designed by Myers and Torrance, (5) Khatena's Training approach, which targets analogies, transposition, synthesis, breaking away from the obvious, and restructuring, and (6) synectics, which is best known for its focus on "making the strange familiar and making the familiar strange." Mansfield et al. concluded that "most evaluation studies of creativity training programs seem to support the view that creativity can be trained" (p. 531). Importantly, they also pointed out that evidence for generalization and maintenance of effect (to other tasks or the natural environment) was weak at best.

There have been so many studies of the enhancement of creativity that meta-analyses have also been conducted. A meta-analysis uses results from individual studies as data. In what was probably the first meta-analysis of creativity enhancement, Rose and Lin (1984) examined investigations that have used the Torrance Tests of Creative Thinking as the criteria of success or training effectiveness. They categorized enhancement efforts into the following:

- Osborn–Parnes creative problem-solving program (or an adaption of it)
- Covington's productive thinking program
- The Purdue creative thinking program
- Multiple-components programs
- School programs
- Kinesthetic, dramatic, or transcendental meditation efforts.

META-ANALYSIS

Meta-analysis uses the statistical results of previous research as data. A meta-analysis is, then, an analysis of previous analyses. Simplifying some, statistical results of previous studies are standardized and then averaged. The result of the meta-analysis is an *effect size.*

Effect size is the statistical result of a meta-analysis. Usually, an effect size of .80 or higher is a large effect and .50 is moderate (Cohen 1977). An effect size of .20 is small. The effect size (often "eta") indicates the average impact of training across all previous studies. The previous studies may be of various sorts. The individual effects are standardized and then compared and averaged. The individual effects originally may be in the form of means and standard deviations from control and experimental groups or from pretreatment and posttreatment, or they may be originally in the form of a statistic, such as an F-test, t-ratio, or z-score. Each of these can be converted into a standard effect size, which is then averaged in the meta-analysis. Details are given by Cohen (1977), Cooper and Hedges (1994, pp. 232–239), and Wortman and Bryant (1985).

The average overall effect size was .47. There were differences in that the effects were clearer and more profound when the criterion was verbal rather than visual or figural, but of course this makes sense given the nature of the enhancement efforts. The actual enhancement interventions were largely verbal. The most dramatic effects were apparent in the Osborn–Parnes programs (eta = .63). This is a respectable effect size.

These results do not necessarily imply that only verbal creativity is sensitive to training. As a matter of fact, Moga et al. (2000) conducted a meta-analysis that uncovered a significant correlation between art study and figural creativity. There was no impact on the measures of verbal creativity.

Swanson and Hoskyn (1998) also reported a meta-analysis of enhancement efforts but they included only previous studies, which attempted to facilitate the creativity of learning-disabled persons. Their results indicated that the average effect size in this population was comparable to that reported earlier, for other populations. Eta was again approximately .70. Swanson and Hoskyn had very few studies (only three) in their meta-analysis, but what is more important is how many criterion variables are involved. One study can produce more than one effect if it has more than one criterion. If a study measures the impact of enhancement on divergent thinking, for example, there might be a result for ideational fluency, and another for ideational flexibility, and yet another for ideational originality, three effects that can be included in a meta-analysis, all from one study. Swanson and Hoskyn had 11 results or effects in their meta-analysis.

Unfortunately, most of these meta-analyses use different categories when compiling the previous effects. This makes it difficult to compare them. One of the most recent meta-analyses simplified the categories and offered what are probably the clearest conclusions. Scott et al. (2004a) used only four categories. These targeted one of the following for enhancement: (1) divergent thinking (e.g., fluency, flexibility, elaboration, and originality), (2) problem solving (emphasizing actual solutions to problems), (3) production and actual performance, or (4) attitudinal improvement. The resulting overall effect size obtained was .68, but there was quite a bit of variation, implied by a standard deviation of .65. Scott et al. (2004b) reported a meta-analysis that examined 11 types of training: imagery, analogy, open idea production, interactive idea production, creative process, computer-based production, structured idea production, analytical or critical/creative thinking, situated idea production, and conceptual combination. Finally Scott et al. used meta-analysis to assess the effectiveness of each type of training. The average effect size was .78.

One important determinant of the effectiveness of training or enhancement is treatment duration. Clearly, a short training period may have different effects from a longer one! With this in mind Scope (1998) examined 40 effect sizes (from 30 investigations). The average effect size was quite impressive (eta = .90) but most important was that the effect was unrelated to the duration of the training. This relationship was analyzed statistically, the resulting correlation being a nonsignificant .06.

Ma (2006) was also precise in his meta-analysis, for he compared enhancement efforts that either tied creativity to some sort of evaluation or relegated evaluation. Brainstorming, with its explicit requirement that participants postpone evaluation, exemplifies the latter, and problem solving, where good or effective solutions are required, exemplifies the former. Ma also examined the duration of the training as well as the ages of the individuals being trained. He found 34 relevant studies, which gave him 268 effect sizes. The overall average effect size was .77, but again the variation was notable (standard deviation .74). The result of .77 is very close to a large effect size (Cohen 1977). Apparently training can be quite effective.

Ma (2006) reported that the duration of training was unrelated to the effectiveness of training. Enhancement efforts were, on the other hand, more effective with older participants. Ma suggested that older participants responded better to enhancement efforts because of their mature cognitive capacities. The lack of effect for duration is a bit puzzling, but it may be that there was simply too little variation among the various training efforts. Perhaps if training that took place during one school day was compared with training that covered a school year, significant difference might be uncovered and duration would be important. Along the same lines, duration itself is not the only temporal factor. Learning theory suggests that humans learn best from displaced practice, which means that we should study something (or receive training), but then put it aside and do something else, and then come back to the study (or training). Displacement is very important for learning, but it was not involved in the previous studies. Future research might even find that training can be of some short duration if the practice is displaced. Very likely, that would be more effective than any enhancement effort that does not utilize displacement.

CONCLUSIONS

Creativity can be encouraged in many ways in various settings. Yet it may not actually be fulfilled unless it is encouraged on both micro- and macro-levels. Tactics certainly help on the micro-level. They can be taught in the classroom, are easy to learn, and broadly applicable. But there is much more to actually fulfilling potential than just cognitive techniques and problem solving. Creativity will be fulfilled only if it is valued within culture, on the social or macro-level as well.

On the macro-level, creativity can be enhanced by maximizing the benefits and minimizing the costs. Creativity also requires tolerance (Florida 2002; Rubenson and Runco 1995). These are each reflections of cultural values and *zeitgeist,* which we found to be quite powerful in the discussion of the historical perspective on creativity. *Zeitgeist* is abstract but manifests itself in the schools, the home, and organizations. It influences everything within a culture, including views about creative product and creative people.

On a more concrete level, enhancement also involves teaching, encouragement, rewards, and models. These may have maximal impact when they target the attitudes about creativity and when they teach and reinforce specific tactics. These tactics must be appropriate for the age group and domain, but there are a large number of tactics from which to choose.

It might help at this point to offer a framework for the tactics. One framework categorizes tactics along the following dimensions:

- Tactics may focus on problem finding or problem solving.
- Tactics may involve assimilation or accommodation.
- Tactics may be best for children or adults.
- Tactics may be literal (e.g., "change your perspective") or metaphorical ("dig elsewhere").

- Tactics may be forceful and intentional ("make it happen") or passive ("let it happen").
- Tactics may focus on particular stages of the creative process (e.g., incubation, verification).

Not everyone believes that creative talents can be enhanced. There are two reasons for this pessimistic view. One is a misunderstanding of human behavior. Virtually all human behaviors are flexible. They each have a range of reaction. The range is genetically determined, and the skill or behavior is a reaction to the experiences that influence that potential. It is very much like exercising. Not everyone will be an outstanding weight-lifter, but everyone can build muscle. The amount of muscle built will depend on genetic potentials and the amount of exercise. Creative talents depend on the same two things. Weight-lifting may not do much for creativity, but the programs and techniques listed throughout this chapter will very likely increase the likelihood that the individual will behave in a creative fashion.

A second criticism emphasizes the role of spontaneity in creative achievements. This is a viable perspective; spontaneity is often vital for creativity. It was emphasized in Rogers' (1995) theory of self-actualization and often included in descriptions of the creative personality. It is also one of the salient characteristics of children at play. It is logically connected to creative efforts in that individuals are most likely to be themselves if they are spontaneous. They are less likely to be inhibited and more likely to follow intrinsic interests. They are probably also in a mood that allows them to play with ideas and take intellectual risks on original ideas. The problem is that if creativity is self-expression, the self is all important and any extrinsic factors or guidance (even tactics) may bias the process such that it is not truly spontaneous and creative. Tactics are used intentionally and deliberately when the person is trying to solve a problem or find a creative idea.

Then again, recall here the idea of "let it happen" tactics. In fact, this concept can be expanded such that there is a continuum of creative behaviors, with entirely spontaneous actions at one extreme and entirely deliberate and intentional creativity at the other. In between are efforts that recognize the importance of spontaneity but are also deliberate. They are intended to allow spontaneous creative thinking. They are intentional but focus on removing barriers and blocks in order to allow spontaneous creativity to occur. These are, then, less forceful than other tactical efforts. The so-called avoidance tactics are also relevant here, for they too imply that creativity will occur if all the blocks to it are removed. Many of these blocks were mentioned in this chapter, including squelchers and the barriers and inhibitors in the organizational assessments of Amabile and Gryskiewicz (1989), Witt and Boerkrem (1989), and Rickards and Jones (1991).

A Continuum of Effort

Spontaneity...	Let it Happen...	Deliberate Creativity
(Self-expression & Self-actualization)	(by removing barriers)	("make it happen" with tactics)

Let-it-happen tactics recognize that creative thinking may sometimes be best encouraged when it is left alone, or at least allowed to take its own course. Daydreaming is often tied to creative insights, and it can be encouraged or supported. The improvisation suggested by

Lemons (2005) may have the same benefit. He described how improvisation can be used to enhance creativity in educational settings (also see Sawyer 1992).

Another example of let-it-happen creativity is suggested by what Wittgenstein (quoted by Runco 1994a) called "the disappearance of the problem." This often has been reported by creative people who are intensely interested in their work, or some particular task, and as a result become immersed in it. They apparently lose sight of their problems. More accurately, the problems become a part of themselves. The problem is no longer "out there" but is a part of one's being. But problems are still solved; they do not just go away. They change their location, almost as if internalized. Root-Bernstein et al. (1993, 1995) described something like this as a kind of *empathizing*. In their words, "personal identification with the elements of a problem releases the individual from viewing the problem in terms of its previously analyzed elements. A chemist makes a problem familiar to himself [or herself] through equations combining molecules and the mathematics of the phenomenological order. On the other hand, to make a problem strange the chemist may personally identify with the molecules in action" (p. 37). It is likely that problems will disappear (or never really be seen as problems) if the individual follows intrinsic interests. Immersion is likely, and sometimes unintentional, and spontaneity may not be hindered.

This line of thought assumes that what are sometimes called "the object" and "the self" are not separated. They are not placed in separate categories. This also implies that something can be done intentionally, for categories can be manipulated. They can be used in a flexible way. Langer (1989) has demonstrated this several times in her research on *mindfulness*, with improvements in creative thinking and health. Something similar is suggested by Csikszentmihalyi's (1996) description of the *flow* state, and by the Zen view of creative thinking (Pritzker 1999). Simplifying a great deal, a Zen view is that categories should be avoided and that we should instead focus on feelings and direct experiences. This worldview can be nurtured.

Recall here Pasteur's statement that "chance favors the prepared mind." This is directly relevant to the present discussion. It suggests how creativity can be a result of both tactical creativity and serendipitous, accidental, and chance encounters. Deliberate creativity does not preclude serendipity, nor do the various serendipitous discoveries in history (e.g., the Post-It note) mean that creative work cannot be intentional and tactical. How can ideas be both deliberate and accidental? Experience cannot be completely controlled; chance always plays a role. Yet the individual can be intentionally open to surprise and the unexpected. That is one of the benefits of the tactics and deliberate efforts outlined above—a prepared mind. If environments and experiences are carefully chosen and constructed, the prepared mind will value creativity and enjoy new and original things, in addition to having procedures and heuristics for dealing with challenges and problems in a creative fashion.

Conclusion: What Creativity is and What it is Not

INTRODUCTION

A few years ago I suggested that everyone avoid the term *creativity* altogether. I proposed this because the term is used in so many ways, and yet has a great deal of uncertainty. I did not suggest that all forms of the word be avoided, just creativity as a noun. I was really just asking for more precision, and thus suggested that we instead use "creative"—the adjective—as in creative art, creative products, creative behavior, creative thinking, creative geniuses, creative eras, and so on.

I am less enthusiastic about dropping the term creativity after reading Bryson's (2003) *Short History of Nearly Everything*. This is because he reminded me how much ambiguity exists in all sciences, even the hard sciences. The ambiguity that is apparent in definitions of creativity is not any more dramatic than that which you find in physics, chemistry, and biology. Ambiguity in fact may be inherent in scientific work; after all, we are exploring a complex universe replete with unknown qualities. Further, ambiguity has its advantages. It may allow wider consideration or application, for example, and it may be a kind of catalyst for further research. The present chapter explores connections between creativity and innovation, imagination, intelligence, originality, problems solving, and so on. Each is associated with creativity, but each is also distinct. Much can be learned by attempting to pinpoint the overlap and distinctiveness.

Some of the critical distinctions were covered in earlier chapters. Chapter 1, for example, went into some detail about the relationships between creativity and problem solving, and creativity and traditional intelligence. The second of these is one of the more significant distinctions because if creativity were merely a kind of intelligence, there would be little need to study creativity. Everything we knew about intelligence would apply to creativity. Additionally, there would be no need to target creative talents or encourage creative students or employees. Basic intelligence could be encouraged and creative talent would tag along. Similarly, managers could just hire the brightest, and since they would be intelligent, they would also be creative. But the data suggest that there may be a threshold, such that creativity and intelligence are related only at the lower levels. The data also suggest that much depends on how "creativity" and "intelligence" are defined and measured (Runco & Albert 1986b; Sosik et al. 1998). It may be that what was said about creativity as a noun also applies to intelligence. It is safe to say that creativity tends to be independent of traditional intelligence, but there are also measures and data that suggest an interplay (e.g., "creative intelligence").

This kind of interplay has been examined in several recent studies. Runco and Smith (1992), for example, developed various measures of judgmental or evaluative skill. These tapped what might be called critical thinking, though the actual judgments might not have been literally critical. They could be appreciative as well. These judgments concerned the originality and creativity of ideas. Examinees were not required to generate ideas but instead were asked to evaluate them. Results indicated that various groups (e.g., parents, teachers) were only moderately accurate when identifying and rating the originality and creativity of ideas. They were not much more accurate when judging their own ideas! Accuracy ranged from about 20% (meaning that 20% of the original ideas were identified as such) to just about 50%. Significantly, people who gave more original ideas were also better at recognizing original ideas. This is one example of an interplay of skills.

The overarching purpose of this chapter is to draw from the previous chapters, and research summarized therein, in order to offer a theory of what creativity is, and what it is not. We begin by addressing the following questions: How is creativity related to intelligence, originality, discovery, and adaptability? Another set of questions also helps to define what creativity is and is not, including these: Does creativity require unconscious processes, or can it be deliberate? What role does chance play? We then turn to issues of distribution. Is everyone creative?

IMAGINATION

Imagination is frequently associated with creativity. Yet there is a distinction. This is suggested by Singer's (1999) definition of imagination as a special feature or form of human thought characterized by the ability of the individual to reproduce images or concepts originally derived from basic senses but now reflected in one's consciousness as memories, fantasies, or future plans. These sensory derived images ('pictures in the mind's eye'), mental conversations, or remembered or anticipated smells, touches, tastes, or movements can be reshaped and recombined into new images or possible featured dialogues that may range all the way from regretful ruminations to rehearsals or practical planning for upcoming job interviews or other social interactions and, in some cases, to the production of creative works of art that occur in literature and science (pp. 13–14).

Creative efforts may be independent of images and imagery.

An interplay between creativity and imagination can be seen in the recent work of Root-Bernstein and Root-Bernstein (2006). They examined the *worldplay* of several groups, including winners of a MacArthur Award (the so-called "genius grants"). College students represented a control group. Worldplay was defined as a kind of imagined location, which was often inhabited by imagined beings or people. Some people explore such imaginary worlds regularly. In fact, the Root-Bernsteins included persistence in their definition. Individuals who employed or enjoyed worldplay did so on a regular basis. They may have also used that worldplay in their lives. It was not just childhood fancy.

Imaginary worlds are sometimes known as *paracosms*. These are probably most common around nine years of age and typically fade in the teenage years. Root-Bernstein et al. (1995) referred to five kinds of paracosms, including those which include (1) places, (2) toys, (3) languages and documents, (4) imagined countries, islands, and peoples, and (5) "idyllic worlds" (p. 5). There are sex differences, with girls often focusing on relationships and personal interactions and boys focusing on histories, and interactions less tied to emotional events.

Paracosms and worldplay have at least five benefits. They

- exercise the imagination,
- exercise playfulness,
- contribute to problem-solving capacity,
- allow people to revisit and control their experiences, and
- suggest to the individual that there are possibilities beyond reality and beyond what is given.

Worldplay "should not be confused with the disturbing fantasies of some psychotic children and teens but belongs to children who clearly distinguish what is imagined and what is real." (p. 4). Note the key role of discretion in this definition. Worldplay is used intentionally and is a matter of choice. That is a critical point, as we will see later.

Interestingly, Root-Bernstein and Root-Bernstein (2006) felt that:

children who create make believe worlds frequently do so in ways that are materially inventive. They document and formalize what is playfully imagined by composing alphabets and languages, writing down stories and histories, and drawing pictures and maps. Such documentation may, in fact, be regarded as a sine qua non for world play in its most recognizable guise, thus differentiating it from other forms of creative play involving imaginative re-enactment, imaginary friends, or daydreams (p. 406).

Root-Bernstein and Root-Bernstein (2006) found that approximately 40% of the winners of a MacArthur Award reported inventing imaginary worlds during their childhood. This was, however, a self-report. Somewhat surprisingly, approximately the same number of students from Michigan State University recorded having experienced worldplay in childhood. When more stringent criteria were applied to the data, these figures were cut nearly in half, with only approximately 20% of the imaginary worlds qualifying. Indeed, after various adjustments, Root-Bernstein et al. concluded that the most accurate frequency of worldplay was somewhere between 5 and 26%.

Worldplay was more likely in some domains than others to be retained and used in adulthood. It was most common (58%) in individuals working in the humanities, somewhat common in social scientists (46%), and less frequent and common in artists (30%) and publications professionals (31%). These figures were very different from the domain differences in the control group of college students: Students majoring in the arts were the most likely to have worldplay (50%).

Creativity and imagination are also both apparent when an individual has an imaginary friend. They may see the friend, for example, or have other sensory evidence of the friend, and children who have them seem to test higher in creative potential (Schaefer & Anastasi 1968; Taylor 1999).

CREATIVE VERSUS VIRTUAL IMAGINATION

Stravinsky (1970) distinguished between *creative imaginative* and *virtual imagination*. The latter is entirely private and often ephemeral. The former allows this to become articulated and communicated, and perhaps formalized. It usually has a concrete medium such as scientific work or artistic endeavor.

The imagination is used for more than just imaginary friends. One category of play is labeled imaginary play. It is distinct from sociodramatic play, parallel play, and solitary play. It may be somewhat cognitively demanding. Children do not play imaginatively until the age of two years. This may be because imaginative play relies on symbolic schema. The same cognitive abilities that allow a child to learn and use language—translating a symbol into meaning—may allow a child to pretend (e.g., be creative in their pretending to use a bar of soap as a ray gun, or dress up like mom and dad).

Imagination might most simply be defined in terms of a transcendence of reality. Creativity, because it must be effective as well as original, may rely less on transcendence than does imagination, though it is quite possible that imagination feeds the first part of creativity, but later judgments and discretion come into play to insure that an idea or solution is effective (and if both original and effective, "creative").

Dewey (1910) saw a connection of imagination with reflective thinking. More recent theories tend to recognize two different categories: reproductive imagination and creative imagination (e.g., Betts 1916; Colello 2007). Reproductive imagination is characterized by the capability to reproduce mental images described by others or images from less accurate recollections of reality. This type of imagination is comprised of four characteristics, namely crystallization, dialectics, effectiveness, and transformation (Liang et al. 2012). In contrast, creative imagination focuses on the attributes of initiation and originality. This type of imagination is composed of six characteristics, namely exploration, focusing, intuition, novelty, productivity, and sensibility (Liang et al. 2012).

Imagination is especially important to fields where a vision is useful, such as film and theater. No wonder there is quite a bit of research in these fields devoted to imagination. Laurier and Brown (2012), for instance, described how "imagination, in the context of video/film production, can be perceived as the inter-subjective task of seeing the film-that-is-to-come through what is currently completed, what is missing, and what needs to be added."

ORIGINALITY

Originality is more difficult to separate from creativity. This is because creative things are always original. They are more than just original, but they must be in some way original. That originality may take the form of novelty, uniqueness or unusualness, or unconventionality.

Recall, however, the question of whether or not ideas, products, and solutions can actually be original. There are two sides to this question.

- Has everything been thought (and perhaps put into words) before, by others?
- Are all our ideas, even the seemingly new (original) ones, tied to other ideas? If so, they are not entirely original but merely extensions of thought.

The question of originality goes back thousands of years, at least to Plato. His discussion with Meno covers the question of "Where does knowledge come from?" Also, "How can new knowledge be created from existing knowledge?" Plato's ideas were speculative, however, and in some ways metaphysical. They were not what we might consider to be scientific.

A more recent take on this is presented by Hausman (1989), who implied that we cannot really be creative but instead merely adapt old ideas into seemingly new ones.

The distinction between "thought before" and "put into words" really complicates things. There would be no way, of course, to check what has been thought before! Thoughts can be quite fleeting. Then there is the problem of self-awareness: We often don't realize where our thoughts come from, and sometimes we don't ourselves remember the thoughts we already had! B. F. Skinner expressed great frustration, late in his life, because his memory deteriorated and he would apparently often work on exciting new projects, only to discover, after investing huge amounts of time, that he had already explored that line of thought in his youth! He just did not remember doing it! He referred to it as a kind of plagiarism, albeit plagiarism of himself.

The second issue is also quite difficult. After all, what constitutes a truly original idea? How different does it need to be from other ideas to be "original?" And even if something is related to what came before, surely it can itself be original. This is a practical issue, because many tactics direct individuals to "mere extensions" of existing ideas. In Chapter 12, for example, there are tactics for "turning a problem on its head," minifying the situation, magnifying, looking to nature, finding an analogy, and many others that imply that you start with a given but then find new ideas by changing that given. The originality of the results might be questioned. Then again, many famous creators have done exactly this. They in some way have "borrowed, adapted, or stolen" from others. Shakespeare apparently did not develop all the plots in his plays, though his characterization and language was incredibly creative. Benjamin Franklin is famous in part for his aphorisms (e.g., "an apple a day," "a penny saved," "early to bed"). Yet many of these were a part of dialogue at this time; he just found a good phrasing and printed the suggestions.

Welling (2007) seemed to think that extensions, adaptations, and analogies might be original in their own right. He coined the label *application* to explain this: "A creative cognitive operation that is often mentioned in the literature on creativity might be identified as *application:* the adaptive use of existing knowledge in its habitual context …. This operation consists of the creative adaptation of existing conceptual structures to fit normally occurring variations."

The opposite view is also possible. Mandler (1995), for example, suggested that "no repetition is very truly entirely that; there is always something novel in whatever we do or say" (p. 11). Thus everything is original! That view is consistent with Runco's (1996d) idea that creativity always depends on personal interpretations of experience, though in this theory there are creative and uncreative ideas and actions. Recall also Weisberg's (1986) idea that creative thinking is not really different from other kinds of problem solving.

Cropley et al. (2008) insisted on effectiveness in their definition of functional creativity. They noted that "for a product to be regarded as creative, it must possess not only novelty, but also relevance and effectiveness. In other words, a creative product must be not only original and surprising (novelty); it must also satisfy the need for which it was created" (Cropley et al. 2008). This view applies very broadly to any unambiguous creativity, for all creativity must have some fit, appropriateness, or effectiveness, along with originality. Runco (1988) referred to it as utility, a label chosen because it has been operationalized in one branch of the social and behavioral sciences (i.e., economics). Without utility or effectiveness, an idea is just original and it may be bizarre and worthless, which means uncreative.

Frequently the criteria of originality and effectiveness are applied to products rather than performances or people. Indeed, this leads us to one of the concepts that overlaps with creativity but should be kept distinct. I am referring to *innovation*. How exactly is innovation related to creativity?

There are problems with the definition of creativity that emphasizes originality and appropriateness. Originality, for example, always begs the question of "in which context" or "against which standards?" What is original for one person, in one context or setting, may not be original for all persons or in other settings. This problem may not come up when studying eminent levels of creative achievement; these are often original regardless of context. The problem arises when thinking about any other level of creative behavior. It is especially obvious when a child is original, but only in the sense that he or she has an idea or finds a solution that is personally new but not original against more general norms or standards. Surely that child *is* original and is showing his or her creative potential even if the idea or solution is not unique in the history of the world.

Another problem is suggested by the fact that things change. In fact, original things may start out being new but then become part of the status quo. Hausman and Anderson (2012, last page of body of chapter) described how

> Einstein's hypotheses were inappropriate in the context of what was expected, that is, in terms of Newtonian assumptions. Cezanne's advances beyond impressionism were inappropriate in terms of the context of painting styles in the latter part of the nineteenth century—that is, before Cezanne created new kinds of style or new ways of being appropriate and which initially even critics who accepted his innovations were at a loss to find adequate descriptive terms—thus they resorted to metaphors ("architectonic" and

"plasticity") that were later accepted as showing some of the appropriateness of Cezanne's way of paint-ing... . It is the individualized character of the creation that prompts us to regard it as a new kind of thing—just as Cezanne's style in his earliest period, a period of unbroken color areas, among other things, evolved into a new style. Cezanne created a new kind of painting, a new way of painting, and he did so by the indi-vidual qualities of brush strokes and broken outlines. In short, an outcome is a creation by virtue of its exhibiting something intelligible in a way that was unprecedented. And it gained its intelligibility through breaking with formerly known ways of making things intelligible, things that were intelligible through knowledge of common properties or characteristics that were repeated and thus identifiable in terms of formerly known kinds.

INNOVATION AND CREATIVITY

Creative things are always original, but originality is not sufficient for creativity. There must be some usefulness as well. Creative things solve a problem or have some utility of some sort. Yet this also describes innovation. How is creativity related to innovation? (Box 13.1).

There are several ways to distinguish creativity from innovation. Of course, there is likely to be some overlap, and individuals who want innovative employees certainly should hire prospects with creative potential. They should also encourage creative thinking. Yet creative thinking is not necessarily innovative. You might say that innovation represents one application of creative thinking.

Innovation has been defined as "the intentional introduction and application within a job, work-team, or organization of ideas, processes, products, or procedures, that are new to that job, work-team, or organization that are designed to benefit that job, work-team, or organiza-tion" (West & Rickards 1999). West and Farr (1991, p. 16) similarly defined innovation as "the intentional introduction and application within a role, group, or organization of ideas, pro-cesses, products or procedures, new to the relevant unit of adoption, designed to significantly benefit role performance, the group, the organization or the wider society. The element need not be entirely novel or unfamiliar to members of the group, but it must involve some dis-cernable change or challenge to the status quo." There are commonalities in these two defini-tions, but the second includes "designed specifically to benefit role performance, the group, the organization, or the wider society." This suggests one difference between creativity and innovation. Creative efforts are often self-expressive and intrinsically motivated.

Of relevance to this last point, Clydesdale (2006) distinguished creativity from innovation by suggesting that the former is driven by intrinsic motives, whereas the latter is driven by extrinsic incentives and "the need to surpass previous standards" (p. 21). West (2002, p. 356) stated the matter quite explicitly: "Creativity is the development of ideas, while innovation ... is the application of [those] ideas." Sometimes "application" is called implementation or even exploitation (Bledow et al. 2009; Roberts 1988) (Boxes 13.2 and 13.3).

Another difference between creativity and innovation is the amount of constraint. Because innovations are always implemented, there is more constraint. In fact, there is often a con-sumer! It is almost as if businesses interested in innovation are microcosms of the more gen-eral cultural microcosm sometimes described in terms of the tension and interplay of "stability and change."

It is possible that innovative products, more often than not, are initiated by someone at a fairly low level of the organizational hierarchy, while process innovations (or at least

BOX 13.1

CREATIVITY IN THE MOVIES—AND IN YOUR PASSWORD!

Are directors more or less creative today, compared with 20 and 30 years ago? If we compare the number of movie-goers today with the 1960s and 1970s, we see an upward trend, and if we are not careful this might be taken to indicate that there is more draw today, due to an increase in talent. Another quantitative but misleading indicator is "gross" profit. Again, there is no comparison: Today's movies (and the individuals involved in making them) make much more money. Is this because they are better films? You actually could argue precisely the opposite, namely, that today's films are less creative. After all, think of the number of remakes in the theaters today! *Batman*, *Superman*, and *Cat Woman* have all been remade (and they were originally TV shows), along with *Mr. Deeds*, *Guess Who's Coming to Dinner*, *The Longest Yard*, *Bewitched*, and innumerable others (Figure 13.1). Surely a remake is not as original as the original. Yet they make more money and have more viewers. If we use such indicators of creativity (fame, profit, impact, reputation, attributions), we would be misled.

This does become a complicated line of argument, in part because actors may be creative in their interpretation of a part (Nemiro 1999). Or consider the musical domain: Someone may write a song, and another person may perform it, but surely the performer can be creative in his or her interpretation and the specifics of the performance. This would be most obvious in improvisational performances (Sawyer 1992) but is probably true of anything short of mimicry. Similarly, in the theater, a remake may have an unoriginal plot and so on, but it may still present original (and potentially creative) performances.

Even the Beatles produced creative works that were not entirely original, as does any musician who sings a song written by someone else. Their early records included mostly remakes (e.g., *Rollover Beethoven*) (Clydesdale 2006). Perhaps a remake can present a creative interpretation of the original. Perhaps remakes in the movies and music allow creative interpretations, even if the lyrics or plot is unoriginal.

Sometimes a similar lack of originality is actually costly. Data scientist Nick Berry described a "staggering lack of imagination" when people selected their PINs and passwords.

> Nearly 11% of the 3.4 million four-digit passwords he analyzed were 1234. The second most popular PIN in is 1111 (6% of passwords), followed by 0000 (2%). Last year SplashData compiled a list of the most common numerical and word-based passwords and found that "password" and "123456" topped the list. … People have even less imagination in choosing five-digit passwords—28% use 12345. The fourth most popular seven-digit password is 8675309, inspired by the Tommy Tutone song. People love using couplets for their PINs: 4545, 1313, etc. And for some reason, they don't like using pairs of numbers that have larger numerical gaps between them. Combinations like 45 and 67 occur much more frequently than 29 and 37. The 17th most common 10-digit password is 3141592654 (for those of you who are not math nerds, those are the first digits of Pi) (Scherzer 2012).

There are times, like finding names, passwords, and PINs, where originality is of huge importance.

FIGURE 13.1 There have been quite a number of movies about RMS *Titanic*, the ship that sank in 1912. *Source: Wikimedia Commons. This media file is in the public domain in the United States. This applies to U.S. works where the copyright has expired, often because its first publication occurred prior to January 1, 1923. http://commons.wikimedia.org/wiki/ File:TitanicNew_York_Herald_front_page.jpeg.*

BOX 13.2

EFFECTIVE BUT UNORIGINAL PUBLIC SPEAKING

Abraham Lincoln's Gettysburg Address was a masterpiece. It was short, original, and poignant. His speech delivered at Cooper Union in New York City, in 1860, was quite different. Unlike the Gettysburg Address, it immediately impressed the audience. More importantly, it was highly effective, but not very original.

Rhodehamel (2005) described Lincoln's intention in this fashion: "What had the Framers of the Constitution intended? Did they mean to give Congress power to regulate slavery in the territories?" To answer this Lincoln "immersed himself in the journals of the Constitutional Convention and the proceedings of early Congresses. What he found in the historical record allowed him ... to retrospectively recruit the founding fathers, including those who had owned slaves, to the antislavery cause." His speech went a long way to aiding his election. Apparently, "when this 'weird, rough, and uncultivated' Westerner began to speak, he was transformed. The audience was carried away with admiration for the 'iron chain of his argument,' his 'unanswerable disposition of the great agitating questions.'" For 90 minutes "he held his audience in the hollow of his hand."

His speech was highly effective but not very original. Little that Lincoln said that night was new, but the audience (and, more important, the hundreds of thousands who soon read the speech in newspapers and pamphlets) agreed that no one had ever put the antislavery message more clearly or forcefully. When he finished, the ovation was "wild and prolonged." Perhaps all public speaking is like that: Effectiveness is vital, and originality secondary.

---

innovations in administrative procedure) tend to start at higher levels of the organization (Damanpour & Evan 1984).

We might use our own "borrow and adapt" tactic, as described in Chapter 12, and infer that there is a threshold of creativity that is necessary for innovation. Innovation certainly requires some level of originality, but not maximal novelty, whereas creative efforts may benefit from extreme originality. As a matter of fact, Runco (2006a) suggested that innovation is different from creativity in the balance of originality-to-effectiveness (Figure 13.2; Box 13.5). Innovation often requires that the result is maximally effective (it should sell or be publicly useful). Originality is secondary, though necessary. In creative performances that are not innovative, such as the arts, originality may be much more important, whereas effectiveness is secondary. There novelty and self-expression may be much more important than public effectiveness.

One of the myths about both creativity and innovation is that they necessarily lead to a product. Though sometimes true, this is not always the case. Look back at the definition of innovation, with its recognition of "ideas, processes, products, or procedures." Similarly, creativity is sometimes self-expression, and there is no tangible product. Although creativity may lead to a product, it may not.

One of the major approaches to the study of creativity emphasizes products (the other major perspectives focus on the creative personality, process, or place). O'Quin and Besemer

BOX 13.3

INNOVATION, ENTREPRENEURSHIP, AND CREATIVITY

Nystrom (1995) suggested that creativity is distinct from both innovation and entrepreneurship. He viewed innovation as "the result and implementation of creativity. It is the process of bringing new ideas into use" (p. 66). Entrepreneurship, in contrast, was defined as "the visualization and realization of new ideas by insightful individuals, who were able to use information and mobilize resources to implement their visions" (p. 67). Significantly, Nystrom implied that entrepreneurs may not be outstandingly creative. His view "does not require entrepreneurs to be highly skilled in generating new ideas, but instead emphasizes the promotion and implementation of radical change" (p. 67). For Nystrom, an entrepreneur might revise and implement but need not be creative; the creativity may come from other individuals. He claimed that entrepreneurs "just as often base their entrepreneurship on the ideas of others" (p. 67). Nystrom also brought invention into the mix, for he believes that, unlike entrepreneurs, inventors may "lack the entrepreneurial skills necessary to evaluate and promote their ideas" (p. 68). Theories of entrepreneurship often do emphasize talents such as risk tolerance and sound judgment

about opportunities. It may be that a minimum level of creative talent is necessary, much like the threshold of intelligence that is necessary but not sufficient for creativity (Runco & Albert 1986b). It of course would be a threshold of creative potential (cf. Ames & Runco 2005).

It also would be wise to view entrepreneurship as a complex, given that requisite creative talents, judgment of opportunities, and risk tolerance may each be involved.

Jeraj and Antoncic (in press) distinguished *entrepreneurial curiosity* from other kinds of curiosity (e.g., social, epistemic, sensory, curiosity involvement). This distinction was validated with two samples of actual entrepreneurs, one from the United States and one from Slovenia. Jeraj and Antoncic (in press) justified this research in part by citing previous empirical results (Baptista & Thurik 2007), as well as the *Schumpeter Effect*. The Schumpeter Effect describes how increased employment and economic growth follow from increases in rates of entrepreneurship. Jeraj and Antoncic (in press) argued that this sort of thing would be the most likely if we are better able to understand the entrepreneurial process, including the role of curiosity.

FIGURE 13.2 Proposed continuum allowing a balance of originality and effectiveness in creative efforts.

(1989) developed a sophisticated rubric for evaluating the creativity of products, and many definitions of creativity emphasize products. This approach is quite objective, and often useful, but there is a better, more parsimonious way to view creative products and inventions.

And of course they may result from the creative process or the innovation process. The relationship between inventiveness and creativity is explored later.

PERSON, PROCESS, PRODUCT, PLACE, PERSUASION, AND POTENTIAL

The major approaches to creativity are *person* (or *personality*), *process*, *product*, or *place* (or *press*) (see Rhodes 1961; Richards 1999; Runco 2004). Simonton (1990a) added *persuasion*, the idea being that creative people change the way other people think, and Runco (2003c) lobbied for *potential* in an attempt to redirect research and educational attention back to "the people that need us the most," namely those with potential but lacking the skills to express themselves.

Once again, care must be taken with the word "creativity." It is imprecise. It either should be avoided as a noun and used only in its adjectival form (e.g., "creative products"), or at least be used with much more precision. Cropley et al. (2008) seemed to feel this way when they described functional creativity. In their words, "for a product to be regarded as creative, it must possess not only novelty, but also relevance and effectiveness. In other words, a creative product must be not only original and surprising (novelty); it must also satisfy the need for which it was created" (Cropley et al. 2008). They concluded that "without relevance and effectiveness, the product is merely aesthetic." This is quite helpful because creative things may have aesthetic utility, at least for the individual. That is where personally creative behaviors show their effectiveness. Of course, the definition presented by Cropley et al. does not require that all creativity leads to products. Sadly, some definitions of creativity do imply just that. Several of these are presented in Box 13.4.

BIASES IN THE CREATIVITY LITERATURE—AND IN PRACTICE?

- *Art Bias*: The misunderstanding of creativity that equates it with artistic talent. The result: Only individuals with artistic talent are labeled creative. This of course would be a problem in the classroom.

- *Product Bias*: The assumption that all creativity (or all innovation, for that matter) is manifested in a tangible product. It may be best to view products as inventions, though the process leading up to them may be creative or innovative.

Bandura (1997) implied that creativity is what comes first, and is highly personal, and innovation may follow if the individual is persistent. In his words,

BOX 13.4

PRODUCT DEFINITIONS

- A "creative idea will be defined simply as one that is both novel and useful (or influential) in a particular social setting …. The definition captures the cultural relativity of creativity (using a lever to move a rock might be judged novel in a Cro-Magnon civilization, but not in a modern one), and it also captures the distinction between the creative and the merely eccentric or mentally ill (novelty without utility)" (Flaherty 2005, p. 147).
- "Creativity involves an original approach to a problem or product within a given domain of study" (Solomon et al. 1999, p. 273).
- "One essential component of creativity is *originality* …. A second component of creativity is *utility* …. A final component of creativity is that it must lead to a *product* of some kind" (Andreasen 2005).
- "Even though creativity begins as an inner process—a feeling or an idea—it must also produce an observable result …. Just being oneself is not being creative. Children's thoughts and feelings may be interesting and important but

thoughts and feelings are not creative per se. There must be a product that expresses those thoughts and feelings" (Bean 1992, p. 3).
- Creativity is "defined solely by its end product" (Halpern 2003, p. 193).
- "The only coherent way in which to view creativity is in terms of the production of valuable products" (Bailin 1988).
- "Over the course of the last decade, we have seemed to reach a general agreement that creativity involves the production of novel, useful products" (Mumford 2003).

These definitions lead to a highly objective view of creativity, but a view that is biased toward products and biased against individuals who have potential but are not yet expressing it or not expressing it in widely recognized ways. With all due respect to those scholars, they exemplify a product bias. It may be more parsimonious to view creative products as inventions, and the process leading up to them as creative or innovative.

Creativity constitutes one of the highest forms of human expression. Innovativeness largely involves restructuring and synthesizing knowledge into new ways of thinking and of doing things. It requires a good deal of cognitive facility to override established ways of thinking that impede exploration of novel ideas and search for new knowledge. But above all, innovativeness requires an unshakeable sense of efficacy to persist in creative endeavors (p. 239).

Psychoeconomic theory (and the more general economic theory, for that matter) relies on optima. Figure 13.3 for instance, suggests an optimal level of costs and benefits.

Higgins (1995) distinguished four types of innovation:

- Product innovation
- Process innovation
- Marketing innovation
- Management innovation.

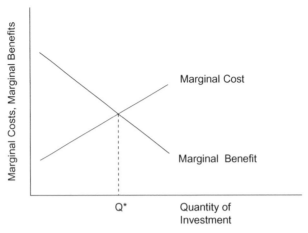

Q* = Equilibrium Rate of Investment.

FIGURE 13.3 The point at which the curves for marginal cost and marginal benefit meet indicates the optimum. *From Rubenson and Runco (1992b).*

BOX 13.5

A BALANCED RATIO THEORY OF CREATIVITY AND INNOVATION

Runco (2006a) attempted to capture both originality and effectiveness in his work on innovation and creativity. He proposed a continuum, with originality at one extreme and effectiveness at the other. Potentially creative products and behaviors can be placed somewhere on that continuum. Truly creative products and behaviors reflect a balance, meaning that they are somewhere in the middle of the continuum. They therefore have some originality but also some effectiveness. Products or behaviors at either extreme are not creative. Someone may act in an entirely effective and efficient fashion, for example, but with very little mindfulness and no originality. They may imitate someone else or just remember what they did before. They may be following routine or relying on "automaticity." All of these preclude creativity though they each can solve a problem or allow efficient action. At the other extreme someone may be extremely original, but if it is not in some way effective, it is merely original—or even psychotic. It is not creative. Psychotic may sound like an exaggeration, but here it is intended to mean "out of touch with reality."

Products and behaviors that do have some balance of originality and effectiveness, in contrast, are innovative (more effectiveness than originality) or creative (more original than effective). "Balance" is not a perfect descriptor, but the point is that both originality and effectiveness are apparent.

Other factors are involved, many of them social. Often the effectiveness of an innovation

(Continued)

BOX 13.5 (*Continued*)

is obvious to some public or business or audience. The effectiveness of creative things, on the other hand, may be personal and a matter of self-expression. Imagine an artist who works on some technical detail or personal disturbance for a long time, but eventually finds a way to capture the idea or solve the technical problem. He or she may be the only one to know that some new perspective is in fact effective. Figure 13.2 shows the proposed continuum.

This view is entirely consistent with theories of organizational creativity that contrast creative organizations with efficient organizations (March 1978). Still, in some situations it may be best to use two continua, one representing high and low originality, and the perpendicular one representing high and low levels of effectiveness.

Note, then, that the product resulting from innovation is not necessarily an object. It can be a strategy or technique.

Higgins (1995) went on to tie innovation to profit. This is how he separated creativity from innovation: "Innovation is how a firm or an individual makes money from creativity" (p. 9). This may seem materialistic, but then again there are creative things that are not intended to sell, but in fact are products. I am thinking here of artwork.

Another important distinction is between social and technological innovation (Gardner et al. 2007; Simms 2006; Marcy & Mumford 2007; Mumford 2002; Mulgan 2006; Bulut et al. in press). Bulut et al. (in press) named "fighting global climate change and reducing poverty or as small-scale as creating a small community garden" as examples of social innovations. Mulgan (2006) recognized intentions as the defining characteristic, the idea being that social innovations are always motivated by public considerations, rather than person considerations, business profits, or technological advance. It might help to consider the 10 social innovations Mumford (2002) found in the oeuvre of Benjamin Franklin: social clubs (juntos), police force, subscription library, fire department, paper currency, Philadelphia hospital, paving and lighting, printing business, the University of Pennsylvania, and the Albany Plan of Union (one government for all American colonies—proposed in 1754!).

Yet another view is that innovation more than creativity depends on previous work and in some ways, innovations are extensions and modifications of what existed previously. Creative things, in this sense, may be more truly original and "out of the blue." There is, however, a controversy over whether or not anything can be truly original (Hausman 1989). There are also a number of tactics and cognitive processes that allow the individual to adapt or borrow ideas for creative problem solving. It is very difficult to judge some originality because an analogy may be involved, and the origin of that analogy or the degree to which it has been retained in the final product is quite difficult to determine. Creative products may seem original but in fact may be related in some analogous or associative fashion to things that came before. They may also appear to be merely analogous, but in fact have an original etiology (Box 13.6).

INNOVATION FOR PROFIT

Much of the management literature defines innovation in terms of commercialization. This might distinguish some creativity from innovation, though creative efforts do sometimes turn a profit. Commercialization does raise the issue of entrepreneurship. Schumpeter (1934) tied innovation specifically to entrepreneurship (also see Bulut et al. in press).

Apparently the concept of entrepreneurship has been around for a long time. Bulut et al. (in press) pointed to Cantillon (1755) as the first to define entrepreneurship. This early definition was paraphrased to describe "an entrepreneur is the person who takes necessary risks in order to provide a profit in return." Bulut et al. elaborated on this such that "an entrepreneur is an individual who pursues the creation, growth, or expansion of a process, business, venture, or procedure, which can lead to the realization of that individual's dream" (cf. Carland & Carland 1997). Carland et al. (1984) distinguished entrepreneurs from business owners, which is important but not difficult, the former necessarily being innovative, and the latter only sometimes creative. Recall here the position offered herein, that creativity feeds innovation. They are related to one another but extricable. If an entrepreneur is necessarily innovative, creative talent is assumed. Innovation depends on creativity. It does not work the other way, however, for the creative process is not always innovative (e.g., when there is no product and when originality is more important than effectiveness, or when the effectiveness of the creative insight is personal or highly aesthetic rather than social and pragmatic).

Before leaving entrepreneurship, the newer idea of *intrapreneurship* should be defined and distinguished (Antoncic & Hisrich 2001). It refers to innovative work, aimed at much the same objectives as entrepreneurship (e.g., originality and profit), but within rather than across organizations. Simplifying, it is entrepreneurship within one organization. This kind of thing is increasingly common with larger organizations and with their specialized departments.

BOX 13.6

A DAY IN THE LIFE, OR, IF YOU WORK FOR THE IRS DO NOT READ THIS

Years ago I subscribed to the *LA Times*, and then wrote it off on my taxes. I was audited that year and the IRS accepted my rationale: I read and wrote about creative people who were described or interviewed in the *Times*. I used the *Times* for my work. Recently I have been thinking about writing everything off! To understand why, consider a day in the life—a day in your own life. Creativity abounds. How often do you hear music during the day? If you watch TV, you hear it (and have other forms of creativity as well), and if you drive you may have the radio on. Even ads have music, as do cell phones (ringers), elevators, and many reception areas. How often do you see or read an advertisement, or use the Internet? How often do you use paperclips, clothes, any technology, or any invention whatsoever? Virtually each moment of every day we experience creativity.

INVENTION VERSUS CREATIVITY

*Everything that can be invented has been invented. **Charles Duell, Head of U.S. Patent Office (1899, quoted by Bryson 1994, p. 93)***

This quotation makes slightly more sense if we take the *zeitgeist* of 1899 into account. At that time, life in the United States was booming. The patent office was quite busy. There was even a need to change the criteria being used such that a new product or device had to be useful as well as new. In a word, it had to have some creativity. How exactly is invention related to creativity?

The definitions offered here have invention as leading to a product. The process leading up to the invention may very well involve creativity. Several studies of the invention process have presented descriptions of the invention process. Rossman (1964), for example, questioned over 700 inventors, each holding an average 39.3 patents. He proposed the following steps to the inventive process:

1. Observation of a need or difficulty.
2. Analysis of the need.
3. A survey of all available information.
4. A formulation of all objective solutions.
5. A critical analysis of these solutions for their advantages and disadvantages.
6. The birth of the new idea—the invention.
7. Experimentation to test out the most promising solution, and the selection and perfection of the final embodiment by some or all of the previous steps (p. 57).

Rossman (1964) was explicit that invention is "not necessarily limited to developments in the physical sciences or in the industries, as it is ordinarily assumed. The term invention embraces all new developments in the social, administrative, business, technical, scientific, and esthetic fields" (p. 8). His inclusion of "embodiment" implies that he, too, requires that invention leads to a product. Additional descriptions of process can be found in Chapter 12 and the tactics presented there that specifically targeted invention. Chapter 7 explored the very interesting question, "Are inventions inevitable?"

Invention may be more dependent on traditional intelligence than other expressions of creativity. Consider the longitudinal study of intellectually precocious youth in the United States (Wai et al. 2005). The authors identified young persons who represented the upper 1% of SAT scores—when they were 13 years of age. The SAT is usually given to high school seniors at approximately 17 or 18, which is why these youths were considered precocious. Not only were they in the top 1%, they were also earning top scores several years before most adolescents even take the test! The longitudinal report discussed data collected when the sample was 33 years of age. It was, then, a 20-year follow-up. Wai et al. were interested in the predictions from the SAT with these criteria: earning a doctorate, patents, tenure at a university in the United States, and income. (Tenure had to be at a university ranked in the top 50 nationwide.) They found that the youth who had scored in the top 1% in the SAT tests were significantly more likely to earn doctorates at high-quality universities, and more likely to obtain patents, tenure, and high income. They believed that patents and tenure, at least, are related to creative potential. This is an important point because the SAT is a test of general aptitude, and not a test of creativity per se.

BOX 13.7

CREATIVITY AND PATENTED INVENTIONS

Huber (1998a) explained the creativity of patents:

> To be patented, inventions must satisfy a widely accepted definition. A patent as a creative output is not a matter of opinion; it is a fact and a matter of law. The principal criteria for an invention to receive a patent is that it be new, useful, and unobvious ... In patents, these terms take on more precise and selective meanings than they have in general use. To be new, the invention must be new to the world, not just new to the individual, new to the domain, or new to the field. To be useful, it must have some economic merit, not just relevance to a domain.

In the field of creativity, if in a less restrictive form. Among authors in the field of creativity, only a few ... have used the patent office definition of new, useful, and unobvious as their definition of creativity. There is general agreement among authors about the requirements of new and useful (or the close synonyms of original and appropriate). Several authors have chosen a third criterion that is very similar to unobvious. (p. 232)

Actually, Bruner (1962a) captured this idea of unobvious creativity with his definition of creativity as "effective surprise." Also see O'Quin and Besemer (1999).

Many cultural differences support the idea that invention, innovation, and creativity are distinguishable and extricable. Evans' (2005) comparisons of the United States and Great Britain discussed in Chapter 8, for example, suggest that the United States is highly innovative, but Great Britain is more inventive. Importantly, Evans acknowledged that innovators are remarkable individuals who are "heroes and benefactors, but they are not saints" (quoted by Lord 2005, p. r6). This is an important point because creative individuals, and apparently inventors and innovators alike, are often viewed as extraordinary, and through history their warts may disappear. Actually, they are just human, warts and all. If we forget this and view them as extraordinary, we might assume that they had something that the rest of us do not. This could keep us from fulfilling our potential and using the creative talents that we do have. Creative people, innovators, and inventors may do extraordinary things, but they are certainly human. This is especially clear in that many of them made notorious mistakes, and some were definitely a few bubbles off plumb. The idea of creativity and deviance is explored later in this chapter. First, a few more details about invention should be reviewed.

Huber (1998a) examined a small group of highly talented inventors from one company, and later (Huber 1998b) tested a larger group of less productive inventors. He examined four patterns of *inventivity:*

- Learning, with increased output over time.
- Senescence, indicated by decreased output over time.
- Control, with a patterned or nonrandom output, perhaps indicating work toward particular objectives.
- Breakthroughs, with peaks or bursts of output.

Each of these models was rejected; the data suggested a random pattern of invention. This supports theories that acknowledge chance factors. This does not necessarily distinguish creativity from what he called inventivity. Huber (1998b) did offer a distinction between the two, using patents (Box 13.7).

DISCOVERY AND CREATIVITY

Another obvious correlate of creativity is that of discovery. This is sometimes easy to distinguish from creativity, at least when discovery involves a kind of geographic exploration. In fact, all active discovery assumes a kind of search. This is clear in Boorstin's (1983) wonderful tome, *The Discoverers*, which has the subtitle, *Man's Search of His World and Himself*. Boorstin devoted chapters to the solar system, time, the oceans and routes around the world, animals, evolution, and writing, just to name a few discoveries. Heroes of discovery include James Cook and Columbus, as well as Copernicus and Galileo.

Some discoveries thus have nothing to do with geography. They are explorations of our world, and the "world" is defined such that it includes subatomic particles and other invisible domains, as well as our own psychological and even spiritual existence (e.g., consciousness). Think of it this way: Scientists often are discovering things, and they study just about everything! Frequently creativity is involved in one fashion or another. What is unique to discovery is that something is found, but the thing found can be a new technique, process, or idea. Even when the discovery does uncover a particular thing, the thinking that led to it or recognizes its value may depend a great deal on creativity. Recall here Root-Bernstein's (1989) ideas about discovery (see Chapter 12); there the connection with creativity was especially clear. It may be best to leave it at that: Discovery often leads to some finding rather than abstract creation, but it often depends heavily on creative thinking and the creative process.

DISCOVERY OF CHAOS

A good example of discovery is that surrounding chaos (Box 13.8). The idea of chaos was a discovery of patterns found in weather, economic trends, and throughout nature. Of course, you might suggest that the interpretation of these phenomena was a creative one, and of course it was, and there is no argument against the idea that discovery and invention often involve creative thinking. "Discovery" implies that there is something out there that is found or identified.

Significantly, a number of tactics (including some described in Chapter 12) were used in the discovery and development of chaos. The discovery of the *butterfly effect* by Edward Lorenz in 1961, for example, was greatly facilitated by his changing the representation of his data. Lorenz had a great deal of numeric data about the weather, but at one point he changed the numbers to graphs and used a particular code. He then quickly found the butterfly effect (where small changes may have enormous effects). The butterfly effect is known in more technical terms as "sensitive dependence on initial conditions."

Chaos theory also shows the power and impact of new technologies and tools. The computer was very helpful, and perhaps even necessary, in finding the butterfly effect in those weather patterns. This is interesting, especially because in 1961, when Lorenz found the weather patterns and the butterfly effect, "virtually all serious scientists mistrusted computers" (Gleick 1987, p. 13). Lorenz was questioning assumptions about computers. He was a contrarian.

The discovery and development of chaos theories also shows how professional marginality may be useful for individuals and their insights. This is very true of the mathematician Benoit Mandelbrot. As a matter of fact, he apparently wrote this description for a Who's Who of Science: "Science would be ruined if (like sports) it were to put competition above

BOX 13.8

CHAOS IN CREATIVITY

Chaos theory has been applied to many fields, and very recently it has shown its utility for creative studies. It is especially useful there because it offers a perspective on process and not just a description of static states. As Gleick (1987) put it (p. 5), "to some physicists chaos is a science of process rather than state, a becoming rather than being." That applies well to creativity. Indeed, the creative process frequently appears to be chaotic, but there may be order in the disorder. Gleick noted that structure and order and meaning may be "masquerading as randomness" (p. 22). Creative ideas that come out of nowhere that reflect intuition or a huge leap, may in fact merely reflect chaos at work within our thinking.

Then there is the creativity of chaos: "Those studying chaotic dynamics discovered that the disorderly behavior of simple systems acted as a creative process. It generated complexity, ritual organized patterns, sometimes stable and sometimes unstable, sometimes finite and sometimes infinite, but always with a fascination of living things" (Gleick 1987, p. 43).

A number of similar perspectives have been developed in the last few years. McCarthy (1993) and Goswami (1995), for example, have presented theories of creativity that draw directly from quantum and indeterminacy theory. Zausner (1998) drew extensively from nonlinear theories in her work on creativity and health. Bohm and Peat (1987) also used quantum theory, and in particular, Heisenberg and Schrodinger's theories to explain creativity, and also the creativity of scientists and the scientific method.

Richards (1997) extended chaos theory such that the concept of "strange attractors" could help to explain how art and creative works allow us to appreciate our place in nature and increase our conscious awareness (p. 60). She also described how creative individuals often prefer complexity and tied this idea to the concept from the chaos theory of fractals. Perhaps most important is Richards' argument that creative art and all forms of beauty have adaptive value and contribute to our evolution.

---

everything else and if it were to clarify the rules of competition by withdrawing entirely into narrowly defined specialties. The rare scholars who are nomads by choice are essential to the intellectual welfare of the subtle disciplines" (Gleick 1987, p. 90). "Nomads by choice" I take to refer to contrarians and individuals who might be professionally marginal.

Chaos theory has been a great help to physicists and biologists, as well as epidemiologists and ecologists. Apparently it has been used to help explain a measles epidemic in New York City as well as fluctuations of various mammal populations, including that of the Canadian lynx. Molecular biologists see chaos as a way of explaining and understanding systems of proteins. Chaos theory has been used to explain irregularities in lightning, clouds, and, on another scale, in stars and blood vessels. It helps us to understand turbulence found in all forms, including fluids. It works independently of scale, which is also a tactic for creative thinking because there are benefits to changing the scale or level of analysis.

Chaos theory has been particularly helpful in developing our understanding of the weather on the red spot on Mars, as well as weather in the Atlantic Ocean and the Gulf Stream. Apparently these cannot be well explained in terms of standard theories and linear logic and mathematics, but instead are nonlinear and chaotic, although stable. It has also been useful for astronomers studying the orbits of galaxies, and for electrical engineers attempting to model electronic circuitry.

There is often resistance to creative ideas. In fact, some people believe that all important creative ideas at first meet with resistance. Gleick (1987) wrote, "to some the difficulty of communicating the new ideas [of chaos theory] and the ferocious resistance from traditional quarters showed how revolutionary the new science was. Shallow ideas can be assimilated; ideas that require people to reorganize their picture of the world promote hostility" (p. 38).

The people studying chaos took risks.

> Often a revolution has an interdisciplinary character—its central discoveries often come from people straying outside the normal bounds of their specialties. The problems that obsessed these theorists are now recognized as legitimate lines of inquiry; the theorists themselves are not sure whether they would recognize the answer if they saw it. They accept risk to their careers. A few free thinkers working alone, unable to explain where they are heading, afraid even to tell their colleagues what they are doing—that romantic image lies at the heart of Kuhn's scheme. Every scientist who turned to chaos early had a story to tell of discouragement or open hostility (Gleick 1987, p. 37).

Kuhn is indeed a good example of marginality and resistance in science. Now famous for his ideas about paradigm shifts and scientific revolutions, apparently his work (and in particular the ideas of science not being linear progression and gradual accumulation of knowledge) "drew as much hostility as admiration when he first published them in 1962" (Gleick 1987, p. 36).

Serendipity also is found in the story of chaos. Indeed, according to Gleick (1987, p. 21), the butterfly effect was discovered by accident. Fortunately, Lorenz pursued the idea and continued to examine the data, often with new representations and perspectives. "Lorenz saw more than a randomness embedded in his model. He saw a fine geometrical structure, order masquerading as randomness. He was a mathematician, a meteorologist, after all, and now he began to live a double life. He would write papers that were pure meteorology. But he would also write papers that were pure mathematics, with a slightly misleading dose of weather talk as a preface. Eventually the prefaces would disappear altogether" (Gleick 1987, p. 22). Notice the professional marginality there as well as serendipity and a willingness to take risks. Notice also Lorenz's correct assumption that new ideas about order within disorder would be met with resistance.

One aside: The father of computer science is often thought to be John von Neumann. Alan Turing is also given much credit, but von Neumann was, if nothing else, "the intellectual father" of computer science (Gleick 1987, p. 18). Interestingly, von Neumann's ambition was actually to control the weather. He may have succeeded if it were not for chaos and instability permeating weather data, and weather itself.

SERENDIPITY AND CHANCE

> Some of the most important determinants of life paths often arise through the most trivial of circumstances (Box 13.9). Although the separate chains of events in a chance encounter have their own causal determinants, their intersection occurs fortuitously, rather than through deliberate plan. *Bandura (1982, p. 749)*

BOX 13.9

SERENDIPITY IN DISCOVERY

The soft tissue of Tyrannosaurus rex was found in 2005. Soft tissue means it was not fossilized bone—the tissue is 70 million years old! It was found only by "an accident of fieldwork" (Hotz 2005). "The tissue specimen was extracted from a fossil femur chiseled from 1,000 cubic yards of rock in the Hell Creek Formation at the Charles M. Russell National Wildlife Refuge in Montana. The bones belonged to a fairly complete skeleton of a 40-foot-tall Tyrannosaurus Rex that died when it was about 18 years old. It took field researchers three years to dig out all the bones. So remote was the site that the fossils could only be removed by helicopter .... The remains of the dinosaur were encased in thick jackets of plaster and were so heavy that fieldworkers had to break the thighbone in two places to load it aboard the aircraft. They also did not treat it with the customary chemical preservatives." In addition to the possibility of cloning Tyrannosaurus rex and solving the puzzle about the relationship of dinosaurs and birds, this finding forces paleontologists to revise their theories. "Until now, scientists have believed that bones fossilized when minerals gradually replaced organic material. Under current theories, organic molecules should not last more than 100,000 years. 'Our theories don't allow for this,'" said one researcher.

Discovery usually involves an active search of some sort. What of things that are found when the discoverer is not actively searching? These are best labeled *serendipitous*. Many examples were given in Chapter 7; many discoveries have been serendipitous. These include dynamite, nitroglycerin, X-rays, the microwave oven, dyes for fabrics, and coffee (Foltz 1999). The butterfly effect was found serendipitously (see the preceding section). (Some of the findings listed by Foltz, like buttons on jacket sleeves, followed from intentional design, but the initial purpose was not the final purpose. That final purpose is unintentional, though not entirely a mistake.)

Some care should be taken when interpreting accidental discoveries. There are several reasons for this. First, discoveries are not necessarily creative. If I lose a book, but then happen upon it while looking for my reading glasses, there is little or no creativity. Second, serendipitous discoveries are almost certainly not representative of all discoveries. Just as the "mad genius" might not be representative of all creative persons, and just as those mad geniuses might attract undue attention because they are mad and thus salient, so too is it interesting to think that discovery can be accidental.

SERENDIPITY AND THE FLYNN EFFECT

An example of serendipity very close to home, at least for students of the social and behavioral sciences, was reported by Flynn (1999). He is famous for his interpretation of IQ data and the suggestion that IQs are on the rise. They are indeed increasing, but there are various interpretations of the data. People could be getting smarter, for example, or they could be better at taking IQ tests ("test wise"). Of most relevance is Flynn's admission that his inference about IQ gains "was more a product of accident than perspicacity" (1999, p. 5).

Intentions must be taken into account to understand discovery and creativity. Intentions may not sound like the appropriate subject matter of an objective science, but actually they are respected in the behavioral sciences. Studies of moral reasoning, for example, use intentionality to explain age differences and objective versus subjective moral reasoning. These differ precisely in that the latter uses intentions. If someone behaves in an immoral fashion, but does so unintentionally, it is very different from the person who violates the same moral expectation but does so intentionally.

Albert (1992) foresaw the need to recognize intentions when he distinguished between eminence (as achievement) and creativity. In his words,

> One way of explaining such differences is to say that one person is more creative than another or has more creativity. But the fact is there is little agreement as to what being "creative" and having "creativity" mean …. Some persons believe that to label someone or some product "creative" is simply to evaluate it according to some social standard …. This would, I believe, make it and "eminence" the products of social attribution. And this approach would make the final, if not the only, arbiters of what is creative and/or eminent those persons and institutions who judge the product. Even though this is usually not done arbitrarily, so heavy an emphasis on the judgment of others in determining what is or is not creative puts too much stress and interest on the end product and social values …. What is needed is a definition of creative behavior that does not depend on failure or success but on intention and effort. (p. 7)

Albert (1990b) also tied intentions to choice and decision making:

> Creativity begins with and is expressed through the decisions one makes, not through the particular media used or the products generated …. An individual's knowledge of self and particular aspects of his or her world is the ultimate medium of creative behavior, for knowledge determines decisions as much as opportunities. In fact, it is on the basis of one's knowledge that one can perceive and identify one's opportunities. To the extent that deliberate efforts and decisions have to be made in career choices and performances, then to that degree one can say that personalized knowledge is a major component of creative and eminence-achieving work.

Runco et al. (1993) identified dozens of examples of choice influencing the development and expression of creativity. Most of these choices lead the individual toward investments of time and energy that eventually pay off in the sense of notable creative talent. Other choices are quite simple and allow the individual to employ problem-solving tactics that also pay off but in the sense of facilitating creative ideation and problem solving. These ideas about intentions and choice are of critical importance because they suggest that much of our creativity is under our own control. Each of us inherits genetic boundaries, but as noted again and again in Chapter 12, each of us has potential that can be fulfilled. To do so we must choose to develop and express creative behavior.

CREATIVITY AS IRRATIONAL OR RATIONAL

> Consciously or unconsciously, artists pursue not only aesthetic but psychological goals. *Kavaler-Adler (1993, p. 5)*

Intentions may be important for creative efforts, but they do not explain all creative efforts. Intentions reflect one part of the creativity complex, but the complex also includes unconscious, emotional, and seemingly irrational processes. These are often beyond our control and in that sense unintentional. Too frequently, behavioral scientists studying creativity dichotomize such that creativity is viewed as either rational or irrational. Of course this reflects the classic either/or fallacy, where things are seen in black or white with no shades of gray. The first view, that creativity is rational, is quite broad and is apparent in theories that creativity is just an expression of problem-solving skill (instead of a special kind of problem solving or something much more general than problem solving). This perspective also includes theories explaining creativity in terms of knowledge or expertise (Ericsson 1996; Hayes 1989; Simon & Chase 1973). These views of creativity as in some way rational parallel the earlier theory that most of the process is a conscious one.

The idea that creativity is rational is also connected to the notion that original insights reflect existing knowledge. They do not appear out of the blue but are instead a result of information generation processes. As Simonton (2007) put it, "Most new ideas are assumed to represent recombinations of previous ideas, either in whole or in part" (p. 332). No wonder, then, that Weisberg (1995a) looked to precursors and early influences on even significant creative achievements. Even Picasso's *Guernica* is in some ways tied to earlier works. The same is true of the artwork of Goya and, very likely, all other artists.

The alternative is that the unconscious plays a significant role, and that creativity is therefore in some ways irrational. This, too, is an umbrella concept and includes theories of creativity as unpredictable, inexplicable, chaotic (Finke et al. 1992), nonlinear (Zausner 1999), and divergent (Runco 1991b). Simonton (2007) tied this view to the Freudian view and to primary process (Hoppe & Kyle 1990). As such it is also related to the "magic synthesis" (Hoppe & Kyle 1990) and "sometimes even autistic thinking" (e.g., Eysenck 1995; Root-Bernstein & Root-Bernstein 1999). Certain associative tendencies would also suggest an irrational process (James 1880; Mednick 1962), as would the Darwinian perspective, at least in the sense that the variations that make up the first part of the process (the second part being selective) are blind (Campbell 1960; Simonton 1999e, 2007). Experimental support for the role of preconscious processes is available in the work on preinventive forms (Finke 1997), Janusian and homospatial thinking (Rothenberg 1999), and intuition (Bowers et al. 1990; Martindale 1990).

A great deal depends on how the terms are defined. Rationality, for example, is sometimes equated with traditional logic, but it can also be defined such that it leads to unconventional and creative decisions (Runco 2005). If there is a need for creativity, and creativity benefits from unconventional and nontraditional logic, it is rational to behave in an unconventional fashion.

This meshes nicely with the idea of emotional creativity. Averill (1999a, 1999b, 2000) gave three criteria for emotional creativity: originality, effectiveness, and authenticity. Original behaviors are novel, and "a novel emotional response is a new response that deviates from an individual's typical way of responding in everyday life (e.g., behaving in a new way toward a close friend that strengthens friendship), or one that deviates significantly from conventional ways of behaving" (Fuchs et al. 2007). Effectiveness may be defined in terms of oneself or other people. "It is possible that a response benefiting the larger group may be harmful to self (e.g., acts of heroism). Also, a response that is detrimental in the short term may turn out to be beneficial in the long term and vice-versa (e.g., waging a war)." Authenticity is recognized by those studying creativity and self-actualization, as well as emotional creativity. An act is authentic if it is a reflection of one's true self and not imitation or the like. It must be consistent with personal values.

Clearly, there is a rationality to creative thinking, even if it is unconventional.

PSEUDO-CREATIVITY

It is fairly easy to distinguish between intentional creativity and those parallel behaviors that are original or innovative but not really creative. This kind of uncreative behavior has been called *pseudo-creativity* (Cattell & Butcher 1968), which is defined as potentially original but occurs because of luck or a mere lack of inhibition. This is an important idea because a lack of inhibition is sometimes helpful for creative thinking, but it can also lead to criminal efforts! It may not lead to successful crime, however. Eisenman (1999) found many incarcerated persons to exhibit low levels of creative potential. Perhaps they just appear to be creative because they are uninhibited, but actually that is all they are—uninhibited. This would be the most parsimonious interpretation of their behavior. Simple explanations and definitions are always best.

The creativity that results from luck has been explained in terms of *blind chance* (Austin 1978). Here the individual plays no role at all. He or she just happens to be at the right place in the right time (also see Cropley et al. 2008). This is not unlike serendipity, where the person is looking for one thing but finds another. Austin also mentioned diligence, where the individual finds something while looking but does not find it in the expected place, and self-induced luck, which is of course consistent with Pasteur's quip that "chance favors the prepared mind."

Runco (1999b) referred to something very similar to the lack of inhibitions, just described, as contrarianism merely for the sake of contrarianism. Here the individual is just trying to be different; they are not solving problems or expressing themselves. No doubt they obtain a great deal of attention for contrarianism, and many people observing them may incorrectly attribute creativity to the contrarian. But actually this is blind nonconformity and a rejection of everything that exists just for the sake of rejection and not for creativity. If labeled creative, it is an incorrect attribution.

Quasi-creativity, originally defined by Heinelt (1974), has what Cropley (2006) called "a high level of fantasy—but only a tenuous connection with reality" (p. 392). Cropley cited daydreams as examples of quasi-creativity. Recall that Cropley did also identify effective creativity. This involves originality and adaptiveness.

This takes us to one of the most critical concepts in the creativity literature, namely adaptation (or adaptability). It is critical for several reasons. First, it is a part of definitions, like Cropley's (2006), and often is seen as a prerequisite for truly or effectively creative behavior. Second, a discussion of adaptation really brings home the possible role of chance and intentionality. Third, adaptation is a good reminder that creative behavior is not merely reactive. It is sometimes proactive instead. Adaptability, like innovation, inventivity, and discovery, can be distinguished from creativity.

Adaptation and Creativity

Having completed the formation of the earth, on the seventh day the Lord rested. Then on the eighth day, the Lord said, "Let there be problems." And there were problems. Cartoon from the New Yorker Magazine *(October 18, 1993, p. 90)*

> The world is not full of standard problems amenable to standard solutions. Everybody needs to be somewhat creative simply to get through a typical day and deal with the innumerable shifts from the ordinary that arise. *Schank & Cleary (1995, p. 229, quoted by Welling, 2007)*

Life is filled with challenges. Some are minor hassles and annoyances, others are stressful and potentially depressing. The worst are the challenges that are beyond our control. Life is in this sense much like driving a car. We can control many things and avoid some annoyances (e.g., a speeding ticket, by driving slowly), but some hassles occur even when we are on the defensive. Accidents sometimes happen to the most careful driver. They may be less likely, but they do happen on occasion. You just cannot completely avoid all problems and hassles. That's life.

You can, however, react such that hassles have minimal impact. This is where adaptability comes in. Adaptability allows the individual to adjust and cope and minimize negative effects. Some adaptability is behavioral. Using the driving metaphor again, you might hydroplane one day and narrowly avoid an accident, but the next day you take a different route to avoid the ice on the road. Adaptability is also cognitive and emotional. It can be creative, if it is original (rather than routine or habitual) and effective.

No wonder so many theorists have tied creativity to adaptability. As a matter of fact, evidence for the value of creative adaptations can be found on virtually every level of analysis. On the most global level, creativity contributes to what might be called societal adaptations and evolution. Consider again Boorstin's (1992) detailed history titled *The Creators*. He found that one of the most important influences on creativity through history was conflict and turbulence. He thought that turbulent situations often created opportunities. This is especially interesting because he took the long view and attempted to cover all of human history. Hunter et al. (2007) found much the same in a meta-analysis of organizational influences on creativity. Instead of looking across humanity and history, they looked within specific organizations and within relatively small groups, including teams within organizations, and found turbulence to be one of the most accurate predictors of creative performance. They also found competitive and high-pressure environments to elicit creativity, but each of these can be functionally tied to turbulence and conflict.

Moving into the personal level of analysis, Runco (1998) summarized a sizable portion of the psychological literature suggesting that individuals often respond to turbulence and conflict by being creative (also see Cohen 1989; Flach 1990). Along the same lines, Singer (1999) suggested that make-believe play has an adaptive function, whereas Campbell (1960) used an evolutionary theory to explain creative thinking and ideation (also see Albert 2012; Simonton 1997b). In this view there is a blind variation of ideas and a selective retention of those that are the most meaningful. This is just how Darwin described adaptations: They depend on variations and selections.

Clearly, even if many creative behaviors result from adaptations, there can be too much turbulence, and challenges that are too large. These ideas about adaptations, therefore, do not suggest that children should be challenged as much as possible. As is the case with virtually all influences on creative development and expression, there are optimal levels. These vary from person to person and age to age. Although many people respond to challenges with creative adaptations, others do not respond well at all. Their creativity may be hindered by even moderate turbulence and tension (Box 13.10).

BOX 13.10

OPTIMA AND CREATIVITY

Happy in that we are not overhappy
On fortune's cap
We are not the very button.
                    Shakespeare's Hamlet
Moderation in all things.
                              Plato

Many of the factors that contribute to creativity require optimization. Optimization in fact is a major theme within creative studies, it applies so broadly. Important optima include knowledge (for too much leads to inflexibility and rigidity), boredom and arousal (Csikszentmihalyi 1990a), divergence of thought, education (Simonton 1984), age, and motivation. Also consider this:

- Independence is good for creativity, but only up to a point. Too much and it

would be impossible to communicate and share one's ideas.

- Critical thinking is good, but only up to a point. It is good to select good ideas, but if you are too critical, even the best ideas will be rejected.

- Turbulence and tension can stimulate creativity, but only up to a point. Beyond that point it would be difficult to survive, let alone think in an original fashion.

Statisticians explain optima very easily, in terms of curvilinear relationships. In the most simple case—a bivariate relationship, for example, between the level of tension and the resulting creativity—the optimum would be apparent as a peak in the curve or function.

Evolutionary Theories

Evolution is so creative. That is how we got giraffes. *Kurt Vonnegut, Jr. (1991, p. E11)*

Theories of evolution are extremely useful. They have what good theories are supposed to have: (a) they are logical; (b) they are consistent with data; (c) they are parsimonious; (d) they explain a wide range of behaviors; and (e) they are elegant. *Elegance*, in this context, is a kind of simplicity. That in turn implies that there are few exemptions to the theory. It applies broadly.

Evolutionary theory is relevant to creativity on several levels. First is a functional level. Many creative achievements seem to have evolved, and they therefore can be understood by applying evolutionary terms and theory. Along the same lines, creative thinking sometimes can be described in evolutionary terms. Campbell (1960), for instance, described "blind variations and selective retention," which parallels Darwin's ideas about the two key aspects of evolution (variation and selection). As a matter of fact, this suggests a third connection between creativity and evolution. Darwin's work was itself creative, and Darwin often is studied as a prototypical creative individual. Howard Gruber's (1981a) *Darwin on Man* is a must-read for students of creativity.

Evolutionary theory relies on variations, some of which arise from mutations. Mutations imply that there is a random or chance component to the process. Evolutionary theories might therefore seem to support explanations of creativity involving chance more than those that emphasize intentions. Then again, it is possible to choose a path for evolution. It cannot be completely controlled, but it can be nudged. This is what is involved in proactive creativity.

Simonton (2007) identified three misconceptions about evolutionary theories of creative thinking, or at least concerning the blind variation models:

> First, contrary to what opponents believe, a blind-variation selective-retention model of creativity does not assume that the ideational variants emerge sans antecedents or de novo. Quite the opposite: Most new ideas are assumed to represent recombinations of previous ideas, either in whole or in part (cf. the primary role of genetic variation in biological evolution) …. Second, a Darwinian theory does not require that the creator always produce a tremendous superfluity of variants with respect to a particular idea. Instead, the theory only mandates the existence of two or more distinguishable variations that represent alternative directions for future development of an incipient idea …. Third, a variation-selection account of creativity does not mandate that the ideational variants be completely unrestricted. On the contrary, it is assumed that the vast majority of variations will fall into a certain well-defined range (cf. the analogous restrictions on both genetic recombination and mutation in biological evolution). It is for this reason that this model holds that creativity constitutes what has been called a "constrained stochastic process."

Evolutionary theories vary slightly. Even Darwin's theory has been modified and extended. Gould (1991), for example, described how evolution might have starts and stops. He referred to this as *punctuated equilibrium*, the idea being that changes sometimes may occur rapidly, but during periods of equilibrium, it may appear to slow down. Other differences are apparent in the evolutionary theories of Simonton (2007), Gabora and Aerts (2005), Dasgupta (2004), and Eysenck (1995).

CREATIVITY AND MEMES

Evolution is also relevant in the sense of *memes* (Lumsden & Findlay 1988). These are units of information that are passed from generation to generation. This is a cultural evolutionary process rather than a biological one, and as such it is Lamarckian rather than Darwinian. This means that it works very quickly. Once memes are proposed, they stick around.

The benefits of adaptability are not limited to cognition and problem solving. Some of the most important benefits are physical and emotional. Consider how your health might suffer if, for example, you have certain pressures and do not respond in an adaptive fashion. It might not cause problems if you experience the stress or anxiety that results from pressure (when you do not truly adapt) in the short run, but those pressures may take a huge toll as they accumulate over the long run. The creatively adaptable person will live each day relatively free of stress and anxiety, but the unadaptable person may very well experience a moderate amount of stress and anxiety day in and day out, year after year.

ART AND MATING DISPLAY AND THE REPRODUCTIVE BENEFITS

Speaking of benefits, one recent line of research suggests that there is a sexual benefit to creative behavior. In the vernacular, this indicates an evolutionary benefit to artistic creativity. Actually, the reasoning is more circuitous, but it is entirely consistent with evolutionary logic. It starts with the question of why schizotypy (the traits that reflect a potential toward actual schizophrenic behavior of some sort) has not become extinct nor at least shown signs of decreasing. After all, schizophrenics often have indications of ill-health and short life expectancy. According to G. F. Miller (2000, 2001) and Nettles and Clegg (2006), schizophrenia remains stable in the population because there is an association with artistic creativity, and artistic creativity in turn provides evolutionary benefits. This line of thought leads to the most interesting hypothesis that "successful engagement in artistic production should be correlated with achieved number and/or quality of sexual partners" (Nettles & Clegg 2006, p. 611).

Nettles and Clegg (2006) tested this hypothesis with 452 British adults (both men and women) who were sampled such that they might be fairly representative of the general population. To insure that notable artistic talent was represented in the sample, some of the participants were recruited via ads in art and poetry magazines, and a few solicited via *Who's Who in Poetry*. They each completed a questionnaire (which was returned through the mail) that asked about their talents and mating histories. Control variables were also studied, including education, social class, and income. Each person completed a life history measure that could be used to estimate schizotypy. Keep in mind that schizotypy is not manifest schizophrenia. It is indicative of potentials or a proneness.

There were two questions about mating: "Since you were 18, how much of the time have you been in a steady relationship?" and "Since you were 18, how many different partners have you had (please include all your relationships, however, short)?" (p. 612). Nettles and Clegg (2006) discussed the alternatives, including one in which a person is involved in many short relationships (quantity) rather than few steady relationships (quality). Careful statistical analyses indicated that one aspect of schizotypy (i.e., a history of unusual experiences, such as unusual perceptions or "magical ideation"), for both men and women, was significantly related to creative activity and "in turn has a significant positive effect on number of partners" (p. 613). Another aspect of schizotypy, namely *impulsive nonconformity,* was unrelated to creative activity but was directly associated with attainment (forgive the term) of a number of sexual partners. A third aspect of schizotypy, namely *introvertive anhedonia,* was negatively related to creative activity and the number of sexual partners. If I did not know that genetic theories are best applied to populations and not individuals, I would offer some advice about relationships at this point.

These results were interpreted as consistent with Miller's (2000, 2001) view that "artistic creativity functions as a mating display" (p. 613). As such it attracts sexual partners and the probability of reproductive success is increased. (Perhaps this should be on the back cover of the present book and in all sales brochures. Enrollment in creativity classes might increase.) These ideas take on even more importance if we reflect on Kaun's (1991) findings about the ill-health and short longevity of writers. As he put it in the title of his paper, "writers die young." One reason is that they may have unhealthful lifestyles. Why? Well mating displays, of course. There is a huge reward to behaving as if you are creative: More relationships.

Kanazawa (2000) offered a similar argument for scientific discoveries, so it may be creativity in general and not artwork alone that is beneficial to courtship. Still, there are numerous qualifications about this research (small samples, self-report measures) and replications are absolutely necessary.

GENETIC POTENTIALS

Genes provide potentials—only potentials. Some, like those related to schizotypy, might indicate a proneness to manifest schizophrenia. Quoting Nettles and Clegg (2006), "what is inherited is best described as a diathesis or vulnerability that may or may not lead to actual illness, and whose progression is affected by environmental factors" (p. 611).

Evolution of Aesthetics

Evolutionary theory has been applied to specific aspects of the creative process, including aesthetics (Berlyne 1971; Lowis 2004; Martindale 1990). Martindale, for example, gleaned from various historical and experimental analyses that supported a "psychological theory of aesthetic evolution." Martindale's premise is that artistic change is predictable. (For this reason the title of his book is *The Clockwork Muse*.) It is predictable because there is a canon that governs all art. Somewhat ironically, that canon is, "rules must be broken … laws must be disobeyed" (p. 11). The relevant law reflects the universal need for novelty. This is expressed in different ways at different times. Sometimes it leads to outrageous styles, sometimes to the fairly mundane or sedate. Behind it all is the need for novelty, which is in turn a reflection of the need for arousal.

FLEXIBILITY

Adaptability may depend, in certain contexts, on flexibility. One kind of flexibility results from the capacity for divergent thinking. Flexible ideation is apparent in the variety of ideas produced and it prevents the individuals from relying on one perspective or routine. This is known as *functional fixity*, or *fixedness* (Smith & Blankenship 1991). Flexibility might also result from the use of particular tactics (e.g., "work backwards, think like a child, incubate"), or it may result from a sensitivity to different perspectives and subliminal or affective processes. If the person is sensitive to various perspectives, he or she might be aware of what is obvious from his or her own point of view, but also aware of how others view the situation at hand. Those are the alternatives, and having them available makes the person flexible and able to choose from various alternatives. Another way of describing this is that the person is open to experience, including personal experience. However the options arise, they allow the individual to choose and select from a range of possibilities. This is connection to adaptability. Flexibility supports adaptability by providing options.

PROACTIVE CREATIVITY

The novelist is a capitalist of the imagination. He or she invents a product which consumers didn't know they wanted until it was made available. *David Lodge, Nice Work (1988, p. 21)*

One of the more important messages within this chapter is that creativity is partly intentional, partly a matter of choice. Obviously great care must be taken with the choices each of us makes. This warning applies very generally to the environments in which we choose to live, the friends we choose to keep, and the lifestyles we choose to follow, but it also applies specifically to choices that have direct bearing on the development and expression of our creative talents. Pseudo-creativity should be avoided; effective creativity should be chosen.

This can be quite difficult. Several things work against it:

- Some choices involve long-term investments with ambiguous benefits, and benefits that will not be available until well into the future. This is especially true of creative skills, which depend on particular forms of expertise. That expertise may take time (some estimate at least 10 years) to develop.
- Like most investments of time and energy, there are opportunity costs. If we invest in creative skills, we may not have time or energy to invest in other skills. (This book might be judged in this fashion: It persuades some readers that choices toward creative behaviors are worth the investment.)
- Creative behavior can be unconventional and sometimes has stigma attached to it. Investing in your own creative talent is not the best way to insure that you will fit in with everyone around you. It might be better to develop impression management skills and to conform if fitting in is your top priority.
- To make matters worse, it is easy to confuse creative achievement with other forms of accomplishment and recognition. Creativity and recognition are even sometimes blurred within the field of creative studies! Recall here the overlap and confusion that exists between innovation, invention, and creativity, as suggested by a large number of definitions of creativity (see Box 13.4). There are even recommendations that individuals invest in impression management to better their creativity. This recommendation was addressed in Chapter 5.

Note that these ideas reinforce the idea that creativity is distinct from adaptability. It might be more adaptable to conform to convention and invest in socially acceptable behaviors. Yet creative behavior is a kind of nonconformity. Creativity must be original and unconventional, and that requires nonconformity. It is also typically intrinsically motivated and rarely extrinsically motivated.

The separation between adaptability and creativity is also obvious from other perspectives, namely, by looking at creative people. They do not always behave in an adaptive fashion. Sometimes it would be most adaptable to fit in and conform, but the creative person leans to contrarianism, nonconformity, and autonomy. Some of them pay dearly for this. Galileo, for example, was under house arrest for many years. It could have been worse: he was very nearly put to death.

Adaptive and proactive creativity can also be distinguished by their intentions. The latter is directed toward originality, and perhaps self-expression. It is not always an easy choice or the only effective choice. Hopefully the intentions and choices are also toward actions that are moral and socially responsible (Gruber 1997; Richards 1990). This is increasingly important for each of us and for our survival as a species. The demands placed upon us are growing at a faster and faster rate. Barron (1995), Wilson (1975), and Bruner (1962a) each noted the accelerated rate of change within Western culture.

Higgins (1995) suggested much the same about the need for innovation. He pinpointed the following reasons:

- The accelerated rate of cultural change
- Increasing competition
- The globalization of business competition
- Rapid technological change, and related to this, technological discontinuity
- An increasingly diverse workforce
- Resource shortages
- The transition from industrial to knowledge based society
- Unstable economic and market conditions
- Increased demands
- Increased complexity within the environment.

DISTRIBUTION OF CREATIVE TALENTS

This chapter focuses on "what creativity is and what it is not." So far intelligence, imagination, originality, innovation, and various kinds of pseudo-creativity have all been distinguished from true creativity. There is another way of specifying "what creativity is and what it is not." This involves the distribution of creativity. Is it widely distributed? Is creativity universal? Is it something we all share? Or is it found only in talented persons?

One way to answer this question is to cite the copious research on domain differences. These have been reported throughout the creativity literature. A sample of the recognized domains is presented in Table 13.1. This list does not include what is probably the best-known theory of domain differences, namely that of Howard Gardner (1983, 1993a; Solomon et al. 1999). This includes the verbal, mathematical, bodily kinesthetic, spatial, musical, interpersonal, intrapersonal, and naturalistic domains. Each of these is tied to a particular section of the brain, and each distinguishable experimentally, psychometrically, and developmentally. Additionally, each domain has a core characteristic. The verbal domain relies on the processing of symbols, for example, and the musical domain relies heavily on sensitivity to rhythm and tempo. The naturalist apparently is sensitive to flora and fauna. This is an especially interesting domain because it reinforces the cross-cultural applicability of Gardner's theory of multiple intelligences. It definitely covers talent in a much broader sense than conventional views of creativity and intelligence. In the United States, for example, schools probably target verbal and mathematical skills significantly more than those in any other domain. But in other cultures, other domains may be more important. This may be especially clear if you consider pre-technological societies where spatial or bodily skills may be more important than symbolic or mathematical skills. It is especially easy to see the naturalist in cultures outside of the United States. It may be that the word *Aloha*, for example, is a reflection of naturalistic skills.

TABLE 13.1 Domains Studied

Domain	Reference
Academic Ability	DeMoss, Milich, & DeMers (1993); Burleson (2005)
Advertising	Reid et al. (1998); El-Murad & West (2003); Hackley & Kover (2007)
Architecture	Dudek & Hall (1991); MacKinnon (1965); Katz (1986); Moore (1970)
Art	Martindale (1990); Rothenberg (1979); Gridley (2006)
Cinematography	Domino (1974)
Comedy	Pritzker (1999); Pritzker & Runco (1997)
Cooking and the Culinary Arts	Horng & Hu (2008)
Dance	Alter (1989)
Design	Goldschmidt (1999); Curşeu (2006)
Engineering	Charyton & Snelbecker (2007); Lehman (1966); Shaw (1989); Blicblau & Steiner (1998); Clapham & Schuster (1992); Court (1998); Perkins (1988)
Invention	Huber (1998b); Hertz (1999); Hadamard (1945); Weber (1996); Gorman et al. (1998); Martinsen & Diseth (2011)
Jazz	Berliner (1994); Sawyer (1992)
Leadership	Mumford et al. (2002); Jung et al. (2003); Simonton (1984)
Learning systems	Burleson (2005)
Mathematics	Livne & Milgram (2006); Sak & Maker (2006); Katz (1986); Hadamard (1949); Mann (2009)
Music	Alter (1989); Sawyer (1992); Schlaug et al. (1995a, 1995b); López-González & Limb (2012); Hass & Weisberg (2009); Piirto (1991); Crow (2006); Charyton & Snelbecker (2007)
Painting	Roe (1975)
Patent-holders	Albaum & Baker (1977)
Performing Arts	Nemiro (1999)
Photography	Domino & Giulani (1997); Dollinger et al. (1999)
Physics	Miller (2009); McCarthy (1993); Diakidoy & Constantinou (2001); Goswami (1996)
Poetry	Patrick (1935, 1937, 1938, 1941); Sundararajan (2002); Rosengren (1985)
Public Relations	Lesly (1966); Marken (1991)
Science	Cropley (1967b); Simonton (1988); Rothenberg (1979)
	Runco (1990b); Runco & Bahleda (1987b); Katz (1986)
Screenwriting	Iglesias (2001)

(Continued)

TABLE 13.1   Continued

Domain	Reference
Teaching	Chambers (1973); Grahm et al. (1989); Rushton et al. (1983); Davidovitch & Milgram (2006)
Technology	Yu-Chu Yeh & Wu (2006); Lubart (2005); Bruce (1989); Elam & Mead (1990); Edwards (2001); Marakas & Elam (1997); MacCrimmon & Wagner (1994); Johnson & Carruthers (2006)
Writing	Taylor et al. (2003); Mohan & Tiwana (1987); Post (1996); Djikic et al. (2006); Barron (1968); Pohlman (1996)

ALOHA

The Hawaiian word *aloha* has many meanings, including "hello," "goodbye," and "affection." Literally it refers to someone "with the breath," the idea being that some people give back to nature what they took from her—they release their breath. When you say "aloha," exhale sharply! AloHA! Then there are *haoles*. Note the prefix there (ha) is the same as the suffix in aloha. Haoles do not "have the breath." They do not respect nature, as evidenced by their not returning to nature what they took from her. The Navajos have a similar concept, namely, *hozho*. No doubt these cultures would respect naturalistic talents most highly. That is why "with aloha" is a kind and polite thing to say to someone (Figure 13.4).

Other domains do not meet these criteria (brain localization, experimental, psychometric, and developmental distinctiveness). Still, it is sometimes useful to distinguish subdomains (e.g., the writing of poetry from the writing of situation comedy). Not all writers are the same, by any means. This is especially true in the clinical research on creativity. Ludwig (1995) reported that poets are more likely to experience depression and psychosis than any other career areas. He used Holland's (1961) widely respected career classification system. Jamison (1989) reported that poets tend toward bipolar disorders. Post (1994) concurred, with poets likely to experience bipolar disorders and unlikely to experience affective and personality disorders—at least relative to playwrights and writers of fiction.

Not all scientists are alike, either. Roe (1983), for instance, looked specifically at researchers working in the physical sciences. She did not, then, clump all scientists together, but rather recognized that the behavioral sciences, or the social sciences, may differ from the hard sciences. Of course there are certain commonalities, which may be shared among the sciences, or theoretically across creative personalities. Roe did find creative individuals to be observant, open to experience, curious, capable of accepting opposites and ambiguities, independent, self-reliant, perseverant, and appreciative of complexity.

One very important domain is not listed in Table 13.1, and only recently gained any attention. This is the moral domain (Gruber 1993; McLaren 1993).

FIGURE 13.4 In Hawaii, the word *aloha* and the lei are poignant, in more ways than one. The lei in the photo is made from the plumeria flower. *Source: Wikimedia Commons. http://en.wikipedia.org/wiki/File:Canoe_lei.jpg.*

Runco (2003b) both acknowledged differences among domains and pointed to the interpretive capacity of humans as necessary for creativity. The view that everyone is creative is also implied by Rogers' (1995) ideas of self-actualization. "Self-actualization or health must ultimately be defined as the coming to pass of the fullest humanness, or as the 'Being' of the person, it is as if SA creativity were almost synonymous with, or *a defining characteristic of, essential humanness*" (p. 145, emphasis added). Of course this does not mean that everyone is equally creative. Maslow (1968) acknowledges differences when he wrote, "I found it necessary to distinguish 'special talent creativeness' from 'self-actualizing (SA) creativeness' which sprang much more directly from the personality, and which showed itself widely in the ordinary affairs of life, for instance, in certain kinds of humor. It looked like a tendency to do *anything* creatively: e.g., housekeeping, teaching, etc." (p. 137). Commonalities among all creative behaviors do not imply that there are no differences among domains. There are, then, clear domain differences as well as possible commonalities.

The other distribution question concerns levels of ability. Consider in this regard Toynbee's (1964) claim that "to give a fair chance to potential creativity is a matter of life and death for any society. This is all-important, because the outstanding creativity of a fairly small percentage of the population is mankind's ultimate capital asset." He thus assigned creativity to "a fairly small percentage of the population." This view is consistent with Lotka's law, which states that a tiny proportion of the population accounts for the vast majority of creative works and ideas (Simonton 1984). That law is in turn consistent with observations in economics, for a large portion of the wealth in the country is held by a small portion of the population. It applies in many other areas as well, but it may not apply to creative potentials.

In his well known book, *Society of Mind,* Minsky (1988) suggested that creativity of the eminent is similar to that of everyone else. In his words,

> I don't think that there is a process of creativity in these people that is terribly different from ordinary people and my position is that people just don't have enough self-respect. We talk and we each make a new sentence that perhaps no one has ever said, and we think it is all right because anyone can make a sentence … but I think the average person is almost indistinguishable from Mozart and Beethoven. An ordinary person

solves new problems every day just getting across the street with a crowd of people without hitting them, and making new sentences, and describing new experiences. It's just that our humanistic stance is such that we are always looking for heroes, but the amount of machinery it takes to do this sort of thing that everyone does all the time is immense. You know, 100 billion brain cells are involved in talking and thinking and we take that for granted (Evans & Deehan 1989, pp. 157–158).

Language is truly a wonderful example of everyday creativity—maybe the best example, in fact.

The notion of different levels of ability is used by educational programs specifically for gifted children. Research on gifted children has identified a number of idiosyncrasies (e.g., Albert 1992; Davidson & Sternberg 1984; Milgram 1990; Runco 1986b). These characterize gifted and even exceptionally gifted children (Albert 1980). Prodigies also confirm that there are different levels of ability, even at early ages (Morelock & Feldman 1999). Prodigies are found only in certain domains, however, which implies that some domains require a large investment of time (and a large knowledge base). By the time the individual has invested that much time, they are no longer young and not really a prodigy. Most disturbing is the fact that there may be prodigies in certain fields (e.g., morality) but we are not looking for them. Prodigies depend on the *zeitgeist* and current cultural values.

NOMOTHETIC AND IDIOGRAPHIC APPROACHES TO CREATIVITY

The *nomothetic* approach to creativity focuses on universals. The *idiographic* focuses on individual differences. Fortunately, a choice between these two perspectives is required only when actually collecting data. If data are to be collected, they tend to test either some nomothetic hypothesis (e.g., "all or typical students experience a fourth-grade slump" [Runco 1999b; Torrance 1972]) or an idiographic hypothesis (e.g., "persons with notable divergent thinking skills solve problems better than other individuals" [Guilford 1968; Runco 1999a]). When standing back and integrating empirical findings into theory, rather than collecting data, both perspectives can be used. Indeed, this is likely to be the most realistic approach to creativity: It involves certain universals and certain individual differences.

Certain definitions of creativity lend directly to a decision about its distribution. Consider, for example, the claim of Newell et al. (1962), that creativity is merely a "special class of problem-solving activity characterized by novelty, unconventionality, persistence, and difficulty in problem formation" (p. 66). If creativity is merely problem solving, it is likely that most everyone, or even everyone, is creative. There are many criticisms of the theory that creativity is equivalent to problem solving (see especially Csikszentmihalyi 1988a; Runco 1994a).

The domains being recognized and the stereotypes of "creative people" depend on *zeitgeist*, cultural value, and even technology. Certain talents may not be recognized, then, until "the time is right." A seven-foot tall individual may excel in basketball right now, given men's and women's professional leagues and the current interest in that sport—many of the players are quite creative and improvisational with the ball—but in other eras there was no basketball, no court, and no game. Any seven-foot tall individual may have been viewed without much respect, and indeed may have been hard-pressed to fit into society. Technology is indirectly relevant to this example with basketball and professional sports and is more directly relevant to other fields. Consider, for instance, photography. Talented photographers had no medium in which to express their creativity until the advent of modern cameras and developers and so on. Of course, they may have found other media in which to express themselves, at least if theories of the generality of creative talent are correct. If these theories are incorrect, talents may be domain-specific and talents may go unfulfilled unless a domain is ripe for expression and development.

Everyday creativity recently has received a great deal of attention (Minsky 1988; Runco & Richards 1997). It also does not satisfy the criteria given earlier for a legitimate domain (Gardner 1983), but it is conceptually useful—and practically important. Its practicality lies in the fact that for many people it is the area in which they are the most likely to be creative. They may dress creatively, cook creatively, teach or parent creatively, and although these actions do not fit neatly into the typical domain theory, they can be original and useful—they can be creative.

CONCLUSIONS

That last point is an appropriate one on which to conclude. In fact, several related points should be underscored. One is that creativity can be used every day. It may be that it must be used every day if we are to fulfill our potential! Second is that there is a need for creativity, and in particular a need for proactive creativity. Hopefully that will be used in the moral domain and current political and environmental problems can be addressed in a creative fashion.

This chapter suggested what creativity is and what it is not. It is not the same thing as intelligence, originality, innovation, nor invention. It may, however, play a role in each. Distinguishing creativity from these things is necessary for good science (e.g., parsimony and discriminant validity), but it is not just an academic exercise. It is often practical. We can best fulfill potentials if we are specific about what is involved. If, by chance, you want your child to be creative, think about originality and self-expression when you are in the toy store or the bookstore. It is not enough to stimulate your child's intelligence. You must specifically target creativity. Creative potentials are the most likely to be fulfilled if they are intentionally chosen and reinforced.

There are three important implications of this emphasis on intentions and choice. The first is that it gives humans a real advantage when it comes to creative behavior. In other words, computers probably cannot be creative. That is certainly debatable. Simon (1988) demonstrated that computers can replicate certain creative discoveries in science. Then again, they were replicating previous discoveries, and the necessary information was provided. They did not seek that information out, nor identify the important problems for themselves (Csikszentmihalyi 1988). Recall also that discovery is not creativity, and many creative performances depend heavily on affect and motivation. This last point might be reworded so as to emphasize that computers do not have the intentionality that instigates and guides creative efforts.

The second implication of the ideas herein, and especially the ideas of intentionality and choice, concerns children. After all, they lack meta-cognitive skills and some aspects of self-awareness and self-monitoring. How then can they recognize the need for the right choices? Some people believe that children are less creative than adults, and perhaps cannot be creative at all. Others believe that children and adults each have the potential to be creative—that there is no group difference reflecting age. Yet others believe that children are more creative than adults.

To answer the question of children's creativity we must decide exactly which traits and tendencies are included in the creativity complex. Creativity is a complex or syndrome with certain traits or tendencies, and some of these may allow for children's creativity whereas others may preclude them. A good example of this has to do with social and communication skills. Children may not be very social and may not express some of their original insights or may not know how to express them, so if the creativity complex includes such expressive skills children would be excluded. They would not have what it takes and the answer to the previous question would be "no, children are not creative." Yet as noted earlier, parsimony suggests that social expressive skills be excluded from the creativity complex. After all, expressive skills are by definition social skills, and there is no reason to assume that all creativity must be social. Parsimony suggests that the creativity complex include only traits that are vital to all creativity.

Very likely the debate about children's creativity exists because it can be so difficult to judge children's thinking. They are cognitive aliens and think in a fashion that differs dramatically from the thinking of adolescents and adults. For this reason we may not recognize children's creative ideas when we see them. It works both ways: Dudek (1974) felt that many things labeled creative by adults were actually mistakes. She suggested that adults are expecting one answer, but a child may surprise us just because they think differently. The child may also lack information and thus surprise us with their answers and statements. The adult may hear the surprising answer, and because it is a surprise, it is labeled "creative." This is one part of the theory that children are not creative.

Perhaps children are creative in one way, and adults in another. Indeed, adults might learn a great deal about creativity from children. They are spontaneous, playful, uninhibited, and often mindful. They do not rely on routine and past experience. They thus have a great deal going for them; each of these things can contribute to creativity. Recall also that Gardner (1993a) and Runco (1996d) have suggested that there are benefits to behaving (or at least thinking) in a child-like fashion. Adults do have the advantage of perspective. They have huge knowledge bases. They have meta-cognitive capacities that allow them to compensate for their lack of spontaneity by tactically finding original ideas and solutions. Their intentionality allows them to use tactics. It also benefits them when they are child-like. Playfulness, for example, might be a good thing for an adult, at the right time, and if it is intended to facilitate creativity. At other times it might not be the best idea.

The third implication of the emphasis on intentions and choice is that there are many reasons to be optimistic about creativity. The fact that creativity is largely intentional supports the notions that "we can do something about creativity." It is not fixed at birth, nor necessarily lost in midlife or late adulthood. Many adults may lose the spontaneity that allows children to be creative, but those same adults can compensate by employing an intentional tactic and by choosing to renew their spontaneity.

None of this means that all creativity is deliberate. Far from it. Look back at Table 7.2, "Accidental Discoveries," or just watch any four-year-old child. At that age, children are quite spontaneous and usually uninhibited. Those tendencies allow the child to do and say surprising and sometimes creative things. They are not doing these things intentionally. Intentions, tactics, and other deliberate or proactive efforts contribute to many but not all creative performances. Indeed, the idea of intentions should not be taken too far. They are not all-important but instead rely on other parts of the creativity complex. Someone could have strong intentions to be creative but not yet have the tactics and knowledge, in which case unambiguous creativity is unlikely.

FINAL COMMENTS

The optimism just mentioned may be social and communal. Here I am referring to the possibility that intentional creativity can help us to construct a better world. Without a doubt we can and should apply creative tactics to ethical issues (Gruber 1993; Richards 1997; Stein 1993). We can also apply creative tactics to evolution, and take control of it. Ornstein and Ehrlich (1989) referred to something like this as conscious evolution. The best place to start this is locally, by working to fulfill our own creative potentials.

References

Abele, A. (1992a). Positive and negative mood influences on creativity: Evidence for asymmetrical effects. *Polish Psychological Bulletin, 23*, 203–221.

Abele, A. (1992b). Positive versus negative mood influences on problem solving: A review. *Polish Psychological Bulletin, 23*, 187–202.

Abra, J. (1988). *Assaulting Parnassus: Theoretical views of creativity*. Washington, DC: University Press of America.

Abra, J. (1995). Do the muses dwell in Elysium? Death as a motive for creativity. *Creativity Research Journal, 8*(3), 205–217.

Abra, J. (1997). *The motive for creative work*. Cresskill, NJ: Hampton Press.

Abra, J., & Valentine-French, S. (1991). Gender differences in creative achievement: A survey of explanations. *Genetic, Social, and General Psychology Monographs, 117*, 235–284.

Abrams, M. H. (1953). *The mirror and the lamp: Romantic theory and the critical tradition*. New York: Norton.

Adams, J. (1974). *Conceptual blockbusting*. New York: Norton.

Adams-Byers, J., Whitsell, S. S., & Moon, S. M. (2004). Gifted students' perceptions of the academic and social/emotional effects of homogenous and heterogeneous grouping. *Gifted Child Quarterly, 48*, 7–20.

Adorno, T., Frenkel-Brunswik, E., Levinson, D., & Sanford, N. (1950). The authoritarian personality. *Studies in prejudice series* (Vol. 1). New York: Harper & Row.

Agnew, R. (1989). Delinquency as a creative enterprise: A review of the recent evidence. *Criminal Justice and Behavior, 16*, 98–113.

Albaum, P. K., & Baker, K. (1977). Cross validation of a creativity scale for the adjective check list. *Educational Psychological Measurement, 37*, 1057–1061.

Albert, R. S. (1971). Cognitive development and parental loss among the gifted, the exceptionally gifted, and the creative. *Psychological Reports, 29*, 15–26.

Albert, R. S. (1975). Toward a behavioral definition of genius. *American Psychologist, 30*, 140–151.

Albert, R. S. (1978). Observations and suggestions regarding giftedness, familial influence and the achievement of eminence. *Gifted Child Quarterly, 22*, 201–211.

Albert, R. S. (1980). Family position and the attainment of eminence: A study of special family positions and special family experiences. *Gifted Child Quarterly, 24*, 87–95.

Albert, R. S., (Ed.), (1983). *Genius and eminence*. New York: Pergamon.

Albert, R. S. (1988). How high should one climb to find common ground? *Creativity Research Journal, 1*, 52–59.

Albert, R. S. (1990a). Identity, experiences, and career choice among the exceptionally gifted and eminent. In M. A. Runco & R. S. Albert (Eds.), *Theories of creativity* (pp. 11–34). Newbury Park, CA: Sage.

Albert, R. S. (1990b). Real world creativity and eminence: An enduring relationship. *Creativity Research Journal, 3*, 1–5.

Albert, R. S. (1991). People, processes, and developmental paths to eminence: A developmental-interactional model. In R. M. Milgram (Ed.), *Counseling gifted and talented children* (pp. 75–93). Norwood, NJ: Ablex.

Albert, R. S. (1992). A developmental theory of eminence. In R. S. Albert (Ed.), *Genius and eminence* (pp. 3–18). (2nd ed.) Oxford: Pergamon.

Albert, R. S. (1994). The contribution of early family history to the achievement of eminence. In N. Colangelo, S. Assouline & D. L. Ambroson (Eds.), *Talent development* (Vol. 2, pp. 311–360). Dayton, OH: Ohio Psychology Press.

Albert, R. S. (1996). What the study of eminence can teach us. *Creativity Research Journal, 9*, 307–315.

Albert, R. S. (2012). The achievement of eminence as an evolutionary strategy. In M. A. Runco (Ed.), *Creativity research handbook* (Vol. 2, pp. 95–156). Cresskill, NJ: Hampton Press.

Albert, R. S., & Elliot, R. C. (1973). Creative ability and the handling of personal and social conflict among bright sixth graders. *Journal of Social Behavior and Personality, 1*, 169–181.

Albert, R. S., & Runco, M. A. (1986). The achievement of eminence: A model of exceptionally gifted boys and their families. In R. J. Sternberg & J. E. Davidson (Eds.), *Conceptions of giftedness* (pp. 332–357). New York: Cambridge University Press.

Albert, R. S., & Runco, M. A. (1987). The possible different personality dispositions of scientists and nonscientists. In D. N. Jackson & J. P. Rushton (Eds.), *Scientific excellence: Origins and assessment* (pp. 67–97). Newbury Park, CA: Sage.

Albert, R. S., & Runco, M. A. (1989). Independence and cognitive ability in gifted and exceptionally gifted boys. *Journal of Youth and Adolescence, 18*, 221–230.

Albert, R. S., & Runco, M. A. (1990). Observations, gaps, and conclusions. In M. A. Runco & R. S. Albert (Eds.), *Theories of creativity*. Newbury Park, CA: Sage.

Albert, T., Pantey, C., Wiendruch, C., Rockstroh, B., & Taub, E. (1995). Increased cortical representation of the fingers of the left hand in string players. *Science, 270*, 305–307.

Alter, J. (1989). Creativity profile of university and conservatory music students. *Creativity Research Journal, 2*, 184–195.

Altshuller, G. S. (1986). *To find an idea: Introduction to the theory of solving problems of inventions*. Novosibirsk: Nauka.

Amabile, T. M. (1990). Within you, without you: Towards a social psychology of creativity, and beyond. In M. A. Runco & R. S. Albert (Eds.), *Theories of creativity*. Newbury Park, CA: Sage.

Amabile, T. M. (2001). Beyond talent: John Irving and the passionate craft of creativity. *American Psychologist, 56*, 333–336.

Amabile, T. M., & Gryskiewicz, N. D. (1989). The creative environment scales: Work environment inventory. *Creativity Research Journal, 2*, 231–253.

Amabile, T. M., Goldfarb, P., & Brackfield, S. C. (1990). Social influences on creativity: Evaluation, coaction and surveillance. *Creativity Research Journal, 3*, 6–21.

Amabile, T. M., Phillips, E., & Collins, M. A. (1933). Creativity by contract: Social influences on the creativity of professional fine artists. *Paper presented at the meeting of the American Psychological Association, Toronto*.

Amabile, T. M., Shatzel, E. A., Moneta, G. B., & Kramer, S. J. (2004). Leader behaviors and the work environment for creativity: Perceived leader support. *Leadership Quarterly, 15*, 5–33.

Ames, M., & Runco, M. A. (2005). Predicting entrepreneurship from ideation and divergent thinking. *Creativity and Innovation Management, 14*, 311–315.

Amos, S. P. (1978). Personality differences between established and less-established male and female creative artists. *Journal of Personality Assessment, 42*, 374–377.

Anderson, C. C., & Cropley, A. J. (1966). Correlates of originality. *Australian Journal of Psychistry, 18*, 218–227.

Anderson, R. E., Arlett, C., & Tarrant, L. (1995). Effects of instructions and mood on creative mental synthesis. In G. Kaufmann, T. Helstrup, & K. H. Teigen (Eds.), *Problem solving and cognitive processes* (pp. 183–195). Bergen, Norway: Fagbokforlaget.

Andreasen, N. C. (1987). Creativity and mental illness: Prevalence rates in writers and their first-degree relatives. *American Journal of Psychiatry, 144*, 1288–1292.

Andreasen, N. C. (1997). Creativity and mental illness: Prevalence rates in writers and their first-degree relatives. In M. A Runco & R. Richards (Eds.), *Eminent creativity, everyday creativity, and health* (pp. 7–18). Greenwich, CT: Ablex (Original work published in 1987).

Andreasen, N. C. (2005). *The creating brain*. New York: Dana Press.

Annett, M., & Kelshaw, D. (1983). Mathematical ability and lateral asymmetry. *Cortex, 18*, 547–568.

Anterion, C., Honore-Masson, S., Dirson, S., & Laurent, B. (2002). Lonely cowboy's thought. *Neurology, 59*, 1812.

Antoncic, B., & Hisrich, R. D. (2001). Intrapreneurship construct refinement and cross-cultural validation. *Journal of Business Venturing, 16*, 495–527.

Aol (2004). *The top 3 most hated inventions*. <http://channels.netscape.com/ns/tech/package.jsp? name=fte/hated-inventions/hatedinventions>.

Ardena, R., Chavez, R. S., Grazioplene, R., & Jung, R. E. (2010). Neuroimaging creativity: A psychometric view. *Behavioural Brain Research, 214*, 143–156.

Arieti, S. (1976). *Creativity: The magic synthesis*. New York: Basic Books.

Arlin, P. (1975). Cognitive development in adulthood: A fifth stage? *Developmental Psychology, 11*, 602–626.

Arndt, J., Greenberg, J., Solomon, S., Pyszcynski, T., & Schimel, J. (1999). Creativity and terror management: Evidence that creative activity increases guilt and social projection following mortality salience. *Journal of Personality and Social Psychology, 77*, 19–32.

Arndt, J., Routledge, C., Greenberg, J., & Sheldon, K. M. (2005). Illuminating the dark side of creative expression: Assimilation needs and the consequences of creative action following mortality salience. *Personality and Social Psychology Bulletin, 31*, 1327–1339.

Arnold, K., & Subotnik, R. (1999). Special issue: Longitunal studies of creativity. *Creativity Research Journal, 12*(2)

Aronson, E. (1980). *The social animal*. San Francisco: WH Freeman.

Ashby, F. G., Isen, A. M., & Turken, U. (1999). A neurophysiological theory of positive affect and its influence on cognition. *Psychological Review, 106*, 529–550.

Ashton, M., & McDonald, R. (1985). Effects of hypnosis on verbal and non-verbal creativity. *International Journal of Clinical and Experimental Hypnosis, 33*, 12–26.

Asimov, I. (1959). *Breakthroughs in science*. Boston: Houghton Mifflin.

Atchley, R. A., Keeney, M., & Burgess, C. (1999). Cerebral hemispheric mechanisms linking ambiguous word meaning retrieval and creativity. *Brain and Cognition, 40*, 479–499.

Austin, J. H. (1978). *Chase, chance, and creativity*. New York: Columbia University Press.

Avarim, A., & Milgram, R. (1977). Dogmatism, locus of control, and creativity in children educated in the Soviet Union, the United States, and Israel. *Psychological Reports, 40*, 27–34.

Averill, R. J. (1999a). Individual differences in emotional creativity: Structure and correlates. *Journal of Personality, 6*, 342–371.

Averill, R. J. (1999b). Creativity in the domain of emotion. In T. Dalgleish & M. J. Power (Eds.), *Handbook of cognition and emotion* (pp. 765–782). New York: John Wiley & Sons.

Averill, R. J. (2000). Intelligence, emotion, and creativity. In R. Bar–On & J. D. A. Parker (Eds.), *Handbook of emotional intelligence: Theory, development, assessment, and application at home, school, and in the workplace* (pp. 277–298). San Francisco, CA: Jossey-Bass.

Averill, R. J. (2002). Emotional creativity: Toward spiritualizing the passions. In C. R. Snyder & S. J. Lopez (Eds.), *Handbook of positive psychology* (pp. 172–185). New York: Oxford University Press.

Averill, R. J., & Nunley, E. P. (1992). *Voyages of the heart: Living an emotionally creative life*. New York: Free Press.

Aviram, A., & Milgram, R. M. (1977). Dogmatism, locus of control, and creativity in children educated in the Soviet Union, the United States, and Israel. *Psychological Reports, 40*, 27–34.

Axelrod, B. N., Jiron, C. C., & Henry, R. R. (1993). Performance of adults ages 20 to 90 on the abbreviated Wisconsin card sorting test. *Clinical Neuropsychology, 7*, 205–209.

Ayman-Nolley, S. (1992). Vygotsky's perspective on the development of imagination and creativity. *Creativity Research Journal, 5*, 101–109.

Bachtold, L. M. (1973). Personality characteristics of creative women. *Perceptual and Motor Skills, 36*, 311–319.

Baer, J. (1994). Divergent thinking is not a general trait: A multidomain training experiment. *Creativity Research Journal, 7*, 35–46.

Baer, J. (1998a). The case for domain specificity of creativity. *Creativity Research Journal, 11*, 173–177.

Baer, J. (1998b). Gender differences in the effects of extrinsic motivation on creativity. *Journal of Creative Behavior, 32*, 18–37.

Baer, J. (2012). Sex differences in creativity. In M. A. Runco (Ed.), *Creativity research handbook* (Vol. 3, pp. 215–250). Cresskill, NJ: Hampton Press.

Bailin, S. (1984). Can there be creativity without creation? *Interchange, 12*, 13–22.

Bailin, S. (1988). *Achieving extraordinary ends: An essay on creativity*. Boston, MA: Kluwer Academic.

Baldwin, A. Y. (2003). Understanding the challenge of creativity among African Americans. *Inquiry: Critical Thinking Across the Disciplines, 22*, 13–18.

Bandura, A. (1982). The psychology of chance encounters and life paths. *American Psychologist, 37*, 747–755.

Bandura, A. (1997). *Self-efficacy: The exercise of control*. New York: Freeman.

Baptista, R., & Thurik, A. R. (2007). The relationship between entrepreneurship and unemployment: Is Portugal an outlier? *Technological Forecasting and Social Change, 74*, 75–89.

Barrett, J. D., Peterson, D. R., Hester, K. S., Robledo, I. C., Day, E. A., Hougen, D. P., et al. (2013). Thinking about applications: Effects on mental models and creative problem-solving. *Creativity Research Journal, 25*, 199–212.

Barron, F. (1955). The disposition towards originality. *Journal of Abnormal and Social Psychology, 51*, 478–485.

Barron, F. (1963a). *Creativity and psychological health*. New York: Van Nostrand.

Barron, F. (1963b). The need for order and for disorder as motives in creative activity. In C. W. Taylor & F. Barron (Eds.), *Scientific creativity: Its recognition and development* (pp. 153–160). New York: Wiley.

Barron, F. (1964). The relationship of ego diffusion to creative perception. In C. W. Taylor (Ed.), *Widening horizons in creativity* (pp. 80–86). New York: Wiley.

Barron, F. (1968). *Creativity and personal freedom*. New York: Van Nostrand.

Barron, F. (1969). *Creative person and creative process*. Montreal: Holt, Rinehart & Winston.

Barron, F. (1972). Twin resemblances in creative thinking and aesthetic judgment. In F. Barron (Ed.), *Artists in the making* (pp. 174–181). New York: Seminar.

Barron, F. (1988). Putting creativity to work. In R. J. Sternberg (Ed.), *The nature of creativity* (pp. 76–98). New York: Cambridge University Press.

Barron, F. (1993). Controllable oddness as a resource in creativity. *Psychological Inquiry, 4*, 182–184.

Barron, F. (1995). *No rootless flower: An ecology of creativity.* Cresskill, NJ: Hampton Press.

Barron, F., & Bradley, P. (1990). The clash of social philosophies and personalities in the nuclear arms control debate: A healthful dialectic? *Creativity Research Journal, 3*, 237–246.

Barron, F., & Harrington, D. (1981). Creativity, intelligence, and personality. *Annual Review of Psychology, 32*, 439–476.

Barron, F., & Parsi, P. (1977). Twin resemblances in expressive behavior. *Acta Genetica Medicae et Gemello Logiae, XXIII*, 27–37.

Basadur, M. S. (1994). Managing the creative process in organizations. In M. A. Runco (Ed.), *Problem finding, problem solving, and creativity.* Norwood, NJ: Ablex.

Basadur, M., & Hausdorf, P. A. (1996). Measuring divergent thinking attitudes related to creative problem solving and innovation management. *Creativity Research Journal, 9*(1), 21–32.

Basadur, M. S., Wakabayashi, M., & Taki, J. (1993). Training effects on the divergent thinking attitudes of Japanese managers. *International Journal of Intercultural Relations, 16*, 329–345.

Basadur, M., Runco, M. A., & Vega, L. (2000). Understanding how creative thinking skills, attitudes, and behaviors work together: A causal process model. *Journal of Creative Behavior, 34*, 77–100.

Basadur, M., Pringle, P., & Kirkland, D. (2001). Crossing cultures: Training effects on the divergent thinking attitudes of Spanish speaking South American managers. *Creativity Research Journal, 14*, 395–408.

Bauer, G. H. (1981). Mood and memory. *American Psychologist, 36*, 129–148.

Baughman, W. A., & Mumford, M. D. (1995). Process analytic models of creative capacities: Operations influencing the combination and reorganization process. *Creativity Research Journal, 8*, 37–62.

Bean, R. (1992). *How to develop your children's creativity.* Los Angeles, CA: Price Stern Sloan Adult.

Bechara, A., Damasio, H., Damasio, A. R., & Lee, G. P. (1999). Different contributions of the human amygdala and ventromedial prefrontal cortex to decision-making. *Journal of Neuroscience, 19*, 5473–5481.

Bechara, A., Damasio, H., & Damasio, A. R. (2000). Emotion, decision making and the orbitofrontal cortex. *Cerebral Cortex, 10*, 295–307.

Becker, E. (1973). *The denial of death.* New York: Free Press.

Becker, G. (1978). *The mad genius controversy: A study in the sociology of deviants.* Beverly Hills, CA: Sage.

Becker, G. (2000–2001). The association of creativity and psychopathology: Its cultural-historical origins. *Creativity Research Journal, 13*, 45–53.

Becker, M. (1995). 19th century foundations of creativity research. *Creativity Research Journal, 8*, 219–229.

Beghetto, R. (2006). Creative self–efficacy: Correlates in middle and secondary students. *Creativity Research Journal, 18*, 447–457.

Bekhtereva, N. P., Starchenko, M. G., Klyucharev, V. A., Vorob'ev, V. A., Pakhomov, S. V., & Medvedev, S. V. (2000). Study of the brain organization of creativity II: Positron emission tomography data. *Human Physiology, 26*, 516–522.

Bekhtereva, N. P., Dan'ko, S. G., Starchenko, M. G., Pakhomov, S. V., & Medvedev, S. V. (2001). Study of the brain organization of creativity III: Brain activation assessed by local cerebral blood flow and EEG. *Human Physiology, 27*, 390–397.

Belcher, T. L. (1975). Modeling original divergent response: An initial investigation. *Journal of Educational Psychology, 67*, 351–358.

Bell, D. (1999). The divine gift of melody. *Interview. Clarity Magazine, 2*, 8–10.

Bem, S. (1986). *The psychology of sex roles.* Action, MA: Copley Publishing.

Benedek, M., Bergner, S., Konen, T., Fink, A., Aljoscha, C., & Neubauer, A. C. (2011). EEG alpha synchronization is related to top-down processing in convergent and divergent thinking. *Neuropsychologia, 49*, 3505–3511.

Benedict, R. (1989). *Patterns of culture.* Wilmington, MA: Mariner Books (Originally published 1934).

Bennis, W., Heil, G., & Stephens, D. C. (2000). *Douglas McGregor, revisited: Managing the human side of the enterprise.* New York: John Wiley and Sons.

Berg, D. H. (1995). The power of playful spirit at work. *Journal for Quality and Participation, 18*(4), 32–39.

Bergson, H. (2007). *The creative mind.* Mineola, NY: Dover.

Berliner, P. (1994). *Thinking in jazz: The infinite art of improvisation.* Chicago: University of Chicago Press.

Berlyne, D. E. (1960). *Conflict, arousal and curiosity.* New York: McGraw-Hill.

Berlyne, D. E. (1969). Laughter, humor, and play. In G. Lindzey & E. Aronson (Eds.), *The handbook of social psychology* (pp. 795–852). (2nd., pp) New York: Addison-Wesley.

Berlyne, D. E. (1971). *Aesthetics and psychobiology.* New York: Appleton Century Crofts.

Berlyne, D. E. (1974). *Studies in the new experimental aesthetics.* Washington, DC: Hemisphere.

Betts, G. H. (1916). Imagination. In G. H. Betts (Ed.), *The mind and its education* (pp. 112–127). New York: D. Appleton and Co.

Bilotta, J., & Lindauer, M. S. (1980). Artistic and nonartistic backgrounds as determinants of the cognitive response to the arts. *Bulletin of the Psychonomic Society, 15,* 354–356.

Binet, A., & Simon, T. (1905). The development of intelligence in children. *L'Année Psychologique, 11,* 163–191.

Bledow, R., Frese, M., Anderson, N., Erez, M., & Farr, J. (2009). Extending and refining the dialectic perspective on innovation: There is nothing as practical as a good theory; nothing as theoretical as a good practice. *Industrial and Organizational Psychology, 2,* 363–373.

Blicblau, A. S., & Steiner, J. M. (1998). Fostering creativity through engineering projects. *European Journal of Engineering Education, 23,* 55–65.

Bloom, H. (2002). *Genius: A mosaic of one hundred exemplary minds.* New York: Warner.

Boden, M. (1999). Computer models of creativity. In R. S. Sternberg (Ed.), *Handbook of creativity* (pp. 341–372). Cambridge: New York.

Boden, M. A. (1998). Creativity and artificial intelligence. *Artificial intelligence, 103,* 347–356.

Bogen, J. (1969). The other side of the brain II: An appositional mind. *Bulletin of the Los Angeles Neurological Society, 34,* 135–162.

Bogen, J. E., & Bogen, G. M. (1969). The other side of the brain III: The corpus callosum and creativity. *Bulletin of the Los Angeles Neurological Society, 34,* 191–220.

Bogen, J. E., & Bogen, G. M. (1988a). Creativity and the corpus callosum. *Psychiatric Clinics of North America, 11,* 293–301.

Bogen, J., & Bogen, G. (1988b). Creativity and the corpus callosum. In K. Hoppe (Ed.), *Hemispheric specialization* (pp. 293–301). Philadelphia, PA: Saunders.

Bogen, J., DeZure, R., TenHouten, W., & Marsh, J. (1972). The other side of the brain IV: The A/P ratio. *Bulletin of the Los Angeles Neurological Society, 37,* 49–59.

Bohm, D., & Peat, F. D. (1987). *Science, order, and creativity.* Toronto: Bantam Books.

Bohm, D. (1983). *Wholeness and the implicate order.* London: Ark Paperbacks (Original work published 1980).

Bologh, R. W. (1976). On fooling around: A phenomenological analysis of playfulness. *Annals of Phenomenological Sociology, 1,* 113–125.

Boorstin, D. J. (1983). *The discoverers: Man's search of his world and himself.* New York: Random House.

Boorstin, D. J. (1992). *The creators: A history of heroes of the imagination.* New York: Random House.

Boring, E. (1950). The dual role of the zeitgeist in scientific creativity. *Scientific Monthly, 80,* 101–106.

Boring, E. G. (1971). Dual role of the zeitgeist in scientific creativity. In V. S. Sexton & H. K. Misiak (Eds.), *Historical perspectives in psychology: Readings* (pp. 54–65). Belmont, CA: Brooks/Cole (Originally published in 1955).

Bouleau, C. (1963). *The painter's secret geometry: The study of composition in art.* London: Thames and Hudson.

Bourassa, M., Akhawayn, A., & Morocco, I. (2001). Effects of marijuana use on divergent thinking. *Creativity Research Journal, 13,* 411–416.

Bowden, C. L. (1994). Bipolar disorder and creativity. In M. P. Shaw & M. A. Runco (Eds.), *Creativity and affect* (pp. 73–86). Norwood, NJ: Ablex.

Bowden, E. M., & Jung-Beeman, M. (2003). Normative data for 144 compound remote associate problems. *Behavior Research Methods, Instruments, and Computers, 35,* 634–639.

Bower, G. H. (1981). Mood and memory. *American Psychologist, 36,* 129–148.

Bowers, K. (1968). Hypnosis and creativity: A preliminary investigation. *International Journal of Clinical and Experimental Hypnosis, 16,* 38–52.

Bowers, K. (1971). Sex and susceptibility as moderator variables in the relationship of creativity and hypnotic susceptibility. *Journal of Abnormal Psychology, 78,* 93–100.

Bowers, K., & van der Meulen, S. (1970). Effect of hypnotic susceptibility on creativity test performance. *Journal of Personality and Social Psychology, 14,* 247–256.

Bowers, K. S., Regehr, G., Balthazard, C., & Parker, K. (1990). Intuition in the context of discovery. *Cognitive Psychology, 22*, 72–110.

Bowers, K. S., Farvolden, P., & Mermigis, L. (1995). Intuitive antecedents of insight. In S. Smith, T. B. Ward, & R. A. Finke (Eds.), *The creative cognition approach* (pp. 27–52). Cambridge, MA: MIT Press.

Bowers, M. T., Green, B. C., & Chalip, L. (2012). *Assessing the relationship between youth sport participation settings and creativity in adulthood.* Unpublished manuscript.

Bowers, P. (1978). Hypnotizability, creativity, and the role of effortless experiencing. *International Journal of Clinical and Experimental Hypnosis, 26*, 184–202.

Bowers, P. G. (1967). Effects of hypnosis and suggestions of reduced defensiveness on creativity test performance. *Journal of Personality, 23*, 311–322.

Bowers, P. G. (1979). Hypnosis and creativity. *Journal of Abnormal Psychology, 88*, 564–572.

Brady, J. (1979). *Bad boy: The life and politics of Lee Atwater.* New York: Addison Wesley.

Bransford, J. D., & Stein, B. S. (1993). *The ideal problem solver.* New York: Freeman.

Briggs, J. (2000). *Fire in the crucible: Understanding the process of creative genius.* New York: St. Martin's.

Brockman, J. (1993). *Creativity.* New York: Touchstone Books.

Brophy, D. R. (2001). Comparing the attributes, activities, and performance of divergent, convergent, and combination thinkers. *Creativity Research Journal, 13*(3/4), 439–455.

Brower, R. (1999). Dangerous minds: Eminently creative people who spent time in jail. *Creativity Research Journal, 12*, 3–13.

Brower, R. (2003). Constructive repetition, time, and the evolving systems approach. *Creativity Research Journal, 15*, 27–61.

Brown, J. W. (2007). Commentary to: Vandervert et al., working memory, cerebellum and creativity. *Creativity Research Journal, 19*, 25–29.

Brown, R. (1973). Development of the first language in the human species. *American Psychologist, 28*, 97–106.

Brown, V. R., & Paulus, P. B. (2002). Making group brainstorming more effective: Recommendations from an associative memory perspective. *Current Directions in Psychological Science, 11*, 208–212.

Bruce, R. (1989). Creativity and instructional technology: Great potential imperfectly studied. *Contemporary Educational Psychology, 14*, 241–256.

Bruch, C. B. (1975). Assessment of creativity in culturally different children. *Gifted Child Quarterly, 19*, 169–174.

Bruininks, R. H., & Feldman, D. H. (1970). Creativity, intelligence and achievement among disadvantaged children. *Psychology in the Schools, 7*, 260–264.

Bruner, J. (1962a). The conditions of creativity. In J. Bruner (Ed.), *On knowing: Essays for the left hand.* Cambridge, MA: Harvard University Press.

Bruner, J. S. (1962b). The conditions of creativity. In H. Gruber, G. Terrell, & M. Wertheimer (Eds.), *Contemporary approaches to creative thinking* (pp. 1–30). New York: Atherton.

Bruner, J. (1965). The growth of mind. *American Psychologist, 20*, 1007–1017.

Bruner, J. S. (1966). *Toward a theory of instruction.* Cambridge, MA: Harvard University Press.

Bryson, B. (1990). *The mother tongue.* New York: William Morrow.

Bryson, B. (1994). *Made in America.* New York: HarperCollins.

Bryson, B. (2003). *A short history of nearly everything.* New York: Broadway Books.

Bulick, B. (2005). Creating creative space, before it's too late. *The Oregonian*, March 11. <http://www.oregonian.com/newsroom/newshome.html>.

Bullough, V., Bullough, B., & Mauro, M. (1980). History and creativity. *Journal of Creative Behavior, 15*(2), 102–116.

Bulut, C., Eren, H., & Halac, D. S. (2013). Which one triggers the other? Technological and social innovations. *Creativity Research Journal, 25*, 436–445.

Burke, B., Chrisler, J., & Devlin, A. (1989). The creative thinking, environmental frustration, and self-concept of left- and right-handers. *Creativity Research Journal, 2*, 279–285.

Burke, J. (1995). *Connections.* Boston, MA: Little, Brown.

Burke, R. J., Maier, N. R. F., & Hoffman, J. R. (1966). Functions of hints in individual problem-solving. *American Journal of Psychology, 79*, 389–399.

Burkhart, R. C. (1960). The creativity–personality continuum based on spontaneity and deliberateness in art. *Studies in Art Education, 2*, 43–65.

Burleson, W. (2005). Developing creativity, motivation, and self-actualization with learning systems. *International Journal of Human-Computer Studies, 63*, 436–451.

Burt, R. S. (2004). Structural holes and good ideas. *American Journal of Sociology, 110,* 349–399.

Butcher, J., & Niec, L. (2005). Disruptive behaviors and creativity in childhood: The importance of affect regulation. *Creativity Research Journal, 17,* 181–193.

Butterfield, H. (1931). *The Whig interpretation of history.* London: Bell.

Buzan, T. (1991). *Use both sides of your brain.* New York: Plume Books.

Bybee, R. (1980). Creativity nurture and stimulation. *Science and Children, 17,* 7–9.

Byrne, B. (1974). Handedness and musical ability. *British Journal of Psychology, 65,* 279–281.

Cameron, N. (1938). Reasoning, repression, and communication in schizophrenics. *Psychological Monographs, 50,* 1–33.

Cameron, N., & Margaret, A. (1951). *The psychology of behavioral disorders.* Boston: Houghton Mifflin.

Campbell, D. T. (1960). Blind variation and selective retention in creative thought as in other knowledge processes. *Psychological Review, 67,* 380–400.

Campbell, J. A., & Willis, J. (1978). Modifying components of creative behavior in the natural environment. *Behavior Modification, 2,* 549–564.

Campos, A., & González, M. A. (1994). Influence of creativity on vividness of imagery. *Perceptual Motor Skills, 78,* 1067–1071.

Campos, A., & González, M. A. (1995). Effects of mental imagery on creative perception. *Journal of Mental Imagery, 19*(1,2), 67–76.

Campos, A., González, M. A., & Pérez, M. J. (1997). Mental imagery and creative thinking. *Journal of Psychology, 131,* 357–364.

Cantillon, R. (1755). *An essay on economic theory.* <http://mises.org/books/Essay_on_economic_theory_cantillon.pdf>.

Capra, F. (1975). *The tao of physics. An exploration of the parallels between modern physics and eastern mysticism.* Boulder, CO: Shambhala.

Carland, J. W., Jr. & Carland, J. C. (1997). Entrepreneurship: An American dream. *Journal of Business and Entrepreneurship, 9,* 33–45.

Carland, J. W., Hoy, F., Boulton, W. R., & Carland, J. A. C. (1984). Differentiating entrepreneurs from small business owners: A conceptualization. *Academy of Management Review, 9,* 354–359.

Carlson, W. B. (2000). Invention and evolution: The case of Edison's sketches of the telephone. In J. Ziman (Ed.), *Technological innovation as an evolutionary process* (pp. 137–158). Cambridge: Cambridge University Press.

Carlsson, I. (2002). Anxiety and flexibility of defense related to high or low creativity. *Creativity Research Journal, 14,* 341–349.

Carlsson, I., Wendt, P. E., & Risberg, J. (2000). On the neurobiology of creativity: Differences in frontal activity between high and low creative subjects. *Neuropsychologia, 38,* 873–885.

Carnevale, P. J. D., & Isen, A. M. (1986). The influence of positive affect and visual access on the discovery of integrative solutions in bilateral negotiation. *Organizational Behavior and Human Decision Processes, 37,* 1–13.

Carroll, J. B. (1968). Review of the nature of human intelligence. *American Educational Research Journal, 5,* 249–256.

Carson, D. K., & Runco, M. A. (1999). Creative problem solving and problem finding in young adults: Interconnections with stress, hassles, and coping abilities. *Journal of Creative Behavior, 33,* 167–190.

Carson, S. H., Peterson, J. B., & Higgins, D. M. (2003). Decreased latent inhibition is associated with increased creative achievement in high-functioning individuals. *Journal of Personal and Social Psychology, 85,* 499–506.

Carson, S., Peterson, J. B., & Higgins, D. M. (2005). Reliability, validity, and factor structure of the creative achievement questionnaire. *Creativity Research Journal, 17,* 37–50.

Cattell, R., & Butcher, H. J. (1968). *The prediction of achievement and creativity.* Indianapolis, IN: Bobbs Merrill.

Cerf, C., & Navasky, V. (1984). *The experts speak.* New York: Pantheon Books.

Chadwick, W., & de Courtivron, I. (1993). *Significant others: Creativity and intimate partnership.* New York: Thames and Hudson.

Chae, S. (2003). Adaptation of a picture-type creativity test for pre-school children. *Language Testing, 20,* 178–188.

Chambers, J. A. (1964). Relating personality and biographical factors to scientific creativity. *Psychological Monographs: General and Applied, 78,* 1–20.

Chambers, J. A. (1973). College teachers: Their effect on creativity of students. *Journal of Educational Psychology, 65,* 326–339.

Chan, D. W., & Chan, L.-K. (1999). Implicit theories of creativity: Teachers' perception of student characteristics in Hong Kong. *Creativity Research Journal, 12,* 185–195.

Chan, D. W., Cheung, P. C., Lau, S., Wu, W. Y., Kwong, J. M., & Li, W. L. (2001). Assessing ideational fluency in primary students in Hong Kong. *Creativity Research Journal, 13*, 359–365.

Chand, I., & Runco, M. A. (1992). Problem finding skills as components in the creative process. *Personality and Individual Differences, 14*, 155–162.

Chandler, A. (1962). *Strategy and structure.* Cambridge, MA: MIT Press.

Channon, S., & Crawford, S. (1999). Problem-solving in real-lifetype situations: The effect of anterior and posterior lesions on performance. *Neuropsychologia, 37*, 757–770.

Charyton, C., & Snelbecker, G. E. (2007a). General, artistic and scientific creativity attributes of engineering and music students. *Creativity Research Journal, 19*, 213–225.

Charyton, C., & Snelbecker, G. E. (2007b). General, artistic and scientific creativity attributes of engineering and music students. *Creativity Research Journal, 19*, 213–225.

Cheek, J. M., & Stahl, S. (1986). Shyness and verbal creativity. *Journal of Research in Personality, 20*, 51–61.

Chein, M.-F. (1983). Creative thinking abilities of gifted children in Taiwan, Republic of China. *Bulletin of Educational Psychology, 15*, 97–110.

Chessare, J. B., Weaver, M. T., & Exley, A. R. (1993). Attention deficit hyperactivity disorder, creativity and the effects of methylphenidate. *Pediatrics, 91*, 816–819.

Cheung, C., & Scherling, S. A. (1999). Job satisfaction, work values, and sex differences in Taiwan's organizations. *Journal of Psychology, 133*, 563–575.

Cheung, P. C., & Lau, S. (2010). Gender differences in the creativity of Hong Kong school children: Comparison by using the new electronic Wallach–Kogan creativity tests. *Creativity Research Journal, 22*, 194–199.

Cheung, P. C., Lau, S., Chan, D. W., & Wu, W. Y. H. (2004). Creative potential of school children in Hong Kong: Norms of the Wallach-Kogan creativity tests and their implications. *Creativity Research Journal, 16*, 69–78.

Child, I. L. (1972). Aesthetics. In P. H. Mussen & M. R. Rosenzweig (Eds.), *Annual Review of Psychology.* Palo Alto, CA: Annual Review.

Choi, J. N. (2004). Individual and contextual predictors of creative performance: The mediating role of psychological processes. *Creativity Research Journal, 16*, 187–199.

Chomsky, N. (1965). *Aspects of the theory of syntax.* Cambridge, MA: MIT Press.

Chown, S. M. (1961). Age and the rigidities. *Journal of Gerontology, 16*, 353–362.

Christensen, B. T. (2005). Spontaneous access and analogical incubation. *Creativity Research Journal, 17*, 207–220.

Christie, A. (1963). *The clocks.* New York: Simon & Schuster.

Clapham, M. M. (1997). Ideational skills training: A key element in creativity training programs. *Creativity Research Journal, 10*, 33–44.

Clapham, M. M., & Schuster, D. H. (1992). Can engineering students be trained to think more creatively? *Journal of Creative Behavior, 26*, 156–162.

Clare, S., & Suter, S. (1983). Drawing and the cerebral hemispheres: Bilateral EEG alpha. *Biological Psychology, 16*, 15–27.

Clark, R. D., & Rice, G. A. (1982). Family constellations and eminence: The birth orders of Nobel prize winners. *Journal of Psychology, 110*, 281–287.

Clements, D. H. (1991). Enhancing creativity in computer environments. *American Educational Research Journal, 28*, 173–187.

Clements, D. H. (1995). Teaching creativity with computers. *Educational Psychology, 7*, 141–161.

Cliatt, M. J., Shaw, J. M., & Sherwood, J. M. (1980). Effects of training on the divergent thinking abilities of kindergarten children. *Child Development, 51*, 1061–1064.

Clickenbeard, P. R. (1991). Unfair expectations: A pilot study of middle school students' comparisons of gifted and regular classes. *Journal for the Education of the Gifted, 15*, 56–63.

Clinton, W. (2012). *Transcript of Bill Clinton's remarks at Democratic National Convention.* Detroit Free Press. <http://www.freep.com/print/article/20120906/NEWS15/120906019/Transcript-of-Bill-Clinton-s-remarks-at-Democratic-National-Convention>.

Clydesdale, G. (2006). Creativity and competition: The beatles. *Creativity Research Journal, 18*, 129–139.

Cohen, I. (1961). Adaptive regression, dogmatism, and creativity. *Dissertation Abstracts, 21*, 3522–3523.

Cohen, J. (1977). *Statistical power analysis for the behavioral sciences.* New York: Academic Press.

Cohen, L. M. (1989). A continuum of adaptive creative behaviors. *Creativity Research Journal, 2*, 169–183.

Cole, J., & Zuckerman, H. (1987). Marriage, motherhood, and research performance in science. *Scientific American,* 119–125.

Colello, S. M. G. (2007). *Imagination in children's writing: How high can fiction fly?* <http://www.hottopos.com/notand14/silvia.pdf>.

Collingwood, R. G. (1938). *The principles of art.* Oxford: Oxford University Press.

Collins, R. (2000). *The sociology of philosophies: A global theory of intellectual change.* Cambridge, MA: Belknap Press of Harvard University.

Comadena, M. E. (1984). Brainstorming groups: Ambiguity tolerance, communication, apprehension, task attraction, and individual productivity. *Small Group Behavior, 15,* 251–264.

Cooper, H., & Hedges, L. V. (1994). *Research synthesis as a scientific enterprise.* New York: Russell Stage Foundation.

Corbin Sicoli, M. L. (1995). Life factors common to women who write popular songs. *Creativity Research Journal, 8,* 265–276.

Corliss, R. (2003). Art Carney. *Time, 162*(21), 23.

Cornelius, G. M., & Yawkey, T. D. (1986). Imaginativeness in preschoolers and single parent families. *Journal of Creative Behavior, 19,* 56–66.

Court, A. W. (1998). Improving creativity in engineering design education. *European Journal of Engineering Education, 23,* 141–154.

Cousins, N. (1990). *Head first: The biology of hope and the healing power of the human spirit.* New York: Dutton.

Cox, A., & Leon (1999). Negative schizotypal traits in the relation of creativity to psychopathology. *Creativity Research Journal, 12,* 25–36.

Cox, C. M. (1983). The early mental traits of 300 geniuses. In R. S. Albert (Ed.), *Genius and eminence: The social psychology of creativity and exceptional achievement* (pp. 46–51). Oxford: Pergamon.

Cox, G. (1995). *Solve that problem.* London: Pitman Publishing.

Cramond, B. (1994). Attention deficit hyperactivity disorder and creativity: What is the connection? *Journal of Creative Behavior, 28,* 193–210.

Cramond, B., & Martin, C. E. (1987). Inservice and preservice teachers' attitudes toward the academically brilliant. *Gifted Child Quarterly, 31,* 15–19.

Cramond, B., Matthews-Morgan, J., Bandalos, D., & Zuo, L. (2005). A report on the 40-year follow-up of the Torrance test of creative thinking: Alive and well in the new millennium. *Gifted Child Quarterly, 49,* 283–291.

Cravats, M. (1990). Creativity and the visually impaired. *Creative Child and Adult Quarterly, 15,* 52–53.

Crawford, R. P. (1954). *The techniques for creative thinking.* New York: Hawthorn.

Croce, B. (1909). *Aesthetic: As science of expression and general linguistic* (D. Ainslie, Trans.). London: Macmillan.

Cropley, A. J. (1967a). *Creativity.* London: Longmans, Green.

Cropley, A. J. (1967b). Divergent thinking and science specialists. *Nature, 215,* 671–672.

Cropley, A. J. (1973). Creativity and culture. *Educational Trends, 1,* 19–27.

Cropley, A. J. (1990). Creativity and mental health in everyday life. *Creativity Research Journal, 3,* 167–178.

Cropley, A. J. (1992). *More ways than one: Fostering creativity.* Norwood, NJ: Ablex.

Cropley, A. (1997a). Creativity: A bundle of paradoxes. *Gifted and Talented International, 12,* 8–14.

Cropley, A. J. (1997b). Creativity and mental health in everyday life. In M. A. Runco & R. Richards (Eds.), *Eminent creativity, everyday creativity, and health* (pp. 231–246). Greenwich, CT: Ablex.

Cropley, A. J. (1999). Definitions of creativity. In M. A. Runco & S. R. Pritzker (Eds.), *Encyclopedia of creativity* (Vol. 1, pp. 511–524). San Diego, CA: Academic Press.

Cropley, A. J. (2001). *Creativity in education and learning: A guide for teachers and educators.* London: Kogan Page.

Cropley, A. (2006). In praise of convergent thinking. *Creativity Research Journal, 18,* 391–404.

Cropley, D., & Cropley, A. (2012). A psychological taxonomy of organizational innovation: Resolving the paradoxes. *Creativity Research Journal, 24,* 29–40.

Cropley, D. H., Kaufman, J. C., & Cropley, A. J. (2008). Malevolent creativity: A functional model of creativity in terrorism and crime. *Creativity Research Journal, 20,* 105–115.

Cropley, D. H. Cropley, A. J. Kaufman, J. C. & Runco, M. A., (Eds.), (2010). *The dark side of creativity.* New York: Cambridge University Press.

Crow, B. (2006). Musical creativity and the new technology. *Music Education Research, 8,* 121–130.

Crozier, R. (1999). Age and individual differences in artistic productivity: Trends within a sample of british novelists. *Creativity Research Journal, 12,* 197–204.

Crutchfield, R. S. (1962). Conformity and creative thinking. In H. E. Gruber, G. Terell, & M. Wertheimer (Eds.), *Contemporary approaches to creative thinking: A symposium held at the University of Colorado.* New York: Atherton.

Csikszentmihalyi, M. (1988a). The dangers of originality: Creativity and the artistic process. In M. M. Gedo (Ed.), *Psychoanalytic perspectives on art* (pp. 213–224). Hillsdale, NJ: Analytic Press.

Csikszentmihalyi, M. (1988b). Motivation and creativity: Toward a synthesis of structural and energistic approaches to cognition. *New Ideas in Psychology, 6*, 159–176.

Csikszentmihalyi, M. (1990a). The domain of creativity. In M. A. Runco & R. S. Albert (Eds.), *Theories of creativity* (pp. 190–212). London: Sage.

Csikszentmihalyi, M. (1990b). *Flow: The psychology of optimal experience*. New York: Harper Collins.

Csikszentmihalyi, M. (1996). *Creativity: Flow and the psychology of discovery and invention*. New York: HarperCollins.

Csikszentmihalyi, M. (1999). Implications of a systems perspective for the study of creativity. In R. J. Sternberg (Ed.), *Handbook of creativity* (pp. 313–335). New York: Cambridge University Press.

Csikszentmihalyi, M. (2000). *Beyond boredom and anxiety: Experiencing flow in work and play*. San Francisco: Jossey-Bass.

Csikszentmihalyi, M., & Getzels, J. W. (1971). Discovery-oriented behavior and the originality of creative products: A study with artists. *Journal of Personality and Social Psychology, 19*, 47–52.

Csikszentmihalyi, M., & Sawyer, K. (1995). Creative insight: The social dimension of a solitary moment. In R. J. Sternberg, & J. E. Davidson (Eds.), *The nature of insight* (pp. 329–361). Cambridge, MA: MIT Press.

Cubbs, J. (1994). Rebels, mystics, and outcasts: The romantic artist outsider. In M. D. Hall & E. W. Metcalf (Eds.), *The artist outsider: Creativity and the boundaries of culture* (pp. 76–95). Washington, DC: Smithsonian Books.

Cutler, A. (2003). *The seashell on the mountaintop: A story of science, sainthood, and the humble genius who discovered a new history of the earth*. New York: Dutton.

Cupchik, G. (1999). Perception and creativity. In M. A. Runco & S. R. Pritzker (Eds.), *Encyclopedia of creativity* (pp. 355–360). San Diego, CA: Academic Press.

Curnow, K. E., & Turner, E. T. (1992). The effect of exercise and music on the creativity of college students. *Journal of Creative Behavior, 26*, 50–52.

Curra, J. (1994). *Understanding social deviance: From the near side to the outer limits*. New York: Harper Collins College.

Curşeu, P. L. (2006). Emergent states in virtual teams. A complex adaptive systems perspective. *Journal of Information Technology, 21*, 249–261.

Dacey, J. S. (1989a). Discriminating characteristics of the families of highly creative adolescents. *Journal of Creative Behavior, 23*, 263–271.

Dacey, J. S. (1989b). *Fundamentals of creative thinking*. Lexington, MA: Lexington Books.

Dacey, J. S., Lennon, K., & Fiore, L. (1998). *Understanding creativity: The interplay of biological, psychological and social factors*. San Francisco: Jossey-Bass.

Damanpour, F., & Evan, W. M. (1984). Organizational innovation and performance: The problem of organizational lag. *Administrative Science Quarterly, 29*, 392–409.

Damásio, A. R. (1994). *Descartes' error: Emotion, reason and the human brain*. New York: Grosset-Putnam.

Damásio, A. R. (1995). *The feeling of what happens: Body and emotion in the making of consciousness*. New York: Harcourt-Brace.

Damásio, A. R. (2001). Some notes on brain, imagination and creativity. In K. H. Pfenninger & V. R. Shubik (Eds.), *The origins of creativity* (pp. 59–68). Oxford: Oxford University Press.

Damásio, A. R. (2002). *Conference proceedings: Neuroethics. Mapping the field*. New York: Dana.

Dane, E. (2010). Reconsidering the trade-off between expertise and flexibility: A cognitive entrenchment perspective. *Academy of Management Review, 35*, 579–603.

Dansky, J. L. (1999). Play. In M. A. Runco, & S. R. Pritzker (Eds.), *Encyclopedia of creativity* (pp. 393–408). San Diego, CA: Academic Press.

Darwin, C. (1964). *On the origin of species*. Cambridge, MA: Harvard University Press (Original work published in 1859).

Dasgupta, S. (2004). Is creativity a Darwinian process? *Creativity Research Journal, 16*, 403–413.

Davidovitch, N., & Milgram, R. M. (2006). Creative thinking as a predictor of teacher effectiveness in higher education. *Creativity Research Journal, 18*, 385–390.

Davidson, J. E., & Sternberg, R. J. (1984). The role of insight in intellectual giftedness. *Gifted Child Quarterly, 28*, 58–64.

Davidson, J. E., & Sternberg, R. J. (1986). What is insight? *Educational Horizons, 64*, 177–179.

Davis, G. A. (1973). *Psychology of problem solving*. New York: Basic Books.

Davis, G. A. (1975). In frumious pursuit of the creative person. *Journal of Creative Behavior, 9*, 75–87.

Davis, G. (1999). Barriers to creativity and creative attitudes. In M. A. Runco & S. R. Pritzker (Eds.), *Encyclopedia of creativity* (pp. 165–174). San Diego, CA: Academic Press.

Davis, S. N., Keegan, R. T., & Gruber, H. (2012). Creativity as purposeful work: The evolving systems approach. In M. A. Runco (Ed.), *Creativity research handbook* (Vol. 2, pp. 199–232). Cresskill, NJ: Hampton Press.

Dawkins, R. (1976). *The selfish gene*. Oxford: Oxford University Press.

Dawson, V. L., D'Andrea, T., Affinito, R., & Westby, E. L. (1999). Predicting creative behavior: A reexamination of the divergence between traditional and teacher-defined concepts of creativity. *Creativity Research Journal, 12*, 57–66.

Day, S. X. (2002). Make it uglier. Make it hurt. Make it real. The generation and maintenance of the creative writer's identity. *Creativity Research Journal, 14*, 127–136.

De Bono, E. (1968). *New think: The use of lateral thinking in the generation of new ideas*. New York: Basic Books.

De Bono, E. (1970). *Lateral thinking: Creativity step by step*. New York: Harper and Row.

De Bono, E. (1992). *Serious creativity: Using the power of lateral thinking to create new ideas*. New York: Harper Collins.

De Rosa, D. M., Smith, C. L., & Hantula, D. A. (2007). The medium matters: Mining the long-promised merit of group interaction in creative idea generation tasks in a meta-analysis of the electronic group brainstorming literature. *Computers in Human Behavior, 23*, 1549–1581.

Deci, R. L., & Ryan, R. M. (1985). *Intrinsic motivation and self-determination in human behavior*. New York: Springer.

De Cock, C. (1996). Thinking creatively about creativity: What can we learn from recent developments in the philosophy of science? *Creativity and Innovation Management, 5*, 204–211.

DeMoss, K., Milich, R., & DeMers, S. (1993). Gender, creativity, depression, and attributional style in adolescents with high academic ability. *Journal of Abnormal Child Psychology, 21*, 455–467.

Dennis, W. (1955). Variations in productivity among creative workers. *Scientific Monthly, 80*, 277–278.

Derrida, J. (1981). Economimesis. *Diacritics, 11*, 3–25.

Dewey, J. (1910). *How we think*. New York: Heath.

DeYoung, C. G. (2006). Higher-order factors of the Big Five in a multi-informant sample. *Journal of Personality and Social Psychology, 91*, 1138–1151.

DeYoung, C. G., Peterson, J. B., & Higgins, D. M. (2002). Higher-order factors of the Big Five predict conformity: Are there neuroses of health? *Personality and Individual Differences, 33*, 533–552.

DeYoung, C. G., Peterson, J. B., & Higgins, D. M. (2005). Sources of openness/intellect: And neuropsychological correlates of the fifth factor of personality. *Journal of Personality, 73*, 825–858.

Diakidoy, I.-A.N., & Constantinou, C. P. (2001). Creativity in physics: Response fluency and task specificity. *Creativity Research Journal, 13*, 401–410.

Diamond, A. (1986). The life-cycle research prod. of math and scientists. *Gerontology, 41*, 520–525.

Diamond, M., Scheibel, A., Murphy, G., & Harvey, T. (1985). On the brain of a scientist: Albert Einstein. *Experimental Neurology, 88*, 198–204.

Diaz de Chumaceiro, C. L. (1996). Freud, poetry and serendipitous paradoxes. *Journal of Poetry Therapy, 9*, 227–234.

DiCyan, E. (1971). Poetry and creativeness: With notes on the role of psychedelic agents. *Perspectives in Biology and Medicine, 14*, 639–650.

Diehl, M., & Stroebe, W. (1987). Productivity loss in brainstorming groups: Toward the solution of the riddle. *Journal of Personality and Social Psychology, 53*, 497–509.

Diehl, M., & Stroebe, W. (1991). Productivity loss in idea generating groups: Tracking down the blocking effect. *Journal of Personality and Social Psychology, 61*, 392–403.

Dietrich, A. (2004). The cognitive neuroscience of creativity. *Psychonomic Bulletin and Review, 11*, 1011–1026.

Digman, J. M. (1997). Higher-order factors of the Big Five. *Journal of Personality and Social Psychology, 73*, 1246–1256.

Djikic, M., Oatley, K., & Peterson, J. B. (2006). The bitter-sweet labor of emoting: The linguistic comparison of writers and physicists. *Creativity Research Journal, 18*, 191–197.

Dogan, M. (1999). Marginality. In M. A. Runco & S. R. Pritzker (Eds.), *Encyclopedia of creativity* (pp. 179–184). San Diego, CA: Academic Press.

Dogan, M., & Pahre, R. (1990). *Creative marginality: Innovation at the intersections of social sciences*. Boulder, CO: Westview Press.

Dollinger, S. J., Robinson, N. M., & Ross, V. J. (1999). Photographic individuality, breadth of perspective, and creativity. *Journal of Personality, 67*, 623–644.

Dollinger, S. J., Urban, K. K., & James, T. J. (2004). Creativity and openness: Further validation of two creative product measures. *Creativity Research Journal, 16*, 35–48.

Dollinger, S., Burke, P. A., & Gump, N. W. (2007). Creativity and values. *Creativity Research Journal, 19*, 91–103.

Dollinger, S. J., Burke, P. A., & Gump, N. W. (2010). Creativity and values. *Creativity Research Journal, 19*, 91–103.

Domino, G. (1974). Assessment of cineamatographic creativity. *Personality and Social Psychology, 30*, 150–154.

Domino, G. (1976). Primary process thinking in dream reports as related to creative achievement. *Journal of Counseling and Clinical Psychology, 44*, 929–932.

Domino, G. (1988). Attitudes towards suicide among highly creative college students. *Creativity Research Journal, 1*, 92–105.

Domino, G. (1989). Synesthesia and creativity in fine arts students: An empirical look. *Creativity Research Journal, 2*, 17–29.

Domino, G. (1994). Assessment of creativity with the ACL: An empirical comparison of four scales. *Creativity Research Journal, 7*, 21–33.

Domino, G., & Giulani, I. (1997). Creativity in three samples of photographers: A validity of the adjective check list creativity scale. *Creativity Research Journal, 10*, 193–200.

Dreistadt, R. (1969). The use of analogies and incubation in obtaining insights in creative problem solving. *Journal of Psychology, 71*, 159–175.

Dreman, D. (1982). *The new contrarian strategy*. New York: Random House.

Drevdahl, J. E., & Cattell, R. B. (1958). Personality and creativity in artists and writers. *Journal of Clinical Psychology, 14*, 107–111.

Drucker, P. F. (1985). *Innovation and entrepreneurship*. London: Heinemann.

Dudek, S. Z. (1974). Creativity in young children: Attitude or ability? *Journal of Creative Behavior, 8*, 282–292.

Dudek, S. Z. (2012). Art and aesthetics: Toward a multiparadigmatic approach. In M. A. Runco (Ed.), *Creativity research handbook* (Vol. 3, pp. 1–60). Cresskill, NJ: Hampton Press.

Dudek, S. Z., & Cote, R. (1994). Problem finding revisited. In M. A. Runco (Ed.), *Problem finding, problem solving, and creativity* (pp. 130–150). Norwood, NJ: Ablex.

Dudek, S. Z., & Hall, W. (1991). Personality consistency: Eminent architects 25 years later. *Creativity Research Journal, 4*, 213–232.

Dudek, S., & Marchand, P. (1983). Artistic style and personality in creative painters. *Journal of Personality Assessment, 47*, 139–142.

Dudek, S. Z., & Verreault, R. (1989). The creative thinking and ego functioning of children. *Creativity Research Journal, 2*, 64–86.

Dudek, S. Z., Strobel, M. G., & Runco, M. A. (1993). Cumulative and proximal influences on the social environment and children's creative potential. *Journal of Genetic Psychology, 154*, 487–499.

Dudek, S. Z., Strobel, M., & Runco, M. A. (1994). Cumulative and proximal influences of the social environment on creative potential. *Journal of Genetic Psychology, 154*, 487–499.

Dugosh, K. L., & Paulus, P. B. (2005). Cognitive and social comparison processes in brainstorming. *Journal of Experimental Social Psychology, 41*, 313–320.

Dunbar, K. (1995). How scientists really reason: Scientific reasoning in real-world laboratories. In R. J. Sternberg & J. E. Davidson (Eds.), *The nature of insight* (pp. 365–395). Cambridge, MA: MIT Press.

Dunbar, K. (1997). How scientists think: On-line creativity and conceptual change in science. In T. B. Ward, S. M. Smith, & S. Vaid (Eds.), *Conceptual structures and processes: Emergence, discovery, and change* (pp. 461–493). Washington, DC: Amerian Psychological Association.

Duncker, K. (1945). On problem-solving. *Psychological Monographs, 58*, 1–112.

Durrheim, K., & Foster, D. (1997). Tolerance of ambiguity as a content specific construct. *Personality and Individual Differences, 5*, 741–750.

Dykes, M., & McGhie, A. (1976). A comparative study of attentional strategies of schizophrenic and highly creative normal subjects. *British Journal of Psychiatry, 128*, 50–56.

Dyson, F. (1995). The scientist as rebel. In J. Cornwell (Ed.), *Nature's imagination: The frontiers of scientific vision* (pp. 1–11). Oxford: Oxford University Press.

Eccles, J. C. (1958). The physiology of imagination. *Scientific American, 199*, 135–146.

Edwards, B. (1979). *Drawing on the right side of the brain*. Los Angeles: Tarcher.

Edwards, S. M. (2001). The technology paradox: Efficiency versus creativity. *Creativity Research Journal, 13*, 221–228.

Eiduson, B. T. (1966). Productivity rates in research science. *American Scientist, 54*, 57–63.

Einstein, A. (1905). Zur elektrodynamik bewegter Körper. *Annalen der Physik, 17*, 891–921.

Einstein, A. (1956). *Lettres à Maurice Solovine*. Paris: Gauthier-Villars.

Einstein, A. (1961). The experimental confirmation of the general theory of relativity. In A. Einstein (Ed.), *Relativity: A special and general theory* (pp. 123–132). New York: Crown Publishers.

Einstein, A., & Infeld, L. (1938). *The evolution of physics.* New York: Simon and Schuster.

Eisen, M. L. (1989). Assessing differences in children with learning disabilities and normally achieving students with a new measure of creativity. *Journal of Learning Disabilities, 22,* 462–464.

Eisenberger, R., & Shanock, L. (2003). Rewards, intrinsic motivation, and creativity: A case study of conceptual and methodological isolation. *Creativity Research Journal, 15,* 121–130.

Eisenman, R. (1990). Creativity, preference for complexity, and physical and mental illness. *Creativity Research Journal., 3,* 231–236.

Eisenman, R. (1992). Creativity in prisoners: Conduct disorders and psychotics. *Creativity Research Journal, 5,* 175–181.

Eisenman, R. (1994–1995). *Contemporary social issues: Drugs, crime, creativity, and education.* Ashland, OH: Bookmasters.

Eisenman, R. (1997). Creativity, preference for complexity, and physical and mental health. In M. A. Runco & R. Richards (Eds.), *Eminent creativity, everyday creativity, and health* (pp. 99–106). Norwood, NJ: Ablex.

Eisenman, R. (1999). Creative prisoners: Do they exist? *Creativity Research Journal, 12,* 205–210.

Eisenman, R. (2008). Malevolent creativity in criminals. *Creativity Research Journal, 20,* 116–119.

Eisenman, R., Runco, M. A., Kritsonis, W., & Savoie, J. (1994). What college students do not like about college: Suggestions for college administrators and faculty. *National Forum of Educational Administration and Supervision Journal, 11,* 74–77.

Ekvall, G., & Ryhammar, L. (1999). The creative climate: Its determinants and effects at a Swedish University. *Creativity Research Journal, 12,* 303–310.

Elam, J. J., & Mead, M. (1990). Can software influence creativity? *Information Systems Research, 1,* 1–22.

Elkind, D. (1981). *Children and adolescence.* New York: Oxford University Press.

Ellen, P. (1982). Direction, past experience, and hints in creative problem solving: A reply to Weisberg and Alba. *Journal of Experimental Psychology: General, 111,* 316–325.

Elliott, A. & Dweck, C., (Eds.), (2005). *Handbook of achievement motivation and competence.* New York: Guilford Press.

Elliott, P. C. (1986). Right (or left) brain cognition, wrong metaphor for creative behavior: Is it prefrontal lobe volition that makes the (human/humane) difference in release of creative potential? *Journal of Creative Behavior, 20,* 202–214.

Ellis, J. J. (2007). *American creation: Triumphs and tragedies at the founding of the republic.* New York: Knopf.

Elms, A. (1999). Sigmund Freud. In M. A. Runco & S. R. Pritzker (Eds.), *Encyclopedia of creativity* (pp. 745–751). San Diego, CA: Academic Press.

El-Murad, J., & West, D. C. (2003). Risk and creativity in advertising. *Journal of Marketing Management, 19,* 657–673.

Epstein, R. (1987). The spontaneous interconnection of four repertoires of behavior in a pigeon. *Journal of Comparative Psychology, 101,* 197–201.

Epstein, R. (1990). Generativity theory. In M. A. Runco & R. S. Albert (Eds.), *Theories of creativity* (pp. 116–140). Newbury Park, CA: Sage.

Epstein, R. (1996). How to get a great idea. In R. Epstein (Ed.), *Creativity, cognition, and behavior* (pp. 51–60). New York: Praeger.

Ericsson, K. A. (1996). *The road to excellence.* Mahwah, NJ: Lawrence Erlbaum Associates.

Ericsson, K. A. (2002). Attaining excellence through deliberate practice: Insights from the study of expert performance. In M. Ferrari (Ed.), *The pursuit of excellence through education* (pp. 21–55). Mahwah, NJ: Lawrence Erlbaum Associates.

Ericsson, K. A. (2003a). The acquisition of expert performance as problem solving. In J. E. Davidson & R. J. Sternberg (Eds.), *The psychology of problem solving* (pp. 31–83). Cambridge: Cambridge University Press.

Ericsson, K. A. (2003b). The search for general abilities and basic capacities: Theoretical implications from the modifiability and complexity of mechanisms mediating expert performance. In R. J. Sternberg & E. I. Grigorenko (Eds.), *The psychology of abilities, competencies, and expertise* (pp. 93–125). Cambridge: Cambridge University Press.

Ericsson, K. A., & Charness, W. (1994). Expert performance: Its structure and acquisition. *American Psychologist, 49,* 725–747.

Erikson, E. H. (1958). *Young man Luther: A study in psychoanalysis.* New York: Norton.

Esgalhado, B. D. (1999). Fernando Pessoa, Alberto Caeiro, Alvar de Campos, Bernardo Soares, Ricardo Reis. In M. A. Runco & S. R. Pritzker (Eds.), *Encyclopedia of creativity* (pp. 377–380). San Diego, CA: Academic Press.

Estrada, C. A., Isen, A. M., & Young, M. J. (1994). Positive affect improves creative problem solving and influences reported source of practice satisfaction in physicians. *Motivation and Emotion, 18*, 285–299.

Evans, H. (2005). *They made America: From the steam engine to the search engine: Two centuries of innovators.* Boston, MA: Little, Brown.

Evans, P., & Deehan, G. (1989). *The keys to creativity.* Grafton Press.

Everett, E. M. (1983). *Diffusion of innovations* (3rd ed.). New York: Free Press.

Ewing, J. H., Gillis, C. A., Scott, D. G., & Patzig, W. J. (1982). Fantasy processes and mild physical activity. *Perceptual and Motor Skills, 54*, 363–368.

Eysenck, H. (1988). Health's character. *Psychology Today*, December, 26–35.

Eysenck, H. J. (1995). *Genius: The natural history of creativity.* Cambridge: Cambridge University Press.

Eysenck, H. J. (1997a). Creativity and personality. In M. A. Runco (Ed.), *Creativity research handbook.* Cresskill, NJ: Hampton Press.

Eysenck, H. J. (1997b). The future of psychology. In R. L. Solso (Ed.), *Mind and brain sciences in the 21st century* (pp. 270–301). Cambridge, MA: MIT Press.

Eysenck, H. (2003). Creativity, personality, and the convergent-divergent continuum. In M. A. Runco (Ed.), *Critical creative processes* (pp. 95–114). Cresskill, NJ: Hampton Press.

Fabricatore, C., & Lopez, X. (in press). Fostering creativity through educational video game development projects: A study of contextual and task characteristics. *Creativity Research Journal.*

Family, G. (1993). The moral responsibility of the artist. *Creativity Research Journal, 6*, 83–88.

Farmer, S. M., Tierney, P., & Kung-McIntyre, K. (2003). Employee creativity in Taiwan: An application of role identity theory. *Academy of Management Journal, 46*, 618–630.

Fasko, D. Jr., (1999). Associative theory. In M. A. Runco & S. R. Pritzker (Eds.), *Encyclopedia of creativity* (Vol. 1, pp. 135–146). San Diego, CA: Academic Press.

Feist, G. (1991). Synthetic and analytic thought: Similarities and differences among art and science students. *Creativity Research Journal, 4*, 145–155.

Feist, G. (1998). A meta-analysis of personality in scientific and artistic creativity. *Personality and Social Psychology Review, 4*, 290–304.

Feist, G. J., & Barron, F. X. (2003). Predicting creativity from early to late adulthood: Intellect, potential and personality. *Journal of Research in Personality, 37*, 62–88.

Feist, G., & Runco, M. A. (1993). Trends in the creativity literature: An analysis of research published in the *Journal of Creative Behavior* (1967–1989). *Creativity Research Journal, 6*, 271–286.

Feldhusen, J. F., & Goh, B. E. (1995). Assessing and accessing creativity: An integrative review of research, development. *Creativity Research Journal, 8*, 231–247.

Feldman, D. H. (1994). *Beyond universals in cognitive development* (2nd ed.). Norwood, NJ: Ablex.

Feldman, D. H., Marrinan, B. M., & Hartfeldt, S. D. (1972). Transformational power as a possible index of creativity. *Psychological Reports, 30*, 335–338.

Festinger, L. (1962). Cognitive dissonance. *Scientific American, 207*, 93–102.

Fine, R. (1990). *The history of psychoanalysis.* New York: Continuum.

Fink, A., & Neubauer, A. C. (2006). EEG alpha oscillations during the performance of verbal creativity tasks: Differential effects of sex and verbal intelligence. *International Journal of Psychophysiology, 62*, 46–53.

Finke, R. (1990). *Creative imagery: Discoveries and inventions in visualization.* Hillsdale, NJ: Erlbaum.

Finke, R. A. (1995). Creative realism. In S. M. Smith, T. B. Ward, & R. A. Finke (Eds.), *The creative cognition approach* (pp. 27–52). Cambridge, MA: MIT Press.

Finke, R. A. (1996). Imagery, creativity, and emergent structure. *Consciousness and Cognition, 5*, 381–393.

Finke, R. A. (1997). Mental imagery and visual creativity. In M. A. Runco (Ed.), *Creativity research handbook* (Vol. 1, pp. 120–183). Cresskill, NJ: Hampton Press.

Finke, R. A., Ward, T. B., & Smith, S. M. (1992). *Creative cognition: Theory, research, and application.* Cambridge, MA: MIT Press.

Firestien, R., & McCowan, R. J. (1988). Creative problem solving and communication behaviors in small groups. *Creativity Research Journal, 1*, 106–114.

Fisher, B. J., & Specht, D. K. (1999). Successful aging and creativity in later life. *Journal of Aging Studies, 13*, 457–472.

Flach, F. (1990). Disorders of the pathways involved in the creative process. *Creativity Research Journal, 3*, 158–165.

Flach, F. (1997). Disorders of the pathways involved in the creative process. In M. A. Runco & R. Richards (Eds.), *Eminent creativity, everyday creativity, and health* (pp. 179–189). Greenwich, CT: Ablex (Original work published in 1990).

Flaherty, A. W. (2005). Frontotemporal and dopaminergic control of idea generation and creative drive. *Journal of Comparative Neurology, 493*, 147–153.

Flaherty, M. A. (1992). The effects of a holistic creativity program on the self-concept and creativity of third graders. *Journal of Creative Behavior, 26*, 165–171.

Florida, R. (2002). *The rise of the creative class: And how it's transforming work, leisure, community and everyday life*. New York: Basic Books.

Florida, R. (2005). *The flight of the creative class*. New York: HarperCollins.

Florida, R. (2011, October 4). The world's leading creative class countries. <www.theatlanticcities.com/jobs-and-economy/2011/10/worlds-leading-creative-class-countries/228/#slide>.

Flynn, J. R. (1999). Searching for justice: The discovery of IQ gains over time. *American Psychologist, 54*, 5–20.

Foltz, C. (1999). *Accidents may happen: Fifty inventions discovered by mistake*. New York: Delacorte Press.

Forgas, J. P. (2000). *Feeling and thinking: The role of affect in social cognition*. Paris: Cambridge University Press.

Fortner, V. L. (1986). Generalization of creative productive-thinking training to LD students' written expression. *Learning Disability Quarterly, 9*, 274–284.

Frenkel-Brunswick, E. (1949). Intolerance of ambiguity as an emotional and perceptual personality variable. *Journal of Personality, 18*, 108–143.

Freud, S. (1966). *The standard edition of the complete psychological works of Sigmund Freud*. London: Hogarth.

Freud, S. (1989). *Leonardo Da Vinci and a memory of his childhood*. New York: Norton (Originally published 1910).

Friedel, R. (1992). Perspiration and perspective: Changing perceptions of genius and expertise in American invention. In R. J. Weber, & D. N. Perkins (Eds.), *Inventive minds: Creativity in technology* (pp. 11–26). New York: Oxford University Press.

Friedman, H. S., Tucker, J. S., Schwartz, J. E., Tomlinson-Keasey, C., Martin, L. R., Wingard, D. L., et al. (1995). Psychosocial and behavioral predictors of longevity: The aging and death of the termites. *American Psychologist, 50*, 69–78.

Friedman, R. S., & Förster, J. (2000). The effects of approach and avoidance motor actions on the elements of creative insight. *Journal of Personality and Social Psychology, 79*, 477–492.

Friedman, R. S., & Förster, J. (2002). The influence of approach and avoidance motor actions on creative cognition. *Journal of Experimental Social Psychology, 38*, 41–55.

Friedman, R. S., Fishbach, A., Förster, J., & Werth, L. (2003). Attentional priming effects on creativity. *Creativity Research Journal, 15*, 277–286.

Friedman, R. S., Förster, J., & Denzler, M. (2007). Interactive effects of mood and task framing on creative generation. *Creativity Research Journal, 19*, 141–162.

Fryer, M., & Collings, J. A. (1991). British teachers views of creativity. *Journal of Creative Behavior, 25*, 75–81.

Fuchs, J. L., Kumar, V. K., & Porter, J. (2007). Emotional creativity, alexithymia, and styles of creativity. *Creativity Research Journal, 19*, 233–245.

Fulgosi, A., & Guilford, J. P. (1968). Short-term incubation in divergent production. *American Journal of Psychology, 81*, 241–246.

Fulgosi, A., & Guilford, J. P. (1973). A further investigation of short-term incubation. *Acta Instituti Psychologie Universitatis Zabrebtensis, 70*, 67–70.

Furnham, A. (1994). A content correlational and factor analytic study of four tolerance of ambiguity questionnaires. *Personality and Individual Differences, 16*, 403–410.

Furnham, A., & Avison, M. (1997). Personality and preference for surreal paintings. *Personality and Individual Differences, 23*, 923–935.

Furnham, A., & Ribchester, T. (1995). Tolerance of ambiguity: A review of the concept, its measurement and applications. *Current Psychology, 14*, 179–199.

Furnham, A., Zhang, J., & Chamorro-Premuzic, T. (2006). The relationship between psychometric and self-estimated intelligence, creativity, personality, and academic achievement. *Imagination, Cognition and Personality, 25*, 119–145.

Gabora, L., & Aerts, D. (2005). Creative thought as a nondarwinian evolutionary process. *Journal of Creative Behavior, 39*, 262–283.

Galton, F. (1869). *Hereditary genius*. New York: Macmillan.

Gamwell, L., (Ed.), (2005). *Exploring the invisible: Art, science, and the spiritual*. Princeton, NJ: Princeton University Press.

Garcia, J. H. (2003). Nurturing creativity in Chicano populations: Integrating history, culture, family, and self. *Inquiry: Critical Thinking Across the Disciplines, 22*, 19–24.

Gardner, C. A., Acharya, T., & Yach, D. (2007). Technological and social innovation: A unifying new paradigm for global health. *Health Affairs, 26*, 1052–1061.

Gardner, H. (1973). *The arts and human development: A psychological study of the artistic process.* New York: Wiley & Sons.

Gardner, H. (1982). *Art, mind, and brain: A cognitive approach to creativity.* New York: Basic Books.

Gardner, H. (1983). *Frames of mind: The theory of multiple intelligences.* New York: Basic Books.

Gardner, H. (1988). Creativity: An interdisciplinary perspective. *Creativity Research Journal, 1*, 8–26.

Gardner, H. (1993a). *Creating minds: An anatomy of creativity seen through the lives of Freud, Einstein, Picasso, Stravinsky, Eliot, Graham, and Gandhi.* New York: Basic Books.

Gardner, H. (1993b). Mahatma Gandhi: A hold upon others. *Creativity Research Journal, 6*, 29–44.

Gardner, H., & Nemirovsky, R. (1991). From private intuitions to public symbol systems: An examination of the creative process in Georg Cantor and Sigmund Freud. *Creativity Research Journal, 4*, 1–22.

Gardner, H., & Wolf, C. (1988). The fruits of asynchrony: A psychological examination of creativity. *Adolescent Psychiatry, 15*, 96–120.

Gaynor, J. L. R., & Runco, M. A. (1992). Family size, birth order, age-interval, and the creativity of children. *Journal of Creative Behavior, 26*, 108–118.

Gazzaniga, M. S. (2000). Cerebral specialization and interhemispheric communication: Does the corpus callosum enable the human condition? *Brain, 123*, 1293–1326.

Gedo, J. (1997). The healing power of art: The case of John Ensor. In M. A. Runco & R. Richards (Eds.), *Eminent creativity, everyday creativity, and health* (pp. 191–212). Greenwich, CT: Ablex.

Gedo, M. M. (1980). *Picasso: Art as autobiography.* Chicago, IL: University of Chicago Press.

Gehlbach, R. D. (1991). Play, Piaget, and creativity: The promise of design. *Journal of Creative Behavior, 25*, 137–144.

Gendrop, S. C. (1996). Effect of an intervention in synectics on the creative thinking of nurses. *Creativity Research Journal, 9*, 11–19.

Gentner, D., Loewenstein, J., & Thompson, L. (2003). Learning and transfer: A general role for analogical encoding. *Journal of Educational Psychology, 95*, 393–408.

George, J. M., & Zhou, J. (2001). When openness to experience and conscientiousness are related to creative behavior: An interactional approach. *Journal of Applied Psychology, 86*, 513–524.

Gerrard, L. E., Poteat, G. M., & Ironsmith, M. (1996). Promoting children's creativity: Effects of competition, self-esteem, and immunization. *Creativity Research Journal, 9*, 339–346.

Getz, I., & Lubart, T. (1997). Emotion, metaphor, and the creative process. *Creativity Research Journal, 10*, 285–301.

Getz, I., & Lubart, T. (2000). An emotional, experiential perspective on creative, symbolic, metaphorical processes. *Consciousness and Emotion, 1*, 89–118.

Getzels, J. W. (1975). Problem finding and the inventiveness of solutions. *Journal of Creative Behavior, 9*, 12–18.

Getzels, J. W., & Csikszentmihalyi, M. (1976). Problem finding and creativity. In *The creative vision: A longitudinal study of problem finding in art* (pp. 236–251). New York: Wiley.

Getzels, J. W., & Jackson, P. W. (1962). *Creativity and intelligence: Explorations with gifted students.* New York: Wiley.

Getzels, J. W., & Smilansky, J. (1983). Individual differences in pupil perceptions of school problems. *British Journal of Educational Psychology, 53*, 307–316.

Ghiselin, B. (1963a). Ultimate criteria for two levels of creativity. In C. W. Taylor & F. Barron (Eds.), *Scientific creativity: Its recognition and development* (pp. 30–43). New York: Wiley.

Ghiselin, B. (1963b). The creative process and its relation to the identification of creative talent. In C. W. Taylor, & F. Barron (Eds.), *Scientific creativity: Its recognition and development* (pp. 355–364). New York: Wiley.

Gibart–Eaglemont, J. E., & Foddy, M. (1994). Creative potential and the sociometric status of children. *Creativity Research Journal, 7*, 47–57.

Gibbs, R. Jr., (1999). Metaphors. In M. A. Runco, & S. R. Pritzker (Eds.), *Encyclopedia of creativity* (pp. 209–219). San Diego, CA: Academic Press.

Gibbs, R. (2006). *Embodiment and cognitive science.* New York: Cambridge University Press.

Gick, M. L., & Holyoak, K. J. (1980). Analogical problem solving. *Cognitive Psychology, 12*, 306–355.

Gick, M. L., & Lockhart, R. S. (1995). Cognitive and affective components of insight. In R. J. Sternberg & J. E. Davidson (Eds.), *The nature of insight* (pp. 197–228). Cambridge, MA: MIT Press.

Gilchrist, M. B. (1982). Creative talent and academic competence. *Genetic Psychology Monographs, 106*, 261–318.

Gillies, J., & Campbell, S. (1985). Conservatism and poetry preferences. *British Journal of Social Psychology, 24*, 223–227.

Gilson, L. L., & Shally, C. E. (2004). A little creativity goes a long way: an examination of teams' engagement in creative processes. *Journal of Management, 30*, 453–470.

Glasgow, M. R., & Cartier, A. M. (1985). Conservatism, sensation-seeking, and music preferences. *Personality and Individual Differences, 6*, 393–395.

Gleick, J. (1987). *Chaos: Making a new science*. New York: Penguin Books.

Gleick, J. (2000). *Faster: The acceleration of just about everything*. New York: Vintage.

Glover, J., & Gary, A. L. (1976). Procedures to increase some aspects of creativity. *Journal of Applied Behavior Analysis, 9*, 79–84.

Goel, V., & Grafman, J. (2000). The role of the right prefrontal cortex in ill-structured problem solving. *Cognitive Neuropsychology, 17*, 415–436.

Goel, V., & Vartanian, O. (2005). Dissociating the roles of right ventral lateral and dorsal lateral prefrontal cortex in generation and maintenance of hypotheses in set-shift problems. *Cerebral Cortex, 15*, 1170–1177.

Goertzel, V., & Goertzel, M. G. (1962). *Cradles of eminence*. Boston, MA: Little, Brown.

Golann, S. E. (1962). The creative motive. *Journal of Personality, 30*, 588–600.

Golann, S. E. (1963). Psychological study of creativity. *Psychological Bulletin, 60*, 548–565.

Gold, J. B., & Houtz, J. C. (1984). Enhancing the creative problem-solving skills of educable mentally retarded students. *Perceptual and Motor Skills, 58*, 247–253.

Goldapple, K., Segal, Z., Garson, C., Lau, M., Bieling, P., Kennedy, S., et al. (2004). Modulation of cortical-limbic pathways in major depression: Treatment-specific effects of cognitive behavior therapy. *Archives of General Psychiatry, 61*, 34–41.

Goldberg, E., Podell, K., & Lovell, M. (1994). Lateralization of frontal lobe functions and cognitive novelty. *Journal of Clinical and Experimental Neuropsychiatry, 22*, 56–68.

Goldenberg, J., Mazursky, D., & Solomon, S. (1999). Creative sparks. *Science, 285*, 1495–1496.

Goldschmidt, G. (1999). Design. In M. A. Runco & S. R. Pritzker (Eds.), *Encyclopedia of creativity* (pp. 525–535). San Diego, CA: Academic Press.

Goleman, D. (1995). *Emotional intelligence*. New York: Bantam Books.

Goleman, D., Kaufman, P., & Ray, M. (1992). *The creative spirit*. New York: Penguin/Plume.

Gondola, J. C. (1986). The enhancement of creativity through long and short term exercise programs. *Journal of Social Behavior and Personality, 1*, 77–82.

Gondola, J. C. (1987). The effects of a single bout of aerobic dancing on selected tests of creativity. *Journal of Social Behavior and Personality, 2*, 275–278.

Gondola, J. C., & Tuckman, B. W. (1985). Effects of a systematic program of exercise on selected measures of creativity. *Perceptual and Motor Skills, 60*, 53–54.

Goodwin, D. W. (1988). *Alcohol and the writer*. New York: Penguin.

Goodwin, D. W. (1992). Alcohol as muse. *American Journal of Psychotherapy, 46*, 422–433.

Gordon, W. J. J. (1961). *Synectics: The development of creative capacity*. New York: Harper & Row.

Gordon, W. J. J. (1972). On being explicit about the creative process. *Journal of Creative Behavior, 6*, 295–300.

Gordon, W. J. J. (1976). Metaphor and invention. In A. Rothenberg & C. R. Hausman (Eds.), *The creativity question* (pp. 250–255). Durham, NC: Duke University Press.

Gordon, W. J. J., & Poze, T. (1981). Conscious/subconscious interaction in a creative act. *Journal of Creative Behavior, 15*, 1–10.

Gorman, M. E., Plucker, J., & Callahan, C. M. (1998). Turning students into inventors: Active learning modules for secondary students. *Phi Delta Kappan*, 530–535.

Goswami, A. (1995). *The self aware universe*. New York: Tarcher.

Goswami, A. (1996). Creativity and the quantum: A unified theory of creativity. *Creativity Research Journal, 9*, 47–61.

Gough, H. G. (1975). *The California psychological inventory*. Palo Alto, CA: Consulting Psychologists Press.

Gough, H., & Heilbrun, A. R. (1975). *The adjective check list manual*. Palo Alto, CA: Consulting Psychologists Press.

Gough, H. G., & Woodworth, D. G. (1960). Stylistic variations among professional research scientists. *Journal of Psychology, 49*, 87–98.

Gough, H., Hall, W., & Bradley, P. (1996). Forty years of experience with the Barron-Welsh art scale. In A. Montuori (Ed.), *Unusual associates*. Cresskill, NJ: Hampton Press.

Gould, S. J. (1989). *The structure of evolutionary theory*. Cambridge, MA: Belknap/Harvard University Press.

Gould, S. J. (1991). *Bully for brontosaurus*. New York: Norton.

Grahm, B. C., Sawyers, J. K., & DeBord, K. B. (1989). Teachers' creativity, playfulness, and style of interaction with children. *Creativity Research Journal, 2*, 41–50.

Gray, C. E. (1966). A measurement of creativity in Western civilization. *American Anthropology, 68*, 1384–1417.

Greenacre, P. (1957). The childhood of the artist: Libidinal phase development and giftedness. *Psychoanalytic Study of the Child, 12*, 47–52.

Greene, T. R., & Noice, H. (1988). Influence of positive affect upon creative thinking and problem solving in children. *Psychological Reports, 63*, 895–898.

Greengross, G., & Miller, G. F. (2009). The Big Five personality traits of professional comedians compared to amateur comedians, comedy writers, and college students. *Personality and Individual Differences, 47*, 79–83.

Gridley, M. C. (2006). Preferred thinking styles of professional fine artists. *Creativity Research Journal, 18*, 247–248.

Griffin, M., & McDermott, M. R. (1998). Exploring a tripartite relationship between rebelliousness, openness to experience, and creativity. *Social Behavior and Personality, 26*, 347–356.

Grossman, J. C., Goldstein, R., & Eisenman, R. (1974). Openness to experience and marijuana use in college students. *Psychiatric Quarterly, 48*, 86–92.

Gruber, H. E. (1981a). *Darwin on man: A psychological study of scientific creativity*. Chicago: University of Chicago Press.

Gruber, H. E. (1981b). On the relation between a-ha experiences and the construction of ideas. *History of Science, 19*, 41–59.

Gruber, H. E. (1988). The evolving systems approach to creative work. *Creativity Research Journal, 1*, 27–51.

Gruber, H. E. (1993). Creativity in the moral domain: Ought implies can implies create. *Creativity Research Journal, 6*, 3–15.

Gruber, H. (1996). The life space of a scientist: The visionary function and other aspects of Jean Piaget's thinking. *Creativity Research Journal, 9*, 251–265.

Gruber, H. E. (1997). Creative altruism, cooperation, and world peace. In M. A. Runco & R. Richards (Eds.), *Eminent creativity, everyday creativity, and health* (pp. 463–479). Norwood, NJ: Ablex.

Gruber, H. E., & Davis, S. N. (1988). Inching our way up Mount Olympus: The evolving-systems approach to creative thinking. In R. J. Sternberg (Ed.), *The nature of creativity* (pp. 243–270). New York: Cambridge University Press.

Gruber, H. E.& Wallace, D., (Eds.), (1993). Creativity in the moral domain. *Creativity Research Journal, 6*, 1–200.

Gruber, H. E., & Wallace, D. B. (1999). The case study method and evolving systems approach for understanding unique creative people at work. In R. J. Sternberg (Ed.), *Handbook of creativity* (pp. 93–115). New York: Cambridge University Press.

Guastello, S., Shissler, J., Driscoll, J., & Hyde, T. (1998). Are some cognitive styles more creatively productive than others? *Creativity Research Journal, 32*, 77–91.

Guencer, B., & Oral, G. (1993). Relationship between creativity and nonconformity to school discipline as perceived by teachers of Turkish elementary school children, by controlling for their grade and sex. *Journal of Instructional Psychology, 20*, 208–214.

Guilford, J. P. (1950). Creativity. *American Psychologist, 5*, 444–454.

Guilford, J. P. (1962). Creativity: Its measurement and development. In J. J. Parnes & H. F. Harding (Eds.), *A source book for creative thinking*. New York: Scribners.

Guilford, J. P. (1965). Frames of reference for creative behavior in the arts. In *Presented at the conference on creative behavior in the arts*. Los Angeles, CA: University of California.

Guilford, J. P. (1967). *The nature of human intelligence*. New York: McGraw-Hill.

Guilford, J. P. (1968). *Creativity, intelligence, and their educational implications*. San Diego, CA: EDITS/Knapp.

Guilford, J. P. (1975). Creativity: A quarter century of progress. In I. A. Taylor & J. W. Getzels (Eds.), *Perspectives in creativity* (pp. 37–59). Chicago, IL: Aldine.

Guilford, J. P. (1979). Some incubated thoughts on incubation. *Journal of Creative Behavior, 13*, 1–8.

Guilford, J. P. (1986). *Creative talents: Their nature, uses and development*. Buffalo, NY: Bearly.

Gur, R. C., & Rayner, J. (1976). Enhancement of creativity via free-imagery and hypnosis. *American Journal of Clinical Hypnosis, 18*, 237–249.

Gutbezahl, J., & Averill, R. J. (1996). Individual differences in emotional creativity as manifested in words and pictures. *Creativity Research Journal, 9*, 327–337.

Hackley, C., & Kover, A. J. (2007). The trouble with creatives: Negotiating creative identity in advertising agencies. *International Journal of Advertising, 26*, 63–78.

Hadamard, J. (1945). *The psychology of invention in the mathematical field*. New York: Dover.

Hadamard, J. (1949). *The psychology of invention in the mathematical field*. Princeton, NJ: Princeton University Press.

Hajcak, F. J. (1976). *The effects of alcohol on creativity. Dissertation Temple University.* Ann Arbor, Michigan: UMI, Dissertation Services.

Hall, B. S. (2002). *Weapons and warfare in renaissance Europe: Gunpowder, technology, and tactics.* Baltimore, MD: Johns Hopkins University Press.

Hall, W., & MacKinnon, M. (1969). Personality inventory correlates of creativity among architects. *Journal of Applied Psychology, 53,* 322–326.

Hallman, R. J. (1970). Toward a Hindu theory of creativity. *Educational Theory, 20,* 368–376.

Hallowell, E. M., & Ratey, J. J. (1994). *Driven to distraction: Recognizing and coping with attention deficit disorder from childhood to adulthood.* New York: Simon and Schuster.

Halpern, D. (2003). Thinking critically about creative thinking. In M. A. Runco (Ed.), *Critical creative processes* (pp. 189–208). Cresskill, NJ: Hampton Press.

Hampton, J. (1987). Inheritance of attributes in natural concept conjunctions. *Memory and Cognition, 15,* 55–71.

Haner, U.-E. (2005). Spaces for creativity and innovation in two established organizations. *Creativity and Innovation Management, 14,* 288–298.

Hann, C. M. (1994). Fast forward: The great transformation realized. In C. M. Hann (Ed.), *When history accelerates: Essays on rapid social change, complexity, and creativity* (pp. 1–22). London: Athlone.

Harman, W., & Rheingold, H. (1984). *Higher creativity: Liberating the unconscious for breakthrough insights.* New York: Penguin Putnam.

Harnad, S. (1972). Creativity, lateral saccades and the nondominant hemisphere. *Perceptual and Motor Skills, 34,* 653–654.

Harpaz, I. (1990). Asymmetry of hemispheric functions and creativity: An empirical examination. *Journal of Creative Behavior, 24,* 161–170.

Harrington, D. M. (1975). Effects of explicit instructions to be creative on psychological meaning of divergent thinking test scores. *Journal of Personality, 43,* 434–454.

Harrington, D. M. (1980). Creativity, analogical thinking, and muscular metaphors. *Journal of Mental Imagery, 4,* 13–23.

Harrington, D. M. (1981). Creativity, analogical thinking, and muscular metaphors. *Journal of Mental Imagery, 6,* 121–126.

Harrington, D. M. (1990). The ecology of human creativity: A psychological perspective. In M. A. Runco & R. S. Albert (Eds.), *Theories of creativity* (pp. 143–169). Newbury Park, CA: Sage.

Harrington, D. M., Block, J., & Block, J. H. (1983). Predicting creativity in preadolescence form divergent thinking in early childhood. *Journal of Personality and Social Psychology, 45,* 609–623.

Harrington, D. M., Block, J. H., & Block, J. (1987). Testing aspects of Carl Rogers' theory of creative environments: Child rearing antecedents of creative potential in young adolescents. *Journal of Personality and Social Psychology, 52,* 851–856.

Harrison, I. (2004). *The book of invention: How'd they come up with that?* Washington, DC: National Geographic.

Hasenfus, N., Martindale, C., & Birnbaum, D. (1983). Psychological reality of cross-media artistic styles: Human perception and performance. *Journal of Experimental Psychology, 9,* 841–863.

Hass, R. W., & Weisberg, R. W. (2009). Career development in two seminal American songwriters: A test of the equal odds rule. *Creativity Research Journal, 21,* 183–190.

Hassler, M. (1990). Functional cerebral asymmetries and cognitive abilities in musicians, painters, and controls. *Brain and Cognition, 13,* 1–7.

Hassler, M. (1992). Creative musical behavior and sex hormones: Musical talent and spatial ability in the two sexes. *Psychoneuroendocrinology, 17,* 55–70.

Hattie, J., & Fitzgerald, D. (1983). Do left-handers tend to be more creative? *Journal of Creative Behavior, 17,* 269.

Hausman, C. (1979). Criteria of creativity. *Philosophical and Phenomenological Research, 40,* 237–249.

Hausman, C. R. (1980). Creativity and rationality. In A. Rothenberg & C. R. Hausman (Eds.), *The creativity question* (pp. 343–351). Durham, NC: Duke University Press.

Hausman, C. (1989). *Metaphor and art.* New York: Cambridge University Press.

Hausman, C., & Anderson, D. (2012). Philosophical approaches to creativity. In M. A. Runco (Ed.), *Creativity research handbook* (Vol. 2, pp. 79–94). Cresskill, NJ: Hampton Press.

Hayes, R. R. (1989). Cognitive processes in creativity. In J. A. Glover, R. R. Ronning & C. R. Reynolds (Eds.), *Handbook of creativity* (pp. 135–145). New York: Plenum.

He, W., & Wong, W. (2011). Gender differences in creative thinking revisited: Findings from analysis of variability. *Personality and Individual Differences, 51,* 807–811.

Healy, D. (2005). *Attention deficit hyperactivity disorder and creativity: An investigation into their relationship.* New Zealand: Dissertation, University of Canterbury.

Heckert, D. R. (2000). Positive deviance. In P. A. Adler & P. Adler (Eds.), *Constructions of deviance: Social power, context, and interaction* (3rd edn). Scarborough, ON: Wadsworth.

Heilman, K. M., Nadeau, S. E., & Beversdorf, D. O. (2003). Creative innovation: Possible brain mechanism. *Neurocase, 9,* 369–379.

Heinelt, G. (1974). *Kreative Lehrer/kreative Schüler [Creative teachers/creative students].* Freiburg: Herder.

Heinzen, T. (1994). Situational affect: Proactive and reactive creativity. In M. Shaw & M. A. Runco (Eds.), *Creativity and affect* (pp. 127–146). Norwood, NJ: Ablex.

Helson, R. (1973). Personality characteristics of women of distinction. *Psychology of Women Quarterly, 3,* 70–78.

Helson, R. (1990). Creativity in women: Inner and outer views over time. In M. A. Runco & R. S. Albert (Eds.), *Theories of creativity* (pp. 46–58). Newbury Park, CA: Sage.

Helson, R. (1996). Arnheim award address to division 10 of the American Psychological Association: In search of the creative personality. *Creativity Research Journal, 9,* 295–306.

Helson, R. (1999). Institute of personality assessment and research. In M. A. Runco & S. R. Pritzker (Eds.), *Encyclopedia of creativity* (pp. 71–79). San Diego, CA: Academic Press.

Helson, R., Roberts, B., & Agronick, G. (1995). Enduringness and change in creative personality and prediction of occupational creativity. *Journal of Personality and Social Psychology, 69,* 1173–1183.

Hemingway, E. (2005). Quoted by the *LA Times,* May 14. <http://www.latimes.com/classified/automotive/highway1/la-hy-nei111may11,0,262461.story? coll=la-home-highway1>.

Hendron, G. (1989). Using sign language to access right brain communication: A tool for teachers. *Journal of Creative Behavior, 23,* 116–120.

Hennessey, B. A. (1989). The effect of extrinsic constraints on children's creativity while using a computer. *Creativity Research Journal, 2,* 151–168.

Hennessey, B. (1994). The consensual assessment technique: An examination of the relationship between ratings of product and process creativity. *Creativity Research Journal, 6,* 193–208.

Hennessey, B. A., & Zbikowski, S. M. (1993). Immunizing children against the negative effects of reward: A further examination of intrinsic motivation training techniques. *Creativity Research Journal, 6,* 297–307.

Hennessey, B. A., Amabile, T. M., & Martinage, M. (1989). Immunizing children against the negative effects of reward. *Contemporary Educational Psychology, 14,* 212–227.

Hequet, M. (1995). Doing more with less. *Training, 32,* 76–82.

Herman, J. (1993). Hay fever's dramatic cure. *Los Angeles Times,* F1–F17 (9 April).

Hermann, N. (1996). *The whole brain business book.* New York: McGraw-Hill.

Herman-Toffler, L. R., & Tuckman, B. W. (1998). The effects of aerobic training on children's creativity, self-perception, and aerobic power. *Sports Psychiatry, 7,* 773–790.

Hershman, D. J., & Lieb, J. (1998). *Manic depression and creativity.* Amherst, NY: Prometheus Books.

Hertz, M. (1999). Invention. In M. A. Runco & S. R. Pritzker (Eds.), *Encyclopedia of creativity* (Vol. 2, pp. 95–102). San Diego, CA: Academic Press.

Hesslow, G. (2002). Conscious thought as simulation of behaviour and perception. *Trends in Cognitive Sciences, 6,* 242–247.

Hewlett, S. A., Luce, C. B., & Servon, L. J. (2008). Stopping the exodus of women in science. *Harvard Business Review, 86,* 22–24.

Higgins, J. (1994). *101 creative problem solving techniques: The handbook of new ideas for business.* Winter Park, FL: New Management Publishing Company.

Higgins, J. M. (1995). *Innovate or evaporate: Test and improve your organization's I.Q—its innovations quotient.* Winter Park, FL: New Management Publishing Company.

Higgins, J. M. (1996). Innovate or evaporate: Creative techniques for strategists. *Long Range Planning, 29,* 370–380.

Hilburn, R. (2004). Rock's enigmatic poet opens a long-private door. *LA Times Calendar,* April 4. <http://www.calendarlive.com/music/pop/cl-ca-dylan04apr04,0,3583678.story>.

Hines, D., & Martindale, C. (1974). Induced lateral eye-movements and creative and intellectual performance. *Perceptual and Motor Skills, 39,* 153–154.

Hines, T. (1991). The myth of right hemisphere creativity. *Journal of Creative Behavior, 25,* 223–227.

Hirt, E. R. (1999). Mood. In M. A. Runco & S. R. Pritzker (Eds.), *Encyclopedia of creativity* (Vol. 2, pp. 241–250). San Diego, CA: Academic Press.

Hoffman, A. (1994). While we waltz off on a book tour. *Los Angeles Times Book Review*, 10 (June 19).

Hofstadter, D. (1985). *Metamagical themas: Questing for the essence of mind and patterns*. New York: Bantam Books.

Hofstede, G. (1991). *Culture's consequences*. Beverly Hills, CA: Sage.

Holguin, O., & Sherrill, C. (1990). On motor creativity, age, and self-concept, in young learning disabled boys. *Creativity Research Journal, 3*, 293–294.

Holland, J. L. (1961). Creative and academic achievement among talented adolescents. *Journal of Educational Psychology, 52*, 136–147.

Holland, J. L. (1996). A psychological classification scheme for vocations and major fields. *Journal of Counseling Psychology, 13*, 278–288.

Holland, J. L. (1997). *Making vocational choices: A theory of vocation-personalities and work environments* (3nd ed.). Odessa, FL: Psychological Assessment Resources.

Hollingworth, L. S. (1942). *Children above 180 IQ Stanford-Binet: Origin and development*. Yonkers, NY: World Book.

Holmes, F. L. (1999). Hans Adolf Krebs (1900–1981): Biochemist and discoverer of the urea cycle and the citric acid cycle. In M. A. Runco & S. R. Pritzker (Eds.), *Encyclopedia of creativity* (pp. 131–138). San Diego, CA: Academic Press.

Holmes, T. H., & Rahe, R. H. (1967). The social readjustment rating scale. *Journal of Psychosomatic Research, 11*, 213–218.

Holton, G. (1973). *Thematic origins of scientific thought: Kepler to Einstein*. Cambridge, MA: Harvard University Press.

Holton, G. (1978). *The scientific imagination: Case studies*. Cambridge: Cambridge University Press.

Holton, G. (1979). Constructing a theory: Einstein's model. *American Scholar, 48*, 309–339.

Hoppe, K., & Kyle, N. (1990). Dual brain, creativity, and health. *Creativity Research Journal, 3*, 150–157.

Hoppe, K. (1977). Split brains and psychoanalysis. *Psychoanalytic Quarterly, 46*, 220–224.

Hoppe, K. (1988). Hemispheric specialization and creativity. In K. Hoppe (Ed.), *Hemispheric specialization* (pp. 303–315). Philadelphia, PA: Saunders.

Horan, R. (2007). The relationship between creativity and intelligence: A combined yogic-scientific approach. *Creativity Research Journal, 19*, 179–202.

Horan, R. (2009). The neuropsychological connection between creativity and meditation. *Creativity Research Journal, 2*, 199–222.

Horng, J. S., & Hu, M. L. (2008). The mystery in the kitchen: Culinary creativity. *Creativity Research Journal, 20*, 221–230.

Hotz, R. E. (2005). *Soft tissue discovered in bone of a dinosaur*, March 25. <http://www.latimes.com/news/science/la-sci-tyrann025mar25,0,7641410.story? coll=la-home-headlines>.

Hough, L. M. (1992). The Big Five personality variables—construct confusion: Description versus prediction. *Human Performance, 5*, 139–155.

Houtz, J. C., & Frankel, A. (1992). Effects of incubation and imagery training on creativity. *Creativity Research Journal, 5*, 183–189.

Howkins, J. (2001). *The creative economy: How people make money from ideas*. London: Penguin Global.

Hu, M. et al. (in press). A structural relationship of teacher encouragement and student creativity. *Creativity Research Journal*.

Huber, J. C. (1998a). Invention and inventivity is a random, poisson process: A potential guide to analysis of general creativity. *Creativity Research Journal, 11*, 231–241.

Huber, J. C. (1998b). Invention and inventivity as a special kind of creativity, with implications for general creativity. *Journal of Creative Behavior, 32*, 58–72.

Hui, A., & Rudowicz, E. (1997). Creative personality versus Chinese personality: How distinctive are these two personality factors? *Psychologia, XL*(4), 277–285.

Hull, D. L., Tessner, P. D., & Diamond, A. M. (1978). Planck's principle: Do younger scientists accept new scientific ideas with greater alacrity than older scientists? *Science, 202*, 717–723.

Hulsheger, U. R., Anderson, N., & Salgado, J. F. (2009). Selecting for innovation: What is good for job performance is not necessarily good for innovative performance. In: Paper presented at the EAWOP conference, Santiago de Compostela, May 2009.

Hunter, S. T., Bedell, K. E., & Mumford, M. D. (2007). Climate for creativity: A quantitative review. *Creativity Research Journal, 19*, 69–90.

Huntley, H. L. (1970). *The divine proportion: A study in mathematical beauty*. New York: Dover.

Hurlock, E. G., & Burstein, M. (1932). The imaginary playmate: A questionnaire study. *Journal of Genetic Psychology, 41,* 380–392.

Iglesias, K. (2001). *The 101 habits of highly successful screenwriters.* Avon, MA: Adams Media Corporation.

Ione, A. (1999). Multiple discovery. In M. A. Runco & S. R. Pritzker (Eds.), *Encyclopedia of creativity* (pp. 261–271). San Diego, CA: Academic Press.

Ippolito, M. F., & Tweney, R. D. (2003). The journey to Jacob's Room: The network of enterprise of Virginia Woolf's first experimental novel. *Creativity Research Journal, 15,* 25–43.

Ippolito, M. R. (1999). Virginia Woolf. In M. A. Runco & S. R. Pritzker (Eds.), *Encyclopedia of creativity* (pp. 709–714). San Diego, CA: Academic Press.

Isaksen, S. G., Lauer, K. J., Ekvall, G., & Britz, A. (2000–2001). Perceptions of the best and worst climates for creativity: Preliminary validation evidence for the situational outlook questionnaire. *Creativity Research Journal, 13,* 171–184.

Isen, A. M. (1993). Positive affect and decision making. In M. Lewis & J. Haviland (Eds.), *Handbook of emotions* (pp. 261–277). New York: Guilford.

Isen, A. M. (1999). On the relationship between affect and creative problem solving. In S. W. Russ (Ed.), *Affect, creative experience and psychological adjustment* (pp. 3–17). Philadelphia, PA: Brunner/Mazel.

Isen, A. M., & Baron, R. A. (1991). Positive affect as a factor in organizational behavior. *Research in Organizational Behavior, 13,* 1–53.

Isen, A. M., & Daubman, K. A. (1984). The influence of affect on categorization. *Journal of Personality and Social Psychology, 47,* 1206–1217.

Isen, A. M., Johnson, M. M., Mertz, E., & Robinson, G. F. (1985). The influence of positive affect on the unusualness of word associations. *Journal of Personality and Social Psychology, 48,* 1413–1426.

Isen, A. M., Daubman, K. A., & Nowicki, G. P. (1987). Positive affect facilitates creative problem solving. *Journal of Personality and Social Psychology, 52,* 1122–1131.

Ito, M. (1993). Movement and thought: Identical control mechanisms by the cerebellum. *Trends in Neurosciences, 16,* 448–450.

Ito, M. (1997). Cerebellar microcomplexes. In J. D. Schmahmann (Ed.), *The cerebellum and cognition* (pp. 475–487). New York: Academic Press.

Jackson, S. E. (1996). The consequences of diversity and multi disciplinary work teams. In M. West (Ed.), *Handbook of work psychology* (pp. 53–76). Chichester: Wiley.

Jakobs, P. L. (1999). Wilbur and Orville Wright. In M. A. Runco & S. Pritzker (Eds.), *Encyclopedia of creativity* (pp. 721–726). San Diego, CA: Academic Press.

James, W. (1880). Great men, great thoughts, and the environment (lecture delivered before the Harvard Natural History Society). *Atlantic Monthly* October, 1880. Reproduced in <http://www.emory.edu/EDUCATION/mfp/jgreatmen.html>.

James, W. (1950). *The principles of psychology* (authorized ed.). New York: Dover (Original work published in 1890).

Jamison, K. R. (1989). Mood disorders and patterns of creativity in British writers and artists. *Psychiatry, 52,* 125–134.

Jamison, K. R. (1993). *Touched by fire: Manic depressive illness and the artistic temperament.* New York: Free Press.

Jamison, K. R. (1997). Mood disorders and patterns of creativity in British writers and artists. In M. A. Runco, & R. Richards (Eds.), *Eminent creativity, everyday creativity, and health* (pp. 19–31). Greenwich, CT: Ablex.

Jansson, D. G., Condoor, S. S., & Brock, H. R. (1993). Cognition in design: Viewing the hidden side of the design process. *Environment and Planning B, Planning and Design, 20,* 257–271.

Jaquish, G. A., & Ripple, R. E. (1984). A life-span developmental cross-cultural study of divergent thinking abilities. *Human Development, 20,* 1–11.

Jauk, E., Benedek, M., Dunst, B., & Neubauer, A. C. (2013). The relationship between intelligence and creativity: New support for the threshold hypothesis by means of empirical breakpoint detection. *Intelligence, 41,* 212–221.

Jausovec, N. (1989). Affect in analogical transfer. *Creativity Research Journal, 2,* 255–266.

Jausovec, N. (1991). Flexible strategy use: A characteristic of gifted problem solving. *Creativity Research Journal, 4,* 349–366.

Jaussi, K. S., Randel, A. E., & Dionne, S. D. (2007). I am, I think I can, and I do: The role of personal identity, self-efficacy, and cross-application of experiences in creativity at work. *Creativity Research Journal, 19,* 247–258.

Jay, E., & Perkins, D. (1997). Creativity's compass: A review of problem finding. In M. A. Runco (Ed.), *Creativity research handbook* (Vol. 1, pp. 257–293). Cresskill, NJ: Hampton Press.

Jeffrey, L. (1999). William Wordsworth. In M. A. Runco & S. R. Pritzker (Eds.), *Encyclopedia of creativity* (pp. 715–720). San Diego, CA: Academic Press.

Jellen, H. U., & Urban, K. (1989). Assessing creative potential worldwide: The first cross-cultural application of the test for creative thinking-drawing production (TCT-DP). *Gifted Education, 6*, 78–86.

Jenkins, J. E., Hedlund, D. E., & Ripple, R. E. (1988). Parental separation effects on children's divergent thinking abilities and creative potential. *Child Study Journal, 18*, 149–159.

Jensen, A. (1980). *Bias in mental testing*. New York: Free Press.

Jeraj, M., & Antoncic, B. (in press). Toward a conceptualization of entrepreneurial curiosity and construct development: A multi-country empirical validation. *Creativity Research Journal*.

Jerison, H. (1974). *Evolution of the brain and intelligence*. San Diego, CA: Academic Press.

John, O. P., & Srivastava, S. (1999). The Big Five trait taxonomy: History, measurement, and theoretical perspectives. In L. Pervin & O. P. John (Eds.), *Handbook of personality: Theory and research* (pp. 102–138). New York: Guilford Press.

Johnson, D., Runco, M. A., & Raina, M. K. (2003). Parents' and teachers' implicit theories of children's creativity: A cross-cultural perspective. *Creativity Research Journal, 14*, 427–438.

Johnson, H., & Carruthers, L. (2006). Supporting creative and reflective processes. *International Journal of Human-Computer Studies, 64*, 998–1030.

Johnson, L. D. (1985). Creative thinking potential: Another example of U-shaped development? *Creative Child and Adult Quarterly, 10*, 146–159.

Johnson, R. A. (1990). Creative thinking in mentally retarded deaf adolescents. *Psychological Reports, 66*, 1203–1206.

John-Steiner, V. (1989). Anais Nin. In D. Wallace & H. E. Gruber (Eds.), *Creative people at work*. New York: Oxford University Press.

John-Steiner, V. (1997). *Notebooks of the mind*. Oxford: Oxford University Press.

Jones, E. (1997). The case against objectifying art. *Creativity Research Journal, 10*, 207–214.

Jones, K., Runco, M. A., Dorinan, C., & Freeland, D. C. (1997). Influential factors in artists' lives and themes in their art work. *Creativity Research Journal, 10*, 221–228.

Jost, J. T., Glaser, J., Kruglanski, A. W., & Sulloway, F. J. (2003). Political conservatism as motivated social cognition. *Psychological Bulletin, 129*, 339–375.

Joussemet, M., & Koestner, R. (1999). Effect of expected rewards on children's creativity. *Creativity Research Journal, 12*, 231–239.

Jowett, B. (1937). *The dialogues of Plato*. New York: Random House.

Jung, C. G. (1923). On the relation of analytic psychology to poetic art. *British Journal of Medical Psychology, 3*, 213–231.

Jung, C. G. (1962). *Psychological types*. New York: Pantheon.

Jung, C. (1964). *Man and his symbols*. New York: Doubleday.

Jung, D. I. (2000–2001). Transformational and transactional leadership and their effects on creativity in groups. *Creativity Research Journal, 13*, 185–195.

Jung, D. I., Chow, C., & Wu, A. (2003). The role of transformational leadership in enhancing organizational innovation: Hypotheses and some preliminary findings. *The Leadership Quarterly, 14*, 525–544.

Jung-Beeman, M., Bowden, E. M., Haberman, J., Frymiare, J. L., Arambel-Greenblatt, R., Reber, P. J., et al. (2004). Neural activity people solve verbal problems with insight. *PLoS Biol, 2*, E97.

Kabaler-Adler, S. (1993). *The compulsion to create: A psychoanalytic study of women artists*. New York: Routledge.

Kaizer, C., & Shore, B. (1995). Strategy flexibility in more and less competent students on mathematical word problems. *Creativity Research Journal, 8*, 77–82.

Kanazawa, S. (2000). Scientific discoveries as cultural displays: A further test of Miller's courtship model. *Evolution and Human Behavior, 21*, 317–321.

Kanazawa, S. (2003). Why productivity fades with age: The crime-genius connection. *Journal of Research in Personality, 37*, 257–272.

Kant, I. (1781/2008). *Critique of pure reason*. New York: Penguin.

Kao, J. J. (1991). *Managing creativity*. Englewood Cliffs, NJ: Prentice Hall.

Kaplan, A., Middleton, M. J., Urdan, T., & Midgley, C. (2002). Achievement goals and goal structures. In C. Midgley (Ed.), *Goals, goal structures and patterns of adaptive learning* (pp. 21–54). Mahwah, NJ: Lawrence Erlbaum.

Karau, S. J., & Kelly, J. R. (1992). The effects of time scarcity and time abundance on group performance and interaction. *Journal of Experimental Social Psychology, 28*, 542–571.

Kashdan, T. B., & Fincham, F. D. (2002). Facilitating creativity by regulating curiosity. *American Psychologist, 57,* 373–374.

Kasof, J. (1995). Explaining creativity: The attributional perspective. *Creativity Research Journal, 8,* 311–366.

Kasof, J. (1997). Creativity and breadth of attention. *Creativity Research Journal, 10,* 303–315.

Katz, A. (1978). Creativity and the right cerebral hemisphere: Towards a physiologically based theory of creativity. *Journal of Creative Behavior, 12,* 253–264.

Katz, A. (1980). Do left-handers tend to be more creative? *Journal of Creative Behavior, 14,* 271.

Katz, A. (1983). Creativity and individual differences in asymmetric hemispheric functioning. *Empirical Studies of the Arts, 1,* 3–16.

Katz, A. N. (1986). The relationship between creativity and cerebral hemisphericity for creative architects, scientists, and mathematicians. *Empirical Studies of the Arts, 4,* 97–108.

Katz, A. N. (1997). Creativity in the cerebral hemispheres. In M. A. Runco (Ed.), *Creativity research handbook* (pp. 203–226). Cresskill, NJ: Hampton Press.

Katz, A., & Thompson, M. (1993). On judging creativity: By one's acts shall ye be known. *Creativity Research Journal, 6,* 345–364.

Katz, J. J. (1964). Semi-sentences. In J. A. Fodor & J. J. Katz (Eds.), *Structure of language* (pp. 400–416). Englewood Cliffs, NJ: Prentice Hall.

Katz, R. (1982). The effect of group longevity on project communication and performance. *Administrative Science Quarterly, 27,* 81–104.

Katz-Buonincontro, J. (2012). Creativity at the crossroads: Pragmatic versus humanist claims in education reform speeches. *Creativity Research Journal, 24,* 257–265.

Kaufman, J. C. (2006). Self-reported differences in creativity by ethnicity and gender. *Applied Cognitive Psychology, 20,* 1065–1082.

Kaufmann, G., & Vosburg, S. K. (1997). Paradoxical mood effects on creative problem solving. *Cognition and Emotion, 11,* 151–170.

Kaufmann, G., & Vosburg, S. K. (2002). Mood effects in early and late idea production. *Creativity Research Journal, 14,* 317–330.

Kaufmann, G. (1979). The explorer and the assimilator: A cognitive style distinction and its potential implications for innovative problem solving. *Scandinavian Journal of Educational Research, 23,* 101–108.

Kaufmann, G. (2003). The effect of mood on creativity in the innovative process. In L. V. Shavinina (Ed.), *International handbook on innovation* (pp. 191–203). Mahwah, NJ: Lawrence Erlbaum Associates.

Kaun, D. E. (1991). Writers die young: The impact of work and leisure on longevity. *Journal of Economic Psychology, 12,* 381–399.

Kavaler-Adler, S. (1993). *The compulsion to create: A psychoanalytic study of women artists.* New York: Routledge.

Kavolis, V. (1966). Community dynamics and artistic creativity. *American Sociological Review, 31,* 208–217.

Keegan, R. (1999). Charles Darwin. In M. A. Runco & S. R. Pritzker (Eds.), *Encyclopedia of creativity* (pp. 493–500). San Diego, CA: Academic Press.

Keegan, J. (2003). *Intelligence in war: Knowledge of the enemy from Napoleon to al-Qaeda.* New York: Knopf.

Kehagia, A. A. (2009). Anais Nin: A case study of personality disorder and creativity. *Personality and Individual Differences, 46,* 800–808.

Keller, F. (1968). Goodbye teacher. *Journal of Applied Behavior Analysis, 1,* 79–89.

Kelly, K., & Kneipp, L. B. (2009). You do what you are: The relationship between the scale of creative attributes and behavior and vocational interests. *Journal of Instructional Psychology, 36,* 79–83.

Kennett, K. F., & Cropley, A. J. (1975). Uric acid and divergent thinking: a possible relationship. *British Journal of Psychology, 66,* 175–180.

Kershner, J., & Ledger, G. (1985). Effect of sex, intelligence, and style of thinking on creativity: A comparison of gifted and average IQ children. *Journal of Personality and Social Psychology, 48,* 1033–1040.

Khandwalla, P. N. (1993). An exploratory investigation of divergent thinking through protocol analysis. *Creativity Research Journal, 6,* 241–259.

Kharkhurin, A. V., & Samadpour Motalleebi, S. N. (2008). The impact of culture on the creative potential of American, Russian, and Iranian college students. *Creativity Research Journal, 20,* 404–411.

Khasky, A. D., & Smith, J. C. (1999). Stress, relaxation states, and creativity. *Perceptual and Motor Skills, 88,* 409–416.

Khatena, J. (1971). *Something about myself: Norms—technical manual.* Huntington, WV: Marshall University.

Khatena, J. (1975). Creative imagination imagery and analogy. *Gifted Child Quarterly, 19,* 149–160.

Kim, J., & Michael, W. B. (1995). The relationship of creativity measures to school achievement and to preferred learning and thinking styles in a sample of Korean high school students. *Educational and Psychological Measurement, 55*, 60–74.

Kim, K.-H. (2011). The creativity crisis: The decrease in creative thinking scores on the Torrance tests of creative thinking. *Creativity Research Journal, 23*, 285–295.

Kimura, D. (1964). Left–right differences in the perception of melodies. *Quarterly Journal of Experimental Psychology, 16*, 355–358.

King, L. A., McKee Walker, L., & Broyles, S. J. (1996). Creativity and the five-factor model. *Journal of Research in Personality, 30*, 189–203.

Kinney, D., Richards, R., Lowing, P. A., LeBlanc, D., Zimbalist, M. E., & Harlan, P. (2000–2001). Creativity in offspring of schizophrenic and control parents: An adoption study. *Creativity Research Journal, 13*, 17–25.

Kinsbourne, M. (1974). Direction of gaze and distribution of cerebral thought processes. *Neuropsychologica, 12*, 279–281.

Kirton, M. J. (1980). Adaptors and innovators in organizations. *Human Relations, 33*, 213–224.

Klein, C. M. (1968). Creativity and incidental learning as functions of cognitive control of attention deployment. *Dissertation Abstracts, 28*(11-B), 4747–4748.

Koberg, D., & Bagnall, J. (1976). *The universal traveller*. Los Altos, CA: William Kaufmann.

Koberg, D., & Bagnall, J. (1991). *The universal traveler: A soft-systems guide to creativity, problem-solving and the process of reaching goals*. Menlo Park, CA: Crisp Publications.

Koestler, A. (1964). *The act of creation*. New York: Macmillan.

Kogan, N., & Pankove, E. (1974). Long-term predictive validity of divergent thinking tests: Some negative evidence. *Journal of Educational Psychology, 66*, 802–810.

Kohlberg, L. (1987). The development of moral judgment and moral action. In L. Kohlberg (Ed.), *Child psychology and childhood education: A cognitive developmental view*. New York: Longman.

Kohler, W. (1925). *The mentality of the apes*. New York: Harcourt Brace.

Konecni, V. J. (2003). The golden section: Elusive, but detectable. *Creativity Research Journal, 15*, 267–275.

Kozbelt, A. (2008). E. H. Gombrich on creativity: A cognitive–historical case study. *Creativity Research Journal, 20*, 93–104.

Kraemer, D., Macrae, C. N., Green, A., & Kelly, W. (2005). Sound of silence activates auditory cortex. *Nature, 434*, 158.

Kraepelin, E. (1976). Manic depressive illness and paranoia (R. M. Barclay, trans.). In G. M. Robertson (Ed.), *Classics in psychiatry* (pp. 1–43). New York: Arno Press (Original work published in 1921).

Kraft, A. (2003). The limits to creativity and education: Dilemmas for the educator. *Journal of Educational Studies, 51*, 113–127.

Krippner, S. (1965). Hypnosis and creativity. *American Journal of Clinical Hypnosis, 8*, 94–99.

Krippner, S. (1968). The psychedelic state, the hypnotic trance and the creative act. *Journal of Humanistic Psychology, 8*, 49–67.

Kris, E. (1950). Preconscious mental processes. *Psychoanalytic Quarterly, 19*, 539–552.

Kris, E. (1952). *Psychoanalytic explorations in art*. New York: International Universities Press.

Kris, E. (1971). *Psychoanalytic explorations in art*. New York: International Universities Press (Original work published in 1952).

Kroeber, A. L. (1944). *Configurations of cultural growth*. Berkeley, CA: University of California Press.

Krull, K. (1993). *Lives of the musicians: Good times, bad times, and what the neighbors thought*. San Diego, CA: Harcourt.

Krull, K. (1994). *Lives of the writers: Comedies, tragedies, and what the neighbors thought*. San Diego, CA: Harcourt.

Krull, K. (1995). *Lives of the artists: Masterpieces, messes, and what the neighbors thought*. San Diego, CA: Harcourt Brace.

Kubie, L. (1958). *Neurotic distortion of the creative process*. Lawrence, KS: University of Kansas Press.

Kuhn, T. (1957). *The Copernican Revolution*. Cambridge, MA: Harvard Press.

Kuhn, T. S. (1962). *Structure of scientific revolutions*. Chicago: University of Chicago Press.

Kuhn, T. (1963). The essential tension: Tradition and innovation in scientific research. In C. W. Taylor & F. Barron (Eds.), *Scientific creativity: Its recognition and development* (pp. 341–354). New York: Wiley.

Kumar, G. (1978). Creativity functioning in relation to personality, value-orientation and achievement motivation. *Indian Educational Review, 13*, 110–115.

Kumar, V. K., Holman, E. R., & Rudegeair, P. (1991). Creativity styles of freshman students. *Journal of Creative Behavior, 25*, 320–323.

Kumar, V. K., Kemmler, D., & Holman, E. R. (1997). The creativity styles questionnaire—revised. *Creativity Research Journal, 10,* 51–58.

Kurtzberg, T. R. (2005). Feeling creative, being creative: An empirical study of diversity and creativity in teams. *Creativity Research Journal, 17,* 51–65.

Kurz, E. M. (1996). Marginalizing discovery: Karl Popper's intellectual roots in psychology; or, how the study of discovery was banned from science studies. *Creativity Research Journal, 9,* 173–187.

Kwang, N. (2002). *Why Asians are less creative than Westerners.* Singapore: Prentice Hall.

Kwang, N. A., & Rodrigues, D. (2002). A big-five personality profile of the adapter and innovator. *Journal of Creative Behavior, 36,* 254–268.

Kwang, N. A., Ang, R. P., Ooi, L. B., Shin, W. S., Oei, T. P. S., & Leng, L. (2005). Do adaptors and innovators subscribe to opposing values? *Creativity Research Journal, 17,* 273–281.

Lachmann, F. M. (2005). Creativity, perversion, and the violations of expectations. *International Forum of Psychoanalysis, 14,* 162–165.

Lack, S. A., Kumar, V. K., & Arevalo, S. (2003). Fantasy proneness, creative capacity, and styles of creativity. *Perceptual and Motor Skills, 96,* 19–24.

Lajoie, D., & Shapiro, S. (1992). Definitions of transpersonal psychology: The first twenty-three years. *Journal of Transpersonal Psychology, 24,* 79–98.

Lamb, D., & Easton, S. (1984). *Multiple discovery.* Wiltshire, England: Avebury.

Langan-Fox, J., & Shirley, D. A. (2003). The nature and measurement of intuition: cognitive and behavioral interests, personality, and experiences. *Creativity Research Journal, 15,* 207–222.

Langer, E. (1989). *Mindfulness.* Reading, MA: Addison-Wesley.

Langer, E., Hatem, M., Joss, J., & Howell, M. (1989). Conditional teaching and mindful learning: The role of uncertainty in education. *Creativity Research Journal, 2,* 139–150.

Langly, P., & Jones, R. (1988). A computational model of scientific thought. In R. J. Sternberg (Ed.), *The nature of creativity: Contemporary psychological perspectives* (pp. 340–361). Cambridge: Cambridge University Press.

Larey, T., & Paulus, P. (1999). Group preference and convergent tendencies in small groups: A content analysis of group brainstorming performance. *Creativity Research Journal, 12,* 175–184.

Lasswell, H. D. (1959). The social setting for creativity. In H. H. Anderson (Ed.), *Creativity and its cultivation* (pp. 203–221). New York: Harper.

Lau, S. (2005). *The zero.* Taipei, Taiwan: Presented at Nanyang University.

Lau, S., & Cheung, P. C. (2010). Developmental trends of creativity: What twists of turn do boys and girls take at different grades? *Creativity Research Journal, 22,* 329–336.

Lau, S., & Li, W.-L. (1996). Peer status and perceived creativity: Are popular children viewed by peers and teachers as creative? *Creativity Research Journal, 9,* 347–352.

Laurier, E., & Brown, B. (2012). The mediated work of imagination in film editing: Proposals, suggestions, re-iterations, directions and other ways of producing possible sequences. In M. Broth, E. Laurier, & L. Mondada (Eds.), *Video at work.* New York: Routledge.

Lazarus, R. S. (1991). Cognition and motivation in emotion. *American Psychologist, 46,* 352–367.

Le Corbusier (1954). *The modulor* (C. E. Jeanneret-Gris, Trans.). London: Faber & Faber.

Lee, E. A., & Seo, H. A. (2006). Understanding of creativity by Korean elementary teachers in gifted education. *Creativity Research Journal, 18,* 237–242.

Lee, P. M. (1999). *Object to be destroyed: The work of Matt-Clark.* Cambridge, MA: MIT Press.

Lee, S. A., & Dow, G. T. (2011). Malevolent creativity: Does personality influence malicious divergent thinking? *Creativity Research Journal, 23,* 73–82.

Lehman, H. C. (1953). *Age and achievement.* Princeton, NJ: Princeton University Press.

Lehman, H. C. (1960). The age decrement in outstanding scientific creativity. *American Psychologist, 15,* 128–134.

Lehman, H. C. (1966). The most creative years of engineers and other technologists. *Journal of Genetic Psychology, 108,* 263–277.

Leiner, H., & Leiner, A. (1997). How fibers subserve computing capabilities: Similarities between brains and machines. In J. D. Schmahmann (Ed.), *The cerebellum and cognition* (pp. 535–553). New York: Academic Press.

Leiner, H., Leiner, A., & Dow, R. (1986). Does the cerebellum contribute to mental skills? *Behavioral Neuroscience, 100,* 443–454.

Leiner, H., Leiner, A., & Dow, R. (1989). Reappraising the cerebellum: What does the hind-brain contribute to the forebrain? *Behavioral Neuroscience, 103,* 998–1008.

Lemons, G. (2005). When the horse drinks: Enhancing everyday creativity using elements of improvisation. *Creativity Research Journal, 17*, 25–36.

Lepper, M. R., Greene, D., & Nisbett, R. E. (1973). Undermining children's intrinsic interest with extrinsic reward: A test of the overjustification hypothesis. *Journal of Personality and Social Psychology, 28*, 129–137.

Lesly, P. (1966). Real creativity in public relations. *Public Relations Quarterly, 8*, 13–16.

Lester, D. (1993). *Studies in creative women.* Commack, NY: Nova Science.

Lester, D. (1999). Sylvia Plath. In M. A. Runco & S. R. Pritzker (Eds.), *Encyclopedia of creativity* (pp. 387–392). San Diego, CA: Academic Press.

Levine, S.-H. (1984). A critique of the Piagetian presuppositions of the role of play in human development and a suggested alternative: Metaphoric logic which organizes the play experience is the foundation for rational creativity. *Journal of Creative Behavior, 18*, 90–108.

Levy-Agresti, J., & Sperry, R. (1968). Differential perceptual capacities in major and minor hemispheres. *Proceedings of the National Academy of Sciences of the USA, 61*, 1151.

Lewis, G. (1991). The need to create: Constructive and destructive behavior in creatively gifted children. *Gifted Education International, 7*, 62–68.

Lezak, M. (1983). *Neuropsychological assessment* (2nd ed.). New York: Oxford University Press.

Liang, C., Chang, C.-C., Chang, Y., & Lin, L.-J. (2012). The exploration of imagination indicators. *Turkish Online Journal of Educational Technology, 11*, 366–374.

Lieberman, J. N. (1977). *Playfulness.* New York: Academic Press.

Lifton, R. J. (1973). The sense of immortality: On death and the continuity of life. *American Journal of Psychoanalysis, 33*, 3–15.

Lifton, R. J. (1979). *The broken connection.* New York: Simon & Schuster.

Lillard, A. S. (1993). Pretend play skills and children's theory of mind. *Child Development, 64*, 348–371.

Lim, W., & Plucker, J. A. (2001). Creativity through a lens of social responsibility: Implicit theories of creativity with Korean samples. *Journal of Creative Behavior, 35*, 115–130.

Limb, C. J. (2006). Structural and functional neural correlates of music perception. *Anatomical Record Part A, 288*, 435–446.

Limb, C. J., Kemeny, S., Ortigoza, E. B., Rouhani, S., & Braun, A. R. (2006). Left hemispheric lateralization of brain activity during passive rhythm perception in musicians. *Anatomical Record Part A, 288*, 382–389.

Lindauer, M. S. (1977). Imagery from the point of view of psychological aesthetics, the arts, and creativity. *Journal of Mental Imagery, 1*, 343–362.

Lindauer, M. (1991). Physiognomy and verbal synesthesia. *Metaphor and Symbolic Activity, 6*, 183–202.

Lindauer, M. S. (1992). Creativity in aging artists: Contributions from the humanities to the psychology of aging. *Creativity Research Journal, 5*, 211–232.

Lindauer, M. S. (1999). Old-age style. In M. A. Runco & S. R. Pritzker (Eds.), *Encyclopedia of creativity* (pp. 311–318). San Diego, CA: Academic Press.

Lindauer, M., Orwoll, L., & Kelley, C. (1997). Aging artists on the creativity of their old age. *Creativity Research Journal, 10*, 133–152.

Lindsay, P., & Norman, D. (1977). *Human information processing* (2nd ed.). New York: Harcourt.

Lines, R., & Grohaug, K. (2004). Rational processes vs. creative context in strategy formulation. In W. Haukedal & B. Kuvaas (Eds.), *Creativity and problem solving in the context of business management* (pp. 164–185). Bergen, Norway: Fagbokforlaget.

Linfield, S. (1998). Inside the outlaws of modern music. *Los Angeles Times*, April 15, E6.

Livne, N. L., & Milgram, R. M. (2006). Academic versus creative abilities in mathematics: Two components of the same construct? *Creativity Research Journal, 2*, 199–212.

Locher, P. J., Smith, J. K., & Smith, L. F. (2001). The influence of presentation format and viewer training in the visual arts on the perception of pictorial and aesthetic qualities of paintings. *Perception, 30*, 449–465.

Lodge, D. (1988). *Nice work.* New York: Viking.

Loehle, C. (1994). Discovery as a process. *Journal of Creative Behavior, 28*, 239–250.

Logsdon, T. (1993). *Breakthrough: Creative problem solving using six suggested strategies.* New York: Addison-Wesley.

Logsdon, T. (1994). Turning ideas into action: Insights: Creative solutions: Imaginative solutions to the city's problems. *Los Angeles Times*, (July 17), S1.

Lopez, E. C., Esquivel, G. B., & Houtz, J. C. (1993). The creative skills of culturally and linguistically diverse gifted students. *Creativity Research Journal, 6*, 401–412.

López-González, M., & Limb, C. J. (2012). Musical creativity and the brain. *Cerebrum* (Epub 2012 February 22).

Lord, M. G. (2005). Their Yankee ingenuity helped change the world: Review of H. Evans' they made America. *Los Angeles Times Review of Books, 10*, r6 (March 6).

Los Angeles Times, 2004. Running strong. Half a century later, that magic time—3:59.4—still stands out. May 2, D1. <http://www.latimes.com/sports/la-sp-roger2may02,1,846168.story?coll=la-headlines-sports>.

Low, M. B., & Abrahamson, E. (1977). Movements, bandwagons, and clones: Industry, evolution, and the entrepreneurial process. *Journal of Business Venturing, 12*, 435–457.

Lowis, M. J. (2002). Music as a trigger for peak experiences among a college staff population. *Creativity Research Journal, 14*, 351–359.

Lowis, M. J. (2004). A novel methodology to study the propensity to appreciate music. *Creativity Research Journal, 16*, 105–111.

Lubart, T., & Getz, I. (1997). Emotion, metaphor, and the creative process. *Creativity Research Journal, 10*, 285–301.

Lubart, T. (2005). How can computers be partners in the creative process: Classification and commentary on the special issue. *International Journal of Human-Computer Studies, 63*(4–5), 365–369.

Lubart, T. I. (1994). Creativity. In R. J. Sternberg (Ed.), *Thinking and problem solving* (pp. 289–332). New York: Academic Press.

Luchins, A. (1942). Mechanization in problem solving: The effect of einstellung. *Psychological Monographs, 54*, 248.

Ludwig, A. M. (1992). Culture and creativity. *American Journal of Psychotherapy, 46*, 454–469.

Ludwig, A. M. (1995). *The price of greatness*. New York: Guilford Press.

Ludwig, A. M. (1997). Creative achievement and psychopathology: Comparison among professions. In M. A Runco & R. Richards (Eds.), *Eminent creativity, everyday creativity, and health* (pp. 33–63). Greenwich, CT: Ablex (Original work published in 1992).

Ludwig, A. (1998). Method and madness in the arts and sciences. *Creativity Research Journal, 11*, 93–101.

Lumsden, C. J., & Findlay, S. C. (1988). Evolution of the creative mind. *Creativity Research Journal, 1*, 75–92.

Lunchins, A. S., & Lunchins, E. H. (1959). *Rigidity of behavior*. Eugene, OR: University of Oregon Press.

Luo, J., & Niki, K. (2003). Function of hippocampus in insight of problem solving. *Hippocampus, 13*, 316–323.

Lykken, D. T. (1981). Research with twins: The concept of emergenesis. *Society for Psychophysical Research, 19*, 361–372.

Ma, H.-H. (2006). A synthetic analysis of the effectiveness of single components and packages in creativity training programs. *Creativity Research Journal, 18*, 435–446.

MacCrimmon, K. R., & Wagner, C. (1994). Stimulating ideas through creativity software. *Management Information Systems, 40*, 1514–1532.

MacDonald, A. P. (1970). Revised scale for ambiguity tolerance: Reliability and validity. *Psychological Reports, 26*, 791–798.

Machotka, P. (1999). Paul Cézanne. In M. A. Runco, & S. R. Pritzker (Eds.), *Encyclopedia of creativity* (pp. 251–257). San Diego, CA: Academic Press.

Mackeith, S. A. (1982). Paracosms and the development of fantasy in childhood. *Imagination, Cognition, and Personality, 2*, 261–267.

MacKinnon, D. W. (1960). The highly effective individual. In R. S. Albert (Ed.), *Genius and eminence: The social psychology of creativity and exceptional achievement* (pp. 114–127). Oxford: Pergamon.

MacKinnon, D. W. (1962). The nature and nurture of creative talent. *American Psychologist, 17*, 484–495.

MacKinnon, D. W. (1963). Creativity and images of the self. In R. W. White (Ed.), *The study of lives* (pp. 252–278). New York: Atherton Press.

MacKinnon, D. (1965). Personality and the realization of creative potential. *American Psychologist, 20*, 273–281.

MacKinnon, D. W. (1975). IPAR's contribution to the conceptualization and study of creativity. In I. A. Taylor, & J. W. Getzells (Eds.), *Perspectives in creativity* (pp. 1–31). Chicago: Aldine.

Magyari-Beck, I. (1991). Identifying the blocks to creativity in Hungarian culture. *Creativity Research Journal, 4*, 419–427.

Maier, N. R. F. (1931). Reasoning in humans II: The solution of a problem and its appearance in consciousness. *Journal of Comparative Psychology, 12*, 181–194.

Maier, N. R. F. (1940). The behavior mechanisms concerned with problem solving. *Psychological Review, 47*, 43–58.

Maital, S., & Seshadri, D. V. R. (2007). *Innovation management: Strategies, concepts and tools for growth and profit*. London: Response Books.

Malkiel, B. G. (1990). *A random walk down wall street*. New York: Norton.

Mandelbrot, B. B. (1982). *The fractal geometry of nature*. San Francisco: W. H. Freeman.

Mandler, G. (1995). Origins and consequences of novelty. In S. M. Smith, T. B. Ward, & R. A. Finke (Eds.), *The creative cognition approach* (pp. 9–25). Cambridge, MA: MIT Press.

Mankiewicz, F. (1997). Pygmalion. *Los Angeles Times Book Review*, 4–5 (January 19).

Manmiller, J., Kumar, V. K., & Pekala, R. J. (2005). Hypnotizability, creativity styles, absorption, and phenomenological experience during hypnosis. *Creativity Research Journal, 17*, 9–24.

Mann, E. (2009). The search for mathematical creativity: Identifying creative potential in middle school students. *Creativity Research Journal, 21*, 338–348.

Mann, S., & Cadman, R. (2013). Does being bored make us more creative? Presented at the British Psychological Society's Division of Occupational Psychology Annual Conference, January 13.

Manosevitz, M., Fling, S., & Prentice, N. M. (1977). Imaginary companions in young children: Relationships with intelligence, creativity, and waiting ability. *Journal of Child Psychology and Psychiatry, 18*, 73–78.

Mansfield, R. S., Busse, T. V., & Kreplka, E. J. (1978). The effectiveness of creativity training. *Review of Educational Research, 48*, 517–536.

Marakas, G. M., & Elam, J. J. (1997). Creativity enhancement in problem-solving: Through software or process? *Management Science, 43*, 1136–1146.

March, J. G. (1971). The technology of foolishness. *Sivil konomen, 18*, 4–12.

March, J. G. (1978). Bounded rationality, ambiguity and the engineering of choice. *Bell Journal of Economics, 9*, 587–608.

March, J. G. (1987). The technology of foolishness. In J. G. March & J. P. Olsen (Eds.), *Ambiguity and choice in organizations* (pp. 69–81). Bergen, Norway: Universitets-Forlaget.

Marcy, R. T., & Mumford, M. D. (2007). Social innovation: Enhancing creative performance through causal analysis. *Creativity Research Journal, 19*, 123–140.

Margolis, H. (1987). *Patterns, thinking and cognition*. Chicago: University of Chicago Press.

Marken, G. A. (1991). Nurturing creativity in a productive society. *Public Relations Quarterly, 36*, 31–32 (Winter).

Marschark, M., & Clark, D. (1987). Linguistic and nonlinguistic creativity of deaf children. *Developmental Review, 7*, 22–38.

Martin, L. L., & Stoner, P. (1996). Mood as input: What we think about how we feel determines how we think. In L. L. Martin, & A. Tesser (Eds.), *Striving and feeling: Interactions among goals, affect, and self-regulation* (pp. 279–301). Mahwah, NJ: Lawrence Erlbaum Associates.

Martin, R. L., & Osberg, S. (2007). Social entrepreneurship: The case for definition. *Stanford Social Innovation Review* (Spring).

Martindale, C. (1975). *Romantic progression: The psychology of literary history*. Washington, DC: Hemisphere.

Martindale, C. (1977–1978). Creativity, consciousness, and cortical arousal. *Journal of the Altered States of Consciousness, 3*, 69–87.

Martindale, C. (1984). The pleasures of thought: A theory of cognitive hedonics. *Journal of Mind and Behavior, 5*, 49–80.

Martindale, C. (1988). Aesthetics, psychobiology and cognition. In F. H. Farley & R. Neperud (Eds.), *The foundations of aesthetics in art and art education*. New York: Praeger.

Martindale, C. (1989). Personality, situation, and creativity. In J. A. Glover, R. R. Ronning, & C. R. Reynolds (Eds.), *Handbook of creativity* (pp. 211–232). New York: Plenum.

Martindale, C. (1990). *The clockwork muse: The predictability of artistic change*. New York: Basic Books.

Martindale, C. (1995). Creativity and connectionism. In S. M. Smith, T. B. Ward, & R. A. Finke (Eds.), *The creative cognition approach* (pp. 249–268). Cambridge, MA: MIT Press.

Martindale, C. (1999). The biological basis of creativity. In R. J. Sternberg (Ed.), *Handbook of creativity* (pp. 137–152). Cambridge: Cambridge University Press.

Martindale, C., & Dailey, A. (1996). Creativity, primary process cognition and personality. *Personality and Individual Differences, 20*, 409–414.

Martindale, C., & Fischer, R. (1977). The effects of psilocybin on primary process content in language. *Confinia Psychiatrica, 20*, 195–202.

Martindale, C., & Hasenfus, N. (1978). EEG differences as a function of creativity, stage of the creative process, and effort to be original. *Biological Psychology, 6*, 157–167.

Martindale, C., & Hines, D. (1975). Creativity and cortical activation during creative, intellectual and EEG feedback tasks. *Biological Psychology, 3*, 91–100.

Martindale, C., Hines, D., Mitchell, L., & Covello, E. (1984). EEG alpha asymmetry and creativity. *Personality and Individual Differences, 5,* 77–86.

Martindale, C., Koss, M., & Miller, I. (1985). Measurement of primary process content in paintings. *Empirical Studies of the Arts, 3,* 171–177.

Martindale, C., Covello, E., & West, A. (1986). Primary process and hemispheric asymmetry. *Journal of Genetic Psychology, 147,* 79–87.

Martinsen, O. (1994). Insight problems revisited: The influence of cognitive styles and experience on creative problem solving. *Creativity Research Journal, 6,* 435–447.

Martinsen, O. (1995). Cognitive styles and experience in solving insight problems: Replication and extension. *Creativity Research Journal, 8,* 291–298.

Martinsen, O., & Diseth, A. (2011). The assimilator–explorer cognitive styles: Factor structure, personality correlates, and relationship to inventiveness. *Creativity Research Journal, 23,* 273–283.

Marx, M., & Hillix, W. A. (1987). *Systems and theories in psychology* (4th ed.). New York: McGraw-Hill.

Mashal, N., Faust, M., Hendler, T., & Jung-Beeman, M. (2007). An fMRI investigation of the neural correlates underlying the processing of novel metaphoric expressions. *Brain and Language, 100,* 115–126.

Maslow, A. (1968). Creativity in self–actualizing people. In *Toward a psychology of being* (pp. 135–145). New York: Van Nostrand Reinhold.

Maslow, A. (1994). *Religions, values and peak experiences.* New York: Penguin Books.

Maslow, A. H. (1970). *Motivation and personality.* New York: Harper & Row.

Maslow, A. H. (1971). *The farther reaches of human nature.* New York: Viking.

Masten, W. (1989a). Learning style, repeated stimuli, and originality in intellectually gifted adolescents. *Psychological Reports, 65,* 751–754.

Masten, W. G. (1989b). Creative self-perceptions of Mexican-American children. *Psychological Reports, 64,* 556–558.

Mathisen, G. E., & Einarsen, S. (2004). A review of instruments assessing creative and innovative environments within organizations. *Creativity Research Journal, 16,* 119–140.

May, R. (1975/1994). *The courage to create.* New York: Norton (Originally published in 1975).

May, R. (1996). *The meaning of anxiety.* New York: Norton (Originally published in 1950).

Mayer, R. E. (1983). *Thinking, problem solving, creativity.* New York: Freeman.

McAllister, P., & Anderson, A. (1991). Conservatism and the comprehension of implausible texts. *European Journal of Social Psychology, 21,* 147–164.

McCann, S. J. H. (2011). Conservatism, openness, and creativity: Patents granted to residents of American states. *Creativity Research Journal, 23,* 339–345.

McCarthy, K. C. (1993). Indeterminacy and consciousness in the creative process: What quantum physics has to offer. *Creativity Research Journal, 6,* 201–219.

McCoy, J. M., & Evans, G. W. (2002). The potential role of the physical environment on fostering creativity. *Creativity Research Journal, 14,* 409–426.

McCrae, R. R. (1987). Creativity, divergent thinking, and openness to experience. *Journal of Personality and Social Psychology, 52,* 1258–1265.

McCrae, R. R., & Costa, P. T. (1987). Validation of the five-factor model of personality across instruments and observers. *Journal of Personality and Social Psychology, 52,* 81–90.

McCrae, R. R., & Sutin, A. R. (2009). Openness to experience. In M. R. Leary & R. H. Hoyle (Eds.), *Handbook of individual differences in social behavior* (pp. 257–273). New York: Guilford Press.

McCrae, R. R., Arenberg, D., & Costa, P. T. Jr., (1987). Declines in divergent thinking with age: Cross-sectional, longitudinal, and cross-sequential analyses. *Psychology of Aging, 2,* 130–137.

McIntyre, P. (2008). Creativity and cultural production: A study of contemporary western popular music songwriting. *Creativity Research Journal, 20,* 40–52.

McLaren, R. B. (1993). The dark side of creativity. *Creativity Research Journal, 6,* 137–144.

McLaughlin, N. (2000). Book review of the sociology of philosophies: A global theory of intellectual change. *Journal of the History of the Behavioral Sciences, 36,* 171–175.

McLemee, S. (2006, November 5). Everyman's philosopher: Review of William James: In the Maelstrom of American Modernism by Robert D. Richardson. *Los Angeles Times Book Reviews.* <http://articles.latimes.com/2006/nov/05/books/bk-mclemee5>.

Mead, M. (1959). Creativity in cross-cultural perspective. In H. H. Anderson (Ed.), *Creativity and its cultivation: Addresses presented at the interdisciplinary symposia on creativity* (pp. 222–235). New York: Harper & Row.

Meadows, D. H., Meadows, D. L., Randers, J., & Brehens, W. W. III, (1972). *The limits to growth*. New York: Signet.

Mednick, M. T., Mednick, S. A., & Mednick, E. V. (1964). Incubation of creative performance and specific associative priming. *Journal of Abnormal and Social Psychology*, 69–88.

Mednick, S. A. (1962). The associative basis for the creative process. *Psychological Bulletin, 69*, 220–232.

Memmertt, D. (2007). Can creativity be improved by an attention-broadening training program? An exploratory study focusing on team sports. *Creativity Research Journal, 19*, 281–291.

Menand, L. (2001). *The metaphysical club: A story of ideas in America*. New York: Farrar, Straus, and Giroux.

Mendelsohn, G., & Griswold, B. (1964). Differential use of incidental stimuli in problem solving as a function of creativity. *Journal of Abnormal and Social Psychology, 68*, 431–436.

Mendelsohn, G., & Griswold, B. (1966). Assessed creative potential, vocabulary level, and sex as predictors of the use of incidental cues in verbal problem solving. *Journal of Personality and Social Psychology, 4*, 423–431.

Mendelsohn, G. A. (1976). Associative and attentional processes in creative performance. *Journal of Personality, 44*, 341–369.

Meneely, J., & Portillo, M. (2005). The adaptable mind in design: Relating personality, cognitive style, and creative performance. *Creativity Research Journal, 17*, 155–166.

Merrotsy, P. (2013). Tolerance of ambiguity: A trait of the creative personality? *Creativity Research Journal, 25*, 232–237.

Merten, T. (1995). Factors influencing word association: A re-analysis. *Creativity Research Journal, 8*, 249–263.

Merton, R. (1961). Singletons and multiples in scientific discovery. *Proceedings of the American Philosophical Society, 105*, 470–486.

Merton, R. (1968). The Matthew effect in science. *Science, 159*, 56–63.

Metcalfe, J. (1986). Feelings of knowing in memory and problem solving. *Journal of Experimental Psychology: Learning, Memory, and Cognition, 12*, 288–294.

Metcalfe, J., & Wiebe, D. (1987). Intuition in insight and non-insight problem solving. *Memory and Cognition, 15*, 238–246.

Michael, W. (1999). Guilford's view. In M. A. Runco & S. R. Pritzker (Eds.), *Encyclopedia of creativity* (pp. 785–797). San Diego, CA: Academic Press.

Michalko, M. (1991). *Thinkertoys*. Berkeley, CA: 10 Speed Press.

Micklus, C. S., & Micklus, S. W. (1994). *Competition stimulates creativity*. Glassboro, NJ: Creative Competitions.

Middlekauff, R. (1982). *The glorious cause: The American revolution, 1763–1789*. New York: Oxford University Press.

Milgram, R. M. (1990). Creativity: An idea whose time has come and gone? In M. A. Runco & R. S. Albert (Eds.), *Theories of creativity* (pp. 215–233). Newbury Park, CA: Sage.

Milgram, R. M., & Feingold, S. (1977). Concrete and verbal reinforcement in creative thinking of disadvantaged students. *Perceptual and Motor Skills, 45*, 675–678.

Milgram, R. M., & Hong, E. (1999). Creative out-of-school activities in intellectually gifted adolescents as predictors of their life accomplishment in young adults: A longitudinal study. *Creativity Research Journal, 12*, 77–87.

Milgram, R., & Milgram, N. (1976). Creative thinking and creative performance in Israeli children. *Journal of Educational Psychology, 68*, 255–259.

Milgram, R. M., & Rabkin, L. (1980). Developmental test of Mednick's associative hierarchies of original thinking. *Developmental Psychology, 16*, 157–158.

Millar, G. W. (1995). *E. Paul Torrance: The creativity man*. Norwood, NJ: Ablex.

Miller, A. I. (2009). *Deciphering the cosmic number: The strange friendship of Wolfgang Pauli and Carl Jung*. New York: Norton.

Miller, A. I. (1996). Metaphors in creative scientific thought. *Creativity Research Journal, 9*, 113–130.

Miller, A. I. (1992). Scientific creativity: A comparative study of Henri Poincaré and Albert Einstein. *Creativity Research Journal, 5*, 385–418.

Miller, A. I. (1996). *Insight of genius: Imagery and creativity in science and art*. New York: Springer-Verlag.

Miller, A. I. (2005). *Empire of the stars: Obsession, friendship, and betrayal in the quest for black holes*. New York: Houghton Mifflin.

Miller, B., Ponton, M., Benson, D., Cummings, J., & Mena, I. (1996). Enhanced artistic creativity with temporal lobe degeneration. *Lancet, 348*, 1744–1755.

Miller, B. L., Cummings, J., Mishkin, F., Boone, K., Prince, F., Ponton, M., et al. (1998). Emergence of artistic talent in frontotemporal dementia. *Neurology, 51*, 978–982.

Miller, B., Boone, K., Cummings, J., Read, S., & Mishkin, F. (2000). Functional correlates of musical and visual ability in frontotemporal dementia. *British Journal of Psychiatry, 176*, 458–463.

Miller, D., & Porter, C. (1988). Errors and biases in the attribution process. In L. Y. Abramson (Ed.), *Social cognition and clinical psychology: A synthesis.* New York: Guilford.

Miller, G. F. (2000). *The mating mind: How mate choice shaped the evolution of human nature.* New York: Doubleday.

Miller, G. F. (2001). Aesthetic fitness: How sexual selection shaped artistic virtuosity as a fitness indicator and aesthetic preference as mate choice criteria. *Bulletin of Psychological Arts, 2*, 20–25.

Miller, H. B., & Sawyers, J. K. (1989). A comparison of self and teachers ratings of creativity in fifth grade children. *Creative Child and Adult Quarterly, XIV*, 179–185, 229.

Miller, N., & Karl, S. (1993). Religious language as a transformational phenomena. *Creativity Research Journal, 6*, 99–110.

Millward, L., & Freeman, H. (2002). Role expectations as constraints to innovation: The case of female managers. *Creativity Research Journal, 14*, 93–109.

Minsky, M. (1988). *Society of mind.* New York: Simon & Schuster.

Misra, I. (2003). Openness to experience: Gender differences and its correlates. *Journal of Personality and Clinical Studies, 19*, 141–151.

Mistry, J., & Rogoff, B. (1985). A cultural perspective on the development of talent. In F. Horowitz & M. O'Brien (Eds.), *The gifted and talented: Developmental perspectives* (pp. 125–145). Washington, DC: American Psychological Association.

Mockros, C. A., & Csikszentmihalyi, M. (1999). The social construction of creative lives. In A. Montouri (Ed.), *Social creativity* (pp. 175–218). Cresskill, NJ: Hampton Press.

Moga, E., Burger, K., Hetland, L., & Winner, E. (2000). Does studying the arts engender creative thinking? Evidence for near but not far transfer. *Journal of Aesthetic Education, 34*, 91–104.

Mohan, J., & Tiwana, M. (1987). Personality and alienation of creative writers: A brief report. *Personality and Individual Differences, 9*, 449.

Molle, M., Marshall, L., Lutzenberger, W., Pietrowsky, R., Fehm, H. L., & Born, J. (1996). Enhanced dynamic complexity in the human EEG during creative thinking. *Neuroscience Letters, 208*, 61–64.

Molle, M., Marshall, L., Wolf, B., Fehm, H. L., & Born, J. (1999). EEG complexity and performance measures of creative thinking. *Psychophysiology, 36*, 95–104.

Moneta, G., & Siu, C. (2002). Trait intrinsic and extrinsic motivations, academic performance, and creativity in Hong Kong college students. *Journal of College Student Development, 43*, 664–683.

Moore, G. T. (1970). Creativity and the prediction of success in architecture. *Journal of Architectural Education, 24*, 28–32.

Moran, J. D., & Liou, E. Y. Y. (1982). Effects of reward on creativity in college students of two levels of ability. *Perceptual and Motor Skills, 54*, 43–48.

Morelock, M. J., & Feldman, H. D. (1999). Prodigies. In M. A. Runco & S. R. Pritzker (Eds.), *Encyclopedia of creativity* (Vol. 2, pp. 449–456). San Diego, CA: Academic Press.

Morgan, C. E., & Murray, H. A. (1935). A method for investigating fantasies: The thematic apperception test. *Archives of Neurology and Psychiatry, 34*, 289–306.

Morgan, D. (1953). Creativity today. *Journal of Aesthetics and Art Criticism, 12*, 1–24.

Morris, D. (1997). *Behind the oval office: Winning the Presidency in the 90s.* New York: Random House.

Morrison, D. (1999). Lewis Carol (aka Charles Lutwidge Dodgson). In M. A. Runco & S. R. Pritzker (Eds.), *Encyclopedia of creativity* (pp. 245–249). San Diego, CA: Academic Press.

Morrison, R. G., & Wallace, B. (2001). Imagery vividness, creativity and the visual arts. *Journal of Mental Imagery, 25*(3/4), 135–152.

Motley, M. (1986). Slips of the tongue. *Scientific American*, 116–126.

Mouchiroud, C., & Lubart, T. (2001). Children's original thinking: An empirical examination of alternative measures derived from divergent thinking tasks. *Journal of Genetic Psychology, 162*, 382–401.

Mount, M. K., & Barrick, M. R. (1995). The Big Five personality dimensions: Implications for research and practice in human resource management. *Research in Personnel and Human Resources Management, 13*, 153–200.

Mraz, W., & Runco, M. A. (1994). Suicide ideation and creative problem solving. *Suicide and Life Threatening Behavior, 24*, 38–47.

Mueller, J. S., Melwani, S., & Goncalo, J. A. (2012). The bias against creativity: Why people desire but reject creative ideas. *Psychological Science, 23*, 13–17.

Mulgan, G. (2006). The process of social innovation. *Innovations*, 145–162 (Spring).

Mullen, B., Johnson, C., & Salas, E. (1991). Productivity loss and brainstorming groups: A meta-analytic integration. *Basic and Applied Social Psychology, 12*, 3–23.

Mumford, M. D. (2002). Social innovation: Ten cases from Benjamin Franklin. *Creativity Research Journal, 14*, 253–266.

Mumford, M. D. (2003). Where have we been, where are we going? Taking stock in creativity research. *Creativity Research Journal, 15*, 107–120.

Mumford, M. D., & Gustafson, S. B. (1988). Creativity syndrome: Integration, application, and innovation. *Psychological Bulletin, 103*, 27–43.

Mumford, M. D., & Mobley, M. (1989). Creativity, biology, and culture: Further comments on the evolution of the creative mind. *Creativity Research Journal, 2*, 87–101.

Mumford, M. D., & Moertl, P. (2003). Cases of social innovation: Lessons from two innovations in the 20th century. *Creativity Research Journal, 15*, 261–266.

Mumford, M. D., & Porter, P. P. (1999). Analogies. In M. A. Runco & S. R. Pritzker (Eds.), *Encyclopedia of creativity* (Vol. 1, pp. 71–77). San Diego, CA: Academic Press.

Mumford, M. D., Mobley, M. I., Uhlman, C. E., Reiter-Palmon, R., & Doares, L. M. (1991). Process analytic models of creative capacities. *Creativity Research Journal, 4*, 91–122.

Mumford, M. D., Costanza, D. P., Baughman, W. A., Threlfall, K. V., & Fleishman, E. A. (1994). Influence of abilities on performance during practice: Effects of massed and distributed practice. *Journal of Educational Psychology, 86*, 134–144.

Mumford, M., Baughman, W., Maher, M., Costanza, D., & Supinski, E. (1997). Process-based measures of creative problem-solving skills: IV. Category combination. *Creativity Research Journal, 10*, 59–71.

Mumford, M. D., Scott, G. M., Gaddis, B., & Strange, J. M. (2002). Leading creative people: Orchestrating expertise and relationships. *The Leadership Quarterly, 13*, 705–750.

Murphy, G. (1958). The creative eras. In G. Murphy (Ed.), *Human potentials* (pp. 142–157). New York: Basic Books.

Murphy, M., Runco, M. A., Acar, S., & Reiter-Palmon, R. (2013). Reanalysis of genetic data and rethinking dopamine's relationship with creativity. *Creativity Research Journal, 25*, 147–148.

Murray, H. A. (1959). Vicissitudes of creativity. In H. H. Anderson (Ed.), *Creativity and its cultivation* (pp. 203–221). New York: Harper.

Myers, I. B., & McCaulley, M. H. (1985). *Manual: A guide to the development and use of the Myers-Briggs type indicator.* Palo Alto, CA: Consulting Psychologists Press.

Nakamura, J., & Csikszentmihalyi, M. (2002). Catalytic creativity: The case of Linus Pauling. *American Psychologist, 56*, 337–341.

Nardini, B. (1999). *Michelangelo: Biography of a genius.* Florence-Milan: Giunti.

Naroll, R., Benjamin, E. C., Fohl, F., Hildreth, R., & Shaefer, J. (1971). Creativity: A cross cultural pilot study. *Journal of Cross Cultural Psychology, 2*, 181–188.

Nebes, (1977). Man's so-called minor hemisphere. In M. C. Wittrock (Ed.), *The human brain* (pp. 97–106). Englewood Cliffs, NJ: Prentice Hall.

Necka, E., & Hlawacz, T. (2013). Who has an artistic temperament? Relationships between creativity and temperament among artists and bank officers. *Creativity Research Journal, 25*, 182–188.

Neisser, U. (1967). *Cognitive psychology.* New York: Meredith.

Neisser, U. (1994). Multiple systems: A new approach to cognitive theory. *European Journal for Cognitive Psychology, 6*, 225–241.

Nemiro, J. (1999). Acting. In M. A. Runco, & S. R. Pritzker (Eds.), *Encyclopedia of creativity* (pp. 1–8). San Diego, CA: Academic Press.

Nemiro, J. (2002). The creative process in virtual teams. *Creativity Research Journal, 14*, 69–83.

Neperud, R. W. (1986). The relationship of art training and sex differences to aesthetic valuing. *Visual Arts Research, 12*, 1–9.

Nettles, D., & Clegg, H. (2006). Schizotypy, creativity and mating success in humans. *Proceedings of the Royal Society B, 273*, 611–615.

Newell, A., & Simon, H. A. (1972). *Problem solving; Human information processing.* Englewood Cliffs, NJ: Prentice-Hall.

Newell, A., Shaw, J., & Simon, H. (1962). The processes of creative thinking. In H. Gruber, G. Terrell, & M. Worthier (Eds.), *Contemporary approaches to creative thinking* (pp. 63–119). New York: Atherton.

Nicholls, J. C. (1983). Creativity in the person who will never produce anything original or useful. In R. S. Albert (Ed.), *Genius and eminence: A social psychology of exceptional achievement* (pp. 265–279). New York: Pergamon.

Nichols, R. C. (1978). Twin studies of ability, personality, and interest. *Homo, 29,* 158–173.

Nickles, T. (1994). Enlightenment versus romantic models of creativity in science—and beyond. *Creativity Research Journal, 7,* 277–314.

Nickles, T. (1999). Paradigm shifts. In M. A. Runco & S. R. Pritzker (Eds.), *Encyclopedia of creativity* (pp. 335–346). San Diego, CA: Academic Press.

Nicol, J. J., & Long, B. C. (1996). Creativity and perceived stress of female music therapists and hobbyists. *Creativity Research Journal, 9,* 1–10.

Niederland, W. G. (1973). Psychoanalytic concepts of creativity and aging. *Journal of Geriatric Psychiatry, 6,* 160–168.

Nietzsche, F. (1886/1973). *Beyond good and evil.* Middlesex, England: Penguin (Original work published 1886).

Nisbett & Wilson, T. D (1977). Telling more than we know: Verbal reports on mental processes. *Psychological Review, 84,* 231–259.

Nisbett, R., & Ross, L. (1980). *Human inference: Strategies and shortcomings.* Englewood Cliffs, NJ: Prentice Hall.

Niu, W. (2003). Ancient Chinese views of creativity. *Inquiry: Critical Thinking Across the Disciplines, 22,* 29–36.

Niu, W., & Sternberg, R. J. (2001). Cultural influences on artistic creativity and its evaluation. *International Journal of Psychology, 36,* 225–241.

Niu, W., & Sternberg, R. J. (2003). Societal and school influences on student creativity: The case of China. *Psychology in the Schools, 40,* 103–114.

Noble, E. P. (2000). Addiction and its reward process through polymorphisms of the D2 dopamine receptor gene: A review. *European Psychiatry, 15,* 79–89.

Noble, E. P., Runco, M. A., & Ozkaragoz, T. Z. (1993). Creativity in alcoholic and nonalcoholic families. *Alcohol, 10,* 317–322.

Nolan, V. (1987). *The innovator's handbook.* London: Sphere Books.

Noppe, L. D. (1996). Progression in the service of the ego, cognitive styles, and creative thinking. *Creativity Research Journal, 9,* 369–383.

Norden, M. J., & Avery, D. H. (1993). A controlled study of dawn simulation in subsyndromal winter depression. *Acta Psychiatrica Scandinavica, 88,* 67–71.

Norlander, T., & Gustafson, R. (1996). Effects of alcohol on scientific thought during the incubation phase of the creative process. *Journal of Creative Behavior, 30,* 231–248.

Norlander, T., & Gustafson, R. (1997). Effects of alcohol on picture drawing during the verification phase of the creative process. *Creativity Research Journal, 10,* 355–362.

Norlander, T., & Gustafson, R. (1998). Effects of alcohol on a divergent figural fluency test during the illumination phase of the creative process. *Creativity Research Journal, 11,* 365–374.

Norlander, T., Bergman, H., & Archer, T. (1998). Effects of flotation rest on creative problem solving and originality. *Journal of Environmental Psychology, 18,* 399–408.

Norton, R. W. (1975). Measurement of ambiguity tolerance. *Journal of Personality Assessment, 39,* 607–612.

Noy, P. (1969). A revision of the psychoanalytic theory of the primary process. *International Journal of Psychoanalysis, 50,* 155–178.

Nystrom, H. (1995). Creativity and entrepreneurship. In C. M. Ford, & D. A. Gioia (Eds.), *Creative action in organizations: Ivory tower visions and real world voices* (pp. 65–70). Thousand Oaks, CA: Sage.

O'Quin, K., & Besemer, S. (1989). The development, reliability, and validity of the revised creative product semantic scale. *Creativity Research Journal, 2,* 268–278.

O'Quin, K., & Besemer, S. P. (1999). Creative products. In M. A. Runco & S. R. Pritzker (Eds.), *Encyclopedia of creativity* (Vol. 1, pp. 413–422). San Diego, CA: Academic Press.

O'Quin, K., & Derks, P. (1997). Humor and creativity: A review of the empirical literature. In M. A. Runco (Ed.), *Creativity research handbook* (Vol. 1, pp. 227–256). Cresskill, NJ: Hampton Press.

O'Reilly, T., Dunbar, R., & Bentall, R. (2001). Schizotypy and creativity: An evolutionary connection? *Personality and Individual Differences, 31,* 1067–1078.

Obama, B. (2010, March 11). Remarks by the President at the Export–Import Bank's annual conference. <http://www.whitehouse.gov/the-press-office/remarks-president-export-import-banks-annual-conference>.

Odom, R. D. (1967). Problem solving strategies as a function of age and socio-economic level. *Child Development, 38,* 753–764.

Ogburn, W. F., & Thomas, D. (1922). Are inventions inevitable? *Political Science Quarterly, 37,* 83.

Ohlsson, S. (1984a). Restructuring revisited I: Summary and critique of the Gestalt theory of problem solving. *Scandinavian Journal of Psychology, 25,* 65–78.

Ohlsson, S. (1984b). Restructuring revisited II: An information processing theory of restructuring and insight. *Scandinavian Journal of Psychology, 25,* 117–129.

Okuda, S. M., Runco, M. A., & Berger, D. E. (1991). Creativity and the finding and solving of real-world problems. *Journal of Psychoeducational Assessment, 9,* 45–53.

Olton, R. M., & Johnson, D. M. (1976). Mechanisms of incubation in creative problem solving. *American Journal of Psychology, 89,* 617–630.

Oral, G. (2003). Creativity in Turkey: The gemstone shadowed by poor regime. *Inquiry: Critical Thinking Across the Disciplines, 22,* 25–28.

Orbach, I., Bar-Joseph, H., & Dror, N. (1990). Styles of problem solving in suicidal individuals. *Suicide and Life-Threatening Behavior, 20,* 56–64.

Ornstein, R., & Ehrlich, P. (1989). *New world, new mind.* Cambridge, MA: Malor Books.

Osborn, A. F. (1963). *Applied imagination* (3rd ed.). New York: Charles Scribner.

Osgood, C. E., May, W. H., & Miron, M. S. (1975). *Cross-cultural universals of affective meaning.* Champaign, IL: University of Illinois Press.

Osowski, J. (1989). Ensembles of metaphor in the psychology of William James. In D. Wallace & H. E. Gruber (Eds.), *Creative people at work* (pp. 127–145). New York: Oxford University Press.

Owen, S. (1992). *Readings in Chinese literary thought.* Cambridge, MA: Harvard University Asia Center Press.

Paine-Clemes B. 2008. *Creative synergy: A causal or idealist view of creativity.* Unpublished manuscript.

Pais, A. (1982). *Subtle is the Lord.* Oxford: Oxford University Press.

Paramesh, C. R. (1971). Value orientation of creative high school students. *Journal of the Indian Academy of Applied Psychology, 8,* 46–49.

Pariser, D. (1991). Normal and unusual aspects of juvenile artistic development in Klee, Lautrec, and Picasso. *Creativity Research Journal, 4,* 51–65.

Parloff, M. D., & Handlon, D. H. (1964). The influence of criticalness on creative problem solving. *Psychiatry, 27,* 17–27.

Parnes, S. J. (1966). *Instructor's manual for institutes and courses in creative problem solving.* Buffalo, NY: Creative Education Foundation.

Parnes, S. J. (1967). *Creative behavior guidebook.* New York: Scribners.

Parnes, S. J. (1999). Programs and course in creativity. In M. A. Runco & S. R. Pritzker (Eds.), *Encyclopedia of creativity* (Vol. 2, pp. 465–477). San Diego, CA: Academic Press.

Parnes, S. J., & Meadow, A. (1959). Effects of brainstorming on creative problem solving by trained and untrained subjects. *Journal of Educational Psychology, 50,* 171–176.

Parnes, S. J., & Noller, R. B. (1972a). Applied creativity: The creative studies project: I. The development. *Journal of Creative Behavior, 6,* 11–22.

Parnes, S. J., & Noller, R. B. (1972b). Applied creativity: The creative studies project: II. Results of the two-year program. *Journal of Creative Behavior, 6,* 164–186.

Parrott, C. A., & Strongman, K. T. (1985). Utilization of visual imagery in creative performance. *Journal of Mental Imagery, 9,* 53–66.

Patrick, C. (1935). Creative thought in poets. *Archives of Psychology, 26,* 1–74.

Patrick, C. (1937). Creative thought in artists. *Journal of Psychology, 5,* 35–73.

Patrick, C. (1938). Scientific thought. *Journal of Psychology, 5,* 55–83.

Patrick, C. (1941). Whole and part relationship in creative thought. *American Journal of Psychology, 54,* 128–131.

Paulus, P. (1999). Group creativity. In M. A. Runco & S. R. Pritzker (Eds.), *Encyclopedia of creativity* (pp. 779–784). San Diego, CA: Academic Press.

Paulus, P. B., & Dzindolef, M. T. (1993). Social influence processes in group brainstorming. *Journal of Personality and Social Psychology, 64,* 575–586.

Paulus, P. B. & Nijstad, B. A., (Eds.), (2003). *Group creativity: Innovation through collaboration.* New York: Oxford University Press.

Pennebaker, J. W. (1997). Writing about emotional experiences as a therapeutic process. *Psychological Science, 8,* 162–166.

Pennebaker, J. W., & Seagal, J. D. (1999). Forming a story: The health benefits of narrative. *Journal of Clinical Psychology, 55*, 1243–1254.

Pennebaker, J., Kiecolt-Glaser, J. K., & Glaser, R. (1988). Confronting traumatic experience and immunocompetence. *Journal of Consulting and Clinical Psychology, 56*, 638–639.

Pennebaker, J. W., Kiecolt-Glaser, J. K., & Glaser, R. (1997). Disclosure of trauma and immune functioning: Health implications for psychotherapy. In M. A. Runco & R. Richards (Eds.), *Eminent creativity, everyday creativity, and health* (pp. 287–302). Norwood, NJ: Ablex.

Pérez Reverte, A. (2002). *The queen of the south.* New York: Putnam.

Perez-Fabello, M. J., & Campos, A. (2007). Influence of training in artistic skills on mental imaging capacity. *Creativity Research Journal, 19*, 227–232.

Perkins, D. N. (1981). *The mind's best work.* Cambridge, MA: Harvard University Press.

Perkins, D. N. (1988). The possibility of invention. In Robert J. Sternberg (Ed.), *The nature of creativity.* Cambridge: Cambridge University Press.

Perls, F. (1978). *The gestalt approach and eye witness to therapy.* London: Bantam Books.

Perry, C., Wilder, S., & Appignanesi, A. (1973). Hypnotic susceptibility and performance on a battery of creativity measures. *American Journal of Clinical Hypnosis, 15*, 170–180.

Peterson, J., & Lansky, L. (1977). Left-handedness among architects: Partial replication and some new data. *Perceptual and Motor Skills, 45*, 1216–1218.

Petroski, H. (2003). Polymath's progress (Review of Silverman's Lightning Man). *Los Angeles Times Review of Books,* R7 (October 24).

Petsche, H. (1996). Approaches to verbal, visual, and musical creativity by EEG coherence analysis. *International Journal of Psychophysiology, 24*, 145–159.

Phares, E. J. (1986). *Introduction to personality* (2nd ed.). Glenview, IL: Scott, Foresman & Co.

Piaget, J. (1952). *The origins of intelligence in the child.* New York: International University Press (Original work published in 1936).

Piaget, J. (1962). *Play, dreams and imitation in childhood.* New York: Basic Books.

Piaget, J. (1968). *Genetic epistemology.* New York: Columbia University Press.

Piaget, J. (1970). Piaget's theory. In P. H. Mussen (Ed.), *Carmichael's handbook of child psychology* (pp. 703–732). (3rd ed.) New York: Wiley.

Piaget, J. (1972). *The psychology of the child.* New York: Basic Books.

Piaget, J. (1976). *To understand is to invent.* New York: Penguin.

Piaget, J. (1981). Foreword. In H. Gruber's (Ed.), *Darwin on man: A psychological study of scientific creativity.* Chicago, IL: Chicago University Press.

Piechowski, M. (1993a). Origins without origins: Exceptional abilities explained away. *Creativity Research Journal, 6*, 465–469.

Piechowski, M. (1993b). Is inner transformation a creative process? *Creativity Research Journal, 6*, 89–98.

Piirto, J. (1991). Why are there so few (creative women: visual artists, mathematicians, musicians)? *Roeper Review, 13*, 142–147.

Pine, R., & Holt, R. (1960). Creativity and primary process: A study of adaptive regression. *Journal of Abnormal and Social Psychology, 61*, 370–379.

Platt, J. M., & Janeczko, D. (1991). Adapting art instruction for students with disabilities. *Teaching Exceptional Children, 24*, 10–12.

Plucker, J. (1998). Beware of simple conclusions: The case for content generality of creativity. *Creativity Research Journal, 11*, 179–182.

Plucker, J. A. (1999). Reanalyses of student responses to creativity checklists: Evidence of content generality. *Journal of Creative Behavior, 33*, 126–137.

Plucker, J. A., & Dana, R. Q. (1999). Drugs and creativity. In M. A. Runco & S. R. Pritzker (Eds.), *Encyclopedia of creativity* (pp. 607–611). San Diego, CA: Academic Press.

Plucker, J., & Runco, M. A. (1999). Deviance. In M. A. Runco & S. R. Pritzker (Eds.), *Encyclopedia of creativity* (pp. 541–545). San Diego, CA: Academic Press.

Plucker, J. A., Beghetto, R. A., & Dow, G. T. (2004). Why isn't creativity important to educational psychologists? Potential pitfalls, and future directions in creativity research. *Educational psychologist, 39*, 83–96.

Plucker, J., Runco, M. A., & Lim, W. (2006). Predicting ideational behavior from divergent thinking and discretionary time on task. *Creativity Research Journal, 18*, 55–63.

Pohlman, L. (1996). Creativity, gender, and the family: A study of creative writers. *Journal of Creative Behavior, 30*, 1–24.

Pollick, M. F., & Kumar, V. K. (1997). Creativity styles of supervising managers. *Journal of Creative Behavior, 31*, 260–270.

Pornrungroj, C. (1992). *A comparison of creativity test scores between Thai children in a Thai culture and Thai-American children who were born and reared in an American culture.* Unpublished doctoral dissertation, Illinois State University, Normal, IL.

Porter, C. A., & Suefeld, P. (1981). Integrative complexity in the correspondence of literary figures: Effects of personal and social stress. *Journal of Personality and Social Psychology, 40*, 321–330.

Post, F. (1994). Creativity and psychopathology: A study of 291 world-famous men. *British Journal of Psychiatry, 165*, 22–34.

Post, F. (1996). Verbal creativity, depression and alcoholism: An investigation of one hundred American and British writers. *British Journal of Psychiatry, 168*, 545–555.

Pratt, C. (1961). Aesthetics. In P. H. Mussen & M. R. Rosenzweig (Eds.), *Annual review of psychology.* Palo Alto, CA: Annual Reviews.

Prentky, R. A. (2000–2001). Mental illness and roots of genius. *Creativity Research Journal, 13*, 95–104.

Press, C. (2002). *The dancing self.* Cresskill, NJ: Hampton Press.

Preston, S. H. (1984). Children and elderly in the U.S. *Scientific American, 251*, 44–49.

Pribram, K. H. (1999). Brain and creative activity. In M. A. Runco & S. R. Pritzker (Eds.), *Encyclopedia of creativity* (pp. 213–217). San Diego, CA: Academic Press.

Pritzker, S. (1999). Zen. In M. A. Runco & S. R. Pritzker (Eds.), *Encyclopedia of creativity* (pp. 745–753). San Diego, CA: Academic Press.

Pritzker, S. (2011). Zen. In M. A. Runco & S. R. Pritzker (Eds.), *Encyclopedia of creativity* (Vol. 2, pp. 539–543). San Diego, CA: Academic Press.

Pritzker, S., & Runco, M. A. (1997). The creative decision-making process in group situation comedy writing. In K. Saywer (Ed.), *Creativity in performance* (pp. 115–141). Greenwich, CT: Ablex.

Pruhbu, V., Sutton, C., & Sauser, W. (2008). Creativity and certain personality traits: understanding the mediating effect of intrinsic motivation. *Creativity Research Journal, 20*, 53–66.

Pryor, K. W., Haig, R., & O'Reilly, J. (1969). The creative porpoise: Training for novel behavior. *Journal of Applied Behavior Analysis, 12*, 653–661.

Putman, V. L., & Paulus, P. B. (2009). Brainstorming, brainstorming rules and decision making. *Journal of Creative Behavior, 43*, 23–39.

Pyryt, M. C. (1999). Effectiveness of training children's divergent thinking: A meta-analytic review. In A. S. Fishkin, B. Cramond, & P. Olszewski-Kubilius (Eds.), *Investigating creativity in youth: Research and methods* (pp. 351–365). Cresskill, NJ: Hampton Press.

Raina, M. K. (1968). A study into the effects of competition on creativity. *Gifted Child Quarterly, 12*, 217–220.

Raina, M. K. (1975). Parental perception about ideal child. *Journal of Marriage and the Family, 37*, 229–232.

Raina, M. K. (1989). *Social change and changes in creative functioning.* New Delhi: National Council of Educational Research and Training.

Raina, M. K. (1997). Most dear to all the Muses: Mapping Tagorean networks of enterprise. *Creativity Research Journal, 10*, 153–173.

Raina, T. N., & Raina, M. K. (1971). Perception of teacher-educators in India about the ideal pupil. *Journal of Educational Research, 64*, 303–306.

Raina, M. (2013). Construction of a creative and self-transcending life: George Sudarshan's conception and experience of creativity. *Creativity Research Journal, 25*, 369–387.

Raina, M. K., Srivastava, A. K., & Misra, G. (2001). Explorations in literary creativity: Some preliminary observations. *Psychological Studies, 46*, 148–160.

Raina, P. (2003). On Moore's Schrödinger: Life and thought. *Creativity Research Journal, 15*, 303–307.

Raina, T. N., & Raina, M. K. (1971). Perception of teacher-educators in India about the ideal pupil. *Journal of Educational Research, 64*, 303–306.

Ramachandran, V. S., & Hirstein, W. (1999). The science of art: A neurological theory of aesthetic experience. *Journal of Consciousness Studies, 6*, 15–51.

Ramachandran, V. S., & Ramachandran, D. R. (1996). Denial of disabilities in anosognosia. *Nature, 382*, 501 (August 8).

Ramey, C. H., & Weisberg, R. W. (2004). The "poetical activity" of Emily Dickinson: A further test of the hypothesis that affective disorders foster creativity. *Creativity Research Journal, 16*, 173–185.

Rank, O. (1941). *Beyond psychology.* New York: Dover.

Rank, O. (1989). *Art and artist: Creative urge and personality development.* New York: Norton.

Rapp, F., & Wiehl, R. (1990). *Whitehead's metaphyics of creativity.* Albany, NY: SUNY Press.

Rawlings, D. (1985). Psychoticism, creativity and dichotic shadowing. *Personality and Individual Differences, 6*, 737.

Rawlings, D., Barrantes–Vidal, N., & Furnham, A. (2000). Personality and aesthetic preference in Spain and England: Two studies relating sensation seeking and openness to experience to liking for painting and music. *European Journal of Personality, 14*, 553–576.

Redmond, M. R., Mumford, M. D., & Teach, R. (1993). Putting creativity to work: Effects of leader behavior on subordinate creativity. *Organizational Behavior and Human Decision Processes, 55*, 120–151.

Reese, H. W., & Parnes, S. J. (1970). Programming creative behavior. *Child Development, 40*, 413–423.

Reese, H. W., Parnes, S. J., Treffinger, D. J., & Kaltsounis, G. (1976). Effects of creative studies program on structure-of-intellect factors. *Journal of Educational Psychology, 68*, 401–410.

Reese, H. W., Lee, L., Cohen, S. H., & Puckett, J. M. Jr., (2001). Effects of intellectual variables, age, and gender on divergent thinking in adulthood. *International Journal of Behavioral Development, 25*, 491–500.

Reid, L. N., King, K. W., & DeLorme, D. E. (1998). Top level agency creatives look at advertising creativity then and now. *Journal of Advertising, 27*, 1–15.

Reiter-Palmon, R., Mumford, M. D., Boes, J. O., & Runco, M. A. (1997). Problem construction and creativity: The role of ability, cue consistency, and active processing. *Creativity Research Journal, 9*, 9–23.

Rejskind, F. G., Rapagna, S. O., & Gold, D. (1992). Gender differences in children's divergent thinking. *Creativity Research Journal, 5*, 165–174.

Renzulli, J. (1978). What makes giftedness? Re-examining a definition. *Phi Delta Kappan, 60*, 180–184.

Renzulli, J. S. (1992). A general theory for the development of creative productivity through the pursuit of ideal acts of learning. *Gifted Child Quarterly, 36*, 170–182.

Reuter, M., Panksepp, J., Schnabel, N., Kellerhoff, N., Kempel, P., & Hennig, J. (2005). Personality and biological markers of creativity. *European Journal of Personality, 19*, 83–95.

Reuter, M., Roth, S., Holve, K., & Hennig, J. (2006). Identification of a first candidate gene for creativity: A pilot study. *Brain Research, 1069*, 190–197.

Reynold, F. (2003). Conversations about creativity and chronic illness I: Textile artists coping with long-term health problems reflect on the origins of their interest in art. *Creativity Research Journal, 15*, 393–407.

Reznikoff, M., Domino, G., Bridges, C., & Honeyman, M. (1973). Creative abilities in identical and fraternal twins. *Behavior Genetics, 4*, 365–377.

Rhodehamel, J. (2005). How Lincoln wowed 'em. Review of Lincoln at Cooper Union: The speech that made Abraham Lincoln president, by Harold Holzer. <http://www.latimes.com/features/printedition/books/la-bk-rhode-hame13ju103,1,3637090. story? coll=la-headlines-bookreview>.

Rhodes, C. (1997). Growth from deficiency creativity to being creativity. In M. A. Runco & R. Richards (Eds.), *Eminent creativity, everyday creativity, and health* (pp. 247–263). Greenwich, CT: Ablex (Original work published in 1990).

Rhodes, M. (1961). An analysis of creativity. *Phi Delta Kappan, 42*, 305–310.

Rich, J. D., & Weisberg, R. A. (2004). Creating all in the family: A case study in creative thinking. *Creativity Research Journal, 16*, 247–259.

Richards, R. (1990). Everyday creativity, eminent creativity, and health: Afterview for Creativity Research Journal issues on creativity and health. *Creativity Research Journal, 3*, 300–326.

Richards, R. (1991). A new aesthetic for environmental awareness: Chaos theory, the beauty of nature, and our broader humanistic identity. *Journal of Humanistic Psychology, 41*, 59–95.

Richards, R. (1996). Does the lone genius ride again? Chaos, creativity, and community. *Journal of Humanistic Psychology, 36*, 44–60.

Richards, R. (1997). Conclusions: When illness yields creativity. In M. A. Runco & R. Richards (Eds.), *Eminent creativity, everyday creativity, and health* (pp. 485–540). Greenwich, CT: Ablex.

Richards, R. (1999). The subtle attraction: Beauty as a force in awareness, creativity, and survival. In S. W. Russ (Ed.), *Affect, creative experience, and psychological adjustment* (pp. 195–219). Philadelphia, PA: Brunner/Mazel.

Richards, R. (2001a). Millennium as opportunity: Chaos, creativity, and Guilford's structure of intellect model. *Creativity Research Journal, 13*, 249–266.

Richards, R. (2001b). A new aesthetic for environmental awareness: Chaos theory, the beauty of nature, and our broader humanistic identity. *Journal of Humanistic Psychology, 41,* 59–95.

Richardson, A. G. (1986). Two factors of creativity. *Perceptual and Motor Skills, 63,* 379–384.

Rickards, T. (1975). Brainstorming: An examination of idea production rate and level of speculation in real managerial situations. *R&D Management, 6,* 11–14.

Rickards, T. (1994). Whitehead revisited: A rediscovered founding father of creativity studies. *Creativity Research Journal, 7,* 85–86.

Rickards, T., & Jones, L. J. (1991). Toward the identification of situational barriers to creative behaviors: The development of a self-report inventory. *Creativity Research Journal, 4,* 303–316.

Rickards, T., & De Cock, C. (2012). Understanding organizational creativity: Toward a multiparadigmatic approach. In M. A. Runco (Ed.), *Creativity research handbook* (Vol. 2, pp. 1–32). Cresskill: NJ. Hampton Press.

Rieker, H.-U. (1971). *The yoga of light.* Los Angeles, CA: Dawn Horse Press.

Rietzschel, E. F., Nijstad, B. A., & Stroebe, W. (in press). Effects of problem scope and creativity instructions on idea generation and selection. *Creativity Research Journal.*

Rietzschel, E. F., Nijstad, B. A., & Stroebe, W. (2007). Relative accessibility of domain knowledge and creativity: The effects of knowledge activation on the quantity and originality of generated ideas. *Journal of Experimental Social Psychology, 43,* 933–946.

Rietzschel, E. F., Nijstad, B. A., & Stroebe, W. (2010). The selection of creative ideas after individual idea generation: Choosing between creativity and impact. *British Journal of Psychology, 101,* 47–68.

Ripple, R. (1999). Teaching creativity. In M. A. Runco & S. R. Pritzker (Eds.), *Encyclopedia of creativity* (Vol. 2 (I–Z), pp. 629–638). San Diego, CA: Academic Press.

Ritter, S. M., Kühn, S., Müller, B. C. N., van Baaren, R. B., Brass, M., & Ap Dijksterhuis (in press). The creative brain: Co-representing schema-violations enhances TPJ activity and boosts cognitive flexibility. *Creativity Research Journal.*

Roberts, B. (1988). Managing invention and innovation. *Research-Technology Management, 33,* 1–19.

Rock, I. (1997). *Eye and brain* (5th ed.). Princeton, NJ: Princeton University Press.

Roe, A. (1975). Painters and painting. In I. A. Taylor & J. W. Getzels (Eds.), *Perspectives in creativity.* Aldine de Gruyter: Hawthorne, NY.

Roe, A. (1983). Family background of eminent scientists. In R. S. Albert (Ed.), *Genius and eminence: The social psychology of creativity and exceptional achievement* (pp. 170–181). Oxford: Pergamon (Originally published 1953).

Rogers, C. R. (1954/1959). Toward a theory of creativity. In H. H. Anderson (Ed.), *Creativity and its cultivation: Addresses presented at the interdisciplinary symposia on creativity* (pp. 69–82). New York: Harper and Row.

Rogers, C. R. (1980). *A way of being.* Boston, MA: Houghton-Mifflin.

Rogers, C. R. (1995). *On becoming a person: A therapist's view of psychotherapy.* Boston, MA: Houghton-Mifflin (Original work published in 1961).

Root-Bernstein, M., & Root-Bernstein, R. (2003). Martha Graham, dance, and the polymathic imagination: A case for multiple intelligences or universal thinking tools? *Journal of Dance Education, 3,* 16–27.

Root-Bernstein, M., & Root-Bernstein, R. (2006). Imaginary worldplay in childhood and maturity and its impact on adult creativity. *Creativity Research Journal, 18,* 405–425.

Root-Bernstein, R. (1997). For the sake of science, the arts deserve support. *Chronicle of Higher Education, 43,* 15.

Root-Bernstein, R. (1999). Discovery. In M. A. Runco & S. R. Pritzker (Eds.), *Encyclopedia of creativity* (Vol. 1, pp. 559–571). San Diego, CA: Academic Press.

Root-Bernstein, R. S. (1984). Creative process as a unifying theme of human cultures. *Daedalus, 113,* 197–219.

Root-Bernstein, R. S. (1987). Tools for thought: Designing an integrated curriculum for lifelong learners. *Roeper Review, 10,* 17–21.

Root-Bernstein, R. S. (1989). *Discovering: Inventing and solving problems at the frontier of scientific research.* Cambridge, MA: Harvard University Press.

Root-Bernstein, R. S. (1996). The sciences and arts share a common creative aesthetic. In A. I. Tauber (Ed.), *The elusive synthesis* (pp. 49–82). Aesthetics and science, Boston: Kluwer Academic Publishers.

Root-Bernstein, R., & Root-Bernstein, M. (1999). *Sparks of genius: The thirteen thinking tools of the world's most creative people.* New York: Houghton-Mifflin.

Root-Bernstein, R. S., Bernstein, M., & Garnier, H. (1993). Identification of scientists making long-term, high-impact contributions, with notes on their methods of working. *Creativity Research Journal, 6,* 320–343.

Root-Bernstein, R. S., Bernstein, M., & Garnier, H. (1995). Correlations between avocations, scientific style, work habits, and professional impact of scientists. *Creativity Research Journal, 8*, 115–137.

Rose, L. H., & Lin, H.-T. (1984). A meta-analysis of long-term creativity training programs. *Journal of Creativity Behavior, 18*, 11–22.

Rosenblatt, A., Greenberg, J., Solomon, S., Pyszczynski, T., & Lyon, D. (1989). Evidence for terror management theory: I. The effects of mortality salience on reactions to those who violate or uphold cultural values. *Journal of Personality and Social Psychology, 57*, 681.

Rosenblatt, E., & Winner, E. (1988). The art of children's drawings. *Journal of Aesthetic Education, 22*, 3–15.

Rosengren, K. E. (1985). Time and literary fame. *Poetics, 14*, 157–172.

Rosenthal, R. (1991). Teacher expectancy effects: A brief update 25 years after the Pygmalion experiment. *Journal of Research in Education, 1*, 3–12.

Rosenthal, R. (1992). *Pygmalion in the classroom: Teacher expectation and pupils' intellectual development*. Irvington, NY: Irvington Publishers.

Ross, R. J. (1976). The development of formal thinking and creativity in adolescence. *Adolescence, 11*, 609–617.

Ross, V. E. (2005). *A model for inventive ideation in a physio-mechanical context*. PhD thesis, University of Pretoria, South Africa, unpublished.

Rossman, J. (1964). *The psychology of the inventor: A study of the patentee*. Washington, DC: Inventors Publishing.

Roth, J. K., & Sontag, F. (1988). *The questions of philosophy*. Belmont, CA: Wadsworth.

Rothenberg, A. (1979). *The emerging goddess: The creative process in art, science, and other fields*. Chicago: University of Chicago Press.

Rothenberg, A. (1990). Creativity, mental health, and alcoholism. *Creativity Research Journal, 3*, 179–201.

Rothenberg, A. (1996). The Janusian process in scientific creativity. *Creativity Research Journal, 9*, 207–231.

Rothenberg, A. (1999). Janusian processes. In M. A. Runco & S. R. Pritzker (Eds.), *Encyclopedia of creativity* (pp. 103–108). San Diego, CA: Academic Press.

Rotton, J. (1992). Trait humor and longevity: Do comics have the last laugh? *Health Psychology, 11*, 262–266.

Routledge, C., & Arndt, J. (2007). Self-sacrifice as self-defence: Mortality salience increases efforts to affirm a symbolic immortal self at the expense of the physical self. *European Journal of Social Psychology, 38*, 531–541.

Rubenson, D. L., & Runco, M. A. (1992a). The economics of creativity, and the psychology of economics: A rejoinder. *New Ideas in Psychology, 10*, 173–178.

Rubenson, D. L., & Runco, M. A. (1992b). The psychoeconomic approach to creativity. *New Ideas in Psychology, 10*, 131–147.

Rubenson, D. L., & Runco, M. A. (1995). The psychoeconomic view of creative work in groups and organizations. *Creativity and Innovation Management, 4*, 232–241.

Rubin, W. Seckel, H. & Cousins, J., (Eds.), (2004). *Les demoiselles d'Avignon*. New York: Museum of Modern Art.

Rubin, Z. (1982). Does personality really change after 20? In K. Gardner (Ed.), *Readings in developmental psychology* (pp. 425–432). Boston, MA: Little, Brown.

Rubinstein, G. (2003). Authoritarianism and its relation to creativity: A comparative study among students of design, social science and law. *Personality and Individual Differences, 34*, 695–705.

Rudowicz, E. (2003). Creativity and culture: Two way interaction. *Scandinavian Journal of Educational Research, 47*, 273–290.

Rudowicz, E. (2004). Applicability of the test of creative thinking-drawing production for assessing creative potential of Hong Kong adolescents. *Gifted Child Quarterly, 48*, 202–218.

Rudowicz, E., & Hui, A. (1996). Creativity and a creative person: Hong Kong perspective. *Australasian Journal of Gifted Education, 5*, 5–11.

Rudowicz, E., & Hui, A. (1997). The creative personality: Hong Kong perspective. *Journal of Social Behavior and Personality, 12*, 139–157.

Rudowicz, E., & Hui, A. (1998). Hong Kong Chinese people's view of creativity. *Gifted Education International, 13*, 159–174.

Rudowicz, E., & Yue, X. D. (2000). Concepts of creativity: Similarities and differences among Hong Kong, Mainland and Taiwanese Chinese. *Journal of Creative Behavior, 34*, 175–192.

Rudowicz, E., & Yue, X. D. (2002). Compatibility of Chinese and creative personalities. *Creativity Research Journal, 14*, 387–394.

Rudowicz, E., Lok, D., & Kitto, J. (1995). Use of the Torrance test of creative thinking in an exploratory study of creativity in Hong Kong primary school children: A cross-cultural comparison. *Journal of Psychology, 30*, 417–430.

Runco, J. (1999). Developmental trends in creative abilities and potentials. In M. A. Runco & S. R. Pritzker (Eds.), *Encyclopedia of creativity* (pp. 537–559). San Diego, CA: Academic Press.

Runco, M. A. (1984). Teachers' judgments of creativity and social validation of divergent thinking tests. *Perceptual and Motor Skills, 59*, 711–717.

Runco, M. A. (1985). Reliability and convergent validity of ideational flexibility as a function of academic achievement. *Perceptual and Motor Skills, 61*, 1075–1081.

Runco, M. A. (1986a). Predicting children's creative performance. *Psychological Reports, 59*, 1247–1254.

Runco, M. A. (1986b). The discriminant validity of gifted children's divergent thinking test scores. *Gifted Child Quarterly, 30*, 78–82.

Runco, M. A. (1986c). Divergent thinking and creative performance in gifted and nongifted children. *Educational and Psychological Measurement, 46*, 375–384.

Runco, M. A. (1986d). Maximal performance on divergent thinking tests by gifted, talented, and nongifted children. *Psychology in the Schools, 23*, 308–315.

Runco, M. A. (1986e). Flexibility and originality in children's divergent thinking. *Journal of Psychology, 120*, 345–352.

Runco, M. A. (1987a). The generality of creative performance in gifted and nongifted children. *Gifted Child Quarterly, 31*, 121–125.

Runco, M. A. (1987b). Interrater agreement on a socially valid measure of students' creativity. *Psychological Reports, 61*, 1009–1010.

Runco, M. A. (1988). Creativity research: Originality, utility, and integration. *Creativity Research Journal, 1*, 1–7.

Runco, M. A. (1989a). Parents' and teachers' ratings of the creativity of children. *Journal of Social Behavior and Personality, 4*, 73–83.

Runco, M. A. (1989b). The creativity of children's art. *Child Study Journal, 19*, 177–189.

Runco, M. A. (1990a). Creativity and health (Editorial). *Creativity Research Journal, 3*, 81–84.

Runco, M. A. (1990b). Creativity and scientific genius (Review of Simonton's Scientific genius). *Imagination, Cognition and Personality, 10*, 201–206.

Runco, M. A. (1990c). The divergent thinking of young children: Implications of the research. *Gifted Child Today, 13*, 37–39.

Runco, M. A. (1990d). Implicit theories and creative ideation. In M. A. Runco & R. S. Albert (Eds.), *Theories of creativity* (pp. 234–252). Newbury Park, CA: Sage.

Runco, M. A. (1990e). Mindfulness and personal control (Review of Langer's Mindfulness). *Imagination, Cognition and Personality, 10*, 107–114.

Runco, M. A. (1991a). Metaphors and creative thinking. *Creativity Research Journal, 4*, 85–86.

Runco, M. A., (Ed.), (1991b). *Divergent thinking*. Norwood, NJ: Ablex.

Runco, M. A. (1991c). Creativity and human capital. *Creativity Research Journal, 5*, 373–378.

Runco, M. A. (1991d). The evaluative, valuative, and divergent thinking of children. *Journal of Creative Behavior, 25*, 311–319.

Runco, M. A. (1991e). On economic theories of creativity. *Creativity Research Journal, 4*, 198–200.

Runco, M. A. (1991f). On investment and creativity: A response to Sternberg and Lubart. *Creativity Research Journal, 4*, 202–205.

Runco, M. A. (1992a). *Creativity as an educational objective for disadvantaged students*. Storrs, CT: National Research Center on the Gifted and Talented.

Runco, M. A. (1992b). Children's divergent thinking and creative ideation. *Developmental Review, 12*, 233–264.

Runco, M. A. (1992c). Creativity and human capital. *Creativity Research Journal, 5*, 373–378.

Runco, M. A. (1993a). Moral creativity: Intentional and unconventional. *Creativity Research Journal, 6*, 17–28.

Runco, M. A. (1993b). On reputational paths and case studies. *Creativity Research Journal, 6*, 487–488.

Runco, M. A. (1993c). Creativity, causality, and the separation of personality and cognition. *Psychological Inquiry, 4*, 221–225.

Runco, M. A. (1993d). Divergent thinking, creativity, and giftedness. *Gifted Child Quarterly, 37*, 16–22.

Runco, M. A. (1993e). Operant theories of insight, originality, and creativity. *American Behavioral Scientist, 37*, 59–74.

Runco, M. A., (Ed.), (1994a). *Problem finding, problem solving, and creativity*. Norwood, NJ: Ablex. pp. 40–76

Runco, M. A. (1994b). Cognitive and psychometric issues in creativity research. In S. G. Isaksen, M. C. Murdock, R. L. Firestien, & D. J. Treffinger (Eds.), *Understanding and recognizing creativity* (pp. 331–368). Norwood, NJ: Ablex.

Runco, M. A. (1994c). Creativity and its discontents. In M. P. Shaw & M. A. Runco (Eds.), *Creativity and affect* (pp. 102–123). Norwood, NJ: Ablex.

Runco, M. A., (Ed.), (1994d). *Problem finding, problem solving, and creativity.* Norwood, NJ: Ablex.

Runco, M. A. (1994e). Conclusions concerning problem finding, problem solving, and creativity. In M. A. Runco (Ed.), *Problem finding, problem solving, and creativity* (pp. 272–290). Norwood, NJ: Ablex.

Runco, M. A. (1994f). Creative thinking, *Encyclopedia of human behavior* (vol. 2, pp. 5346–5368). San Diego, CA: Academic Press.

Runco, M. A. (1994g). Giftedness as critical creative thought. In N. Colangelo, S. Assouline, & D. L. Ambroson (Eds.), *Talent development* (Vol. 2, pp. 239–249). Dayton, OH: Ohio Psychology Press.

Runco, M. A. (1995a). The creativity and job satisfaction of artists in organizations. *Empirical Studies of the Arts, 13,* 39–45.

Runco, M. A. (1995b). Creativity and the future. In G. T. Kurian & G. T. T. Molitor (Eds.), *Encyclopedia of the future* (Vol. 1, pp. 156–157). New York: Macmillan.

Runco, M. A. (1995c). Insight for creativity, expression for impact. *Creativity Research Journal, 8,* 377–390.

Runco, M. A. (1995d). New dimensions in creativity. *Understanding Our Gifted, 7,* 12–15.

Runco, M. A. (1996a). Creativity and development: Recommendations. *New Directions for Child Development, 72,* 87–90 (Summer).

Runco, M. A. (1996b). Creativity need not be social. In A. Montuori & R. Purser (Eds.), *Social creativity* (Vol. 1). Cresskill, NJ: Hampton Press.

Runco, M. A. (1996c). Objectivity in creativity research. In M. Montuori (Ed.), *Unusual associates: Essays in honor of Frank Barron* (pp. 69–79). Cresskill, NJ: Hampton Press.

Runco, M. A. (1996d). Personal creativity: Definition and developmental issues. *New Directions for Child Development, 72,* 3–30 (Summer).

Runco, M. A., (Ed.) (1997a). *Critical creative processes.* Cresskill, NJ: Hampton Press.

Runco, M. A. (1997b). Is every child gifted? *Roeper Review, 19,* 220–224.

Runco, M. A. (1998). Suicide and creativity: The case of Sylvia Plath. *Death Studies, 22,* 637–654.

Runco, M. A. (1999a). The fourth-grade slump. In M. A. Runco & S. R. Pritzker (Eds.), *Encyclopedia of creativity* (pp. 743–744). San Diego, CA: Academic Press.

Runco, M. A. (1999b). Misjudgment. In M. A. Runco & S. R. Pritzker (Eds.), *Encyclopedia of creativity* (pp. 235–240). San Diego, CA: Academic Press.

Runco, M. A. (1999c). Tension, adaptability, and creativity. In S. W. Russ (Ed.), *Affect, creative experience, and psychological adjustment* (pp. 165–194). Philadelphia, PA: Taylor & Francis.

Runco, M. A. (1999d). Divergent thinking. In M. A. Runco & S. R. Pritzker (Eds.), *Encyclopedia of creativity* (pp. 577–582). San Diego, CA: Academic Press.

Runco, M. A. (Ed.) (1999e). Longitudinal studies of creativity: Special issue of the Creativity Research Journal. *Creativity Research Journal.* 12.

Runco, M. A. (2001a). Creativity as optimal human functioning. In M. Bloom (Ed.), *Promoting creativity across the lifespan* (pp. 17–44). Washington, DC: Child Welfare League of America.

Runco, M. A. (2001b). The intersection of creativity and culture: Foreword. In N. A. Kwang (Ed.), *Why Asians are less creative than Westerners.* Singapore: Prentice Hall.

Runco, M. A. (2003a). Discretion is the better part of creativity: Personal creativity and implications for culture. *Inquiry: Critical Thinking Across the Disciplines, 22,* 9–12.

Runco, M. A. (2003b). Creativity, cognition, and their educational implications. In J. C. Houtz (Ed.), *The educational psychology of creativity* (pp. 25–56). Cresskill, NJ: Hampton Press.

Runco, M. A. (2003c). Education for creative potential. *Scandinavian Journal of Education, 47,* 317–324.

Runco, M. A. (2003d). Where will we hang all of the paintings? Introduction to the Festschrift for Howard Gruber. *Creativity Research Journal, 15,* 1–2.

Runco, M. A., (Ed.) (2003e). *Critical creative processes.* Cresskill, NJ: Hampton Press.

Runco, M. A. (2004). Personal creativity and culture. In S. Lau, A. N. N. Hui, & G. Y. C. Ng (Eds.), *Creativity when East meets West* (pp. 9–22). New Jersey: World Scientific.

Runco, M. A. (2005). Motivation, competence, and creativity. In A. Elliott & C. Dweck (Eds.), *Handbook of achievement motivation and competence* (pp. 609–623). New York: Guilford Press.

Runco, M. A. (2006a, January). What the recent creativity research suggests about innovation and entrepreneurship. In *Annual Norwegian Business Economics and Finance Conference.* Norway: Bergen.

Runco, M. A. (2006b). Reasoning and personal creativity. In J. C. Kaufman & J. Baer (Eds.), *Knowledge and reason in cognitive development* (pp. 99–116). Cambridge: Cambridge University Press.

Runco, M. A. (2007). A hierarchical framework for the study of creativity. *New Horizons in Education, 55,* 1–9.

Runco, M. A. (2008). Creativity and education. *New Horizons in Education, 56*(1), 107–115.

Runco, M. A. (2010a). Creativity has no dark side. In D. H. Cropley, A. J. Cropley, J. C. Kaufman, & M. A. Runco (Eds.), *The dark side of creativity* (pp. 15–32). New York: Cambridge University Press.

Runco, M. A. (2010b). Education based on a parsimonious theory of creativity. In R. A. Beghetto & James C. Kaufman (Eds.), *Nurturing creativity in the classroom* (pp. 235–251). New York: Cambridge University Press.

Runco, M. A. (2010c). Parsimonious creativity and its measurement. In E. Villalba (Ed.), *Proceedings of European council meeting on creativity and innovation. Brussels, Belgium.*

Runco, M. A. (2011). Contrarianism. In M. A. Runco & S. R. Pritzker (Eds.), *Encyclopedia of creativity* (pp. 261–263). (2nd ed.) San Diego, CA: Elsevier.

Runco, M. A. (2012). Creativity, stress, and suicide. In M. A. Runco (Ed.), *Creativity research handbook* (Vol. 3, pp. 163–192). Cresskill, NJ: Hampton Press.

Runco, M. A. (2013a, September). *Is there a creativity crisis?* Presentation to the Mississippi Association for Gifted Children, Hattiesburg, MS.

Runco, M. A., (Ed.), (2013b). *Divergent thinking and creative potential.* Cresskill, NJ: Hampton Press.

Runco, M. A. (in press). Misleading implications of the Big C, Little c distinction. *Creativity Research Journal.*

Runco, M. A., & Acar, S. (2010). Do tests of divergent thinking have an experiential bias? *Psychology of Art, Creativity, and Aesthetics, 4,* 144–148.

Runco, M. A., & Albert, R. S. (1985). The reliability and validity of ideational originality in the divergent thinking of academically gifted and nongifted children. *Educational and Psychological Measurement, 45,* 483–501.

Runco, M. A., & Albert, R. S. (1986a). Exceptional giftedness in early adolescence and intra-familial divergent thinking. *Journal of Youth and Adolescence, 15,* 333–342.

Runco, M. A., & Albert, R. S. (1986b). The threshold hypothesis regarding creativity and intelligence: An empirical test with gifted and nongifted children. *Creative Child and Adult Quarterly, 11,* 212–218.

Runco, M. A., & Albert, R. S. (1997). *Theories of creativity* (rev. ed.). Cresskill, NJ: Sage.

Runco, M. A., & Albert, R. S. (2005). Parents' personality and the creative potential of exceptionally gifted boys. *Creativity Research Journal, 17,* 355–368.

Runco, M. A., & Bahleda, M. D. (1987a). Birth order and divergent thinking. *Journal of Genetic Psychology, 148,* 119–125.

Runco, M. A., & Bahleda, M. D. (1987b). Implicit theories of artistic, scientific, and everyday creativity. *Journal of Creative Behavior, 20,* 93–98.

Runco, M. A., & Basadur, M. (1993). Assessing ideational and evaluative skills and creative styles and attitudes. *Creativity and Innovation Management, 2,* 166–173.

Runco, M. A., & Catalan, S. M. (2013, August). Assessing transformational capacity with divergent thinking tests. In *Accepted presentation for the annual meeting of the American Psychological Association, Washington, DC.*

Runco, M. A., & Cayirdag, N. (2012a). The theory of personal creativity and implications for the fulfillment of children's potentials. In O. N. Saracho (Ed.), *Contemporary perspectives on research in creativity in early childhood education* (pp. 31–43). Charlotte, NC: Information Age Publishing.

Runco, M. A., & Cayirdag, N. (2012b). The development of children's creativity. In O. N. Saracho & B. Spodek (Eds.), *Handbook of research on the education of young children* (pp. 102–114). (3rd ed.) Philadelphia, PA: Taylor & Francis.

Runco, M. A., & Chand, I.. In M. A. Runco (Ed.), (1994). *Problem finding, problem solving, and creativity.* Norwood, NJ: Ablex.

Runco, M. A., & Chand, I. (1995). Cognition and creativity. *Educational Psychology Review, 7,* 243–267.

Runco, M. A., & Charles, R. (1993). Judgments of originality and appropriateness as predictors of creativity. *Personality and Individual Differences, 15,* 537–546.

Runco, M. A., & Charles, R. (1997). Developmental trends in creativity. In M. A. Runco (Ed.), *Creativity research handbook* (Vol. 1, pp. 113–150). Cresskill, NJ: Hampton Press.

Runco, M. A., & Jaeger, G. (2012). The standard definition of creativity. *Creativity Research Journal, 24,* 92–96.

Runco, M. A., & Johnson, D. J. (2002). Parents' and teachers' implicit theories of children's creativity: A cross-cultural perspective. *Creativity Research Journal, 14,* 427–438.

Runco, M. A., & Gaynor, J. L. R. (1993a). Creativity as optimal development. In J. Brzezinski, S. DiNuovo, T. Marek, & T. Maruszewski (Eds.), *Creativity and consciousness: Philosophical and psychological dimensions* (pp. 395–412). Amsterdam/Atlanta: Rodopi.

Runco, M. A., & Gaynor, J. L. R. (1993b). Creativity as optimal development. In J. Brzezinski, S. DiNuovo, T. Marek, & T. Maruszewski (Eds.), *Creativity and consciousness: Philosophical and psychological dimensions* (pp. 395–412). Amsterdam/Atlanta: Rodopi.

Runco, M.A., & Kaufman, J. (2006). *Reputational paths: Preliminary data.* Unpublished manuscript.

Runco, M. A., & Kim, D. (2013). The 4Ps of creativity. In I. Dubina (Ed.), *Encyclopedia of creativity, invention, innovation, and entrepreneurship* (pp. 755–759). New York: Springer.

Runco, M. A., & Mraz, W. (1992). Scoring divergent thinking tests using total ideational output and a creativity index. *Educational and Psychological Measurement, 52,* 213–221.

Runco, M. A., & Nemiro, J. (1994). Problem finding, creativity, and giftedness. *Roeper Review, 16,* 235–241.

Runco, M. A., & Okuda, S. M. (1988). Problem-discovery, divergent thinking, and the creative process. *Journal of Youth and Adolescence, 17,* 211–220.

Runco, M. A., & Okuda, S. M. (1991). The instructional enhancement of the ideational originality and flexibility scores of divergent thinking tests. *Applied Cognitive Psychology, 5,* 435–441.

Runco, M. A., & Okuda Sakamoto, S. (1993). Reaching creatively gifted children through their learning styles. In R. M. Milgram, R. Dunn, & G. E. Price (Eds.), *Teaching and counseling gifted and talented adolescents: An international learning style perspective* (pp. 103–115). New York: Praeger.

Runco, M. A., & Pezdek, K. (1984). The effect of radio and television on children's creativity. *Human Communications Research, 11,* 109–120.

Runco, M. A. & Richards, R., (Eds.), (1997). *Eminent creativity, everyday creativity, and health.* Norwood, NJ: Ablex.

Runco, M. A., & Sakamoto, S. O. (1996). Optimization as a guiding principle in research on creative problem solving. In T. Helstrup, G. Kaufmann, & K. H. Teigen (Eds.), *Problem solving and cognitive processes: Essays in honor of Kjell Raaheim* (pp. 119–144). Bergen: Fagbokforlaget Vigmostad and Bjorke.

Runco, M. A., & Sakamoto, S. O. (1999). Experimental research on creativity. In R. S. Sternberg (Ed.), *Handbook of human creativity.* New York: Cambridge University Press.

Runco, M. A., & Schreibman, L. (1983). Parental judgments of behavior therapy efficacy with autistic children: A social validation. *Journal of Autism and Developmental Disorders, 13,* 237–248.

Runco, M. A., & Schreibman, L. (1987). Socially validating behavioral objectives in the treatment of autistic children. *Journal of Autism and Developmental Disorders, 17,* 141–147.

Runco, M. A., & Schreibman, L. (1988). Children's judgments of autism and social validation of behavior therapy efficacy. *Behavior therapy, 19,* 565–576.

Runco, M. A., & Shaw, M. P. (1994). Conclusions concerning creativity and affect. In M. P. Shaw & M. A. Runco (Eds.), *Creativity and affect* (pp. 261–270). Norwood, NJ: Ablex.

Runco, M. A., & Smith, W. R. (1992). Interpersonal and intrapersonal evaluations of creative ideas. *Personality and Individual Differences, 13,* 295–302.

Runco, M. A., & Thurston, B. J. (1987). Students' ratings of college teaching: A social validation. *Teaching of Psychology, 14,* 89–91.

Runco, M. A., & Vega, L. (1990). Evaluating the creativity of children's ideas. *Journal of Social Behavior and Personality, 5,* 439–452.

Runco, M. A., Charlop, M. H., & Schreibman, L. (1986). The occurrence of autistic children's self-stimulation as a function of familiar versus unfamiliar stimulus conditions. *Journal of Autism and Developmental Disorders, 16,* 31–44.

Runco, M. A., Okuda, S. M., & Thurston, B. J. (1987). The psychometric properties of four systems for scoring divergent thinking tests. *Journal of Psychoeducational Assessment, 5,* 149–156.

Runco, M. A., Noble, E. P., & Luptak, Y. (1990). Agreement between mothers and sons on ratings of creative activity. *Educational and Psychological Measurement, 50,* 673–680.

Runco, M. A., Ebersole, P., & Mraz, W. (1991a). Self-actualization and creativity. *Journal of Social Behavior and Personality, 6,* 61–167. (Also appears in Jones, A., & Crandall, R. (Eds.), Handbook of self-actualization. Corte Madera, CA: Select Press.)

Runco, M. A., Okuda, S. M., & Thurston, B. J. (1991b). A social validation of college examinations. *Educational and Psychological Measurement, 51,* 463–472.

Runco, M. A., Okuda, S. M., & Thurston, B. J. (1991c). Environmental cues and divergent thinking. In M. A. Runco (Ed.), *Divergent thinking* (pp. 79–85). Norwood, NJ: Ablex.

Runco, M. A., Johnson, D., & Baer, P. (1993). Parents' and teachers' implicit theories of children's creativity. *Child Study Journal, 23,* 91–113.

Runco, M. A., McCarthy, K. A., & Svensen, E. (1994). Judgments of the creativity of artwork from students and professional artists. *Journal of Psychology, 128,* 23–31.

Runco, M. A., Nemiro, J., & Walberg, H. (1997). Personal explicit theories of creativity. *Journal of Creative Behavior, 31,* 43–59.

Runco, M. A., Johnson, D., & Gaynor, J. R. (1999). Judgmental bases of creativity and implications for the study of gifted youth. In A. Fishkin, B. Cramond, & P. Olszewski-Kubilius (Eds.), *Creativity in youth: Research and methods* (pp. 113–141). Cresskill, NJ: Hampton Press.

Runco, M. A., Jilles, J. J., & Reiter-Palmon, R. (2005a). Explicit instructions to be creative and original: A comparison of strategies and criteria as targets with three types of divergent thinking tests. *Korean Journal of Thinking and Problem Solving, 15*, 5–15.

Runco, M. A., Illies, J. J., & Eisenman, R. (2005b). Creativity, originality, and appropriateness: What do explicit instructions tell us about their relationships? *Journal of Creative Behavior, 39*, 137–148.

Runco, M. A., Dow, G., & Smith, W. R. (2006). Information, experience, divergent thinking: An empirical test. *Creativity Research Journal, 18*, 269–277.

Runco, M. A., Cramond, B., & Pagnani, A. (2010). Sex differences in creative potential and creative performance. In J. C. Chrisler, & D. McCreary (Eds.), *Handbook of gender research in psychology* (Vol. 2, pp. 343–357). New York: Springer.

Runco, M. A., Noble, E. P., Reiter-Palmon, R., Acar, S., Ritchie, T., & Yurkovich, J. M. (2011). The genetic basis of creativity and ideational fluency. *Creativity Research Journal, 23*, 376–380.

Runco, M. A., Lubart, T., & Getz, I. (2012). Creativity from the economic perspective. In M. A. Runco (Ed.), *Creativity research handbook* (Vol. 3, pp. 173–198). Cresskill, NJ: Hampton Press.

Runco, M. A., Acar, S., Kaufman, J., & Halladay, L. R. (2012). Changes in reputation and associations with fame and biographical data. Manuscript submitted for publication.

Ruse, M. (1979). *The Darwinian revolution*. Chicago, IL: University of Chicago Press.

Rushton, P., Murray, H. G., & Paunonen, S. V. (1983). Personality, research creativity, and teaching effectiveness. In R. S. Albert (Ed.), *Genius and eminence* (pp. 281–301). Oxford: Pergamon Press.

Russ, S. W., & Schafer, E. D. (2006). Affect in fantasy play, emotion and memories, and divergent thinking. *Creativity Research Journal, 18*, 346–354.

Russ, S. W. (1993). Affect and creativity. In *Affect and creativity: The role of affect and play in the creative process* (pp. 1–16). Hillsdale, NJ: Lawrence Erlbaum Associates.

Russ, S. W. (1998). Play, creativity, and adaptive functioning: Implications for play interventions. *Journal of Clinical Child Psychology, 27*, 469–480.

Russ, S., (Ed.), (1999). *Affect, creative experience, and psychological adjustment*. Philadelphia, PA: Taylor & Francis.

Russ, S. W. (2001). Primary process thinking and creativity: Affect and cognition. *Creativity Research Journal, 13*, 27–35.

Russo, C. F. (2004). A comparative study of creativity and cognitive problem-solving strategies of high-IQ and average students. *Gifted Child Quarterly, 48*, 179–190.

Ryhammar, L., & Smith, G. J. W. (1999). Creative and other personality functions as defined by percept-genetic techniques and their relation to organizational conditions. *Creativity Research Journal, 12*, 277–286.

Sacks, O. (1996). *An anthropologist on Mars*. New York: Vintage Books.

Safire, W. (1990). *Fumblerules*. New York: Doubleday.

Sagiv, L. (2002). Vocational interests and basic values. *Journal of Career Assessment, 10*, 233–257.

Sak, U., & Maker, C. J. (2006). Developmental variation in children's creative mathematical thinking as a function of schooling, age, and knowledge. *Creativity Research Journal, 18*, 279–291.

Saldivar, T. (1992). *Silvia Plath: Confessing the fictive self*. New York: Peter Lang.

Salovey, P., & Mayer, J. D. (1990). Emotional intelligence. *Imagination, Cognition, and Personality, 9*, 185–211.

Sang, B., Yu, J., Zhang, Z., & Yu, J. (1992). A comparative study of the creative thinking and academic adaptability of ADHD and normal children. *Psychological Science, 25*, 31–33.

Sanguinetti, C., & Kavaler-Adler, S. (1999). Anne Sexton. In M. A. Runco & S. R. Pritzker (Eds.), *Encyclopedia of creativity* (pp. 551–557). San Diego, CA: Academic Press.

Sass, L. (2000–2001). Schizophrenia, modernism, and the "creative imagination": On creativity and psychopathology. *Creativity Research Journal, 13*, 55–74.

Sass, L. A., & Schuldberg, D. (2000–2001). Introduction to the special issue: Creativity and the schizophrenic spectrum. *Creativity Research Journal, 13*, 1–4.

Savransky, S. (2000). *Engineering of creativity: Introduction to TRIZ methodology of inventive problem solving*. Florida: CRC Press.

Sawyer, K. (1992). Improvisational creativity: An analysis of jazz performance. *Creativity Research Journal, 5*, 253–263.

Sayed, F. M., & Mohamed, A. H. H. (2013). Gender differences in divergent thinking: Use of the test of creative thinking–drawing production on an Egyptian sample. *Creativity Research Journal, 25*, 222–227.

Scarr, S., & McCartney, K. (1983). How people make their environments: A theory of genotype–environment effects. *Child Development, 54*, 424–435.

Schack, G. D. (1989). Self-efficacy as a mediator in the creative productivity of gifted children. *Journal of the Education of the Gifted, 12*, 231–249.

Schaefer, C. E. (1969). Imaginary companions and creative adolescents. *Developmental Psychology, 1*, 747–749.

Schaefer, C., & Anastasi, A. (1968). A biographical inventory for identifying creativity in adolescent boys. *Journal of Applied Psychology, 54*, 42–48.

Schank, R. C., & Cleary, C. (1995). Making machines creative. In S. M. Smith, T. B. Ward, & R. A. Finke (Eds.), *The creative cognition approach* (pp. 229–247). Cambridge, MA: MIT Press.

Scharfenberg, J. (1994). Creativity and religious symbols. In M. P. Shaw & M. Runco (Eds.), *Creativity and affect* (p. 251). Norwood, NJ: Ablex.

Scheerer, M. (1963). Problem solving. *Scientific American, 208*, 118–128.

Scheibel, A. B. (1999). *Creativity and the brain.* <http://www.pbs.org/teachersource/scienceline/archives/sept99/sept99.shtm>.

Scherzer, L. (2012). *Cracking your PIN code: Easy as 1-2-3-4.* <http://finance.yahoo.com/blogs/the-exchange/cracking-pin-code-easy-1-2-3-4-130143629.html>.

Schickel, R. (1973). *Hitchcock: Master of suspense. Winstar Studios.* Produced, written, and directed by Richard Schickel, produced by American Cinemtcheque, Center of music and drama.

Schiff, S. (2005). *A great improvisation: Franklin, France, and the birth of America.* New York: Henry Holt and Co.

Schilling, M. A. (2005). A "small-world" network model of cognitive insight. *Creativity Research Journal, 17*, 131–154.

Schlaug, G. (2001). The brain and musicians: A model for functional and structural plasticity. *Annals of the New York Academy of Science, 930*, 281–299.

Schlaug, G., Jancke, L., Huang, Y., Staigar, J. F., & Steinnetz, H. (1995a). Increased corpus callosum size in musicians. *Neuropsychologia, 33*, 1047–1055.

Schlaug, G., Jancke, L., Huang, Y., & Steinmetz, H. (1995b). In vivo evidence of structural brain asymmetry in musicians. *Science, 267*, 699–701.

Schneider, F., Gur, R. E., Alavi, A., Seligman, M. E., Mozley, L. H., Smith, R. J., et al. (1996). Cerebral blood flow changes in limbic regions induced by unsolvable anagram tasks. *American Journal of Psychiatry, 153*, 206–212.

Schooler, J. W., & Melcher, J. (1995). The ineffability of insight. In S. M. Smith, T. B. Ward, & R. A. Finke (Eds.), *The creative cognition approach* (pp. 97–133). Cambridge, MA: MIT Press.

Schooler, J. W., Fallshore, M., & Fiore, S. M. (1995). Epilogue: Putting insight into perspective. In R. J. Sternberg & J. E. Davidson (Eds.), *The nature of insight* (pp. 559–587). Cambridge, MA: MIT Press.

Schooler, J. W., Ohlsson, S., & Brooks, K. (1993). Thoughts beyond words: When language overshadows insight. *Journal of Experimental Psychology: General, 122*, 166–183.

Schotte, D., & Clum, G. A. (1982). Suicide ideation in a college population: A test of a model. *Journal of Consulting and Clinical Psychology, 5*, 690–696.

Schotte, D., & Clum, G. (1987). Problem-solving skills in suicidal psychiatric patients. *Journal of Consulting and Clinical Psychology, 1*, 49–54.

Schreibman, L., Runco, M. A., Mills, J. I., & Koegel, R. L. (1982). Teachers' judgments of improvements in autistic children in behavior therapy: A social validation. In R. L. Koegel, A. Rincover, & A. L. Egel (Eds.), *Educating and understanding autistic children* (pp. 78–87). San Diego, CA: College-Hill Press.

Schrodinger, E. (1992). *What is life? With mind and matter and autobiographical sketches.* Cambridge: Cambridge University Press (Originally published 1946).

Schuldberg, D. (1990). Schizotypal and hypomanic traits, creativity and psychological health. *Creativity Research Journal, 3*, 218–230.

Schuldberg, D. (1994). Giddiness and horror in the creative process. In M. P. Shaw & M. A. Runco (Eds.), *Creativity and affect* (pp. 87–101). Norwood, NJ: Ablex.

Schuldberg, D. (2001). Six subclinical spectrum traits in normal creativity. *Creativity Research Journal, 13*, 5–16.

Schumpeter, J. A. (1934). *The theory of economic development, an inquiry into profits, capital, credit, interest, and the business cycle.* Cambridge, MA: Harvard University Press.

Schunn, C. D., Crowley, K., & Okada, T. (1998). The growth of multidisciplinarity in the cognitive science society. *Cognitive Science, 22*, 107–130.

Schwebel, M. (1993). Moral creativity as artistic transformation. *Creativity Research Journal, 6*, 65–82.

Schwinger, J. (1999). *Einstein's legacy*. New York: Scientific American Books.

Science News (2001). Power of waves inspires ingenuity. *Science News, 159* (April 14), 235.

Scope, E. E. (1998). Meta-analysis of research on creativity: The effects of instructional variables. Unpublished doctoral dissertation, Fordham University, New York.

Scott, G., Leritz, L. E., & Mumford, M. D. (2004a). The effectiveness of creativity training: A quantitative review. *Creativity Research Journal, 16*, 361–388.

Scott, G., Leritz, L. E., & Mumford, M. D. (2004b). Types of creativity training: Approaches and their effectiveness. *Journal of Creative Behavior, 38*, 150–179.

Scott, G. M., Lonergan, D. C., & Mumford, M. D. (2005). Conceptual combination: Alternative knowledge structures, alternative heuristics. *Creativity Research Journal, 17*, 79–98.

Scott, M. E. (1985). How stress can affect gifted/creative potential: Ideas to better insure realization of potential. *Creative Child and Adult Quarterly, 10*, 240–249.

Segal, L. (1996). A dance with difficulty. *Los Angeles Times* (January 2), F1–F11.

Seitz, J. (2003). The political economy of creativity. *Creativity Research Journal, 15*, 385–392.

Sela, M. (1994). A personal view of molecular immunology. *Creativity Research Journal, 7*, 327–339.

Sen, A. K., & Hagtvet, K. A. (1993). Correlations among creativity, intelligence, personality, and academic achievement. *Perceptual and Motor Skills, 77*, 497–498.

Serba, J. (2012). *Nature wars: The incredible story of how wildlife comebacks turned backyards into battlegrounds*. New York: Crown.

Sergent, J., Zuck, E., Terriah, S., & MacDonald, B. (1992). Distributed neural network underlying musical sight-reading and keyboard performance. *Science, 257*, 106–109.

Seyle, H. (1988). Creativity in basic research. In F. Flach (Ed.), *Creative mind* (pp. 243–268). Buffalo, NY: Bearly Limited.

Shalley, C. E., & Oldham, G. R. (1997). Competition and creative performance: Effects of competitor presence and visibility. *Creativity Research Journal, 10*, 337–345.

Shapiro, R. J. (1970). The criterion problem. In P. E. Vernon (Ed.), *Creativity* (pp. 257–269). New York: Penguin.

Shaw, E. D., Mann, J. J., Stokes, P. E., & Manevitz, A. Z. (1986). Effects of lithium carbonate on associative productivity and idiosyncrasy in bipolar outpatients. *American Journal of Psychiatry, 143*, 1166–1169.

Shaw, G. A., & Brown, G. (1991). Laterality, implicit memory, and attention disorder. *Educational Studies, 17*, 15–23.

Shaw, M. (1989). The eureka process: A structure for the creative experience in science and engineering. *Creativity Research Journal, 2*, 286–298.

Shaw, M. P. & Runco, M. A., (Eds.) (1994). *Creativity and affect*. Norwood, NJ: Ablex.

Shepard, R. (1982). *Mental images and their transformation*. Cambridge, MA: Bradford Books.

Shlain, L. (1991). *Art and physics: Parallel visions in space, time and light*. New York: Quill/Morrow.

Shou, M. (1979). Artistic productivity and lithium. *British Journal of Psychiatry, 135*, 97–103.

Sifneos, P. E. (1973). The prevalence of alexithymic characteristics in psychosomatic patients. *Psychotherapy and Psychosomatics, 22*, 255–262.

Silverman, K. et al. (1995). Giftedness and gender. In K. Noble, K. Arnold, & R. Subotnik (Eds.), *Remarkable women*. Cresskill, NJ: Hampton Press.

Silverman, K. (2003). *Lightning man: The accursed life of Samuel F. B. Morse*. New York: Knopf.

Simms, J. R. (2006). Technical and social innovation determinants of behavior. *Systems Research and Behavioral Science, 23*, 383–393.

Simon, H. A. (1973). Does scientific discovery have a logic? *Philosophy of Science, 40*, 471–480.

Simon, H. A. (1981). *Sciences of the artificial*. Cambridge, MA: MIT Press.

Simon, H. A. (1988). Creativity and motivation: A response to Csikszentmihalyi. *New Ideas in Psychology, 6*, 177–181.

Simon, H. A. (1995). Machine discovery. *Foundations of Science, 1*, 171–200.

Simon, H. A., & Chase, W. (1973). Skill in chess. *American Scientist, 61*, 394–403.

Simon, H. A., & Chase, W. G. (1977). Skill in chess. In I. L. Janis (Ed.), *Current trends in psychology: Readings from American Scientist* (pp. 194–203). Los Altos, CA: William Kaufmann.

Simon, R. S. (1979). *Jungian types and creativity of professional fine artists*. Unpublished doctoral dissertation. United States International University. Available from University Microfilms, as 7924570.

Simonton, D. K. (1979). Was Napoleon a military genius? Score: Carlyle 1, Tolstoy 1. *Psychological Reports, 44*, 21–22.

Simonton, D. K. (1983). Creative productivity and age: A mathematical model based on a two-step cognitive process. *Developmental Review, 3*, 97–111.

Simonton, D. K. (1984). *Genius, creativity, and leadership.* Cambridge, MA: Harvard University Press.

Simonton, D. K. (1985). Quality, quantity, and age: The careers of ten distinguished psychologists. *International Aging and Human Development, 21,* 241–254.

Simonton, D. K. (1987a). Multiples, chance, genius, creativity, and zeitgeist. In D. N. Jackson & J. P. Rushton (Eds.), *Scientific excellence: Origins and assessment* (pp. 98–128). Beverly Hills, CA: Sage.

Simonton, D. K. (1987b). Musical aesthetics and creativity in Beethoven: A computer analysis of 106 compositions. *Empirical Studies of the Arts, 5,* 87–104.

Simonton, D. K. (1988). *Scientific genius.* New York: Cambridge University Press.

Simonton, D. K. (1989). The swan-song phenomenon: Last-works effects for 172 classical composers. *Psychology and Aging, 4,* 42.

Simonton, D. K. (1990a). History, chemistry, psychology, and genius: An intellectual autobiography of historiometry. In M. A. Runco & R. S. Albert (Eds.), *Theories of creativity* (pp. 61–91). Newbury Park, CA: Sage.

Simonton, D. K. (1990b). Political pathology and social creativity. *Creativity Research Journal, 3,* 85–99.

Simonton, D. K. (1994). *Greatness: Who makes history and why.* New York: Guilford Press.

Simonton, D. K. (1995). Exceptional personal influence: An integrative paradigm. *Creativity Research Journal, 8,* 371–376.

Simonton, D. K. (1997a). Creative productivity: A predictive and explanatory model of career trajectories and landmarks. *Psychological Review, 104,* 66–89.

Simonton, D. K. (1997b). Creativity as variation and selection: Some critical constraints. In M. A. Runco (Ed.), *Critical creative processes* (pp. 3–18). Cresskill, NJ: Hampton Press.

Simonton, D. K. (1997c). Political pathology and societal creativity. In M. A. Runco & R. Richards (Eds.), *Eminent creativity, everyday creativity, and health* (pp. 359–377). Greenwich, CT: Ablex.

Simonton, D. K. (1998). Achieved eminence in minority and majority cultures: Convergence versus divergence in the assessments of 294 African Americans. *Journal of Personality and Social Psychology, 74,* 804–817.

Simonton, D. K. (1999a). Historiometry. In M. A. Runco & S. R. Pritzker (Eds.), *Encyclopedia of creativity* (pp. 815–822). San Diego, CA: Academic Press.

Simonton, D. K. (1999b). William Shakespeare. In M. A. Runco & S. R. Pritzker (Eds.), *Encyclopedia of creativity* (pp. 559–563). San Diego, CA: Academic Press.

Simonton, D. K. (1999c). *Origins of genius: Darwinian perspectives on creativity.* New York: Oxford University Press.

Simonton, D. K. (1999d). Matthew effects. In M. A. Runco & S. R. Pritzker (Eds.), *Encyclopedia of creativity* (pp. 185–192). San Diego, CA: Academic Press.

Simonton, D. K. (1999e). Creativity as blind variation and selective retention: Is the creative process Darwinian? *Psychological Inquiry, 10,* 309–328.

Simonton, D. K. (2007). The creative process in Picasso's Guernica sketches: Monotonic improvements versus non-monotonic variants. *Creativity Research Journal, 19,* 329–344.

Singer, D. G., & Singer, J. L. (1992). *The house of make-believe: Children's play and the developing imagination.* Cambridge, MA: Harvard University Press.

Singer, J. L. (1975). Navigating the stream of consciousness: Research in daydreaming and related inner experiences. *American Psychologist, 30,* 727–738.

Singer, J. L. (1999). Imagination. In M. A. Runco & S. R. Pritzker (Eds.), *Encyclopedia of creativity* (pp. 13–25). San Diego, CA: Academic Press.

Singer, J., & Singer, D. (2012). Imagining possible worlds to confront and to create new realities. In M. A. Runco (Ed.), *Creativity research handbook* (Vol. 3, pp. 193–214). Cresskill, NJ: Hampton Press.

Singh, L., & Gupta, G. (1977). Creativity: As related to the values of Indian adolescent students. *Indian Psychological Review, 14,* 73–76.

Singh, R. P. (1987). Parental perception about creative children. *Creative Child and Adult Quarterly, 12,* 39–42.

Singh, S. (2005). The whole truth about the real star-wars cast (Review of A. I. Miller's Empire of the Stars). *Los Angeles Times Book Review,* R8 (May 8).

Skinner, B. F. (1956). A case study in the scientific method. *American Psychologist, 11,* 211–233.

Skinner, B. F. (1968). *The technology of teaching.* Upper Saddle River, NJ: Prentice Hall.

Skinner, B. F. (1972). Creating the creative artist. In B. F. Skinner (Ed.), *Cumulative record* (pp. 333–344). New York: Appleton-Century-Crofts.

Skinner, B. F. (1983). Intellectual self-management in old age. *American Psychologist, 38,* 239–244.

Skinner, B. F. (1985). *Enjoy old age.* New York: Norton.

Skinner, B. F. (2005). *Walden Two*. Hacket Publishing (Originally published 1948).

Sligh, A. C., Conners, F., & Roskos-Ewoldsen, B. (2005). Relation of creativity to fluid and crystallized intelligence. *Journal of Creative Behavior, 39*, 123–136.

Smith, G. J. W. (1994). The internal breeding ground of creativity. *Paper presented as part of the symposium on creativity and cognition, October, Venice.*

Smith, G. J. W., & Amner, G. (1997). Creativity and perception. In M. A. Runco (Ed.), *Creativity research handbook* (Vol. 1, pp. 67–82). Cresskill, NJ: Hampton Press.

Smith, G. J. W., & van der Meer, G. (1997). Creativity in old age. In M. A. Runco & R. Richards (Eds.), *Eminent creativity, everyday creativity, and health* (pp. 333–353). Greenwich, CT: Ablex.

Smith, G. J. W., Carlsson, I., & Andersson, G. (1989). Creativity and the subliminal manipulation of projected self-images. *Creativity Research Journal, 2*, 1–16.

Smith, K. L. R., Michael, W. B., & Hocevar, D. (1990). Performance on creativity measures with examination-taking instructions intended to induce high or low levels of test anxiety. *Creativity Research Journal, 3*, 265–280.

Smith, S. M. (1995). Fixation, incubation, and insight in memory and creative thinking. In S. M. Smith, T. B. Ward, & R. A. Finke (Eds.), *The creative cognition approach* (pp. 135–156). Cambridge, MA: MIT Press.

Smith, S. M., & Blankenship, S. E. (1991). Incubation and the persistence of fixation in problem solving. *American Journal of Psychology, 104*, 61–87.

Smith, S. M., & Dodds, R. A. (1999). Incubation. In M. A. Runco & S. R. Pritzker (Eds.), *Encyclopedia of creativity* (Vol. 1, pp. 39). San Diego, CA: Elsevier.

Smith, W. W. (1988). *Creativity and handwriting: A study of the relationship between handwriting and creativity in fifth-grade children*. Ed.D. Dissertation ATT-8612087, Amherst: University of Massachusetts.

Smolucha, L., & Smolucha, F. (1986). A fifth Piagetian stage. *Poetics, 15*, 475–491.

Sneed, C., & Runco, M. A. (1992). The beliefs adults and children hold about television and video games. *Journal of Psychology, 126*, 273–284.

Snow, C. P. (1963). *The two cultures and the scientific revolution*. New York: Cambridge University Press.

Snyder, A., & Thomas, M. (1997). Autistic savants give clues to cognition. *Perception, 26*, 93–96.

Snyder, A. W., Mulcahy, E., Taylor, J. L., Mitchell, D. J., Sachdev, P., & Gandevia, S. C. (2003). Savant-like skills exposed in normal people by suppressing the left fronto-temporal lobe. *Journal of Integrative Neuroscience, 2*, 149–158.

Solomon, A. O. (1974). Analysis of creative thinking of disadvantaged children. *Journal of Creative Behavior, 8*, 293–295.

Solomon, B., Powell, K., & Gardner, H. (1999). Multiple intelligences. In M. A. Runco & S. R. Pritzker (Eds.), *Encyclopedia of creativity* (pp. 259–273). San Diego, CA: Academic Press.

Sosik, J. J., Kahai, S. S., & Avolio, B. J. (1998). Transformational leadership and dimensions of creativity: Motivating idea generation in computer-mediated groups. *Creativity Research Journal, 11*, 111–121.

Souder, W., & Ziegler, R. (1977). A review of creativity and problem-solving techniques. *Research Management, 20*, 34–42.

Spearman, C. (1927). *The abilities of man: Their measurement in nature*. New York: Macmillan.

Sperling, O. E. (1954). An imaginary companion, representing a prestage of the superego. *Psychoanalytic Study of the Child, 9*, 252–258.

Sperry, R. (1964). The great cerebral commissure. *Scientific American, 210*, 42–52.

Spiel, C., & von Korff, C. (1998). Implicit theories of creativity: The conceptions of politicians, scientists, artists and school teachers. *High Ability, 9*, 43–58.

Springer, S. P., & Deutsch, G. (1998). *Left brain, right brain* (5th ed.). San Francisco, CA: W. H. Freeman.

Spurling, H. (1998). *The unknown Matisse: A life of Henri Matisse: The early years, 1869–1908*. Los Angeles: University of California Press.

Srivastava, B. (1982). A study of creative abilities in relation to socioeconomic status and culture. *Perspectives in Psychological Researches, 5*, 37–40.

Starbuck, W. H., & Webster, J. (1991). When is play productive. *Accounting, Management, and Information Technology, 1*, 71–90.

Stavridou, A., & Furnham, A. (1996). The relationship between psychoticism, trait creativity and the attention mechanism of cognitive inhibition. *Personality and Individual Differences, 21*, 143–153.

Stein, M. I. (1953). Creativity and culture. *Journal of Psychology, 36*, 311–322.

Stein, M. I. (1975). *The physiognomic cue test*. New York: Behavioral Publications.

Stein, M. I. (1993). Moral issues facing intermediaries between creators and the public. *Creativity Research Journal, 6*, 197–200.

Steinberg, H., Sykes, E. A., Moss, T., Lowery, S., LeBoutillier, N., & Dewey, A. (1997). Exercise enhances creativity independently of mood. *British Journal of Sports Medicine, 31*, 240–245.

Sternberg, R. J. (1977). Component processes in analogical reasoning. *Psychological Review, 84*, 353–378.

Sternberg, R. J. (1985). Implicit theories of intelligence, creativity, and wisdom. *Journal of Personality and Social Psychology, 49*, 607–627.

Sternberg, R. J. (1986). A triarchic theory of intellectual giftedness. In R. J. Sternberg & J. E. Davidson (Eds.), *Conceptions of giftedness* (pp. 223–243). Cambridge, MA: Cambridge University Press.

Sternberg, R. J., (Ed.), (1999a). *Handbook of creativity*. Cambridge, MA: Cambridge University Press.

Sternberg, R. J. (1999b). A propulsion model of types of creative contributions. *Review of General Psychology, 3*, 83–100.

Sternberg, R. J. & Davidson, J. E., (Eds.), (1995). *The nature of insight*. Cambridge, MA: MIT Press.

Sternberg, R. J., & Lubart, T. I. (1995). *Defying the crowd: Cultivating creativity in a culture of conformity*. New York: Free Press.

Sternberg, R. J., & Lubart, T. I. (1996). Investing in creativity. *American Psychologist, 51*, 77–88.

Stevens, G., & Burley, B. (1999). Creativity + business discipline = higher profits faster from new product development. *Journal of Product Innovation Management, 16*, 455–468.

Stillinger, J. (1991). *Multiple authorship and the myth of solitary genius*. New York: Oxford University Press.

Stokes, P. D., & Balsam, P. (2003). The effects of constraint on response variability. *Creativity Research Journal, 15*, 331–341.

Stokes, T. F., & Baer, D. M. (1977). An implicit technology of generalization. *Journal of Applied Behavior Analysis, 10*, 349–367.

Stokols, D., Clitheroe, C., & Zmuidzinas, M. (2002). Qualities of work environments that promote perceived support for creativity. *Creativity Research Journal, 14*, 137–147.

Stoycheva, K. (2003a). *Tolerance for ambiguity* (Tolerantnostta kam neopredelenost.). Pleven, Bulgaria: Lege Artis.

Stoycheva, K. (2003b). Talent, science and education: How do we cope with uncertainty and ambiguities? In P. Csermely, & L. Lederman (Eds.), *Science education: Talent recruitment and public understanding* (pp. 31–43). Amsterdam, The Netherlands: IOS Press. (NATO Science Series, Volume V/38.)

Stravinsky, I. (1970). *Poetics of music in the form of six lessons* (A. Knodel, & I. Dahl, Trans.). Cambridge, MA: Harvard University Press (Original work published 1942).

Suler, J. R. (1980). Primary process thinking in creativity. *Psychological Bulletin, 88*, 144–165.

Sulloway, F. (1987). Birth order and scientific revolutions. *Paper presented at the University of Hawaii, Hilo, January*.

Sulloway, F. (1996). *Born to rebel*. New York: Pantheon.

Sundararagan, L. (2002). The vail and veracity of passion in Chinese poetics. *Consciousness and Emotion, 3*, 231–262.

Sundararajan, L. (2004). 24 poetic moods: Poetry and personality and (or in) Chinese aesthetics. *Creativity Research Journal, 16*, 201–214.

Sutton, R. L. (2001). *The weird rules of creativity: You know how to manage for efficiency and productivity, but if it's creativity you want, chances are you're doing it all wrong*. September: Harvard Business Review. pp. 94–103

Suzuki, S. (1969). *Nurtured by love*. Hicksville, NY: Exposition Press.

Svenssen, N., Archer, T., & Norlander, T. (2006). A Swedish version of the regressive imagery dictionary: Effects of alcohol and emotional-enhancement on primary-secondary process relations. *Creativity Research Journal, 18*, 459–470.

Swanson, H. L., & Hoskyn, M. (1998). Experimental intervention research on students with learning disabilities: A meta-analysis of treatment outcomes. *Review of Educational Research, 68*, 277–321.

Swensen, E. (1978). Teacher-assessment of creative behavior in disadvantaged children. *Gifted Child Quarterly, 22*, 338–343.

Szasz, T. S. (1984). *The myth of mental illness: Foundations of a theory of personal conduct* (rev. ed.). New York: Harper.

Taft, R. (1971). Creativity: Hot and cold. *Journal of Personality, 39*, 345–361.

Tahir, L. (1999). George Bernhard Shaw. In M. A. Runco, & S. R. Pritzker (Eds.), *Encyclopedia of creativity* (pp. 565–570). San Diego, CA: Academic Press.

Tang, T. L., & Baumeister, R. F. (1984). Effects of personal values, perceived surveillance, and task labels on task preference: The ideology of turning play into work. *Journal of Applied Psychology, 69*, 99–105.

Tate, K., & Domb, E. (1997a). *40 inventive principles with examples.* <www.triz-journal.com/archives/1997/07/b/index.html>.

Tate, K., & Domb, E. (1997b). How to help TRIZ beginners succeed. *TRIZ Journal* (April). <http://www.triz-journal.com/archives/1997/04/a/index.html>.

Taylor, C. W. & Barron, F., (Eds.), (1963). *Scientific creativity: Its recognition and development.* New York: Wiley.

Taylor, D., Berry, P., & Block, C. (1958). Does group participation when using brainstorming facilitate or inhibit creative thinking? *Administrative Science Quarterly, 3*, 323–347.

Taylor, G. J. (1984). Alexithymia: Concept, measurement, and implications for treatment. *American Journal of Psychiatry, 141*, 725–782.

Taylor, M. (1999). *Imaginary companions and the children who create them.* New York: Oxford University Press.

Taylor, M. (2011). Imagination (2nd ed.). In M. A. Runco & S. R. Pritzker (Eds.), *Encyclopedia of creativity* (Vol. 1, pp. 637–643). San Diego, CA: Elsevier.

Taylor, M., Cartwright, B. S., & Carlson, S. M. (1993). A developmental investigation of children's imaginary companions. *Developmental Psychology, 29*, 276–285.

Taylor, M., Hodges, S. D., & Kohanyi, A. (2003). An illusion of independent agency: Do adult fiction writers experience their characters as having minds of their own? *Imagination, Cognition, and Personality, 22*, 361–380.

Tegano, D. W. (1990). Relationship of tolerance of ambiguity and playfulness to creativity. *Psychological Reports, 66*, 1047–1056.

Tegano, D. W., & Moran, J. D. (1989). Sex differences in the original thinking of preschool and elementary school children. *Creativity Research Journal, 2*, 102–110.

Tegano, D., Fu, V., & Moran, J. (1983). Divergent thinking and hemispheric dominance for language function among preschool children. *Perceptual and Motor Skills, 56*, 691–698.

TenHouten, W. (1994). Creativity, intentionality, and alexithymia: A graphological analysis of split-brained patients and normal controls. In M. A. Runco & M. P. Shaw (Eds.), *Creativity and affect.* Norwood, NJ: Ablex.

Tenner, E. (1996). *Why things bite back: Technology and the revenge of unintended consequences.* New York: Random House.

Tett, R. P. (1998). Is conscientiousness always positively related to job performance? *Industrial–Organizational Psychologist, 36*, 24–29.

Thackray, J. (1995). That vital spark (creativity enhancement in business). *Management Today, 56*, 56–58.

Therriault, D. J. (2013). The cognitive underpinnings of creative thought: A latent variable analysis exploring the roles of intelligence and working memory in three creative thinking processes. *Intelligence, 41*, 306–320.

Thomas, K., Crowl, S., Kaminsky, D., & Podell, M. (1996). *Educational psychology: Windows on teaching.* Madison: Brown and Benchmark.

Thomas, N. G., & Burke, L. E. (1981). Effects of school environments on the development of young children's creativity. *Child Development, 52*, 1153–1162.

Thurston, B. (1999). Marie Sklodowska Curie. In M. A. Runco & S. R. Pritzker (Eds.), *Encyclopedia of creativity* (pp. 465–468). San Diego, CA: Academic Press.

Thurstone, L. L. (1952). *The scientific study of inventive talent.* Chicago: Chicago University Press.

Tierney, P., & Farmer, S. M. (2002). Creative self-efficacy: Its potential antecedents and relationship to creative performance. *Academy of Management Journal, 45*, 1137–1148.

Tierney, P., & Farmer, S. M. (2004). The Pygmalion process and employee creativity. *Journal of Management, 30*, 413–432.

Tinklenberg, J. R., Darley, C. F., Roth, W. T., Pfefferbaum, A., & Kopell, B. S. (1978). Marijuana effects on associations to novel stimuli. *Journal of Nervous and Mental Disease, 166*, 264–362.

Tobar, H. (2012, December 7). Nature Wars details an uneasy relationship. *Los Angeles Times Review of Books.* <http://articles.latimes.com/2012/dec/07/entertainment/la-ca-jc-jim-sterba-20121209>.

Tomas, V. (1958). Creativity in art. *Philosophical Review, 4*, 1–15.

Toplyn, G., & Maguire, W. (1991). The differential effect of noise on creative task performance. *Creativity Research Journal, 4*, 337.

Torrance, E. P. (1962). *Guiding creative talent.* Englewood Cliffs, NJ: Prentice Hall.

Torrance, E. P. (1963a). The creative personality and the ideal pupil. *Teachers College Record, 65*, 220–226.

Torrance, E. P. (1963b). *Education and the creative potential.* Minneapolis: University of Minnesota Press.

Torrance, E. P. (1965). *Rewarding creative behavior: Experiments in classroom creativity.* Englewood Cliffs, NJ: Prentice Hall.

Torrance, E. P. (1968a). Finding hidden talents among disadvantaged children. *Gifted Child Quarterly, 12,* 131–137.

Torrance, E. P. (1968b). A longitudinal examination of the fourth-grade slump in creativity. *Gifted Child Quarterly, 12,* 195–199.

Torrance, E. P. (1971). Are the Torrance tests of creative thinking biased against or in favor of "disadvantaged" groups? *Gifted Child Quarterly, 15,* 75–80.

Torrance, E. P. (1972). Can we teach children to think creatively? *Journal of Creative Behavior, 6,* 114–143.

Torrance, E. P. (1973). Cross-cultural studies of creative development in seven selected societies. *Educational Trends, 8,* 28–38.

Torrance, E. P. (1974). *Torrance tests of creative thinking: Directions guide and scoring manual.* Boston, MA: Personal Press.

Torrance, E. P. (1979a). *The search for satori and creativity.* Buffalo, NY: Creative Education Foundation.

Torrance, E. P. (1979b). Unique needs of the creative child and adult. In A. H. Passow (Ed.), *The gifted and talented: their education and development. 78th NSSE Yearbook* (pp. 352–371). Chicago: National Society for the Study of Education.

Torrance, E. P. (1983). Role of mentors in creative achievement. *Creative Child and Adult Quarterly, 3,* 8–18.

Torrance, E. P. (1987). Teaching for creativity. In S. G. Isaksen (Ed.), *Frontiers of creativity research.* Buffalo, NY: Bearly Limited.

Torrance, E. P. (1988). The nature of creativity as manifested in testing. In R. J. Sternberg (Ed.), *Nature of creativity* (pp. 43–75). New York: Cambridge University Press.

Torrance, E. P. (1995). *Why fly?* Norwood, NJ: Ablex.

Torrance, E. P. (2003). Reflection on emerging insights on the educational psychology of creativity. In J. Houtz (Ed.), *The educational psychology of creativity* (pp. 273–286). Cresskill, NJ: Hampton Press.

Torrance, E., & Mourad, S. (1979). Role of hemisphericity in performance on selected measures of creativity. *Gifted Child Quarterly, 23,* 44–55.

Torrance, E. P., & Presbury, J. (1984). The criteria of success used in 242 recent experimental studies of creativity. *Creative Child and Adult Quarterly, 9,* 238–242.

Torrance, E. P., Clements, C. B., & Goff, K. (1989). Mind-body learning among the elderly: Arts, fitness, incubation. *Educational Forum, 54,* 123–133.

Toynbee, A. (1964). Is America neglecting her creative minority? In C. W. Taylor (Ed.), *Widening horizons in creativity: The Proceedings of the Fifth Utah Creativity Research Conference* (pp. 3–9). New York: Wiley.

Treffert, D. A., & Wallace, G. L. (2004). Islands of Genius. *Scientific American, 14,* 14–23. (special ed.)

Treffinger, D. J. (1987). Research on creativity assessment. In S. G. Isaksen (Ed.), *Frontiers of creativity research* (pp. 103–109). Buffalo, NY: Bearly.

Treffinger, D., Tallman, M., & Isaksen, S. G. (1994). Creative problem solving: An overview. In M. A. Runco (Ed.), *Problem finding, problem solving, and creativity* (pp. 223–236). Norwood, NJ: Ablex.

Triandis, H. C. (1995). *Individualism and collectivism.* Boulder, CO: Westview.

Triandis, H. C. (1996). The psychological measurement of cultural syndromes. *American Psychologist, 51,* 407–415.

Tsoukas, H. (1989). The validity of idiographic research explanations. *Academy of Management Review, 24,* 551–561.

Twain, M. (1999). *Adventures of Tom Sawyer.* New York: Scholastic (Originally published in 1876).

Tweney, R. D. (1996). Presymbolic processes in scientific creativity. *Creativity Research Journal, 9,* 163–172.

Twiss, B. C. (1986). *Managing technological innovation* (3rd ed.). London: Pitman Publishing.

Ulin, D. L. (1992). An appetite for rehash (Review of D. Stern's Twice upon a time). *Los Angeles Times Book Review, 3,* 5 (December 13).

Ulin, D. L. (2005). Older and bleaker (Review of Kurt Vonnegut's A Man Without a Country). *Los Angeles Times, E1,* E10–E11 (September 10).

Ulin, D. L. (2012). Caltech physicist Sean Carroll makes the search for the Higgs boson a scientific detective story. (Review of *Particle at the end of the universe.*) *Los Angeles Times.* http://latimes.com/features/books/jacketcopy/la-ca-jc-sean-carroll-20121202,0,4799148.story.

Urban, K. K. (1991). On the development of creativity in children. *Creativity Research Journal, 4,* 177–191.

Vaillant, G. E. (2002). *Aging well.* Boston: Little, Brown.

Valkenburg, P. M., & van der Voort, T. H. A. (1994). Influence of TV on daydreaming and creative imagination: A review of research. *Psychological Bulletin, 116,* 316–339.

Valliant, G. E., & Valliant, C. O. (1990). Determinants and consequences of creativity in a cohort of gifted women. *Psychology of Women, 14,* 607–616.

Van Andel, P. (1992). Serendipity: Expect the unexpected. *Creativity and Innovation Management, 1*, 20–32.

Van Gundy, A. B. (1992). *Idea power*. New York: American Management Association.

Van Maanen, J. (1995). Style as theory. *Organization Science, 6*, 133–143.

Vandervert, L. (2003). How working memory and cognitive modeling functions of the cerebellum contribute to discoveries in mathematics. *New Ideas in Psychology, 21*, 159–175.

Vandervert, L. (Ed.) (1997). Understanding tomorrow's mind: Advances in chaos theory, quantum theory, and consciousness in psychology [Special issue]. *The Journal of Mind and Behavior, 18(2, 3)*.

Vandervert, L. (in press). Creativity: The blending of cerebellar cognitive models in the cerebral cortex. *Creativity Research Journal*.

Vandervert, L. R., Schimpf, P. H., & Liu, H. (2007). How working memory and the cerebellum collaborate to produce creativity and innovation. *Creativity Research Journal, 19*, 1–18.

VanTassel-Baska, J. (1999). The Bronte sisters. In M. A. Runco & S. R. Pritzker (Eds.), *Encyclopedia of creativity* (pp. 229–233). San Diego, CA: Academic Press.

Vartanian, O., & Goel, V. (2005). Neural correlates of creative cognition. In C. Martindale, P. Locher, & V. Petrov (Eds.), *Evolutionary and neurocognitive approaches to aesthetics, creativity and the arts*. Amityville, NY: Baywood Publishing.

Vartanian, O., Martindale, C., & Kwiatkowski, J. (2003). Creativity and inductive reasoning: The relationship between divergent thinking and performance on Wason's 2–4–6 task. *Quarterly Journal of Experimental Psychology, 56A*, 641–655.

Verhaeghen, P., Joorman, J., & Khan, R. (2005). Why we sing the blues: The relation between self-reflective rumination, mood, and creativity. *Emotion, 5(2)*, 226–232.

Vernon, P. E. (1970). *Creativity: Selected readings*. Middlesex: Penguin.

Vernon, P. E. (1989). The nature-nurture problem in creativity. In J. A. Glover, R. R. Ronning, & C. R. Reynolds (Eds.), *Handbook of creativity* (pp. 93–110). New York: Plenum Press.

Victor, H., Grossman, J., & Eisenman, R. (1973). Openness to experience and marijuana use in high school students. *Journal of Consulting and Clinical Psychology, 41*, 38–45.

Vidal, F. (1989). Self and oeuvre in Jean Piaget's youth. In D. Wallace & H. E. Gruber (Eds.), *Creative people at work* (pp. 189–208). New York: Oxford University Press.

Von Oech, R. (1983). *A whack on the side of the head*. New York: Warner Communications.

Voneche, J. (2003). The changing structure of Piaget's thinking: Invariance and transformations. *Creativity Research Journal, 15*, 3–9.

Vonnegut, K. (1991). *Fates worse than death*. New York: Putnam.

Vosburg, S. K., & Kaufmann, G. (1999) In S. W. Russ (Ed.), *Affect, creative experience and psychological adjustments* Philadelphia, PA: Brunner/Mazel.

Vosburg, S. K. (1998a). The effects of positive and negative mood on divergent thinking performance. *Creativity Research Journal, 11*, 165–172.

Vosburg, S. K. (1998b). Mood and the quantity and quality of ideas. *Creativity Research Journal, 11*, 315–324.

Vygotsky, L. S. (1997). *Educational psychology*. Boca Raton, FL: St. Lucie Press (Original work published 1926).

Wai, J., Lubinski, D., & Benbow, C. B. (2005). Creativity and occupational accomplishment among intellectually precocious youths: An age 13 to age 33 longitudinal study. *Journal of Educational Psychology, 97*, 484–492.

Wakefield, J. (1992). *Creative thinking: Problem solving skills and the arts orientation*. Norwood, NJ: Ablex.

Walberg, H. J. (1988). Creativity and talent as learning. In R. J. Sternberg (Ed.), *The nature of creativity: Contemporary psychological perspectives* (pp. 340–361). Cambridge: Cambridge University Press.

Walberg, H. J., & Stariha, W. E. (1992). Productive human capital: Learning, creativity, and eminence. *Creativity Research Journal, 5*, 323–340.

Wallace, D. B. (1991). The genesis and microgenesis of sudden insight in the creation of literature. *Creativity Research Journal, 4*, 41–50.

Wallace, D. B., & Gruber, H. E. (1989). *Creative people at work*. New York: Oxford University Press.

Wallach, M. A., & Kogan, N. (1965). *Modes of thinking in young children*. New York: Holt, Rinehart, & Winston.

Wallach, M. A., & Wing, C. (1969). *The talented student*. New York: Holt, Rinehart & Winston.

Wallas, G. (1926). *The art of thought*. New York: Harcourt Brace and World.

Waller, N. G., Bouchard, T. J., Lykkens, D. T., Tellegen, A., & Blacker, D. M. (1993). Creativity, heritability, familiality: Which word does not belong? *Psychological Inquiry, 4*, 235–237.

Ward, C. D. (1996). Adult intervention: Appropriate strategies for enriching the quality of children's play. *Young Children*, 20–25.

Ward, T. B. (1994). Structured imagination: The role of category structure in exemplar generation. *Cognitive Psychology, 27*, 1–40.

Ward, T. B., Smith, S. M., & Finke, R. A. (1999). Creative cognition. In R. J. Sternberg (Ed.), *Handbook of creativity* (pp. 189–212). New York: Cambridge University Press.

Ward, T. B., Patterson, M. J., Sifonis, C. M., Dodds, R. A., & Saunders, K. N. (2002). The role of graded category structure in imaginative thought. *Memory and Cognition, 30*, 199–216.

Ward, T. B., Patterson, M. J., & Sifonis, C. M. (2004). The role of specificity and abstraction in creative idea generation. *Creativity Research Journal, 16*, 1–9.

Ward, W. C., Kogan, N., & Pankove, E. (1972). Incentive effects in children's creativity. *Child Development, 43*, 669–676.

Watson, J. D. (1968). *The double helix*. New York: Signet Books.

Watts, D. J., & Strogatz, S. H. (1998). Collective dynamics of small-world networks. *Nature, 393*, 440–442.

Weber, R. (1996). Toward a language of invention and synthetic thinking. *Creativity Research Journal., 9*, 353–367.

Weber, R., & Perkins, D. N. (1992). *Inventive minds*. New York: Oxford University Press.

Wechsler, S. M., Medeiros Vendramini, C. M., & Oakland, T. (2012). Thinking and creative styles: A validity study. *Creativity Research Journal, 24*, 235–242.

Weckowitz, T., Fedora, O., Mason, J., Radstaak, D., Bay, K., & Yonge, K. (1975). Effect of marijuana on divergent and convergent production cognitive tests. *Journal of Abnormal Psychology, 84*, 386–398.

Weightman, G. (2007). *The industrial revolutionaries*. New York: Grove Press.

Weinstein, E., Clark, Z., DiBartolomeo, D. J., & Davis, K. (in press). A decline in creativity? It depends on the domain. *Creativity Research Journal*.

Weisberg, R. W. (1986). *Creativity: Genius and other myths*. New York: Freeman and Co.

Weisberg, R. W. (1988). Problem solving and creativity. In R. J. Sternberg (Ed.), *The nature of creativity: Contemporary psychological perspectives* (pp. 148–176). Cambridge, MA: University Press.

Weisberg, R. W. (1994). Genius and madness? A quasi-experimental test of the hypothesis that manic-depression increases creativity. *Psychological Science, 5*, 361–367.

Weisberg, R. W. (1995a). Case studies of creative thinking: Reproduction versus restructuring in the real world. In S. M. Smith, T. B. Ward, & R. A. Finke (Eds.), *The creative cognition approach* (pp. 53–72). Cambridge, MA: MIT Press.

Weisberg, R. W. (1995b). Prolegomena to theories of insight in problem solving: Definition of terms and a taxonomy of problems. In R. J. Sternberg, & J. E. Davidson (Eds.), *The nature of insight* (pp. 157–196). Cambridge MA: MIT Press.

Weisberg, R. W. (1999). Creativity and knowledge: A challenge to theories. In R. J. Sternberg (Ed.), *Handbook of creativity* (pp. 226–250). Cambridge: Cambridge University Press.

Weisberg, R. W., & Alba, J. W. (1981). An examination of the alleged role of fixation in the solution of several insight problems. *Journal of Experimental Psychology: General, 110*, 169–192.

Weisberg, R., & Haas, R. (2007). We are all partly right: Comment on Simonton. *Creativity Research Journal, 19*, 345–360.

Weiss, D. S. (1981). A multigroup study of personality patterns in creativity. *Perceptual and Motor Skills, 52*, 735–746.

Welling, H. (2005). The intuitive process: The case of psychotherapy. *Journal of Psychotherapy Integration, 15*, 19–47.

Welling, H. (2007). Four mental operations in creative cognition: The importance of abstraction. *Creativity Research Journal, 19*, 163–177.

Wertheim, M. (2006). Complicated copernicus. Review of William Woolmann's uncentering the earth: Copernicus and the revolution of the heavenly spheres. *Los Angeles Times Book Review, 5*, R2 (February 5).

Wertheimer, M. (1950). Laws of organization in perceptual forms (Untersuchungen zur Lehre von der Gestalt II. Psychologische Forschungen trans. 4, 301–350). In W. Ellis (Ed.), *A source book of Gestalt psychology* (pp. 71–88). New York: Humanities Press (Original work published in 1923).

Wertheimer, M. (1982). *Productive thinking*. Chicago, IL: Univeristy of Chicago Press (Original work published in 1945).

Wertheimer, M. (1991). Max Wertheimer: Modern cognitive psychology and the Gestalt problem. In A. Kimble, M. Wertheimer, & C. White (Eds.), *Portraits of pioneers in psychology* (Vol. 1, pp. 189–207). Hillsdale, NJ: Lawrence Erlbaum.

West, A., Martindale, C., Hines, D., & Roth, W. T. (1983). Marijuana-induced primary process content in the TAT. *Journal of Personality Assessment, 47*, 466–467.

West, M. A. & Farr, J. L., (Eds.), (1991). *Innovation and creativity at work*. Chichester: Wiley.

West, M. A., & Rickards, T. (1999). Innovation. In M. A. Runco & S. R. Pritzker (Eds.), *Encyclopedia of creativity* (Vol. 2, pp. 35–43). San Diego, CA: Academic Press.

West, M. A. (2002). Sparkling fountains or stagnant ponds: An integrative model of creativity and innovation implementation in work groups. *Applied Psychology: An International Review, 51*, 355–424.

Westby, E. L., & Dawson, V. L. (1995). Creativity: Asset or burden in the classroom? *Creativity Research Journal, 8*, 1–10.

White, P. (1981). *Flaws in the glass: A self-portrait*. London: Jonathan Cape.

Whyte, L. L. (1983). *The unconscious before Freud*. London: Pinter.

Wilber, K. (1996). Transpersonal art and literary theory. *Journal of Transpersonal Psychology, 28*, 63–91.

Wild, C. (1965). Creativity and adaptive regression. *Journal of Personality and Social Psychology, 2*, 161–169.

Willerman, L. (1979). *The psychology of individual and group differences*. San Francisco, CA: Freeman.

Williams, F. (1980). *Creativity Assessment Packet: Manual*. East Aurora, NY: DOK Publishers.

Williams, F. E. (1991). *Creativity assessment packet: Test manual*. Austin, TX: Pro–Ed.

Wilson, E. O. (1975). *On human nature*. Cambridge, MA: Harvard University Press.

Wilson, G. D., Ausman, J., & Mathews, T. R. (1973). Conservatism and art preferences. *Journal of Personality and Social Psychology, 25*, 286–288.

Witt, L. A., & Beorkrem, M. (1989). Climate for creative productivity as a predictor of research usefulness and organizational effectiveness in an R&D organization. *Creativitiy Research Journal, 2*, 30–40.

Wittgenstein, L. (1965). *The blue and brown books*. New York: Harper Torchbooks.

Wittkower, R. (1973). Genius: Individualism in art and artists. In P. P. Wiener (Ed.), *Dictionary of the history of ideas* (pp. 297–312). New York: Scribner's.

Wittkower, R., & Wittkower, M. (1963). *Born under Saturn*. London: Shenval.

Wolford, G., Miller, M. B., & Gazzaniga, M. (2000). The left hemisphere's role in hypothesis formation. *Journal of Neuroscience, 20*, RC64.

Wolfradt, U., & Pretz, J. E. (2001). Individual differences in creativity: Personality, story writing, and hobbies. *European Journal of Personality, 15*, 297–310.

Woodman, R. W., & Schoenfeldt, L. F. (1990). An interactionist model of creative behavior. *Journal of Creative Behavior, 24*, 279–291.

Woodmansee, M. (1994). *The author, art, and the market: Rereading the history of aesthetics*. New York: Columbia University Press.

Woolley, J. D., & Phelps, K. E. (1994). Young children's practical reasoning about imagination. *British Journal of Developmental Psychology, 12*, 53–67.

Wortman, P. H., & Bryant, F. B. (1985). School desegregation and black achievement: An integrative review. *Sociological Methods and Research, 13*, 289–324.

Wotiz, J. H., & Rudofsky, S. (1954). Kekulé's dream: Fact or fiction? *Chemistry in Britain, 20*, 720–723.

Wurman, R. (1989). *Information anxiety*. New York: Doubleday.

Yalom, I. D. (1980). *Existential psychotherapy*. New York: Basic Books.

Yalow, R. (1986). Peer review and science revolutions. *Biological Psychiatry, 21*, 1–2.

Yeh, Yu-Chu, & Wu, Jing-Jyi (2006). The cognitive processes of pupils' technological creativity. *Creativity Research Journal, 18*, 213–227.

Yutang, L., (Ed.), (1942). *The wisdom of China and India*. New York: Random House.

Zachopoulou, E., & Makri, A. (2005). A developmental perspective of divergent movement ability in early young children. *Early Child Development and Care, 175*, 85–95.

Zajonc, R. B., & Markus, G. B. (1975). Birth order and intellectual development. *Psychological Review, 82*, 74–88.

Zajonc, R. B. (1976). Family configuration and intelligence. *Science, 92*, 227–236.

Zausner, T. (1998). When walls become doorways: Creativity, chaos theory, and physical illness. *Creativity Research Journal, 11*, 21–28.

Zausner, T. (1999). Georgia O'Keeffe. In M. A. Runco & S. R. Pritzker (Eds.), *Encyclopedia of creativity* (pp. 305–310). San Diego, CA: Academic Press.

Zemore, S. E. (1995). Ability to generate mental images in students of art. *Current Psychology: Developmental, Learning, Personality, Social, 14,* 83–88.

Zenhausern, R., & Kraemer, M. (1991). The dual nature of lateral eye movements. *International Journal of Neuroscience, 56,* 169–175.

Zha, P., Walczyk, J. J., Griffith-Ross, D. A., Tobacyk, J. J., & Walczyk, D. F. (2006). The impact of culture and individualism-collectivism on the creative potential and achievement of American and Chinese adults. *Creativity Research Journal, 18,* 355–366.

Zhang, X., & Bartol, K. M. (2010a). Linking empowering leadership and employee creativity: The influence of psychological empowerment, intrinsic motivation, and creative process engagement. *Academy of Management Journal, 53,* 107–128.

Zhang, X., & Bartol, K. M. (2010b). The influence of creative process engagement on employee creative performance and overall job performance: A curvilinear assessment. *Journal of Applied Psychology, 95,* 862–873.

Zimmerman, B. J., & Dialessi, F. (1973). Modeling influences on children's creative behavior. *Journal of Educational Psychology, 65,* 127–134.

Zoglin, R. (2004). 10 questions for George Carlin. *Time Magazine,* (March 29), p. 8.

Zuckerman, H. (1977). *Scientific elite.* New York: Free Press.

Zysberg, L., & Schenk, T. (2013). Creativity, religiosity, and political attitudes. *Creativity Research Journal, 25,* 228–231.

Index

Printed in the United States
By Bookmasters